THE PRACTICE OF INTERNATIONAL AND NATIONAL COURTS AND THE (DE-)FRAGMENTATION OF INTERNATIONAL LAW

In recent decades there has been a considerable growth in the activities of international tribunals and the establishment of new tribunals. Furthermore, supervisory bodies established to control compliance with treaty obligations have adopted decisions in an increasing number of cases. National courts further add to the practice of adjudication of claims based on international law.

While this increasing practice of courts and supervisory bodies strengthens the adjudicatory process in international law, it also poses challenges to the unity of international law. Most of these courts operate within their own special regime (functional, regional, or national) and will primarily interpret and apply international law within the framework of that particular regime. The role of domestic courts poses special challenges, as the powers of such courts to give effect to international law, as well as their actual practice in applying such law, largely will be determined by national law. At the same time, both international and national courts have recognised that they do not operate in isolation from the larger international legal system, and have found various ways to counteract the process of fragmentation that may result from their jurisdictional limitations.

This book explores how international and national courts can, and do, mitigate fragmentation of international law. It contains case studies from international regimes (including the WTO, the IMF, investment arbitration and the ECtHR) and from various national jurisdictions (including Japan, Norway, Switzerland and the UK), providing a basis for conclusions to be drawn in the final chapter.

Volume 40 in the series Studies in International Law

Studies in International Law
Recent titles in this series

State Liability in Investment Treaty Arbitration:
Global Constitutional and Administrative Law in the BIT Generation
Santiago Montt

Reappraising the Resort to Force: International Law, *Jus ad Bellum* and the War on Terror
Lindsay Moir

International Law and Dispute Settlement: New Problems and Techniques
Edited by Duncan French, Matthew Saul and Nigel White

The Democratic Legitimacy of International Law
Steven Wheatley

Reflections on the UN Declaration on the Rights of Indigenous Peoples
Edited by Stephen Allen and Alexandra Xanthaki

Contracting with Sovereignty:
State Contracts and International Arbitration
Ivar Alvik

Multi-Sourced Equivalent Norms in International Law
Edited by Yuval Shany and Tomer Broude

The Distinction and Relationship between *Jus ad Bellum* and *Jus in Bello*
Keiichiro Okimoto

International Humanitarian Law and Terrorism
Andrea Bianchi and Yasmin Naqvi

The Militarisation of Peacekeeping in the Twenty-First Century
James Sloan

Accounting for Hunger: The Right to Food in the Era of Globalisation
Edited by Olivier De Schutter and Kaitlin Y Cordes

Promises of States under International Law
Christian Eckart

Multilevel Regulation of Military and Security Contractors:
The Interplay between International, European and Domestic Norms
Edited by Christine Bakker and Mirko Sossai

Europe and Extraterritorial Asylum
Maarten den Heijer

For the complete list of titles in this series, see

'Studies in International Law' link at
www.hartpub.co.uk/books/series.asp

The Practice of International and National Courts and the (De-)Fragmentation of International Law

Edited by

Ole Kristian Fauchald

and

André Nollkaemper

HART PUBLISHING

OXFORD AND PORTLAND, OREGON

2012

Published in the United Kingdom by Hart Publishing Ltd
16C Worcester Place, Oxford, OX1 2JW
Telephone: +44 (0)1865 517530
Fax: +44 (0)1865 510710
E-mail: mail@hartpub.co.uk
Website: http://www.hartpub.co.uk

Published in North America (US and Canada) by
Hart Publishing
c/o International Specialized Book Services
920 NE 58th Avenue, Suite 300
Portland, OR 97213-3786
USA
Tel: +1 503 287 3093 or toll-free: (1) 800 944 6190
Fax: +1 503 280 8832
E-mail: orders@isbs.com
Website: http://www.isbs.com

British Library Cataloguing in Publication Data
Data Available

ISBN: 978-1-84946-247-1

Typeset by Hope Services, Abingdon

Preface

This volume was prepared as part of two research projects. The International Law in Domestic Courts (ILDC) project is hosted at the Amsterdam Center for International Law (ACIL) and implemented in cooperation with international partners. This project has resulted in what has become the ILDC module of the Oxford Reports on International Law, which provides access to a large number of domesic cases on international law, with expert commentary. Based on the newly-acquired information on cases, the project also sought to enhance our academic understanding of such cases for international law.

This project has been carried out with the support of COST Action IS0602 International Law in Domestic Courts. COST is an intergovernmental framework for European Co-operation in the field of Scientific and Technical Research, allowing the co-ordination of nationally-funded research on a European level. COST Action IS0602 has substantially facilitated the networking between European partners, both for the reporting on national case-law (for European states), and for the academic research. The present volume is the result of this cooperation carried out in the framework of COST IS0602.

The 'International tribunals: legalization and constitutionalization – implications for national constitutional structures' project, funded by the Research Council of Norway, is hosted by the University of Oslo, Department of Public and International Law. The project has as its main focus international tribunals in the fields of human rights, international crimes, international trade and investment, and environmental protection, and studies their relationship with domestic courts.

The premise underlying the volume, as a joint enterprise between these two research projects, is that the increasing activities of national courts in the application of international law is part of a wider phenomenon of an increasing role of courts – both national and international. One of the many dimensions of this increasing practice of courts is that it poses challenges to the unity of international law, as most courts operate within their own special regime (functional, regional, or national) and will primarily interpret and apply international law within the framework of that particular regime. This book explores how international and national courts have sought to counteract the process of fragmentation that may result from jurisdictional limitations.

Most chapters in this volume were orginally presented as papers at the conference 'Unity or Fragmentation of International Law – the Role of

International and National Tribunals' (Second ILDC Colloquium), held 14–15 May 2009 in Oslo. The chapters were substantially revised in the light of the discussion at the Conference and on the basis of comments provided by the editors.

We thank Geir Ulfstein and Erika de Wet, co-organisers of the 2009 Conference and as such jointly responsible for developing the theme of the Conference and the present volume. We also thank Ralph Janik, Anna Marhold and Scarlet Wagner, research assistants at ACIL, for editorial work, and Martine van Trigt for organising the COST Action at ACIL, as a result of which, the volume was produced.

Ole Kristian Fauchald and André Nollkaemper
February 2012

Contents

Preface v
Abbreviations vii

Part One International Courts 1

1 **Introduction** 3

2 **One Law to Rule Them All: Should International Courts Be Viewed as Guardians of Procedural Order and Legal Uniformity?** 15
Yuval Shany

3 **Customary Rules of Interpretation in the Practice of WTO Dispute Settlement Bodies** 35
Lukasz Gruszczynski

4 **IMF-WTO Interaction: Institutional, Jurisdictional and Procedural Aspects** 57
Claus D Zimmermann

5 **Sources of Law and Arbitral Interpretations of *Pari Materia* Investment Protection Rules** 87
Martins Paparinskis

6 **The ECHR and its Normative Environment: Difficulties Arising from a Regional Human Rights Court's Approach to Systemic Integration** 117
Ragnar Nordeide

Part Two National Courts 139

7 **The Systemic Integration of International Law by Domestic Courts: Domestic Judges as Architects of the Consistency of the International Legal Order** 141
Jean d'Aspremont

8 **Legal Integration through Judicial Dialogue** 167
Tor-Inge Harbo

9 **Judicial Dialogue in Multi-level Governance: The Impact of the *Solange* Argument** 185
Antonios Tzanakopoulos

10 Flux and Fragmentation in the International Law of State Jurisdiction: The Synecdochal Example of Canada's Domestic Court Conflicts over Accountability for International Human Rights Violations 217
Robert J Currie and Hugh M Kindred

11 Immunities and Human Rights: Dissecting the Dialogue in National and International Courts 245
Philippa Webb

12 Transjudicial Dialogue and Consistency in Human Rights Jurisprudence: A Case Study on Diplomatic Assurances against Torture 267
Aristoteles Constantinides

13 Racial Discrimination in Japan: Unity, Diversity and International Law 295
Timothy Webster

14 Subtle but Enduring – The Role of Domestic Courts in the Shaping of International Economic Law through Proper Interpretation of Domestic Law: The WTO Agreement before Swiss Courts 321
Andreas R Ziegler

15 Conclusions 343
Ole Kristian Fauchald and André Nollkaemper

Abbreviations

ACIL	Amsterdam Center for International Law
ADI	Anuario de Derecho Internacional
AFDI	Annuaire Français de Droit International
Afr J Int'l & Comp L	African Journal of International and Comparative Law
AJP	Aktuelle Juristische Praxis
Am J Comp L	American Journal of Comparative Law
Am J Int'l L	American Journal of International Law
Am U Int'l L Rev	American University International Law Review
Am U J Int'l L & Pol'y	American University Journal of International Law and Policy
AöR	Archiv des öffentlichen Rechts
Arb Int'l	Arbitration International
Arch Phil Droit	Archives de philosophie du droit
Asian-Pac L & Pol'y J	Asian-Pacific Law and Policy Journal
AsianYBIL	Asian Yearbook of International Law
ASIL Proceedings	American Society of International Law, Proceedings of the Annual Meeting
ASIL Discussion Paper Series	American Society of International Law, Discussion Paper Series
Austl J Asian L	Australian Journal of Asian Law
AustYBIL	Australian Yearbook of International Law
BaltYIL	Baltic Yearbook of International Law
BerGesVR	Berichte der Deutschen Gesellschaft für Völkerrecht
Berkeley J Int'l L	Berkeley Journal of International Law
BGBl	Bundesgesetzblatt (Federal Official Journal) Germany
BIICL	British Institute for International and Comparative Law
Buff Hum Rts L Rev	Buffalo Human Rights Law Review
BYIL	British Yearbook of International Law
Brooklyn J Int'l L	Brooklyn Journal of International Law
Cal L Rev	California Law Review
Can-US LJ	Canada-United States Law Journal
CFI	Court of First Instance (since 30 November 2009 renamed to European General Court, EGC)
Chi J Int'l L	Chicago Journal of International Law
Chinese J Int'l L	Chinese Journal of International Law

Colum J Asian L	Columbia Journal of Asian Law
Colum J Transnat'l L	Columbia Journal of Transnational Law
CM L Rev	Common Market Law Review
Cornell Int'l LJ	Cornell International Law Journal
Decision and Reports	Decision and Reports – European Commission of Human Rights
Denv J Intl'l L & Pol'y	Denver Journal of International Law and Policy
Duke J Comp & Int'l L	Duke Journal of Comparative and International Law
BVerfGE	Entscheidungen des Bundesverfassungsgerichts
ECJ	European Court of Justice
ECtHR	European Court of Human Rights
Eur	Europarecht
Eur Const L Rev	European Constitutional Law Review
Eur J Int'l L	European Journal of International Law
Eur J Legal Studies	European Journal of Legal Studies
Eur J Migration & L	European Journal of Migration and Law
EJIL: Talk!	European Journal of International Law: Talk! (available at)
Eur LJ	European Law Journal
FinnishYBIL	Finnish Yearbook of International Law
Fordham Int'l LJ	Fordham International Law Journal
Fordham L Rev	Fordham Law Review
Foreign Inv LJ	Foreign Investment Law Journal
GA Res	United Nations General Assembly Resolution
Geo LJ	Georgetown Law Journal
Geo Wash Int'l L Rev	George Washington International Law Revue
Ger LJ	German Law Journal
GYIL	German Yearbook of International Law
Hamline J Pub L & Pol'y	Hamline Journal of Public Law and Policy
Hastings Int'l & Comp L Rev	Hastings International and Comparative Law Review
Hastings LJ	Hastings Law Journal
Harv Int'l LJ	Harvard International Law Journal
Harv L Rev	Harvard Law Review
Hebr U Int'l L Research Paper	Hebrew University International Law Research Papers
Hous J Int'l L	Houston Journal of International Law
Hum R L Rev	Human Rights Law Review
Hum Rts Q	Human Rights Quarterly
ICJ	International Court of Justice
ICJ Reports	Annual Reports of the International Court of Justice

ICTR	International Criminal Tribunal for Rwanda
ICTY	International Criminal Tribunal for the Former Yugoslavia
Int'l & Comp L Q	International and Comparative Law Quarterly
IILJ Working Paper	International Law and Justice Working Papers
ILR	International Law Reports
Ind J Global Legal Stud	Indiana Journal of Global Legal Studies
Int'l Comm L Rev	International Community Law Review
Int'l J Const L	International Journal of Constitutional Law
Int'l J Legal Info	International Journal of Legal Information
Int'l J Refugee L	International Journal of Refugee Law
Int'l Org L Rev	International Organization Law Review
Int'l Law	The International Lawyer
International Organization	International Organization
Int'l Rev Red Cross	International Review of the Red Cross
Is L Rev	Israel Law Review
ITLOS	International Tribunal for the Law of the Sea
Japanese Ann Int'l L	Japanese Annual of International Law
J Legal Stud	Journal of Legal Studies
J Int'l Arb	Journal of International Arbitration
J Int'l Crim Just	Journal of International Criminal Justice
J Int'l Econ L	Journal of International Economic Law
JORF	Journal Officiel de la République Française
Justice J	The Justice Journal
J World Trade	Journal of World Trade
JZ	Juristenzeitung
Ky LJ	Kentucky Law Journal
Law & Prac Int'l Cts & Tribunals	The Law and Practice of International Courts and Tribunals
Law & Soc Inq	Law and Social Inquiry
Leiden J Int'l L	Leiden Journal of International Law
Loy U Chi Int'l L Rev	Loyola University Chicago International Law Review
Loy LA Int'l & Comp L Rev	Loyola of Los Angeles International and Comparative Law Review
McGill LJ	McGill Law Journal
Melbourne J Int'l L	Melbourne Journal of International Law
Mich J Int'l L	Michigan Journal of International Law
Mich L Rev	Michigan Law Review
Minn L Rev	Minnesota Law Review
Modern L Rev	Modern Law Review
MPEPIL	Max Planck Encyclopedia of Public International Law online edition, available at www.mpepil.com

NILR	Netherlands International Law Review
Neth YB Int'l L	
NJW	Neue Juristische Wochenschrift
Nordic J Int'l L	Nordic Journal of International Law
Nw J Int'l L & Bus	Northwestern Journal of International Law and Business
NRC Handelsblad	Nieuwe Rotterdamse Courant, Daily Paper
NYU J Int'l L & Pol	New York University Journal of International Law and Politics
NYU L Rev	New York University Law Review
N Y U IILJ Working Paper	New York University International Law and Justice Working Papers
OMPI	Organisation Mondiale de la Propriété Intellectuelle
Osgoode H LJ	Osgoode Hall Law Journal
ORIL	Oxford Reports on International Law
Oxford J Legal Stud	Oxford Journal of Legal Studies
Pac Rim L & Pol'y J	Pacific Rim Law and Policy Journal
RBDC	Revue belge de droit constitutionnel
RBDI	Revue belge de droit international
RDI	Rivista di Diritto Internazionale
RDDI	Revista de Derecho Internacional
Recueil des Cours	The Hague Academy (Académie de droit international) Collected Courses
RFDC	Revue Française de Droit Constitutionelle
RGDIP	Revue Générale de Droit International Public
RIAA	Reports of International Arbitral Awards
RSDIE	Revue Suisse de Droit International et Européen
SC Res	United Nations Security Council Resolution
SSRN	Social Science Research Network, available at www.ssrn.com
Stan L Rev	Stanford Law Review
Stan J Int'l L	Stanford Journal of International Law
Statute L Rev	Statute Law Review
STL	Special Tribunal for Lebanon
SZIER	Schweizerische Zeitschrift für internationales und europäisches Recht
TDM	Transnational Dispute Management
Tulane J Int'l & Comp L	Tulane Journal of International and Comparative Law
Tex Int'l LJ	Texas International Law Journal
Tulsa LJ	Tulsa Law Review (64-2001, thereafter review)
UC Davis L Rev	UC Davis Law Review
UCLA L Rev	UCLA Law Review

UN	United Nations
UN Doc	United Nations Document
U Miami L Rev	University of Miami Law Review
U Pa L Rev	University of Pennsylvania Law Review
U Pa J Int'l Econ L	University of Pennsylvania Journal of International Economic Law [Until volume 28 volume 29–32: University of Pennsylvania Journal of International Law, U Pa J Int'l L]
U Rich L Rev	University of Richmond Law Review
Vand L Rev	Vanderbilt Law Review
Va J Int'l L	Virginia Journal of International Law
WTO	World Trade Organization
WTO AB	Appellate Body of the World Trade Organization
Yale Hum Rts & Dev LJ	Yale Human Rights and Development Law Journal
Yale J Int'l L	Yale Journal of International Law
Yale LJ	Yale Law Journal
YBILC	Yearbook of the International Law Commission
ZaöRV	Zeitschrift für ausländisches öffentliches Recht und Völkerrecht

Part One

International Courts

1

Introduction

IN RECENT DECADES there has been a considerable growth in the activities of international tribunals. We have seen an increase in the case-load of existing tribunals and the establishment of new tribunals. The practice of the International Court of Justice (ICJ), the dispute settlement mechanism of the World Trade Organization (WTO), investment arbitration (mainly through the International Centre for Settlement of Investment Disputes), the International Tribunal for the Law of the Sea and regional human rights courts illustrates the trends. Furthermore, supervisory bodies that have been established to control compliance with treaty obligations in respect of human rights, multilateral environmental agreements and international labour law, have adopted decisions in an increasing number of specific cases. National courts further add to the practice of adjudication of claims based on international law.

From one perspective, the increasing practice of courts and supervisory bodies strengthens the adjudicatory process in international law, and may be seen as strengthening the international rule of law. International law is more likely now than ever before to be followed up through formalised procedures designed to ensure that the law is applied in specific cases.

From another perspective, this development poses challenges to the unity of international law. Most of these courts operate within their own special regime (functional, regional, or national) and will primarily interpret and apply international law within the framework of that particular regime. While they may and often do apply rules of general international law, their powers to do so and the interpretations that they offer will be limited and coloured by that particular regime. The role of domestic courts poses special challenges, as the powers of such courts to give effect to international law, as well as their actual practice in applying such law, will be coloured by national law.

The challenge that the practice of (international) tribunals poses for the unity of international law is part of a much broader phenomenon of fragmentation, which also relates to such phenomena as relatively autonomous international organisations, regionalism, unilateralism and bilateralism.[1]

[1] B Simma, D Pulkowski, 'Of Planets and the Universe: Self-contained Regimes in International Law' (2006) 17 *Eur J Int'l L* 483; N Thomas, *Governance and Regionalism in Asia* (New York, Routledge, 2009); AJ Grant and F Söderbaum, *The New Regionalism in Africa*

Increasingly specialised treaty regimes and international organisations with differing memberships and overlapping jurisdictions[2] may not sufficiently take account of one another, and thus may produce inconsistencies within the general international order.[3]

Of course, fragmentation is not at all a new phenomenon. It stems from a multitude of factors that are familiar to traditional international law, including sovereign equality of states, the lack of centralised organs, specialisation of law, different structures of legal norms (for example, hierarchical and non-hierarchical), parallel and sometimes competing regulations, an expanding scope of international law, and different dynamics for rule development.[4]

The proliferation and increasing activity of international courts and compliance mechanisms have provided new dimensions to the phenomenon of fragmentation.[5] While the increasing use of international tribunals can be seen as a function of the expansion and maturity of international law,[6] it may lead to further fragmentation. Globally dispersed courts, tribunals, arbitration panels and alternative dispute resolution bodies are so closely coupled with their own specialised regimes, both in terms of organisation and self-perception, that they are likely to contribute to fragmentation.[7]

The fragmentation of international law through the operation of tribunals has institutional, procedural and substantive aspects. At an institutional level, the proliferation of tribunals and compliance organs for specific treaty regimes has given rise to a concern over deviating jurisprudence and forum-shopping. At the one extreme is the ICJ with its broad substantive jurisdiction combined with specific compulsory jurisdiction

(London, Ashgate Aldershot, 2003); D Bodansky, 'What is So Bad about Unilateral Action to Protect the Environment?' (2000) 11 *Eur J Int'l L* 339; G Blum, 'Bilateralism, Multilateralism, and the Architecture of International Law' (2008) 49 *Harv Int'l LJ* 323; A Reich, 'Bilateralism versus Multilateralism in International Economic Law' (2010) 60 *U Toronto LJ* 263.

[2] EU Petersmann, 'De-Fragmentation of International Economic Law through Constitutional Interpretation and Adjudication with Due Respect for Reasonable Disagreement' (2008) 6 *Loy U Chi Int'l L Rev* 209, 210.

[3] International Law Commission (ILC), Fragmentation of International Law: Difficulties Arising from the Diversification and Expansion of International Law (ILC Fragmentation Report), UN Doc A/CN.4/682 (2006) (finalised by Martti Koskenniemi).

[4] C Leathley, 'An Institutional Hierarchy to Combat the Fragmentation of International Law: Has the ILC Missed an Opportunity?' (2007) 40 *NYU J Int'l L & Pol* 259; AC Martineau, 'The Rhetoric of Fragmentation: Fear and Faith in International Law' (2009) 22 *Leiden J Int'l L* 1.

[5] Leathley, ibid 265.

[6] PS Rao, 'Multiple International Judicial Forums: A Reflection of the Growing Strength of International Law or Its Fragmentation?'(2004) 25 *Mich J Int'l L* 929.

[7] A Khrebtukova, 'A Call to Freedom: Towards a Philosophy if International Law in an Era of Fragmentation' (2008) 4 *J Int'l L & Int'l Rel* 55; G Hafner, 'Pros and Cons of Ensuing from Fragmentation of International Law' (2004) 25 *Mich J Int'l L* 849, 857.

as set out in certain treaties.[8] At the other extreme are investment tribunals which are established *ad hoc* and which may or may not have an institutional affiliation.[9] The rights and obligations of legal subjects may depend on which body is seized to recognise them.[10]

At the procedural level, the procedures to be followed by the tribunals differ significantly and may or may not be conducive to their coordination with other tribunals. Of particular interest are the rules on the applicable law and on interpretation. It has been suggested that procedures to seek information from, informal or formal advice from, or formal decisions by, organs established under other treaties may improve the prospects for coordination.[11]

At the substantive level, problems consist of the emergence of 'special laws', treaty-regimes, and functional clusters of rules and specialised branches of international law that raise questions in terms of their relationship *inter se* and to general international law.[12] These are factors that may lead to substantive inconsistencies in jurisprudence. Even in cases where the same case is argued on the basis of almost identical rules before tribunals following almost identical procedures, the results may differ significantly.[13] The lack of specific rules concerning the methodology to be used in the mandates of most tribunals means that they are potentially open to a very broad range of interpretive arguments. Given the significant human and economic resources available to most parties to cases before international tribunals, we observe that such tribunals are being

[8] See, *inter alia*, art 38 of the Convention Relating to the Status of Refugees (28 July 1951) 189 UNTS 150.

[9] OK Fauchald, 'The Legal Reasoning of ICSID Tribunals – An Empirical Analysis' (2008) 19 *Eur J Int'l L* 301.

[10] One frequently cited example is the *Sword Fish* case between Chile and the European Commission, which was brought before the International Tribunal of the Law of the Sea by Chile (available at www.itlos.org/cgi-bin/cases/case_detail.pl?id=6&lang=en) and before dispute settlement under the WTO by the European Communities (available at www.wto.org/english/tratop_e/dispu_e/cases_e/ds193_e.htm) (both last visited 1 June 2011). None of these cases were pursued beyond the preliminary stage.

[11] M Koskenniemi and P Leino, 'Fragmentation of International Law? Postmodern Anxieties' (2002) 15 *Leiden J Int'l L* 553, 553–56.

[12] ILC Fragmentation Report (n 3), para 489. One frequently cited example is the *MOX Plant* case, which was brought before two separate arbitration tribunals of the Permanent Court of Arbitration; one according to the United Nations Convention on the Law of the Sea (10 December 1982) (available at www.pca-cpa.org/showpage.asp?pag_id=1148), and one according to the OSPAR Convention for the Protection of the Marine Environment of the North-East Atlantic (22 September 1992) (available at www.pca-cpa.org/showpage.asp?pag_id=1158) (both last visited 1 June 2011), as well as the European Court of Justice (*European Commission v Ireland*, Case C-459/03).

[13] An obvious example is an investor–state dispute raised by the same investor on the basis of the same facts against the Czech Republic before two different investment tribunals, *CME Czech Republic BV v Czech Republic and Lauder v Czech Republic*. Both tribunals were established under the UNCITRAL Arbitration Rules, considered almost identical rights and duties under two distinct bilateral investment treaties, but came to very different conclusions.

subjected to broad ranges of such arguments, which frequently result in lengthy and complex decisions.[14]

The extent to which the current level of fragmentation is problematic is contested. It may well be argued that overall, the different international tribunals share a coherent understanding of international law. Moreover, the fundamentals of general international law tend to remain the same regardless of which tribunal is deciding the issue. The risk of conflicting judgments is largely a theoretical problem and whilst there are instances of overlapping jurisdiction between tribunals which share the same competence to settle disputes on the basis of international law, this does not generally lead to disagreement or disorder.[15]

It can even be argued that it is through the decisions of the national and regional tribunals that we are witnessing a progressive development and application of international standards. These tribunals generally act more as agents and instruments for the unity and integrity of international law than as sources of its fragmentation.[16] Some authors have also downplayed the problems of fragmentation on the ground that competition for influence among institutions as a generative and market-like pluralism has produced more progress toward integration and democratisation than could have been achieved through more formal means.[17] Charney has noted that the alternative fora that complement the work of the ICJ strengthen the system of international law, notwithstanding some loss of uniformity. Even different approaches adopted in relation to the same subject may only represent a healthy 'level of experimentation in a collective effort to find the best rule to serve the international community as a whole'.[18]

[14] The length and complexity of decisions of international tribunals have increased significantly in the past decades, and this is particularly visible in cases relating to international trade and investment law.

[15] M Prost and P Kingsley Clark, 'Unity, Diversity and the Fragmentation of International Law: How Much Does the Multiplication of International Organizations Really Matter?' (2006) 5 *Chinese J Int'l L* 341. Also T Treves, 'Judicial Lawmaking in an Era of "Proliferation" of International Courts and Tribunals: Development or Fragmentation of International Law?' in R Wolfrum and V Röben (eds), *Developments of International Law in Treaty* Making (Berlin, Heidelberg, New York, Springer, 2005) 587; PS Rao, 'Multiple International Judicial Forums: A Reflection of the Growing Strength of International Law or Its Fragmentation?' (2004) 25 *Mich J Int'l L* 929.

[16] Rao (n 15), 958–59. See also A Reinisch, 'The Proliferation of International Dispute Settlement Mechanisms: The Threat of Fragmentation vs. the Promise of a More Effective System? Some Reflections From the Perspective of Investment Arbitration' in I Buffard, J Crawford, G Hafner and A Pellet (eds), *International Law between Universalism and Fragmentation: Festschrift in Honour of Gerhard Hafner* (Leiden, Brill, 2008) 107.

[17] See, eg: Treves (n 15); J Pauwelyn, 'Bridging Fragmentation and Unity: International Law as a Universe of Inter-Connected Islands' (2004) 25 *Mich J Int'l L* 903.

[18] JI Charney, 'Is International Law Threatened by Multiple International Tribunals?' (1998) 271 *Recueil des Cours* 101, 354. See also WT Worster, 'Competition and Comity in the Fragmentation of International Law' (2008) 34 *Brook J Int'l L* 119.

Still others have challenged the view of fragmentation as a negative development and a threat to the legal system, by suggesting that international law is not fragmenting, but rather is being transformed into a pluralist system. Instead of being undermined by fragmentation, the rules, institutions, and practices of the international legal order can be strengthened by the emergence of an international legal pluralism. It has been argued that the 'respect of legitimate difference inherent in such a pluralist conception may actually enhance the effectiveness of international law by increasing the legitimacy and political acceptability of international legal rules.'[19]

On the other hand, presidents of the ICJ, including Jennings, Schwebel and Guillaume, have pointed to problematic aspects of fragmentation among international tribunals. Judge Guillaume emphasised that the prospect of forum-shopping may generate unwanted confusion and distort the operation of justice. Such concerns were followed by suggestions to facilitate the resort to advisory opinions from the ICJ.[20]

It has been pointed out that differences in the development of dispute settlement mechanisms in various areas of international law may lead to careful consideration of some interests while other interests are regarded as irrelevant or not accorded corresponding weight. Such concerns are particularly relevant where a limited range of interests is protected through mandatory dispute settlement. One example is the discussion of how the dispute settlement mechanism and the rules of the WTO could be reformed to strike an appropriate balance between trade and other interests.[21]

Others have argued that fragmentation may sabotage the evolution of a more democratic and egalitarian international regulatory system. Benvenisti and Downs have emphasised three main reasons why we should consider fragmentation to be a serious problem, all of which are relevant in the context of international tribunals. They have suggested that fragmentation limits the opportunities for weaker actors to build the cross-issue coalitions that could potentially increase their bargaining power and influence, that it increases the transaction costs that international legal bodies must incur in trying to reintegrate or rationalise the legal order, and that it creates a regulatory order that reflects the interests of the powerful.[22]

[19] WW Burke-White, 'International Legal Pluralism' (2004) 25 *Mich J Int'l L* 963, 978. See also SR Ratner, 'Regulatory Takings in Institutional Context: Beyond the Fear of Fragmented International Law' (2008) 102 *Am J Int'l L* 475.

[20] M Koskenniemi and P Leino, 'Fragmentation of International Law? Postmodern Anxieties' (2002) 15 *Leiden J Int'l L* 553, 553–56.

[21] See JP Trachtman, 'The Domain of WTO Dispute Resolution' (1999) 40 *Harvard Int'l LJ* 2, 333, 364 and 376.

[22] E Benvenisti and GW Downs, 'The Empire's New Clothes: Political Economy and the Fragmentation of International Law' (2007) 60 *Stan L Rev* 595, 597–98.

While the debate on the question whether fragmentation on the whole is a positive or negative force in international law is thus ongoing, and more work certainly needs to be done, in this volume we approach the issue of fragmentation from a different angle. There is a need to move beyond general statements and assumptions concerning the links between tribunals and fragmentation of international law and to increase our understanding of these links by examing in depth the practices and dilemmas within the various legal regimes.

On the whole, not much thought has been given to the question of how specific (international) courts and institutions do contribute to, or can counteract problems of fragmentation.[23] It is noteworthy that the International Law Commission in its work on fragmentation did not make any proposals as to how international courts could function, alone or in cooperation, to that end.[24] It did observe, however, that international law's traditional 'fragmentation' has already equipped practitioners with techniques to deal with rules and rule-systems that point in different directions.[25] Specific manifestations of functionally discrete international courts as well as national courts raise the question of how these techniques can be applied as part of the judicial function. With the exception of a few contributions dealing with human rights courts and the WTO, little is known as to the practices of particular courts and tribunals, whether individually or from a comparative perspective. In particular, little attention has been given to the powers and practices of international courts to counteract fragmenting patterns, and contribute to the unity and coherence of international law.[26]

National courts face an increasingly complex web of national and international rules that will be relevant for their decision-making. As international legal regimes, in general, lack effective enforcement mechanisms, to some extent they depend on national courts for their effective application. The increase in the application of international law in national courts raises the question whether this practice further contributes to a fragmentation of international law, or whether national courts seek ways to

[23] Major contributions to this discussion were published as parts of 25(4) *Mich J Int'l L* (2003–04) publishing the proceedings from the symposium 'Diversity or Cacophony: New Sources of Norms in International Law'.

[24] C Leathley, 'An Institutional Hierarchy to Combat the Fragmentation of International Law: Has the ILC Missed an Opportunity?' (2007) 40 *NYU J Int'l L & Pol* 259.

[25] ILC Fragmentation Report (n 3), para 20.

[26] One notable exception is the publication of the proceedings from a symposium on fragmentation of international law and international tribunals in vol 31 of the *New York University Journal of International Law & Policy* (1999). In the foreword, Kingsbury notes that 'the initial question confronted by the contributors is whether the proliferation of international courts and tribunals, in a horizontal legal arrangement lacking in hierarchy and sparse in any formal structure of relations among these bodies, is fragmenting or system-building in its effects on international law'. B Kingsbury, 'Foreword: Is the Proliferation of International Courts and Tribunals a Systemic Problem?' (1999) *NYU J Int'l L & Pol* 679, 680.

maintain some form of unity in the interpretation and application of international law.

Even when the standards of judicial independence are satisfied, and we discount differences in interpretation due to an open political and nationalistic bias of national courts, national judicial practice may diffuse a more or less clear international standard into a multitude of particular meanings that may differ between courts of different states and even between different courts in one state.[27]

Divergence in the interpretation and application of international law at the national level is not a new phenomenon. International law consists to a large extent of a process of continuous interpretation and application, rather than a set of abstract rules.[28] That process has been determined by auto-interpretation of international law. This phenomenon has always led to national colour and interpretative distortions between states.[29]

While auto-interpretation is as enduring as international law itself, the role of national courts in the adjudication of international claims leads to a special situation. It should be recalled that while states have the right of auto-interpretation, they do not have the right of auto-decision. Their interpretation and application of international law are 'neither final nor binding upon the other parties'.[30] There is a difference of degree between a situation which is characterised by auto-interpretation by the state as such or its political organs, and the situation in which national courts engage in interpretation and application of international law. The degree of auto-interpretation in the various situations depends in particular on national rules concerning the relationship between domestic and international law and on the characteristics of the international legal regime in question.

While most authors have limited the term 'fragmentation' to refer to horizontal fragmentation between institutions and functional regimes within the international legal order,[31] there is no need to confine the

[27] RA Müllerson, *Ordering Anarchy: International Law in International Society* (Leiden, Martinus Nijhoff Publishers, 2000) 199; A Reinisch, 'Should Judges Second-Guess the UN Security Council?' (2009) 6 *Int'l Org L Rev* 257, 284.

[28] M Koskeniemmi, *From Apology to Utopia: The Structure of International Legal Argument*, 2nd edn (Cambridge, Cambridge University Press, 2006) 135; M Koskenniemi, 'Lauterpacht: The Victorian Tradition in International Law' (1997) 8 *Eur J Int'l L* 215, 218 f.

[29] M McDougal, 'The Impact of International Law Upon National Law: A Policy-oriented Perspective' (1959) 4 SD L Rev 25; reprinted in McDougal & Associates, *Studies in World Public Order* (New Haven, Yale University Press, 1960) 225.

[30] L Gross, 'States as Organs of International Law and the Problem of Autointerpretation' in GA Lipsky (ed), *Law and Politics in the World Community* (Berkeley and Los Angeles, University of California Press, 1953) 59, 76 f.

[31] See, eg: *Conclusions of the Work of the Study Group on the Fragmentation of International Law: Difficulties Arising from the Diversification and Expansion of International Law*, para 24 in ILC, 'Report of the ILC on its 58th Session – Suppl No 10' (1 May–9 June and 3 July–11 August 2006) UN Doc A/61/10, 416; M Koskenniemi, 'Fragmentation of International Law? Postmodern Anxieties' (2002) 15 *Leiden J Int'l L* 553. See also: AL Paulus, 'Subsidiarity, Fragmentation and Democracy: Towards the Demise of General International Law?' in

concept of fragmentation to this meaning. In view of the interplay between domestic and international law, and the engagement of national courts in the international legal order, national judicial practice is a central factor for the level and characteristics of the fragmentation of international law.[32] Even more than fragmentation between different international legal regimes, the fragmentation caused by divergent national receptions of international law is a reflection of a more fundamental, multi-dimensional fragmentation of global society itself.[33] Further, it should be asked which role domestic tribunals can play in efforts to counteract negative effects of fragmentation of international law.

While a large body of literature exists on the practice of national courts in general, hardly anything has been written on the specific issue of how national courts impact fragmentation.[34]

Against the spectrum of differing assessments of empirical material and different normative appraisals on the phenomenon of fragmentation, this book aims to enhance our understanding of how international and national courts can, and do, contribute to or mitigate problems associated with fragmentation.

This book takes as its starting point that better insight in particular cases can help strengthen the empirical basis for assessment of fragmentation and related trends. Our objectives are to provide a contribution that is firmly based on some 15 years of scholarly debate and studies of the practice of international tribunals.[35] On this basis, we will bring case studies from international regimes and, importantly, from various national jurisdictions, providing an improved basis for our assessment to be undertaken in the concluding chapter. Finally, we intend to contribute to the discussion of principles and techniques that international and national courts have applied to counter-act negative effects of fragmentation. Such techniques are not really new.

T Broude and Y Shany (eds), *The Shifting Allocation of Authority in International Law: Considering Sovereignty, Supremacy and Subsidiarity: Essays in Honour of Professor Ruth Lapidoth* (Oxford, Hart Publishing, 2008) 99; Hafner (n 7), J Pauwelyn (n 17); AK Björklund, 'Private Rights and Public International Law: Why Competition Among International Economic Tribunals is not Working' (2007) 59 *Hastings LJ* 241, 259.

[32] See examples given in: P Trimble, 'Review Essay: International Law, World Order, and Critical Legal Studies' (1990) 42 *Stanford L Rev* 811, 836 f. The connection between the role of national courts and fragmentation is noted by: A Kunzelmann, 'An Australian International Law: The Impact of Australian Courts on the Fragmentation of International Law' (2008) 27 *AustlYIL* 225, 248.

[33] The phrase is taken from A Fischer-Lescano and G Teubner, 'Regime-Collisions: The Vain Search for Legal Unity in the Fragmentation of Global Law' (2004) 25 *Mich J Int'l L* 999, 1004, who used this in a different context. See also VJ Jackson, *Constitutional Engagement in a Transnational Era* (Oxford, Oxford University Press, 2010) 50 f.

[34] A rare exception is: Kunzelmann (n 32). See also E Benvenisti and G Downs, 'National Courts, Domestic Democracy, and the Evolution of International Law' (2009) 20 *EJIL* 59.

[35] A proper starting date for the current scholarly debate is the 1999 special issue of *NYU J Int'l L & Pol.*

The book contains 13 contributions that support these aims.

Shany's contribution raises the fundamental question whether we should expect international tribunals to fulfil a role as guardians of procedural order and legal uniformity. It maps the main different judicial functions of the three principal categories of international courts: classic inter-state courts focused on dispute settlement, regime-supporting courts designed to sustain a contractual and institutional equilibrium between the regime's Member States and institutions and to encourage cooperation among the relevant stakeholders, and compliance-inducing courts expected to advance the enforcement of important international norms. It then identifies possible tensions between the functions that can be served by jurisdictional regulation and norm-harmonisation, on the one hand, and other judicial functions on the other. In the process, some possible justifications for prioritising the courts' jurisdictional-regulation and norm-harmonisation functions at the expense of their other functions are discussed.

The subsequent chapters discuss more specific approaches by which international courts and tribunals can and do seek to counteract the effects of fragmentation, although the extent that they can do may well depend on the conflicting functions identified by Shany in chapter one. Gruszczynski discusses the compatibility of WTO practice with the interpretative rules provided for in the Vienna Convention on the Law of Treaties (1969) and identifies instances where WTO dispute settlement bodies have diverged from Vienna Convention on the Law of Treaties provisions. He demonstrates that functional regimes such as that of the WTO can indeed see a reason to diverge from the general rules on interpretation. The chapter connects the issue of interpretation with the problem of fragmentation/unity of international law as a whole, and proposes some tentative observations with regard to WTO practice.

Zimmermann analyses various institutional, jurisdictional and procedural aspects of the interaction between the International Monetary Fund (IMF) and the WTO. This includes a discussion of how issues of jurisdictional overlap between the two organisations are decided. The IMF-WTO relationship is an interesting illustration of policy-coordination and resolution of jurisdictional issues between two international organisations of which one (the WTO) has a highly elaborated and efficient dispute settlement system whereas the other (the IMF) relies on a quite unique set of institutional mechanisms for overseeing compliance. Selected comparative institutional and procedural elements, drawn from the interaction of the international trading and monetary systems with the realms of international environmental, labour and investment protection, are used to put the IMF-WTO relationship into a larger perspective as part of the debate on unity or fragmentation of international law.

Paparinskis considers whether and how decisions by arbitral tribunals that discuss bilateral investment treaties are legally relevant for interpreting corresponding treaty rules in other (investment) treaties. This area is of particular relevance for the book as these tribunals are not engaged in diverse interpretations of a single treaty, but rather in the interpretation of a variety of different, but in substance overlapping treaties. Against the background of a complex mix between continuities, discontinuities and innovations, the contribution focuses on interpretative practices and considers whether they can be explained in traditional terms or require a formulation of a new framework of analysis.

Nordeide explores the European Court of Human Rights' approach to the interface between the European Convention for the Protection of Human Rights and Fundamental Freedoms (1950) and other rules of international law through treaty interpretation. The contribution explores what the Court's approach tells us about the challenges of integrating a regional human rights treaty into the wider system of international law. It focuses in particular on the Court's use of Article 31(3)(c) of the Vienna Convention on the Law of Treaties.

D'Aspremont sets the stage for the second part of the book which focuses on domestic courts. He examines whether international law contains some prescriptions regarding its interpretation by domestic courts. He zeroes in particularly on the extent to which domestic courts presuppose that international law constitutes a coherent and systemic set of rules, and apply the principle of systemic integration of international law enshrined in the Vienna Convention on the Law of Treaties. The contribution simultaneously aims at appraising whether domestic courts, because of different legal and institutional constraints, construe the systemic character of the international legal order differently from international courts and international legal scholars.

Tzanakopoulos traces the development, parameters, and effects of the *Solange* argument – an argument relevant to the book as it provides a normative justification for (national) courts to refrain from doing what is assumed to be the normal situation: following a prior binding decision of an international courts or decision of an international organisation as required by international law. The contribution traces the impact of the argument on various courts in their adoption of a deferential or defiant stance towards the international organisation which exercises conferred governmental powers. It concludes that by using the *Solange* argument, domestic courts, being agents of state practice, assert the existence of a list of 'core' or 'fundamental' rights which must be substantively and procedurally protected at whatever level the exercise of governmental powers takes place.

Harbo examines whether and to what degree national courts have entered into a judicial dialogue with the European Court of Human Rights, using as a case study the practice of the courts of the United Kingdom (UK) and Norway with regard to the proportionality analysis.

Whereas the Court is applying this proportionality analysis as an instrument of judicial review, UK and Norwegian courts have traditionally applied different assessment schemes. While it might be expected that the degree to which these national courts adopt proportionality analysis in law relevant to the Convention could be the consequence of judicial dialogue with the Court, an inquiry into relevant case law reveals, however, that the respective national courts have been reluctant to take on the proportionality analysis in human rights law. Furthermore, to the extent the respective national courts have taken on proportionality analysis this may not exclusively be a consequence of judicial dialogue.

Currie and Kindred illustrate the flux and fragmentation in the principles of state jurisdiction by examining Canada's treatment of the prevention, punishment and reparation of international human rights law violations. Canadian courts have recently issued a number of decisions that reflect the struggle over jurisdictional issues. In the public law case of *R v Hape* and subsequent decisions, the Supreme Court of Canada refused to apply Canada's international human rights obligations extraterritorially, arguing that to do so would violate the principle of foreign state sovereignty. In *Bouzari v Iran*, a leading appellate court declined jurisdiction in a private law suit involving serious human rights violations that took place abroad, based on traditional readings of the limitations of territorial jurisdiction and the privileges of state sovereignty. In each case, there are international law precedents or instruments that suggest a contrary result, but it cannot be said that there is a solid principle demanding it.

Webb considers how national courts are engaged in dialogue on immunities, examining the circumstances that encourage a high level of dialogue and those that discourage it. The contribution reviews the dialogue among international courts, including their use of national decisions to identify international custom.

Constantinides discusses the main justifications and patterns of transjudicialism and its relevance to the coherence of international law and jurisprudence. He presents a case study on transjudicial dialogue on diplomatic assurances against torture with a view to testing the theoretical propositions put forward. The practice of diplomatic assurances involves the return of aliens to their home country despite the prohibition on nonrefoulement, on the basis of assurances that the returnee will receive humane treatment, most notably that she/he will not be subjected to torture. There is a burgeoning international and domestic jurisprudence on the topic despite the lack of any specific international legal norm regulating it. The concluding remarks stress both the positive and negative aspects of transjudicialism, in particular the need not to lose sight of the interests of justice in transjudicial dialogue's quest for consistency.

Webster focuses on the concepts of unity and fragmentation as they emerge in the application of international human rights law by the courts of Japan. In his contribution, unity refers to relatively strong adherence to the letter of international treaty law, as well as relatively close conformity with the legal practices of other courts around the world. In the absence of such unity, one faces fragmentation of international law, when domestic practice deviates significantly from international practices or trends. Both elements, unity and fragmentation, are critical for understanding Japan's engagement with the international normative community, as the Japanese judiciary's response to these norms and obligations have been mixed. For example, international standards of criminal justice have had an impact on Japanese conceptions of certain trial rights. But there is less consistency on issues such as the right to equality and minority rights.

Ziegler addresses the application of WTO law in domestic courts, mainly on the basis of experiences in Swiss jurisprudence. The fact that WTO law is increasingly defining substantive rules regarding domestic administrative law has led to important changes in the relevance of WTO law for domestic courts. Nevertheless, absolute numbers of cases remain relatively low as domestic courts in most countries remain reluctant to use WTO law as a legal basis for their decisions. The contribution observes that domestic courts seem to be increasingly open to preferring an interpretation of domestic law that is compatible with a country's WTO obligations to one that leads to incoherence. It seems that slowly the concept of multilayered governance is being accepted by courts, but that interpretation of domestic legal sources in accordance with existing obligations is still preferred to giving priority to international obligations over domestic law.

In the concluding chapter, we draw on the main elements of the contributions and examine the extent to which, and in particular how, international and national courts contribute to or counteract negative effects of fragmentation in the international legal order.

2

One Law to Rule Them All: Should International Courts Be Viewed as Guardians of Procedural Order and Legal Uniformity?

YUVAL SHANY*

I. INTRODUCTION

COMMENTATORS CONCERNED WITH the increased fragmentation of international law into specialised legal regimes often view international courts and tribunals as a potential barrier against the dynamics of normative fragmentation. Indeed international courts can, and sometimes do, act as agents of legal unity (just as their domestic counterparts often serve as agents of legal unity within national legal systems).[1] They can minimise jurisdictional conflicts between different legal institutions purporting to render distinct authoritative normative statements relating to the same issues, reduce fragmentation by interpreting the rules of one legal regime in accordance with the rules of other legal regimes and general international law, follow consistent lines of jurisprudence within their own legal regime, and monitor the application of international law by national courts (for example, through EC Treaty, Article 234 (or Article 267 of the Treaty on the Functioning of the

* Hersch Lauerpacht Chair in Public International Law, Faculty of Law, Hebrew University of Jerusalem; Board of Directors, Project on International Court and Tribunals. The paper was prepared with the support of the European Research Council Starting Grant for Frontier Research. I thank Erin Gray for her research assistance, and Professor André Nollkaemper, Professor Ole Kristian Fauchald and Professor Geir Ulfstein for their comments on earlier drafts.

[1] See, eg: AH Putney, *United States Constitutional Law vol II: State Constitutions, Statutory Constructions* (Cleveland, Cree Publishing House, 1908) 285 ('The Courts make every effort to harmonize all existing portions of the law'); A Barak, *The Judge in a Democracy* (Princeton, Princeton University Press, 2006) 140 f (the objective interpretation of statutes requires integrating specific statutes within a broader normative environment).

EU) preliminary ruling types of procedure).[2] The question which this chapter seeks to examine is not whether international courts *could* invoke conflict-regulating and law-harmonising tools; it is rather whether international courts are likely to do so and if so, under what circumstances.

Significantly, the resort to jurisdiction-regulation rules and norm-harmonising techniques may interfere with some other functions entrusted to international courts, such as the provision of prompt and effective dispute resolution services (which may militate against a stay of proceedings in favour of other, more appropriate parallel procedures, or long and complicated 'comparative' studies of other branches of law), or the advancement of the specific goals of the regime under which the respective court operates (for example, excessive coordination and harmonisation with other regimes may dilute the normative and institutional impact of the court's own regime).[3] Moreover, legal pluralism may, at times, serve a useful purpose. International courts seeking to improve state compliance with international norms in the field of human rights, for example, may be inclined to provide their Member States with a margin of appreciation when applying the norms in question, rather than insisting on rigid legal uniformity.[4] In other words, reducing fragmentation and increasing normative harmony across international regimes may conflict with the other missions occupying international courts; or, put differently, expose conflicts of interest between the different sets of constituencies that the courts are serving – the immediate parties to the dispute, the state parties to the specific regime under which the court operates, and other national and international stakeholders – who may be pulling international courts in different directions. Any pro-coordination or pro-harmonisation agenda is likely to meet only some of the needs, interests and expectations of the aforementioned constituencies.

As a result, calling upon international courts to assume a more robust jurisdiction-regulating and norm-harmonising role should arguably be based on a theory that recognises and explains the different functions of international courts, establishes methods for reconciling tensions arising between their competing functions, and offers guiding principles as to when, and for what purpose, one judicial function (jurisdictional coordination or norm-harmonisation for example) should trump other functions. Moreover, different courts have unique judicial functions, or prioritise

[2] See, eg: A Arnull, *The European Union and its Court of Justice*, 2nd edn (Oxford, Oxford University Press, 2006) ch 4.

[3] See for a discussion of the policy considerations militating against jurisdictional regulation and normative harmonisation: Y Shany, *Regulating Jurisdictional Relations between National and International Courts* (Oxford, Oxford University Press, 2007) 109, 178 f, 190 f.

[4] See, eg: M Burstein, 'The Will to Enforce: An Examination of the Political Constraints Upon a Regional Court of Human Rights' (2006) 24 *Berkeley J Int'l L* 423, 439; D Shelton, 'The Boundaries of Human Rights Jurisdiction in Europe' (2003) 13 *Duke J Comp & Int'l L* 95, 134 f; WM Carter, Jr, 'A Reality Check: Rethinking Subsidiarity in International Human Rights Adjudication' (2008) 30 *Hamline J Pub L & Pol'y* 319, 319.

specific judicial functions. Consequently, the expounded theory must be flexible enough to accommodate different types of international courts (understood in this chapter as independent judicial bodies, created by an international instrument, and invested with the authority to apply international law to specific cases brought before them),[5] and to explore how the application of more robust jurisdiction-regulation and norm-harmonisation by international courts could be legitimised in different institutional contexts – if indeed it can be.

Although this chapter does not purport to present a coherent or comprehensive theory on the prioritising judicial functions, it hopes to encourage more thinking on the matter and to propose some future scholarship directions. Section II of this chapter maps, in very general terms, the main different judicial functions of the three principal categories of international courts: classic inter-state courts focused on dispute settlement (such as the International Court of Justice (ICJ) and the International Tribunal for the Law of the Sea (ITLOS)); regime-supporting courts designed to sustain a contractual and institutional equilibrium between the regime's Member States and institutions and to encourage cooperation among the relevant stakeholders (such as the European Court of Justice (ECJ) and the World Trade Organization (WTO)); and compliance-inducing courts expected to advance the enforcement of important international norms (such as the European Court of Human Rights (ECtHR) and the International Criminal Court (ICC)). I will then identify, in section III, possible tensions between the functions that can be served by jurisdiction-regulation and norm-harmonisation, on the one hand, and other judicial functions on the other. In the process, some possible justifications for prioritising the courts' jurisdiction regulation and norm-harmonisation functions at the expense of their other functions will be discussed. This analysis will facilitate some general observations and conclusions (expounded in sections IV and V), pertaining to the circumstances under which it may be legitimate and reasonable to expect international courts to engage in jurisdiction-regulation and norm-harmonisation.

[5] Romano defines an international judicial body as a body entrusted with five features: a) permanence; b) established by an international instrument; c) decides cases on the basis of international law; d) decides cases according to pre-existing rules of procedure; and e) a process leading to a binding decision. See: C Romano, 'The Proliferation of International Judicial Bodies: The Pieces of the Puzzle' (1999) 31 *NYU J Int'l L & Pol* 709, 712. See also: E Voeten, 'The Politics of International Judicial Appointments' (2009) 9 *Chi J Int'l L* 387, 389 (international courts are created 'by definition' by multiple governments); J Alvarez, *International Organizations As Law-Makers* (Oxford, Oxford University Press, 2006) 458; C Tomuschat, 'International Courts and Tribunals' in R Wolfrum (ed), *Max Planck Encyclopedia of Public International Law* (2008) (online edition, available at www.mpepil.com, last visited 1 June 2011) (defining international courts and tribunals as 'permanent judicial bodies made up of independent judges which are entrusted with adjudicating international disputes on the basis of international law according to a pre-determined set of rules of procedure and rendering decisions which are binding on the parties').

II. THE FUNCTIONS OF INTERNATIONAL COURTS

Courts are social institutions established within states in order to fulfil certain functions of governance: they settle disputes; interpret the law; and apply it to specific fact patterns. By providing an orderly outlet for conflict resolution, courts reduce violence and reaffirm the rule of law in society.[6] In international life, courts have fulfilled analogous functions, although given the volatility of international politics they have traditionally focused more on dispute settlement (that is, on actually resolving conflicts as a method of war-prevention), and less on a systematic development of the law in a manner that may exceed what is actually needed for the disposition of the immediate case.[7] As a result, it has not been uncommon for international courts to embrace pragmatic 'half-way' solutions in their judgments that are likely to please all litigants to some degree, or that otherwise appear to provide a fair basis for settlement.[8] With the gradual shift in international law's focus from the law of co-existence to the law of cooperation however,[9] the centre of gravity of international courts' work has also changed in ways that emphasise their norm elaboration (or, formally speaking, law-interpretation), and law-application functions.[10]

Although the lumping together of international courts offers us a general perspective on the contribution that international courts make to the world of international dispute settlement and institutional governance, adopting such a broad view naturally obscures many of the particular features of different international courts, and overlooks some of their unique missions and actual functions. In fact, the very existence of 'international courts' as an institutional category may suggest normative implications, as it emphasises the shared normative origin of the different courts (international law), their comparable constituency (states and other international actors), and their common mission (the settlement of international disputes, and international law-interpretation and application).

A somewhat more sophisticated analysis of the field of international adjudication would divide international courts into categories, according to

[6] See generally: S Shetreet (ed), *The Role of Courts in Society* (Dordrecht, Martinus Nijhoff Publishers, 1988); C Albiston, 'The Rule of Law and the Litigation Process: The Paradox of Winning by Losing' in HM Kritzer and SS Silbey (eds), *In Litigation*, (Stanford, Stanford University Press, 2003) 168, 200 f.

[7] See for a discussion: Y Shany, 'No Longer a Weak Department of Power? Reflections on the Emergence of a New International Judiciary' (2009) 20 *Eur J Int'l L* 73.

[8] See for a discussion: G Abi-Saab, 'Fragmentation of Unification: Some Concluding Remarks' (1999) 31 *NYU J Int'l L & Pol* 919, 930; Y Shany, 'Bosnia, Serbia and the Politics of International Adjudication' (2008) 45 *Justice* 21.

[9] See: WG Friedmann, *The Changing Structure of International Law* (New York, Columbia University Press, 1964) 60 ff.

[10] See for a survey of these developments: Y Shany (n 7).

the different models of functional combination and function-prioritisation they represent. Such models underscore the point that different courts have different dominant missions which may be incompatible, to a greater or lesser extent, with the protection of the systemic interests facilitated by jurisdictional coordination and norm-harmonisation. As a result, some types of courts may be more readily available than others for curbing the fragmentation of international law and promoting unity therein.

One could argue, for example, that 'classic' international courts (such as the ICJ and ITLOS), and inter-state arbitration tribunals have traditionally focused on settling disputes between states (with adjudication serving in this instance as a law-based alternative to diplomatic forms of dispute settlement such as mediation or conciliation), and that their law-interpretation and law-application functions, while important, are secondary in nature.[11] As a result, depending on the degree to which promoting systemic unity through jurisdictional coordination and norm-harmonisation complicates the resolution of specific disputes (for example, by introducing procedural delays, or expanding the scope of the contested legal issues), tensions may arise.[12]

At the same time, trade liberalisation and economic integration courts such the WTO Appellate Body (AB) and the ECJ appear to engage in the functions of dispute settlement, norm elaboration and compliance monitoring on a more or less equal basis – that is, they sustain cooperative relations among their Member States by resolving potentially destabilising conflicts; providing ongoing normative guidance which adapts the legal equilibrium underlying the regime to changing circumstances; and offering robust enforcement avenues – thereby strengthening the credibility of the parties' original undertakings and reducing the incentive for defections from the relevant regime.[13] Still, the specific functions of

[11] See, eg: D Shelton, 'Form, Function, and the Powers of International Courts' (2009) 9 *Chi J Int'l L* 537, 542 ('Some of the courts, like the ICJ and the International Tribunal for the Law of the Sea (ITLOS), are primarily intended to settle disputes between states'); AS Muller, D Raič and JM Thuránszky, 'The International Court of Justice: Its Future after Fifty Years – Editorial Introduction' in AS Muller, D Raič and JM Thuránszky (eds), *The International Court of Justice: Its Future after Fifty Years* (The Hague, Martinus Nijhoff Publishers, 1997) xxv, xxix; N Klein, *Dispute Settlement in the UN Convention on the Law of the Sea* (Cambridge, Cambridge University Press, 2005) 24 f. See also: Charter of the United Nations (UN Charter), art 33 (listing the ICJ as a dispute settlement mechanism to be considered in situations in which international peace and security are threatened); United Nations Convention on the Law of the Sea (10 December 1982) 1833 UNTS 396, art 287 (listing ITLOS in a 'menu' of dispute settlement procedures).

[12] See for a discussion: Shany (n 3) 178 f.

[13] See, eg: G Sacerdoti, 'The Role of Lawyers in the WTO Dispute Settlement System' in R Yerxa and B Wilson (eds), *Key Issues in WTO Dispute Settlement: The First Ten Years* (Cambridge, Cambridge University Press, 2005) 125, 127; SA Ghias, 'A Theoretical and Political Analysis of the WTO Appellate Body' (2006) 24 *Berkeley J Int'l L* 534, 548; P Van Den Bossche, *The Law and Policy of the World Trade Organisation*, 2nd edn (Cambridge, Cambridge University Press, 2008) 182 f; J Hunt, 'The European Court of Justice and the Court of First Instance' in A Warleigh (ed), *Understanding European Union Institutions* (London, Routledge,

economic courts must be viewed against the background of the specific legal regime to which they belong.[14] Arguably, a regime's goals, structures, and procedures shape and control the judicial functions of international courts belonging to that regime to a considerable degree. To the extent that promoting systemic interests through jurisdictional coordination and norm-harmonisation affects the dispute settling functions of economic courts and dilutes their regime norm-interpretation and application missions, frictions may arise here too.

Finally, international human rights courts and international criminal courts, such as the ECtHR and the ICC, seem to focus their energies on promoting state compliance with specific treaty norms (which are, in turn, reflective of important international societal values).[15] In this context, the introduction of jurisdictional coordination and norm-harmonisation measures may weaken the influence of the aforementioned courts (for example, by removing certain cases from the courts' docket) and reduce the impact of the relevant treaty norms.[16] In other words, pursuing systemic goals may adversely affect the compliance-inducing mission of 'humanitarian' courts.

Besides the three functional categories identified above, one may note that many international courts also perform unique functions other than dispute settlement, law-interpretation and law-application (these functions are normally prescribed in the relevant court's constitutive

2002) 103, 114; Arnull (n 13) 44; DS Law, 'A Theory of Judicial Power and Judicial Review' (2009) 97 *Geo LJ* 723, 760 ff. See also: Understanding on Rules and Procedures Governing the Settlement of Disputes (DSU), Marrakech Agreement Establishing the World Trade Organisation, Annex 2, Legal Instruments – Results of the Uruguay Round (15 April 1994) 33 ILM 1123, art 3(2); Treaty Establishing the European Community, 25 March 1957 (Consolidated Version) OJ C 325 (24 December 2002), art 220 ('The Court of Justice and the Court of First Instance, each within its jurisdiction, shall ensure that in the interpretation and application of this Treaty the law is observed'). But see: WTO Panel Report, *EC – Bananas III* (25 September 1997) WT/DS27/AB/R (suggesting that the principal function of the DSB Panels is dispute resolution).

[14] Regimes have been defined by one influential writer as 'sets of implicit or explicit principles, norms, rules, and decision-making procedures around which actors' expectations converge in a given area of international relations': SD Krasner, 'Structural Causes and Regime Consequences: Regimes as Intervening Variables' (1982) 36 *International Organization* 186.

[15] See, eg: Shelton (n 11) 542; SC Greer, *The European Convention on Human Rights: Achievements, Problems and Prospects* (2006) 166; Romano (n 5) 750. See also: European Convention on Human Rights and Fundamental Freedoms (4 November 1950) ETS 5, art 19 ('To ensure the observance of the engagements undertaken by the High Contracting Parties in the Convention and the Protocols thereto, there shall be set up a European Court of Human Rights.'); Rome Statute of the International Criminal Court (Rome Statute) (17 July 1998) 2187 UNTS 90, preamble (stating that the Court's mission is ending impunity).

[16] See, eg: *Al-Adsani v UK*, App No 35763/97, ECHR 2001-XI (ECtHR Grand Chamber holding that State immunity rules limit the application of the European Convention on Human Rights); *R (Al-Jedda) v Secretary of State for Defence* [2007] UKHL 58 (Security Council Resolution 1546 overrides the terms of the European Convention for Human Rights).

instruments.) Hence, for example: international criminal courts may be expected to generate long-term deterrence,[17] and to contribute to national reconciliation and the restoration of the rule of law in devastated societies;[18] the ECtHR is arguably expected to contribute to the 'achievement of greater unity' [19] among the Member States of the Council of Europe; the WTO Dispute Settlement Body (DSB) is expected to contribute to 'the effective functioning of the WTO and the maintenance of a proper balance between the rights and obligations of Members';[20] one of the primary missions of the ECJ is to ensure the uniform application of EC law across the EU;[21] and one of the primary missions of the European Free Trade Area (EFTA) Court is to harmonise EFTA/EEA law with EC law.[22]

It is therefore fair to say that many international courts serve at least two principal normative/political constituencies, as follows: 1) they serve the international community by comprising part of international law – mainly by virtue of the international law framework which directly or indirectly governs their creation and operation (international courts are typically created by international instruments governed by international law; the regimes establishing them are also created and governed, to some extent, by international law);[23] 2) they serve the stakeholders of a particular regime through comprising part of a specific treaty regime which addresses certain states only. In addition, courts serve a third, more limited constituency – the immediate parties to the dispute – whose needs and interests may only partly overlap with those of the two aforementioned broader constituencies. As the next section illustrates, instances of jurisdictional competition and normative fragmentation may put functions associated with the needs and interests of the three aforementioned constituencies in direct conflict with one another.

III. JURISDICTIONAL COMPETITION, NORMATIVE DISHARMONY AND CONFLICTING FUNCTIONS

According to parts of the literature on competing jurisdictions, a jurisdictional conflict between two international sets of proceedings may arise if

[17] Rome Statute, preamble ('*Determined* to put an end to impunity for the perpetrators of these crimes and thus to contribute to the prevention of such crimes') (emphasis added).

[18] Statute of the International Criminal Tribunal for Rwanda (ICTR), Annex to SC Res 955 (1994), preamble ('Prosecution of persons responsible for serious violations of international humanitarian law would . . . contribute to the process of national reconciliation and to the restoration and maintenance of peace').

[19] European Convention on Human Rights and Fundamental Freedoms, preamble.

[20] DSU, art 3(3).

[21] *R (ABNA Ltd) v Secretary of State for Health and Food Standards Agency*, C-435/03, 2005 ECR I-10423, para 104.

[22] *Norway v ESA* (Judgment) E-6/98 (20 May 1999), para 40.

[23] See: n 5.

the proceedings involve the same parties, and raise the same issues.[24] When parallel proceedings occur, jurisdiction-regulating principles designed to prevent procedural disorder and reduce the risk of conflicting judgments (such as exclusive jurisdiction provisions and the *lis alibi pendens* and *res judicata* rules) may be invoked. In many other instances, when the strict conditions ('same parties and same issues') that underlie most of the aforementioned rigid jurisdiction-regulating rules are not met, it has been argued that softer principles of judicial comity and *abus de droit* should be employed in order to minimise tensions between the competing procedures.[25] So, for example, it has been suggested that the latter-seized, or less-appropriate court, may stay proceedings in order to allow the other court to 'take a first bite at the apple' – that is, to engage in fact-finding, offer a legal analysis of the issues at stake, and attempt to resolve the pending dispute.[26]

In the same vein it has been proposed that international courts should, as much as possible, take cognisance of the decisions of their counterparts, and strive to follow their specific findings of fact and law when hearing related cases[27] (anticipating such cross-reliance, international courts may be well advised to formulate their decisions in ways that invite deference by other international courts – for example, couched in language that has a broad appeal outside the 'four corners' of any specific regime).[28] More generally, some writers have argued that international courts should assume the role of systemic coherence-generating agents, and strive to make their decisions conform to a principle of systemic integration that encourages, in turn, the building of bridges between their specific applicable law and the broader international law normative framework.[29]

The policy considerations that support at least some level of jurisdiction-regulation among courts are relatively straightforward. First, when viewed behind a 'veil of ignorance', there is little question that litigating the very same dispute before different international courts – a situation capable of

[24] See, eg: Y Shany, *The Competing Jurisdictions of International Courts and Tribunals* (Oxford, Oxford University Press, 2003); A Reinisch, 'The Use and Limits of Res Judicata and Lis Pendens as Procedural Tools to Avoid Conflicting Dispute Settlement Outcomes' (2004) 3 *Law & Prac Int'l Cts & Tribunals* 37.

[25] Shany (n 3) 165.

[26] See, eg: Shany (n 24) 147 f.

[27] ibid 124. See for a discussion of recent cross-reference trends: R Teitel and R Howse, 'Cross-Judging: Tribunalization in a Fragmented but Interconnected Global Order' (2009) 41 *NYU J Int'l L & Pol* 959.

[28] See: Shany (n 24). Similar principles may apply in the relations between national and international courts; see: Shany (n 3).

[29] See, eg: International Law Commission (ILC), Fragmentation of International Law: Difficulties Arising from the Diversification and Expansion of International Law (ILC Fragmentation Report), UN Doc A/CN.4/682 (2006) (finalised by Martti Koskenniemi) 206 ff; Shany (n 24) 120 ff.

giving rise to inconsistent judgments and excessive litigation costs[30] – is generally at odds with the cumulative interests of the immediate parties to dispute. Other considerations of judicial economy also militate in favour of some orderly division of labour between the different international courts. Moreover, opting for increased inter-regime coordination facilitates a comprehensive approach towards resolving complicated international disputes, which may also be viewed in line with the long-term interests of many disputing parties. Arguably, such an approach is more consistent with the interconnectedness of issues in the 'real world' than the alternative approach of disintegrating disputes into mini-disputes arising under specific regimes.[31]

Systemic interests – first and foremost, the need to maintain the unity of international law – militates in favour of a robust regulation of jurisdictional overlaps. Coordinating the work of different international courts litigating similar or related international problems strengthens normative links between the different legal regimes to which the courts belong, and contributes to the development and maintenance of a common normative international law 'umbrella'. Hence, engaging courts with one another's work and encouraging them to refrain from generating inconsistent decisions may minimise legal fragmentation[32] and underline the common projects of the international judiciary.

These diverse policy considerations not only support coordination between overlapping proceedings, they also support adopting a liberal definition of what constitutes the 'same dispute' standards – a determination that would invite the application of general jurisdiction-regulating rules, such as *lis alibi pendens*, or treaty-based exclusive jurisdiction provisions.[33] So, in illustration, the fact that two distinct rules belonging to two or more different legal regimes govern the same transaction or situation, should not necessarily entail the conclusion that the disputes governed by such rules are not the same. Everything would depend on the substantive degree of similarity between the contents of the parallel rules in question (that is, whether they 'point in the same direction', contain the same legal elements, are governed by comparable secondary rules, etc).[34]

30 See: J Pauwelyn and LE Salles, 'Forum Shopping Before International Tribunals: (Real) Concerns, (Im)Possible Solutions' (2009) 42 *Cornell Int'l LJ* 77, 83 ('The biggest concern with forum shopping among international tribunals seems to be, therefore, the concern of inconsistent rulings'). See for a more general discussion of the link between authority fragmentation and norm fragmentation: T Broude, 'Principles of Normative Integration and the Allocation of International Authority: The WTO, the Vienna Convention on the Law of Treaties, and the Rio Declaration' (2008) 6 *Loy U Chi Int'l L Rev* 173, 179 ff.

31 See for a discussion: Shany (n 3) ch 3.

32 ILC Fragmentation Report (n 29) paras 47–48.

33 See for a discussion: Shany (n 3) 133.

34 See for a discussion: T Broude and Y Shany, 'The International Law and Policy of Multi-Sourced Equivalent Norms' in T Broude and Y Shany, *Multi-Sourced Equivalent Norms in*

Of course, the aforementioned party-centred, institutional and systemic interests support not only jurisdictional coordination, but also, more generally, norm-harmonisation – that is, the evolution over time of generally consistent lines of jurisprudence before different international courts.[35] Such harmonisation may improve conditions by: meeting the legitimate expectation of parties that international laws and institutions produce consistent outcomes; enabling courts to save precious time and resources by relying on the work of their judicial counterparts; and fostering, more generally, legal coherence. Hence, courts may be well advised to embrace, whenever possible, legal interpretations that are consistent with the case law of other courts, and even more generally, with other sources of international law (such as other specific regimes, or general international law), and to develop robust norm-harmonising interpretive strategies.[36]

As compelling as these policy considerations may be, the fact of the matter is that many courts are reluctant to apply jurisdiction-regulating rules, and demonstrate relatively little interest in making their work conform to the related jurisprudence of other international courts and tribunals.[37] Hence, for instance, the WTO DSB refused to defer jurisdiction in favour of Southern Common Market (MERCOSUR) and North American Free Trade Agreement (NAFTA) dispute settlement procedures;[38] ITLOS declined to stay proceedings in *MOX* and *Southern Bluefin Tuna* despite parallel proceedings before regional dispute settlement bodies;[39] and many panels of the International Centre for Settlement of Investment Disputes (ICSID) have circumvented the application of contractual provisions referring investment disputes exclusively to local courts (provisions that may be understood as a form of jurisdiction-regulation).[40] In the same vein, the ECJ, for example, does not tend to cite the case law of other international courts (except the ECtHR and the EFTA Court);[41] and in *Tadić* the International Criminal Tribunal for the Former Yugoslavia (ICTY) refused

International Law (Oxford, Hart Publishing, 2011) 1.

[35] See for a discussion: C Brown, *A Common Law of International Adjudication* (Oxford, Oxford University Press, 2009) 232; Shany (n 24) 117 ff.

[36] See: ILC Fragmentation Report (n 29) 24 ('it may also be rationalized in terms of a *political obligation* on law-appliers to make their decisions cohere with the preferences and expectations of the community whose law they administer') (emphasis added).

[37] EU Petersmann, 'Justice as Conflict Resolution: Proliferation, Fragmentation, and Decentralization of Dispute Settlement in International Trade' (2006) 27 *U Pa J Int'l Econ L* 273, 283 ('most international judicial bodies operate in "splendid isolation", without explicit regulation of the jurisdictional interaction between international courts and with little, if any, regard for the jurisprudence of other international tribunals').

[38] WTO AB Report, *Mexico – Tax Measures on Soft Drinks and Other Beverages* (6 March 2006) WT/DS308/AB/R; Panel Report, *Argentina – Definitive Anti-Dumping Duties on Poultry from Brazil* (22 April 2003) WT/DS241/R.

[39] *Southern Bluefin Tuna (Australia and New Zealand v Japan)* (2000) 39 ILM 1359, Order of 27 August 1999; *MOX Plant (Ireland v UK)* (2003) 42 ILM 1187, Order of 3 December 2001.

[40] Shany (n 24) 70.

[41] C Baudenbacher, 'Globalisation of the Judiciary' (2003) 38 *Tex Int'l LJ* 397, 401.

to apply the ICJ case law on attribution of responsibility.[42] Of course, many other examples of lack of jurisdictional-coordination[43] and norm-harmonisation may be cited.[44]

While it may be possible to criticise, at times, such a lack of openness to other procedures and jurisprudence as a form of 'regime chauvinism', legal ignorance, or intellectual laziness, it appears that more fundamental considerations may be at play here.[45] Arguably, at the heart of the reluctance of international courts to coordinate their norms procedures with other international norms and procedures, one may find a strong sense that accommodating other regimes, the common international umbrella, and even the long-term interests of the disputing parties may compromise the unique and independent functions of the court in question.[46] At an even more fundamental level, one may even detect a rejection of the vision of a unified and coherent international legal framework that underlies jurisdictional coordination and norm-harmonisation:[47] if courts perceive their role as having been entrusted with giving expression to a specific agreement between a distinct group of sovereign states, then stepping

[42] *Prosecutor v Tadić* (Judgment) (15 July 1999) para 115.

[43] See, eg: Judge G Guillaume, 'The Proliferation of International Judicial Bodies: The Outlook for the International Legal Order' Speech to the Sixth Committee of the General Assembly of the United Nations (29 November 2000) available at www.icj-cij.org/court/index.php?pr=85&pt=3&p1=1&p2=3&p3=1 (last visited 1 June 2011).

[44] See for a thorough, although not fully current, analysis of inconsistencies in the case law of international courts: J Charney, 'Is International Law Threatened by Multiple International Tribunals?' (1998) 271 *Recueil des Cours* 101. See for more current assessments of normative fragmentation in international jurisprudence: WT Worster, 'Competition and Comity in the Fragmentation of International Law' (2008) 34 *Brooklyn J Int'l L* (2008) 119, 119 f. But see: R Higgins, 'A Babel of Judicial Voices? Ruminations from the Bench' (2006) 55 *Int'l & Comp L Q* 791; B Simma, 'Fragmentation in a Positive Light' (2004) 25 *Mich J Intl L* 845.

[45] See, eg: G de Burca, 'The European Court of Justice and the International Legal Order After Kadi' (2010) 51 *Harv Int'l LJ* 1, 3 f (referring to the language of the ECJ's *Kadi* judgment as 'chauvinistic' and 'parochial'). *cf* A Bayefsky and J Fitzpatrick, 'International Human Rights Law in US Courts: A Comparative Perspective' (1992) 14 *Mich J Int'l L* 1, 27 f (describing reluctance of US courts to embrace international human rights law as 'born partly because of unfamiliarity and perhaps a degree of intellectual laziness'). But see: M Tushnet, 'When is Knowing Less Better Than Knowing More? Unpacking the Controversy over Supreme Court Reference to Non-US Law' (2006) 90 *Minn L Rev* 1275, 1288 (suggesting that haphazardly citing the decisions of other courts is a form of intellectual laziness).

[46] See: C Romano, 'Patterns, Possibilities, and Problems: Deciphering the Grammar of the International Jurisprudential Dialogue' (2009) 41 *NYU J Int'l L & Pol* 755, 758 ('There are powerful constraints built into international courts' statutes that limit where judges can look for applicable law. Most international courts are by design self-contained legal islands. Moreover, a certain sense of pride and desire to defend one's own judicial turf are also important factors that prevent international judges from paying too much deference to their peers in other courts. Relying too much on other courts' jurisprudence is tantamount to abdicating one's own role').

[47] See: M Koskenniemi and P Leino, 'Fragmentation of International Law? Postmodern Anxieties' (2002) 15 *Leiden J Int'l L* 553. Similarly, Romano dismisses the systemic explanation for judicial-driven coordination and harmonisation, because it is premised on an unrealistic vision of judicial altruism. See, eg: Romano (n 46) 780.

outside the four corners of their explicit mandate could raise serious legitimacy concerns.[48]

The conflict between the unique and more general functions of international courts may be illustrated by some of the reasoning offered by courts when refusing to engage in jurisdiction-regulation or norm-harmonisation. In *Soft Drinks,* the WTO AB explained its refusal to defer jurisdiction to NAFTA in the following terms:

> The Appellate Body has repeatedly ruled that a panel would not fulfil its mandate if it were not to make an objective assessment of the matter. Under Article 11 of the DSU, a panel is, therefore, charged with the *obligation* to 'make an objective assessment of the matter before it, including an objective assessment of the facts of the case and the applicability of and conformity with the relevant covered agreements.' Article 11 also requires that a panel 'make such other findings as will assist the DSB in making the recommendations or in giving the rulings provided for in the covered agreements.' It is difficult to see how a panel would fulfil that obligation if it declined to exercise validly established jurisdiction and abstained from making any finding on the matter before it.[49]

In other words, the special responsibility for ensuring compliance with WTO law seemed to have required the WTO DSB to assume jurisdiction regardless of the alleged superior propriety of the NAFTA dispute settlement machinery.

In *Kadi* (a case dealing not with interaction between international courts, but more generally, with coordination across international regimes), the ECJ explained why it should not give effect to a Regulation implementing a Security Council Resolution in terms which are not dissimilar from the terms used by the WTO AB:

> [T]he Community judicature must, in accordance with the powers conferred on it by the EC Treaty, ensure the review, in principle the full review, of the lawfulness of all Community acts in the light of the fundamental rights forming an integral part of the general principles of Community law, including review of Community measures which, like the contested regulation, are designed to give effect to the resolutions adopted by the Security Council under Chapter VII of the Charter of the United Nations.[50]

The upshot of cases such as *Soft Drinks* and *Kadi* may be that the special functions of international courts might prevent them (or be perceived as

[48] L Scheeck, 'Inter-Judicial Dialogue, Institutional and Functional Legitimacy in Supranational Judiciary Spaces' (2008), 1, available at www.allacademic.com/meta/p251223_index.html (last visited 1 June 2011) ('supranational actors might increase the legitimacy of their *institutions* by importing norms, they also put at risk the legitimacy of their *function*, ie it appears that sometimes cases are decided with regard to institutional interests and precisely aim to "charm" other courts, whereas other legal issues fall into the background'); Romano (n 46) 780.

[49] *Soft Drinks* (n 38) para 51.

[50] *Kadi v Council* (Judgment) C-402/05 P (3 September 2008) para 326.

preventing them) from engaging in meaningful jurisdiction-regulation and normative harmonisation across legal regimes.

The other side of the coin may be that the very establishment of 'regime courts' or courts entrusted with special legal functions may reduce the level of jurisdiction-regulation and norm-harmonisation applied towards them by other courts. This is because the perception of a special court as being driven by idiosyncratic legal agendas may detract from the value of their decisions in the eyes of their international judicial counterparts. This may explain the reluctance of the ITLOS in the *MOX* to defer jurisdiction in favour of parallel dispute settlement procedures, operating under specific treaties or regimes:

> [T]he application of international law rules on interpretation of treaties to identical or similar provisions of different treaties may not yield the same results, having regard to, *inter alia*, differences in the respective contexts, objects and purposes, subsequent practice of parties and *travaux préparatoires*.[51]

In other words, differences in the *anticipated* manner of application of the international law of the sea by ITLOS and the other competent courts underlay the former's decision to regard the parallel proceedings as not involving the same legal issues, and thus to refrain from applying a jurisdiction-regulating rule governing *similar* proceedings.

In the same vein, in *Bosnian Genocide*, the ICJ explained why the ICTY's decision to depart from ICJ jurisprudence on state responsibility should not be followed, in terms that allude to the special criminal law prism employed by the ICTY:

> [T]he Court observes that the ICTY was not called upon in the *Tadić* case, nor is it in general called upon, to rule on questions of State responsibility, since its jurisdiction is criminal and extends over persons only. Thus, in that Judgment the Tribunal addressed an issue which was not indispensable for the exercise of its jurisdiction. As stated above, the Court attaches the utmost importance to the factual and legal findings made by the ICTY in ruling on the criminal liability of the accused before it and, in the present case, the Court takes fullest account of the ICTY's trial and appellate judgments dealing with the events underlying the dispute. The situation is not the same for positions adopted by the ICTY on issues of general international law which do not lie within the specific purview of its jurisdiction and, moreover, the resolution of which is not always necessary for deciding the criminal cases before it.[52]

It thus appears that systemic policy arguments favouring jurisdiction-regulation and norm-harmonisation carry little weight with judicial institutions that do not regard themselves as operating in a unified international legal system, or feel inhibited from resorting to a broad agenda which

[51] *MOX* (n 39) para 51.

[52] *Application of the Convention on the Prevention and Punishment of the Crime of Genocide (Bosnia and Herzegovina v Serbia and Montenegro)* (Judgment) [2007] ICJ Rep 43, para 403.

they were not explicitly authorised to pursue by the states or institutions that created them. One may also refer to concerns about the increased complication of procedures which coordination and harmonisation may entail, and the limited familiarity of many international courts with the operation of, and law applicable before, other judicial institutions. As a result, any call upon international courts to assume a greater jurisdiction-regulating and norm-harmonising role must be based on justifications and a theoretical position that offers guidance as to when, and for what purpose, one set of judicial functions (such as jurisdictional coordination and norm-harmonisation) should trump the other functions fulfilled by international courts.

IV. THE NORMATIVE AND INSTITUTIONAL DILEMMA

The multiplicity of functions of international courts and the divergent expectations of their different constituencies (such as the immediate parties to the dispute, the stakeholders in the regime under which the court operates, and the broader international community) generates chronic tensions which are integral to the decision whether or not to engage in jurisdiction-regulation and norm-harmonisation. Whereas certain functions and certain stakeholder interests clearly support such strategies, other functions and stakeholder interests point in the other direction. The question I address in this section is whether it is reasonable to expect international courts to prioritise their coordination and harmonisation functions over all other judicial functions – and, by necessary implication, to accord preference to the needs and expectations of some constituencies over those of others.

Elsewhere I have taken a strong position in favour of encouraging all international courts to engage in jurisdiction-regulation and norm-harmonisation.[53] Among the arguments I raised at the time, the following points were included: a) that international law ultimately serves as a legitimating factor for all specific regimes. As a result, the long-term interest in legitimacy of all specific regimes should support jurisdictional coordination and norm-harmonisation if it contributes to the 'systemic wellbeing' of general international law; b) that the weakness of the dispute-settling structures that are in place at the international level (especially, the lack of strong enforcement agencies) places a particular responsibility on international courts to conduct their business in ways that would be conducive to the disputing parties' long-term interest in effective resolution of the

[53] Shany (n 24). See also: C Leathley, 'An Institutional Hierarchy to Combat the Fragmentation of International Law: Has The ILC Missed an Opportunity?' (2007) 40 *NYU J Int'l L & Pol* 259, 299.

dispute; and c) that general international law – a body of law which is applied by most international courts – has a pro-systemic bias, which should impact on the manner of its application.[54]

Whilst I have not reversed my basic position on the subject, recent cases such as *Kadi* and *Bosphorus*[55] have demonstrated that expecting courts to engage in jurisdiction-regulation or norm-harmonisation without strong support for such an approach from the regimes in which they operate, may be too much to ask for. All stakeholders have expectations from international courts. Such expectations are often reflected explicitly in the courts' constitutive instruments which may limit the courts' ability to invoke general international law[56] or prioritise specific sets of considerations.[57] At times, such expectations are conveyed to the courts via more circumspect methods, such as informal communications.[58] Still, some stakeholders are more 'equal' than others. Arguably, with regard to 'regime courts', the overarching regime stakeholders (that is, the dominant political institutions of the regime in which the court functions such as the Commission and Council in the case of the ECJ), and the Member States participating in the regime, exert the strongest pressure on the courts. The courts are financed by the overarching regime, their judges and other senior officials are elected by Member States of the regime or by other regime institutions, and the judges and other court officials interact extensively (formally and informally) with individuals working for the other regime institutions and the Member States. All of these regime stakeholders may try to influence the court's work so as to advance their idiosyncratic interests and preferences (which may conflict with one

[54] See for a comparable argument, identifying a normative penumbra, governing the manner of application of international law: A Nollkaemper, 'The International Quality of Domesticated International Norms' in T Broude and Y Shany (eds), *Multi-Sourced Equivalent Norms in International Law* (Oxford, Hart Publishing, 2011).

[55] *Bosphorus v Ireland*, App No 45036/98, ECHR 2005-VI.

[56] See, eg: DSU, art 3(2) ('Recommendations and rulings of the DSB cannot add to or diminish the rights and obligations provided in the covered agreements').

[57] See, eg: Rome Statute, art 22(2) ('The definition of a crime shall be strictly construed and shall not be extended by analogy. In case of ambiguity, the definition shall be interpreted in favour of the person being investigated, prosecuted or convicted').

[58] See for an example of an indirect conveyance of expectations about the limits of a court's function: C Del Ponte, *Madame Prosecutor* (New York, Other Press, 2009) 68 ('No one in NATO ever pressured me to refrain from investigating the bombing campaign or from undertaking a prosecution based upon it. But I quickly concluded that it was impossible to investigate NATO, because NATO and its member states would not cooperate with us. They would not provide us access to the files and documents. Over and above this, however, I understood that I had collided with the edge of the political universe in which the Tribunal was allowed to function'). See also: AM Danner, 'When Courts Make Law: How the International Criminal Tribunals Recast the Laws of War' (2006) 59 *Vand L Rev* 1, 48 f ('The ICTY, therefore, can also be seen as a quite sophisticated agent – one that understood the tacit message of the Security Council and stayed within the boundaries desired by the principal's key members').

another).[59] In addition, the professional background of the judges and their future career paths normally places them well within an epistemological and political community that prioritises the same set of goals and values that the regime promotes (such as trade liberalisation, criminal deterrence, human rights promotion, etc).[60] As a result, judges sitting on specific courts enjoy, in Slaughter and Helfer's words, only 'constrained independence' vis-a-vis the overarching regime,[61] and it would be anything but surprising if the ultimate loyalty of judges sitting in regime courts would not rest within their 'own' specific regime.

If judges do indeed tend, as an empirical matter, to prefer regime interests over the interests of the international community as a whole (a hypothesis which is supported by the anecdotal cases discussed above, but would need further empirical substantiation),[62] then courts operating outside specific treaty regimes are more likely to apply jurisdiction-regulation rules and norm-harmonisation principles than courts operating within such regimes. So, for example, one would expect the ICJ to be more open to the systemic concerns underlying jurisdiction-regulation and norm-harmonisation than the ECJ.[63] This is especially so in light of the designation of the ICJ under the UN Charter as the UN 'principal judi-

[59] See, eg: G Garrett, 'The Politics of Legal Integration in the European Union' (1995) 49 *International Organization* 171, 174 ('if member governments have neither changed nor evaded the European legal system, then . . . it must be the case that the existing legal order furthers the interests of national governments'); LR Helfer and AM Slaughter, 'Toward a Theory of Effective Supranational Adjudication' (1997) 107 *Yale LJ* 273, 333 ('A supranational tribunal can invoke the power of law and the interests of ordinary citizens, but these appeals will be far less persuasive if they do not resonate with domestic political values'). See more generally: W Mattli and AM Slaughter, 'Constructing the European Community Legal System from the Ground Up: The Role of Individual Litigants And National Courts', text accompanying fn 78, available at www.jeanmonnetprogram.org/papers/96/9606ind.html (last visited 1 June 2011) ('judicial decisions that consistently and sharply contradict majority policy preferences are likely to undermine perceptions of judicial legitimacy and can result in legislative efforts to restrict or even curtail judicial jurisdiction – the scope of judicial power over particular classes of cases. An astute judge will anticipate these reactions and seek to avoid them').

[60] See, eg: M Koskenniemi, 'The Politics of International Law – 20 Years Later' (2009) 20 *Eur J Int'l L* 7, 10 ('the centre may have completely collapsed, its place taken by a plethora of specialisations, each with its own preferred idiom, career prospects, and, of course, structural bias').

[61] LR Helfer and AM Slaughter, 'Why States Create International Tribunals: A Response to Professors Posner and Yoo' (2005) 93 *Cal L Rev* 899, 930 f.

[62] See for support: I Canor, 'Between Dédoublement Fonctionnel and Balancing of Values: Three Replies to Pasquale De Sena and Maria Chiara Vitucci' (2009) 20 *Eur J Int'l L* 870, 881 (the distancing of the ECJ in *Kadi* from general international law is indicative of its ultimate loyalty); EA Posner and JC Yoo, 'Judicial Independence in International Tribunals' (2005) 93 *Cal L Rev* 1, 27 ('Tribunals composed of dependent members have a strong incentive to serve the joint interests of the disputing states. Tribunals composed of independent members have a weaker incentive to serve those states' interests').

[63] Still, the ICJ has relied directly on art 31(3)(c) of the Vienna Convention on the Law of Treaties – a key norm-harmonising provision – only in one case: *Oil Platforms (Iran v US)* [2003] ICJ Rep 161, 182.

cial organ'[64] – a position which allegedly confers upon the ICJ the responsibility of addressing the systemic problems arising from the operation of specific courts, with more limited geographical and substantive reach.

In fact, the ICJ's jurisdiction-regulating role has been minor.[65] The lack of rich ICJ jurisprudence on the subject may be explained by the overall limited number of cases referred to that body – a predicament which may have had the double effect of reducing the instances in which the ICJ actually interacts with other legal procedures, and rendering ICJ judges more reluctant to surrender jurisdiction in the event of jurisdictional overlap. Interestingly enough, the record of the Permanent Court of International Justice (PCIJ) on jurisdiction-regulation has been more impressive – a fact related perhaps to the extensive jurisdictional overlap between the various post-First World War adjudicative mechanisms dealing with the war's aftermath.[66] With respect to norm-harmonisation, recent ICJ jurisprudence shows growing awareness of the need to follow the case law of other courts.[67] Still, the refusal of the ICJ in the *Bosnian Genocide* case to embrace the ICTY's *Tadić* standard for attributing responsibility for non-state militia conduct[68] illustrates the limits of the ICJ's norm-harmonising role: the central position of the ICJ in international life generates expectations among ICJ judges that other courts would conform themselves to their case law, and not vice versa.

Another group of adjudicatory bodies, which operate outside the framework of a specific regime, and could thus theoretically have been more amenable to weighing systemic considerations, are international arbitration tribunals. Still, since such tribunals were established by the parties to the dispute, they are likely to prioritise the interests of the parties over those of third parties (including the international community).[69] Hence, they too, like regime courts, are expected to accord only limited relative weight to the interests of the international community in jurisdiction-regulation and norm-harmonisation.

In sum, the institutional constraints under which many international courts operate do not permit them to advance systemic interests via the adoption of jurisdiction-regulating and norm-harmonising measures, notwithstanding the fact that such interests are desirable from a broad international community perspective. The logical conclusion, which is

[64] UN Charter, art 92.

[65] See for a discussion: Shany (n 24) 247 ff.

[66] See, eg: *Mavrommatis Palestine Concessions,* 1924 PCIJ Rep Series A No 2; *Certain German Interests in Polish Upper Silesia,* 1925 PCIJ Rep Series A No 5; *Factory at Chorzów Factory,* 1927 PCIJ Rep Series A No 9; 1928 *Rights of Minorities in Upper Silesia (Minority Schools)*, 1928 PCIJ Rep Series A No 15; *Prince von Pless Administration,* 1933 PCIJ Rep Series A/B No 57.

[67] See, eg: *Legal Consequences of a Wall Constructed in the Occupied Palestinian Territory* [2004] ICJ Rep 136, 179; *Bosnian Genocide* (n 52) paras 188–209. Still, the ICJ has relied directly on art 31(3)(c) of the Vienna Convention on the Law of Treaties only once, see (n 63).

[68] *Bosnian Genocide* (n 52) para 403.

[69] See: Posner and Yoo (n 62) 27.

supported by the anecdotal cases discussed above, is that courts are primarily loyal to the regimes under which they operate (in the case of regime courts) or to immediate parties to the dispute (in the case of international arbitration tribunals). Such international courts are likely to engage in pro-systemic jurisdiction-regulation and norm-harmonising only if they can be convinced that the interests of their more immediate stakeholders would be served by a systemic approach. In other words, the broader 'systemic welfare' interests must be legitimised through appeal to the more specialised interests of the specific regime and parties.

V. THE WAY FORWARD

Although from a normative perspective, a strong case can be made in favour of the proposition that jurisdiction-regulation and norm-harmonisation are worthy functions which all international courts should pursue, most courts face limited institutional incentives to actually employ such strategies. At the end of the day, it seems that the fragmentation of international law can be slowed down or reversed only if stakeholders in specific regimes come to appreciate the long-term problems that fragmentation presents for their own regimes, thus creating for them new incentives to coordinate their courts' procedure and jurisprudence. The experience of the ECJ and ECtHR is particularly interesting from this perspective. The overlapping membership in their treaty regimes, and the expectation of stakeholders in both regimes for coordination and harmonisation – an expectation which is strongly related to the EU's quest for political legitimacy and the Council of Europe's support of European integration – has led the two Courts to embrace reciprocal jurisdiction-regulation and norm-harmonisation strategies.[70] The inclination of the EFTA Court to follow ECJ case law is another example of mutuality of goals leading to improved harmonisation.[71]

However, even when there is an incentive to coordinate judicial activities between two or more related regimes, there may not be a similar incentive to coordinate with other regimes. Again, the ECJ and its different treatment of ECtHR case law on the one hand, and WTO case law and

[70] See, eg: *Bosphorus v Ireland* (n 55). See generally: D Spielmann, 'Human Rights Case Law in Strasbourg and Luxembourg: Conflicts, Inconsistencies and Complementarities' in P Alston et al (eds), *The EU and Human Rights* (Oxford, Oxford University Press, 1999) 757, 772 ff. In the same vein, the Council of Europe's Member States heavy involvement in peacekeeping, may have led the ECtHR to identify with the broader international interests supporting such operations and to release Member States from liability for violations committed in the course of peacekeeping operations. *Behrami v France* (Decision on Admissibility), App No 71412/01 (2 May 2007).

[71] See: C Baudenbacher, 'The EFTA Court: An Actor in the European Judicial Dialogue' (2005) 28 *Fordham Int'l LJ* 353.

Security Council Resolutions on the other hand, is an instructive example of the contingent and political context-based nature of the jurisdiction-regulation and norm-harmonisation efforts. Such differences in treatment may be explained partly through geo-political and cultural factors, but may also be explained through variations in functional overlaps. Courts fulfilling similar functions or belonging to comparable functional models are, for example, more likely to relate to one another's legal experience than another set of courts.

In the same vein, *ad hoc* tribunals established by the parties to the dispute are expected to prioritise the interests of the parties and will embrace jurisdiction-regulation and norm-harmonisation measures only if such a strategy is perceived to serve the parties' best interests (for example, to avert conflicting judgments, reduce the overall costs of litigation, or meet the legitimate expectations of the parties in obtaining consistent outcomes from different international courts). It is interesting to note in this context that whereas ITLOS (which operates within the framework of UNCLOS – a weak treaty regime) refused to apply jurisdiction-regulating rules in the aforementioned *Bluefin Tuna* and *MOX* cases, the two arbitral tribunals to which the cases were ultimately referred have declined jurisdiction in favour of other dispute settlement procedures.[72] This may be indicative of *ad hoc* bodies giving greater weight to the interests of the parties in avoiding conflicting judgments than permanent courts.[73] There may be limits however, to the willingness of arbitral tribunals to prioritise the needs of the disputing parties. When the adoption of jurisdiction-regulating principles would lead to the tribunal's own dissolution, the self-interest of the arbitrators in preserving the process may trump all other considerations.[74] In this respect, the *Bluefin Tuna* and *MOX* awards are quite exceptional.

In sum, the appeal to systemic considerations as the basis of jurisdiction-regulation and norm-coordination measures is unlikely to garner the broad support of international courts in practice, given the institutional incentives to prioritise the expectations of other stakeholders such as the overarching regime or the disputing parties. The academic project of addressing institutional coordination and norm fragmentation at the international level must, as a result, focus greater attention and effort on identifying common interests across stakeholders as a possible way for legitimising jurisdictional coordination and norm-harmonisation by the

[72] *MOX Plant (Ireland v UK)* (n 39); *Southern Bluefin Tuna (Australia and New Zealand v Japan)* (n 39).

[73] The intuition that arbitrators are better situated than courts to prioritise party interests underlies Posner and Yoo's controversial article on effectiveness of international courts; see: Posner and Yoo (n 62).

[74] See, eg: TE Carbonneau, 'The Ballad of Transborder Arbitration' (2002) 56 *U Miami L Rev* 773, 801.

different international courts. Furthermore, since the discussion above suggests that in their current configuration most international courts have only a limited appetite for coordination and harmonisation across legal regimes, other – non-judicial – methods for institutional coordination and normative harmonisation ought to be explored.

3

Customary Rules of Interpretation in the Practice of WTO Dispute Settlement Bodies

LUKASZ GRUSZCZYNSKI*

I. INTRODUCTION

THE INTERPRETATIVE RULES that are used in the adjudicative practice of the World Trade Organization (WTO) have become the object of increasing attention over the last few years. Some scholars and practitioners have voiced a need for special interpretative rules that would reflect the distinctiveness of the WTO system.[1] Others have disagreed, noting that the instructions provided for in Articles 31 to 33 of the Vienna Convention on the Law of Treaties[2] are sufficiently flexible to accommodate any particularities of WTO law.[3] There is also a disagreement among scholars as to the compatibility of the interpretative methods actually used by the WTO dispute settlement bodies with the Vienna Convention on the Law of Treaties. Once again there are those who believe that both the Appellate Body (AB) and panels follow the language of the Vienna Convention,[4] and those who argue that the approach of the WTO dispute settlement bodies is not always compatible with the standards established by Articles 31 to 33.[5] At the same time, many of the latter

* Assistant Professor, Institute of Legal Studies, Polish Academy of Science. I would like to thank Professor Nollkaemper and Professor Fauchald for their valuable comments on the earlier versions of this chapter. Of course all omissions and mistakes remain my sole responsibility. The author may be contacted at Lukasz.Gruszczynski@eui.eu.

[1] *cf* discussion in section II of this chapter.

[2] Vienna Convention on the Law of Treaties (23 May 1969) 1155 UNTS 331.

[3] *cf* discussion in section II of this chapter.

[4] I Van Damme, *Treaty Interpretation by the WTO Appellate Body* (London, Oxford University Press, 2009) 57.

[5] See, eg: F Ortino, 'Treaty Interpretation and the WTO Appellate Body Report in US-Gambling: A Critique' (2006) 9(1) *J Int'l Econ L* 117.

critics fail to identify any specific examples of such divergences in WTO practice.[6]

The application of general/specific rules of interpretation in WTO jurisprudence may also be connected with the broader problem of fragmentation and/or unity of international law. The reliance by the WTO dispute settlement bodies on specific rules, distinct from those that are applied by other international tribunals, will most probably contribute to the fragmentation of international law and play a part in creating self-contained regime, while reliance on the interpretative provisions included in the Vienna Convention on the Law of Treaties (as well as on other generally recognised rules of interpretation that are not codified in the Convention) will have a de-fragmentation effect and lead to greater convergence among different international legal systems. This issue, although sometimes discussed in the literature,[7] appears to be under-investigated.

Taking into account the above context, this chapter discusses the compatibility of WTO practice with the interpretative rules provided for in the Vienna Convention on the Law of Treaties and identifes those instances where WTO dispute settlement bodies have decided to diverge from the Convention's provisions. Based on that, the chapter connects the issue of interpretation with the problem of fragmentation and/or unity of international law as a whole, and proposes some tentative observations with regard to WTO practice. The analysis presented here should not be seen as exhaustive, as it is based on the qualitative assessment of a limited number of cases. Nevertheless, in the opinion of the author the issues identified may reflect broader problems that exist in WTO jurisprudence.

The first section of the chapter describes the general practice of the WTO dispute settlement bodies with regard to the rules provided by the Vienna Convention on the Law of Treaties. The second and third sections concentrate on those instances where the approach of panels and the AB is not entirely compatible with the Vienna Convention. In this context, the chapter identifies two types of situations – relying on overly textual methods, and limiting the role of non-WTO rules in the process of interpretation – and illustrates each of them with relevant examples. The last part of the chapter analyses the significance of those situations for the issue of fragmentation and/or unity of international law.

[6] *cf* S Picciotto, 'The WTO's Appellate Body: Legal Formalism as a Legitimation of Global Governance' (2005) 18(2) *Governance: An International Journal of Policy, Administration, and Institutions* 477.

[7] Notably: International Law Commission (ILC), Fragmentation of International Law: Difficulties Arising from the Diversification and Expansion of International Law (ILC Fragmentation Report), UN Doc A/CN.4/682 (2006) (finalised by Martti Koskenniemi).

II. CUSTOMARY RULES OF INTERPRETATION IN THE WTO JURISPRUDENCE

WTO panels and the AB have progressively recognised the rules of the Vienna Convention on the Law of Treaties as relevant to the process of interpretation of WTO agreements.[8] Pursuant to Article 3(2) of the Understanding on Rules and Procedures Governing the Settlement of Disputes (DSU), dispute settlement bodies are to interpret provisions of WTO agreements in accordance with the customary rules of interpretation of public international law.[9] According to the AB, and in line with the prevailing view in the international community,[10] Articles 31 to 33 of the Vienna Convention on the Law of Treaties provide a codified version of such customary rules of interpretation.[11] The mandatory language used by Article 3(2) of the DSU implies that the WTO dispute settlement bodies are under an actual legal obligation to follow those rules.[12] However, it has also been noted in the literature that due to the status of those rules in the international legal order (being a part of international customary law), even without the explicit reference in Article 3(2) of the DSU, WTO panels and the AB would still be obliged to apply them when interpreting WTO law.[13]

[8] There seems to be a disagreement among scholars as to the nature of arts 31–33 of the Vienna Convention on the Law of Treaties. Some believe that they are nothing more than a methodological device and cannot be regarded as legally binding rules; *cf* Jan Klabber on the Opinio Juris webpage, available at http://opiniojuris.org/tag/gardiner-treaty-interpretation-symposium (last visited 1 June 2011). Others describe them as principles, not rules, that set general guidance, eg: Van Damme (n 4) 56. At the same time, there are number of AB reports that refer to arts 31–33 as legally binding rules giving a rise to specific obligations; *cf* cases referred to in WTO AB Report (n 12). This is also the approach taken in this chapter. Of course this does not mean that arts 31–33 establish rigid and inflexible obligations. On the contrary, the Vienna Convention on the Law of Treaties only provides general rules that leave an interpreter with a considerable margin of discretion.

[9] Understanding on Rules and Procedures Governing the Settlement of Disputes, Marrakesh Agreement Establishing the World Trade Organisation, Annex 2, Legal Instruments – Results of the Uruguay Round (15 April 1994) 33 ILM 1123 (DSU) art 3(2) ('The dispute settlement system of the WTO is a central element in providing security and predictability to the multilateral trading system. The Members recognize that it serves to preserve the rights and obligations of Members under the covered agreements, and to clarify the existing provisions of those agreements in accordance with customary rules of interpretation of public international law').

[10] Van Damme (n 4) 50.

[11] See, eg: WTO AB Report, *Japan – Taxes on Alcoholic Beverages* (1 November 1996) WT/DS8/AB/R, WT/DS10/AB/R, WT/DS11/AB/R, 10; WTO AB Report, *European Communities – Customs Classification of Frozen Boneless Chicken Cuts* (27 September 2005) WT/DS269/AB/R, WT/DS286/AB/R and Corr 1 (27 September 2005) para 282; WTO AB Report, *United States – Standards for Reformulated and Conventional Gasoline* (20 May 1996) WT/DS2/AB/R, para 17.

[12] WTO AB Report, *European Communities – Customs Classification of Certain Computer Equipment* (22 June 1998) WT/DS62/AB/R, WT/DS67/AB/R, WT/DS68/AB/R, para 84.

[13] Van Damme (n 4) 22; CD Ehlermann, 'Six Years on the Bench of the 'World Trade Court'. Some Personal Experience as Member of the Appellate Body of the World Trade Organization' (2002) 36(4) *J World Trade* 605, 617.

Since Articles 31 to 33 of the Vienna Convention on the Law of Treaties do not include all existing customary rules of interpretation of public international law, it was natural for the WTO dispute settlement bodies to rely on other interpretative guidelines. As noted by Lennard, 'they have been treated in WTO fora as emerging naturally from the expressed principles in the Vienna Convention',[14] particularly the good faith principle. This catalogue is broad and includes, among other things, the principle of effective treaty interpretation; the principle in dubio mitius (if the meaning of the term is ambiguous, that meaning is to be preferred which is less onerous to the party assuming an obligation);[15] the presumption of consistency (different terms are understood as having different meanings);[16] and the concept of evolutionary meaning (generic terms may be interpreted in an evolutionary manner).[17] Some calls have been also made urging the development of more specific rules of interpretation which would reflect the special character of WTO obligations, and which may diverge from the principles contained in the Vienna Convention on the Law of Treaties. In particular, the Special Consultative Board to the WTO Director-General noted that 'the customary international law rules of interpretation are, themselves, sometimes questionable when applied in the context of very detailed and intricate economic obligations of the WTO'.[18] The Board also added that 'there are many different techniques that can be used for interpreting a treaty, and the Appellate Body has utilised many of the rules that are necessary'.[19] Unfortunately, the Board neither identified those instances nor proposed any coherent and comprehensive alternatives to the rules of the Vienna Convention on the Law of Treaties.[20] Moreover, if one examines the WTO case law, it is difficult to find any consistent practice that would rely on such special rules of interpretation. In fact, in one of the reports, the AB explicitly refused to recognise the 'interpretative principle directing Panels to bias towards the reduction of tariff commitments'.[21] It is also worth referring here to the statement of the former member of the AB, who observed that WTO case law 'does not reveal any mention of, or reference to, one or more rules of interpretation specific to this particular field that would come to comple-

[14] M Lennard, 'Navigating by the Stars: Interpreting the WTO Agreement' (2002) 5(1) *J Int'l Econ L* 17, 55.

[15] WTO AB Report, *EC Measures Concerning Meat and Meat Products* (13 February 1998) WT/DS26/AB/R, WT/DS48/AB/R, fn 154.

[16] ibid para 164.

[17] WTO AB Report, *United States – Import Prohibition of Certain Shrimp and Shrimp Products* (6 November 1998) WT/DS58/AB/R, 2755, para 153.

[18] WTO, Consultative Board to the Director-General Supachai Panitchpakdi, *The Future of the WTO – Addressing Institutional Challenges in the New Millennium* (Geneva, 2004) para 235.

[19] ibid.

[20] Van Damme (n 4) 59 f.

[21] WTO AB Report, *EC – Chicken Cuts* (n 11) para 189.

ment or substitute for the . . . general rule'.[22] Of course, as was mentioned above, both panels and the AB rely not only on Articles 31 to 33 of the Vienna Convention on the Law of Treaties but also refer to other rules, which nevertheless are to be qualified as general customary international law.

In the WTO context, the text of the treaty remains, in line with the Vienna Convention on the Law of Treaties, a central element of the interpretative process.[23] The normal practice is to contextualise the text of a provision (determined initially on the basis of dictionaries) with the text, preamble and annexes of a particular WTO agreement,[24] as well as any agreement or instrument related to the treaty.[25] WTO case law also recognises the relevance of the good faith requirement in the process of interpretation.[26] In practice, this is sometimes translated into the principle of effective treaty interpretation, which requires the interpreter to read different provisions in a harmonious way so as to give meaning to all of them.[27] Nonetheless, it has been noted in the literature that the application of the good faith principle does not change the 'result found after applying the other interpretative criteria of Article 31, ie wording, context and object and purpose of the treaty'.[28]

Part of the contextualisation is also provided by the purpose and an object of a treaty. Both elements are normally conceptualised as referring to a treaty as a whole and not to a particular term or provision.[29] Arguably, a purpose and an object may be sought not only in the preamble of a particular agreement, but also in the Marrakesh Agreement, which is an umbrella treaty for other WTO agreements. WTO case law, at least in theory, fully accepts the relevance of the elements enumerated in Article 31(3)

[22] G Abi-Saab, 'The Appellate Body and Treaty Interpretation' in G Sacerdoti, A Yanovich and J Bohanes (eds), *The WTO at Ten – The Contribution of the Dispute Settlement System* (Cambridge, Cambridge University Press, 2006) 460.

[23] WTO AB Report, *Japan – Alcoholic Beverages* (n 11) para 12.

[24] See, eg: WTO Panel Report, *European Communities – Customs Classification of Frozen Boneless Chicken Cuts, Complaint by Brazil* (27 September 2005) WT/DS269/R, as modified by AB Report WT/DS269/AB/R, WT/DS286/AB/R, para 7.153.

[25] See, eg: WTO Panel Report, *United States – Section 110(5) of the US Copyright Act* (27 July 2000) WT/DS160/R, para 6.45.

[26] See, eg: WTO AB Report, *United States – Continued Dumping and Subsidy Offset Act of 2000* (27 January 2003) WT/DS217/AB/R, WT/DS234/AB/R, para 296; WTO AB Report, *Japan – Alcoholic Beverages* (n 11) fn 21.

[27] *cf* WTO Panel Report, *United States – Measures Affecting the Cross-Border Supply of Gambling and Betting Services* (20 April 2005) WT/DS285/R, as modified by AB Report WT/DS285/AB/R, para 6.49 (noting 'the requirement that a treaty be interpreted in "good faith" can be correlated with the principle of "effective treaty interpretation", according to which all terms of a treaty must be given a meaning'). However, one may also legitimately argue that this is an application of the rules on contextual interpretation, ensuring consistency within the treaty rather than a subscription to the principle of 'effective treaty interpretation'.

[28] HE Zeitler, '"Good Faith" in the WTO Jurisprudence: Necessary Balancing Element or an Open Door to Judicial Activism' (2005) 8(3) *J Int'l Econ L* 721, 727.

[29] WTO AB Report, *EC – Chicken* Cuts (n 11) para 238.

of the Vienna Convention on the Law of Treaties. According to the AB, in order for subsequent practice to be relevant, there needs to be a concordant, common, and consistent sequence of acts or pronouncements, which imply the agreement of the parties on the interpretation of a treaty.[30] This means that isolated acts do not qualify as subsequent practice. At the same time, it is not necessary that all WTO Members are engaged in a particular practice.[31] Last but not least, the WTO dispute settlement bodies have also sometimes referred to Article 31(3)(c) of the Vienna Convention on the Law of Treaties. In particular, the case law has clarified that rules of international law applicable to relations between the parties include the general principles of international law[32] and the rules of international customary law.[33]

WTO practice, again in line with the Vienna Convention on the Law of Treaties, accepts recourse to Article 32 in those cases when the application of primary rules still leaves the meaning ambiguous or obscure, or leads to a result that is manifestly absurd or unreasonable.[34] Moreover, reference to supplementary means of interpretation is also made in order to confirm the results obtained on the basis of Article 31. The supplementary means include the *travaux preparatoires* and the circumstances of the conclusion of WTO agreements.[35] There are also instances where WTO dispute settlement bodies have relied on Article 33 of the Vienna Convention. The AB, in line with the instruction of the provision, normally tries to reconcile text of a particularly WTO agreement that differs between various authentic language versions.

Despite this explicit recognition of the rules of the Vienna Convention on the Law of Treaties in the WTO context, a closer examination of WTO jurisprudence also reveals cases where WTO dispute settlement bodies favour some elements enumerated in the Convention over others. In this contribution two such situations are identified: interpretation that is dominated by textual analysis (and which may be labelled as extended textualism), and interpretation that tends to limit the relevance of non-WTO rules. Depending on one's understanding of Articles 31 to 33 of the Vienna Convention on the Law of Treaties, such a situation may be regarded either as a deviation from the Convention's rules[36] or merely a permissible

[30] WTO AB Report, *Japan – Alcoholic Beverages* (n 11) para 12.
[31] WTO AB Report, *EC – Chicken Cuts* (n 11) para 257.
[32] WTO AB Report, *US – Shrimp* (n 17) para 158.
[33] *cf* WTO Panel Report, *European Communities – Measures Affecting the Approval and Marketing of Biotech Products* (21 November 2006) WT/DS291/R, WT/DS292/R, WT/DS293/R, Corr 1 and Add 1, 2, 3, 4, 5, 6, 7, 8 and 9 (21 November 2006) para 7.67.
[34] WTO Panel Report, *Japan – Taxes on Alcoholic Beverages* (1 November 1996) WT/DS8/R, WT/DS10/R, WT/DS11/R, as modified by AB Report WT/DS8/AB/R, WT/DS10/AB/R, WT/DS11/AB/R, para 87.
[35] eg: WTO Panel Report, *US – Gambling* (n 27) para 6.114; WTO AB Report, *EC – Chicken Cuts* (n 11) para 283.
[36] *cf* Ortino (n 5) 120.

variation in their application.[37] This chapter subscribes to the first position. Although the rules of the Vienna Convention on the Law of Treaties are general and may accommodate different interpretative methods, the overreliance on a text of a treaty or interpretation that reduces the importance of Article 31(3)(c) can hardly be seen as compatible with the holistic approach that stands behind the Convention. The Vienna Convention on the Law of Treaties recognises a text of a treaty as a central element in the interpretative process, but it also makes clear that the interpretation is not limited to the text alone, and that other elements play an equally important role. Consequently, a text of a provision cannot be detached from its context, the purpose and an object of a treaty, while some other elements that are extrinsic to a treaty also need to be taken into account.[38] Even Klabbers admits that the flexibility, which is embodied in the Vienna Convention on the Law of Treaties, 'does not mean that anything goes: interpretation is not an open-ended "free-for-all"'.[39]

III. TEXTUALISM

As was already mentioned above, WTO jurisprudence generally adheres to the holistic version of the rules contained in the Vienna Convention on the Law of Treaties. As explained by one of the panels:

> [T]he elements referred to in Article 31 – text, context and object-and-purpose as well as good faith – are to be viewed as one holistic rule of interpretation rather than a sequence of separate tests to be applied in a hierarchical order.[40]

The same approach was taken by the AB in *EC – Chicken Cuts*. The AB particularly explained that interpretation pursuant to the customary rules codified in Article 31 of the Vienna Convention on the Law of Treaties is an exercise that should not be mechanically subdivided into rigid components.[41]

Despite the general compatibility of the WTO practice with the Vienna Convention on the Law of Treaties, there are instances when, through the

[37] *cf* a discussion on treaty interpretation on the Opinio Juris webpage. In particular, Jan Klabbers argues that the rules of the Vienna Convention on the Law of Treaties are so flexible that is hard to find a practice that is incompatible with arts 31–33, available at http://opiniojuris. org/tag/gardiner-treaty-interpretation-symposium (last visited 1 June 2011).

[38] Art 31(3) of the Vienna Convention on the Law of Treaties mandates taking into account, together with the context, some other extrinsic elements such as any subsequent agreement between the parties regarding the interpretation of the treaty or the application of its provisions; any subsequent practice in the application of the treaty which establishes the agreement of the parties regarding its interpretation; and any relevant rules of international law applicable to the relationship between the parties.

[39] Klabbers (n 37).

[40] WTO Panel Report, *United States – Sections 301–310 of the Trade Act of 1974* (27 January 2000) WT/DS152/R, para 7.22.

[41] WTO AB Report, *EC – Chicken Cuts* (n 11) para 176.

application of a sequential method or overreliance on dictionaries, the textual determination dominates the entire interpretative process to the exclusion of other elements enumerated in Article 31. This observation is equally true with respect to the reports of panels as well as the practice of the Appellate Body. Although there are some indications in the WTO jurisprudence that the recent case law subscribes more strictly to the holistic approach,[42] instances of extended textualism may be still detected.

In practice, the different techniques used by the WTO dispute settlement bodies tend to promote the text of a treaty. In particular, the AB and the panels sometimes apply a sequential approach under which the context, object and purpose of a treaty are only examined when textual methods fail to elucidate the meaning of a provision, or are used as a mere confirmation of the results obtained on the basis of purely textual interpretation. The sequential approach is well captured in the *US – Shrimp* report, where the AB held that if

> the meaning imparted by the text itself is equivocal or inconclusive, or where confirmation of the correctness of the reading of the text itself is desired, light from the object and purpose of the treaty as a whole may usefully be sought.[43]

This obviously reduces the importance of the purpose and object of a treaty, as an interpreter is required to consider those elements only in order to confirm the results obtained through purely textual methods or to clarify a text which remains equivocal or inconclusive after the application of textual methods. Note also that such an approach mixes different interpretative guidelines provided by the Vienna Convention on the Law of Treaties. According to Article 31, a text needs to be interpreted in its context and in light of the object and purpose of a treaty. This requirement is not conditioned under the Convention upon the existence of specific circumstances (eg ambiguity or inconclusiveness of a text). Situations that are identified by the AB should rather lead to the application of the rules provided in Article 32, but only after the text is interpreted in its context and taking into account the purpose and object of a treaty.

The same method was used by the AB in *US – Gambling* when it inquired into the character of online gambling and betting services. In short, the AB had to decide whether such services were to be regarded as sporting activities rather than other recreational services. This was an important question as the US in its Schedule of Commitments did not make any concessions for sporting activities. The AB first concentrated on the text of the

[42] AH Quereshi, *Interpreting WTO Agreements. Problems and Perspectives* (Cambridge, Cambridge University Press, 2006) 15 (arguing that 'the overwhelming authority and weight in the WTO is given to the view that the correct approach is the holistic approach' but also recognising that a part of the case law relies on the sequential methods).

[43] WTO AB Report, *US – Shrimp* (n 17) para 114.

Schedule and found that the language was inconclusive.[44] In the second step of its analysis, the AB examined the context and concluded that it did not clearly reveal the scope of US concessions. Only then did the AB 'turn to the object and purpose of the GATS to obtain further guidance for our interpretation'.[45] As noted by one scholar, the approach of the AB may be summarised as follows:

> [S]ince the 'text' and 'context' are not helpful, let us look at the 'object and purpose'. A holistic approach to treaty interpretation would require reaching a conclusion on the ordinary meaning of the term at issue only upon the examination of all the relevant elements [taken as a whole], rather than examining each element in turn until the meaning of the term at issue is revealed.[46]

Another example may be found in the panel report in *EC – Chicken Cuts*. In particular, the panel observed that 'the object and purpose should be considered after the treaty interpreter had determined the meaning of the words constituting the treaty obligation in question when read in their context'.[47] Although the panel recognised that the treaty terms had to be interpreted in their context, the object and purpose were conceptualised as subsequent steps of the interpretative act. Again, this seems to deviate from the holistic understanding of the rules of the Vienna Convention on the Law of Treaties. As noted in the literature, while it is necessary to 'proceed in stages (usually from "text" to "context" and then to "object and purpose"), this does not mean that the interpretative process is not one and one only'.[48] In other words, it is not really possible to determine the meaning of the words without proper consideration of the purpose and the object of the treaty.

The textual approach is also visible in the extensive recourse of the WTO dispute settlement bodies to dictionaries. In this context, it was even anecdotally noted in the literature that panels and the AB had already transformed the Oxford English Dictionary into one of the covered agreements.[49] This approach poses three distinct problems. First, overreliance on dictionaries sometimes leads to unsatisfactory interpretative outcomes. Second, the over-emphasis on the text can mask normative choices made by the WTO dispute settlement bodies in the process of interpretation. In such cases, textualism is only a formal tool which allows for formulation of the rationale, while the real normative decisions are either hidden or arbitrary. The examples provided below illustrate both types of prob-

[44] WTO AB Report, *United States – Measures Affecting the Cross-Border Supply of Gambling and Betting Services* (20 April 2005) WT/DS285/AB/R, para 166.

[45] ibid para 187.

[46] Ortino (n 5) 131.

[47] WTO Panel Report, *EC – Chicken Cuts* (n 11) para 7.92. It is also worth noting that the AB, when reviewing the panel's report, adopted an approach which follows the instructions of the Vienna Convention on the Law of Treaties.

[48] Ortino (n 5) 130.

[49] Quereshi (n 42) 17.

lems.[50] Last but not least, the over-reliance on dictionaries may also have an impact on the fragmentation/unity of international law. I will come back to this issue in the last section of the chapter.

The first type of problem outlined above is well illustrated by the reasoning of the AB in *EC – Hormones*. When analysing two definitions of risk assessment that are provided by the Agreement on Application of Sanitary and Phytosanitary Measures (SPS Agreement), the AB found that the first one (quarantine risk assessment) required evaluation of the likelihood of entry, establishment or spread of a pest or disease, while the second (food-borne risk assessment) spoke merely about the potential for adverse effects. The AB referred to the ordinary meaning of those terms and equated likelihood with probability, while potential was understood as a mere possibility.[51] Consequently, the first category required a higher level of 'probability' than the second one (arguably a quantitative determination). Therefore, in the case of pest and disease risk assessment 'it is not sufficient that a risk assessment conclude that there is a possibility of entry, establishment or spread of diseases'.[52] A panel should rather look for the '"probability" of entry, establishment or spread of diseases'.[53] Establishing a mere possibility is obviously an easier process than determining a probability. While from a textual point of view the interpretation proposed by the AB is fully acceptable, it also results in a strange outcome. The AB, by establishing different thresholds for each risk assessment, provided importing countries with greater discretion in the case of food-borne risk as compared to quarantine risks. However, since both types of risk may relate to the life and health of humans and animals, there would seem to be no compelling reasons for differentiating between these two situations.[54] A contextual and more teleological reading would require disregarding textual differences and adopting the same threshold for both types of risk assessment.[55] Moreover, the interpretation proposed by the AB may also be viewed as disregarding another preambular state-

[50] There are also other examples, see: WTO AB Report, *EC Measures Concerning Meat and Meat Products (Hormones)* (16 January 1998) WT/DS26/AB/R, WT/DS48/AB/R, para 181 (rejecting on textual grounds a distinction between risk assessment and risk management); WTO AB Report, *European Communities – Anti-Dumping Duties on Malleable Cast Iron Tube or Pipe Fittings from Brazil* (18 August 2003) WT/DS219/AB/R (and the criticism by: P Mavroidis, 'Legal Eagles?: The WTO Appellate Body's First Ten Years' in ME Janow, V Donaldson and A Yanovich (eds), *The WTO: Governance, Dispute Settlement, and Developing Countries* (Huntington, Juris Publishing, 2008) 345).

[51] WTO AB Report, *EC – Hormones* (n 50) para 184. The same approach was adopted by the AB in *Australia – Salmon*: WTO AB Report, *Australia – Measures Affecting Importation of Salmon* (6 November 1998) WT/DS18/AB/R.

[52] WTO AB Report, *Australia – Salmon* (n 51) para 123.

[53] ibid.

[54] See also the argument made by the EC in *Australia – Salmon*: WTO AB Report, *Australia – Salmon* (n 51) third participant's submission of the European Communities, para 7.

[55] One of the goals (recital no 2 of the preamble) of the SPS Agreement is to improve human health, animal health and the phytosanitary situation in all WTO Members.

ment of the SPS Agreement, which provides that the agreement does not '[require] Members to change their appropriate level of protection of human, animal or plant life or health'.[56]

Another example in the more recent case law can be found in the *Biotech* panel report. The panel, when examining the conditions of applicability of the SPS Agreement, was required to interpret various terms of the SPS Annex A. Among other things, the panel considered whether crops grown for purposes other than human or animal consumption (eg cotton or plants grown as a material for biofuels) can be regarded as 'food', and in consequence fall within the ambit of the SPS Agreement. The panel referred to the Oxford English Dictionary and found that 'food' is a substance taken into the body to maintain life and growth. This allowed the panel to classify a genetically modified crop that was grown for a different purpose, but which could be eaten by animals (including wild fauna), as 'food' for those animals. According to the panel, this included both genetically modified crops consumed by insects and genetically modified plants consumed by non-target animals such as insects, deer, rabbits or other wild fauna. The panel reached the same conclusion with respect to genetically modified seeds used for sowing purposes, because it found that these seeds could be spilled next to a field or on a farm and subsequently eaten by birds. As the result of such interpretation, the panel came up with a definition of 'food' which is completely unrelated to its understanding in the SPS field, where food is always defined in reference to human consumption. Interestingly, the panel's understanding of various other terms included in Annex A was also different from those contained in the documents of the specialised international organisations (ie the Codex Alimentarius, the World Organization for Animal Health and the International Plant Protection Convention).[57]

The second type of situation (over-reliance on text masking normative choices) is exemplified by the AB report in *EC – Sardines*.[58] One of the issues disputed between the parties, was the meaning of the term 'standard' as used in the Agreement on Technical Barriers to Trade (TBT Agreement). According to the EC, only standards that were adopted by international standardisation bodies by consensus could qualify as

[56] L Gruszczynski, *Regulating Health and Environmental Risks under WTO Law. A Critical Analysis of the SPS Agreement* (London, Oxford University Press, 2010) 116 (explaining how introduction of a probability threshold limits the ability of WTO Members to establish their appropriate level of protection).

[57] Essentially the same approach was adopted by the *Biotech* panel with respect to other terms that are found in Annex A of the SPS Agreement (eg: WTO Panel Report, *EC – Biotech Products* (n 33) paras 7.297–7.301 (with respect to the term 'additive'), para 7.240 ('pest'), para 7.313 ('contaminant')).

[58] WTO AB Report, *European Communities – Trade Description of Sardines* (23 October 2002) WT/DS231/AB/R, para 278.

international standards.[59] That was an important point as the standard relied on by Peru did not meet this requirement. The AB decided the issue by the application of different textual techniques and without reference to any other elements such as the context, the purpose or object of the TBT Agreement, and held that no consensus was required.[60] The same approach was applied by the AB in the interpretation of the expression 'as a basis for', which appears in the context of the obligation to base national technical measures on international standards. Again the AB, employing a textual analysis, held that the expression connoted a substantive relationship between an international standard and a national measure.[61] Note, however, that in both cases the text permitted different interpretative outcomes that depended more on the normative stance held by the interpreter than on the text alone (eg, it was possible to interpret the expression 'as a basis for' as a procedural requirement). This in turn creates an impression that either the AB was arbitrary in its choice between competing options, or relied on some normative factors that were not disclosed in the report. As correctly noted in the literature, such an approach is problematic as it lacks an

> overreaching vision of the [TBT] agreement that guides the AB in this determination concerning the details . . . As a consequence there is a risk of a tyranny of the 'incremental steps', whereby the cumulative effect of the often reasonable incremental decision is to substantially restrict WTO Members' regulatory sovereignty without such an outcome ever being explicitly analyzed by the AB.[62]

IV. THE LIMITED RELEVANCE OF NON-WTO RULES

The Vienna Convention on the Law of Treaties recognises the relevance of other international rules in the process of treaty interpretation. Article 31(3)(c) specifically mandates an interpreter to take into account, together with the context, any relevant rules of international law applicable to the relations between the parties. How do WTO dispute settlement bodies respond to this instruction? The jurisprudence again seems to point in different and conflicting directions. On one hand, the AB has confirmed that WTO law cannot be read in clinical isolation from public international

[59] The relevant provision of the TBT Agreement provides: 'For the purpose of this Agreement standards are defined as voluntary and technical regulations as mandatory documents. Standards prepared by the international standardization community are based on consensus. This Agreement covers also documents that are not based on consensus'.

[60] WTO AB Report, *EC – Sardines* (n 58) para 227.

[61] ibid para 248.

[62] H Horn and JH Weiler, 'European Communities – Trade Description of Sardines: Textualism and its Discontent' in H Horn and PC Mavroidis (eds), *The WTO Case Law of 2002* (Cambridge, Cambridge University Press, 2006). A similar problem may be also identified in the reasoning of the AB in *EC – Hormones*: WTO AB Report, *EC – Hormones* (n 50) para 163 (defining the expression 'based on' in the SPS Agreement).

law.[63] As was mentioned in section II, both general principles of international law and rules of customary international law are identified as relevant for the purpose of interpretation.[64] Other types of extraneous normative materials have also been used by the dispute settlement bodies. Interestingly this was done without reference to Article 31(3)(c) of the Vienna Convention on the Law of Treaties. First, such materials assisted panels and the AB in ascertaining the ordinary meaning of terms. In other words, they were used not so much as a source of binding law but as a kind of dictionary which reveals the internationally agreed-upon meaning of specific terms.[65] Second, the extraneous rules were also applied through reference to Article 32, as part of the historical background leading to the conclusion of WTO agreements.[66] Third, some international treaty rules were identified as rules of customary international law.[67] This allowed the AB to overcome the problem of the consent of all WTO Members that emerges under Article 31(3)(c).

On the other hand, there are also reports where Article 31(3)(c) was interpreted very narrowly or disregarded. The decisions in *EC – Hormones* and *EC – Biotech Products* are instructive in this regard as in both cases the external rules were effectively disregarded. The panel report in *EC – Biotech Products* is particularly important here. Although the panel formally recognised the relevance of Article 31(3)(c), it also adopted such an interpretation of this provision that minimises the relevance of any international treaty rules in the WTO context (at least under Article 31(3)(c) of the Vienna Convention on the Law of Treaties).

In *EC – Hormones*, the EC argued that the precautionary principle has become a customary rule of international law (or at least a recognised general principle of law). According to the EC, the application of the principle in the context of the SPS Agreement would have an impact on the interpretation of its specific obligations.[68] The panel, when discussing the issue of precaution and its relevance under the SPS Agreement, did not really address the arguments of the EC and only broadly stated that the principle could not override the explicit language of the agreement (particularly Article 5(1) and (2)). The AB confirmed those findings. It observed, first, that the status of the precautionary principle as a general principle or rule of customary international law was unclear. Although

[63] WTO AB Report, *US – Gasoline* (n 11) para 17.

[64] eg: WTO AB Report, *US – Shrimp* (n 17) para 158.

[65] *cf* materials referred by the AB in *US – Shrimp*: WTO AB Report, *US – Shrimp* (n 17).

[66] eg: WTO AB Report, *European Communities – Measures Affecting the Importation of Certain Poultry Products* (23 July 1998) WT/DS69/AB/R, paras 77–85.

[67] WTO AB Report, *US – Shrimp* (n 17) fn 110.

[68] WTO Panel Report, *European Communities – Measures Concerning Meat and Meat Products (Hormones), Complaint by the United States* (13 February 1998) WT/DS26/R/USA, as modified by AB Report, WT/DS26/AB/R, WT/DS48/AB/R, para 124 (eg this would require granting a greater discretion to the WTO Members as how to perform risk assessment).

the AB refrained from taking a position on that issue, it found that the status of the principle in international law was an abstract problem without consequence for the dispute.[69] The AB also observed that 'the precautionary principle has not been written into the *SPS Agreement* as a ground for justifying SPS measures that are otherwise inconsistent with the obligations of Members set out in particular provisions of that Agreement'.[70] Finally, the AB added that without clear textual formulation in the SPS Agreement, the precautionary principle does not 'relieve a panel from the duty of applying normal (ie customary international law) principles of treaty interpretation'.[71]

The same problem resurfaced 10 years later in *EC – Biotech Products*, when the EC again argued that the precautionary principle has become a general principle of international law.[72] The panel, when addressing the EC's arguments, followed the same reasoning as the AB. First it noted that there was still disagreement on the status and the meaning of the precautionary principle in international law. The panel recognised that the principle was reflected in numerous international environmental agreements, and frequently applied in the domestic context of some WTO Members. Simultaneously however, the panel observed that the content of the principle remained unclear, and that a number of authors questioned its status.[73] On that basis, without any detailed analysis, the panel concluded that 'prudence suggests . . . not [to] attempt to resolve this complex issue' and added that there was no need to decide this issue for the purposes of the case.[74]

The approach of the AB (and the *Biotech* panel) is confusing. On the one hand, the AB refused to assess the status of the precautionary principle under international law. Yet on the other hand, the AB instructed the panel to apply normal rules of treaty interpretation. As mentioned above, Article 31(3)(c) of the Vienna Convention on the Law of Treaties requires the taking into account, in the process of interpretation, of relevant rules of international law applicable in the relations between the parties. These 'rules' also include the rules of customary international law (and general principles of international law). Consequently, the status of the precau-

[69] WTO AB Report, *EC – Hormones* (n 50) para 123.

[70] ibid para 124; as noted by Howse, the approach of the AB also confuses the issue of conflict between different rules of international law with the use of extraneous rules in the process of interpretation (R Howse, 'The Use and Abuse of Other 'Relevant Rules of International Law' in Treaty Interpretation: Insight from WTO Trade/Environment Litigations' (2007) 1 *IILJ Working Paper* 7).

[71] WTO AB Report, *EC – Hormones* (n 50) para 124.

[72] WTO Panel Report, *EC – Biotech Products* (n 33) para 4.523 (as noted by the panel, the EC used a somewhat imprecise expression, since the theory and practice of international law refer to rules of international customary law and general principles of law recognised by nations).

[73] ibid para 7.88.

[74] ibid para 7.89.

tionary principle in international law could hardly be seen an abstract question without relevance for the outcome of the interpretation, that is, if the precautionary principle is a rule of international customary law it should be taken into account when interpreting WTO provisions. It would seem that this issue could have been handled in a better way. The AB could, for example, have taken conservative view and recognised the precautionary principle as an evolving principle of international law that had not yet attained the status of customary rule of international law. As an evolving principle, it would be irrelevant from the perspective of the Vienna Convention on the Law of Treaties (since if it is not qualified as a rule of international law it cannot fall into the ambit of Article 31(3)(c)). Such an approach would lead to the same result as reached by the AB, but at the same time it would be compatible with the prescriptions of the Vienna Convention.

The other example of the limited role of non-WTO rules may be found again in *EC – Biotech Products*. The panel analysed the relevance of the rules of the Convention on Biological Diversity and the Cartagena Protocol on Biosafety (Cartagena Protocol) in the context of WTO law. Following a position expounded in some circles in the literature,[75] it adopted a very narrow interpretation of Article 31(3)(c) of the Vienna Convention on the Law of Treaties and found that the expression 'applicable in the relations between the parties' required that the treaty (for example, the Cartagena Protocol), in order to be relevant for the purpose of the SPS Agreement, had to be applicable to all WTO Members.[76] The panel based its finding on three arguments. First, it used the textual argument and found that the Vienna Convention used the expression 'parties' in reference to the parties of a treaty and not to a dispute.[77] Second, the panel emphasised that its approach was motivated by the desire to 'ensure . . . or enhance . . . the consistency of the rules of international law applicable to these States'.[78] However, this consistency was understood as concerning only WTO law. Third, it referred to the consent argument and stressed that the parties could not be bound by rules which they did not expressly accept.[79]

This position was, however, mitigated as the panel noted a few lines later that its interpretation did not exclude the possibility of considering the rules of another treaty applicable to all the parties to a particular dispute, if all parties to the dispute agreed that a WTO agreement should be interpreted in the light of these other rules of international law.[80] The structure of the panel's reasoning seems to be logically flawed. Its earlier

[75] eg: M Lennard (n 14) 36.
[76] Panel Report, *EC – Biotech Products* (n 33) para 7.70.
[77] ibid para 7.68.
[78] ibid para 7.70.
[79] ibid para 7.71; also *cf* art 34 of the Vienna Convention on the Law of Treaties.
[80] Panel Report, *EC – Biotech Products* (n 33) para 7.72.

requirement that all WTO Members have to be parties to a treaty logically excludes the possibility of accepting such a treaty as relevant even if it binds all parties to the dispute and those parties express their desire to use such rules in the interpretation of WTO provisions. Note also that this second finding is incompatible with two considerations that motivated the panel to reject a broad interpretation of Article 31(3)(c) of the Vienna Convention on the Law of Treaties (that is, textual basis in the Convention and consistency in application of WTO law).[81]

In this context, it is also worth noting that overall the arguments put forward by the panel are not entirely persuasive. As noted in the literature, the text of the Vienna Convention on the Law of Treaties is ambiguous and may equally support the conclusion that the expression 'parties' used in Article 31(3)(c) refers to parties to a dispute.[82] McGrady, in particular, notes that the expression 'parties' is used in the Vienna Convention on the Law of Treaties in at least three different ways: as parties to a dispute, all parties to a treaty, and some subset of parties. There are also 12 instances where reference to 'all parties' is made.[83] If the notion of 'parties' as used in Article 31(3)(c) by definition encompassed all the parties, then the expression 'all parties' would become superfluous. This leads to the conclusion, contrary to the panel's finding, that the text of Article 31(3)(c) actually does not unequivocally determine the meaning of the term. Secondly, as has been convincingly argued by Pauwelyn,[84] WTO agreements mainly consist of bilateral (or reciprocal) rather than collective obligations.[85] The object of WTO law (trade, which remains bilateral business), its origin (concessions negotiated on the bilateral basis), objective (trade liberalisation, which is not a genuine collective interest), and the enforcement procedure (bilateral enforcement, including bilateral suspensions) all indicate that WTO obligations are predominantly of a bilateral nature. The SPS Agreement is no exception. Although the SPS Agreement 'set out minimum standards that WTO Members must meet, irrespectively of their actual or potential trade impact in (bilateral) relations with other WTO Members'[86] this does not change the bilateral character of its obligations. Breach of the SPS Agreement affects one or more WTO Members, and not the collective obligations owed to all WTO Members. As summarised by Pauwelyn, 'the mere fact that they are regulatory in nature – and thus substantially the same bundles for all

[81] Note that the panel did not take into account any case law from other tribunals regarding the interpretation of art 31(3)(c) of the Vienna Convention on the Law of Treaties.

[82] Howse (n 70) 24.

[83] B McGrady, 'Fragmentation of International Law or Systemic Integration of Treaty Regimes: EC – Biotech Products and the Proper Interpretation of art 31(3)(c) of the Vienna Convention on the Law of Treaties' (2008) 42(4) *J of World Trade* 589, 594 f.

[84] See generally: J Pauwelyn, 'A Typology of Multilateral Treaty Obligations: Are WTO Obligations Bilateral or Collective in Nature' (2003) 14(5) *Eur J Int'l L* 907.

[85] But *cf* C Carmody, 'WTO Obligations as Collective' (2006) 17(2) *Eur J Int'l L* 419.

[86] Pauwelyn (n 84) 938.

WTO Members – does not suddenly transform them into constitutional-type norms in the interest of some global common'.[87] Consequently, if one subscribes to the view of WTO rules (including SPS rules) as bilateral obligations, divergence in their interpretation, depending on the parties to the dispute, does not necessarily create the problems that the panel was concerned with. Countries, as actors in international relations, may take up different obligations arising from different treaties and conventions. To separate one set of bilateral rights and obligations and disregard others (vis-a-vis another country) constitutes interference with the sovereign decisions of the states that agreed to be bound by a number of different international rules.[88] This observation is also connected with the third argument used by the panel (ie the requirement of consent). Again, it seems that the panel did not sufficiently think over its argument. *EC – Biotech Products* was technically only a single dispute between four parties while legally there were three disputes (*EC v Canada, EC v US,* and *EC v Argentina*) merged into a single proceeding. The DSU makes clear that a single panel examining different complaints organises its examination and presents its findings to the DSB in such a manner that the rights which the parties to the dispute would have enjoyed, had separate panels examined the complaints, are in no way impaired.[89] Thus, the panel should have addressed the question of consent in relation between the EC and each of the complainants. Although none of the complainants was a party to the Cartagena Protocol, both Canada and Argentina were parties to the Convention on Biological Diversity. Moreover, if WTO obligations are conceptualised as bilateral, the problem of consent only becomes relevant with regard to the parties to a specific dispute.

In this context, one should also examine an additional argument that is sometimes advanced in the literature and which seems to support the panel's position. Some scholars are concerned that a broad reading of Article 31(3)(c) of the Vienna Convention on the Law of Treaties will result in great uncertainty as to the nature of WTO rights and obligations and will reduce the precedential character of AB rulings. Although this is an important objection, its relevance should not be overstated. The WTO case law shows only a small number of instances where the need to take extraneous treaty rules into account was argued by the parties.[90] This, in turn, indicates that the risk of reducing the precedential nature of AB

[87] ibid 939 f; McGrady also notes that art 31(3)(c) lays down general interpretative rules as well as rules for resolution of disputes, consequently the phrase 'the parties to a dispute' would not be appropriate in the context of this provision: McGrady (n 83) 598.

[88] *cf* ILC Fragmentation Report (n 7), para 472 ('although this creates a possibility of eventually divergent interpretations that would simply reflect the need to respect (inherently divergent) party's will').

[89] DSU, art 9(2).

[90] Of course, it may be argued that litigation strategies of parties result from the approach of dispute settlement bodies. However, as the current approach of the case law is not consistent, one should not expect any consistency in these litigation strategies.

decisions may be limited.[91] This risk is further minimised by the current WTO practice of regarding particular provisions of an extraneous treaty as a rule of customary international law, or considering such a treaty as a form of dictionary (instead of applying Article 31(3)(c) of the Vienna Convention on the Law of Treaties). Under this approach, a particular rule is applicable to all WTO Members and does not negatively impact the consistency of WTO jurisprudence.

V. TREATY INTERPRETATION AND THE UNITY/FRAGMENTATION OF INTERNATIONAL LAW – SOME OBSERVATIONS

In general, the dispute settlement bodies follow the instructions of Article 31 to 33 of the Vienna Convention on the Law of Treaties. The customary rules that are embodied in these articles constitute a point of reference for both panels and the AB in their interpretation of WTO provisions. The same is true for other non-codified customary rules of interpretation (eg the principle of effectiveness or *in dubio mitius*). It is also difficult to find in WTO jurisprudence, any consistent interpretative approach that would be characteristic only for the trade legal system.

Such an approach has a clear de-fragmentation effect. First of all, it acknowledges the applicability of other rules of international law in the WTO context. As explained by the WTO Director-General Pascal Lamy, the reliance of WTO dispute settlement bodies on rules of the Vienna Convention on the Law of Treaties constitutes 'a clear confirmation that the WTO wants to see itself as being as fully integrated into the international legal order as possible'.[92] WTO law, despite its particularities, is therefore seen as an integral part of the broader system of international law, rather than a type of self-contained regime. Second, one may also expect that the use of the same methodological devices by different international tribunals (including panels and the AB) will lead to a greater convergence in their interpretative results, or at least it will create a common ground for a judicial dialogue between various international entities. This may also be seen as an element that contributes to the unity of international law.

At the same time, this chapter has identified a number of instances where the WTO dispute settlement bodies appear to deviate from the holistic approach that is promoted by the Vienna Convention on the Law of Treaties. The extensive reliance on text, combined with an interpretative approach that limits the relevance of non-WTO rules of international law in the process of interpretation, arguably contribute to the fragmenta-

[91] Lennard (n 14) 38.

[92] P Lamy, 'The Place of the WTO and its Law in the International Legal Order' (2006) 17(5) *Eur J Int'l L* 969, 979.

tion of international law. Indeed, it has been noted in the literature that the AB textualism results in the emergence of 'a wide gap between the jurisprudence of the World Court [the International Court of Justice] and that of the World Trade Court [the AB]. The former is no less skilled or sophisticated in its hermeneutics – without, however, a reductionist textualism'.[93]

The fragmentation effect is particularly visible when technical terms that have acquired an internationally agreed-upon meaning are interpreted by WTO dispute settlement bodies solely on the basis of dictionaries. As discussed in the section III of this chapter, the *Biotech* panel defined a number of technical terms using only the Oxford English Dictionary. As a consequence, it came up with meanings that did not correspond to their understanding in the SPS field. However, one needs to realise that the SPS Agreement (as well as some other WTO agreements) is a legal instrument that regulates highly technical issues and the meaning of some of its terms cannot be simply established on the basis of dictionaries. Such terms have their own specific sense, which can be determined only within a particular technical or scientific discipline. In this context, the documents produced by specialised international agencies such as the Food and Agriculture Organization or the World Health Organization, may constitute a useful reference point.[94] Technically speaking, these documents may be regarded as a kind of glossary which reveals the meaning ascribed to specific technical terms by the international community.[95] Such an approach would clearly contribute to the unity of international law by integrating different legal instruments (including soft law) into one system (here the WTO).

In this context, it should be also noted that this kind of approach is not alien to the WTO dispute settlement bodies, which sometimes use extraneous normative (or quasi-normative) materials in order to identify the 'ordinary meaning' of words used in WTO law.[96] For example the AB in *US – Shrimp*, when defining the expression 'exhaustible natural resource', referred to a number of different legal instruments, including the United Nations Convention on the Law of the Sea, the Convention on Biological Diversity, and Agenda 21 of the United Nations Conference on Environment

[93] Horn and Weiler (n 62) 253.

[94] eg: *International Animal Health Code*, 2002, Codex General Standard for Contaminants and Toxins in Food, Codex General Standard for Food Additives.

[95] *cf* Howse (n 70) 15. Although it may look as if the *Biotech* panel followed such an approach, the ultimate outcome of its analysis indicates that the meaning of the terms used in Annex A(1) of the SPS Agreement was determined solely on the basis of dictionaries.

[96] eg: WTO Decision by the Arbitrators, *Brazil – Export Financing Programme for Aircraft – Recourse to Arbitration by Brazil under Article 22.6 of the DSU and Article 4.11 of the SCM Agreement* (28 August 2000) WT/DS46/ARB, fn 48; WTO AB Report, *US – Shrimp* (n 17) para 130; *cf* also: C McLachlan, 'The Principle of Systemic Integration in Treaty Interpretation and Article 31(3)(c) of the Vienna Convention' (2005) 54 *Int'l & Comp L Q* 279, 315.

and Development.[97] The same approach was used to determine whether the US importation ban could be regarded as relating to the conservation of natural resources. Again the AB looked at other international instruments in order to establish the consensus of the international community (ie whether turtles could be regarded as an endangered species).[98] In this way, the AB was able to integrate different legal instruments, without departing from the instructions of the Vienna Convention on the Law of Treaties.

The occasional over-reliance by the WTO dispute settlement bodies on the text of a treaty (to the exclusion of other elements) should not come as a surprise. The WTO, as a relatively young international organisation, is particularly vulnerable to the accusation of overstepping its mandate. The establishment and maintenance of authority (of the AB as an international adjudicating body in trade matters and WTO law as system of reference for such controversies) seem to be more important in the early years of a particular organisation than later. If one adds to this the fact that a considerable number of disputes which emerge in the WTO context relate to highly sensitive issues, the caution expressed by the panels and the AB is even more understandable. This is particularly true with respect to cases which involve regulatory issues pertaining to public health (eg *EC – Hormones*) or public morals (eg *US – Gambling*), matters that are at the core of sovereign prerogatives of each national state. An additional difficulty is added by the fact that the WTO system remains to great extent a type of unfinished contract. Specific provisions are formulated in general language, while the system as such has numerous gaps that have to be filled in by the WTO dispute settlement bodies. Employment of strictly textual methods may be seen as a way which helps to defend against charges of having exceeded their authority to act, particularly if a dispute is highly politicised. At the same time, the interpretative results obtained through such a method seem to be more easily acceptable by WTO Members as compared to other methods. As expressly admitted by a former member of the AB, 'the heavy reliance on the "ordinary meaning to be given to the terms of the treaty" has protected the Appellate Body from criticism that its reports have added to or diminished the rights and obligations provided in the covered agreements'.[99]

In other words, deciding disputes at a technical level, with text playing the central (or even exclusive) role in the interpretative process, allows the AB, at least on its face, to depoliticise the controversy. Such an approach denies the relevance of policy considerations in the dispute settlement process, since it assumes that a particular issue is decided on the basis of a neutral text and does not require the dispute settlement bodies to make

[97] AB Report, *US – Shrimp* (n 17) para 130.

[98] ibid para 132 (referring to the Convention on International Trade in Endangered Species of Wild Fauna and Flora).

[99] Ehlermann (n 13) 617.

difficult normative decisions. The logical consequence of strict textualism is to deny any policy-making role to dispute settlement bodies. In consequence, textualism acts as a shield against the governments of WTO Members. A similar observation is made by Van Damme, who notes the AB's 'excessive use of dictionaries . . . was probably instigated by the need to assert its judicial function against the backdrop of a not fully-developed institutional model and under-developed procedural rules in the DSU'.[100] One may also expect that once the WTO becomes more mature, its dispute settlement system will depart more and more from strict textualism, openly accepting the existence of a political dimension to its decisions, and becoming more receptive to other rules of international law. There is indeed some evidence of movement in this direction. As has been noted by one scholar, 'since the very beginning of its mandate, the Appellate Body has been very adamant in strengthening its legitimacy underpinnings (eg, by adopting the very narrow textualist approach to treaty interpretation from which it is now trying to emancipate).'[101] This is also reflected in the more recent practice of the AB, where the reference to dictionaries, although present, is not as frequent as previously. The practice of the panels still seems to fall behind, but here too, changes are visible.[102]

As far as the second type of situation (ie, interpretation that limits the relevance of other rules of international law) is concerned, the answer is not straightforward. While the refusal of the AB and the panel to assess the status of the precautionary principle within WTO law clearly does not contribute to unity of international law, the narrow interpretation of Article 31(3)(c) of the Vienna Convention on the Law of Treaties has a more ambiguous character. On the one hand, it has a fragmentation effect as it transforms WTO law into a quasi self-contained regime by limiting the possibility of taking into account, at least under subparagraph (c) of Article 31(3) of the Vienna Convention, other international treaties. This effect has recently provoked a bitter comment from the International Law Commission, which observed that such an approach is 'contrary to the legislative ethos behind most of multilateral treaty-making and, presumably, with the intent of most treaty-makers'.[103] On the other hand, a broad reading of Article 31(3)(c) of the Vienna Convention on the Law of Treaties (interpreting 'parties' as the parties to the dispute), would enhance the substantive unity for some of parties (ie parties to the dispute) while undermining the unity of a particular system (ie the WTO) by emphasising the 'existence of bilateral relationships within the multilateral

[100] Van Damme, in a discussion on treaty interpretation on the Opinio Juris webpage (n 37).
[101] Ortino (n 5) 129.
[102] JH Weiler, 'Constituting a Global Economic Public Space' Robert Hudec Lecture, Second Biennial Global Conference of the Society of International Economic Law (Barcelona, 8–10 July 2010).
[103] *cf* ILC Fragmentation Report (n 7) para 472.

context'.[104] This problem, however, disappears under a middle ground approach, which concentrates on a common intention of the parties (ie, common understanding among the parties of a particular treaty as to the meaning of a specific term), without requiring all of them to be parties to a specific non-WTO agreement.[105] This would guarantee the consistency of WTO law and maintain the precedential nature of AB decisions. At the same time, such an approach would also contribute to the unity of international law as it would allow for broader consideration in the interpretive process of extrinsic legal materials. Interestingly, the middle ground position seems to correspond closely with the approach of the AB in *US – Shrimp*, where extrinsic legal materials were used as an aid in determination of the 'ordinary' meaning of terms used in WTO law.

Despite the above observations, the analysis of WTO practice shows a clear tendency on the part of the dispute settlement bodies to interpret WTO provisions in accordance with the methods established by the Vienna Convention on the Law of Treaties. Deviations from its model are not frequent and appear to be less visible in the more recent case law. Future WTO jurisprudence will show whether this is a permanent trend.

[104] McGrady (n 83) 598.

[105] ibid 592; Howse (n 70) 35; however, it may be argued that such a reading of art 31(3)(c) is incompatible with the textual basis and also raises the problem of a party's consent. This drawback may be somewhat overcome by examining the extent to which that other treaty was implicitly accepted or at least tolerated by other parties.

4

IMF-WTO Interaction: Institutional, Jurisdictional and Procedural Aspects

CLAUS D ZIMMERMANN*

I. INTRODUCTION

INTERNATIONAL TRADE AND the international monetary regime have often been described as two sides of a single coin. The convertibility of national currencies is the counterpart of the liberalisation of international trade on a non-discriminatory basis. Liberalising commercial transactions becomes futile if the liberalisation of the corresponding payment flows does not keep pace. This intrinsic unity would logically have advocated the creation of a one-stop shop after the Second World War, in other words, to entrust a single international organisation with the various challenges arising from the linkages between trade and money.[1] However, under the constraints of political feasibility a different approach was chosen. On the one side, the International Monetary Fund (IMF or Fund) was put in charge of overseeing the international monetary regime. On the other side, the liberalisation of international trade was given to the International Trade Organization (ITO) (with only the General Agreement on Tariffs and Trade (GATT) entering into force on a provisional basis) and, more recently,[2] the World Trade Organization (WTO).

This chapter analyses various institutional, jurisdictional and procedural aspects of the interaction between the IMF and the WTO. This

* LL.M. 2007 (Yale), Doctoral Candidate 2012 (University of Oxford). I am deeply indebted to Deborah Siegel for many insightful discussions and her advice on many of the issues addressed in this chapter. I would also like to thank Amy Porges, Vilaysoun Loungnarath as well as my doctoral supervisor, Dan Sarooshi, for highly valuable comments. I am of course solely responsible for any of the chapter's shortcomings. Please note that the detailed analysis of various issues related to GATT art XV included in this chapter is a significantly extended version of part VI of the following article: CD Zimmermann, 'Exchange Rate Misalignment and International Law' (2011) 105 *Am J Int'l L* 423.

[1] See: D Carreau and P Juillard, *Droit international économique*, 3rd edn (Paris, Dalloz, 2007) 358 ff.

[2] After the end of the Uruguay Round and entry into force on 1 January 1995 of the Marrakesh Agreement Establishing the World Trade Organization, signed on 15 April 1994.

includes, but is not limited to, analysing how issues of jurisdictional overlap between the two organisations are decided. The IMF-WTO relationship is an interesting illustration of policy-coordination and resolution of jurisdictional issues between two international organisations of which only one (the WTO) disposes of a highly elaborated and widely respected dispute settlement system whereas the other (the IMF) relies on a quite unique set of institutional mechanisms for overseeing compliance with the underlying treaty framework. In order to put the IMF-WTO relationship into a broader perspective as part of this book's general focus on unity or fragmentation of international law, this chapter also takes a look at several comparative institutional and procedural issues related to the interaction of the international trading and monetary regimes with the realms of international environmental, labour and investment protection.

Most of the rules that address the relationship between the IMF and the WTO do so in a quite general manner. For instance, Article III:5 of the Marrakesh Agreement Establishing the World Trade Organization (WTO Agreement) provides:[3]

> With a view to achieving greater coherence in global economic policy-making, the WTO shall cooperate, as appropriate, with the International Monetary Fund and with the International Bank for Reconstruction and Development [ie the World Bank] and its affiliated agencies.

In a similar manner, Paragraph 5 of the Declaration on the Contribution of the World Trade Organization to Achieving Greater Coherence in Global Economic Policymaking (Declaration on Coherence in Economic Policymaking) states in relevant part:[4]

> The interlinkages between different aspects of economic policy require that the international institutions with responsibilities in each of these areas follow consistent and mutually supportive policies. The World Trade Organization should therefore pursue and develop cooperation with the international organizations responsible for monetary and financial matters, while respecting the mandate, the confidentiality requirements and the necessary autonomy in decision-making procedures of each institution, and avoiding the imposition on governments of cross-conditionality or additional conditions.

The Articles of Agreement of the International Monetary Fund (IMF Agreement/Fund's Articles)[5] contain similarly general statements. Article

[3] Marrakesh Agreement Establishing the World Trade Organization (15 April 1994) in WTO Secretariat, *The Results of the Uruguay Round of Multilateral Trade Negotiations, The Legal Texts* [hereinafter: *Legal Texts*] (WTO and Cambridge University Press, Geneva, 1999) 4. Also available online at www.wto.org/english/docs_e/legal_e/legal_e.htm (last visited 1 June 2011).

[4] Declaration on the Contribution of the World Trade Organization to Achieving Greater Coherence in Global Economic Policymaking (15 April 1994) in WTO Secretariat, *Legal Texts* (n 3) 386.

[5] Articles of Agreement of the International Monetary Fund (22 July 1944), 60 Stat. 1401, 2 UNTS 39, as effectively amended through 10 August 2009, available at www.imf.org/

X of the IMF Agreement states, *inter alia*, that 'The Fund shall cooperate with public international organizations having specialized responsibilities in related fields'. The IMF Agreement lacks any more specific cooperation provisions with respect to the former GATT or even the WTO.[6]

In 1996, in an attempt to formalise their cooperation, the WTO and the IMF signed the Agreement between the International Monetary Fund and the World Trade Organization (IMF-WTO Cooperation Agreement).[7] This Agreement is based on the authority and mandate to cooperate as spelt out in the previously mentioned parts of the respective treaties. It contains various provisions on document exchange, consultations between the WTO Secretariat and the Fund's staff, attendance at each other's meetings, and deals with other routine bureaucratic matters that are thought to facilitate cooperation between the two organisations at various levels.[8]

The key provision for IMF-WTO interaction, in particular with a view to avoiding inconsistent rights and obligations for members common to both organisations, is Article XV of the GATT 1994,[9] which has been the key provision for the relationship of the two organisations ever since entry into force of the GATT and the IMF Agreement. Most notably, as will be analysed in detail in this chapter, this provision establishes both the obligation for the WTO to consult with the IMF in monetary and exchange matters and establishes the legal value of the findings delivered by the Fund in the context of such consultations.

This chapter starts with an analysis of the scope of the WTO's obligation to consult with the IMF in exchange matters (section II) before examining the role and legal value of IMF findings in the context of consultations with the WTO and related procedural aspects (section III). Subsequently, the chapter assesses the legal value of GATT Article XV:4 (section IV).

external/pubs/ft/aa/index.htm (last visited 1 June 2011). The IMF Agreement, which entered into force on 27 December 1945, was adopted on 22 July 1944, at the United Nations Monetary and Financial Conference held at Bretton Woods, New Hampshire (US).

[6] See for detail on this point and for an insightful historic overview: Dukgeun Ahn, 'Linkages Between International Financial and Trade Institutions: IMF, World Bank and WTO' (2000) 34 *J World Trade* 1.

[7] Agreement between the International Monetary Fund and the World Trade Organization, adopted by WTO General Council Decision WT/L/194 (18 November 1996) as well as by IMF Executive Board Decision No 11381-(96/105) (25 November 1996). See for the IMF-WTO Cooperation Agreement and both related Decisions: IMF, *Selected Decisions and Selected Documents of the International Monetary Fund* [hereinafter: *Selected Decisions*] (34th issue, Washington DC, 31 December 2009) 858.

[8] See: D Siegel, 'Legal Aspects of the IMF/WTO Relationship: The Fund's Articles of Agreement and the WTO Agreement' (2002) 96 *Am J Int'l L* 561, 568.

[9] General Agreement on Tariffs and Trade 1994 (15 April 1994) in WTO Secretariat, *Legal Texts* (n 3) 17. Please note that, for the sake of improved readability, the remainder of this chapter, when quoting specific provisions in the GATT 1994, will mostly refer to the GATT 1994 as 'GATT'. This does not give rise to ambiguity since the rules that were contained in the GATT 1947 have been incorporated by reference into the GATT 1994 according to para 1(a) of the introductory text of the GATT 1994. All GATT arts that were originally contained in the GATT 1947 can be easily recognised by their Roman numerals (I, II, III, etc).

Finally, the chapter looks into several comparative institutional and procedural issues related to the interaction of the international trading and monetary systems with the realms of international environmental, labour and investment protection (section V) and concludes (section VI).

II. THE SCOPE OF THE WTO'S OBLIGATION TO CONSULT WITH THE IMF IN EXCHANGE MATTERS

GATT Article XV provides in relevant part:

> 2. In all cases in which the [WTO][10] [is] called upon to consider or deal with problems concerning monetary reserves, balances of payments or foreign exchange arrangements, [it] shall consult fully with the International Monetary Fund.

Whether WTO dispute settlement panels or the WTO Appellate Body are firmly required to consult with the IMF as opposed to having the mere option to do so when considering a measure falling within the scope of GATT Article XV:2 is not entirely clear despite the firm language employed ('shall consult'). This is due to the fact that Article XV:2 broadly obliges *the WTO* to fully consult with the IMF on the matters listed, without further specification whether or not this obligation extends to dispute settlement proceedings.

In particular with respect to one of the subject matters listed in GATT Article XV:2 – balances of payments – the precise meaning of the WTO agreements remains ambiguous and lends at least some support to interpreting the WTO's obligation to 'consult fully with the IMF' as extending merely to the consultations carried out by the competent WTO body, the Committee on Balance-of-Payments Restrictions, according to GATT Articles XII and XVIII,[11] the Understanding on the Balance-of-Payments Provisions of the General Agreement on Tariffs and Trade 1994,[12] the

[10] This quotation of GATT art XV has been adapted according to art 2(a) of the introductory text of the GATT 1994, which stipulates that all references to 'contracting party' in the now incorporated provisions of the GATT 1947 shall be deemed to read 'Member' (emphasis added). In addition, the quoted parts of GATT art XV are among those provisions for which, according to art 2(b) of the introductory text of the GATT 1994, references to the Contracting Parties acting jointly shall be deemed to be references to the WTO. Subsequent quotes of GATT provisions in this chapter will have included these changes without further express notice.

[11] Any WTO member applying new balance-of-payments restrictions or substantially intensifying existing ones is obliged to consult with the WTO Committee on Balance-of-Payments Restrictions (according to GATT arts XII:4(a) and XVIII:12(a)). Any member maintaining such restrictions is required to consult with the Committee annually (art XII:4(b)) or biennially (art XVIII:12(b)). A third type of consultations may be initiated on the basis of a complaint by a member adversely affected by restrictions maintained by another, if these restrictions are inconsistent with the relevant legal provisions (arts XII:4(d) and XVIII:12(d)).

[12] Understanding on the Balance-of-Payments Provisions of the General Agreement on Tariffs and Trade 1994 (15 April 1994) in WTO Secretariat, *Legal Texts* (n 3) 22.

Declaration on Trade Measures Taken for Balance-of-Payments Purposes, adopted on 28 November 1979,[13] as well as the relevant consultation procedures.[14] Such a reading of GATT Article XV is supported by the provision in the General Agreement on Trade in Services (GATS)[15] dealing with balance-of-payments restrictions in the context of trade in services, GATS Article XII. After stating, in Article XII:5(a), the obligation for WTO members making use of balance-of-payments restrictions to consult with *the Committee on Balance-of-Payments Restrictions*, paragraph 5(e) of the same Article further specifies, in language extremely close to GATT Article XV:2:

> *In such consultations*, all findings of statistical and other facts presented by the International Monetary Fund relating to foreign exchange, monetary reserves and balance-of-payments, shall be accepted and conclusions shall be based on the assessment by the Fund of the balance-of-payments and the external financial situation of the consulting Member.[16]

Unfortunately, this obvious ambiguity created by the corresponding GATT and GATS provisions is not limited to scenarios of balance-of-payments-restrictions, but also concerns all other subject matters addressed in GATT Article XV, that is, also those for which the Fund does not merely provide a technical service to the WTO as is the case for trade restrictions to safeguard the balance of payments, but for which conflicting rights and duties of members common to both organisations might arise.[17]

The IMF-WTO Cooperation Agreement of 1996 would have been a great opportunity to formally clarify whether the WTO's obligation to consult the Fund in exchange matters extends to dispute settlement proceedings or not. And at first sight, it appears that the drafters of the IMF-WTO Cooperation Agreement intended to provide at least some degree of clarification in this matter, since paragraph 8 of the IMF-WTO Cooperation Agreement states in relevant part:

[13] Declaration on Trade Measures Taken for Balance-of-Payments Purposes (28 November 1979) BISD 26S/205-209.

[14] The so-called 'full consultation procedures' (BISD 18S/48-53) and 'simplified consultation procedures' (BISD 20S/47–49).

[15] General Agreement on Trade in Services (15 April 1994) in WTO Secretariat, *Legal Texts* (n 3) 284.

[16] GATS art XII:5(e) (emphasis added).

[17] As pointed out perfectly by Deborah Siegel, trade restrictions imposed to safeguard a member's balance-of-payments do not involve a jurisdictional overlap between the Fund and the WTO, since these restrictions do not involve *exchange* measures subject to Fund jurisdiction. In balance-of-payments matters the Fund is consulted for its recognised technical expertise in the subject matter, therewith providing a service to the WTO, not in order to avoid conflicting rights and obligations for members common to both organisations as in other scenarios. See: Siegel (n 8) 576.

> The Fund shall inform in writing the relevant WTO body (*including dispute settlement panels*) considering exchange matters within the Fund's jurisdiction whether such measures are consistent with the Articles of Agreement of the Fund.[18]

However, in a separate decision on the implementation and interpretation of the IMF-WTO Cooperation Agreement,[19] the WTO General Council specified, among many other things:

> 4(b) In light of, . . . in particular, [GATT] Article XV:2 and [GATS] Articles XI and XII . . .[:] whenever the IMF wishes to submit its views to a panel on whether an exchange measure within its jurisdictions is consistent with the IMF's Articles of Agreement, it shall submit these views by directing a letter containing those views to the Chairman of the DSB. The Chairman of the DSB shall inform the chairman of the panel of the availability of this communication which, unless the panel decides otherwise, shall remain confidential to the panel and to the parties to the dispute.
>
> Nothing in this Decision nor in the Agreement shall affect the rights and obligations of Members under the Dispute Settlement Understanding, including those provided in Article 13 thereof.

This specification given by the WTO General Council, in particular the explicit reference to Article 13 of the Dispute Settlement Understanding (DSU)[20] (stating, *inter alia*, that 'Each panel shall have the right to seek information and technical advice from any individual or body which it deems appropriate') seems to indicate that, although it does not say so explicitly, the WTO General Council considers that WTO panels are *allowed* to, but are *not obliged* to consult the IMF under GATT Article XV:2 and GATS Article XII.

Although the IMF has never made an official statement as to whether it considers that the consultation requirement extends to WTO dispute settlement proceedings, it appears nevertheless to have been concerned about the position taken by the WTO General Council, since it formulated its own approval[21] (postdating the WTO's) of the IMF-WTO Cooperation Agreement in the following terms:

> The Executive Board approves the [IMF-WTO Cooperation Agreement] . . . on the understanding that decisions taken by either party for the implementation of the [IMF-WTO Cooperation Agreement] will not prevent [its] effective application in accordance with its provisions.

[18] Emphasis added.

[19] WT/L/194 (18 November 1996), available online at http://docsonline.wto.org (last visited 1 June 2011).

[20] Understanding on Rules and Procedures Governing the Settlement of Disputes (15 April 1994) in WTO Secretariat, *Legal Texts* (n 3) 354.

[21] IMF Executive Board Decision No 11381-(96/105) (25 November 1996) in IMF, *Selected Decisions* (n 7) 858.

Unfortunately, WTO dispute settlement has not contributed, at least not so far, to clarifying this persisting ambiguity in the legal texts, and this despite the fact that the consultation requirement under GATT Article XV:2 has already been covered three times by panel proceedings.

The first relevant dispute, *Argentina – Textiles and Apparel*, involved, among other measures, an import surcharge which was claimed to violate GATT Article VIII:1(a) but which Argentina argued was part of the commitments it had undertaken in the context of its IMF adjustment programme and should therefore not lead to a finding of breach under WTO rules. However, the Appellate Body found that Argentina had not demonstrated an 'irreconcilable conflict between the provisions of its "Memorandum of Understanding" with the IMF and the provisions of Article VIII of the GATT 1994' and thus upheld 'the Panel's implicit finding that Argentina failed to demonstrate that it had a legally binding commitment to the IMF that would somehow supersede Argentina's obligations under Article VIII of the GATT 1994'.[22] As a consequence, the issue of a potential exemption for Argentina from its obligations under GATT Article VIII did not have to be resolved in this dispute since there were no conflicting obligations in the first place, contrary to what had been claimed by Argentina.

With respect to the consultation requirement under GATT Article XV:2, Argentina had argued on appeal that the Panel had failed to make 'an objective assessment of the matter', as required by DSU Article 11, 'by not acceding to the request of the parties to seek information from, and consult with, the IMF so as to obtain its opinion on specific aspects of the matter concerning the statistical tax'.[23] The Appellate Body upheld the Panel's finding and recalled that there is a requirement for the WTO to consult on the matters specified in GATT Article XV:2, but that measures included in an economic adjustment programme sponsored by the IMF are not among them.[24] The Appellate Body observed, however, that 'it might perhaps have been useful for the Panel to have consulted with the IMF on the legal character of the relationship or arrangement between Argentina and the IMF in this case',[25] which it could have done based on its discretionary right under DSU Article 13 to seek information and technical advice. Unfortunately, all this merely confirmed issues that had already been well understood before that dispute and did not contribute to a clarification of the consultation requirement as set forth in GATT Article XV:2.

Before moving on, it should be noted briefly that Argentina's defence in this dispute would have had to fail in any event, that is, even if the

[22] WTO AB Report, *Argentina – Measures Affecting Imports of Footwear, Textiles, Apparel and other Items (Argentina – Textiles and Apparel)* (22 April 1998) WT/DS56/AB/R and Corr 1, para 69.
[23] ibid para 82.
[24] ibid para 84.
[25] ibid para 86.

contested measure had been part of its IMF adjustment programme. This is because stand-by arrangements, the main instruments of Fund conditionality, have always been analysed as lacking the character of international agreements. Alain Pellet, for example, regards them as unilateral decisions creating the one-sided obligation for the IMF to grant the member in question access to its financial resources as long as the latter conforms to the relevant programme conditionality.[26] For Pellet, and this perfectly corresponds to the official IMF position,[27] the non-respect of conditionality by an IMF member does not give rise to a formal breach of its obligations towards the Fund. The only consequence for the member concerned is a suspension of its access to IMF resources. This line of thought has been further elaborated on by Jean-Marc Sorel who analyses the various documents that constitute a stand-by arrangement (letter of intent, memorandum of economic and financial policy, technical memorandum on the one side and the Fund's approval on the other) convincingly as parallel, unilateral acts that converge in their finality.[28] Hence, policy measures undertaken as part of an IMF adjustment programme cannot lead to conflicting obligations in a legal sense since, strictly speaking, they do not constitute formal obligations owed to the Fund.

Independent of this formal legal assessment, it is obviously in both the IMF's and WTO's interest to avoid from the outset one of their common members initiating policies as part of an IMF adjustment programme that might violate WTO rules. Paragraph 10 of the IMF-WTO Cooperation Agreement therefore imposes a very sensitive consultation requirement for the staff of both organisations:

> The Fund's staff shall consult with the WTO Secretariat on issues of possible inconsistency between measures under discussion with a common member and that member's obligations under the WTO Agreement. The WTO Secretariat shall consult with the Fund's staff on issues of possible inconsistency between measures under discussion with a common member and that member's obligations under the Fund's Articles of Agreement.

Returning to the consultation requirement in GATT Article XV:2, the next relevant dispute, *India – Quantitative Restrictions*, concerned quantitative restrictions imposed by India due to alleged balance-of-payments difficulties. In this dispute, the issue of whether or not the requirement under

[26] See: A Pellet, 'Le financement dans le cadre du Fonds monétaire international' in P Daillier, H Ghérari and G de la Pradelle (eds), *Droit de l'économie internationale* (Paris, Pedone, 2004) 224, 227.

[27] The IMF's guidelines on conditionality recall without ambiguity: 'Fund arrangements are not international agreements': IMF, 'Guidelines on Conditionality', voted by the IMF Executive Board on 25 September 2002 and replacing an older version of 1979, available at www.imf.org/External/np/pdr/cond/2002/eng/guid/092302.pdf (last visited 1 June 2011).

[28] See: JM Sorel, 'La puissance normative des mesures de suivi au sein du FMI et de la Banque Mondiale' in H Ruiz Fabri et al (eds), *L'efficacité des organisations internationales: Mécanismes de suivi et de contrôle* (Athens/Paris, Pedone, 2000) 197, 203.

GATT Article XV:2 extends to panels had been debated at length before the Panel and the parties had expressed divergent views on the issue. As summarised by the Panel:

> The United States was of the opinion that the Panel had before it sufficient evidence, but should consult the IMF if the Panel had any doubts. For the United States, the terms of Article XV:2 of GATT 1994 require the WTO to consult with the IMF in specific matters, *and the WTO includes panels*. For India, on the contrary, to interpret the terms of Article XV to refer to panels ignores the division of functions between the different bodies of the WTO, and only the General Council and BOP Committee are covered by this provision.[29]

In the end, the Panel circumvented the crucial issue and explicitly stated that it did not find it necessary, for the purposes of this dispute, to decide whether or not the consultation requirement under GATT Article XV:2 extends to panel proceedings.[30] Instead, the Panel decided to consult the IMF 'as a recognized body with extensive expertise in [balance-of-payments] matters',[31] based on its discretionary authority under DSU Article 13. The Appellate Body abstained from taking any position on this issue since it was not appealed.[32]

It is not so much the practical result in this dispute – the Panel did consult with the IMF regarding India's balance-of-payments situation – but the legal reasoning put forward by the Panel that needs to be criticised. As has been pointed out plainly elsewhere,[33] in conformity with the logic followed by the Panel in *India – Quantitative Restrictions*, that is, consultation merely on the basis of the discretionary authority under DSU Article 13, in the future a panel might choose not to consult the Fund at all or, which would be in open conflict with GATT Article XV:2, to consult the IMF but without accepting its findings.

In a more recent dispute, however, *Dominican Republic – Import and Sale of Cigarettes*, the Panel resisted the temptation to take the easy path and to consult the IMF merely under DSU Article 13.[34] The Panel in this dispute was the first to consult with the IMF on the basis of GATT Article XV:2. It explained its move as follows:

[29] WTO Panel Report, *India – Quantitative Restrictions on Imports of Agricultural Textile and Industrial Products (India – Quantitative Restrictions)* (22 September 1999) WT/DS90/R para 5.11 (emphasis added); upheld by WTO AB Report WT/DS90/AB/R.

[30] ibid para 5.13.

[31] ibid para 5.12.

[32] WTO AB Report, *India – Quantitative Restrictions* (n 29) para 152.

[33] See: Siegel (n 8) 581.

[34] In this dispute, the Panel found that the imposition by the Dominican Republic of a foreign exchange fee on imports of cigarettes was not justifiable as an exchange restriction within the meaning of GATT art XV:9(a) but that it constituted 'another charge or duty' inconsistent with GATT art II:1(b). For a succinct discussion of relevant aspects of this dispute, see, eg, Annamaria Viterbo, 'Dispute Settlement of Exchange Measures Affecting Trade and Investments: The Overlapping Jurisdictions of the IMF, WTO and the ICSID', SIEL Online Proceedings Working Paper no 34/08, 14, available at http://papers.ssrn.com/sol3/papers.cfm?abstract_id=1154673 (last visited 1 June 2011).

> The Panel *considered* during the proceedings *that it needed to seek more information* on the precise legal nature and status of the foreign exchange fee measure in the stand-by arrangement between the IMF and the Dominican Republic. Secondly, since the Dominican Republic argues that the fee is an exchange restriction and it is imposed in accordance with the Articles of Agreement of the IMF, the Panel *considered that it needed to consult with the IMF based on paragraph 2 of Article XV to verify such an argument for a determination by the Panel* on whether the measure is justified under [GATT] Article XV:9(a). The core issue in this regard is whether the foreign exchange measure constitutes an 'exchange restriction' in the package of the stand-by arrangement. If the answer is positive, the next issue then is whether the foreign exchange fee is 'in accordance with' the Articles of Agreement of the IMF and hence justified under [GATT] Article XV:9(a).[35]

Unfortunately, the language employed by the Panel leaves some doubt. What would the Panel have done had it *considered that it did not need more information* on the precise legal nature of the foreign exchange fee at issue? Would it then still have *considered that it needed to consult* with the IMF? It seems that although the Panel in this dispute formally opted to consult the IMF on the basis of GATT Article XV:2, it did so without considering that it was obliged to do so. In other words, although the Panel formally consulted under GATT Article XV:2, it appears to have reasoned as if it were proceeding on the basis of its discretionary authority under DSU Article 13.

Overall, all three of these disputes, in particular the latter two, should be regarded as having underlined the urgent need for a concerted clarification, by the WTO and the IMF, of whether or not the consultation requirement in GATT Article XV:2 and the analogous requirement in GATS Article XII extend to dispute settlement proceedings and to draw a clear line between such consultations and a panel's discretionary right under DSU Article 13 to seek information and technical advice from any individual or body deemed appropriate. As has been argued convincingly by the United States in *India – Quantitative Restrictions*, accepting an interpretation of GATT Article XV:2 that would leave panels less constrained by the rules of the GATT 1994 than other WTO bodies (like notably the Committee on Balance-of-Payments Restrictions) might be regarded as introducing inconsistency between panels and the rest of the WTO.[36] In any event, it should be stressed that it is not the dispute settlement mechanism's role to amend poor treaty drafting and to provide coherence to an openly ambiguous rule, but that it is the responsibility of the membership to shed light on inherently unclear treaty provisions.

[35] WTO Panel Report, *Dominican Republic – Measures Affecting the Importation and Internal Sale of Cigarettes (Dominican Republic – Import and Sale of Cigarettes)* (19 May 2005) WT/DS302/R, para 7.139 (emphasis added); modified by Appellate Body Report, WT/DS302/AB/R.

[36] WTO Panel Report, *India – Quantitative Restrictions* (n 29) para 3.309.

Once the IMF has been consulted under GATT Article XV:2 or GATS Article XII, the question of the legal value of the responses given by the IMF arises. This question as well as additional procedural issues will now be addressed.

III. ROLE AND LEGAL VALUE OF IMF FINDINGS IN THE CONTEXT OF CONSULTATIONS WITH THE WTO AND RELATED PROCEDURAL ASPECTS

Even assuming that the WTO's obligation under GATT Article XV:2 to consult with the IMF in exchange matters extends to dispute settlement proceedings, this requirement does not imply that the WTO has to hand over its complete decisional power to the Fund with respect to the issues covered by such consultations.[37] As set forth in GATT Article XV:2:

> In such consultations, the [WTO] shall accept all findings of statistical nature and other facts presented by the Fund relating to foreign exchange, monetary reserves and balances of payments, and shall accept the determinations of the Fund as to whether action by a [Member] in exchange matters is in accordance with the Articles of Agreement of the International Monetary Fund, or with the terms of a special exchange agreement between that [Member] and the [WTO]. The [WTO] in reaching [a] final decision in cases involving the criteria set forth in paragraph 2(a) of Article XII or in paragraph 9 of Article XVIII, shall accept the determination of the Fund as to what constitutes a serious decline in the [Member's] monetary reserves, a very low level of its monetary reserves, and as to the financial aspects of other matters covered in consultation in such cases. [38]

The determinations made by the Fund in response to a consultation are thus to be treated by the WTO as either a factual or a legal finding depending on the context in which the IMF has been consulted.[39] The WTO needs factual information, like for example the level of a state's foreign exchange reserves, in order to apply correctly the balance-of-payments exception set forth in GATT Article XII. In such a scenario, the IMF is consulted for its special expertise due to the regular and detailed statistical work it undertakes on the subject matter. The Fund's task in this scenario is not to rule whether the balance-of-payments exception of Article XII applies, but to provide the factual basis for the legal assessment that will be undertaken independently by the competent WTO panel.[40]

In contrast, any determination by the Fund on whether or not a specific action or policy in exchange matters is consistent with the IMF Agreement has to be regarded as a legal finding. Other WTO rules, aiming at avoiding

[37] See: Siegel (n 8) 570.
[38] Emphasis added.
[39] See: Siegel (n 8) 571.
[40] ibid 571, 582–83.

inconsistent legal rulings and conflicting rights and obligations for members common to both organisations, depend upon such case-by-case determinations by the Fund.[41] The best-known of these provisions is the one for trade in goods, GATT Article XV:9, which states in relevant part:

> Nothing in this Agreement shall preclude:
>
> (a) the use by a [Member] of exchange controls or exchange restrictions in accordance with the Articles of Agreement of the International Monetary Fund or with that [Member's] special exchange agreement with the [WTO][.]

For the realm of trade in services an essentially equivalent provision can be found in GATS Article XI:2:

> Nothing in this Agreement shall affect the rights and obligations of the members of the International Monetary Fund under the Articles of Agreement of the Fund, including the use of exchange actions which are in conformity with the Articles of Agreement, provided that a Member shall not impose restrictions on any capital transactions inconsistently with its specific commitments regarding such transactions, except under Article XII or at the request of the Fund.

For a complete understanding of the above provisions it needs to be recalled at this stage that under IMF Article VIII:2(a), the main multilateral provision for freeing the means of payments for international trade, IMF members are prohibited from imposing restrictions on the making of payments and transfers for current international transactions[42] without approval of the Fund.[43] In order to provide guidance on the correct application of this important rule, the IMF has defined what constitutes an exchange restriction. This definition, set forth in a 1960 decision by the IMF Executive Board, relies entirely on a technical criterion asking 'whether [a measure] involves a direct governmental limitation on the availability or use of exchange as such'.[44] The underlying purpose or the economic effects of a measure are thus entirely irrelevant for deciding whether an exchange measure amounts to an exchange restriction under the Fund's Articles.[45] It follows that, unless a restriction on the making of payments and transfers for current international transactions has been

[41] ibid 571.

[42] As defined, in relevant part, by IMF art XXX(d): 'Payments for current transactions means payments which are not for the purpose of transferring capital, and includes, without limitation: (1) all payments due in connection with foreign trade, other current business, including services, and normal short-term banking and credit facilities; (2) payments due as interest on loans and as net income from other investments; (3) payments of moderate amount for amortization of loans or for depreciation of direct investments; and (4) moderate remittances for family living expenses'.

[43] See for a detailed analysis of the precise terms of the provisions contained in arts VIII and XIV of the IMF Agreement: Siegel (n 8) 584 ff.

[44] IMF, Decision No 1034-(60/27) (1 June 1960), IMF, *Selected Decisions* (n 7) 517, 518, available at www.imf.org/external/pubs/ft/sd/index.asp?decision=1034-(60/27) (last visited 1 June 2011).

[45] See for detail on this point: Siegel (n 8) 586.

approved by the Fund under Article VIII:2(a) or is being maintained under the transitional provisions of Article XIV of the IMF Agreement, it constitutes a breach of the Fund's Articles and would thus definitely not be covered by the exception under GATT Article XV:9(a).

However, as noted above, the exception under GATT Article XV:9(a) does not only embrace IMF-consistent 'exchange *restrictions*' but also 'exchange *controls*' that are used in accordance with the Fund's Articles. This category of IMF-consistent 'exchange controls' in the sense of GATT Article XV:9(a) includes all exchange measures whose use is in accordance with the Fund's Articles,[46] but which are non-restrictive.[47]

The restrictive and non-restrictive measures that an IMF member might employ in order to regulate international capital movements, would amount either to an 'exchange restriction' or to an 'exchange control' for the purposes of GATT Article XV:9(a), although ultimately, this distinction would be irrelevant. Whereas payments and transfers for current transactions may not be restricted without the approval of the Fund (except under the transitional provisions of IMF Article XIV), IMF members have retained a vast right, according to IMF Article VI:3,[48] to impose both exchange controls and restrictions on international capital movements, covering both in- and outflows.[49] It is commonly accepted that this provision authorises the regulation of international capital movements through both restrictive and non-restrictive exchange measures, both of which are covered by the term 'controls of capital transfers' as employed

[46] It should be noted at this point that the GATS contains a similar exception which, however, is not framed in precisely the same terms. Whereas the exception under GATT art XV:9(a) covers 'the use . . . of exchange controls or exchange restrictions in accordance with the [IMF Agreement]', the first part of GATS art XI:2 refers to 'the use of exchange *actions* which are in conformity with the [IMF Agreement]' (emphasis added). Providing a detailed analysis of this issue would go well beyond the scope of this chapter. It appears quite safe, however, to say that, although it would obviously have been ideal if the drafters of GATS art XI:2 had employed the same terms as those that already existed in the corresponding provision under the GATT, the difference appears to be essentially one of semantics. The term 'exchange actions' under GATT art XI:2 appears to be identical in scope to the exchange measures referred to under GATT art XV:9(a), ie restrictive exchange measures ('exchange restrictions') plus non-restrictive exchange measures ('exchange controls'). However, since both GATT art XV:9(a) and GATS art XI:2 have never been subject to interpretation in the context of dispute settlement, one cannot but acknowledge that the issue remains at least to some extent uncertain. See for a detailed analysis of the exception under GATS art XI:2, including of its second part which limits the scope of the exception with respect to certain restrictions on capital transactions: Siegel (n 8) 596 ff.

[47] See for a detailed analysis: Siegel (n 8) 589 f.

[48] IMF art VI:3, establishing only minor limits for IMF members in their regulation of international capital movements, reads as follows: 'Members may exercise such controls as are necessary to regulate international capital movements, but no member may exercise these controls in a manner which will restrict payments for current transactions or which will unduly delay transfers of funds in settlement of commitments, except as provided in [art VII:3(b)] [dealing with the scarcity of the Fund's holdings] and in [art XIV:2] [transitional provisions]'.

[49] See for detail on this point: F Gianviti, 'The IMF and the Liberalization of Capital Markets' (1997) 19 *Hous J Int'l L* 773, 775 f.

in the Fund's Articles.[50] As a consequence, the use of exchange controls and restrictions on capital in- and outflows will in most instances be perfectly consistent with the rights and obligations under the IMF Agreement and would hence fall into the scope of the exception under GATT Article XV:9(a).

Unfortunately, the case law on the issue raises the question whether the distinction between the Fund's factual determinations (which will flow into a panel's independent legal assessment) and the Fund's legal findings on the consistency of a contested exchange measure with the Fund's Articles (from which, according to GATT Article XV:2, the WTO cannot deviate) has been properly understood. Only two panel reports, both from disputes discussed earlier in this chapter, *India – Quantitative Restrictions* and *Dominican Republic – Import and Sale of Cigarettes* are relevant here.

The Panel in *India – Quantitative Restrictions*, by circumventing GATT Article XV:2 and consulting the IMF on the basis of DSU Article 13 as noted earlier, not only eluded the question whether or not the requirement to consult the IMF extends to WTO panels, but also the question whether a panel would have to regard as dispositive the determinations made by the IMF.[51] In contrast, and as discussed above, the Panel in *Dominican Republic – Import and Sales of Cigarettes*, did at least formally consult the IMF on the basis of GATT Article XV:2. However, the relevant passage in the Panel Report, though not affecting the overall correct findings in this dispute, points to a wrong understanding of the legal value of the determinations made by the Fund:

> The Panel *fully agrees with the opinion of the IMF. . . . [C]onsidering the opinion expressed by the IMF, the Panel finds* that the foreign exchange fee measure as it is currently applied by the Dominican Republic does not constitute an 'exchange restriction' within the meaning of Article XV:9(a) of the GATT 1994.[52]

As alluded to previously, although formally consulting the IMF under GATT Article XV:2, the Panel in *Dominican Republic – Import and Sales of Cigarettes* appears to have attached to the IMF's findings no greater legal value than to the type of information panels may obtain based on their discretionary right under DSU Article 13. This stands in implicit contrast to the language of GATT Article XV:2 ('shall accept the determination of the Fund'). Unfortunately, this issue was not appealed.

[50] See, eg in this sense: RM Lastra, *Legal Foundations of International Monetary Stability* (Oxford, Oxford University Press, 2006) 396; C Lichtenstein, 'International jurisdiction over international capital flows and the role of the IMF: plus ça change . . .' in M Giovanoli (ed), *International Monetary Law – Issues for the New Millennium* (Oxford, Oxford University Press, 2000) 61, 66; Siegel (n 8) 590.

[51] WTO Panel Report, *India – Quantitative Restrictions* (n 29) paras 5.12–5.13.

[52] WTO Panel Report, *Dominican Republic – Import and Sale of Cigarettes* (n 35) para 7.145 (emphasis added).

In light of the major consequences under GATT Article XV:9(a) and GATS Article XI:2 for the consistency with WTO law of an exchange measure, a few words at least need to be said on how the Fund reaches its findings when consulted by the WTO. Both the relevant Articles of the GATT 1994 and the GATS as well as the IMF-WTO Cooperation Agreement speak only quite generally of 'the Fund' or 'the International Monetary Fund' when it comes to the consultation requirement. As explained perfectly elsewhere, any such general reference to the IMF points to 'formal contact on an institutional level'.[53] Before being submitted on behalf of the IMF, any response to a consultation request from the WTO would be subject to review and formal approval by the Executive Board,[54] the organ of the Fund that conducts the organisation's every-day business.[55]

Furthermore, the question as to whether the IMF is obliged to respond to a formal WTO consultation as opposed to having the option to do so, is equally important. The Fund is commonly regarded as having originally undertaken the obligation to respond to a consultation request in a 1947 exchange of letters, under which, according to Deborah Siegel, 'several consultations ha[d] occurred and a regular practice ha[d] developed'.[56] Today, the IMF-WTO Cooperation Agreement has replaced this exchange of letters as the legal basis for the Fund's obligation to respond to WTO consultation requests regarding exchange measures within the Fund's jurisdiction.[57] As noted earlier, paragraph 8 of the IMF-WTO Cooperation Agreement states explicitly:

> The Fund shall inform in writing the relevant WTO body (including dispute settlement panels) considering exchange measures within the Fund's jurisdiction whether such measures are consistent with the Articles of Agreement of the Fund.

In the past, some authors have defended the view that a formal obligation for the Fund to respond could only originate from the Fund's Articles, which would require their amendment.[58] Whereas this point of view might be formally correct, it appears that, in light of the difficulty of achieving an amendment of a multilateral international treaty, the incorporation of the relevant obligation into the IMF-WTO Cooperation

53 Siegel (n 8) 569.

54 See ibid.

55 According to IMF art XII:2(b), 'the Board of Governors may delegate to the Executive Board authority to exercise any powers of the Board of Governors, except the powers conferred directly by this Agreement on the Board of Governors'. In addition, IMF art XII:3(a) states: 'the Executive Board shall be responsible for conducting the business of the Fund, and for this purpose shall exercise all the powers delegated to it by the Board of Governors.

56 Siegel (n 8) 569.

57 See ibid.

58 This hypothesis has been advanced, notably, by Frieder Roessler, the former director of the GATT Legal Division, in a discussion of the above-mentioned exchange of letters: F Roessler, 'Selective Balance-of-Payments Adjustment Measures Affecting Trade: The Roles of the GATT and the IMF' (1975) 9 *J World Trade* 622, 644.

Agreement has still provided a sufficiently stable basis for the Fund's obligation to respond. Admittedly, that obligation has not yet been seriously tested in practice.

Additional complexity arises from the fact that the exception under GATT Article XV:9(a) is introduced by the words 'Nothing in this Agreement'. There is no doubt that prior to the entry into force of the WTO Agreement on 1 January 1995, the term 'this Agreement' in GATT Article XV:9(a) referred exclusively to the GATT 1947, which at the time was the only multilateral agreement on trade in goods.

Since the WTO came into being, however, the body of multilateral WTO rules on trade in goods emerges from 13 different agreements on trade in goods included in Annex 1A to the WTO Agreement, with the GATT 1994 being only one of them. None of the other 12 multilateral agreements on trade in goods contains a provision similar to the one in GATT Article XV:9(a) aimed at avoiding conflicting rights and obligations of members common to both the IMF and the WTO for areas of jurisdictional overlap. What some of the other 12 agreements do is to incorporate by reference parts or all of the exceptions under the GATT;[59] most of the agreements, however, are entirely silent on the issue. A crucial question has thus arisen: despite being introduced by the straightforward words 'Nothing in this Agreement', would the exception under GATT Article XV:9(a) apply to potential violations under other multilateral agreements on trade in goods contained in Annex 1A to the WTO Agreement, including those that are silent on the question as to whether the exceptions contained in the GATT apply to the rights and obligations under that specific agreement?

It has been suggested elsewhere that the Declaration on the Relationship of the World Trade Organization with the International Monetary Fund (Declaration on the WTO-IMF Relationship)[60] should be read as providing sufficient relief to this dilemma.[61] After noting the 'close relationship' between the Contracting Parties to the GATT 1947 and the Fund, and the provisions of the GATT 1947 governing that relationship, especially GATT Article XV, that Declaration:

> reaffirm[s] that, unless otherwise provided for in the Final Act, the relationship of the World Trade Organization with the International Monetary Fund, with

[59] Art 3 of the Agreement on Trade-Related Investment Measures (TRIMS), eg, provides: 'All exceptions under GATT 1994 shall apply, as appropriate, to the provisions of this Agreement': Agreement on Trade-Related Investment Measures (15 April 1994) in WTO Secretariat, *Legal Texts* (n 3) 143.

[60] Declaration on the Relationship of the World Trade Organization with the International Monetary Fund (15 April 1994) in WTO Secretariat, *Legal Texts* (n 3) 391. This ministerial declaration is an integral part of the Final Act embodying the result of the Uruguay Round of multilateral trade negotiations. See for background information on the discussions as a result of which the Declaration on the WTO-IMF Relationship was included into the WTO's Final Act: Siegel (n 8) 593 ff.

[61] See: Siegel (n 8) 594.

> regard to the areas covered by the Multilateral Trade Agreements in Annex 1A of the WTO Agreement, will be based on the provisions that have governed the relationship of the Contracting Parties of the GATT 1947 with the International Monetary Fund.

Strictly legally speaking, in light of the hierarchy of sources of the WTO legal framework, it would be very problematic to maintain that a simple ministerial declaration should have the effect of modifying the substantial scope of the rights and obligations contained in the multilateral trade agreements in Annex 1A of the WTO Agreement. It is broadly accepted that the various Ministerial Decisions and Declarations, like the present one, though all being integral parts of the WTO's Final Act, do not generate specific rights and obligations for WTO members which can be enforced through WTO dispute settlement.[62]

This does not mean, however, that the Declaration on the WTO-IMF Relationship is legally irrelevant. As will be elaborated below, the Declaration would still have to be taken into account as an important element in the interpretation, under the rules of the Vienna Convention on the Law of Treaties,[63] of any WTO rule that concerns the WTO-IMF relationship with respect to the matters covered by the multilateral agreements on trade in goods contained in Annex 1A of the WTO Agreement, like notably GATT Article XV:9(a).

Prior to embarking on this interpretation, it is crucial to recall that, according to Article II:4 of the WTO Agreement, the GATT 1994 is legally distinct from the GATT 1947 which ceased to exist on 31 December 1995, that is, one year after the WTO came into being. Although it incorporates by reference the provisions of the GATT 1947 according to paragraph 1(a) of the introductory text of the GATT 1994, the GATT 1994, in its entirety, entered into force as a new agreement on 1 January 1995,[64] together with all other multilateral agreements contained in Annexes 1, 2, and 3 of the WTO Agreement as integral parts of that treaty.

As a consequence, the interpretation of those provisions of the GATT 1994 that were previously enshrined in the GATT 1947 does not necessarily have to reach the same result as under the former GATT, since these provisions re-entered into force as part of a new treaty, with additional elements having to be taken into account for their interpretation. Furthermore, under the WTO legal framework the GATT 1994 constitutes

[62] See: P van den Bossche, *The Law and Policy of the World Trade Organization*, 2nd edn (Cambridge, Cambridge University Press, 2008) 53.

[63] Vienna Convention on the Law of Treaties (23 May 1969) 1155 UNTS 331. The Vienna Convention on the Law of Treaties entered into force on 27 January 1980, and, as of 1 June 2011, has been ratified by 111 states.

[64] With respect to the provisions contained in GATT art XIX and those in the Agreement on Safeguards, this point has been explicitly confirmed by the WTO Appellate Body in the dispute *Argentina – Footwear (EC)*: WTO AB Report, *Argentina – Safeguard Measures on Imports of Footwear (Argentina – Footwear (EC)* (12 January 2000) WT/DS121/AB/R, para 81.

the *lex generalis* on trade in goods. Both the GATT 1994 and the other multilateral agreements on trade in goods, though enshrined in different agreements, have to be read as complementing each other.[65] It is only when a provision of the GATT 1994 stands in open conflict to a provision contained in one of the other 12 multilateral agreements on trade in goods that the latter will prevail,[66] and this independent of whether it constitutes the more specific provision.

In light of the above, there is little doubt that, for example, the requirement for the WTO to consult with the Fund in exchange matters as enshrined in GATT Article XV:2 applies in the same manner across all multilateral agreements on trade in goods contained in Annex 1A of the WTO Agreement, since none of them contains a provision that would conflict with that general rule governing the WTO-IMF relationship with respect to trade in goods. The Declaration on the WTO-IMF Relationship fully supports this interpretation. However, as alluded to earlier, with respect to the general exception in GATT Article XV:9(a), matters are more complicated because this exception is introduced by the words 'Nothing in this Agreement'. At least arguably, however, sticking to a strictly literal reading of these terms might not be appropriate in light of the rules set forth in the Vienna Convention on the Law of Treaties.

As determined by Article 31(1) of the Vienna Convention on the Law of Treaties, 'A treaty shall be interpreted in good faith in accordance with the ordinary meaning to be given to the terms of the treaty in their context and in the light of its object and purpose'. As further provided by Article 31(2)(a) of the Vienna Convention on the Law of Treaties, 'The context for the purposes of the interpretation of a treaty shall comprise, in addition to the text, including its preamble and annexes[,] any agreement relating to the treaty which was made between all the parties in connection with the conclusion of the treaty'.

It is precisely under Article 31(2)(a) of the Vienna Convention on the Law of Treaties, that is, as context, that the Declaration on the WTO-IMF Relationship might come into play, since that Declaration reaffirms, with explicit reference to GATT Article XV, that the provisions that have governed the GATT-IMF relationship should also govern the WTO-IMF relationship with respect to all 13 multilateral agreements on trade in goods contained in Annex 1A of the WTO Agreement.[67] This would clearly

[65] See: van den Bossche (n 62) 47 f.

[66] According to the General interpretative note to Annex 1A which determines that 'In the event of conflict between a provision of the General Agreement on Tariffs and Trade 1994 and a provision of another agreement in Annex 1A to [the WTO Agreement], the provision of the other agreement shall prevail to the extent of the conflict'. (General interpretative note to Annex 1A (15 April 1994) in WTO Secretariat, *Legal Texts* (n 3) 16).

[67] See for background information on the discussions leading up to the inclusion of the Declaration on the WTO-IMF Relationship into the Final Act supporting this view: Siegel (n 8) 594.

support the view that, for the purposes of GATT Article XV:9(a), the terms 'in this Agreement' should be read as referring to the entire body of multilateral WTO rules on trade in goods, and this despite the fact that these rules emerge from 13 different agreements. The object and purpose of the GATT 1994 with respect to GATT Article XV,[68] namely to avoid inconsistent rights and obligations for members common to both the IMF and the WTO, further sustains such a broad reading of the term 'in this Agreement' in GATT Article XV:9(a).

Adopting the contrary position, that is, limiting the availability of the exception in GATT Article XV:9(a) exclusively to obligations under the GATT 1994, would lead to the paradoxical situation where the consultation requirement under GATT Article XV:2 would apply across all 13 multilateral agreements on trade in goods in Annex 1A of the WTO Agreement, but not the related exception. The obligation for the WTO, under GATT Article XV:2, to accept the determination of the Fund as to whether action by a WTO member in exchange matters is in accordance with the Fund's Articles would be rendered meaningless if an IMF-consistent exchange measure could still be found to violate a provision under any of the multilateral trade agreements that do not explicitly incorporate the exceptions enshrined in the GATT 1994. At least arguably, such an interpretation would run counter to both the fundamental principle in Article 31(1) of the Vienna Convention on the Law of Treaties that treaties be interpreted in good faith and the principle of effective treaty interpretation requiring that a treaty be interpreted in a manner that gives effective meaning to each of its provisions.

If one now has recourse to supplementary means of interpretation according to Article 32 of the Vienna Convention on the Law of Treaties,[69] either in order to confirm the interpretation that the term 'in this Agreement' in GATT Article XV:9(a) has to be read in a broad manner or, in order to determine its meaning if one considers that the interpretation under Vienna Convention on the Law of Treaties Article 31 leaves its meaning ambiguous, it is of utmost importance to take into account the

[68] As determined by the Appellate Body in *US – Shrimp*: 'A treaty interpreter must begin with, and focus upon, the text of the particular provision to be interpreted. It is in the words constituting that provision, read in their context, that the object and purpose of the states parties to the treaty must first be sought. Where the meaning imparted by the text itself is equivocal or inconclusive, or where confirmation of the correctness of the reading of the text itself is desired, light from the object and purpose of the treaty as a whole may usefully be sought'. WTO Appellate Body Report, *United States – Import Prohibition of Certain Shrimp and Shrimp Products (US – Shrimp)* (6 November 1998) WT/DS58/AB/R, para 114 (fn omitted).

[69] As determined by Vienna Convention on the Law of Treaties, art 32, Supplementary means of interpretation: 'Recourse may be had to supplementary means of interpretation, including the preparatory work of the treaty and the circumstances of its conclusion, in order to confirm the meaning resulting from the application of art 31, or to determine the meaning when the interpretation according to art 31: (a) leaves the meaning ambiguous or obscure; or (b) leads to a result which is manifestly absurd or unreasonable'.

circumstances under which the WTO Agreement was concluded with respect to the obligations enshrined in the GATT 1994. If the drafters of the WTO Agreement chose the rather cumbersome way of incorporating by reference the provisions of the GATT 1947 into the GATT 1994 instead of negotiating an entirely new text, they did so in order keep a lid on the many contentious issues relating to the interpretation and application of GATT provisions.[70]

This significantly weakens the view that the reference to 'in this Agreement' in GATT Article XV:9(a) should be read as reflecting the intention of the drafters of the WTO Agreement to limit the availability of this exception to the provisions contained in the GATT 1994 only. Contrary to, for example, the reference to 'this Agreement' in TRIMS Article 3, the term 'in this Agreement' in GATT Article XV:9(a) is not the deliberate result of negotiation during the Uruguay Round; it was merely carried over from the GATT 1947, that is, from an agreement that, in its time, contained the entire set of multilateral rules on trade in goods.

Overall, a holistic interpretation under the rules of the Vienna Convention on the Law of Treaties, strongly supports the view that the exception enshrined in GATT Article XV:9(a) is applicable to all 13 multilateral agreements on trade in goods in Annex 1A of the WTO Agreement unless one of these agreements explicitly excludes such applicability, which is not the case. It still remains the case, of course, that the issue has not yet been subject to WTO dispute settlement. Whether a panel would interpret the term 'in this Agreement' in the way suggested above, is impossible to predict. All that creates additional legal uncertainty for potential WTO disputes involving a jurisdictional overlap between the IMF and the WTO.

The following fourth section of this chapter will look into yet another source of ambiguity arising from GATT Article XV. In addition to the issues addressed already, the IMF-WTO legal relationship is further complicated by the twofold question whether GATT Article XV:4 would prevail over GATT Article XV:9(a) as *lex specialis* and could serve as an independent basis for a WTO dispute.

IV. THE LEGAL VALUE OF GATT ARTICLE XV:4 – AN INDEPENDENT BASIS FOR A LEGAL CLAIM?

GATT Article XV:4 and the related *Ad* note read as follows:

> [Members] shall not, by exchange action, frustrate* the intent of the provisions of this Agreement, nor, by trade action, the intent of the provisions of the [IMF] Agreement.

[70] See: van den Bossche (n 62) 45.

> *Ad Article XV:4*
>
> The word 'frustrate' is intended to indicate, for example, that infringements of the letter of any Article of this Agreement by exchange action shall not be regarded as a violation of that Article if, in practice, there is no appreciable departure from the intent of the Article. Thus, a contracting party which, as part of its exchange control operated in accordance with the Articles of Agreement of the International Monetary Fund, requires payment to be received for its exports in its own currency or in the currency of one or more members of the International Monetary Fund will not thereby be deemed to contravene Article XI or Article XIII. Another example would be that of a contracting party which specifies on an import licence the country from which the goods may be imported, for the purpose not of introducing any additional element of discrimination in its import licensing system but of enforcing permissible exchange controls.

In order to understand this provision, it is of utmost importance to take into account the circumstances under which it was included in the GATT. As described by John Jackson in his seminal treatise on the GATT, the drafters of the GATT, particularly the American delegates, found it important to include in the GATT some degree of protection against the use, for protectionist purposes, of par value manipulation and of exchange controls and restrictions, that is, of exchange action in a broad sense.[71] They therefore included paragraph 4 and some other provisions in GATT Article XV, and this despite the fact that the IMF Agreement, containing explicit provisions to prevent the abuse of monetary practices for trade purposes, had already entered into force when the GATT was drafted in 1946–47. However, not all contracting parties of the GATT were also members of the Fund. It is for this reason that GATT Article XV was not only drafted to coordinate the interaction between the GATT and the IMF, but also, as put by Jackson, 'to establish an independent basis for certain obligations to cover those GATT parties that were not Fund members'.[72]

In the complex legal framework of GATT Article XV, paragraph 4 appears to fulfil the following, important function. According to paragraph 6 of that Article, any WTO member that is not yet a member of the Fund shall join it within a time to be agreed by the WTO after consultation with the Fund. However, in case the member concerned fails to join the Fund, or in case its Fund membership ends, it shall enter into a so-called 'special exchange arrangement' with the WTO, which would thereupon become an integral part of its WTO obligations. Paragraph 7(a) determines that such a special exchange arrangement 'shall provide to the satisfaction of the [WTO] that the objectives of [the GATT] will not be frustrated as a result of action in exchange matters' by any WTO member that is not subject to the obligations of the IMF Agreement. Paragraph 4,

[71] See: JH Jackson, *World Trade and the Law of GATT* (Indianapolis, Bobbs-Merrill, 1969) 479.
[72] ibid 482.

which is framed as a general obligation applicable to all WTO members, independent of whether they are members of the Fund, establishes essentially a very similar obligation, but also covers the potentially extended periods of time during which a special exchange arrangement between the WTO and a member that is not yet or no longer a member of the Fund does not exist.[73]

Interestingly, in the history of the former GATT several Contracting Parties that would normally have had to conclude a special exchange arrangement under GATT Article XV:6 were granted an exemption, this exemption taking the form of either a waiver under GATT Article XXV:5(a) or of a reservation in those contracting parties' protocols of accession to the GATT.[74] Hence, it seems indeed that the draftsmen of the GATT have been well advised to include a generally applicable obligation, with GATT Article XV:4, that exchange action (broadly understood) may not be used at any time to undermine the GATT.

In light of this very special role fulfilled by GATT Article XV:4 in the WTO legal framework, with particular relevance during the early years of the former GATT, it appears extremely uncertain whether this provision could serve as an independent basis for a legal claim, even more so in a dispute between two WTO members that are both also members of the Fund. In the absence of a single panel decision on the matter, the issue remains necessarily somewhat speculative, but it seems that the above-cited explanatory *Ad* Note can be read convincingly in a way that sheds light on this question.

Ad Article XV:4 explicitly states that the word 'frustrate' in GATT Article XV:4 indicates that 'infringements of the letter of any Article [of the GATT] by exchange action shall not be regarded as a violation of that Article if, in practice, there is no appreciable departure from the intent of the Article'. This means that in order for an exchange measure to be found to breach the GATT there needs to be, in the first place, a distinct infringement of the letter of a specific rule contained in the GATT.[75] As a consequence, it emerges from Article XV:4 that a WTO member, independent of whether it is also a member of the IMF, cannot be found to violate a provision con-

[73] Jackson provides a detailed and highly insightful account of the tedious process in the early GATT years to conclude such special exchange arrangements. See: Jackson (n 71) 486 ff.

[74] For detail on this issue and exhaustive references to related GATT documents, see ibid 489–91.

[75] See, eg, in this sense: GC Hufbauer, Y Wong, and K Sheth, *US-China Trade Disputes: Rising Tide, Rising Stakes* (Policy Analyses in International Economics 78, Peterson Institute for International Economics, 2006) 19; Catharina E Koops, 'Manipulating the WTO? Challenging Undervalued Currencies Under WTO Rules' (Amsterdam, Amsterdam Center for International Law Research Paper Series, 2010) 10, available at http://papers.ssrn.com/sol3/papers.cfm?abstract_id=1564093 (last visited 1 June 2011); JP Trachtman, 'Yuan to fight about it? The WTO legality of China's exchange regime' in SJ Evenett (ed), *The US-Sino Currency Dispute: New Insights from Economics, Politics and Law* (VoxEU.org e-book, 2010) 128 f, available at www.voxeu.org/index.php?q=node/4868 (last visited 1 June 2011).

tained in the GATT for employing exchange measures (both IMF-consistent and IMF-inconsistent ones) that infringe upon the literal meaning of that specific GATT provision, but that do not run counter to the intent of that provision, in a way similar to the two examples given by the *Ad* note to Article XV:4.

Overall, GATT Article XV:4, read together with its *Ad* note, seems therefore to have the effect of narrowing, and not of broadening, the possibilities for seeking legal relief under the GATT against contested exchange action understood broadly. This is due to the fact that under the effect of GATT Article XV:4 not every literal infringement, by exchange action, of another GATT provision will amount to a violation. It therefore appears appropriate to conclude that, although GATT Article XV:4 undoubtedly fulfilled an important role during the early years of the former GATT as explained in detail above, it seems highly uncertain that a legal claim could be based on an alleged violation of GATT Article XV:4 alone.

It should be added that it has been argued by a couple of authors that the above interpretation of the term 'frustrate' should not be regarded as the only one possible due to the fact it is introduced, in the *Ad* note to Article XV:4, by the words 'for example'.[76] This argument is not convincing. The use of the words 'for example' in the *Ad* note to Article XV:4, before specifying the meaning of the term 'frustrate', can be explained by the fact that this *Ad* note addresses explicitly only one of the two components of GATT Article XV:4, namely frustration of the intent of the GATT by exchange action. It does not explicitly address frustration of the intent of the IMF Agreement by trade action, for which it can be reasonably assumed that the term 'frustrate' has to be understood in an analogous manner; thus the introduction by the words 'for example'.

It has also been suggested that GATT Article XV:4 should be read as merely giving effect to the principle that treaty obligations be observed and performed in good faith.[77] However, adopting this point of view would amount to rendering Article XV:4 entirely redundant, which would be contrary to the principle of effective treaty interpretation. As explained in detail in the preceding paragraphs, GATT Article XV:4 can indeed be interpreted in an effective, and hence preferable, manner.

Finally, it has not yet been clarified, in the context of WTO dispute settlement,[78] whether GATT Article XV:4 would prevail as *lex specialis* over

[76] See: D Ahn, 'Is the Chinese exchange rate regime "WTO-legal"?' in Evenett (ed) (n 75) 141; J Miranda, 'Currency undervaluation as a violation of GATT Article XV(4)' in Evenett (ed) (n 75) 121 f.

[77] C Proctor, *Mann on the Legal Aspect of Money*, 6th edn (Oxford, Oxford University Press, 2005) 570.

[78] Jackson discusses a GATT case of 1952 involving Greece where the issue arose without being decided by the GATT Contracting Parties. See: Jackson (n 71) 483 ff.

the exception under Article XV:9(a) or vice versa.[79] It certainly seems that the reference in the exception in GATT Article XV:9(a) to 'exchange controls or exchange restrictions in accordance with the [IMF Agreement]' is more specific than the broad reference, in GATT Article XV:4, to 'exchange action' without further specification.[80] However, in the absence of a formal interpretation of the issue we are left with at least some degree of uncertainty. As recalled by Jackson, a special subgroup to the Ninth Session of the GATT Contracting Parties (1954–55) noted that the relationship between paragraphs 4 and 9 of GATT Article XV was troublesome. Unfortunately, the group decided not to lay down general principles on this problem, but to leave that question 'over for empirical consideration if and when particular points arose which had a bearing on it'.[81]

Having completed this *tour d'horizon* of the most relevant legal aspects of GATT Article XV, the key provision of IMF-WTO interaction, it appears appropriate to address some comparative institutional and procedural issues.

V. COMPARATIVE INSTITUTIONAL AND PROCEDURAL PERSPECTIVES

Whereas the IMF and the WTO are by far not the only two international organisations between which conflicting rights and obligations for common members might potentially arise, informal cooperation and unbinding consultation are usually preferred to binding rules on how to decide issues of jurisdictional overlap.

However, a highly interesting exception to this general pattern can be found in the ultimately unsuccessful negotiations on a proposed Multilateral Agreement on Investment (MAI) that were held at the Organisation for Economic Co-operation and Development (OECD) between 1995 and 1998.[82] The draft consolidated treaty text of the MAI[83] contained a temporary safeguard provision for balance-of-payments crises which, like the relevant provisions in the GATT and GATS analysed in this chapter, would

[79] In the earlier-mentioned dispute *Dominican Republic – Import and Sale of Cigarettes*, one of the third parties, China, had expressed her hope that the Panel would provide clarification on the relationship between GATT arts XV:4 and XV:9(a), but the Panel did not address this issue at all in its findings. See: WTO Panel Report, *Dominican Republic – Import and Sale of Cigarettes* (n 35) paras 5.56–5.58.

[80] See: Siegel (n 8) 591.

[81] GATT, 3d Supp BISD 195, 197 (1955) (quoted and discussed in Jackson (n 71) 485 f).

[82] See, eg, for an interesting analysis of the failure of the MAI and its implications: PT Muchlinski, 'The Rise and Fall of the Multilateral Agreement on Investment: Where Now' (2000) 34 *Int'l Law* 1033.

[83] Consolidated draft texts of the MAI as well as commentary documents are available at www.oecd.org/daf/mai (last visited 1 June 2011).

have taken Fund jurisdiction explicitly into account. The consolidated draft text of the MAI reads in relevant part:

> TEMPORARY SAFEGUARD
>
> A Contracting Party may adopt or maintain measures inconsistent with its obligations . . .
>
> in the event of serious balance-of-payments and external financial difficulties or threat thereof; or
>
> where, in exceptional circumstances, movements of capital cause, or threaten to cause, serious difficulties for macroeconomic management, in particular monetary and exchange rate policies.
>
> 2. Measures referred to in paragraph 1:
>   (a) shall be consistent with the Articles of Agreement of the International Monetary Fund;
>
>   shall be temporary and shall be eliminated as soon as conditions permit.
>
>   With regard to measures referred to in paragraph 1
>
>   (b) *The Parties Group shall request an assessment by the International Monetary Fund of the Conditions mentioned under paragraph 1 and of the consistency of any measures with paragraph 2. Any such assessment shall be accepted by the Parties Group.*
>
> Additional Article:
>
> *If a dispute arises under this Article . . ., a Dispute Settlement Panel shall request an assessment by the International Monetary Fund of the consistency of the measures with its Articles of Agreement, of the conditions mentioned under paragraph 1 and of the consistency of any measures as applied with paragraph 2. Any such assessment by the International Monetary Fund shall be accepted by the Panel.*[84]

As becomes obvious at first sight of this draft provision, the IMF would have been granted under the MAI the same jurisdictional deference and the same prominent role regarding legal determinations of consistency of contested exchange measures with the Fund's Articles and regarding factual determinations in the Fund's area of expertise as it possesses in the IMF-WTO relationship. As explained by Sean Hagan, currently IMF General Counsel and Director of the IMF Legal Department, 'The prominent role of the Fund in the implementation of the derogation provisions reflects the fact that the Fund is charged with both assisting countries in the design of programmes that address balance-of-payments problems and providing the financial assistance that is necessary to support these programmes'.[85]

[84] MAI Draft Consolidated Text April 1998, DAFFE/MAI(98)7/REV1, 78 (emphasis added).

[85] S Hagan, 'Transfer of Funds' (2000) *UNCTAD Series on issues in international investment agreements* UNCTAD/ITE/IIT/20, 52, available at http://unctad.org/en/docs/psiteiitd20.en.pdf (last visited 1 June 2011).

Despite the failure of the MAI, it seems likely that further attempts will be undertaken by the international community to establish a coherent set of multilateral rules on foreign investment, including maybe even the creation of a specialised international organisation in this field. It remains to be seen to what extent the drafters of such a future international treaty will adhere to the draft MAI's approach for balance-of-payments derogations with the major role given to IMF jurisdiction as described above. To this author, following the same approach appears desirable, since doing so might ultimately lead to a consistent legal treatment of balance-of-payments derogations across the three traditional pillars of international economic law: trade, investment, and money.

Other areas of concern for which the international community will have to decide between continued 'soft' cooperation and introducing binding rules on how to deal with issues of common concern or even potential jurisdictional overlap are the interaction between the International Labour Organization (ILO) and the WTO as well as between the various multilateral environmental agreements (MEAs)[86] and the WTO. As is well established, states have always shown a certain tendency to invoke the respect of environmental and labour standards not only in order to achieve the primary purposes of these standards, but also out of protectionism.

The common characteristic in these domains of interaction is that only one of the legal frameworks involved, the WTO, can rely on a strong and efficient dispute settlement mechanism. So far, no legal action against trade measures taken under an international environmental agreement or aimed at imposing international labour standards has been brought to the WTO dispute settlement mechanism. It seems safe to say, however, that it is only a matter of time, in particular for the pair trade-environment, until such disputes will arise.

It is therefore not surprising that the WTO's ongoing Doha Development Round initiated negotiations on some related key aspects. Paragraph 31(i) of the 2001 Doha Ministerial Declaration,[87] for instance, mandates WTO members to negotiate on the relationship between WTO rules and specific trade obligations set out in MEAs. Negotiations were also mandated in paragraph 31(ii) on procedures for information exchange between MEAs and the relevant WTO committees, and on the criteria for the granting of

[86] The number of MEAs is impressive and constantly growing. Currently, there appear to be about 200 MEAs dealing with various environmental issues. About 20 of these include provisions that may affect trade. Eg, they authorise states to restrict trade in certain circumstances or ban certain products. Among them figure the Basel Convention on the Trade or Transportation of Hazardous Waste Across International Borders, the Montreal Protocol for the Protection of the Ozone Layer, and the Convention on International Trade in Endangered Species. See, eg, for detailed information: WTO Secretariat, *Trade and Environment at the WTO* (Geneva, WTO, 2004) available at www.wto.org/english/tratop_e/envir_e/envir_wto2004_e.pdf (last visited 1 June 2011).

[87] Doha Ministerial Declaration (14 November 2001) WT/MIN(01)/DEC/1, available at http://docsonline.wto.org (last visited 1 June 2011).

observer status in WTO bodies. As for the entire Doha Round, the outcome remains uncertain. As far as dispute settlement is concerned, it will be interesting to follow whether WTO members will consider the panel's discretionary authority under DSU Article 13 to seek information and technical advice as sufficient for dealing with MEAs on issues of jurisdictional overlap or whether mandatory consultation requirements like the ones analysed in detail in this chapter will be introduced at some point in the future.

By contrast, the relationship between the IMF and the ILO will be unaffected by the outcome of the Doha Round since the Doha Ministerial Declaration merely reaffirms the 1996 Singapore Ministerial Declaration stating rather bluntly in its paragraph 4:

> We renew our commitment to the observance of internationally recognized core labour standards. The [ILO] is the competent body to set and deal with these standards, and we affirm our support for its work in promoting them. We believe that economic growth and development fostered by increased trade and further trade liberalization contribute to the promotion of these standards. We reject the use of labour standards for protectionist purposes, and agree that the comparative advantage of countries, particularly low-wage developing countries, must in no way be put into question. In this regard, we note that the WTO and ILO Secretariats will continue their existing collaboration.[88]

Despite this statement, there is currently no work on the topic of core labour standards in the WTO's Councils and Committees and interaction between the two organisations appears to be limited to the respective Secretariats attending sessions of each other's governing body as observers. As summed up in a telling manner on the WTO website:

> [T]he secretariats of the two organizations work together on technical issues under the banner of 'coherence' in global economic policy-making. However, beyond that it is not easy for them to agree, and the question of international enforcement is a minefield.[89]

Although it might therefore appear entirely unrealistic to hope for the introduction into WTO-ILO interaction of a binding consultation requirement any time soon, WTO members should not underestimate the potential for jurisdictional overlap in this domain and might be well advised to strengthen their efforts to formalise their collaboration with the ILO. For any steps in this direction, the relationship between the IMF and the WTO might serve as an inspiring example, and this despite the persisting ambiguities arising from GATT Article XV and the related case law as addressed in this chapter.

[88] Singapore Ministerial Declaration (13 December 1996) WT/MIN(96)/DEC, available at http://docsonline.wto.org (last visited 1 June 2011).

[89] WTO website, 'Labour standards: consensus, coherence and controversy', available at www.wto.org/english/thewto_e/whatis_e/tif_e/bey5_e.htm (last visited 1 June 2011).

VI. CONCLUSION

This chapter has provided a detailed analysis of the most important institutional, jurisdictional and procedural aspects of the relationship between the IMF and the WTO. The key provision for avoiding conflicting rights and obligations for members common to these two prominent organisations in the field of international economic relations is GATT Article XV. However, an analysis of both the treaty text and relevant WTO disputes reveals persistent ambiguities with respect to the scope and precise legal effect of the consultation requirement in GATT Article XV:2. Notably, it is not entirely clear whether the WTO's obligation to consult the Fund in exchange matters extends to dispute settlement proceedings or not. If it does, as can be argued quite convincingly, then it is important to stress that the consultation requirement has to be regarded as a firm obligation distinct from the discretionary authority of panels under DSU Article 13 to seek information and technical advice from any individual or body deemed appropriate. This chapter has also attempted to shed light on the legal value of GATT Article XV:4 and on the fundamental question as to whether the exception enshrined in GATT Article XV:9(a) is applicable across all multilateral agreements on trade in goods as contained in Annex 1A of the WTO Agreement. Overall, one cannot but admit that all these issues remain fraught with at least some degree of uncertainty due to an inherent ambiguity in the relevant treaty provisions.

As a consequence, the issues discussed in this chapter call for a formal clarification. For two reasons, however, it does not appear ideal to wait until the contested issues need to be explicitly addressed by a panel or the Appellate Body in a future WTO dispute and then to follow that interpretation.

First, although contained exclusively in the treaty framework of only one of the organisations concerned (the WTO), the future coherence of IMF-WTO interaction is clearly an issue that requires a clarification provided jointly by the WTO and the IMF. Initially, this could take the form of an amendment of the IMF-WTO Cooperation Agreement, followed by the necessary amendment of the WTO Agreement.

Second, the WTO dispute settlement mechanism has clearly not been charged by WTO members with amending poor treaty drafting. It is the membership's exclusive responsibility to provide coherence to openly ambiguous provisions and to formally shed light on the issues discussed in this chapter. The fact that IMF-WTO interaction appears to function rather well in practice should not be used as an excuse for not improving obvious deficits in the existing legal framework.

Finally, the brief review towards the end of this chapter of selected comparative institutional and procedural elements drawn from the interaction of the international trading and monetary systems with the realms of international environmental, labour, and investment protection shows that the detailed rules on how to resolve jurisdictional overlap between the IMF and the WTO are still more an exception than the rule. At least for the moment, informal cooperation and consultation continue to be widely preferred by the international community to formal and binding rules for dealing with potential jurisdictional overlap between international organisations.

5

Sources of Law and Arbitral Interpretations of Pari Materia *Investment Protection Rules*

MARTINS PAPARINSKIS*

I. INTRODUCTION

RELIANCE BY INVESTMENT treaty arbitration tribunals on the case law of their predecessors is an empirically well-documented process in contemporary law.[1] This practice has given rise to different attempts of conceptualisation both in the case law itself and in legal writings.[2] It may be useful to put the discussion in perspective. Sir Gerald

* D Phil (Oxon), Junior Research Fellow, Merton College, University of Oxford. At the time of the conference I was an AHRC and Commercial Bar Scholar at the University of Oxford. I also worked on the paper while I was a Hauser Research Scholar at the New York University. Comments and criticisms from Anastasios Gourgourinis, Stephan Schill, the participants of the conference and particularly the editors are greatly appreciated. The views expressed and the errors or omissions made are the responsibility of the author alone. Unless stated otherwise, the investment awards cited are available at http://icsid.worldbank.org/ICSID/Index.jsp, www.investmentlaims.com and http://italaw.com, and the investment treaties cited are available at www.unctadxi.org/templates/DocSearch____779.aspx.

[1] JP Commission, 'Precedent in Investment Treaty Arbitration: A Citation Analysis of a Developing Jurisprudence' (2007) 24 *J Int'l Arb* 2, 129; OK Fauchald, 'The Legal Reasoning of ICSID Tribunals: An Empirical Analysis' (2008) 19 *Eur J Int'l L* 301, 333 ff.

[2] The spectrum is broad: some authorities suggest a duty to follow consistent case law. See, eg: G Kaufmann-Kohler, 'Arbitral Precedent: Dream, Necessity or Excuse?' (2007) 23 *Arb Int'l* 3, 357, 377; *Saipem SpA v Bangladesh* (ICSID Case No ARB/05/07, Decision on Jurisdiction and Recommendation on Provisional Measures, 21 March 2007) para 67; *Victor Pey Casado and President Allende Foundation v Republic of Chile* (ICSID Case No ARB/98/2, Award, 8 May 2008) para 119. Others call for a *jurisprudence constante*. See, eg: *SGS Société Générale de Surveillance SA v Republic of the Philippines* (ICSID Cases No ARB/02/6 and ARB/04/08, Decision of the Tribunal on Objections to Jurisdiction, 29 January 2004) para 97; AK Björklund, 'Investment Treaty Arbitral Decisions as *Jurisprudence Constante*' in CB Picker et al (eds), *International Economic Law: State and Future of the Discipline* (Oxford, Hart Publishing, 2008) 265. Yet others deny any normative or other relevance of earlier cases on the issue; see, eg: *RosInvestCo UK Ltd v Federation of Russia* (SCC V 079/2005, Award on Jurisdiction, November 2008) paras 49, 136–37; *Wintershall Aktiengesellschaft v Argentina* (ICSID Case No ARB/04/14, Award, 8 December 2008) paras 178–84, 194.

Fitzmaurice famously observed in his contribution to *Symbolae Verzijl* that despite the theoretical limitation of international judgments to the particular dispute between particular parties '[i]n practice, it is obvious that neither the United Kingdom nor any other country could now successfully contest the general *principle* of straight base-lines [identified by the International Court of Justice (ICJ) in the *Fisheries* case]'.[3] However, the normative influence of the judgment is limited by reference to the particular rule that it authoritatively explains. As Fitzmaurice added in an important footnote, 'decisions turning on the *interpretation* of treaties or other instruments would not always readily lend themselves to this process'.[4] The commentators of the Iran-US Claims Tribunal's case law clearly appreciated this point, agreeing that cases explaining customary law in principle had general legal relevance while those elaborating the particular treaty in principle did not.[5] In other words, even if the content of a rule is taken from the award, the award still relates to the particular rule. Its broader relevance has to be derived not from its existence but from the relationship to the underlying rules and sources.

This chapter does not address the contribution of case law to the development of international law in general[6] or international investment law in particular.[7] The present analysis instead considers the logically anterior question in the context of investment arbitration, namely whether and how arbitral elaborations in earlier cases of *pari materia* rules from other treaties are legally relevant for interpreting a particular treaty rule. There may be different reasons for an investment tribunal to refer to earlier case law by other tribunals.[8] An earlier award may have explained the application of general concepts in a particular context. For example, the *Compañiá*

[3] G Fitzmaurice, 'Some Problems Regarding the Formal Sources of International Law' in JHW Verzijl, *Symbolae Verzijl* (The Hague, Martinus Nijhoff Publishers, 1958) 170. It is now known that after the *Fisheries* case UK carried out a general re-examination of its territorial sea claims: *Sovereignty over Pedra Branca/Pulau Batu Puten, Middle Rocks and South Ledge (Malaysia/Singapore)* [2008] ICJ Rep 12, para 225.

[4] Fitzmaurice ibid 171.

[5] Even if disagreeing whether particular propositions turned on custom or treaty: G Abi-Saab, 'Permanent Sovereignty over Natural Resources and Economic Activities' in M Bedjaoui (ed), *International Law: Achievements and Prospects* (Paris, UNESCO, 1991) 613; D Magraw, 'The Iran-US Claims Tribunal: Its Contributions to International Law and Practice: Remarks' in R Lefeber, *Contemporary International Law Issues: Opportunities at a Time of Momentous Change* (Dordrecht, Martinus Nijhoff Publishers, 1994) 2 f; J Crook ibid 6; D Caron ibid 6 ff; M Pellonpää ibid 13 f; A Mouri ibid 19 f; CN Brower and JD Bruesckhe, *The Iran-United States Claims Tribunal* (The Hague, Martinus Nijhoff Publishers, 1998) 645 ff.

[6] CJ Tams and A Tzanakopoulos, '*Barcelona Traction*: the ICJ as an Agent of Legal Development' (2010) 23 *Leiden J Int'l L* 4, 781.

[7] CH Schreuer and M Weiniger, 'Conversations Across Cases – Is There a Doctrine of Precedent in Investment Arbitration?' in P Muchlinski, F Ortino and CH Schreuer (eds), *The Oxford Handbook of International Investment Law* (Oxford, Oxford University Press, 2008) 1188; J Paulsson, 'Awards – and Awards' in AK Björklund et al (eds), *Investment Treaty Law: Current Issues III* (London, British Institute for Comparative and International Law, 2008) 95.

[8] Fauchald (n 1) 335 f.

de Aguas del Aconquija SA and Vivendi Universal v Argentina annulment decision is often the starting point of discussing the cause and object in investment treaty claims raising contractual issues.[9] The *CMS Gas Transmission Company v Argentina* annulment decision formulates the framework for discussing primary and secondary rules in investment treaty law.[10] Different views of applicable law, privity, cause and scope of umbrella clauses naturally invite consideration of approaches taken in other cases.[11] The reasoning of the earlier awards may also serve as an inspiration or be applied by analogy.

Still, while there are shades of difference between arguments, there is a point when reliance on earlier awards goes further than that. The case law regarding open-textured substantive rules (particularly most-favoured-nation (MFN) treatment, indirect expropriation and fair and equitable treatment) shows a case-by-case fleshing out and refinement of presumptions, criteria and sub-criteria, often developed on the basis of particular case-specific factual circumstances by references to earlier awards. For example, the *Waguih Elie George Siag and Clorinda Vecchi v Egypt* (*Siag*) tribunal observed that:

> While its [fair and equitable treatment's] precise ambit is not easily articulated, a number of categories of frequent application may be observed from past cases. These include such notions as transparency, protection of legitimate expectations, due process, freedom from discrimination and freedom from coercion and harassment. Claimants submit that Egypt has violated each of the generally recognised 'strands' of the fair and equitable treatment doctrine and the Tribunal upholds this contention.[12]

The approach identifying 'a number of categories of frequent application . . . from past cases', conceptualising them as 'notions' and then finding breaches of these 'generally recognised "strands"' seems to proceed on an implicit premise of the mutual normative relevance of all the arbitral pronouncements.[13]

[9] *Compañiá de Aguas del Aconquija SA and Vivendi Universal v Argentina* (ICSID Case No ARB/97/3, Decision on Annulment, 3 July 2002) paras 94–115.

[10] *CMS Gas Transmission Company v Argentina* (ICSID Case No ARB 01/08, Decision of the *ad hoc* Committee on the Application for Annulment, 25 September 2007) paras 129–34.

[11] *Pan American Energy LLC and others v Argentina* (ICSID Cases No ARB/03/13 and ARB/04/8, Decision on Preliminary Objections, 27 July 2006) paras 99–113.

[12] *Waguih Elie George Siag and Clorinda Vecchi v Egypt* (ICSID Case No ARB/05/15, Award, 1 June 2009) para 450 (internal fnn omitted).

[13] This is not an isolated example of such reasoning. To consider the most recent publicly available awards interpreting clauses on fair and equitable treatment, all tribunals to a greater or lesser degree relied on criteria formulated in earlier cases regarding other treaties to identify the content of the rule, *Rumeli Telekom A.S. and Telsim Mobil Telekomikasyon Hizmetleri AS v Kazakhstan* (ICSID Case No ARB/05/16, Award, 29 July 2008) para 609; *Duke Energy Electroquil Partners & Electroquil SA v Republic of Ecuador* (ICSID Case No ARB/04/19, Award, 18 August 2008) paras 333–44; *Plama Consortium Limited v Republic of Bulgaria* (ICSID Case No ARB/03/24, Award, 27 August 2008) paras 173–78; *National Grid v Republic of Argentina* (UNCITRAL Arbitration, Award, 3 November 2008) paras 172–75; *Jan de Nul NV*

Such a case-by-case identification of different aspects and criteria from the factual mistreatment in particular cases would be unremarkable if all adjudicators interpreted the same rule of law (or at least the rule of law interpreted in other cases was legally relevant for the rule applicable in the particular instance). However, at least *prima facie* that is not the case: the *Siag* tribunal had to interpret a treaty rule on fair and equitable treatment in a 1989 Italy-Egypt Bilateral Investment Treaty (BIT), while the authorities it referred to were a 2000 award interpreting the 1994 North American Free Trade Agreement (NAFTA), a 2003 award interpreting a 1996 Spain-Mexico BIT, a 2006 award interpreting a 1991 Germany-Argentina BIT and a 2007 award interpreting a 1991 US-Argentina BIT.[14] Since the limit of adjudicatory explanation of the content of the rule appears to be logically set by the scope of the rule itself, one is faced with the question of whether and how the interpreter of the Italy-Egypt BIT can attribute such normative importance to 'categories', 'notions' and 'strands' from post-conclusion treaties and awards. As the tribunal in the *Chevron Corporation (USA) and Texaco Petroleum Company (USA) v Ecuador* (*Chevron*) case cautiously noted after setting out the interpretative framework of the Vienna Convention on the Law of Treaties, 'It is not evident whether and if so to what extent arbitral awards are of relevance to the Tribunal's task'.[15]

The interpretative approaches adopted by the investment treaty tribunals need to be situated in the broader context of international courts dealing with fragmentation. The quantitative increase in fragmentation of rules and proliferation of adjudicators seems unquestionable.[16] However, it is less certain that this increase always raises qualitatively new challenges. From the very creation of the Westphalian system by three bilateral treaties,[17] the problems of fragmentation (and later of proliferation) often show a remarkable degree of conceptual continuity to the modern

and Dredging International NV v Egypt (ICSID Case No ARB/04/13, Award, 6 November 2008) paras 185–94; *LESI SpA et ASTALDI SpA c République algérienne démocratique et populaire* (CIRDI No ARB/05/03, Sentence, 12 November 2008) para 151; *EDF (Services) Limited v Romania* (ICSID Case No ARB/05/13, Award, 8 October 2009) paras 216, 218–19; *Joseph Charles Lemire v Ukraine* (ICSID Case No ARB/06/18, Decision on Jurisdiction and Liability, 21 January 2010) paras 259–62, 264. Recent NAFTA tribunals tend to refer only to the classic customary law authorities and earlier NAFTA awards in interpreting art 1005, *Glamis Gold Ltd v US* (UNCITRAL Arbitration, Award, 8 June 2009) paras 598–626; *Merril & Ring Forestry LP v Canada* (UNCITRAL Arbitration, Award, 31 March 2010) paras 182–213; *Chemtura Corporation v Canada* (UNCITRAL Case, Award, 2 August 2010) paras 121, 215.

[14] *Siag* (n 12).

[15] *Chevron Corporation (USA) and Texaco Petroleum Company (USA) v Ecuador* (UNCITRAL Arbitration, Partial Award on the Merits, 30 March 2010) para 163.

[16] Conclusions of the Study Group of the ILC, 'Fragmentation of International Law: Difficulties Arising from Diversification and Expansion of International Law' UN Doc A/CN.4/L.682, para 9.

[17] J Crawford, 'Multilateral Rights and Obligations in International Law' (2006) 319 *Recueil des Cours* 325, 349 ff.

challenges.[18] In investment treaty law and arbitration, despite the factually remarkable developments,[19] it is arguable that the principal features of the regime reflect continuity much more than discontinuity.[20] From a general international law perspective, the justification of claims of conceptual novelty is not self-evident: the language of primary rules in question may be traced back for centuries;[21] the substantive and procedural debates often continue those in the classic law;[22] already in 1907, states negotiated with complete nonchalance treaties providing individuals with access to international courts;[23] and investor-state arbitration is simply a(nother) regime of invocation of state responsibility.[24] While the elegant technical craftsmanship of treaty drafters is admirable, the building blocks themselves are unexceptional elements of the traditional legal order.[25] Against the background of the complex mix between continuities, discontinuities and innovations, the present chapter will focus on interpretative practices and consider whether they can be explained in traditional terms or require a formulation of a new framework of analysis.

The argument will be made in three steps. First of all, a brief historical overview of international investment law will be given, suggesting that the somewhat specific interpretative challenges may be explained by the peculiarities of the post-Second World War investment law-making (section II). Secondly, a number of traditional ways of explaining the relevance of case law on *pari materia* treaties will be considered, discussing the

[18] Y Shany, *The Competing Jurisdiction of International Courts and Tribunals* (Oxford, Oxford University Press, 2003) 230 ff, 239 ff, 247 f.

[19] Acknowledged by those supporting and criticising the investment arbitration regime alike, *cf* J Paulsson, 'Arbitration without Privity' (1995) 10 *ICSID Review – Foreign Inv L J* 232, 256; G van Harten, *Investment Treaty Arbitration and Public Law* (Oxford, Oxford University Press, 2007) particularly ch 5.

[20] J Crawford, 'Continuity and Discontinuity in International Dispute Settlement' in C Binder et al (eds), *International Investment Law for the 21st Century: Essays in Honour of Christoph Schreuer* (Oxford, Oxford University Press, 2009) 802.

[21] The language of most-favoured-nation (MFN) and national treatment clauses may be traced to late-17th century, H Neufeld, *The International Protection of Private Creditors from the Treaties of Westphalia to the Congress of Vienna* (Leiden, AW Sijthoff, 1971) 110 ff. Despite the apparent consensus to the contrary, treaty rules on fair and equitable treatment may also be traced back at least to mid-17th century British treaties. eg, the 1670 Treaty with Denmark (concluded by Cromwell's Commonwealth and re-made by Charles II) in its art 24 required states to 'cause justice and equity to be administered to the subjects and people of each other according to the laws and statutes of either country'. *Ambatielos case (Greece v UK)* ICJ Pleadings 484 (Fitzmaurice): see generally 412 f, 483 f.

[22] Crawford, 'Continuity and Discontinuity' (n 20).

[23] See the discussion regarding the International Prize Court at the 1907 Hague Second Peace Conference: *Deuxième conférence internationale de la paix: La Haye 15 juin–18 octobre 1907: Actes et documents* (The Hague, Tome II, Martinus Nijhoff Publishers, 1909) 789 ff, 811.

[24] J Crawford, 'Treaty and Contract in Investment Arbitration' (2008) 24 *Arbitration International* 351, 355 f.

[25] DM Price, 'Some Observations on Chapter Eleven of NAFTA' (1999–2000) 23 *Hastings Int'l & Comp L Rev* 421, 421; DM Price, 'Chapter 11 – Private Party vs. Government, Investor-State Dispute Settlement: Frankenstein or Safety Valve?' (2000) 26 *Can-US LJ* 107, 107 f; B Legum, 'The Innovation of Investor-State Arbitration' (2002) 43 *Harv Int'l LJ* 531.

arguments of ordinary meaning, generic terms, supplementary means of interpretation and customary law (section III). Thirdly, the possibility of qualitatively new approaches will be addressed (section IV). It will be suggested that even though the traditional approaches cannot fully explain the existing practice, no qualitatively new framework has emerged and therefore a more formalistic or alternatively a more cautious approach to interpretation and sources would be preferable. In particular, to the extent that the anterior adjudicator has explained a rule of customary or treaty law that falls within the admissible interpretative materials of the particular interpretative exercise, reliance on the case law in the manner of *Siag* would be permissible. In the absence of such nexus, direct reliance on earlier awards for case-by-case elucidations would be justified only in limited circumstances.[26]

Before engaging in the analysis, it should be noted what this chapter is not about. It is not disputed that arbitral awards can authoritatively explain international law – they surely represent one of the storehouses[27] from which the material content of rules can be extracted.[28] It is not argued that international adjudications (should) have no relevance in determining the content of the rules of international law. It is not disputed that arbitral awards may be appropriate for elucidating the content of the broadly textured investment protection rules, and that – unless systemic conditions radically change – the most important legal issues will continue to be explained in precisely this manner.[29] The equivalence of investment and trade law will also not be addressed here,[30] limiting the discussion to *pari materia* investment rules. The shade of science and art in the interplay of different admissible interpretative materials will not be dealt with,[31] focusing rather on the anterior question of their admissibility. It is precisely the likely emergence of a clearer and more detailed understanding of the content of the rules that requires a consideration of

[26] M Paparinskis, 'Investment Protection Law and Sources of Law: A Critical Look' (2009) 103 *ASIL Proceedings* 76.

[27] S Rosenne, *The Law and Procedure of the International Court, 1920–2005* (Leiden, Martinus Nijhoff Publishers, 2006) 1551.

[28] G Guillaume, 'Can Arbitral Awards Constitute a Source of International Law under Article 38 of the Statute of the International Court of Justice?' in Y Banifetami (ed), *Precedent in International Arbitration* (New York, Juris Publishing Inc, 2008); see: discussion below at section III.C.

[29] Of course, treaty parties themselves still possess crucial law-making and (re-)interpretative powers that may directly affect the existence and meaning of disputed rules: M Paparinskis, 'Investment Arbitration and the Law of Countermeasures' (2008) 79 *BYIL* 264, 342; A Roberts, 'Power and Persuasion in Investment Treaty Interpretation: the Dual Role of States' (2010) 104 *Am J Int'l L* 179.

[30] M Paparinskis, 'Equivalent Primary Rules and Differential Secondary Rules: Countermeasures in WTO and Investment Protection Law' in T Broude and Y Shany (eds), *Multi-Sourced Equivalent Norms in International Law* (Oxford, Hart Publishing, 2011) 259.

[31] RY Jennings, 'General Course on Principles of Public International Law' (1967) 121 *Recueil des Cours* 323, 544.

the interpretative limits of the international adjudicators: how can the case-by-case elucidation of rules be conceptualised in terms of interpretation and sources when the underlying rules in each case are *prima facie* different?

II. HISTORICAL PERSPECTIVE OF LAW-MAKING

The context of contemporary investment law is shaped by the historical development of the investment law-making and the experiments by states with different types of law-making methods.[32] During the second half of the nineteenth century and the beginning of the last century, the emphasis of law-making efforts in the area of protection of aliens (increasingly including investors) was on the customary law, largely reflected in the collections of state practice and arbitral awards.[33] While rules on investment protection were also included in bilateral treaties, they seemed nearly irrelevant, failing to extend the protection to corporate investors[34] and being used mainly to confirm the customary nature of certain rules.[35] Another element of the pre-Second World War law-making that set the pattern for the further development was the consistent failure of multilateral treaty-making.[36]

Even general customary rules were subject to considerable criticism. While it may have been the case that 'international law in the late nineteenth century *was* what the Western powers said it was',[37] by the 1920s and 1930s the situation had changed. The earlier law-making efforts were now viewed much more critically, 'conceived as misuse of law by former colonial and imperial powers'.[38] The existing state practice and case law on the treatment of aliens were viewed with suspicion, and the attempts to invoke general principles of law were dismissed as externalisation of peculiar domestic conceptions of a limited number of states.[39] The 1930

32 A Newcombe and L Paradell, *Law and Practice of Investment Treaties: Standards of Treatment* (The Hague, Wolters Kluwer, 2009) ch 1.
33 E Borchard, *Diplomatic Protection of Citizens Abroad* (New York, The Banks Law Publishing Co, 1915).
34 H Walker, 'Provisions on Companies in United States Commercial Treaties' (1956) 50 *Am J Int'l L* 373, 379 f.
35 C de Visscher, 'Le déni de justice en droit international' (1935) 52 *Recueil des Cours* 369, 374.
36 JW Cutler, 'Treatment of Foreigners: In Relation to the Draft Convention and Conference of 1929' (1933) 27 *Am J Int'l L* 225; EM Borchard, '"Responsibility of States", at the Hague Codification Conference' (1930) 24 *Am J Int'l L* 517; 'Texts Adopted by the Committee in First Reading as Revised by the Drafting Committee' in S Rosenne (ed), *Conference for the Codification of International Law [1930] vol IV* (New York, Oceana Publications Inc, 1975) 1659 f.
37 M Mendelson, 'The *Cameroon-Nigeria* Case in the International Court of Justice: Some Territorial Sovereignty and Boundary Delimitation Issues' (2004) 75 *BYIL* 223, 232.
38 S Rosenne, 'State Responsibility: *Festina Lente*' (2004) 75 *BYIL* 363, 364.
39 JF Williams, 'International Law and the Property of Aliens' (1928) 9 *BYIL* 1, 19 ff.

Hague Conference on the Codification of International Law took the debate between national treatment and international standards one step further (or perhaps rather back), debating not only the possibility of any rules other than non-discrimination but also the process of international law-making itself through treaty, custom and general principles.[40] Discussions about sources of law took five out of the total of available 12 days, and therefore contributed directly to the failure to reach a consensus on the substantive issues.[41]

Against this rather uninspiring background, the post-Second World War era law-makers continued parallel experiments in the form of customary law, multilateral treaties and bilateral treaties. Step by step, the first two law-making avenues were closed. The attempts at drafting multilateral treaties failed, and the controversies relating to nationalisations carried out by developing, decolonised and Socialist countries made the emergence of any generalised consensus necessary for such treaties unlikely.[42] The customary law avenue was closed by the *Barcelona Traction, Light and Power Company, Limited* case, with the ICJ lamenting 'the intense conflict of systems and interests' that precluded the indispensible 'consent of those concerned' to create customary rules on the protection of investment.[43] When the making of multilateral treaties and general customary law became unfeasible, the only option remaining available for law-makers was bilateral treaty-making (special customary law was *a priori* inappropriate for the task by requiring an opt-out from the general rule).[44] States modernised the Friendship, Commerce and Navigation Treaties, created the first BITs and provided them with investor-State arbitration clauses.[45] However, investors did not fully appreciate the potential of investor-state arbitration until the end of 1990s, and therefore investment protection law lacks the orderly and logical interrelation between law-makers and adjudicators (States creating rules, adjudicators adjudicating upon them, states reflecting upon the judicial interpretation and following it or modifying the rules

[40] As de Ruelle (Belgium) noted in the *Oscar Chinn* case, while all states at the Hague Conference agreed that a state breaching its obligations regarding the treatment of aliens under treaty, custom or general principles would commit a wrongful act, 'il reste à définir les obligations internationales résultant du droit coutumier, ainsi que des principes généraux de droit. On tourne donc ici dans un cercle vicieux'. *Oscar Chinn (UK v Belgium)* PCIJ Rep Series C No 75, 284 f.

[41] Rosenne (n 36) 1442 ff, 1583.

[42] Van Harten (n 19) 19 ff.

[43] *Barcelona Traction, Light and Power Company, Limited (Belgium v Spain) (New Application: 1962) (Second Phase)* [1970] ICJ Rep 3, para 89.

[44] M Mendelson, 'The Formation of Customary International Law' (1998) 272 *Recueil des Cours* 155, 215 ff.

[45] *Barcelona Traction* (n 43) Separate Opinion of President Rivero 57, para 3; F Berman, 'The Relevance of the Law on Diplomatic Protection in Investment Arbitration' in F Ortino et al (eds), *Investment Treaty Law: Current Issues II* (London, BIICL, 2007) 69; M Paparinskis, '*Barcelona Traction*: A Friend of Investment Protection Law' (2008) 8 *BaltYIL* 105, 105 ff.

through state practice and treaties, etc).[46] The historical record rather shows a 30-year long process of bilateral treaty-making creating a considerable number of similarly worded rules, with the adjudications beginning at the stage when a large number of binding rules (that would be complicated to change) already existed with considerable uncertainty about their content.

The move to bilateral treaty-making had obvious advantages and less obvious disadvantages. From the law-making perspective, when an 'intense conflict of systems and interests' precluded the consensus necessary for generating customary law or concluding multilateral treaties, bilateral treaties permitted the creation of nuanced rules that would for different reasons not command sufficient approval of all states.[47] The economical and political developments made the BIT programmes spectacularly successful, especially after the end of the Cold War and the declared departure of the ideas of New International Economic Order.[48] The number of investment protection treaties is nowadays assumed to amount to more than 2,600 BITs and several regional or *ratione materiae* specialised multilateral investment treaties.[49]

From the adjudicative perspective, when rules are expressed in customary law or in a multilateral treaty binding on all the relevant parties, the adjudicator's explanation of the content of the rule is relevant for all parties bound by the rule. However, BITs 'are concluded *intuitu personae*. The limited scope of their personal reach is part of the game'.[50] The adjudicatory explanation of one treaty rule is at least in the first instance not relevant for

[46] In investment law context, changes in BIT practice have taken place after the ICJ judgment in the *ELSI* case and the early NAFTA cases, SM Schwebel, 'The United States 2004 Model Bilateral Investment Treaty and Denial of Justice in International Law' in C Binder and others (eds), *International Investment Law for the 21st Century: Essays in Honour of Christoph Schreuer* (Oxford, Oxford University Press, 2009); LY Fortier, 'The Canadian Approach to Investment Protection: How Far Have We Come' in Binder and others, ibid; www.transnational-dispute-management.com; KJ Vandevelde, *US International Investment Agreements* (Oxford, Oxford University Press, 2009) 64 ff.

[47] Developed traditional home states could be less compromising within a bilateral negotiation than within a multilateral context, see: JE Alvarez and K Khamsi, 'The Argentine Crisis and Foreign Investors: A Glimpse into the Heart of the Investment Regime' (2008–2009) 1 *YB Int'l Inv L & Pol'y* 379, 410 ff.

[48] TW Waelde, 'A Requiem for the "New International Order"' in G Hafner (ed), *Liber Amicorum Professor Ignaz Seidl-Hohenveldern: in Honour of His 80th Birthday* (The Hague, Kluwer Law International, 1998). Calling for a requiem may have been somewhat premature, see: OM Garibaldi, 'Carlos Calvo Redivivus: The Rediscovery of the Calvo Doctrine in the Era of Investment Treaties (2006) *TDM*, and the same applies to describing the Calvo Doctrine 'dead as a door nail' in a Dickensian *Christmas Carol* allusion in 1910, see: 'Intervention for Breach of Contract or Tort where the Contract is Broker by the State or the Tort Committed by the Government or Governmental Agency' (1910) 4 *ASIL Proceedings* 148, 173.

[49] At the end of 2008 there were 2,676 BITs, see: UNCTAD, *Recent Developments in International Investment Agreements* (2008–June 2009) (New York and Geneva, United Nations, 2009) available at www.unctad.org/en/docs/webdiaeia20098_en.pdf, 2 (last visited 1 June 2011).

[50] R Kolb, 'Note: Is an Obligation Assumed by Two Different States in Two Different Treaties Binding between Them?' (2004) 51 *NILR* 185, 191.

other *pari materia* rules binding other parties. It is in this context that the interpretative question has to be asked: how and to what extent can the interpreter of investment treaties incorporate the reasoning of tribunals interpreting broadly similar rules that for the reason of historical developments are set out in different treaties and are binding on different parties?

III. *PARI MATERIA* TREATY RULES AND TRADITIONAL APPROACHES

In practice, when investment tribunals treat arbitral interpretation of *pari materia* rules as directly relevant, the relevance is usually assumed and not demonstrated.[51] While there is some support for the view that a complete substitution of citations for *de novo* analysis is impermissible,[52] the following sections will not address particular ways of framing references to earlier cases but rather the anterior question of their admissibility as interpretative materials in the first place. The simple fact that tribunals have not been explicit in categorising every argument in terms of principles of treaty interpretation does not mean that the argument is wrong *per se* or cannot be made. There are different ways in which rules of international law can play a part in the interpretation of other rules.[53] This section will consider in turn four perhaps most obvious arguments that could justify treating *pari materia* rules (and their arbitral interpretations) as part of relevant interpretative materials.

A. *Pari Materia* Rules and Ordinary Meaning

Article 31(1) of Vienna Convention on the Law of Treaties provides that 'A treaty shall be interpreted in good faith in accordance with the ordinary meaning to be given to the terms of the treaty in their context and in the light of its object and purpose'. If the case law interpreting *pari materia* treaty rules explained the ordinary meaning of the treaty rules,

[51] But see: discussion below section III.C.

[52] In the *MTD* Annulment Proceedings, Chile argued that the arbitral tribunal had manifestly exceeded its power by its excessive reliance on the award in the *Técnicas Medioambientales Tecmed, SA v Mexico* case. The *ad hoc* annulment committee rejected the argument because 'The *TECMED* dictum was cited in support of this standard, not in substitution for it', *MTD Equity Sdn Bhv and MTD Chile SA v Chile* (ICSID Case No ARB/01/07, Decision on annulment, 21 March 2007) para 70. It seems permissible to infer that *a contrario* substitution of an award for the treaty standard could have (manifestly) exceeded the bounds of a proper interpretative exercise.

[53] TW Wälde, 'Interpreting Investment Treaties: Experience and Examples' in C Binder et al (eds), *International Investment Law for the 21st Century: Essays in Honour of Christoph Schreuer* (Oxford, Oxford University Press, 2009) 724.

its use would be permissible for the purposes of interpretation. The argument is unobjectionable in principle and has been accepted in practice,[54] assuming that 'the Parties must have had in contemplation at the time when they concluded the second instrument the meaning which had been attributed to like expressions in the earlier instrument'.[55] The meaning is thus established through the examination of materials extrinsic to particular treaty(-making) but reflecting the generally accepted meaning of the term, somewhat similarly to dictionary definitions. Of relevance to the particular inquiry is that the generally accepted meaning of the earlier treaty instruments may also be established through adjudication. Consequently, to the extent that arbitral interpretations of investment protection rules become generally accepted, they could inform the ordinary meaning of terms and therefore justify their use as interpretative materials.

The ordinary meaning argument has two logical qualifications. The first qualification is of a temporal character: to conclude one treaty with a certain proposition of ordinariness in mind, the other treaty must already be in existence before the conclusion of the first one.[56] The second qualification is of a qualitative character. The meaning of the particular term has to be both sufficiently clear and sufficiently widely accepted to create the background of 'normality' against which treaty-making takes place. In the adjudicative context, the argument would naturally work in a temporally linear setting, courts authoritatively interpreting treaties in a way that forms the background of ordinariness for subsequent treaty-making. In this way, in the *Oil Platforms* case the ICJ implicitly treated the Permanent Court's 1935 *Oscar Chinn* interpretation of 'freedom of commerce' in a 1919 treaty as informing the meaning of 'freedom of trade' in a 1955 treaty.[57] Conversely, in the *Methanex v US* case, the tribunal rejected the claimant's argument that WTO approaches to the interpretation of national treatment may be employed in interpreting NAFTA, pointing out that 'The drafting parties of NAFTA were fluent in GATT law and incorporated, in very precise ways, the term "like goods" and the GATT provisions relating to it when they wished to do so'.[58] The classic proposition that 'words which may have a customary meaning in treaties . . . must be

[54] eg: *SS Wimbledon* [1923] PCIJ Rep Series A No 1 16, 25–28; *Minority Schools in Albania* [1935] PCIJ Rep Series A/B No 64 4, 16–17; *Maritime Delimitation in the Black Sea (Romania v Ukraine)* [2009] ICJ Rep 61, paras 133–34.

[55] E Lauterpacht, 'The Development of the Law of International Organization by the Decisions of International Tribunals' (1976) 152 *Recueil des Cours* 377, 396.

[56] MA Young, 'The WTO's Use of Relevant Rules of International Law: An Analysis of the *Biotech* Case' (2007) 56 *Int'l & Comp L Q* 907, 918 ff.

[57] *Oil Platforms (Iran v US)* (Preliminary Objections) [1996] ICJ Rep 803, para 48; F Berman, 'Treaty Interpretation in a Judicial Context' (2004) 29 *Yale J Int'l L* 315, 318.

[58] *Methanex v US* (UNCITRAL Case, Final Award, 3 August 2005) Part IV – ch B, para 30, also paras 29–37.

understood in that meaning' will also provide interpretative unity for temporally linear law-making in contemporary law.[59]

The temporal and qualitative qualifications seem to render reliance on pre-established meaning inapplicable to most investment arbitrations. In temporal terms, the modern controversies in case law about the meaning of key investment protection law standards have arisen relatively recently, mostly at the beginning of the 2000s. Since a large part of the existing treaties were already concluded, at least their ordinary meaning cannot be influenced by arbitral interpretations taking place after the conclusion. In qualitative terms, the arbitral interpretations of such rules as MFN, indirect expropriation and umbrella clauses is characterised by disagreement rather than consensus.[60] The unsettled nature of the debate makes it increasingly unlikely that states presently concluding treaties – to the extent that they do not expressly pick and choose the preferred approaches – may be deemed to have implicitly accepted any of the contested meanings. Of course, should consistency in case law emerge, the 'ordinary meaning' argument could help to legitimise this consensus for the future treaties.

A final problematic aspect, assuming that consistency exists at the moment of conclusion of treaties and informs the ordinary meaning, relates to the possibility of a radical change in interpretation of the rule explaining 'ordinariness' after the conclusion of the treaty. Had the *Methanex* tribunal accepted the argument that NAFTA incorporated the GATT approach to non-discrimination, it would have been faced with a further question about what 'GATT approach' to apply. The tribunal may have relied on the approach of 1994 (when NAFTA was concluded and GATT panels considered the purpose of the state adopting the allegedly discriminatory measure to be relevant), the second half of the 1990s (when the conduct complained of took place and the WTO Appellate Body considered the purpose of the state to be irrelevant), or the beginning of the 2000s (when it rendered its award and WTO Appellate Body appeared to

[59] AP Higgins (ed), *Hall's Treatise on International Law*, 8th edn (Oxford, Clarendon Press, 1924) 390.

[60] The only points of apparent agreement about MFN clauses and procedural matters – that MFN treatment applied to remove the requirement to litigate in domestic courts for a certain period of time but that it could not create jurisdiction (Newcombe and Paradell (n 32) 205 ff) – have been rejected by recent awards in *Wintershall* (n 2) paras 161–97, and *RosInvestCo* (n 2) paras 130–39, respectively. There are many divergent approaches to indirect expropriation, from emphasising the effect of the measures, see: *LESI* (n 13) paras 131–32, to minimising the relevance of the effect, see: *Saluka Investment BV v Czech Republic* (Partial Award, 17 March 2006) para 255, with different intermediate positions, see: *Continental Casualty Company v Republic of Argentina* (ICSID Case No ARB/03/9, Award, 5 September 2008) para 276. Early disagreements between narrow and broad readings of umbrella clauses have now fractured further into different strands of thinking about the standing, object, applicable law and parties to the agreements: A Sinclair, 'The Umbrella Clause Debate' in AK Bjorklund et al (eds), *Investment Treaty Law: Current Issues III* (London, British Institute for Comparative and International Law, 2009) 275.

be attributing some relevance to the purpose of the state).[61] None of these approaches are persuasive, suggesting respectively an application of a discredited approach, a determination of the content of the rule by a *renvoi* to a different and evolving legal regime and apparent retroactive change of the content of the rule. Such changes in case law are likely to be even more frequent in the decentralised investment protection law context.

B. *Pari Materia* Rules and Generic Terms

The most serious qualification of the ordinary term argument was the inter-temporal one: since most disputes are based on treaties concluded before the arbitral controversies properly began, even subsequent consensus cannot be implied back into the ordinary meaning contemporaneous to conclusion. This objection may be dealt with by reliance on the concept of generic treaty terms having an evolutionary potential of which states are assumed to have necessarily been aware.[62] The conclusion of the treaty for a very long or continuous period[63] and the purpose of the treaty to conclusively resolve controversial matters can support the treating the particular term as evolutionary.[64] As the ICJ recognised in the *Aegean Sea Continental Shelf* case, if a term is a generic one then 'the presumption necessarily arises that its meaning was intended to follow the evolution of the law and to correspond with the meaning attached to the expression by the law in force at any given time'.[65] If investment protection rules were generic terms, then their arbitral interpretations could legitimately follow the evolution of investment protection law so as to correspond with the meaning attached to it at the moment of interpretation, most likely expressed in different arbitral awards.[66]

There are three objections to this argument. First of all, it is not clear whether the most contested investment protection rules are *stricto sensu* generic. The most common BIT practice seems to be to have a fixed period

[61] See the summary of evolving approach to non-discrimination: N DiMascio and J Pauwelyn, 'Nondiscrimination in Trade and Investment Treaties: Worlds Apart or Two Sides of the Same Coin' (2008) 102 *Am J Int'l L* 48, 62 ff.

[62] *Dispute Regarding Navigational and Related Rights (Costa Rica v Nicaragua)* [2009] ICJ Rep 213, paras 66–67, available at www.icj-cij.org/docket/files/133/15321.pdf (last visited 1 June 2011).

[63] ibid para 66.

[64] ibid para 67; *Award in the Arbitration regarding the Iron Rhine ('Ijzeren Rijn') Railway (Belgium/the Netherlands)* (2005) 10 *RIAA* 33 para 83.

[65] *Aegean Sea Continental Shelf (Greece v Turkey)* (Judgment) [1978] ICJ Rep 3 para 77; HWA Thirlway, 'The Law and Procedure of the International Court of Justice 1960–1989. Supplement, 2005: Parts One and Two' (2005) 76 *BYIL* 1, 71 ff; R Gardiner, *Treaty Interpretation* (Oxford, Oxford University Press, 2008) 172 f.

[66] B Simma and T Kill, 'Harmonizing Investment Protection and International Human Rights: First Steps Towards a Methodology' in Binder et al (n 53) 678, 683 ff.

of duration of 10 years with subsequent continuation in force unless notified otherwise.[67] The implications are at best unclear: treaties are concluded for a continuous period and the purpose may be to provide the contemporary level of protection. At the same time, the period is not excessively long and the obligations do not provide for any kind of definite settlement.

Generic terms are 'known legal term[s], whose content the Parties expected would change through time'.[68] Fair and equitable treatment is clearly a known legal term.[69] However, unlike such generic terms as 'territorial status'[70] or 'natural resources' with a clear meaning at the moment of conclusion that has significantly changed,[71] until the beginning of the 2000s there was no significant interest in the meaning of fair and equitable treatment.[72] Since generic meaning is an exception to the normal inter-temporal principle of contemporaneous interpretation, it seems somewhat strained to argue that states have treated a rule as important enough to implicitly create an inter-temporal *renvoi* when before the treaty-making neither debates had taken place nor any consensus been established. MFN clauses themselves are rules by which states link the treaties to further development, so one should perhaps pause before attributing an implicit evolutionary potential to the meaning of a clause that itself operates as an explicit one.[73] Finally, the rules of expropriation can be better explained through the lenses of customary international law rules.[74] In any event, since states have at their disposal more certain tools for linking treaty rules to future developments of international law (MFN clauses and express reference to customary law), caution is needed before implying the less obvious interpretative argument of generic terms.[75]

[67] C McLachlan, L Shore and M Weiniger, *International Investment Arbitration: Substantive Principles* (Oxford, Oxford University Press, 2007) 33–34.

[68] *Kasikili/Sedudu Island (Botswana/Namibia)* (Judgment) [1999] ICJ Rep 1045, Declaration of Judge Higgins 1113, para 2.

[69] *Oil Platforms (Iran v US)* (Preliminary Objections) [1996] ICJ Rep 803, Separate Opinion of Judge Higgins 847, para 39.

[70] *Aegean Sea* (n 65) para 77.

[71] WTO AB Report, *US – Import Prohibition of Certain Shrimps and Shrimp Products* (6 November 1998) WT/DS58/AB/R, para 130.

[72] S Vasciannie, 'The Fair and Equitable Treatment Standard in International Investment Law and Practice' (1999) 70 *BYIL* 99. The divergent views adopted in the first NAFTA arbitrations illustrate the lack of any settled meaning during the earlier law-making processes, see: S Franck, 'The Legitimacy Crisis in Investment Treaty Arbitration: Privatizing Public International Law through Inconsistent Decisions' (2005) 73 *Fordham L Rev* 1521, 1574 ff.

[73] *RosInvestCo* (n 2) para 40; *cf* P Reuter, *Introduction au droit des traites*, 3rd edn (Paris, Presses Universitaires de France, 1995) 98 f.

[74] *Saluka* (n 60) para 254.

[75] Simma and Kill view the practice of reference to customary law as supporting their view that fair and equitable treatment is a generic term. It is complicated to see how an explicit customary *renvoi* could support, rather than undermine, the argument for an implicit treaty *renvoi*, see: Simma and Kill (n 66) 704.

Secondly, the generic term argument is structurally problematic. The contemporary meaning of generic terms has, so far in judicial practice, usually been sought in the understanding reflected in multilateral treaties and customary law, or otherwise through normatively determinable general consensus. Consequently, even if the term is itself capable of being elaborated through the development of the international legal order, it may be questioned whether bilateral elucidations may ever accurately state the general consensus usually reflected in genuinely multilateral rules. In any event, even if the evolution of generic terms through interpretation of bilateral treaties is not theoretically impossible, one would expect a very high degree of consistency over a lengthy period of time that is usually not present.

Thirdly, the generic term argument is also conceptually problematic. To treat investment protection law standards as generic terms in the meaning adopted by the ICJ would distort the clear dichotomy between the source of the argument requiring contemporary meaning ('territorial status', 'environment', 'natural resources') and conclusion of the argument providing it (customary law and generally accepted multilateral documents). This perspective would turn the investment treaty rules into the start and the finish of the analysis, all rules simultaneously being both evolutionary terms requiring contemporary meaning and authoritative statements providing that meaning. In other words, the interpreter would not engage in a one-way intellectual operation of explaining open-textured classic rules through the lens of subsequent developments but rather become part of the ongoing process of the subsequent development itself. The circularity of the argument is qualitatively different from the relatively one-way operation of generic terms, and would probably be a distortion of the traditional understanding of this concept. The application of the concept of generic terms to investment obligations may thus at one level seem to be favourable to the unity of international law in broadening the scope of interpretative authorities that investment tribunals could use; however, at a more profound level it would fragment the universality of the traditional rules of interpretation.

C. *Pari Materia* Rules and Supplementary Means

Article 32 of the Vienna Convention on the Law of Treaties provides that 'Recourse may be had to supplementary means of interpretation, including the preparatory work of the treaty and the circumstances of its conclusion'. The *Canadian Cattlemen for Free Trade v Canada* (*CCFT*) and *Chevron* tribunals have suggested that, since judgments and awards are subsidiary means for the determination of law, they could fit in this non-exhaustive list of supplementary means.[76] Even though the role of Article 32 in the interpretative process is limited, the open-textured nature of most substantive rules in investment treaties would probably be sufficient to characterise them as 'ambiguous and obscure' and therefore justify the application of the case law to 'determine the meaning.'

The *CCFT-Chevron* argument may be criticised on a number of levels. First of all, it is problematic from the perspective of sources. A judgment is one of the subsidiary means for the determination of rules of law, in the sense of not having an *ab initio* binding force independent from the particular rules[77] (even if judgments are often taken as rightly explaining the content of the binding rule).[78] Just as an interpretation of customary law would reflect a synthesis of state practice and *opinio juris,* and interpretation of general principles would extrapolate the rules from principles *in foro domestico* or the general framework of the international legal order, so an interpretation of the treaty would fully follow the required rules of interpretation. The result of the interpretation would not become a part of the rule itself, just as the process of interpretation of customary law or a general principle would not transform an international court's judgment into an element of state practice or domestic rules that constituted the formal source for the rule in the first place. Even though states not parties to the particular dispute could in practice follow the judgment, in technical terms they would follow the rules with content authoritatively reflected in the judgment. Of course, there is nothing to preclude states from relying on the judgment in their subsequent practice or treaty-making so as to technically bring it within the formal rules, but that would be a separate issue not covered by the general proposition.

Secondly, the argument is problematic from the perspective of treaty interpretation.[79] Introducing judgments as elements of treaty interpretation would go against the grain of the model of interpretation reflected in the Vienna Convention on the Law of Treaties that incorporates different authorities reflecting the attitude that states have taken (or implicitly approved) towards the treaty, and not developments completely extrinsic not only to the process of treaty-making itself but also to its parties. Even the broader concept of 'circumstances of conclusion' in Article 32 refers to

[76] *The Canadian Cattlemen for Free Trade v Canada* (UNCITRAL Arbitration, Award on Jurisdiction, 28 January 2008) paras 49–51, 164–69; *Chevron Corporation (USA) and Texaco Petroleum Corporation (USA) v Ecuador* (UNCITRAL Case, Interim Award, 1 December 2008) paras 119–24.

[77] C McLachlan, 'Investment Treaties and General International Law' (2008) 57 *Int'l & Comp L Q* 361, 391 f.

[78] H Lauterpacht, *The Development of International Law by the International Court* (London, Stevens & Sonds Ltd, 1958) 21.

[79] A Orakhelashvilli, 'Principles of Treaty Interpretation in the NAFTA Arbitral Award on *Canadian Cattlemen*' (2009) 26 *J Int'l Arb* 159, 167 ff.

the range of materials and information before the particular parties,[80] and cases arguably hinting at third party practice as other supplementary materials at their strongest (and most controversial) have not gone further than looking at the treaty practice of one party acquiesced by the other one.[81] It is certainly possible that an authoritative judgment becomes relevant in terms of treaty interpretation, in particular through being adopted in subsequent state practice or agreement, or by informing the ordinary meaning of subsequent treaties. However, in such cases the interpretative relevance flows from the conduct (or lack thereof) of the states themselves and not from the judgments *ipso jure*.

Thirdly, even leaving aside the two previous arguments, the *CCFT-Chevron* approach does not seem to lead very far in practice. Conceptualising arbitral awards as supplementary means would not permit a broader reference to third-party treaties. Supplementary means of interpretation logically apply to the particular treaty, and within the four corners of this argument there is nothing that would require generalising supplementary materials amongst all *pari materia* treaties. To the extent that arbitral awards have been rendered regarding the particular treaty, it is more natural to identify their interpretative relevance in terms of Article 31(3)(b) of the Vienna Convention on the Law of Treaties. Reliance by states on awards in their pleadings or failure to object to a consistent line of cases (where objections could reasonably be expected) would provide the legitimising approval or acquiescence in the more certain terms of the primary rule of interpretation. To conclude, the *CCFT-Chevron* does not seem fully persuasive either in terms of sources or of treaty interpretation, and would have limited practical effect in authorising greater references to arbitral interpretations of other treaties.[82] Similarly to the broader readings of generic terms, the seemingly progressive extension of the interpretative authority of investment tribunals could disrupt the unity of traditional rules on sources and interpretation.

[80] Gardiner (n 65) 343 ff.

[81] *Oil Platforms* (n 57) para 30; Separate Opinion of Judge Shahabuddeen 836; Dissenting Opinion of Vice-President Schwebel 882; Berman (n 57) 317; HWA Thirlway, 'The Law and Procedure of the International Court of Justice 1960–1989. Supplement, 2006: Part Three' (2006) 77 *BYIL* 1, 74 ff. It is doubtful whether interpreting arts 31 and 32 *ejusdem generis* permits implying totally unconnected *pari materia* treaties into art 32 as Linderfalk appears to suggest, see: U Linderfalk, 'Doing the Right Thing for the Right Reason – Why Dynamic or Static Approaches Should be Taken in the Interpretation of Treaties' (2008) 10 *Int'l Comm L Rev* 109, 139 f.

[82] Importantly, the *Chevron* tribunal appears to have changed its earlier position of treating awards as subsidiary means of interpretation, *Chevron* Interim Award (n 76) paras 119–24, to explicitly doubting the relevance of earlier decisions and using them without interpretative classification only 'to the extent that it may find that they shed any useful light on the issues that arise for decision in this case', *Chevron* Partial Award (n 15) paras 163–65.

D. *Pari Materia* Rules and Customary Law

Article 31(3)(c) of the Vienna Convention on the Law of Treaties and the customary law it reflects[83] require the interpreter to 'take into account, together with the context . . . any relevant rule of international law applicable in the relations between the parties'. The jurisdictional basis of the treaty arbitrations is treaty law, but the applicable law is not necessarily limited to it, since 'any relevant rule of international law' may include customary international law. To the extent that the investment protection rules can be demonstrated as having made explicit or implicit references to custom, the reliance on case law interpreting third-party treaties would become acceptable. While starting the interpretative process from different treaty rules set out in their respective treaties, all the tribunals would conclude the process by drawing upon the same rule of customary law (leaving aside special customary law).[84] Of course, the question would still remain about whether the interpretation of customary law is persuasive, but different awards could be legitimately incorporated in the analysis as admissible authorities purporting to explain the same legal rule.

There are a number of qualifications to the customary law argument. First of all, this argument can apply only to those treaty rules that have broadly analogous customary rules. Consequently, customary law could not explain the case-by-case developments regarding clauses on national treatment and MFN treatment. The debate about the application of MFN clauses to procedural clauses has largely taken place through the case-by-case consideration of the criteria explained by the *Maffezini v Spain* tribunal, and whether the approach is accepted or rejected the very form of analysis often assumes the legal relevance of distinctions drawn in earlier cases.[85] Customary law cannot explain these developments.

Secondly, because of the bilateral treaty setting, the language of the rules in the treaties is rarely identical, describing broadly similar phenomena in slightly or significantly different terms, in particular regarding indirect expropriation and fair and equitable treatment. The rules on expropriation use apparently different terms like 'expropriation', 'confiscation', 'deprivation', 'dispossession', 'taking' and 'nationalisation.'[86] Similarly, as Newcombe and Paradell note in their research of treaty practice, 'Although the fair and equitable treatment standard is included in

[83] *Certain Questions of Mutual Assistance in Criminal Matters (Djibouti v France)* (Judgment) [2008] ICJ Rep 177, para 112.

[84] S Ratner, 'Regulatory Takings in Institutional Context: Beyond the Fear of Fragmented International Law' (2008) 102 *Am J Int'l L* 475, 524.

[85] R Dolzer and C Schreuer, *Principles of International Investment Law* (Oxford, Oxford University Press, 2008) 253 ff; although see: *Gas Natural SDG, SA v Argentina* (ICSID Case No ARB/03/10, Decision on Preliminary Questions of Jurisdiction, 17 June 2005) para 36.

[86] McLachlan et al (n 67) 274 ff.

the majority of IIAs, there are important variations among IIA texts', both regarding the formulation of the rule and its relationship with other treaty or customary rules.[87]

The uncertainty about the appropriate criteria for distinguishing implicit references to customary law from a conscious exclusion of customary law may be seen in the example of *Saluka v Czech Republic* award. The tribunal accepted the argument that a treaty rule of 'deprivation' made a reference to customary law of expropriation explained in a draft text discussing 'taking', but rejected the argument that the treaty rule of 'fair and equitable treatment' made a reference to the customary minimum standard.[88] In both cases, the treaty rules were structurally analogous to customary rules, and the wording of treaty and custom sufficiently different to raise the possibility of different substantive content. However, the tribunal did not contrast the interpretative arguments and did not explain why 'fair and equitable treatment' was meant to exclude custom while 'deprivation' implicitly referred to the customary law of 'taking'.

The argument of reliance on customary law in investment protection law has three further problematic aspects. The first question is whether the difference in language plays a role in identifying a reference to customary law. The use of different terms could well be read to reflect a different intention regarding the content of the treaty rule, and this intention could be defeated if all the rules referred back to a single rule of customary law of identical content.[89] While customary law is 'any relevant rule', it does not mean that any existing customary law needs to be applied: it is just as plausible that gaps or different emphases in wording have been deliberate.[90]

The second aspect of the problem is whether a reference can be made when the treaty and customary standards are alleged to be different. A number of treaty rules are alleged to provide more stringent obligations than the analogous custom, whether regarding fair and equitable treatment and customary minimum standard, treaty and customary rules on full protection and security, or umbrella clauses and customary law of state contracts.[91] On the one hand, where the difference of content between customary and treaty rules is clearly identifiable (particularly regarding umbrella clauses and customary law of state contracts), it could be argued that *lex generalis* should not be implied back into the *lex specialis* treaty rules that were created precisely to provide qualitatively different treatment. On the

[87] Newcombe and Paradell (n 32) 257.

[88] *Saluka* (n 60) paras 254, 294 f.

[89] In practice, many treaty rules on expropriation use definitions concurrently, implicitly attempting to cover all possible paths to customary law. Still, the question of principle remains, and is relevant in those cases when the treaty terms do differ (as it was in *Saluka*).

[90] M Wood, 'The International Tribunal for Law of the Sea and General International Law' (2007) 22 *Journal of Coastal and Marine Law* 351, 361.

[91] Newcombe and Paradell (n 32) respectively 264 ff, 309 ff, 438 ff.

other hand, where the difference of content is less clear, to reject an interpretative argument because of its presumable result would arguably misapply the requirement of Article 31 to throw all relevant materials into the interpretative 'crucible'[92] and would instead assume the correctness of the meaning before the general rule has been properly followed.

Thirdly, even when customary law exists and can be implied in the treaty, the final question is an inter-temporal one. It could be said (as Sir Gerald Fitzmaurice argued before the ICJ in the *Ambatielos* case) that contemporary customary international law should not be used for interpreting the treaty if there has been a fundamental change in the law since the time of conclusion of the treaty.[93] In other words, the scope of the implicit *renvoi* that the treaty makers presumably make to customary law should be limited to customary law as it *ratione materiae* was at the moment of conclusion or to its the developments that could plausibly have been foreseen at that point. The argument seems particularly attractive in the investment protection context, where some statements of customary law of, for example, indirect expropriation may be read as reflecting a qualitatively new type of analysis, addressing the state's powers to regulate with a significantly higher degree of scrutiny.[94] If that is the case, the principle of contemporaneous interpretation could arguably limit the application of those rules that do not fall within the ambit of logical and predictable development of the customary law contemporaneous to the conclusion of the treaty. Therefore, even though the states themselves would be bound by the modern customary law, it would not be admissible for the interpretation of the particular treaty rule and thus could not be applied by the tribunal.

Bringing customary law into the discussion provides the most persuasive model for conceptualising the developments. However, even this argument is not without limitations and controversies, and its full implications are likely to be fleshed out in future treaty practice and case law, if and to the extent that the issues of applicable law are addressed more directly. The International Law Commission's Study Group has suggested certain criteria that support reliance on customary law: unclear or open-textured nature of the treaty rule;[95] treaty terms having recognised meaning in customary law;[96] and more generally the presumptive will of the parties to refer to customary law for all questions that they do not resolve

[92] Gardiner (n 65) 142.
[93] *Ambatielos Case*, ICJ Pleadings 407–11.
[94] See the classic article on the 'purpose' and 'effect' approaches, describing the more intrusive analysis of the 'sole effect' tribunals: LY Fortier and SL Drymer, 'Indirect Expropriation in the Law of International Investment: I Know It When I See It, or *Caveat Investor*' (2004) 19 *ICSID Rev–Foreign Investment L J* 293.
[95] Conclusions of the Study Group (n 16) para 20.a.
[96] ibid para 20.b.

in express terms.[97] While important, these guidelines are not entirely unproblematic both because they seem to unnecessarily distance themselves from the Vienna Convention on the Law of Treaties by creating new terminology of interpretation and because they seemingly conflate two distinct legal arguments. For example, the concept of 'unclear or open-textured' seems quite close to 'ambiguous or obscure' that Article 32 of the Vienna Convention on the Law of Treaties provides as one of the alternative conditions for its application. As a result, the Study Group may have merged a criterion for application of a part of the primary rule of interpretation with the condition for having resource to supplementary means, effectively collapsing Article 31(3)(c) into Article 32. Moreover, if a treaty term has a 'recognised meaning' in customary law, would it not be more natural to say that reference to customary law *is* the 'ordinary meaning' or 'special meaning' of the particular term?[98] The general presumption for reliance on customary law for matters not resolved expressly may also be contested. The fact that particular matters are not expressly dealt with in a treaty could simply suggest that they do not fall within the intended scope of treaty. Treaty makers are perfectly entitled to draft treaties with narrow scope and fairly abstract content, and there is no presumption towards broader subject matters or more detailed regulation. To use explicit language as a condition for reliance on custom could blur both the application of primary rule with conditions for using supplementary means and admissibility of interpretative materials with their effect in the interpretative process. More generally, Articles 31 and 32 provide treaty makers with a nuanced framework within which particular acts or omissions have predictable consequences. It would be surprising if this otherwise subtle and sophisticated approach to the particular treaty rule would only provide the rather crude tool of a strong one-way presumption for relating it to other rules.

More generally, it could be argued that the problems in the application of Article 31(3)(c) arise from a conflation of two interpretative techniques for bringing customary law into the interpretative process. The first type of argument would rely on the sameness or similarity of the subject matter of treaty and custom to determine the 'relevance' of customary law *qua* admissible interpretative materials. At the same time, the interpretative weight of the admissible customary law will be determined by the *chapeau* of Article 31(3)(c), requiring the interpreter only to 'take [custom] into account, together with context'. The other technique would rely on an express or implicit reference to customary law by the treaty itself, with the

[97] ibid paras 19.a, 20.c.

[98] JE Alvarez, 'The Factors Driving and Constraining the Incorporation of International Law in WTO Adjudication' in ME Janow et al (eds), *The WTO: Governance, Dispute Settlement & Developing Countries* (New York, Juris Publishing Inc, 2008) 622.

interpretative weight of customary law directly affecting the ordinary or special meaning of the term.[99]

The second type of question is fundamentally a question of interpretation, and it could be approached in terms of rules of interpretation. Such a perspective would both systematise the existing practice (that already *sub silentio* adopts some traditional rules of interpretation) and provide a subtler framework for dealing with the question than a general presumption can. Despite certain circularity of argument, Articles 31 and 32 could be applied both to elaborating the content of the particular rule, and to identifying the permissible reference to other rules. In particular, supplementary materials could be useful in confirming the interpretative choice of reference to customary law, both as preparatory materials[100] and as the circumstances of the treaty's conclusion, showing the consistently symbiotic customary and treaty law-making regarding the particular rule of law or even field of law.[101] The ILC has approved a somewhat similar meta-interpretative approach in its work on reservations. Guideline 3.1.6 on 'Determination of the object and purpose of the treaty' (object and purpose itself being an interpretative element) requires the application of all interpretative approaches of Articles 31 and 32 except object and purpose itself.[102] While acknowledging the tautological nature of this approach, the ILC concluded that 'it would appear to be legitimate, *mutatis mutandis*, to transpose the principles in Articles 31 and 32 of the Vienna Conventions applicable to the interpretation of treaties'.[103] The interpretative framework to be applied to bringing customary law into investment treaties could be formulated in similar terms, distinguishing the Article 31(3)(c) argument based on the mere sameness of subject matter and the separate question of a treaty reference, resolved in traditional interpretative terms.

IV. *PARI MATERIA* TREATY RULES AND NEW APPROACHES

The historical development of the investment protection law raises the challenge for the interpreters to explain the considerable importance

[99] M Paparinskis, 'Investment Treaty Interpretation and Customary Law: Preliminary Remarks' in C Brown and K Miles (eds), *International Investment Treaty Law and Arbitration* (Cambridge, Cambridge University Press, 2011) 65.

[100] E Denza and S Brooks, 'Investment Protection Treaties: United Kingdom Experience' (1987) 36 *Int'l & Comp L Q* 908, 912.

[101] See the argument regarding regulatory expropriation: M Paparinskis, 'Regulatory Expropriation and Sustainable Development' in MW Gehring, MC Cordonnier-Segger and A Newcombe (eds), *Sustainable Development in World Investment Law* (The Hague, Kluwer Law International, 2010) 295, 301 ff.

[102] ILC, 'Draft Guidelines on Reservations to Treaties' in *Official Records of the General Assembly, Sixty-First Session, Supplement No 10*, UN Doc A/64/10, Guideline 3.1.6.

[103] ILC, 'Draft Guidelines on Reservations to Treaties' in *Official Records of the General Assembly, Fifty-Ninth Session, Supplement No 10*, UN Doc A/62/10, Guideline 3.1.6, Commentaries 4–7.

attributed to *pari materia* arbitral interpretations. As was suggested in the previous sections, this approach is not easily explainable in terms of rules of treaty interpretation as set out in the Vienna Convention on the Law of Treaties and relevant customary law.[104] Stephan Schill has taken a different view, arguing for the permissibility of interpretative reliance on *pari materia* rules and suggesting that:

> What is decisive in cases of interpretation *in pari materia* is that the treaty for interpretation and the third-party treaty form part of a larger framework or system of treaties. The conclusion to be drawn from the practice of international courts and tribunals is therefore that cross-treaty interpretation is accepted and permissible to the extent that the treaties taken into account form part of a common and treaty-overarching system.[105]

However, the particular instances of practice and case law that Schill relies on do not necessarily support his thesis and may be explained in terms of traditional interpretative approaches outlined in the previous sections.[106] In most cases, the *pari materia* treaties relied on predated the particular instrument and therefore could plausibly be read as simply informing its ordinary meaning.[107] Some cases can be explained in light of the use of the argument by both parties to the treaty, arguably legitimising recourse to such materials through subsequent practice.[108] Other cases interpret ancient treaties or are decided in pre-Vienna Convention on the Law of Treaties time.[109] Both reasons possibly explain a more flexible approach to

[104] AF Lowenfeld, 'Investment Agreements and International Law' (2003–2004) 42 *Colum J Transnat'l L* 123, 129 f.

[105] S Schill, *The Multilateralization of International Investment Law* (Cambridge, Cambridge University Press, 2009) 275.

[106] ibid 270 ff.

[107] See: above section III.A. The Permanent Court of International Justice (PCIJ) interpreted arbitration clauses against the background of 'the movement in favour of general arbitration', moreover explicitly denying that any interpretative relevance could be derived even from a treaty between the same parties: *Case Concerning the Factory at Chorzów (Germany v Poland)* (Claim for Indemnity) (Jurisdiction) [1927] PCIJ Rep Series A No 9, 22, 24. In a different advisory opinion, the PCIJ relied on an earlier treaty on the same topic: *Interpretation of the Convention of 1919 concerning Employment of Women during the Night* (Advisory Opinion) [1932] PCIJ Series Rep A/B No 50 365, 374–76. In a later advisory opinion, the PCIJ interpreted Albanian minority obligations by reference to other minority treaties because the Albanian treaty built on matters 'which had already been agreed upon', *Minority Schools in Albania* (Advisory Opinion) [1935] PCIJ Series Rep A/B No 64 4, 16 (or, in the words of the dissenting judges, the Albanian treaty 'follow[ed] closely the wording' of earlier treaties: Dissenting Opinion of Judges Hurst, Rostworowski and Negulesco 24, 27). The term 'disputes' in an 1836 US-Morocco treaty was interpreted against the background of 17th century France-Morocco and 18th century Great Britain-Morocco treaties, *Case Concerning Rights of Nationals of the United States of America in Morocco (France v US)* (Judgment) [1952] ICJ Rep 176, 189.

[108] *Oil Platforms* (n 57) para 48.

[109] D Greig, 'The Time of Conclusion and the Time of Application of Treaties as Points of Reference in the Interpretative Process' in M Craven, M Fitzmaurice and M Vogiatzi (eds), *Time, History and International Law* (Leiden, Martinus Nijhoff Publishers, 2007) 207 ff.

interpretation.[110] Finally, the cases relying on treaty practice posterior to the particular treaty that cannot be clearly explained in terms of any of the recognised interpretative approaches seem to represent only a minority view.[111] At the end of the day, this practice may be simply an erroneous application of interpretative rules (possible under any regime).[112] If there is a choice of reading these disparate authorities either as reflecting and confirming the existing rules (and misapplying the law in a minority of cases) or as evidencing a fundamental change, it is certainly more natural to explain them in the former way with the grain of the established legal order rather than against it.

The interpretative challenges of the *pari materia* investment treaty rules and decentralised dispute settlement system have led to the development of vernacular *prima facie* reaching further than the traditional approaches. Two approaches have been suggested that may be described as the 'weak' and 'strong' arguments for consistency. While contributing to unity at the level of interpretative authority, they may challenge the unity of the traditional rules of sources and interpretation. The 'weak' consistency argument was made by the *SGS v Philippines* tribunal, seeing 'the applicable law . . . by definition . . . different for each BIT', and therefore arguing for a development of consistent solutions in the form of *jurisprudence con-*

[110] *Kronprins Gustaf Adolf (Sweden v US)* (1932) 2 *RIAA* 1239, 1258–59 (interpreting a 1783 Sweden-US treaty confirmed in 1827 in light of late 18th and early 19th century US treaty practice); although see the subtle and narrow Swedish argument 'turn[ing] to the treaties with France and Prussia, which were made just before and just after this treaty with Sweden, because they throw a great deal of light' on interpretation, *Arbitration between the United States and Sweden under Special Agreement of December 17, 1930: the 'Kronprins Gustaf Adolf' and the 'Pacific': Oral Arguments vol II* (Washington, Government Printing Office, 1934) 1257 (Acheson).

[111] eg: in the *ELSI* case referred to by Schill, only Judge Oda relied on the US treaty practice posterior to the US-Italy FCN Treaty, *Elettronica Sicula SpA (ELSI) (US v Italy)* [1989] ICJ Rep 15, Separate Opinion of Judge Oda 83, 87–88, 90–91. In the early *North Atlantic Coast Fisheries* case where an 1818 Great Britain-US treaty had to be interpreted, the dissenting arbitrator Drago considered that post-1818 British treaties 'may [evolve] the right interpretation' (1910) 9 *RIAA* 203, 206; while the majority used these treaties only to make *de lege ferenda* policy recommendations: *North Atlantic Coast Fisheries (Great Britain v US)* (1910) 9 *RIAA* 173, 199. In investment treaty arbitration, some tribunals have relied on trends of treaty practice in interpretation (particularly in the earlier cases relating to MFN clauses), *Maffezini v Spain* (ICSID Case No ARB/02/1, Decision on Jurisdiction, 25 January 2000) paras 58–61; *Telenor Mobile Communications as v Hungary* (ICSID Case No ARB/04/15, Award, 13 September 2006) para 96; *Vladimir Berschader and Moïse Berschader v Russia* (SCC Case No 080/2004, Award, 21 April 2006) paras 203–05. However, the majority of cases reject the normative relevance of such considerations, *Plama Consortium Limited v Bulgaria* (ICSID Case No ARB/03/24, Decision on Jurisdiction, 8 February 2005) paras 195–96; *Aguas del Tunari SA v Bolivia* (ICSID Case No ARB/02/03, Decision on Respondent's Objections to Jurisdiction, 21 October 2005) para 266; *Berschader* ibid Separate Opinion of Weiler para 24; *RosInvestCo* (n 2) para 38; *cf* Z Douglas, *The International Law of Investment Claims* (Cambridge, Cambridge University Press, 2009) 250 ff.

[112] *Industria Nacional de Alimentos, S.A. and Indalsa Perú, S.A.* (ICSID Case No ARB/03/4, Decision on Annulment, 5 September 2007) Dissenting Opinion of Sir Franklin Berman paras 5–12.

stante.[113] The premise of this argument appears to understate the potential for harmonious development that investment protection law already possesses. It is true that in a treaty dispute applicable law *prima facie* will be different for each treaty. However, it is perfectly possible that Article 31(3)(c) of the Vienna Convention on the Law of Treaties requires the interpreter of the particular treaty to take into account customary law that would then provide (special custom aside) identical law for all such treaties. More broadly, the concept of *jurisprudence constante* does not seem to add much to the analytical tools that the interpreter already possesses regarding applicable law and the application of general concepts (cause, object, etc) to particular rules.

The 'strong' consistency argument was made by the *Saipem v Bangladesh* tribunal, suggesting that 'subject to compelling contrary grounds, it has a duty to adopt solutions established in a series of consistent cases'.[114] Even if the proposition is relatively uncontroversial regarding cases interpreting the same rule of customary or treaty law, to say that interpretation of five or seven unconnected treaties without any express or implicit approval *requires* certain interpretation of more than 2,600 other BITs goes further than *lex lata*. The tribunal's purpose 'to satisfy the legitimate expectations of the community of States and of investors as regards the predictability of the law on these questions' is not very helpful in identifying the normative rationale of the argument.[115] It is not clear why expectations of investors and states, other than the parties to the dispute and the home state, should be of any immediate normative relevance for interpreting the rules in dispute. Conversely, if for some reason they are, it is not clear why international organisations (like the European Union, member of the Energy Charter Treaty) do not have such expectations. Moreover, if 'community of States' alludes to *erga omnes* obligations,[116] it has uncertain application to investment protection law which, even if in its multilateral form amounting to more than multilateral BITs,[117] has not moved beyond bundles of bilateral obligations.[118]

An argument for 'new' rules of interpretation permitting greater flexibility in permissible authorities is certainly unremarkable in principle. Rules of interpretation are only *jus dispositivum* and as such can be modified

[113] *SGS* (n 2) para 97.

[114] *Saipem* (n 2) para 67; *Casado* (n 2) para 119.

[115] ibid.

[116] CJ Tams, *Enforcing Obligations* Erga Omnes *in International Law* (Cambridge, Cambridge University Press, 2005).

[117] *CCFT* (n 76) paras 164–69.

[118] O Schachter, 'Entangled Treaty and Custom' in Y Dinstein and M Tabory (eds), *International Law at a Time of Perplexity – Essays in Honour of Shabtai Rosenne* (Dordrecht, Martinus Nijhoff Publishers, 1998) 735; C Carmody, 'WTO Obligations as Collective' (2006) 17 *Eur J Int'l L* 419 and fnn 76–77; TW Waelde, 'International Investment Law: An Overview of Key Concepts and Methodologies' (2007) 4(4) *TDM* 48 f (n 104); Paparinskis 'Countermeasures' (n 29) 330 f.

through subsequent practice. Still, despite the quantitatively impressive nature of modern developments, the better view is that no special new rules have emerged.[119] The complex parallelism of rules and disputes relating to the property interests of foreigners is not an innovation of the twenty-first century investment law[120] and was known to the ILC during its work on what was eventually to become the Vienna Convention on the Law of Treaties.[121] While some features of the investment protection system could justify changes *de lege ferenda*,[122] the policy desirability cannot on its own change the *lex lata*. Just as in any other case of alleged change of customary or treaty law, the desirable change needs to be demonstrated in terms of actual state practice (that may be reflected in case law).

States argue and tribunals accept the rules of the Vienna Convention on the Law of Treaties.[123] Since the pleadings in most cases are not publicly available, the legal rationale for the invocation of case law by states is uncertain. Still, with all due caution drawing upon the available information, the picture is at best mixed: some states have expressly argued against the normative influence of *pari materia* case law,[124] others appear to have accepted it,[125] while yet others seem to have invoked it as explaining customary law.[126] The case law is by no means unanimous in relying on earlier awards, with equally distinguished tribunals adopting positions from very receptive to deeply sceptical.[127]

When tribunals are conceived as engaging in law-making, the state practice has been disapproving. The response by NAFTA states to perceived

[119] See a discussion of investment law and *lex specialis* in the context of state responsibility: Paparinskis, 'Countermeasures' (n 29) 345 ff.

[120] In the 1903–1905 Venezuelan Arbitrations similar legal issues were arbitrated in parallel bilateral proceedings in Venezuela-US, Belgium, Great Britain (1903–1905) 9 *RIAA* 111–533; Venezuela-France, Germany, Italy, Mexico, Netherlands, Spain, Sweden and Norway Mixed Claims Commissions (1903–1905) 10 *RIAA* 1–770, while the implications of earlier gunboat diplomacy were addressed in both arbitration, *Venezuelan Preferential Case* (1904) 9 *RIAA* 99, and landmark law-making activities: JB Scott, 'The Work of the Second Hague Peace Conference' (1908) 2 *Am J Int'l L* 1, 15. See also: nn 20–25.

[121] Venezuelan cases were extensively discussed in the reports on state responsibility submitted to the ILC at the time, see: FV García-Amador, 'Sixth Report on State Responsibility' in (1961) *YBILC vol II*, A/CN.4/SER.A/1961/Add.1 1 paras 57 (fn 89), 67, 69, 103, 104, 106 (fn 197), 122, 123, 130, 132, 137(fn 244), 142, 150, 153, 161.

[122] Z Douglas, 'The Hybrid Foundations of Investment Treaty Arbitration' (2003) 74 *BYIL* 151, 168.

[123] CH Schreuer, 'Diversity and Harmonization of Treaty Interpretation in Investment Arbitration' (2006) 3 (2) *TDM* 1 f.

[124] *AES Corporation v Argentina* (ICSID Case No ARB/02/17, Decision on Jurisdiction, 26 April 2005) paras 20–22 (Argentina); *MTD* Annulment (n 52) para 63 (Chile); *LLC Amto v Ukraine* (SCC Case No 80/2005, Final Award, 26 March 2008) para 28.iii (Ukraine); *Glamis* (n 13) para 605 (US).

[125] *Rumeli Telekom A.S. and Telsim Mobil Telekomikasyon Hizmetleri A.S. v Kazakhstan* (ICSID Case No ARB/05/16, Award, 29 July 2008) para 609 (Kazakhstan); *Plama Consortium Limited v Bulgaria* (ICSID Case No ARB/03/24, Award, 27 August 2008) para 175 (Bulgaria).

[126] *Saluka* (n 60) para 289 (Czech Republic); *Jan de Nul* (n 13) para 182 (Egypt).

[127] See (n 2).

activist tribunals through Article 1128 submissions, NAFTA Free Trade Commission and changes in subsequent BIT treaty practice support the traditional sources of law in both multilateral and bilateral contexts, emphasising and furthering the classic approaches across-the-board rather than relaxing them.[128] The responses to creative MFN clause interpretations have been similarly negative.[129] Of interest is also the broader systemic scepticism directed at the desirability of the elucidation of investment protection law through investment arbitration. The treaty practice of the United States and Canada now *de facto* internationalises domestic constitutional approaches to regulatory expropriation,[130] and the Norwegian Model BIT (now abandoned) expressly drew upon the experience of human rights law of expropriation.[131] Whatever view one takes about the merits of these changes in treaty practice, they appear to indicate strong dissatisfaction with the overly flexible interpretative practices, rejecting particular criteria, criticising broader normative foundations and searching for more appropriate approaches in other legal regimes and systems.

V. CONCLUSION

The decentralisation of rules and adjudicators in investment law has caused some strain to the traditional approaches to sources and interpretation. There seems to be a normative mismatch between the pragmatic case-by-case identification of criteria of broadly termed *pari materia* obligations and the *prima facie* lack of mutual legal relevance between these elucidations. The issue may be considered on two levels: first of all, whether in descriptive terms the practice can be explained by traditional approaches to sources and interpretation; secondly, whether in normative terms it signifies a change to or at least a reappraisal of the traditional meta-rules of sources and interpretation. From the four arguments reflecting the traditional approaches only reliance on customary law may implicitly explain some parts of the recent practice. However, even though practice sometimes goes further than the traditional understanding of sources and interpretation, it has not resulted in an underlying normative shift of the meta-rules. Most instances of state practice and case law confirm the traditional understanding of sources and interpretation, and the explicit and implicit attempts to change the traditional approaches are

[128] Newcombe and Paradell (n 32) 61, 272 ff.

[129] ibid 223 f.

[130] A Newcombe, 'Canada's New Model Foreign Investment Protection Agreement' (2005) 2 (1) *TDM* 6 f.

[131] 2007 Norway Model BIT, art 6, available at http://italaw.com/documents/NorwayModel2007.doc; Comments on the Model for Future Investment Agreements paras 22–23, available at http://italaw.com/documents/NorwayModel2007-commentary.doc (both last visited 1 June 2011).

neither widespread nor consistent enough to change the Vienna Convention on the Law of Treaties and customary rules on treaty interpretation. There seem to be a number of possible solutions. The interpreters could change their legal argumentation from *verbatim* incorporation of case-by-case elucidated criteria to *de novo* interpretations. The other alternative would be to demonstrate the existence and relevance of customary law (or other kind of interpretative nexus with the rules elaborated in other awards) before the argument is made. More plausibly, tribunals could be explicit about the lack of direct normative relevance in most instances and minimise the approach of explicit substitution and extensive borrowing from earlier case law.

Whatever *a priori* jurisprudential reasons for consistency states may be presumed to have, it is hard to read the practice otherwise as showing the satisfaction of states with the existing sources framework encapsulating the procedurally and substantively decentralised system. Classic approaches already permit certain flexibility, and to the extent that tribunals have attempted to extend it further, the response of states – when expressed in normatively determinable terms – has been sceptical both regarding particular choices and the broader teleology. States have shown little normatively determinable interest to initiate or acquiesce in any radical reforms, in particular through giving the adjudicators a greater harmonising role than they already enjoy *de lege lata*. This system may be far from perfect for ensuring fully harmonious development of law, but it accurately reflects the unified meta-rules on sources and interpretation and is precisely the kind of system that states have crafted in the last 50 years.

The 2010 award in the *Chemtura* case provides an appropriate arbitral postscript for this chapter. Three distinguished arbitrators who had sat on earlier tribunals making landmark pronouncements on sources and interpretation in investment arbitration (Gabrielle Kaufmann-Kohler in *Saipem*, Charles Brower in *Chevron* and James Crawford in *SGS II*) appeared now to take a cautious stance. The *Saipem* tribunal had earlier suggested that 'it *must* pay due consideration to earlier decisions of international tribunals. . . . Subject to compelling contrary grounds, it *has a duty* to adopt solutions established in a series of consistent cases. . . . It *has a duty* to seek to contribute to the harmonious development of investment law'.[132] The language of the *Chemtura* award is slightly but importantly different: 'a tribunal *should* pay due regard to earlier decisions. . . . It *ought* to follow solutions established in a series of consistent cases'.[133] The explanation of the role of earlier decisions trails *Saipem* but the imperative language has been changed into merely suggestive, and the arbitral obligation to harmoniously develop the law is completely dropped. If *Chemtura* is indeed a

[132] *Saipem* (n 2) para 67 (emphasis added).
[133] *Chemtura* (n 13) para 109 (emphasis added).

confirmation of and a (re)turn to the traditional perception of sources and interpretation, it provides a symbolic closure for the investment law's first decade of the third millennium and the imaginative normative innovations that failed to receive the law-making stamp of approval.

6

The ECHR and its Normative Environment: Difficulties Arising from a Regional Human Rights Court's Approach to Systemic Integration

RAGNAR NORDEIDE*

I. INTRODUCTION

A. Fragmentation and Persuasiveness of Legal Reasoning – Exploring a Regional Human Rights Court's Approach to Systemic Integration

AS A CONSEQUENCE of the general debate on fragmentation of international law, an increasingly important element of the persuasiveness of international courts' reasoning in contemporary international law seems to be their ability to navigate their methods of interpretation between the Scylla of unreflective self-containment and the Charybdis of overreaching the mandate given to them in the relevant jurisdiction-endowing treaty. The capability of international courts to face this challenge head-on has benefited from the report of the International Law Commission (ILC) on fragmentation,[1] in which it both identified a legal technique to make use of (Article 31(3)(c) of the Vienna Convention

* Research Fellow/PhD candidate, Department of Public and International Law, University of Oslo and Visiting Fellow, Graduate Institute of International and Development Studies (IHEID), Geneva. This chapter has its origins in a conference paper presented at the Conference 'Unity or Fragmentation of International Law: the Role of International and National Tribunals' organised in Oslo 14–15 May 2009, and was revised during the author's visiting fellowship at IHEID in 2010–11.

[1] ILC, *Fragmentation of International Law: Difficulties Arising from the Diversification and Expansion of International Law*, Report of the Study Group of the International Law Commission (ILC Fragmentation Report), finalised by Martti Koskenniemi, UN Doc A/CN.4/L.682 (2006).

on the Law of Treaties)[2] and articulated the rationale for a greater use of this legal technique (the objective of systemic integration).[3]

When exploring the feasibility of using the ILC's proposed technique in the context of the European Convention on Human Rights,[4] two particular traits of the Convention would seem especially relevant to take into account. First, it has been suggested that although the provisions on treaty interpretation in the Vienna Convention on the Law of Treaties seem to deal with all treaties alike, this should not detract from the fact that human rights treaties nevertheless have a specific object and purpose that make interpretation of these treaties different from other treaties in international law.[5] Hence, the element of relying on the object and purpose of a treaty (articulated in Article 31 of the Vienna Convention on the Law of Treaties) is of particular significance when interpreting human rights treaties.[6] Second, as regards the Convention more specifically, it has been suggested that the European Court of Human Rights[7] – in addition to attaching weight to the fact that it is supervising a human rights treaty – should take into account the Convention's regional character.[8] Both these suggestions find support in the case law of the Court.[9]

The purpose of the present chapter is to explore the Court's approach to the interface between the Convention and other international law through treaty interpretation, and to assess what its approach tells us about the challenges of integrating a regional human rights treaty into the wider system of international law.

B. Mitigating Fragmentation through a Principle of Systemic Integration

In 2006 a study group set up by the ILC to consider the phenomenon of fragmentation of international law delivered its final report.[10] Of principal

[2] Vienna Convention on the Law of Treaties (23 May 1969) 1155 UNTS 331. Art 31(3)(c) of the Vienna Convention on the Law of Treaties reads as follows: '3. There shall be taken into account, together with the context: . . . (c) any relevant rules of international law applicable in the relations between the parties'.

[3] ILC Fragmentation Report (n 1) para 423.

[4] European Convention for the Protection of Human Rights and Fundamental Freedoms (4 November 1950) ETS no 5, 213 UNTS, hereinafter: 'the Convention'.

[5] R Bernhardt, 'Thoughts on the Interpretation of Human Rights Treaties' in F Matscher and H Petzold (eds), *Protecting Human Rights: The European Dimension. Studies in Honour of Gérard J Wiarda* (Cologne, Heymann, 1988) 65 ff.

[6] ibid.

[7] Hereinafter: 'the Court'.

[8] C Ovey, R White and FG Jacobs, *The European Convention on Human Rights*, 4th edn (Oxford, Oxford University Press, 2006) 54.

[9] See, eg: *Belilos v Switzerland* App No 10328/83 (ECtHR, 29 April 1988); *Loizidou v Turkey* (preliminary objections) App No 15318/89 (ECtHR, 23 March 1995) para 85; *Wemhoff v FRG* App No 2122/64 (ECtHR, 27 June 1968) para 8; *Ireland v United Kingdom* App No 5310/71 (ECtHR, 18 January 1978) para 239. See for a discussion of the cases: L Wildhaber, 'The European Convention on Human Rights and International Law' (2007) 56 *Int'l & Comp L Q* 217–32, 227 ff.

[10] ILC Fragmentation Report (n 1).

significance is the report's emphasis on the fundamental importance of applying Article 31(3)(c) of the Vienna Convention on the Law of Treaties as an interpretative tool to avoid problems of fragmentation.[11] In the ILC's view the provision expresses a principle of 'systemic integration' and as such can counter problems of fragmentation, since it entails that 'although a tribunal may only have jurisdiction in regard to a particular instrument, it must always *interpret* and *apply* that instrument in its relationship to its normative environment – that is to say "other" international law'.[12] The ILC's conclusions were based on its view that international law is a legal system, and not a random collection of norms.[13] Hence, 'whatever their subject matter, treaties are a creation of the international legal system and their operation is predicated upon that fact'.[14] The nature of the principle of 'systemic integration' was explained by the ILC as 'the process . . . whereby international obligations are interpreted by reference to their normative environment ("system")'.[15] The ILC therefore argued for enhanced recognition and application of Article 31(3)(c) as an interpretative tool to avoid problems of fragmentation.[16] Article 31(3)(c) of the Vienna Convention on the Law of Treaties requires that 'There shall be taken into account, together with the context: . . . (c) any relevant rules of international law applicable in the relations between the parties'. The increasing treatment of the provision in both theory and practice during the last decade has shown that the proper operation of the provision is by no means straightforward.

The wording gives rise to several questions of interpretation, which for the sake of presentation can be divided into two main parts: 'relevant rules of international law' and 'applicable between the parties'. The first part raises, *inter alia*, questions as to what extent other international law drawn upon must be of the same subject matter as the treaty under interpretation for it to be regarded as 'relevant'; questions regarding intertemporality; and questions regarding the range and status of instruments that can be drawn upon under the rubric 'rules of international law'.[17] The main questions concerning the second part 'relate to whether the rules of international law need to be applicable between all disputants, all parties to the treaty under interpretation, or reflect the common intention of the parties to the treaty under interpretation'.[18]

[11] ibid paras 420, 479–80.
[12] ibid para 423.
[13] Conclusions of the work of the Study Group on the Fragmentation of International Law, *Difficulties arising from the Diversification and Expansion of International Law*; adopted by the International Law Commission at its Fifty-eighth session, 2006, and submitted to the General Assembly as a part of the Commission's report covering the work of that session (ILC Conclusions) UN Doc A/61/10, para 251, conclusion (1).
[14] ILC Conclusions (n 13), conclusion (17).
[15] ILC Fragmentation Report (n 1) para 413.
[16] ILC Fragmentation Report (n 1) para 420, 479–80.
[17] R Gardiner, *Treaty Interpretation* (Oxford, Oxford University Press, 2008) 259 ff.
[18] ibid 361.

The questions raised by the wording have prompted much scholarly debate in recent years, and a *tour d'horizon* of the main arguments will be presented here. It has been argued that non-binding rules cannot be relied upon when making use of the provision.[19] Concerning the questions of the range and status of instruments that can be drawn upon and how to denote the common intentions of the parties, it has been argued that the evidence of such common understanding – in order to be a valid interpretative element under the Vienna Convention on the Law of Treaties Article 31(3)(c) – must either constitute a rule of customary international law or, if not, be sufficiently accepted to constitute an interpretative agreement.[20] This understanding would seem to find support in the practice of some international tribunals. In the *Mox Plant OSPAR Arbitration*, the majority (2–1) held that it could not rely on non-binding or evolving rules, that is, law which was not considered general principles or customary law.[21] That the threshold of the norm constituting a general principle of international law must be met, was also stated in the *Iron Rhine* case[22] and in the *Biotech* case.[23]

The use of the provision has also spurred discussions on the hierarchical nature of Article 31 of the Vienna Convention on the Law of Treaties. Although the ILC in 1966 clearly envisaged Article 31 being applied in a non-hierarchical way,[24] the three paragraphs being only a matter of 'logic',[25] it has been argued that the subsequent practice of international courts shows a different picture.[26]

Recourse to the provision has also prompted reactions focusing on the general limits of treaty interpretation. The argument here is that other international law to be referred to pursuant to Article 31(3)(c) can only assist in giving meaning to the terms used in the treaty, and thus cannot change or overrule those terms.[27] On this basis, the argument goes, a distinction must be made between interpretation of the treaty in the *context of* other international law and application of the treaty *together with* other international law.[28]

[19] ME Villiger, *Commentary on the 1969 Vienna Convention on the Law of Treaties* (Leiden, Martinus Nijhoff Publishers, 2009) 433. See also: A Orakhelashvili, *The Interpretation of Acts and Rules in Public International Law* (Oxford, Oxford University Press, 2008) 366.

[20] R Gardiner, *Treaty Interpretation* (n 17) 275.

[21] Perm Ct Arb, *Ireland v United Kingdom*, Final Award, paras 93–105 (2 July 2003). Documents for arbitrations under the auspices of the Permanent Court of Arbitration are available at http://www.pca-cpa.org.

[22] Perm Ct Arb, *Belgium v Netherlands*, Award, para 59 (24 May 2005).

[23] WTO Panel Report, *European Communities – Measures Affecting the Approval and Marketing of Biotech Products* (21 November 2006) WT/DS291–293/R, paras 7.67–7.72 .

[24] ILC Report 1966, YBILC 1966 vol II, 220, paras 8–9.

[25] ibid.

[26] ME Villiger (n 19) 436, 441. See also: A Orakhelashvili (n 20) 312, 366.

[27] J Pauwelyn, *Conflict of Norms in Public International Law* (Cambridge, Cambridge University Press, 2003) 254.

[28] ibid 272 f.

II. THE COURT'S GENERAL APPROACH: PLACING THE CONVENTION WITHIN THE BROADER SYSTEM OF INTERNATIONAL LAW

The Court has over the years developed a body of case law concerning interpretation of the Convention in light of other international law.[29] From this case law it transpires that the Court has adopted an approach which places the Convention within the broader system of international law. A common formulation of this approach can be found in the *Al-Adsani* case, in which the Court stated that the 'Convention . . . cannot be interpreted in a vacuum' and that it 'should so far as possible be interpreted in harmony with other rules of international law of which it forms part.'[30]

In the more recent *Demir*[31] case rendered by a Grand Chamber, the Court devoted 26 paragraphs to 'the methodology to be adopted' when interpreting 'the Convention in light of other international instruments'.[32] In setting out the 'basis' for its approach, the Court noted its consistent practice since *Golder*[33] of being 'guided mainly' by the rules of interpretation set out in Articles 31 to 33 of the Vienna Convention on the Law of Treaties.[34] Although the Court explicitly referred to Article

[29] Some of the best known, which are also regularly referred to by the Court itself, are: *Al-Adsani v United Kingdom* App No 35763/97 (ECtHR, 21 November 2001); *Loizidou v Turkey* App No 15318/89 (ECtHR, 18 December 1996); *Golder v United Kingdom* App No 4451/70 (ECtHR, 21 February 1975). One could also point to examples of cases within different themes or areas that have arisen in the Court's case law regarding interpretation in light of other international law, *inter alia*: concerning state immunity: *Fogarty v United Kingdom* App No 37112/97 and *McElhinney v United Kingdom* App No 31253/96 (both judgments ECtHR, 21 November 2001); concerning responsibility of acts or omissions following from membership of an international organisation: *Behrami and Behrami v France & Saramati v France, Germany and Norway* App No 13229/03 and 78166/01 (ECtHR 2 May 2007); *Bosphorus Hava Yollari Turizm Ve Ticaret Anonim Sirketi v Ireland* App No 45036/98 (ECtHR 30 June 2005); concerning the concept of 'jurisdiction' in the Convention and in general international law: *Banković and others v Belgium and others* App No 52207/99 (ECtHR Grand Chamber, 12 December 2001); *Cyprus v Turkey* App No 25781/94 (ECtHR Grand Chamber, 10 May 2001); concerning the Convention and International Humanitarian Law: *Kononov v Latvia* App No 36376/04 (Grand Chamber, 17 May 2010); concerning interim measures: *Mamatkulov and Askarov v Turkey* App Nos 46827/99, 46951/9) (ECtHR, 4 February 2005), to name a few.

[30] *Al-Adsani v United Kingdom* (n 29) para 55. The Court's approach in *Al-Adsani* was also among the sources relied on as a basis for the ILC's view of art 31(3)(c) as articulating an objective of systemic integration in its report on the issue of fragmentation of international law (n 1).

[31] *Demir and Baykara v Turkey* App No 34503/97 (ECtHR, 12 November 2008).

[32] See for a general analysis of the case: R Nordeide, 'Demir & Baykara v. Turkey' (2009) 103 *Am J Int'l L* 567–74.

[33] *Golder v United Kingdom* (n 29).

[34] The Court presented the following general account of what this entailed:

> In accordance with the Vienna Convention the Court is required to ascertain the ordinary meaning to be given to the words in their context and in the light of the object and purpose of the provision from which they are drawn . . . Recourse may also be had to supplementary means of interpretation, either to confirm a meaning determined in accordance with the above steps, or to establish the meaning where it would otherwise be ambiguous, obscure, or manifestly absurd or unreasonable. . . . Since the Convention

31(3)(c),[35] it did not embark upon an analysis of the provision itself.[36] Rather, the Court set forth an extended analysis of its own practice of interpreting the Convention in light of other international texts and instruments, in which it presented examples from its own case law of the 'Diversity of international texts and instruments used for the interpretation of the Convention'.[37] And in this subsection on exploring the range of international legal materials that the Court has used to interpret the Convention, the Vienna Convention on the Law of Treaties was invoked nowhere by the Court.[38]

Whilst generally having adopted an integrationist approach to the Convention and the broader system of international law, the Court has also emphasised the implications of the Convention being a human rights treaty, and the fact that it operates in a regional context. Thus, in Loizidou, the Court formulated the following as regards the Convention being a human rights treaty:

> Unlike international treaties of the classic kind, the Convention comprises more than mere reciprocal engagements between Contracting States. It creates, over

is first and foremost a system for the protection of human rights, the Court must interpret and apply it in a manner which renders its rights practical and effective, not theoretical and illusory. The Convention must also be read as a whole, and interpreted in such a way as to promote internal consistency and harmony between its various provisions . . . In addition, the Court has never considered the provisions of the Convention as the sole framework of reference for the interpretation of the rights and freedoms enshrined therein. On the contrary, it must also take into account any relevant rules and principles of international law applicable in relations between the Contracting Parties . . . The Court further observes that it has always referred to the 'living' nature of the Convention, which must be interpreted in the light of present-day conditions, and that it has taken account of evolving norms of national and international law in its interpretation of Convention provisions, *Demir* (n 31) paras 65–68.

[35] The Court made reference to Vienna Convention on the Law of Treaties, art 31(3)(c) in the following way: 'In addition, the Court has never considered the provisions of the Convention as the sole framework of reference for the interpretation of the rights and freedoms enshrined therein. On the contrary, it must also take into account any relevant rules and principles of international law applicable in relations between the Contracting Parties (see *Saadi*, cited above, § 62; *Al-Adsani*, cited above, § 55; and *Bosphorus Hava Yolları Turizm ve Ticaret Anonim Şirketi v Ireland* [GC], no 45036/98, § 150, ECHR 2005-VI; *see also Article 31 § 3 (c) of the Vienna Convention*)', *Demir* (n 31) para 67 (emphasis added).

[36] Other international tribunals seem more inclined to conduct an exploration of the nature and boundaries of Vienna Convention on the Law of Treaties, art 31(3)(c) as such, see: *Oil Platforms (Iran v US)* 2003 ICJ Rep Series 161 para 41 (6 November 2003); ibid 225 paras 45–49 (Separate Opinion of Judge Higgins); ibid 270 paras 21–24, 28 (Separate Opinion of Judge Buergenthal); ibid 324, para 9 (Separate Opinion of Judge Simma); see also: WTO Panel Report, *European Communities – Measures Affecting the Approval and Marketing of Biotech Products* (n 23); *Belgium v Netherlands* (n 22) paras 58, 79; *Ireland v United Kingdom* (n 21) paras 101–05; ibid paras 2(2), 9, 19 (Dissenting Opinion of Arbitrator Griffith).

[37] *Demir* (n 31) paras 69–86.

[38] See: R Nordeide, 'Demir & Baykara v Turkey' (n 32); and R Nordeide, 'Fragmentation and the Leeway of the VCLT: Interpreting the ECHR in Light of Other International Law' (2009; published 2011) 20 *Finnish YBIL* 189–207.

> and above a network of mutual, bilateral undertakings, objective obligations which, in the words of the Preamble benefit from a 'collective enforcement'.[39]

Regarding the Convention's regional character, the Court in *Neulinger and Shuruk* formulated it thus:

> [T]he Court must also bear in mind the special character of the Convention as an instrument of European public order (*ordre public*) for the protection of individual human beings and its own mission, as set out in Article 19, 'to ensure the observance of the engagements undertaken by the High Contracting Parties' to the Convention.[40]

The Court's general approach to the interpretation of the Convention in light of other international law can consequently be described as taking an integrationist starting point, whilst maintaining a certain distance to the express wording of Article 31(3)(c) and preserving the special characteristics of the Convention as a regional human rights treaty. While the Court's general approach therefore gives important pointers on how one can expect the Court to deal with the relationship between the Convention and its normative environment, it provides only limited guidance as to how the Court in fact uses these elements in any given case. In order to attain a more comprehensive understanding of the Court's approach, sections III and IV therefore first set out to provide more substance to the Court's general approach and then assess the implications of these findings.

III. EXPLORING THE SUBSTANCE OF THE COURT'S APPROACH

A. Introduction

In form, and as a starting point, the Court thus no doubt agrees with the relevance and general notion of the legal technique and rationale of systemic integration enshrined in Article 31(3)(c) of the Vienna Convention on the Law of Treaties. The purpose of the present section is to explore how this starting point is brought to bear on different situations of interrelationships between the Convention and other international law, in order to gain an understanding of the substance of the Court's approach. The present section adopts a threefold division of the Court's case law on interpretation of the Convention in light of other international law. The general nature of this division is intentional, since it aims to present, by way of representative cases within each group, the widest possible view of the substance of the Court's approach. The two first groups concern

[39] *Loizidou v Turkey* (preliminary objections) (n 9) para 70 (citing its earlier case law *Ireland v The United Kingdom* (judgment) Series A No 25, 90 (18 January 1978) para 239).

[40] *Neulinger and Shuruk v Switzerland* App No 41615/07 (6 July 2010) para 133.

situations of interface between the Convention and other international law, while the third group involves instances where there is a more evident conflict between the Convention and other international law.

B. Interface with other International Human Rights Law

In addition to its significance for the Court's general approach, the above-mentioned *Demir*[41] case is of particular importance when exploring the interface between the Convention and other international human rights law. Of particular interest is the Court's approach to the question of the inclusion of collective bargaining within Article 11. The Court was here faced with the question of reviewing the merits of its earlier understanding of the inherent rights enshrined in the provision. The Court pointed to various sources: Conventions No 98 and No 151 of the International Labour Organization (ILO); statements by the ILO's Committee of Experts on the interpretation of Convention No 98; the European Social Charter; the European Union's Charter of Fundamental Rights; and the practice of European states.[42] The Court concluded that its case law should be reconsidered in order to take account of the 'perceptible evolution' in both international and domestic law, with the effect that the right to bargain collectively had 'in principle' become one of the 'essential elements' of the rights set forth in Article 11.[43] In its reasoning the Court further observed that 'in searching for common ground among the norms of international law it has never distinguished between sources of law according to whether or not they have been signed or ratified by the respondent State',[44] and that 'when it considers the object and purpose of the Convention provisions, it also takes into account the international law background to the legal question before it'.[45]

A similar wide approach can be found in the recent *Rantsev* case by the Court, in which it posed the question whether 'trafficking itself may be considered to run counter to the spirit and purpose of Article 4'.[46] After going through the relevant instruments and developments regarding the issue, the Court concluded on the following note:

> In view of its obligation to interpret the Convention in light of present-day conditions, the Court considers it unnecessary to identify whether the treatment about which the applicant complains constitutes 'slavery', 'servitude' or 'forced and compulsory labour'. Instead, the Court concludes that trafficking itself,

[41] *Demir and Baykara v Turkey* (n 31).
[42] ibid paras 147–51.
[43] ibid paras 153–54.
[44] ibid para 78.
[45] ibid para 76.
[46] *Rantsev v Cyprus and Russia* App No 25965/04 (ECtHR, 7 January 2010).

within the meaning of Article 3(a) of the Palermo Protocol and Article 4(a) of the Anti-Trafficking Convention, falls within the scope of Article 4 of the Convention.[47]

In *Saadi v UK*[48] the Court was 'called upon for the first time to interpret the meaning of the words in the first limb of Article 5 § 1(f)', which authorises 'the lawful arrest or detention of a person to prevent his effecting an unauthorised entry into the country'.[49] More specifically, the case concerned a claim for asylum by a doctor who had fled the Kurdish Autonomous Region of Iraq after treating members of the Iraqi Workers' Communist Party in the course of his duties as a doctor. As such, the case raised the question of the relationship between the Convention and other instruments of international law concerning the rights of asylum seekers. While the general approach of interpreting the Convention in light of other international was reiterated by the Court,[50] other relevant instruments on the subject matter were absent from the Court's further reasoning. Instead the Court focused on its own case law, both in presenting the starting point of the 'undeniable sovereign right to control aliens' entry into and residence in their territory',[51] and in its further analysis of the 'notion of arbitrary detention in the context of Article 5'[52] and whether the 'applicant's detention was arbitrary'.[53] As the partly dissenting opinion points out, there was plenty of opportunity to consider the provision's relationship to other instruments regarding asylum seekers.

In *Jersild*[54] the Court found that interference with freedom of the press, argued by Denmark to be necessary in order to comply with its obligations under the International Convention on the Elimination of All Forms of Racial Discrimination, constituted a violation of the freedom of expression in Article 10. This was not because the Court did not take into account the Convention on the Elimination of All Forms of Racial Discrimination, but because it was of the opinion that its interpretation of Article 10 'in the present case is compatible with Denmark's obligations under the UN Convention'.[55] Apart from its observation that it would '[bear] in mind the obligations on States under the UN Convention and other international instruments' when evaluating whether the item in question 'had as its purpose the propagation of racist views and ideas',[56] the Court's further consideration is largely based on its own case law, and as such does not

[47] ibid para 282.
[48] *Saadi v United Kingdom* App No 13229/03 (ECtHR, 29 January 2008).
[49] ibid para 61.
[50] ibid para 62.
[51] ibid para 64.
[52] ibid paras 67–74.
[53] ibid paras 75–80.
[54] *Jersild v Denmark* App No 15890/89 (ECtHR, 23 September 1994).
[55] ibid para 30.
[56] ibid para 31.

provide much on the general relationship between the Convention and the Convention on the Elimination of All Forms of Racial Discrimination. However, in this regard it seems reasonable to attach importance to the Court's observation when setting out the basis for its interpretation of Article 10 that 'freedom of expression constitutes one of the essential foundations of a democratic society and that the safeguards to be afforded to the press are of particular importance'.[57]

C. Interface with General International Law

As early as 1975, in the *Golder*[58] case, the Court made a clear statement about the influence general principles of international law would have on the interpretation of Convention provisions. Facing the question whether access to court was to be considered an inherent part of the rights under Article 6, the Court found it 'inconceivable' that the provision should only encompass procedural guarantees without 'first protect[ing] that which alone makes it in fact possible to benefit from such guarantees, that is, access to a court'.[59] A central part of the Court's reaching of this conclusion was its conviction that the Convention had to be read in light of general principles of international law, of which the 'principle whereby a civil claim must be capable of being submitted to a judge ranks as one of the universally "recognised" fundamental principles of law'.[60]

The influence of general principles of international law on the interpretation of the Convention has since had a firm basis in the Court's case law, and not least so in its case law on state immunity. Through this case law the Court has affirmed that the right of access to court is not absolute, but may, for example, be subject to limitations following from measures taken by states 'which reflect generally recognised rules of public international law on State immunity'.[61] In the *Al-Adsani v UK* case,[62] the Court interpreted the right of access to court in Article 6 (concerning a claim for damages for alleged torture committed outside the forum state) in light of general principles on state immunity in international law. The Court observed that 'the grant of immunity is to be seen not as qualifying a substantive right but as a procedural bar on the national courts' power to determine the right',[63] and found that international law did not yet recognise exceptions to the general law of state immunity concerning civil claims.

[57] ibid.
[58] *Golder v United Kingdom* (n 29).
[59] ibid para 35.
[60] ibid.
[61] See, eg: *Al-Adsani v United Kingdom* (n 29) para 56.
[62] ibid.
[63] ibid para 48.

The Court appears moreover to relate such general principles of international law with broader concepts of international law, such as when referring to the 'concept' of 'sovereign immunity', 'developed out of the principle *par in parem non habet imperium*'.[64] Two such broader concepts, which have had a profound impact on the nature of the Convention are the concepts of 'jurisdiction' and 'interim measures' in international law. As regards both concepts, the Court has been highly conscious of its normative environment, whilst also trying to craft what place there should be for the Convention's special character in its understanding of the two concepts.

As regards jurisdiction, two formative cases by the Court are the *Loizidou*[65] and *Bankovic*[66] cases. Of the several fundamental elements guiding the Court in these two cases, for the present purposes, the focus is on some of the Court's most general pronouncements regarding jurisdiction and how they were coupled with the notion as understood in general international law. In *Loizidou* the Court observed, *inter alia*, that the concept of jurisdiction is not restricted to the territory of the High Contracting Parties, and that bearing in mind the object and purpose of the Convention, 'may also arise when as a consequence of military action – whether lawful or unlawful – it exercises effective control of an area outside its national territory'.[67] Absent from this reasoning is any consideration of the concept of jurisdiction in general international law, the Court focusing rather on its own case law.

In contrast, the Court's starting point in *Bankovic* was that 'from the standpoint of public international law, the jurisdictional competence of a State is primarily territorial'.[68] It also (*inter alia* because the applicants had argued that the Court should adopt the same approach as in *Loizidou*) found reason to clarify 'that Article 1 of the Convention must be considered to reflect this ordinary and essentially territorial notion of jurisdiction, other bases of jurisdiction being exceptional and requiring special justification in the particular circumstances of each case'.[69] In an observation clarifying the scope of establishing jurisdiction in order to avoid a gap or vacuum in human rights' protection – but which is also reasonable to understand as having a bearing on the Court's perception of the general character of the Convention – the Court moreover declared that 'the Convention is a multi-lateral treaty operating, subject to Article 56 of the Convention, in an essentially regional context and notably in the legal space (*espace juridique*) of the Contracting States'.[70]

[64] ibid para 43.
[65] *Loizidou v Turkey* (preliminary objections) (n 9).
[66] *Banković and others v Belgium and others* (n 29).
[67] *Loizidou v Turkey* (preliminary objections) (n 9) para 62.
[68] *Banković and others v Belgium and others* (n 29) para 59.
[69] ibid para 61.
[70] ibid para 80 (fn omitted).

As concerns the concept of interim measures, the question of whether these could be binding upon contracting states had been answered in the negative until the Court rendered its judgment in *Mamatkulov*[71] in 2005. The better part of the Court's reasoning leading up to its conclusion that interim measures were in fact binding, and that failing to comply therefore entailed a violation of Article 34, was an examination of recent developments in international law. The Court drew on practice from the UN Human Rights Committee, the UN Committee Against Torture, the Inter American Court of Human Rights, and, not least, the judgment of the International Court of Justice (ICJ) in the *La Grand* case in 2001.[72] Thus, placing much weight on this basis, it found reason to depart from its previous findings regarding interim measures.

D. Conflicting Obligations under the Convention and other International Law

Moving now from the instances where the Convention has an interface with either human rights law or general international law, we come to situations where the Court is faced with the question of Member States' conflicting obligations under the Convention and other international law.

The Court's basis and starting point seems to be clearly articulated in the *Al-Saadoon* case, in which it observed that 'the State is considered to retain Convention liability in respect of treaty commitments subsequent to the entry into force of the Convention', referring, as an example, to the *Soering* case where the obligations of the United Kingdom (UK) under Article 3 of the Convention were held to 'override [its] obligations under the Extradition Treaty it had concluded with the United States in 1972'.[73] Moreover, the Court held that 'it is not open to a Contracting State to enter into an agreement with another State which conflicts with its obligations under the Convention'.[74]

A technique the Court has developed in order to harmonise such conflicting obligations can be found in its case law concerning child abduction. In the recent *Neulinger*[75] judgment, rendered by a Grand Chamber in 2010, the Court sets out its method of considering the relationship between the Convention and the Hague Convention on the Civil Aspects of International Child Abduction. Its starting point was to note that there was 'currently a broad consensus – including in international law – in

[71] *Mamatkulov and Askarov v Turkey* (n 29).

[72] ibid paras 110–17.

[73] *Al-Saadoon and Mufdhi v the United Kingdom* App No 61498/08 (ECtHR, 2 March 2010) para 128.

[74] ibid para 138.

[75] *Neulinger and Shuruk v Switzerland* (n 40) para 133.

support of the idea that in all decisions concerning children, their best interests must be paramount',[76] referring to several international instruments. It then reiterated its own practice of considering the 'child's interest', before observing that the 'same philosophy is inherent in the Hague Convention'.[77] It then proceeded to consider the merits of the case, concluding that a return of the child would not be in the child's best interest, and would thus entail a violation of Article 8 of the Convention.

Perhaps the most difficult questions that have arisen before the Court regarding conflicting obligations are those between the Convention and obligations following from membership of other international organisations. In this area the Court now follows a set of 'established' principles,[78] the basis of which are to be found in the *Bosphorus*[79] and *Behrami and Saramati*[80] cases of 2005 and 2007 respectively. *Bosphorus* concerned the seizure in 1993 by Irish authorities of an aircraft leased by the Turkish airline charter company Bosphorus Airways from Yugoslav Airlines. The seizure was made under EC Council Regulation 990/93 which, in turn, had implemented the UN sanctions regime against the Federal Republic of Yugoslavia. Bosphorus Airways complained that the manner in which Ireland had implemented the sanctions regime to impound its aircraft constituted a violation of the protection of property under the Convention (Article 1 of Additional Protocol I). Thus, the central question concerned the relationship between Ireland's obligations under the Convention and its obligations under EC law (which in turn was based on the obligation to implement the UN sanctions regime). In reiterating its general approach of interpreting the Convention in light of other rules and principles of international, the Court pointed to the principle of *pacta sunt servanda* being one such principle and stated that it had 'long recognised the growing importance of international cooperation and of the consequent need to secure the proper functioning of international organisations'.[81] On account of this, as long as the relevant organisation was considered to have an 'equivalent' protection of fundamental rights to that of the Convention, the 'presumption' would be that the state had not departed from the requirements of the Convention.[82] The Court also pointed out that 'equivalent' was to mean 'comparable', since 'any requirement that the organisation's protection be "identical" could run counter to the interest of international cooperation pursued'.[83] However, if in the circumstances of the case it was considered that the protection afforded was

[76] ibid para 135.
[77] ibid paras 136–37.
[78] *Rambus Inc v Germany* App No 40382/04 (ECtHR, 16 June 2009).
[79] *Bosphorus Hava Yollari Turizm Ve Ticaret Anonim Sirketi v Ireland* (n 29).
[80] *Behrami and Behrami v France & Saramati v France, Germany and Norway* (n 29).
[81] *Bosphorus* (n 29) para 150.
[82] ibid paras 155–56.
[83] ibid.

'manifestly deficient', the Court's presumption could be rebutted and 'the interest of international cooperation would be outweighed by the Convention's role as a "constitutional instrument of European public order" in the field of human rights'.[84]

The *Behrami and Saramati* cases (joined by the Court) raised questions regarding the Respondent States' obligations for actions performed in participation of a UN Security Council mandated operation in Kosovo. The Court dismissed the case because of lack of jurisdiction *ratione personae*, on account of its finding that the operation in Kosovo was directly attributable to the UN; an international organisation not party to the Convention. In the course of its reasoning, however, it responded to the applicants' claims – made in reference to the Court's line of reasoning in *Bosphorus* – that the military (KFOR) authorities in the UN authorised mission in Kosovo did not provide protection 'equivalent' to that of the Convention. The Court's response was that the circumstances of *Behrami and Saramati* were 'clearly distinguishable' from the *Bosphorus* case, but it nonetheless found it necessary to add an observation, which appeared to signal an additional element to the notion of international cooperation it had developed in *Bosphorus*:

> There exists, in any event, a fundamental distinction between the nature of the international organisation and of the international cooperation with which the Court was there concerned and those in the present cases. As the Court has found above, UNMIK was a subsidiary organ of the UN created under Chapter VII and KFOR was exercising powers lawfully delegated under Chapter VII of the Charter by the UNSC. As such, their actions were directly attributable to the UN, an organisation of universal jurisdiction fulfilling its imperative collective security objective.[85]

E. Concluding Remarks

The aim of the present section has been to provide a more comprehensive understanding beyond the main elements that transpire from the Court's general approach. It follows from this exploration that in all three groups of cases the Court in certain situations has been inclined to show openness towards systemic integration, and in other instances not. The next section seeks to assess the reasons and merits of the Court's openness and reticence.

[84] ibid.

[85] *Behrami and Behrami v France & Saramati v France, Germany and Norway* (n 29) para 151.

IV. ASSESSING THE COURT'S OPENNESS AND RETICENCE TOWARDS SYSTEMIC INTEGRATION

A. International Human Rights Law

The *Demir* and *Rantsev* cases saw the Court integrating the Convention into the body of international human rights law. As it stated in *Demir*, the Court does not regard 'the provisions of the Convention as the sole framework of reference for the interpretation of the rights and freedoms enshrined therein'.[86] Two elements of the *Demir* case stand out: first, the way in which the Court does not distinguish between binding and non-binding instruments; secondly, the way in which the Court incorporates other international human rights law when identifying the object and purpose of the relevant Convention provision. A similar wide approach was displayed in *Rantsev*. However, here the Court did not find it necessary to place the notion of 'trafficking' within the express wording of Article 4. Instead, what was important was that the notion of trafficking fell within the 'spirit and purpose' of the Convention provision.[87]

It is quite clear from these cases that the Court sees itself as a guarantor for the continuing development of international human rights law in general. First, incorporating these rights into the supervisory system of the Convention, and not least bringing them within the binding nature of the Court's decisions, undoubtedly has important consequences for how the Member States of the Council of Europe relate to these rights. Secondly, it does not seem unreasonable to view the Court's wide approach in these cases as bordering between interpretation and outright revision of the treaty, which of course make them particularly significant when assessing the wider picture of the Court's approach.

There is a marked difference between the foregoing wide approach and the reasoning of the Court in the *Saadi v UK* case. While the basis of its approach is articulated in a similar manner, any further specific consideration of other relevant human rights instruments in this field was absent from the Court's reasoning. In the dissenting judges' view this should have been done, and by failing to do so the majority's reasoning resulted in the Convention offering a 'lower level of protection' than the UN, the EU, and the Council of Europe.[88] In this sense the majority appears to adopt a highly regional approach, not wanting to engage with other relevant human rights instruments in this field.

[86] *Demir and Baykara v Turkey* (n 31) para 67.
[87] *Rantsev v Cyprus and Russia* (n 46).
[88] *Saadi v United Kingdom* (n 48), Joint Partly Dissenting Opinion of Judges Rozakis, Tulkens, Kovler, Hajiyev, Spielmann and Hirvelä.

The Court's reasoning in *Jersild* can be seen in a similar regional vein. However, this is not because the relevant international human rights instrument was absent from the Court's reasoning, but rather because the fundamental issue for the Court was arguably that 'freedom of expression constitutes one of the essential foundations of a democratic society and that the safeguards to be afforded to the press are of particular importance'.[89] The regional approach in this case is therefore not one of non-engagement with other international instruments, but rather that the Court, in its balancing of two fundamental human rights, in the last resort appears to have been guided by the value of democracy; arguably one of the fundamental values underpinning the whole Convention.[90] If this was indeed the rationale of the Court's balancing, it would however raise the pertinent question of whether the Court perceived the issue of democracy from a perspective that was far too regional.

B. General International Law

It would seem that there was a clear connection between the Court's openness towards general principles of international law and its understanding of the nature of the Convention in the *Golder* case. As the Court observed when concluding its consideration of 'right to access':

> Taking all the preceding considerations together, it follows that the right of access constitutes an element which is inherent in the right stated by Article 6 para 1 (art. 6-1). This is not an extensive interpretation forcing new obligations on the Contracting States: it is based on the very terms of the first sentence of Article 6 para. 1 (art. 6-1) read in its context and having regard to the object and purpose of the Convention, *a lawmaking treaty* (see the Wemhoff judgment of 27 June 1968, Series A no. 7, p. 23, para. 8), and to general principles of law.[91]

The Court had in *Wemhoff* defined the notion of 'lawmaking treaty' in the context of the Convention by observing:

> Given that it is a law-making treaty, it is also necessary to seek the interpretation that is most appropriate in order to realise the aim and achieve the object of the treaty, not that which would restrict to the greatest possible degree the obligations undertaken by the Parties.[92]

This relationship between the nature of the Convention and its openness towards general principles resurfaced in a significant way in the Court's

[89] *Jersild v Denmark* (n 54) paras 30–31.

[90] M Emberland, *The Human Rights of Companies – Exploring the Structure of ECHR Protection* (Oxford, Oxford University Press, 2006) especially ch 2.

[91] *Golder v United Kingdom* (n 29) para 36 (emphasis added).

[92] *Wemhoff v FRG* (n 9) para 8.

landmark judgments concerning state immunity in 2001.[93] Judge Loucaides, who dissented in all three judgments, spelled out his main concern in his dissent in *McElhinney*. On the more general aspect of the influence of general principles on the Convention he argued thus:

> In a case like the one before the Court, the *lex specialis* is the European Convention of Human Rights. General principles of international law are not embodied in the Convention except insofar as reference is expressly made to them by the Convention (see, for example, Articles 15, 35 § 1 and 53 of the Convention and Article 1 of Protocol No. 1). Therefore, one should be reluctant to accept restrictions on Convention rights derived from principles of international law such as those establishing immunities which are not even part of the *jus cogens* norms.[94]

In its now established case law on state immunity, the Court has followed its line of reasoning in these judgments. The reason for mentioning Judge Loucaides' argument in such detail is rather for another reason. It has a resemblance to the approaches found in certain cases decided by the WTO supervisory bodies,[95] which have given rise to much debate as regards the 'closing off' of WTO law from general international law. Thus, although the Court has an established case law on state immunity, it is still worth exploring what these cases imply for the general understanding of the relationship between the nature of the Convention and its openness towards general principles.

In this context it has been argued that *Al-Adsani* signalled a changed course as regards the relationship between the Convention and general international law, since the Court's reasoning seemed to entail less emphasis on the distinctive features of the Convention vis-a-vis other areas of international law, and more emphasis on the importance of harmony in international law.[96] If that is the case, this appears to be precisely the reason for a criticism put forth against the Court's reasoning in *Al-Adsani*.[97] The thrust of the criticism is that the Court did not properly take into account the object and purpose of the Convention, and that it accepted

[93] *Al-Adsani v United Kingdom* (n 29); *McElhinney v United Kingdom* (n 29); *Fogarty v United Kingdom* (n 29). See for a general analysis of the case: M Emberland, 'McElhinney v. Ireland, Al-Adsani v. United Kingdom, Fogarty v. United Kingdom' (2002) 96 *Am J Int'l L* 699.

[94] *McElhinney v United Kingdom* (n 29) (Dissenting Opinion of Judge Loucaides).

[95] WTO Panel Report, *European Communities – Measures Affecting the Approval and Marketing of Biotech Products* (n 23); WTO AB Report, *EC Measures Concerning Meat and Meat Products (Hormones)* (13 February 1998) WT/DS26/AB/R, WT/DS48/AB/R, 135; WTO AB Report, *United States – Import Prohibition of Certain Shrimp and Shrimp Products (Shrimp)* (6 November 1998) WT/DS58/AB/R, 2755; and the discussion of the cases in: R Howse, 'The Use and Abuse of Other "Relevant Rules Of International Law" in Treaty Interpretation: Insights From WTO Trade/Environment Litigation' *NYU IILJ Working Paper* 2007/1.

[96] J Viljanen, *The European Court of Human Rights as a Developer of the General Doctrines of Human Rights Law* (Tampere, Tampere University Press 2003) 81.

[97] A Orakhelashvili, 'Restrictive Interpretation of Human Rights Treaties in the Recent Jurisprudence of the European Court of Human Rights' (2003) 14 *Eur J Int'l L* 529–68.

that general international law alien to the object and purpose of the Convention could override the rights enshrined in it. Moreover, that the Court went beyond the boundaries of interpretation because its reasoning came closer to deciding on the application, or rather non-application, of Article 6 instead of merely clarifying the scope of Article 6 through interpretation.[98] A similar understanding, albeit in a more subtle way, would seem to follow from a comment by the ILC on the case:

> It is useful to note that here the Court might have simply brushed aside State immunity as not relevant to the application of the Convention. But it did not do so. The conflict between article 6 and rules of customary international law on State immunity emerged only because the Court decided to integrate article 6 in its normative environment (doubtless because that is what was claimed by the respondent). The right provided under the European Convention was weighed against the general interest in the maintenance of the system of State immunity. In the end, the Court used article 31(3)(c) so as to set aside, in this case, the rules of the Convention.[99]

The Court's understanding of the relationship between the nature of the Convention and its openness towards systemic integration appears also to be a central theme in its dealings with the concepts of jurisdiction and interim measures. And – as in its approach to general principles – its openness to systemic integration in these areas has led to both the widening and delimiting of Convention protection. Thus, as regards interim measures, the taking into account of developments of this concept by other international bodies lead the Court in *Mamatkulov* to adopt a clear stance on the binding effect of interim measures. This stance had at best been unclear in the Court's previous case law, if not even settled in the opposite.[100] As regards jurisdiction, the openness towards systemic integration led the Court in *Bankovic* to delimit the concept within the meaning of the Convention. This, however, was not due so much to recent developments in international law, but rather to the Court's coupling of its understanding of jurisdiction with that in general international law.

C. Conflicting Obligations

The Court's approach to child abduction cases provides an important technique of harmonisation that supplements the Court's general starting point that it is not open to Member States to enter into agreements that conflict with their obligations under the Convention. By locking on to common

[98] ibid 560.
[99] ILC Fragmentation Report (n 1) para 438.
[100] L Caflisch, 'Provisional Measures in the Protection of Human Rights: The Mamatkulov Case' in PM Dupuy, B Fassbender, MN Shaw, and KP Sommermann (eds), *Common Values in International Law: Essays in Honour of Christian Tomuschat* (Kehl, NP Engel Verlag, 2006).

purposes (the child's best interest) of the Convention and the Hague Convention in these cases, the Court in effect harmonises the otherwise conflicting obligations. A general use of this technique is, however, not without its problems. In relying on what constitutes the purpose of other treaties the Court must at the same time avoid overreaching its mandate, which in its own words entails 'that it is competent to apply only the European Convention on Human Rights, and that it is not its task to interpret or review compliance with other international conventions as such'.[101]

Coming back to the relationship between the nature of the Convention and its openness to systemic integration that we saw was an integral part of the Court's approach to general principles of international law, this consideration is also part of Court's approach to obligations flowing from membership of other international organisations. However, it manifests itself in a different way when the Court deals with this issue. There appear to be two main elements that stand out as regards the Court's approach in *Bosphorus* and *Behrami and Saramati*. First, whereas the Court in *Bosphorus* displayed an approach of both openness and reticence towards systemic integration, in *Behrami and Saramati* the element of reticence seems totally absent. In *Bosphorus*, although the Court underlined its starting point of the interest of international cooperation, it made it clear that this interest could be 'outweighed by the Convention's role as a "constitutional instrument of European public order" in the field of human rights'.[102] This principle of a 'fall-back' on reticence seems nowhere to be found in the Court's reasoning in *Behrami and Saramati*. Secondly, and this might be even more fundamental as regards the Court's approach, is the notion alluded to by the Court in *Behrami and Saramati* that there existed 'in any event, a fundamental distinction between the nature of the international organisation and of the international cooperation'[103] with which the Court was concerned with in the two cases. Since the Court did not elaborate on the normative import of its statement, one can only speculate as to what this really means. It might be seen as a reference to a normative hierarchical order in international law akin to notions of constitutionalism, but if that is the case it seems odd to convey a view on the international normative order of such fundamental importance in such ambiguous terms. An alternative way of understanding the Court may be to couple it with the aforementioned elements of openness or reticence towards systemic integration.

If *Bosphorus* is rightly understood to convey *both* openness and reticence, this might be based on the view by the Court that international cooperation in the context of the relationship between the Convention and the EU operates on a horizontal level, and that as guardian of the Convention it is only natural that the Court operates with a fall-back on

[101] *Somogyi v Italy* App No 67972/01 (18 May 2004) para 62.
[102] *Bosphorus* (n 29) para 156.
[103] *Behrami and Saramati* (n 29) para 151.

reticence in the last instance. Consequently, if *Behrami and Saramati* is rightly understood to convey *only* openness, this might be based on the view that, at the moment, international cooperation in the context of the relationship between the Convention and the UN Security Council operates in a vertical order.

As opposed to inferring from the Court's statements a reference to a normative hierarchical order, this alternative understanding would seem more representative of the current realities of international law, without at the same time shutting the door prematurely to developments of this reality. It would moreover fit better with the broader picture that emerges from the present exploration of the substance of the Court's approach to systemic integration: this is a regional human rights court that places much weight on its structural relationship to other international law, whilst clearly conscious of the far-reaching role the field of human rights plays in the understanding and continuing development of international law.

V. BY WAY OF CONCLUSION: DIFFICULTIES ARISING FROM THE COURT'S APPROACH

As the above exploration has shown, the Court's approach to systemic integration encompasses both a sliding scale of developing Convention-protection and a sliding scale of circumscribing Convention-protection. In other words, understanding the Court's approach to systemic integration becomes a central part of understanding the scope and limits of the rights enshrined in the Convention.

The central insight derived from the present attempt at understanding the Court's approach is that the Court, in a methodological sense, has adopted a multifaceted approach to systemic integration. The study undertaken here of this multifaceted approach reveals difficulties that would seem to have particular implications for the assessment of the Court's contribution to fragmentation or unity of international law. Five difficulties stand out as crucial to address.

First, although the Court, in presenting its general approach, is generally consistent in expressly making reference to the Vienna Convention on the Law of Treaties, the further impact of the Vienna Convention on the Law of Treaties on the substance of the Court's approach is not clear however. Related to the ILC's study on fragmentation, the Court's approach might therefore be described as an openness to the ILC's articulation of the rationale of systemic integration, but a reticence towards engaging in the finer details of the legal technique the ILC identified in Article 31(3)(c) of the Vienna Convention on the Law of Treaties. This would seem to stand in contrast to the approach taken by other international courts.[104]

[104] See: n 36 above.

The Court seems rather to merge the rationale of systemic integration with its own developed methods of interpretation, and this gives rise to the second difficulty to be addressed. The Court has over the years developed a fairly elaborate set of methods of interpretation (no doubt also as a consequence of the enormous amount of decisions and judgments the Court has produced).[105] Basing the substance of its approach on its own developed methods of interpretation rather than an (express at least) exploration of the finer details of the Vienna Convention on the Law of Treaties Article 31(3)(c), thus becomes a central reason for the Court's multifaceted approach to systemic integration. However, many of these developed methods appear to sit uncomfortably with how the technique of systemic integration is articulated in the Vienna Convention on the Law of Treaties Article 31(3)(c). This has two main effects. One is the already mentioned effect of the Court's approach being different from that of other international courts. The other is that it creates problems for assessing whether the Court is operating within the boundaries of the general law on treaty interpretation, and when assessing whether the Court operates within a coherent framework when it interprets the Convention in light of other international law. As to the former point this seems aptly illustrated by *Demir*, through the Court's reliance on non-binding instruments and its observation that the object and purpose of the Convention could also be derived from other international instruments; or from *Mamatkulov*, which prompted the dissenting judges to label the majority's approach *ultra vires*.[106] The difficulties in assessing whether the Court operates within a coherent framework can be illustrated by the different approach it took in *Saadi v UK* as opposed to the *Demir* and *Rantsev* cases.

The third difficulty concerns the Court's understanding of the nature of the Convention when interpreting it in light of other international law. It might be reasonable to say that the three judgments in 2001 regarding sovereign immunity marked a turning point; a point where the Court made a choice of principle as regards the influence of other international law. This openness towards general principles of international law, coupled with the Court's approach of merging systemic integration with its own developed methods, might very well be a central factor in its struggles to articulate its understanding of the concept of jurisdiction.[107] As regards the critique the Court has encountered for its understanding of jurisdiction, this might be caused by what Koskenniemi has described as

[105] Even counting only judgments, the number is astounding for an international court. On 18 September 2008 the Court delivered its 10,000th judgment; see: 'Facts and Figures' on the Court's '50 years site', available at www.echr.coe.int/echr/Homepage_EN.

[106] *Mamatkulov and Askarov v Turkey* (n 29), Joint Partly Dissenting Opinion of Judges Caflisch, Türmen and Kovler.

[107] M Milanovic, 'From Compromise to Principle: Clarifying the Concept of State Jurisdiction in Human Rights Treaties' (2008) 8 *Hum R L Rev* 3.

the core of the problem concerning the fears of fragmentation: 'not so much in the emergence of new sub-systems but in the use of general law by new bodies representing interests or views that are not identical with those represented in old ones'.[108]

The fourth difficulty is connected to the third, and concerns the question of identifying what exactly is the Court's understanding of the Convention's regional character in these cases. It was shown that *Jersild* could be understood as a case in point where the Court made a principled choice based on the Convention's regional character. However, in what appears to be in stark contrast to the European Court of Justice (ECJ) in the *Kadi*[109] case, the combined result of the Court's approach in *Bosphorus* and *Behrami and Saramati* seems to be a blurred conception of the implications of the Convention's regional character.

The fifth and final difficulty relates to these two last mentioned cases, and concerns the broader issue of what conception of legitimacy that guides the Court in its approach to systemic integration. This issue might also be said to have a bearing on all the aforementioned difficulties. Many have been surprised that it was the ECJ and not the Court that would stand up to the Security Council in the name of human rights. This raises the question of whether underlying the Court's multifaceted approach to systemic integration is also a multifaceted conception of legitimacy that is guided by whether the Court operates 'within' or 'outside' the 'four corners' of the Convention. It is not uncommon for the Court to emphasise the Convention's 'special character' when operating *within* the four corners of the Convention,[110] and it is not unreasonable to infer that this is done on the basis that the Convention's legitimacy is dependent on locking on to the 'rights holders' under the treaty. When stepping *outside* the four corners of the Convention, however, the Court's approach to systemic integration might be taken to imply that the Convention's legitimacy in these instances rests upon 'maintaining the credibility of the existing structures of treaty law'.[111]

[108] M Koskenniemi and P Leino, 'Fragmentation of International Law?: Postmodern Anxieties' (2002) 15 *Leiden J Int'l L* 561.

[109] ECJ, *Yassin Abdullah Kadi and Al Barakaat International Foundation v Council of the European Union and Commission of the European Communities*, Joined Cases C-402/05 P and C-415/05 P (3 September 2008). For commentaries on the case, see eg: G de Burca, 'The European Court of Justice and the International Legal Order after Kadi' NYU School of Law Jean Monnet Working Paper 01/09; J Weiler, 'Editorial' (2008) 19 *Eur J Int'l L* 5.

[110] See, eg, in relation to applicants' 'victim' status under the Convention: *Anguelova v Bulgaria* App No 38361/97 (ECtHR, 6 June 2000); *Ahmet Sadik v Greece* App No 18877/91 (ECtHR, 15 November 1996); *Cardot v France* App No 11069/84 (ECtHR, 19 March 1991).

[111] See for a discussion of such 'alternative identities' of human rights treaties: M Craven, 'Legal Differentiation and the Concept of the Human Rights Treaty in International Law' (2000) 11 *Eur J Int'l L* 489–519, 490.

Part Two

National Courts

7

The Systemic Integration of International Law by Domestic Courts: Domestic Judges as Architects of the Consistency of the International Legal Order

JEAN D'ASPREMONT*

I. INTRODUCTION

BECAUSE THERE IS no application of law without interpretation,[1] international law, being increasingly applied by domestic courts, has been subject to their interpretation. This chapter examines whether international law contains some prescriptions regarding its interpretation by domestic courts. It particularly zeroes in on the extent to which domestic courts presuppose that international law constitutes a coherent and systemic set of rules and apply the principle of systemic integration of international law enshrined in the Vienna Convention on the Law of Treaties. The chapter simultaneously aims at appraising whether domestic courts, because of different legal and institutional constraints, construe the systemic character of the international legal order differently from international courts and international legal scholars.

Until recently, questions of interpretation of international law by domestic courts had barely been examined in the international legal scholarship,[2] international legal scholars classically devoting their

* Associate Professor and Senior Research Fellow, Amsterdam Center for International Law (ACIL), University of Amsterdam.

[1] G Scelle, *Précis de droit des gens vol II* (Paris, Sirey, 1932–34) 488. See also G Schwarzenberger, 'Myths and Realities in Treaty Interpretation' (1968) 9 *Va J Int'l L* 1, 8.

[2] Among a few exceptions, see: CH Schreuer, 'The interpretation of treaties by domestic courts' (1971) 45 *BYIL* 255; MA Rogoff, 'Interpretation of international agreements by domestic courts and the politics of international treaty relations: reflections on some recent decisions of the United States Supreme Court' (1996) *Am U J Int'l L & Pol'y* 559; J Bederman, 'Revivalist Canons and Treaty Interpretation' (1993–94) 41 *UCLA L Rev* 953.

attention to the effect of the interpretation of international law *on* domestic law.[3] Modern developments have, however, sweepingly expanded the information available about domestic decisions involving questions of international law.[4] As a result, this classical disinterest for questions of interpretation of international law by domestic courts has been overturned and the manner in which domestic judges deal with international law is nowadays the centre of great scholarly attention. The present chapter aspires to buoy this growing interest for the use of international law by domestic courts by shedding some light on the conception of international law that is promoted by domestic judges.

After recalling the extent to which international law is applied and interpreted by domestic judges (section II), this chapter examines the degree to and the manner in which domestic judges are in a position to make use of the principle of systemic integration of international law (section III). Because the practice analysed here shows an inclination of domestic judges to resort to systemic integration of international law, this chapter discusses the implications of the use of the principle of systemic integration by domestic judges and especially the possibility of using it as a tool to further the integration of the international legal order (section IV).

II. INTERNATIONAL LAW AND DOMESTIC COURTS

International law has long ceased exclusively to govern inter-state relations and has become more regulatory of internal matters and issues affecting individuals. Compliance with international law has accordingly incrementally required the adoption of domestic rules. Even rules regulating inter-state relations have required domestic implementation. The entry of international law in domestic systems is thus a natural consequence of the extension *ratione materiae* of its object.[5]

[3] See the numerous contributions in OE Fitzgerald and E Eid (eds), *The globalized rule of law: relationships between international and domestic law* (Toronto, Irwin Law, 2006); Y Shany, 'How Supreme Is the Supreme Law of the Land?: Comparative Analysis of the Influence of International Human Rights Treaties upon the Interpretation of Constitutional Texts by Domestic Courts' (2006) 31 *Brooklyn J Int'l L* 341, 341 ff; M Arden, 'The Interpretation of UK Domestic Legislation in the Light of European Convention on Human Rights Jurisprudence' (2004) 25 *Statute L Rev* 165, 165 ff; AM Weisburd, 'Using International Law to Interpret National Constitutions: Conceptual Problems: Reflections on Justice Kirby's Advocacy of International Law in Domestic Constitutional Jurisprudence' (2006) 21 *Am U Int'l L Rev* 365–77; JJ Paust, 'Domestic influence of the International Court of Justice' (1998) 26 *Denv J Intl'l L & Pol'y* 787–805; MJ Glennon, 'Interpreting 'Interpretation' 20 *UC Davis L Rev* 913 (1987).

[4] See, eg: *International Law in Domestic Courts* (ILDC) database, available at www.oxfordlawreports.com.

[5] According to Provost and Conforti, 'The truly legal function of international law essentially is found in the internal legal system of States', see: Provost and Conforti, *International Law and the Role of Domestic Legal Systems* (Dordrecht, Martinus Nijhoff Publishers, 1993) 8;

That international law regulates objects traditionally deemed to be of domestic relevance does not, however, suffice to explain the growing presence of international law in domestic legal orders. Because international law only enters domestic legal orders if so allowed by them, the greater presence of international law in the domestic legal orders of states also is the direct consequence of the growing amenability of states towards international law. In this respect, it is not disputed that states have proved less reluctant to let international law pervade and enter their own legal order. The basic manner in which states let international law penetrate their legal order is the adoption of measures of incorporation. Indeed, the abiding divide between legal orders has required that international law, to yield any effect in domestic law, be duly incorporated by each state.[6] Simultaneously, more countries have proved monist and, by pruning the formal domestic requirements of incorporation, have further facilitated the entry of international law in their domestic legal order.

Incorporation has not been the only means by which international law enters the domestic legal order. Indeed, most states in the world instruct their courts to construe domestic law in a manner that is consistent with the international obligations of the state. If international law is not the 'law of the land' because it has not been incorporated, it may still yield effect in the domestic legal order if domestic judges interpret national law by drawing on international law.[7] This is true by virtue of the so-called principle of consistent interpretation. According to that principle – which we will return to in this chapter – domestic courts are obliged to interpret domestic law in a manner consistent with international law. As a result, they necessarily heed international law and give weight to it in the domestic legal order. As such, the application of the principle of consistent interpretation does not endow international law with a self-executing character in domestic law – the question of the self-executing character of an international legal instrument being chiefly a question of international law rather than a question of

JHH Weiler, 'The Geology of International Law: Governance, Democracy and Legitimacy' (2004) 64 *ZaöRV* 547, 559 ff. See also: A von Bogdandy, 'Globalization and Europe: How to Square Democracy, Globalization and International Law' (2004) 15 *Eur J Int'l L* 885, 889; M Kumm, 'The Legitimacy of International Law: A Constitutionalist Framework of Analysis' (2004) 15 *Eur J Int'l L* 917, 917. But see also: Arangio-Ruiz, 'Le domaine reservé. L'organisation internationale et le rapport entre le droit international et le droit interne. Cours général de droit international public' 225 *Recueil des Cours* (1990-VI) 29, especially 435 ff.

6 See: J d'Aspremont and F Dopagne, 'Kadi: the ECJ's Reminder of The Abiding Divide Between Legal Orders' (2008) 5 *Int'l Org L Rev* 371.

7 This is also known as the 'Charming Betsy' principle; see: US Supreme Court, *Murray v The Schooner Charming Betsy* 6 US (2 Cranch) 64 (1804); see also: *Restatement (Third) of Foreign Relations Law*, para 114 (1987). See on the Charming Betsy principle, generally: RG Steinhardt, 'The Role of International Law as a Canon of Domestic Statutory Construction'(1990) 43 *Vand L Rev* 1103; J Turley, 'Dualistic Values in an Age of International Legisprudence' (1993) 44 *Hastings LJ* 185.

domestic law.[8] However, the role that international law can play through interpretation is far from negligible and it surely gives it an indirect effect in domestic law.[9] In the same vein, the principle of consistent interpretation is sometimes a means to bypass missing requirements of incorporation and apply international law short of any measure of incorporation.[10] This is why the principle of consistent interpretation has been dubbed the 'phantom' use of international law by domestic courts,[11] domestic judges making use of it being seen as 'worldly judges'.[12]

The growing effect of international law in the domestic legal order through incorporation and consistent interpretation has been accompanied by a general amenability of domestic judges towards international law as a whole, irrespective of whether it is incorporated and binding upon the state.[13] It seems that nowadays there is a steady appeal of international law to domestic judges who occasionally see themselves as agents of the international legal order and the guardians of the international rule of law.[14] This openness towards international law is remarkable, for it has not been out of a sense of a legal obligation imposed upon them by the domestic legal order but simply rests on the persuasive character of international law. This has also been explained by some authors as a strategy to preserve the space for domestic deliberation.[15] Benefits expected from reciprocity are probably not alien to such growing openness either.[16] Be that is it may, this calling for the 'international' has

[8] PCIJ, Jurisdiction of the Courts of Danzig, 1928 PCIJ Series B, No 15, 17–18. See: J Verhoeven, 'La notion d'applicabilité directe du droit international' 15 *RBDI* 1980–82, 243 ff.

[9] See for instance the House of Lords' decision in: *A (FC) v Secretary of State for the Home Department* (Conjoined Appeals) (2005) UKHL 71; or see also the Indian Supreme Court's decision in: *People's Union for Civil Liberties v Union of India* (1997) 125 ILR 510. See for some insights on the Canadian Practice: R Provost, 'Judging In Splendid Isolation'(2008) 56 *Am J Comp L* 125.

[10] See, eg: in Canada and the comments of J d'Aspremont, 'Du dualisme au monisme. La révolution silencieuse de la Cour suprême du Canada' (2003) *RBDC* 399.

[11] CA Bradley, 'The Charming Betsy Canon and Separation of Powers: Rethinking the Interpretative Role of International Law' (1997–98) 86 *Geo LJ* 479.

[12] K Young, 'The World through the Judge's Eye' 28 *AustYIL* 27, 46.

[13] See generally: Y Shany, 'National Courts as International Actors: Jurisdictional Implications' (October 2008) *Hebr U Int'l L Research Paper* No 22-08. See also: R Provost (n 9). See for an early manifestation of that tendency: Bangalore Principles adopted by the Judicial Colloquium on 'The Domestic Application of International Human Rights Norms', India, 24–26 February 1988, reprinted in (1989) 1 *Afr J Int'l & Comp L* 345. The Bangalore Principles is a set of 10 principles meant to guide the work of domestic judges, including human rights and freedom enshrined in international instruments as well as international jurisprudence.

[14] K Young has qualified this attitude as being that of an 'internationalist judge'. See: K Young, 'The World through the Judge's Eye' 28 *AustYBIL* 27, 42.

[15] This argument is made by E Benvenisti and GW Downs, 'National Courts, Domestic Democracy, and the Evolution of International Law' (2009) 20 *Eur J Int'l L* 59–72.

[16] In China (which remains, as a matter of principle, a dualist country) the Supreme Court issued in 1995 an interesting prescription according to which 'in the handling of cases with foreign elements, on the basis of the principle of reciprocity and mutual benefit, international treaty obligations undertaken by China should be strictly observed'. The text is mentioned

manifested itself in various ways. It has been illustrated by a growing reference to decisions of international courts.[17] To some more limited extent, it has also been reflected in what liberal legal scholars have depicted as the transnational interactions between all courts in the world.[18] One should probably not exaggerate this tendency.[19] It is, however, worthy of mention as it undoubtedly constitutes a new gateway for the entry of international law into domestic law.

It is interesting to realise that domestic judges do not have a monopoly on this growing introduction of international law in domestic legal orders. Indeed, it must be acknowledged that the greater amenability of judges towards international law often ensues after the invocation of international law by the parties to domestic proceedings.[20] Likewise, it is important to stress that the promotion of international law has also been spearheaded by governmental authorities who happen to resort to the 'discourse' of international law for domestic purposes, at least when this is consistent with their political agenda.[21] This use of international law by governmental authorities – and to some more limited extent by legislative bodies[22] – has, in turn, influenced the interpretation of international law by domestic judges; at least in those countries where domestic judges are obliged to abide by the interpretation provided by governmental authorities.[23] The growing place of international law in domestic legal orders is thus not solely an accomplishment of domestic judges.

and translated by X Hanqin and J Qian, 'International Treaties in the Chinese Domestic Legal System' (2009) 8 *Chinese J Int'l L* 299–322, especially 315 f.

[17] For some critical remarks, see DJ Kochan, 'Sovereignty and the American Courts at the Cocktail Party of International Law: The Dangers of Domestic Judicial Invocations of Foreign and International Law' (2006) 29 *Fordham Int'l LJ* 508.

[18] AM Slaughter, 'A Global Community of Courts' (2003) 44 *Harv Int'l LJ* 191.

[19] See for a criticism: E Benvenisti, 'Reclaiming Democracy: The Strategic Uses of Foreign and International Law by National Courts' (2008) 102 *Am J Int'l L* 241.

[20] See for an example: d'Aspremont (n 10).

[21] See for instance the recent dispute between Belgium and the Netherlands on the enlargement of the Schelde River around Antwerp. The Dutch Prime Minister invoked the international agreement with Belgium to proceed with the enlargement which had been opposed (see: 'Coalitie oneens over Westerschelde-zaak' *NRC Handelsblad*, 18 August 2009). See generally on the use of international law in the discourse of governmental authorities: MA Rogoff, 'Interpretation of International Agreements by Domestic Courts and the Politics of International Treaty Relations: Reflections on Some Recent Decisions of the United States Supreme Court' (1996) 11 *Am U J Int'l L & Pol'y* 559, 675 ff.

[22] See the discussion about the weight of the US Senate's discussions around treaty ratification before domestic courts. *cf Coplin v United States*, 6 Cl. Ct. 115, 131, fn 16 (1984) and *Rainbow Navigation, Inc v Department of the Navy*, 686 F Supp 354, 357 and n 17 (DDC 1988).

[23] See, eg: in the US, *Restatement (Third) of the Foreign Relations Law of the United States* (1987), para 326: 'The President has authority to determine the interpretation of an international agreement to be asserted by the United States in its relations with other states. Courts in the United States have final authority to interpret an international agreement for purposes of applying it as law in the United States but will give great weight to an interpretation made by the Executive branch'. See for an example: *Kolovrat v Oregon*, 366 US 187, 194 (1961) or *United States v Curtiss-Wright Export Corp*, 299 US 304, 319–20 (1936). On this question, see WM Reisman, 'Necessary and Proper: Executive Competence to Interpret Treaties' (1990) 15

Whether the entry of international law into the domestic legal orders takes the path of incorporation, consistent interpretation, or simple persuasiveness, and whomever this entry can be traced back to, it is uncontested that international law is more present in the domestic legal orders and is relentlessly resorted to by domestic courts. While some may see this as a positive phenomenon, it surely does not come without problems, especially in terms of the consistency of international law. Indeed, the application and the interpretation of international law by domestic courts is anything but a simple process of transmission[24] and is not at all synonymous with greater homogenisation and uniformisation of international law. The same is true of governmental or legislative authorities making use of international law at the domestic level. On the contrary, the growing application and interpretation of international law – be it by judicial or governmental authorities – can give rise to diverging interpretations. Diverging interpretation and the correlative fragmentation of law that ensues do not constitute a new phenomenon. Given the open texture of law, individual rules in all legal orders have been subject to diverging interpretations that have not always been fixed by supreme judicial authorities.[25] Even though diverging interpretation remains an abiding phenomenon of all legal orders, the contradicting interpretations of international law prove alarming when they rest on diverging visions of the international legal order as a whole and are not limited to the content of a single rule. In other words, when they are not about individual rules of international law but about the international legal order as a whole, conflicting interpretations can cause disquiet.

Among the understandings of the international legal order which may potentially pervade the application and interpretation of international law by domestic courts, one must be carefully examined here with reference to the practice.[26] This is the assumption that international law is a systemic set of rules pertaining to one 'system' of international law. Such a predisposition of domestic judges to construe international law as a consistent system of rules corresponds to the principle of interpretation of international law known as the principle of systemic integration. It is the aim of the following section to analyse to what extent this principle applies before domestic courts.

Yale J Int'l L 316; ER Rostow, 'The Reinterpretation Debate and Constitutional Law' (1989) 137 *U Pa L Rev* 1451; GM Buechler, 'Comment, Constitutional Limits on the President's Power to Interpret Treaties: The Sofaer Doctrine, Biden Condition and the Doctrine of Binding Authoritative Representations' (1990) 78 *Geo LJ* 1983; see also: the criticisms of J Bederman, 'Revivalist Canons and Treaty Interpretation' (1993–94) 41 *UCLA L Rev* 953.

[24] See: K Knop, 'Here and There: International Law in Domestic Courts' (2000) 32 *NYU J Int'l L & Pol* 501, 505 (arguing in particular that the interpretation of international law by domestic courts is not simply 'a conveyor belt that delivers international law to the people').

[25] HLA Hart, *The Concept of Law* (Clarendon, Oxford, 1997) 136.

[26] See: below section III.C.

III. THE PRINCIPLE OF SYSTEMIC INTEGRATION OF INTERNATIONAL LAW BEFORE DOMESTIC COURTS

For the sake of this chapter, a legal order is deemed consistent if it is an order whose rules coexist without conflicting with one another. A legal order can be made consistent not only by actually devising rules which are in tune with one another but also by interpreting them in a systemic manner. Interpretation is the very first technique that a judge can resort to with a view to enhancing the systemic character of the legal order in which the rules that he applies originate. The current techniques of international law designed to solve conflicts of norm only come into play in judicial proceedings if interpretation has not sufficed to lessen an antagonism between two rules.[27] The situation of domestic judges applying international law is not different in this respect. On the contrary, as will be explained below, interpretation techniques prove particularly crucial for domestic judges confronted with questions of international law since they often are ill-equipped to resolve conflicts of international norms contracted by their governments.

It is argued in this section that domestic judges tend to construe the international legal order as a consistent and systemic order. This leaning of domestic judges to interpret international law in a systemic manner and to give it some consistency deserves some attention in that it undoubtedly mirrors the use of the principle of systemic integration of international law which is enshrined in the Vienna Convention on the Law of Treaties and relied upon by international judges. Before dwelling on the actual use systemic integration of international law by domestic judges (section III.C), a few words will need to be said about the principle of systemic integration of international law in general (section III.A) and the extent to which it is a principle of interpretation relevant before domestic courts (section III.B).

A. The Systemic Integration of International Law

The principles of interpretation of international treaties contained in the Vienna Convention on the Law of Treaties provide for an interpretation of

[27] These various conflict of norms-solving mechanisms are based on the different status of norms (*jus cogens*, art 103), specificity (*lex specialis*), temporality (*lex posterior*) of norms. See the conclusions of the ILC Study Group on the Fragmentation of International Law: International Law Commission (ILC), Fragmentation of International Law: Difficulties Arising from the Diversification and Expansion of International Law (ILC Fragmentation Report), UN Doc A/CN.4/682 (2006) (finalised by Martti Koskenniemi). These conflict-solving mechanisms provided by international law can also help domestic judges solve conflicts of international norms with which they are confronted when applying and interpreting international law in the domestic legal order.

treaties that takes into account 'any relevant rules of international law applicable in relations between the parties'.[28] When the provision was included in the Vienna Convention on the Law of Treaties, it echoed the previous teaching of some scholars[29] as well as the position of the *Institut de droit international*.[30] It also furthered the somewhat redundant and circular definition of the concept of treaty provided by the Vienna Convention on the Law of Treaties.[31]

The principle of systemic integration finally enshrined in the Vienna Convention[32] is premised on the *fiction* that, despite international law-making being fragmented and decentralised, any new rule has been made with the awareness of other existing rules. In that sense, the principle of systemic integration presupposes the formal unity of the legal system.[33]

The principle of systemic integration prescribes that a treaty be interpreted by reference to its 'normative environment' which includes all sources of international law. That means that when several norms bear on a single issue, they should, to the greatest extent possible, be interpreted so as to give rise to a single set of compatible obligations. Its application is undoubtedly delicate. It presupposes that the status of the 'normative environment' of the norm be clarified, and, in particular, that the status rule to which it is referred be established. It is only after the scope and the applicability of this other rule of international law is defined that it can be taken into account in the interpretation of the rule at issue.

The difficulty in applying the principle of systemic integration has been magnified by international judges themselves. It is particularly important to note that the use of the principle that was made by the International Court of Justice (ICJ) has not helped clarify what 'taken into account' really means. In what probably constitutes one of the most questionable decisions of the ICJ from the standpoint of legal logic, the principle of systemic integration was expressly relied upon by the Court for the very first

[28] Art 31(3)(c).

[29] AD McNair, *The Law of Treaties* (Oxford: Clarendon Press, 1961) 466; see also: P Verzijl, Georges Pinson case (1927–28) AD No 292, cited by C McLachlan, 'The Principle of Systemic Integration and Article 31(3)(c) of the Vienna Convention' (2005) 54 *Int'l & Comp L Q* 279, 279.

[30] *Annuaire de l'Institut de droit international* (1956) 364–65. See also: www.idi-iil.org.

[31] Art 2(1)(a).

[32] The principle was first designed as a principle of contemporaneity which provided that treaties should be interpreted in the law in force at the time of their adoption. On the drafting history of art 31(3)(c), see: P Merkouris, 'Debating the Ouroboros of International Law: The Drafting History of Article 31(3)(c)' (2007) 9 *Int'l Comm L Rev* 1.

[33] See: P Sands, 'Treaty, Custom and the Cross-Fertilization of International Law' (1998) 1 *Yale Hum Rts & Dev LJ* 85, 95; see also: J Combacau and S Sur, *Droit international public*, 5th edn (Paris, Montchrestien, 2001) 175. On the unity of the legal system, see generally: H Kelsen, 'Les Rapport de système entre le droit interne et le droit international', 'Les rapports de système entre le droit interne et le droit international public' (1926) 14 *Recueil des Cours* (1926-IV) 264 (who argues that the unity of the system rests on the same principle of validity on which all the constitutive elements of the system rest). *cf* PM Dupuy, 'L'unité de l'ordre juridique international, Cours général de droit international public' (2002) 297 *Recueil des Cours* 9–490.

time in its decision in the *Oil Platform* case.[34] On that occasion, the Court resorted to Article 31(3)(c) to apply general rules of international law, including rules pertaining to the use of force, to examine whether the measures taken by the United States were necessary under the Treaty of Navigation and Commerce on the basis of which the Court had jurisdiction.[35] In that particular case, the principle of systemic integration allowed the Court to extend its jurisdiction *ratione materiae* in order to judge the behaviour of the United States in the light of rules for which the Court, strictly speaking, had no jurisdiction. It is not surprising that the decision of the Court stirred some unease, not only among legal scholars,[36] but also among judges themselves.[37] This 'bold use'[38] of the principle of systemic integration led the Court to change the applicable law.[39] It simultaneously proves a makeshift tool to create an opportunity for the Court to say a word about the use of force in the Gulf. It can reasonably be contended that the principle of systemic integration cannot go as far as displacing the applicable law. 'Taking into account' other rules of international law applicable between the parties does not mean that the 'normative environment' of the rule being interpreted can displace the latter, especially before a judge who does not have jurisdiction regarding the former. This decision of the ICJ illustrates the possible praetorian manipulations to which the rule enshrined in Article 31(3)(c) of the Vienna Convention can be subject. The more reasonable use of Article 31(3)(c) in the case *Djibouti v France*[40] has done little to expunge this suspect use of that provision in the *Oil Platform* case.

[34] ICJ, *Oil Platform* (Decision of 6 November 2003) [2003] ICJ Rep.

[35] ibid para 78.

[36] See the criticisms of: P d'Argent, 'Du commerce à l'emploi de la force: l'affaire des plates-formes pétrolières (arrêt sur le fond)' (2003) *AFDI* 655 ff.

[37] See: the Opinion of Judge Buergenthal, Judge Higgins, or the Opinion of Judge Kooijmans.

[38] See: C McLachlan, 'The Principle of Systemic Integration and Article 31(3)(c) of the Vienna Convention' (n 28) 309.

[39] ibid.

[40] ICJ Reports, 1999, paras 113–14:

> The provisions of the 1977 Treaty of Friendship and Co-operation are 'relevant rules' within the meaning of Article 31, paragraph (3)(c), of the Vienna Convention. That is so even though they are formulated in a broad and general manner, having an aspirational character. According to the most fundamental of these rules, equality and mutual respect are to govern relations between the two countries; co-operation and friendship are to be preserved and strengthened. While this does not provide specific operational guidance as to the practical application of the Convention of 1986, that Convention must nevertheless be interpreted and applied in a manner which takes into account the friendship and co-operation which France and Djibouti posited as the basis of their mutual relations in the Treaty of 1977. . . . The Court thus accepts that the Treaty of Friendship and Co-operation of 1977 does have a certain bearing on the interpretation and application of the Convention on Mutual Assistance in Criminal Matters of 1986. But this is as far as the relationship between the two instruments can be explained in legal terms. An interpretation of the 1986 Convention duly taking into account the spirit of friendship and co-operation stipulated in the 1977 Treaty cannot possibly stand in the way of a party to

This being said, the case law of the Court pertaining to Article 31(3)(c) is difficult to evaluate, for the Court has not always been willing to expressly invoke that principle while carrying out an interpretation of the same nature. For instance, the Court impliedly applied a principle of systemic integration in its *Namibia* advisory opinion where it deemed that 'an international instrument has to be interpreted and applied within the framework of the entire legal system prevailing at the time of the interpretation'.[41] In its case law pertaining to the application of human rights obligations, the Court, under the guise of the principle of *lex specialis*, also made use of the principle of systemic integration. Indeed, it actually engaged in an interpretation of the protection of the rights of individuals that reconcile human rights law and international humanitarian law.[42] In these cases, the Court resorted to the principle of *lex specialis* less to solve a conflict of norms than to determine the norm of reference of the normative environment of the obligations at stake.[43]

The principle of systemic integration has also been expressly referred to by regional courts – and especially human rights courts[44] or by international arbitral tribunals – as is illustrated by the 2005 Iron Rhine Railway arbitral award (*Ijzeren Rijn*).[45] The WTO appellate body also applied it in the *EC – Measures Affecting the Approval and Marketing of Biotech Products*.[46] It is worthy

> that Convention relying on a clause contained in it which allows for non-performance of a conventional obligation under certain circumstances. The Court can thus not accede to the far-reaching conclusions on the impact of the Treaty of 1977 upon the Convention of 1986 put forward by the Applicant.

[41] Legal Consequences for States of the Continued Presence of South Africa in Namibia (South West Africa) notwithstanding Security Council Resolution 276 (1970), 21 June 1971, para 53.

[42] See in particular: ICJ, *Legality of the Threat or Use of Nuclear Weapons* (Advisory Opinion) [1996] ICJ Rep, para 25.

[43] See: V Gowlland-Debbas, 'The Right to Life and Genocide: The Court and International Public Policy' in L Boisson de Chazournes and P Sands (eds), *International Law, the International Court of Justice and Nuclear Weapons* (Cambridge, Cambridge University Press, 1999) 315 ff; see also J d'Aspremont, 'Articulating International Human Rights and International Humanitarian Law: Consiliatory Interpretation Under the Guise of Conflict of Norms-Resolution', in M Fitzmaurice and P Merkouris (eds), *The European Convention on the UK Human Rights Act* (Brill, Martinus Nijhoff Publishers, forthcoming).

[44] See, eg: ECtHR, *Golder v United Kingdom* (1975) Series A No 18, 13 f; see also: *Loizidou v Turkey* (1996) Reports 1996-VI, para 44. More recently, see *Al-Adsani v United Kingdom*, App No 35763/97 (2001), ECHR – 2001-XI, 79, *Fogarty v United Kindgdom* App No 37112/97 (2001), ECHR – 2001-XI, 157; *McElhinney v Ireland*, App No 31253/96 (2001), ECHR – 2001-XI, 37; *Bankovic v Belgium and others*, ECHR 2001-XII, 351. See for an insightful analysis of the variations in the use of the principle of systemic integration by the European Court of Human Rights: V Tzevelekos, 'The Use of Article 31(3)(c) of the VCLT in the Case Law of the ECtHR: An Effective Anti-Fragmentation Tool or a Selective Loophole for the Reinforcement of Human Rights Teleology? Between Evolution and Systemic Integration' (2010) 31 *Mich J Int'l L* 621.

[45] Arbitration regarding the *Iron Rhine Railway, Kingdom of Belgium v Kingdom of the Netherlands* (24 May 2005) available at www.pca-cpa.org, para 58, 79. See the remarks of: P d'Argent, 'De la fragmentation à la cohésion systémique: la sentence arbitrale du 24 mai 2005 relative au Rhin de fer (Ijzeren Rijn)' in *Droit du pouvoir, pouvoir du droit, Liber amicorum Jean Salmon* (Bruylant, 2007) 1113–37.

[46] (29 September 2006) WT/DS291/R; WT/DS292/R; WT/DS293/R, para 7.68.

of mention that in all these cases, the normative environment upon which interpretation has been based according to the principle of systemic integration has not always been construed in the same manner, especially regarding the similarity that must exist between the respective memberships to the two instruments at stake.[47] Some of these tribunals have themselves been seesawing between different uses of the principle of systemic integration.[48]

Leaving aside these controversies as to the *material* scope of the principle of systemic integration, it is important, for the sake of this chapter, to say a word on the customary status of the principle of systemic integration. In this respect, it can be defended that the principle of systemic integration is of customary nature. Indeed, Article 31 of the Vienna Convention on the Law of Treaties as a whole is traditionally seen as customary international law.[49] There seems to be no reason why the principle of systemic integration would not be endowed with a customary character, as are all other principles of interpretation contained in Article 31. This seems further underpinned by the numerous abovementioned decisions by international tribunals which have resorted to that interpretative principle without the Vienna Convention on the Law of treaties necessarily being part of the applicable law between the parties. The customary character of the principle of systemic integration is not limited to the interpretation of treaties. Although its conventional consecration is limited to the law of treaties, it does not seem unreasonable to submit that the principles governing the interpretation of customary international law and unilateral acts mirror the interpretative principle devised for international treaties.[50]

[47] See the very restrictive interpretation by the WTO Appellate body in: EC – *Measures Affecting the Approval and Marketing of Biotech Products* (29 September 2006) WT/DS291/R; WT/DS292/R; WT/DS293/R, para 7.68 ('Indeed, it is not apparent why a sovereign State would agree to a mandatory rule of treaty interpretation which could have as a consequence that the interpretation of a treaty to which that State is a party is affected by others of international law which that State has decided not to accept'). On this point, see the remarks of B Simma, 'Universality of International Law from the Perspective of a Practitioner (2009) 20 *Eur J Int'l L* 276–77.

[48] See V Tzevelekos, 'The Use of Article 31(3)(c) of the VCLT in the Case Law of the ECtHR: An Effective Anti-Fragmentation Tool or a Selective Loophole for the Reinforcement of Human Rights Teleology? Between Evolution and Systemic Integration, (2010) 31 *Mich J Int'l L* 621.

[49] See generally: JM Sorel, 'Article 31' in P Klein and O Corten, *Les Conventions de Vienne sur le Droit des Traités. Commentaire article par article* (Bruxelles, Bruylant, 2006) 1289–1334; ME Villiger, *Customary International Law and Treaties: A Study of their Interactions and Interrelations with Special Consideration of the 1969 Vienna Convention on the Law of Treaties* (Dordrecht, Martinus Nijhoff Publishers, 1985) 334 ff; see: ICJ, *Territorial Dispute (Libyan Arab Jamahiriya v Chad)* [1994] ICJ Rep, para 6; *Kasikili/Sedudu Island (Botswana v Namibia)* [1999] ICJ Rep, para 1059; *LaGrand (Germany v United States of America)* [2001] ICJ Rep 501, para 99. See: *Affaire concernant l'apurement des comptes entre le Royaume des Pays-Bas et la République Française en application du Protocole du 25 septembre 1991 additionnel à la Convention relative à la protection du Rhin contre la pollution par les chlorures du 3 décembre 1976 (The Netherlands v France)* (Award of 12 March 2004) UNRIAA, vol XXV, 312, para 103; WTO AB Report, *United States – Standards for Reformulated and Conventional Gasoline* (29 April 1996) WT/DS2/AB/R, 16–17.

[50] See on the principle of interpretation of unilateral acts: J d'Aspremont, 'Les travaux de la Commission du droit international relatifs aux actes unilatéraux des Etats' (2005) *RGDIP* 163.

B. The Relevance of Systemic Integration before Domestic Courts

The determination of the principles governing the interpretation of international law by domestic judges has long been a matter of contention. It is argued here that when applying the rules of another legal order, judges should heed the rules of interpretation of that legal order. In other words, the rules of a given legal order, even when applied by the judiciary of another legal order, should be interpreted according to the principles of interpretation of the legal order in which they originate.[51] Failing to do so, judges would simply apply another rule than the rule originating in that foreign legal order.[52] Such a position seems to have been convincingly supported by the Permanent Court of International Justice (PCIJ) with respect to the application of foreign domestic law.[53] This is true as much for foreign law as for international law when they are applied by domestic courts, as is confirmed by the practice pertaining to the interpretation of international law by domestic judges. Indeed, practice shows that when interpreting international law, domestic judges resort to the rules of interpretation of Article 31 – or the corresponding principles pertaining to customary international law or unilateral acts of states.[54] The absence of incorporation of the principles of interpretation of international law designed by international law in the domestic legal order does not bar their application by domestic judges, for the principle of systemic integration, as was explained above, can be deemed a customary rule of international law and consequently becomes part of domestic law in most states in the world. Even the so-called dualist domestic legal systems have usually endorsed a monist position regarding customary international law.[55] As a result, domestic judges are most of the time in a position to apply the customary principle of systemic integration when applying rules of international law.

[51] See regarding the application of the secondary rules of responsibility by domestic courts in case involving issues of state responsibility: A Nollkaemper, 'Internationally Wrongful Acts in Domestic Courts' 101 *Am J Int'l L* 760 (2007).

[52] See generally: A Nollkaemper, 'The Power of Secondary Rules of International Law to Connect the International and National Legal Orders' Amsterdam Center for International Law, Working Paper 2009, 22, available at www.ssrn.com/abstract=1515771 (last visited 1 June 2011).

[53] See: *Brazilian Loans (France v United States)* (Judgment) PCIJ Rep Series A No 21, para 72 ('Once the Court has arrived at the conclusion that it is necessary to apply the municipal law of a particular country, there seems no doubt that it must seek to apply it as it would be applied in that country. It would not be applying the municipal law of a country if it were to apply it in a manner different from that in which that law would be applied in the country in which it is in force').

[54] See: below section II.C.

[55] See, eg: in the US, US Supreme Court, *The Paquete Habana*, 175 US 677, 678–79 (1900). For a contemporary reexamination of that jurisprudence, see DR Koslosky, 'Ghost of Horace Gray: Customary International Law as Expectation in Human Rights Litigation' (2008–09) 97 *Ky LJ* 615.

The conjugation of customary character of the principle of systemic integration and the idea that the interpretation of a norm should be based on the interpretative principles of its legal order of origin is not the only reason why domestic judges can apply the principle of systemic integration. It is also argued here that the principle of systemic integration can be applied by domestic judges by virtue of the abovementioned principle of *consistent interpretation* of domestic law with international law. Indeed, if read in conjunction with the principle of systemic integration which applies to all rules of international law, the principle of consistent interpretation of domestic law does not only call upon domestic judges to interpret domestic law in conformity with the international obligations of the state but also requires that such interpretation of domestic law rests on an interpretation of international law that does away with conflicts between the obligations of the state and other rules of international law. To correctly understand this articulation between the principle of consistent interpretation and the principle of systemic integration, it is necessary to recall that the principle of consistent interpretation has *spontaneously* been adopted by most domestic legal orders because of fear of a breach of international law that could lead to conflicts with other nations[56] or, because of the fiction that the domestic legislature necessarily takes into account the international obligations of the state when making law.[57] More recently, the principle of consistent interpretation has also been endorsed by virtue of the idea that domestic judges also constitute some sort of agents of the international legal order entrusted with the function of harmonising international law.[58] Whatever its rationale, this principle has classically been rooted in constitutional law.[59] In that sense, the principle of consistent interpretation is imposed upon the judge by the domestic legal order and does not stem from any international legal obligation.[60] And it is no surprise that a similar principle is found in regional legal orders, as is illustrated by the European legal order where European

[56] S Jay, 'The Status of the Law of Nations in Early American Law' (1989) 42 *Vand L Rev* 819, 821.

[57] *Restatement (Third) of Foreign Relations Law*, para 115 (1987). See also: US Supreme Court *Schooner Paulina's Cargo v United States* 11 US (7 Cranch) 52 (1812).

[58] See, eg: *Amerada Hess Shipping Corp v Argentine Republic*, 830 F2d 421 (2nd Cir 1987). See generally the comments of: CA Bradley, 'The Charming Betsy Canon and Separation of Powers: Rethinking the Interpretative Role of International Law' (1997–98) 86 *Geo LJ* 479, 497.

[59] G Betlem and A Nollkaemper, 'Giving effect to Public International Law'(2003) 14 *Eur J Int'l L* 569, especially 573. They argue, however, that international is not completely neutral, see: ibid 574. See also the comments of: A von Bogdandy, 'Pluralism, direct effect, and the ultimate say: On the relationship between international and domestic constitutional law' (2008) *Int'l J Const L* 1–17.

[60] See the decision of the German Federal Court of 14 October 2004 in: *Görgülü* B VerfG, docket number 2 BvR 1481/04, English translation available at www.bverfg.de/entscheidungen/rs20041014_2bvr148104en.html (last visited 1 June 2011).

law ought to be interpreted in conformity with international law.[61] Consequently, domestic judges, being required by their own domestic law to interpret domestic rules in conformity with international law, simultaneously have to ensure that the obligations binding the state – and with which domestic law must be consistently interpreted – are in conformity with other rules of international law. In other words, because of the interaction between the (domestic) principle of consistent interpretation and the (international) principle of systemic integration, domestic judges end up being in charge of the twofold task of construing domestic law in a manner consistent with international law and, *at the same time*, reconciling conflicts between international obligations of the state and other existing international rules. This means that, by virtue of the domestic principle of consistent interpretation of domestic law, it is possible to root the principle of systemic integration in domestic law as well.

It is not entirely certain that application of the principle of systemic integration of international law by domestic judges by virtue of an international obligation (*top-down* application) and as the result of a voluntary choice of the state (*bottom-up* application) always leads to a consistent understanding of its substantive meaning. This means that it cannot be excluded that the manner in which domestic judges construe the source of systemic integration of international law impinges on their actual use of it. Such an assumption is however hard to verify, for domestic judges, as is demonstrated below, often fail to indicate the source of the interpretative principles that they apply. Such an affirmation thus remains mostly speculative. However, it cannot be entirely excluded that, if systemic integration of international law is seen as originating in an obligation imposed upon the state, domestic judges prove less amenable to such an 'obligatory' conception of the international legal order than if it seems to be a voluntary choice of the state.

C. Systemic Integration in the Practice of Domestic Courts

As has already been indicated above, domestic courts commonly ground their interpretation of international law in Article 31 of the Vienna Convention. They expressly do so when they base their interpretation on the object and purpose of the treaty in issue,[62] the ordinary meaning of its

[61] See: Case 41/74 *Van Duyn v Home Office* [1974] ECR 1337; see also *Poulsen and Diva Corp* [1992] ECR-I 6019.

[62] German Federal Constitutional Court, 12 December 2000, *Jorgic Case*, Individual constitutional complaint, BVerfG, 2 BvR 1290/99; ILDC 132 (DE 2000); *Anonymous v Republic of Austria*, 16 December 2004, Final Appeal/Cassation, B 484/03; ILDC 139 (AT 2004); Supreme Court of Benin, 23 July 2003, Legal Opinion on the Compatibility of the Bilateral Agreement Between the Governments and the United States and Benin with Article 98 of the Rome Statute of the International Criminal Court, Case No 029-C; ILDC 844 (BJ 2003); Australian

terms,[63] the principle of good faith,[64] or any subsequent practice.[65] For the sake of this brief study, it is interesting to note that domestic courts are not only in a position to resort to the principle of systemic integration – as was demonstrated in the previous section – but actually engage in a systemic integration of international law. For instance, the Greek Court of Appeal of Piraeus ruled that the International Convention on Civil Liability for Oil Pollution Damage and the International Convention on the Establishment of an International Fund for Compensation for Oil Pollution Damage had to be read as one single instrument.[66] Likewise, the Latvian Constitutional Court decided that the protection owed to diplomatic premises provided for by the Vienna Convention on Diplomatic Relations and the Vienna Convention on Consular Relations did not go as far as to restrict the freedom of assembly.[67] Likewise, the Italian Court of Cassation contended that the (customary) rule of sovereign jurisdictional immunity must be read in conjunction with the European Convention on State Immunity, the Inter-American Draft Convention on Jurisdiction Immunity of States, the 1980 Rome Convention on the Law Applicable to Contractual Obligations which provides for a limitation to foreign state jurisdiction immunity.[68]

As these few cases demonstrate, systemic integration can be witnessed when domestic judges are confronted with a conflict between the international rules which they are asked to apply.[69] In these cases, systemic integration is rarely express and takes the form of a conciliatory interpretation of international legal rules which could otherwise be deemed

High Court, *Povey v Quantas Airways Ltd and British Airways Plc*, Appeal judgment, (2005) HCA 33, ILDC 506 (AU 2005) 216 ALR 427, (2005) 79 ALJR 1215.

[63] Belgian Court of Cassation, 27 June 2006, *Sabanci v Erdal* (Appeal in cassation) No P 05 1491 N, (2006) Journal des Tribunaux 642, ILDC 592 (BE 2006); Dutch Supreme Court, *Secretary of State for Finance v X Inc*, 1 November 2000, Final appeal judgment, Case No 35398; ILDC 1073; Australian High Court, *Povey v Quantas Airways Ltd and British Airways Plc* (Appeal judgment) (2005) HCA 33, ILDC 506 (AU 2005) 216 ALR 427, (2005) 79 ALJR 1215; Indonesian Constitutional Court, 23 October 2007, *Sianturi and ors v Indonesia*, Constitutional Review, Nos 2, 3/PUU-V/2007; ILDC 1041 (ID 2007).

[64] UK House of Lords, 9 December 2004, *Regina (European Roma Rights Centre) v Immigration Officer at Prague Airport and another*, Appeal, (2004) UKHL 55, ILDC 110 (UK 2004); Indonesian Constitutional Court, 23 October 2007, *Sianturi and ors v Indonesia*, Constitutional Review, Nos 2, 3/PUU-V/2007; ILDC 1041 (ID 2007).

[65] Ontario Court of Appeal, 30 June 2004, *Bouzari and ors v Iran*, Appeal decision, 71 OR (3d) 675 (Ont CA); ILDC 175 (CA 2004), (2004) 243 DLR (4th) 406; 2004 CarswellOnt 2681; 122 CRR (2d) 26; (2004) OJ No 2800; 2004 CanLII 871 (ON CA).

[66] Greek Court of Appeals of Piraeus, 16 February 2004, *Marine Environmental Services MC and Environmental Protection Technical SA v International Oil Pollution Compensation Fund 1992*, Appeal Judgment No 103/2004, ILDC 855 (GR 2004).

[67] Latvian Constitutional Court, 23 November 2006, *Assemblies Case, Ageśins and ors v Parliament of Latvia (Saeima)*, Constitutional Review, Case No 2006-03-0106; ILDC 1062 (LV 2006).

[68] Italian Court of Cassation, 22 July 2004, *Verspignani v Bianchi* (Final appeal on a preliminary question) No 13711; ILDC 556 (IT 2004), Foro Italiano I-428 (2005).

[69] Latvian Constitutional Court, (n 67).

contradictory.[70] Systemic integration may thus not always be a goal in itself but results from the attempts of domestic judges to provide consistent interpretation of international law. Yet, the implicit systemic integration of international law by domestic courts is not only a by-product of conciliatory interpretation. Indeed, the systemic integration of international law by domestic courts is not constricted to the law applicable to the case of which they are seized. Interestingly, when domestic courts venture into a systemic integration of international law, they not only take into account the rules binding upon the state but also the rules of international law by which the state is not bound.[71] The fact that they do not balk at taking into account rules that are not applicable in the case shows that the systemic integration of international law by domestic is not only a side-effect of their endeavours to make conciliatory interpretations of international rules. It can also be a more conscious and purposed enterprise.

It is important to note that, in the cases referred to above, the systemic integration was rarely decisive as it was often used to shore up a conclusion already reached by the Court[72] or which could have been reached otherwise. However, this does not thwart the conclusion that domestic courts, while being in a position to make use of the principle of domestic integration, occasionally carry out a systemic integration of international law. Such an integration of international law has usually manifested itself in a conciliatory interpretation of the rules but not exclusively, for domestic judges have occasionally integrated rules which were not applicable to the case of which they were seized. It is the aim of the following section to discuss a few of the implications of this possibility – confirmed by the practice – of domestic judges conducting a systemic integration of international law.

IV. DOMESTIC COURTS AS ARCHITECTS OF THE CONSISTENCY OF THE INTERNATIONAL LEGAL ORDER

As has been famously explained by Lauterpacht, 'it is a fallacy to assume that the existence of [rules of interpretation of international law] is a secure safeguard against arbitrariness and impartiality'.[73] Indeed, the

[70] Greek Court of Appeals of Piraeus, (n 66); Italian Court of Cassation, (n 68); Latvian Constitutional Court, (n 67); Argentinean Supreme Court, 10 May 2005, *Office of the Public Prosecutor v Lariz Iriondo*, Ordinary Appeal Judgment, L.845XL, Vol 328; ILDC 125 (AR 2005); Indonesian Constitutional Court, 23 October 2007, *Sianturi and ors v Indonesia*, Constitutional Review, Nos 2, 3/PUU-V/2007; ILDC 1041 (ID 2007).

[71] Indonesian Constitutional Court, (n 70); Italian Court of Cassation, (n 68).

[72] Argentinean Supreme Court, n 70); Indonesian Constitutional Court, (n 70); Italian Court of Cassation, (n 68).

[73] H Lauterpacht, 'Restrictive Interpretation and the Principle of Effectiveness in the Interpretation of Treaties' (1949) 26 *BYIL* 48, 53.

principles of interpretation of international law provided for by the Vienna Convention on the Law of Treaties do not in any way rein in the open texture[74] of law. Interpretation of law continues to take place in a context to which judges are not completely insensitive.[75] The same is true of the principle of systemic integration which can pave the way for different interpretations of international law, and hence, diverging conceptions of the international legal order (section IV.A). A few words must thus be said about the different constraints which bear upon the interpretation of international law respectively by domestic and international judges and which could lead to different interpretations of that law (section IV.B). Finally, the chapter will elaborate on the theoretical possibility – underpinned by the practice reported above – of domestic courts using the principle of systemic integration as a tool for furthering the integration of international law, for this is not without impact on the function and the role played by domestic judges (section IV.C).

A. Multiple Uses of the Principle of Systemic Integration

The considerable leeway inherent in the principle of systemic integration stems from the choice of the norm of reference on which interpretation will be based. In particular, the determination of the normative environment of the interpreted rule leaves much discretion to the interpreter.

Among the vast array of different interpretations that can be carried out by virtue of the principle of systemic integration, not all necessarily lead to a greater development of international law. Indeed, it is conceivable that international law is interpreted on the premise of its unity and account taken of other rules in force while still providing a very restrictive interpretation of international law. In other words, interconnection between international rules can possibly provide very restrictive readings of each of them.[76] The practice of international tribunals does not offer any such example but this use of the principle of systemic integration is utterly conceivable.[77]

[74] H Hart, *The Concept of Law*, 2nd edn (Oxford, Oxford University Press, 1997) 124 ff.

[75] See generally: G Schwarzenberger, 'Myths and Realities of Treaty Interpretations: Articles 25–29 of the Vienna Draft Convention on the Law of Treaties'(1968) 9 *Va J Int'l L* 1, 15.

[76] While not formally applying the principle of systemic integration, the US Supreme Court, in *Alvarez Machain* gave a very narrow understanding of the Extradition Treaty between Mexico and the US, resorting to other rules of international law to back its contention. For a criticism, see MA Rogoff, 'Interpretation of international agreements by domestic courts and the politics of international treaty relations: reflections on some recent decisions of the United States Supreme Court' (1996) *Am U J Int'l L & Pol'y* 559.

[77] While not providing a clear example of restrictive interpretation of international law, the practice of international tribunals shows that the principle of systemic integration has been applied in a manner that further fragments international law. This has been argued

Even if it is used in a manner favourable to the greater development of international law, there are various degrees of integration which can be achieved through the principle of systemic integration. For instance, the extent to which the principle of systemic integration can be used to reinforce the integration of the international legal order can go as far as the promotion of an international legal order endowed with all the features of a constitutional order that rests on hierarchy in procedures and substantive standards.[78] Such a use of the principle of systemic integration permeates the case law of the European Court of Human Rights.[79] In that sense, the principle of systemic integration can be wielded as a tool that enhances the formal and substantive unity of international law.[80] Yet, this very integrationist use of the principle of systemic integration is not the only manner in which this principle of interpretation can be wielded. Other, less integrationist, uses can be envisaged. Such uses are more in line with the practice reported above, for they will usually not imply any hierarchy of international rules or values. This is not to say that the systemic integration of international law by domestic courts is minimalistic. Indeed, as explained above, domestic courts have happened to conduct systemic integration of rules which were not binding upon the state nor applicable to the case of which they were seized.[81]

B. Dissimilar Constraints on Domestic and International Judges

As has already been mentioned, there are some cogent reasons to consider that when applying and interpreting the rules originating in another legal

with respect to the *Loizidou* decision of the ECHR. See: *Loizidou v Turkey*, 18 December 1996, Reports, 1996-VI, 2216, 2221 ff. See also: *Behrami v France & Saramati v France, Germany and Norway* (Decision as to the admissibility) App Nos 71412/01 & 78166/01, para 129 ff. See on this particular use of systemic integration: V Tzevelekos, 'The Use of Article 31(3)(c) of the VCLT in the Case Law of the ECtHR: An Effective Anti-Fragmentation Tool or a Selective Loophole for the Reinforcement of Human Rights Teleology? Between Evolution and Systemic Integration' (2010) 31 *Mich J Int'l L* 621, 671 f or 677.

[78] See for an analysis of the possible features that make a legal order a constitutional order: B Fassbender, *The United Nations Charter as the constitution of the international community* (Leiden, Martinus Nijhoff Publishers, 2009); B Fassbender, 'The United Nations Charter as constitution of the international community' (1998) 36 *Colum J Transnat'l L* 529–619; *cf* G Arangio-Ruiz, 'The "Federal Analogy" and UN Charter Interpretation: a crucial issue' (1997) 8 *Eur J Int'l L* 1.

[79] See generally: M Koskenniemi, 'The Fate of Public International Law: Between Technique and Politics' (2007) 70 *Modern L Rev* 1, 4.

[80] See generally on the distinction between formal and substantive unity: PM Dupuy, 'L'unité de l'ordre juridique international, Cours général de droit international public' (2002) 297 *Recueil des Cours* 9.

[81] Indonesian Constitutional Court, 23 October 2007, *Sianturi and ors v Indonesia*, Constitutional Review, Nos 2, 3/PUU-V/2007; ILDC 1041 (ID 2007); Italian Court of Cassation, 22 July 2004, *Verspignani v Bianchi* (Final Appeal on a Preliminary Question) No 13711; ILDC 556 (IT 2004), Foro Italiano I-428 (2005).

order, a judge should always interpret these rules according to the principles of interpretation of that other legal order.[82] If this is true, domestic and international judges, when they engage in an interpretation of international law, should use the same principles of interpretation designed by international law. This does not mean, however, that domestic and international judges, although they should be using the same principles of interpretation of international law, will necessarily interpret international law in the same manner. On the contrary, it is argued here that there are various reasons why the systemic interpretation of the international legal order by domestic judges may depart from that by international judges.[83]

In particular, it can hardly be contested that domestic judges are not subject to the same constraints as international judges.[84] International judges are entrusted with the powers that have been granted to them by those have accepted to subject themselves to their authority. As a result, the use that an international judge can make of its powers is certainly not alien to the manner in which the states involved will subsequently perceive international justice and dispute settlement as a whole.[85] This is why international courts – especially since they generally feel themselves entrusted with the role of guardian of international society – can be more amenable to the subtleties of inter-state relations.

Conversely, when they are applying and interpreting international law, domestic courts do not usually see themselves as protector of the political *equilibrium* of the international society. The subtle contingencies of the international society as well as states' sensitivities do not constitute a chief concern for domestic courts,[86] especially since their powers are not based on the consent of those subject to it. Hence, domestic judges commonly feel less constrained than international judges in the interpretation that they give to international law. This does not mean, however, that domestic judges are totally indifferent to contingencies of international relations. They surely heed some of the imperatives dictated by the foreign relations

[82] *cf* above section III.B. as well as nn 52–53.

[83] The differences of interpretation between domestic and international judges has sometimes be dubbed the 'dual-treaty interpretation', see: M Halberstam, 'A Treaty is a Treaty is a Treaty' (1992) 3 *Va J Int'l L* 51 –54.

[84] See generally on the diverging jurisprudential environments of domestic and international courts: MA Rogoff, 'Interpretation of International Agreements by Domestic Courts and the Politics of International Treaty Relations: Reflections on Some Recent Decisions of the United States Supreme Court' (1996) 11 *Am U J Int'l L & Pol'y* 559, 611; see also: J Bederman, 'Revivalist Canons and Treaty Interpretation' (1993–94) 41 *UCLA L Rev* 953.

[85] It is for instance well known that the ICJ was partly boycotted by developing states after its decision in the *South West African* case. It was not until the Court's condemnation of the US in the *Nicaragua* case in 1986 that the suspicions of these countries towards the Court were allayed.

[86] See for a similar argument: E Benvenisti, 'Reclaiming Democracy: The Strategic Uses of Foreign and International Law by National Courts' (n 19); see also: E Benvenisti and GW Downs, 'National Courts, Domestic Democracy, and the Evolution of International Law' (n 16) 68.

between their state and others. Yet, they will usually be less sensitive to the international political contingencies. The possibility for domestic judges to carry out integrationist interpretations of international law, even when they come at the expense of their state's interest, is simultaneously bolstered by the separations of powers enshrined in most domestic orders.

There is another set of factors of differentiation between domestic and international jurisdiction that ought to be mentioned. This relates to the available *material means* when handling cases involving issues of international law. It should not be overlooked that domestic courts are very often ill-equipped to deal with questions of international law in the sense that they may not have the human and scholarly resources to engage in wide-ranging studies of international law. Moreover, when confronted with conflicting obligations contracted by the state, domestic courts will find very little help in the scant and sometimes obscure conflict-solving principles of international law.[87] As a result, they may feel a lot of unease towards any finding of inconsistency between international rules. The scarcity of their international legal expertise for providing a conciliatory interpretation of all the legal obligations contracted by the state may explain why domestic courts prove potentially more inclined to stifle any possible conflict between the rules of international which they are supposed to apply, and especially those binding the state.

There is probably a wide variety of other constraints that affect the use of international law by domestic judges. For the sake of this chapter, the lesser amenability of domestic judges to the political contingencies of the international arena, the separation of powers at the domestic level as well as the scarcity of the international legal expertise at the disposal of domestic judges sufficiently explain why the use of the principle of systemic integration by domestic judges can potentially be more integrationist than that by international courts.

C. Domestic Judges as Agents of the Greater Integration of International Law

The previous sections have shown that domestic judges are in a position to use the principle of systemic integration and carry out a very integrationist interpretation of international law. In doing so, domestic judges can potentially elevate themselves into architects of the consistency of the international legal system. The limited practice mentioned above also underpins that conclusion. Yet, one must acknowledge that the use of the principle of systemic integration by domestic judges can simultaneously yield contradicting interpretations, for each domestic court, as was

[87] *cf* n 30.

explained above, can carry out various systemic integrations of international law. First, because systemic integration can yield very different interpretations, even ones that restrict international law.[88] Second, even systemic integration favourable to the greater development of international law can be of various degrees and lead to different results. Such a risk of diverging systemic integrations of international law is probably higher at the domestic level than at the international level, although, as is demonstrated by the practice, international tribunals have also made diverging uses of the principle of systemic integration.[89] Yet, this possible dissonance among domestic judges engaged in a systemic integration of international law should probably not be exaggerated. The limited practice referred to above points to a rather integrationist interpretation of international law with few obvious divergences.[90]

Be that is it may, the fact that positive law as well as practice show that domestic judges are in a position to integrate international law – with significant room for manoeuvre that can include some bold systematisation of international law – will surely be welcomed by those scholars who have always been sympathetic to constitutionalist understandings of international law. These scholars will hail the possibility to further integrate the international legal system through the systemic interpretation of international law by domestic courts. This is not to say that participating in the greater integration of international law amounts to reinforcing its constitutional character. Constitutionalist accounts of international law – and their idea of transcendental substantive principles – by far surpass the idea that law be made consistently with existing rules of the legal order and rests on the belief in the existence of substantive foundations.[91]

[88] *cf* above section IV.A.

[89] *cf* in particular the 2005 award in the *Iron Rhine* arbitration (n 45) paras 58 and 79 with the ICJ in the *Oil Platforms* case (n 34) para 41. Some international courts have also not been consistent in their use of the principle of systemic integration. A good illustration is provided by the European Court of Human Rights. See on this point: V Tzevelekos, 'The Use of Article 31(3)(c) of the VCLT in the Case Law of the ECtHR: An Effective Anti-Fragmentation Tool or a Selective Loophole for the Reinforcement of Human Rights Teleology? Between Evolution and Systemic Integration' (2010) 31 *Mich J Int'l L* 621.

[90] *cf* above section III.C.

[91] See for a few illustrations: C Tomuschat, 'International Law: Ensuring the Survival of Mankind on the Eve of a New Century, General Course on Public International Law' (1999) 281 *Recueil des Cours* 10, especially 237, 306; E de Wet, 'The International Constitutional Order' (2006) 55 *Int'l & Comp L Q* 51; E de Wet, 'The Emergence of International and Regional Value Systems as a Manifestation of the Emerging International Constitutional Order' (2006) 19 *Leiden J Int'l L* 611; H Mosler, *The International Society As a Legal Community* (Alphen aan den Rijn, Sijthoff & Noordhoff, 1980) 17 f. See also: 'Der "Gemeinschaftliche Ordre Public" in Europäischen Staatengruppen' (1968) *RDDI vol 21*, 523, 532; J Delbrück (ed), *New Trends in International Lawmaking – International 'Legislation' in the Public Interest* (Berlin, Duncker & Humblot) especially 18 f; B Simma, 'From Bilateralism to Community interest' *Recueil des Cours* 1994-VI vol 250, 217 ff, especially 233; A Peters, 'Compensatory Constitutionalism: The Function of Potential of Fundamental International Norms and Structure' (2006) 19 *Leiden J Int'l L* 579; PM Dupuy, 'Some reflections on Contemporary International Law and the Appeal to Universal Values: A Response to Martti Koskenniemi' (2005) 16 *Eur J Int'l L* 131;

However, the systematicity and consistency of international law that can potentially accompany the systemic integration of international law by domestic judges is classically perceived as a necessary condition for international law to witness the emergence of common substantive principles.

Scholars who embrace a very monistic understanding of the relationship between international and domestic law will similarly applaud the integrationist role taken on by domestic judges. It is true that the systemic integration of international law should not be conflated with a monist understanding of international law. One can still further the integration of the international legal order while backing away from a monist vision of international law. However, monism and systemic integration of international law by domestic judges bear some resemblance with respect to the conception of the role of domestic judges. Indeed, according to a purely monist reasoning, the international legal order encompasses the domestic legal orders of Member States and domestic courts naturally are 'agents of the international community' entrusted with the duty to give a systemic and consistent interpretation of international law as a whole.[92] Against this monist backdrop, domestic judges are more inclined to participate in the systematisation of the international legal order to which it belongs.

The possibility of domestic judges playing the role of architects when using the principle of systemic integration of international law may nonetheless not please everyone and some may find this 'integrationist' role slightly unsettling. Such a possible role for domestic judges is especially not self-evident if one assumes that the international legal order and the domestic legal orders are distinct legal orders.[93] There is, *per se*, no reason why judges of a given legal order ought to participate in the systematisation of another legal order. Indeed, it could be argued that domestic judges are solely entrusted with the power to apply the law of the domestic legal

JHH Weiler, 'The Geology of International Law – Governance, Democracy and Legitimacy' (2004) 64 *ZaöRV* 547, especially 556 f; C Walter, 'International Law in a Process of Constitutionalization' in J Nijman and A Nollkaemper (eds), *New Perspectives on the Divide Between National and International Law* (Oxford, Oxford University Press, 2007) 191 ff. It is interesting to note in this respect that in its conclusions, the ILC Study Group on the Fragmentation of International Law alluded to the 'constitutional character of the UN Charter', *Yearbook of the International Law Commission vol II*, part two, para 35. On Constitutionalism in general see: A von Bogdandy, 'Constitutionalism in International Law: Comment on a Proposal from Germany' (2006) 47 *Harv Int'l LJ* 223.

[92] G Scelle, 'Règles générales du droit de la paix' (1933) 46 *Recueil des Cours* 331, 356. See on the Monism of Kelsen according to whom international law ought to have supremacy but is not necessarily endowed with it: H Kelsen, 'Les rapports de système entre le droit interne et le droit international public' (1926) 14 *Recueil des Cours* IV, 276 ff.

[93] See: J d'Aspremont and F Dopagne, 'Kadi: the ECJ's Reminder of The Elementary Divide Between Legal Orders', available at http://papers.ssrn.com/sol3/papers.cfm?abstract_id=1341982 (last visited 1 June 2011) (n 3); see also: G Arangio-Ruiz, 'International Law and Interindividual Law' in Nijman and Nollkaemper (n 91) 39 ff, especially 42.

order which empowers them to do so and do not need to heed the systemic consistency of legal orders distinct from their own.

Domestic judges' possible role as architects can equally be opposed by those who believe that the integration of international law is a function reserved to legal scholarship and not to judges. The role of architects of the consistency of the international legal order that domestic judges can potentially endorse through systemic integration can be seen as an encroachment on what has classically been seen as a task of international legal scholars. Indeed, international legal scholars have usually understood their task as being directed at the depiction and explanation of the rules of international law in a systemic and consistent manner.[94] They have always had the tendency to see international legal order as a legal system.[95] When this is not the case, systematising the international legal order was one of the responsibilities of legal scholars. This is why the 'integrationist' role of domestic judges that could stem from the application of the principle of systemic integration could be perceived as outweighing the classical role of scholars in the systematisation of international law and raise the hackles of those who deem such a task to be the exclusive responsibility of scholars.

The potential involvement of domestic judges in the greater integration of international law by virtue of the principle of systemic integration can thus yield opposing sentiments. Whether domestic judges should or should not engage in furthering the integration of domestic law and endorse the role of an architect boils down to a political question, for it hinges on whether one wants to leave the integration of international law exclusively to international actors and how the latter are to be understood. It is not the aim of this chapter to take a position on whether or not domestic judges should engage in the integration of the international legal order through interpretation of international norms. That is a fundamental theoretical issue that touches upon the organisation of the international law-making and the delineation of the law-making powers of the actors involved which is beyond the ambit of this brief study.

Although it leaves aside the question of whether domestic judges should or should not further the integration of international law, this chapter, drawing on the practice mentioned above, contends that the fact that domestic judges are in a position to promote a very consistent

[94] According to Kelsen, 'Un ordre juridique . . . doit être conçu par la science du droit comme un système de normes placées dans un rapport réciproque, où les unes sont subordonnées aux autres': H Kelsen, 'Théorie du droit international public' (1953) *Recueil des Cours* III, 6; see also: M Virally, *La pensée juridique* (Paris, LGDJ, 1999) XXII f; and the enlightening and famous interpretation of the role of scholars by Reuter, 'Principes de droit international public' (1961) 103 *Recueil des Cours* II, 459.

[95] See the enlightening and insightful comments of J Combacau, 'Le droit international: bric-à-brac ou système' (1986) 31 *Arch Phil Droit* 85.

conception of international law through systemic integration should not be bemoaned. Judges can work well towards the consistency and systemic character of other legal orders whose norms they apply in their own legal order. Likewise, there is no reason why legal scholars should enjoy a monopoly on systemic interpretation of international law.[96] On the contrary, the 'competition' between judges and scholars in terms of consistent and systemic interpretation of international law could surely bring about diversity in the understanding of the international legal system.[97] It could also make those scholars that enthuse about constitutionalist discourses about international law more pragmatic and attuned to the practical solutions of legal problems.[98]

While coming to terms with the possible integration of international law by domestic judges through systemic integration, this chapter ends by formulating a caveat. It is has been demonstrated that systemic interpretation of international law by domestic judges can potentially contribute to the greater integration of the international legal order. As was said, this can foster diversity in the understanding of international law and prod international legal scholars towards more modesty. This is not to say, however, that we should wholeheartedly and unconditionally acclaim the role of architects potentially bestowed upon domestic courts through systemic integration of international law. This is first, because the risk of contradictory systematisations of international law, although widely exaggerated as is illustrated by the – limited – practice mentioned above, continue to lurk behind the growing application of international law by domestic judges. But the attention that is drawn here to the risks inherent to the integrationist role played by domestic judges is not limited to diverging interpretations of international law. Unconstrained by the subtle equilibrium of the international society, domestic judges can also be unaware of dangers and oversimplifications inherent in an *impulsive and unbridled integration* of international law.[99] While domestic judges' contribution to the systematisation of international law may help tone down the idealism that sometimes permeates constitutionalist understanding of international law, it can conversely give undue weight to the pipe dream of a constitutional legal order that rests on allegedly universally accepted global values. When applying the principle of systemic integration,

[96] See on the contemporary self-centrism of international legal scholars: J d'Aspremont, 'Softness in International Law: A Self-Serving Quest for New Legal Materials' (2008) 19 *Eur J Int'l L* 1075.

[97] See the well-known plea for diversity made by Martti Koskenniemi, eg: 'The Fate of Public International Law: Between Technique and Politics' (2007) 70 *Modern L Rev* 1.

[98] See on the need for a more pragmatic legal scholarship: J d'Aspremont, 'La doctrine du droit international face à la tentation d'une juridicisation sans limites' (2008) *RGDIP* 849.

[99] J d'Aspremont, 'International Law in Asia: The Limits to the Western Constitutionalist and Liberal Doctrines' (2008) 13 *AsianYBIL* 89. See: J d'Aspremont, 'The Foundations of the International Legal Order' (2007) 12 *FinnishYBIL* 261.

domestic judges should thus not delude themselves as to the existence of a sweeping substantive and procedural harmony of the international legal order and should instead remain amenable to the realities of international law. While the practice mentioned above does not prove that domestic judges have been lured by the mirage of a fully entirely integrated international legal order, the growing place of international law in domestic legal orders calls for a greater awareness by domestic judges of the risks inherent in an all-out systemic interpretation of international law at the domestic level.

8

Legal Integration through Judicial Dialogue

TOR-INGE HARBO*

I. INTRODUCTION

THIS CHAPTER SETS out to examine whether and to what degree the European Court of Human Rights (ECtHR) has entered into a judicial dialogue with the United Kingdom (UK) and Norwegian courts with regard to proportionality analysis. Whereas the Strasbourg Court is applying proportionality analysis as an instrument of judicial review, UK and Norwegian courts have traditionally applied different assessment schemes. The hypothesis of the article is that the degree to which these two national courts adopt proportionality analysis in Convention-relevant law could be the consequence of judicial dialogue with the Strasbourg Court.

The Strasbourg Court applies proportionality analysis when it assesses whether a national administrative or legislative measure infringing a Convention right is lawful or not. As is well known, most Convention rights are not absolute. This means that exemptions from the rights may be allowed. However, there are limits to the exemptions. According to Articles 8 to 11 of the European Convention on Human Rights, for example, a national measure infringing the respective right is lawful only as long as it constitutes a legitimate reason for exception, that is, it falls within one of the grounds listed in the relevant exception clause, and as long as the exemption does not exceed what is deemed as 'necessary in a democratic society'.[1]

* Dr Dr Tor-Inge Harbo, ARENA Center of European Studies, University of Oslo. I thank the participants at the conference, 'Unity or fragmentation of international law: the role of international and national tribunals', Oslo, 14–15 May 2009 and in particular Professors Erika de Wet and Ole Kristian Fauchald for their comments on earlier drafts of this chapter.

[1] Art 8 of the European Convention on Human Rights concerns right to respect for private and family life; art 9 concerns the freedom of thought, conscience and religion; art 10 concerns the freedom of expression; and art 11 concerns the freedom of assembly and association. The phrase 'necessary in a democratic society' has been rephrased by the Court to mean

Over time the Court has established proportionality analysis as a general head of judicial review.[2] In this effort the Court has elaborated and refined the application of proportionality analysis.[3] Although one may read a proportionality requirement into many of the Convention provisions,[4] the establishment of proportionality analysis as a general head of judicial review in Convention law is to a large degree a Court-created endeavour. This means that the full meaning of proportionality analysis can only be read out of the respective Convention provisions in light of the case law of the Court.

UK and Norwegian courts have traditionally not applied proportionality analysis when assessing whether a legislative or administrative measure infringes individual rights. The reason for this is an assumption that proportionality analysis implies that the substance or merits of the measure is reviewed. Proportionality analysis thus implies that courts will potentially overrule the legislator's or administrator's discretion with regards to the weighting of different values. Granting the judiciary such a powerful tool would be contrary to the established constitutional and legal conceptual understanding in the two countries. The respective national courts have applied a strictly formulated reasonableness test in this regard, reflective of the constitutional/legal conceptual context within which they are operating.

Since, as noted above, proportionality analysis cannot exclusively be read out of the Convention provisions but is to a great degree established by the Human Rights Court, this means that domestic courts in their effort to get the proportionality analysis right have to rely on the jurisprudence of the former. Taking for granted that the application of proportionality analysis does influence the outcome of cases,[5] Contracting Parties' ability to comply with their European Convention obligations may in fact rest on the willingness or ability of domestic courts to apply proportionality

'pressing social need'. Thus, in *Sunday Times* the Court concluded that an article allegedly infringing a provision on contempt of court did not correspond to a social need sufficiently pressing to outweigh the public interest in freedom of expression within the meaning of the Convention; see: *Sunday Times v UK* App No 6538/74 Series A No 30, 38 (26 April 1979) para 67. Arguably, this implies a strict interpretation of the phrase 'necessary in a democratic society' which in effect secures greater protection for the respective Convention right.

[2] MA Eissen, 'The Principle of Proportionality in the Case-Law of the European Court of Human Rights' in R Macdonald et al (eds), *The European System for the Protection of Human Rights* (Dortrecht, Kluwer, 1993) 125 ff.

[3] Although the Strasbourg Court has not been as structured in its approach as the European Court of Justice, it is nevertheless assumed that the Court applies a similar tripartite test, namely the suitability, necessity and *stricto sensu* tests, *cf* J Christoffersen, *Fair Balance: A Study of Proportionality, Subsidiarity and Primarity in the European Convention on Human Rights* (Leiden, Martinus Nijhoff Publishers, 2009).

[4] Arts 8–11 have been mentioned above. In addition, the Court has interpreted as proportionality requirements: 'to the extent strictly required' in art 15, and 'lawfully' in art 5.

[5] See for a discussion on the substantial nature of proportionality analysis: TI Harbo, 'The Function of the Proportionality Principle in EU Law' (2010) 16 *Eur LJ* 158.

analysis. Finally, since the relationship between the domestic courts and the Strasbourg Court is not one of judicial hierarchy, other instruments have to be relied on in order to ensure that domestic courts apply proportionality analysis in conformity with the Strasbourg Court. In this chapter I will discuss the application of the medium of judicial dialogue to this effect.

Whereas judicial dialogue does not necessarily mean that judges enter into a dialogue with each other in the literal meaning of the word, it must, first, imply an element of reciprocity, which means that the parties to the 'dialogue' are taking part on equal terms. A relationship between courts characterised by mutuality and equality, thus, contrasts the unequal relationship between courts which we find in a hierarchical judicial order.[6] Second, the statements uttered within the frames of a judicial dialogue are not legally binding commands but rather opinions or recommendations which the other party may or may not choose to follow on a voluntary basis. Third, judicial dialogue presupposes that there is a direct communicative channel between courts. In case an intermediator such as a legislator interferes with the course of the dialogue, the dialogue is not necessarily distorted but its importance is limited.

In the second section, I will discuss the UK courts' approach to proportionality analysis, and in the third section a similar discussion will be conducted with regard to Norwegian courts. I will in the discussions attempt to highlight issues which are indicative of a judicial dialogue between the Strasbourg Court and the respective national courts. As we shall see, the two national courts' approaches are in many aspects comparable. By including both courts in the study more weight may be given to the conclusions drawn from the discussions.

II. JUDICIAL DIALOGUE BETWEEN THE HUMAN RIGHTS COURT AND UK COURTS

The comparable test applied by UK courts when they review legislative and administrative measures has been referred to as the *Wednesbury* reasonableness test.[7] Accordingly, courts may quash a measure only in exceptional

[6] See: H Kelsen, *Allgemeine Staatslehre* (Berlin, Springer, 1925); H Kelsen, *Reine Rechtslehre* (Leibzig, Franz Deutick, 1934).

[7] *Associated Provincial Picture Houses v Wednesbury Corporation* [1948] 1 KB 223. The case concerned the validity of an administrative measure – more precisely, a decision made by a local authority which was empowered to grant licences for Sunday entertainment. A cinema was licensed subject to the condition that no children under 15 be admitted. The cinema challenged the age restriction as being unreasonable and (thus) *ultra vires*. Lord Green stressed that the court could not substitute its view of that of the empowered local authority, and then proceeded to examine what the term unreasonable meant in this context. GCHQ case *R v Minister for the Civil Service, ex parte Council of Civil Service Unions* [1985] AC 375, 410–11.

cases.[8] With regard to legislative measures one could hold that it follows from the constitutional doctrine of parliamentary sovereignty juxtaposed with the positivist conception of law that courts may not review these at all.[9] There are, however, clear indicators suggesting that UK courts have intensified their review of legislative and administrative measures in certain types of cases more recently. The intensified review is reflected in the courts' application of a moderate version of the *Wednesbury* reasonableness test.[10] The question of interest for this study is whether this shift in approach has come about as a consequence of the UK courts' dialogue with the Strasbourg Court.

In this regard, it should be noted that the shift in approach could already be detected in the 1980s. As the UK began to lose cases before the Strasbourg Court, UK judges came to realise that reliance on common law did not suffice to protect Convention rights.[11] One approach chosen by the courts in their effort to respond to the very clear signal from the Strasbourg Court was to moderate the *Wednesbury* reasonableness test to accommodate stricter scrutiny of legislative and administrative measures and thus a stronger protection of the respective individual right allegedly infringed.

A moderation of the *Wednesbury* reasonableness test is discussed in depth by the law lords in *Brind* from 1991.[12] The case concerned a directive under the Broadcasting Act 1981 requiring the British Broadcasting Corporation (BBC) and other broadcasters to refrain from broadcasting certain matters by persons who represented organisations, which were proscribed under legislation concerning the prevention of (IRA) terrorism. The ambit of this proscription was limited to direct statements made by the members of the organisations. It did not, for example, prevent the broadcasting of such persons on film, provided that there was a voice-over account paraphrasing what had been said. The objective was both to deny such organisations any appearance of political legitimacy and also

[8] The example used by Lord Green in *Wednesbury* (ibid) is that of a schoolteacher being dismissed because she has red hair.

[9] In the words of Dicey, Parliament has, 'under the English constitution, the right to make or unmake any law whatever; and further that no person or body is recognised by the law of England as having a right to override or set aside the legislation of Parliament'. Parliament in Dicey's formulations referred to the constitutional phenomenon known as the 'Queen in Parliament', ie the legislative process by which a Bill approved by the House of Commons and the House of Lords may receive the royal assent and thus become an Act of Parliament: AV Dicey, *Introduction to the Study of the Law of the Constitution* (London, MacMillan & Co Ltd, 1994) 39 f.

[10] P Craig, *Administrative Law*, 5th edn (London, Thomson, Sweet & Maxwell, 2003).

[11] See: *Malone v Metropolitan Police Commissioner* [1979] 2 All ER 620, Chancery Division 344, 379 f. Sir Robert Megarry V-C: 'Certainly in law any "adequate and effective safeguards against abuse" are wanting . . . this is not a subject on which it is possible to feel any pride in English law'. The general attitude in the UK was that there was not really a need for the Human Rights Convention since individual rights were protected through the common law. In the eyes of the British the addressees of the Convention were first of all the earlier dictatorships of Continental Europe.

[12] *R v Secretary of State for the Home Department, ex parte Brind* [1991] 1 AC 696.

to prevent intimidation. The applicants sought judicial review on a number of grounds; one of which was that the directives were disproportionate to the end sought to be attained.

After first having dismissed the strict *Wednesbury* test – 'The subject matter and date of the *Wednesbury* principles cannot in my opinion make it either necessary or appropriate for the courts to judge the validity of an interference with human rights by asking themselves whether the Home Secretary has acted irrationally or perversely'[13] – Lord Bridge, embracing a moderate version of the test, stated that in cases concerned with individual rights the Court must inquire 'whether a reasonable Secretary of State, on the material before him, could reasonably make that primary judgment'.[14] In the reformulation of the *Wednesbury* test, explicit references are made to the intensity of review required under Article 10(2) of the Convention.

Sir Thomas Bingham MR in *Smith* provided a similar reformulation of the *Wednesbury* test.[15] In the case, which concerned the dismissal of personnel from the Royal Air Force because of their homosexuality, the Court of Appeal referred to *Brind* with regard to the assessment scheme and held that 'the court may not interfere with the exercise of an administrative discretion on substantive grounds save where the court is satisfied that the decision is unreasonable in the sense that it is beyond the range of responses open to a reasonable decision-maker'.[16]

It has been argued that the Appeals Court in *Smith* opened up the possibility of scrutinising administrative decisions of the Minister of Defence more intensively than the *Wednesbury* reasonableness test, as moderated in *Brind*, suggested. This possibility lay in the introduction of what has been referred to as the flexible substantive-justification test.[17] In *Smith*, the Court noted that 'in judging whether the decision-maker has exceeded this margin of appreciation the human rights context is important. The more substantial the interference with human rights, the more the court will require by way of justification before it is satisfied that the decision is reasonable in the sense outlined above'.[18]

The Strasbourg Court was, however, not impressed by the standard of review in *Smith*. Thus, when Mr Smith appealed against the Appeal Court's judgment to the Strasbourg Court, the latter found that:

[13] ibid.

[14] ibid. On the other side, Lord Bridge emphasises that there is no entitlement to start from the premise that any restriction of the right to freedom of expression requires to be justified and that nothing less than an important competing public interest will be sufficient to justify it.

[15] *R v Minister of Defense, ex parte Smith and Others* (1996) QB 517.

[16] ibid.

[17] I Leigh, 'The standard of judicial review after the Human Rights Act' in H Fenwick, G Phillipson, and R Masterman (eds), *Judicial Reasoning under the UK Human Rights Act* (Cambridge, Cambridge University Press, 2007) 174 ff, especially 175.

[18] *R v Minister of Defense, ex parte Smith and Others* (n 15).

> [T]he threshold at which the High Court and the Court of Appeal could find the Ministry of Defence policy irrational was placed so high that it effectively excluded any consideration by the domestic courts of the question of whether the interference with the applicants' rights answered a pressing social need or was proportionality to the national security and public order aims pursued, principles which lie at the heart of the Court's analysis of complaints under Article 8 of the Convention.[19]

The high threshold set by the Appeal Court did not only have substantial implications, that is, the violation of Article 8 ECHR, but also procedural implications since under this review regime the applicants had no effective remedy according to Article 13 of the Convention.

The UK courts' response to the Strasbourg Court's judgment can be found in the House of Lords' *Daly* judgment of 2001.[20] In this case the House of Lords was concerned with the proportionality in assessing the legality of the policy for searching prisoners' cells, made pursuant to section 47(1) of the Prison Act 1952. This required staff to examine the prisoners' possessions, including legally privileged correspondence, which was not normally to be read in their absence. Applying the common law of fundamental rights, the House of Lords found the policy to be unlawful. However, they also concluded that the same result would have been reached under the Human Rights Act applying the Convention's Article 8.

In the case Lord Steyn carefully distinguished proportionality from the moderate *Wednesbury* approach and sought to clarify the 'material difference' between the two. The criteria for proportionality were, he argued, 'more precise and sophisticated' in three respects: it required 'the reviewing court to assess the balance which the decision maker has struck, not merely whether it was within the range of rational or reasonable decision', and second, it 'may require attention to be directed to the relative weight accorded to interests and considerations'. The third difference concerned the process of reasoning. Taking Article 8 of the Convention as an example, this required the Court to engage with 'the twin requirements that the limitation of the right was necessary in a democratic society, in the sense of meeting a pressing social need, and the question whether the interference was really proportionate to the legitimate aim being pursued'.[21] He concluded that although in many cases the outcome would be the same regardless of the balancing scheme applied, this was not always the case, and it was 'therefore important that cases involving Convention rights must be analysed in the correct way'.[22]

[19] *Smith and Grady v UK* (27 December 1999) 29 EHRR 413, para 138.

[20] *R (Daly) v Secretary of State for the Home Department* [2001] 2 AC 532.

[21] ibid para 27.

[22] ibid para 28. In *HL v UK* App no 45508/9 (5 October 2004), the Strasbourg Court held that 'anxious scrutiny' was inadequate in that it did not allow the Court to reach its own determination of the lawfulness of the detention of mentally ill persons, in violation of art

Lord Bingham noted that under proportionality review, domestic courts themselves had to form a judgment whether a Convention right had been breached which would include conducting such inquiry of facts and evidence necessary to form that judgment.[23] Traditionally (and according to *Wednesbury*), the task of the court which can hear appeals was limited to the *appeal* and not *review* of a decision, meaning that it would apply the facts found by the first instance court or public body. Thus, proportionality analysis requires that the court in, for example, asylum cases could no longer take for granted the asylum authorities' assessment of whether a given country was a safe country to which to return asylum seekers, but had to make its own independent factual inquiry. Thus, in the *Javed* case, which concerned the return of an asylum seeker to Pakistan, the court concluded, after having made its own assessment with regard to the security situation in Pakistan, that the respective deciding public body had *erred in facts*.[24]

In *Belmarsh*, a majority of the House of Lords found that a measure providing for detention without trial of foreign nationals under the Anti-Terrorism, Crime and Security Act 2001 violated the Convention. Hence, the derogation entered under Article 15 of the Convention by an order under the Human Rights Act was not operative. With that hurdle removed, there was a clear violation of Article 5, since the detention was prior to neither deportation nor to trial – rather it was an alternative to both. The measure infringing Article 5 could not be justified, according to the Court, because it was discriminatory and disproportionate. With regard to the proportionality of the measure, the House pointed to the fact that the UK government was prepared to allow the detainees to regain their liberty and freedom of action if they found another state prepared to accept them. Taking into account that terrorism is a global phenomenon; the judges found that this aspect of the measure cast doubt on the seriousness of the assessment the government had conducted with regard to the measure.

On the reluctance of the relevant public body to apply the proportionality principle (and the Court of Appeal's reluctance to point this out) the House of Lord held:

> The European Court does not approach questions of proportionality as questions of pure fact . . . Nor should domestic courts do so. The greater intensity of review now required in determining questions of proportionality, and the duty

5(4). The domestic proceedings were *R v Bournewood Community and Mental Health NHS Trust*, ex Parte L [1999] AC 458 (HL).

[23] *Daly* (n 20) para 23.

[24] *R (Javel) v Secretary of State for the Home Department* [2001] 3 WLR 323 (CA). Other cases where the Court has found breaches in the factual assessment by the relevant public body are: *R (Farrakhan) v Secretary of State for the Home Department* [2002] QB 1391 paras 72–74, per Lord Phillips MR; *R (Mahmood) v Secretary of State for the Home Department* [2001] 1 WLR 840 (CA); *R (On the Application of Wilkinson) v Broadmoor Special Hospital Authority and Others* [2002] 1 WLR 419 (CA).

> of the courts to protect Convention rights, would in my view be emasculated if a judgment at first instance on such a question were conclusively to preclude any further review. . . . In my opinion, SIAC *erred in law* and the Court of Appeal erred in failing to correct its error.[25]

From the brief discussion above it is clear that the moderation of the *Wednesbury* reasonableness test has come about, at least to a certain degree, as a response to the fact that the Strasbourg Court is applying proportionality analysis. As the UK courts have pointed out, proportionality analysis deviates from the (moderate) *Wednesbury* test both with regards to normative and factual aspects. First, this means that the norm, standard or threshold according to which measures are reviewed differs. Proportionality analysis constitutes, at least, potentially, a stricter review norm than the *Wednesbury* test – even as moderated in *Smith* – which means that individual rights are (potentially) better protected under the former. Secondly, when courts assess the proportionality of a decision, this also includes a review of the weighing of the different interests / rights conducted by the respective public body. How much weight a given interest / right in absolute and relative terms should have is a matter of fact in each case. Thus, when courts apply proportionality analysis they would necessarily also have to dig into the facts of the case. Although courts have to rely heavily in this respect on what is provided by the parties this does not exclude the court from having an independent role in establishing or clarifying the facts.

The House of Lords' elaborations in *Daly* and subsequent cases clearly displays that it has understood that there is a clear difference between the assessment regimes applied by the Strasbourg Court and (traditionally) by UK courts and what this difference entails. The House of Lords' elaboration in *Daly* is, apparently, a response to the Strasbourg Court's dismissal of the test applied by the Appeals Court in *Smith* – at least this is how I have chosen to present it above. In that case one could clearly hold that the relationship could be characterised as one of judicial dialogue, or perhaps rather judicial monologue, since it appears that the Strasbourg Court disregards the UK court's position in this respect. (Apparently, any discussion concerning the margin of appreciation in these cases is a 'dialogue' which the Strasbourg Court has with the national political authorities and not the national courts.)

However, it must be admitted that it is not crystal clear whether the more moderate approach taken by UK courts in *Daly* and subsequent cases is solely a response to the Human Rights Court's judgment in *Smith*. It might also be a response to the UK legislator; specifically, to its enactment of the Human Rights Act of 1998.[26] The Human Rights Act incorpor-

[25] ibid para 44 (emphasis added).

[26] Human Rights Act, adopted 9 November 1998, entered into force 2 October 2000.

ates the Convention into the domestic law of the UK.[27] It requires that courts and other public authorities apply the Convention rights directly within the UK legal system; and it empowers individuals to plead the Convention rights against public authorities in the domestic courts.

Section 2 of the Human Rights Act provides that a court or tribunal determining a question which has arisen under the Human Rights Act in connection with a Convention right must take into account any judgment, decision, etc of the Strasbourg Court and other relevant Strasbourg institutions. UK courts are, in other words, not bound by the jurisprudence of the Strasbourg Court; however, they are under an obligation to take the case law of the Court into account to the extent they believe it to be of relevance to the proceedings before them. If we translate this into judicial dialogue terminology, this would mean that the UK courts are obliged to listen to the Human Rights Court, but not compelled to follow its recommendations. Furthermore, UK courts should not merely play the role of passive receptors of the Human Rights Court's case law. The task is rather to develop a municipal law of human rights by the incremental method of the common law, case by case, taking account of the Strasbourg Court's jurisprudence.[28]

III. JUDICIAL DIALOGUE BETWEEN THE HUMAN RIGHTS COURT AND NORWEGIAN COURTS

Norwegian courts have also been reluctant to review the merits of administrative as well as legislative measures. True, Norwegian courts have, in contrast to their UK counterparts, reviewed the constitutionality of legislative acts for more than 150 years.[29] However, the fact that Norwegian courts have the constitutional institutional competence to review legislative acts does not necessarily say anything about the scope or intensity of this review. At the outset, one must note that the legislator rather than the judiciary is considered the 'guardian' of the Constitution. In practice, this means that the courts, in case of conflict, will grant considerable weight to legislative provisions which allegedly infringe the Constitution, since these are to be regarded as the legislator's interpretation of the Constitution. In *Kløfta* the Supreme Court introduced a so-called 'preferred position principle' suggesting that it would review constitutional provisions concerning rights securing individual freedom and security more intensively than provisions protective of economic and social rights

[27] Some authors do not regard the Human Rights Act 1998 as an incorporating act *stricto sensu*, but merely as an act that gives effect to an international convention in British law. See, eg: R Clayton and H Tomlinson, *The Law of Human Rights* (Oxford, Oxford University Press, 2006).

[28] See: Laws LJ in *Begum v Tower Hamlets LBC* (2002) HRLR 24 para 17.

[29] E Smith, *Høyesterett og folkestyre* (Oslo, Universitetsforlaget, 1993).

or provisions concerning the competences of the different state powers.[30] Although it has referred to this principle in a number of subsequent cases, it is difficult to determine whether courts really apply it.[31]

The courts may initially review all sides of an administrative measure. However, where the administration has applied its discretionary powers, the courts may defer their review of the merits of the measure. More precisely, they will review whether the respective administrative body has operated within the limits of its competences including whether the consequence of the measure is *manifestly unreasonable* for the individual affected by it. The Supreme Court has stated in a judgment from 2008 that this reasonable review includes aspects of proportionality analysis.[32] However, the threshold of the reasonableness test is, as we noted, set so high that one could clearly question whether this type of judicial review constitutes a reality.[33]

In *Foreigners Act I* from 1995, which concerned the expulsion of a foreigner because he had committed a criminal offence, the Supreme Court deferred its review of the proportionality analysis which the administrative body was compelled to conduct according to the provision pursuant to which it had made its decision. The main reason for this was that the Court perceived proportionality analysis to be within the scope of the respective administrative body's discretionary powers. However, in the same judgment, the Court did review whether the same measure was in breach of Article 8 of the European Convention, that is, whether the measure was 'necessary in a democratic society'. This incoherent approach was corrected in the *Foreigners Act II* from 1998 in which the Court decided also to review the proportionality analysis which the respective administrative body had conducted according to the Norwegian provision. The reason for the change in approach was that the Court (eventually) realised that the assessment according to the Foreigners Act was the same as the one the Strasbourg Court performed in similar cases and thus was required according to Article 8 of the Convention.

The Norwegian courts' initial reluctance to conduct proportionality analysis is arguably an important reason why the Strasbourg Court overruled the Norwegian Supreme Court's judgments in a number of cases concerning defamation in the 1990s. In *Bergens Tidende*[34] and *Bratholm*,[35] the Supreme Court interpreted the freedom of expression laid down in

[30] Rt 1976: 1 (*Kløfta*).
[31] Smith (n 29).
[32] Rt. 2008: 560.
[33] Rt. 1997: 1784.
[34] Rt. 1994: 348 (*Bergens tidende/Røv*) concerned a series of newspaper articles, including interviews with a number of unsatisfied patients, shedding critical light on the operation of a plastic surgery clinic.
[35] Rt. 1993: 538 (*Bratholm/Politivold*) concerned statements in a book written by a professor of criminal law about the existence of police violence in the Bergen police department.

paragraph 100 of the Constitution narrowly in order to protect the reputation of others. Paragraph 100 includes a general exemption clause meaning that no explicit reference is made with regard to defamatory statements.[36] The prohibition against defamatory statements was at the time of the incident laid down in the Norwegian Criminal Act, paragraph 247,[37] to which the courts may, according to the 'preferred position principle', not grant very much weight since the freedom of expression is categorised as a right protective of the individual's freedom and security.[38] In both cases, the Supreme Court, nevertheless, decided in favour of the defamed individual.[39]

In both cases, however, the judgments were overruled by the Strasbourg Court. One reason for this was apparently that the Court focused on the importance of the freedom of expression laid down in Article 10 of the Convention, also in securing the general democratic deliberation vital for the sustainability of democratic governance. In balancing the freedom of expression against the protection of the reputation of others, which is explicitly set out in Article 10(2) as a legitimate ground of exemption, the Court applied proportionality analysis. The decisive question was, then, whether a restriction of the freedom of expression (in consideration of the reputation of others) was 'necessary in a democratic society'. Thus, in *Bergens Tidende*[40] the Court found that there was no 'reasonable relationship of proportionality' between the restrictions on the applicant's right to freedom of expression (which followed from the Norwegian Supreme Court judgment) and the aim pursued (to protect the reputation of others) and, accordingly, that there had been a violation of Article 10.[41]

Since the Norwegian Supreme Court in the two judgments referred to above did not explicitly formulate the norm according to which it weighted the two interests/rights in question, it is difficult to assess whether the different outcomes are a question of norms or facts. It could in this regard be noted that in two subsequent cases also concerning defamatory statements – *Nordlandsposten*[42] and *Tønsbergs Blad* – the Supreme Court first made clear references to Article 10 of the Convention in its reasoning. Secondly, the balance conducted between the competing rights/interests in the cases was

[36] A reference to the relevant statutory provision is provided in a footnote.

[37] Defamatory statements were decriminalised in 2009 pursuant to the fragmented entering into force of a new Criminal Statute: Lov on straff, 20 May 2005, no 28.

[38] Rt 1997: 1821 (*Kjuus*).

[39] One could argue that one reason for this decision is that the Supreme Court regards the protection of the reputation of others as a quasi-right to privacy. Thus, in these types of cases two individual rights have to be balanced against each other, as opposed to one individual right and a public interest.

[40] *Bergens tidende and others v Norway* App No 26132/95 (ECtHR 2 May 2000). The appeal case of Mr Bratholm: *Nilsen and Johnson v Norway* (politivold) App no 23119/93 (ECtHR 25 November 1999).

[41] *Bergens tidende* (n 41) para 60.

[42] Rt 2002: 764 (*Nordlandsposten*).

performed with clear reference to the Strasbourg Court's approach in similar cases, including *Bergens Tidende*. It must be noted that there is no guarantee that taking on the same assessment norm as the Strasbourg Court would lead to a particular outcome. Thus, in the *Tønsbergs Blad* appeal case, the Strasbourg Court overruled the respective Norwegian Court's judgment.[43]

In any case, there are indications that the more adoptive approach taken by the Supreme Court in the latter two cases is not merely a consequence of judicial dialogue. One could argue that the dialogue between the Strasbourg Court and the Norwegian Supreme Court in these cases has been 'interrupted' by a third party, namely the legislator. In 1999, prior to the Supreme Court's judgment in the latter two cases, the legislator enacted the Human Rights Act implementing the Convention into Norwegian law. The very rationale of the Human Rights Act was to strengthen the position of international human rights in Norwegian law. This was done most effectively by introducing a clause – paragraph 3 – in the implementation act providing the primacy of provisions laid down in the Human Rights Act over other legislative acts enacted both before and after, giving the Human Rights Act a quasi-constitutional status.

Although the Act does not explicitly require national courts to apply the case law of the Strasbourg Court, it is clear that following the jurisprudence of the Court would facilitate compliance with the treaty obligations. In *Bøhler* the Norwegian Supreme Court stated that it would apply the same methodology as the Strasbourg Court.[44] However, it noted at the same time that it was for the Strasbourg Court to develop the Convention, meaning that Norwegian courts were not to embark upon a dynamic interpretation of the Convention in an effort to avoid its decisions being quashed by the Strasbourg Court. Furthermore, it stated that when Norwegian courts interpret the Convention they may also take into account traditional Norwegian value judgments. Taking a proactive approach, the Court stated that the Norwegian courts should seek interaction with the Strasbourg Court in order to influence its practice.[45]

The priority of the Convention over other statutory law combined with the Supreme Court's promise to apply the same methodology as the Strasbourg Court, one would think, would secure the application of proportionality analysis in Convention relevant law. However, there are indications that the adoption of proportionality analysis in this area of law has not proceeded as smoothly as one could expect. The *TV Vest*[46] judgment of 2004 may be illustrative in this regard. The question raised in the case was whether a legislative ban on political advertising on tele-

[43] And ruled in according to the position of the dissenting judge in the case: *Tønsberg Blad AS and Haukom v Norway* App no 510/04 (ECtHR 1 March 2007).
[44] Rt 2000: 996 (*Bøhler*).
[45] ibid 1008.
[46] Rt 2004: 1737 (*TV Vest*).

vision was contrary to the freedom of speech laid down in the Norwegian Constitution, paragraph 100 and the European Convention's Article 10. The Court chose a two-track approach, first, discussing the legal questions with a basis in Norwegian legal sources (and methodology), and thereafter with regard to the Convention.

In the first discussion the Court concluded (perhaps not surprisingly) in favour of the legislator. With regard to Article 10 of the Convention, the Supreme Court stated that there was no European consensus with regard to political advertising on television. In the Court's opinion then, there must be a wide margin of appreciation for the Contracting Parties in these types of cases. Furthermore, the Court noted that the regulation of political advertising was less about the individual right to freedom of expression, and more about how the political debate should be facilitated and the framing of democratic elections.[47] These considerations would, according to the Court, be best handled by the legislator.

By framing the expression of freedom as a quasi-collective right, the Court could justify taking a deferential approach without compromising the 'preferred position principle' stated in the *Kløfta* judgment.[48] At the same time, the invocation of the margin of appreciation legitimised taking Convention obligations lightly. Leaving the issue to the legislator also meant leaving the balancing of the concrete interests involved (subsumption) to the legislator or whoever administrated the act on its behalf.[49] Thus, the legislator's considerations in these cases should not be questioned by the Court except in cases where the measure must be perceived *unfounded or objectively weak in other ways*.[50]

Taking into account the assessment norm applied by the Supreme Court – unfounded or objectively weak in other ways – it is perhaps no surprise that the Strasbourg Court came to a different conclusion in the appeal case.[51] The Court noted that the freedom of expression as laid down in Article 10 of the Convention is not an absolute right and, thus, can be infringed if justified. Furthermore, it noted that according to Article 10(2) of the Convention, an infringement can be justified if it is found 'necessary in a democratic society', corresponding to a 'pressing social need', that is, whether it is *proportionate to the legitimate aim pursued* and whether the reasons given by the national authorities to justify it are relevant and

[47] ibid para 62. The considerations which found the basis for para 100 are those of truth-seeking, individual autonomy, and the protection of democratic institutions.

[48] Rt 1976: 1 (*Kløfta*). In the case the Supreme Court stated that the type of right was divisive for the intensity of the judicial review.

[49] ibid para 62.

[50] ibid para 62: 'Stortingets hensiktsmessighetsskjønn bør legges til grunn med mindre – slik som I Kjuus saken – det fremstår som ufundert eller saklig sett svakt på annen måte' ('The Parliament's assessment must be taken as point of departure unless – as in the *Kjuus* case – the assessment appears to be unfounded or deficient in other ways'; translation provided by the author).

[51] *TV Vest AS & Rogaland Pensjonistparti v Norway* App no 21132/05 (11 December 2008).

sufficient.[52] The Court noted that in assessing whether such a 'need' existed, the national authorities are given a certain margin of appreciation:[53] 'the Contracting States enjoy a wide margin of appreciation in striking *a fair balance* between, on the one hand, freedom of expression and, on the other hand, the need to place restrictions thereon in order to secure the free expression of the opinion of the people is the choice of the legislator'.[54] At the same time it noted that this margin of appreciation is not unlimited, and that there is, according to the Court's case law under Article 10(2) of the Convention, little scope for restrictions on political speech.[55] 'The political nature of the advertisements that were prohibited', it noted, 'calls for a *strict scrutiny* on the part of the Court and a correspondingly circumscribed national margin of appreciation with regard to the *necessity* of the restriction'.[56]

The Court 'did not find it appropriate in the present case to attach much weight to the various justifications for allowing States a wide margin of appreciation'.[57] It noted that it was clear that the ban on political advertising on television was of an absolute, permanent nature, and not, as the Court had accepted before, applied in a short timeframe before elections.[58] Thus, according to the Court, the permanent ban 'might lead to results incompatible with the privileged position of free political speech under Article 10'.[59]

Addressing the arguments of the Norwegian government, the Court held that in order to reach the subordinated aim of securing a level playing field for all the political parties, it was 'not persuaded that the ban had the desired effect'.[60] It noted that while the Pensioners Party fell within the category of parties that were the primary targets of the prohibition, it proved that paid advertising on television had become the only way for the same party to get its message across to the public. And since the Pensioners Party was not given attention in the edited television coverage, as all major parties were, this was its only chance of obtaining the same advantage – equal treatment – as that of the major parties. The Court concluded that there was not '*a reasonable relationship of proportionality* between the legitimate aim pursued by the prohibition on political advertising and the means deployed to achieve that aim'.[61]

[52] ibid para 58, with references to *Sunday Times v the United Kingdom* (n 1) para 62.
[53] ibid para 62: the Court holds that in sum its 'task in exercising its supervisory function is not to take the place of the national authorities but rather to review under Article 10, in the light of the case as a whole, the decisions they have taken pursuant to their power of appreciation'.
[54] ibid para 65.
[55] ibid para 59.
[56] ibid para 64.
[57] ibid para 66.
[58] *Bowman v United Kingdom* (Judgment, 19 February 1998).
[59] *TV Vest* (n 52) para 66.
[60] ibid para 73.
[61] ibid para 78.

One could hold that the reason why the Strasbourg Court reached a different conclusion than the Norwegian Supreme Court is that the former balanced the pending rights and interests differently. It is clear that the Supreme Court did not apply the proportionality analysis scheme to this effort. The assessment test applied by the Supreme Court – 'unfounded or objectively weak in other ways' – does not reflect the 'strict scrutiny' which the Strasbourg Court suggests is appropriate in the particular case – although one could argue that the latter does not apply its strictest test either. Thus, although the Strasbourg Court notes that it will scrutinise the measure strictly, the test provided in the case is nevertheless formulated as 'a reasonable relationship of proportionality' which reflects a rather lenient necessity test. However, it is clear that the test applied by the Strasbourg Court is nevertheless stricter than that applied by the Norwegian Supreme Court.

Another reason for the divergent reasoning and conclusions could also be a consequence of the Supreme Court's two-track approach, implying that it first, and as a separate issue, discussed the legal question with reference to Norwegian legal sources and methodology and thereafter discussed the question in relation to Convention law. One could hold that this approach is problematic from a legal integrational point of view because this first discussion will tend to be exclusively based on national legal sources reflecting a traditional methodological approach, and moreover, that this initial discussion will tend to influence the second discussion concerning whether the measures comply with the Convention in the name of coherence. Underpinning this view is the way in which the Norwegian Court frames the relationship between the constitutional right and the statutory measure, namely as one of balancing rather than infringement. As we have seen, the Strasbourg Court frames the relationship as one of infringement rather than balancing, which grants the freedom of expression an *a priori* stronger position.

IV. CONCLUSIONS

The discussion in this chapter demonstrates that there are elements of judicial dialogue characterising the relationship between the Strasbourg Court, on the one side, and the respective national courts, on the other. When I refer to elements, I have in mind first of all the voluntariness which characterises judicial dialogue. For one could question whether the reciprocal element as well as the direct communicative element of judicial dialogue is really part of the relationship. Rather, it appears that the dialogue is actually more of a monologue. What we have is then an issue of judicial governance on part of the Strasbourg Court. Furthermore, it appears that the Strasbourg Court and the courts included in this study are not communicating directly with each other. In both cases, the legislator has interfered in a way which one cannot exclude has had an important influence on the national courts relationship with the Strasbourg Court. In both the UK and the Norwegian examples, the legislator has played an essential role as facilitator and arguably also as a participant in the 'dialogue' with the Human Rights Court with regard to proportionality analysis. By enacting statutes implementing human rights into domestic law, the legislator has provided national courts with a solid legal basis with which they can handle Convention provisions as well as the Strasbourg Court's jurisprudence.

This could clearly lead us to question whether UK and Norwegian courts are really about to become 'important actors in their own right in the process in which European law becomes effective in national legal orders'.[62] Perhaps the courts do not agree that they have 'a powerful interest in closely monitoring the Strasbourg Court's activity, and in staying one step ahead of the latter when it comes to developing standards of rights protection'.[63] The first part of the quotation presupposes that the courts are 'international' actors independent of the legislator, which clearly is contrary to the institutional constitutional regime of the two countries. The latter part of the sentence suggests that national courts should actively contribute to the development of the Convention by applying the same dynamic approach as the Strasbourg Court. This latter approach has firmly been rejected by the Norwegian Supreme Court, as noted above.[64]

Proportionality review implies, as I have noted above, 'second guessing' with regard to how different interests and values are to be weighted against each other. These are, in both countries, perceived as being questions of a political nature, which according to conceptualisation of law and politics should best be conducted by the democratically elected legislator or whoever it has delegated the power to, typically the executive branch. This understanding of democratic legitimacy can, of course, be questioned, since it tends to presuppose a republican/majoritarian rather than a pluralist/liberal conceptualisation of democracy. In the latter understanding of democracy, the judiciary may be granted a more important role as protectors of individual and group rights according to an assumption that these cannot be sufficiently protected by the democratic majority. However, this assumption, perhaps paradoxically, presupposes a fear of the establishment of a 'tyranny of the majority' which again pre-

[62] H Keller and A Stone Sweet, 'Introduction: The reception of the ECHR in national legal orders' in H Keller and A Stone Sweet (eds), *A Europe of Rights: The Impact of the ECHR on National Legal Systems* (Oxford, Oxford University Press, 2008) 3; see also: AM Slaughter, *A New World Order* (Princeton, Princeton University Press, 2004) ch 2.

[63] H Keller and A Stone Sweet, 'Assessing the Impact of the ECHR on National Legal Systems' in *A Europe of Right* (n 62) 687.

[64] ibid Rt. 2000: 996 (*Bøhler*), 1008.

supposes a republican/majoritarian understanding of democracy. Taking a consistent approach, we should accept the pluralist/liberal claim that it is not possible to form a tyranny of the majority because of the plurality of different opinions and interests which are present in Parliament and society at large and therefore that the need for judicial check in this regard is perhaps not so great after all.[65]

However one may perceive this, it is interesting to note the recent change which has taken place in the UK court system. The House of Lords, previously the highest court of the land, has been replaced by the Supreme Court.[66] One important reason for this replacement has been to secure the separation between the legislative and the judicial branches. As is well known, the House of Lords was also the Second Chamber of the Parliament. A Supreme Court independent from the legislative branch may well prove to be a more self-confident and constructive dialogue partner for the Strasbourg Court.

[65] See: R Dahl, *Preface of Democratic Theory* (Chicago, Chicago University Press, 1956).

[66] The Supreme Court was established by Part 3 of the Constitutional Reform Act 2005 and commenced its work on 1 October 2009.

9

Judicial Dialogue in Multi-level Governance: The Impact of the Solange *Argument*

ANTONIOS TZANAKOPOULOS*

I. INTRODUCTION

THE CONFERRAL OF powers by states to international organisations in a small number of instances allows an international organisation to make decisions which are binding on states and which interfere with individual rights, such as the right of access to a court, the right to property, the freedom of movement, and others. To the extent that an international organisation has been given the power to make decisions with such wide-ranging effects, directly affecting persons within state jurisdiction, the organisation is exercising 'governmental' or 'sovereign' power. Examples include the power of the United Nations (UN) Security Council to make binding decisions under Chapter VII of the Charter of the United Nations (UN Charter), and the power of the European Union (EU) to make Regulations that are directly applicable in the legal order of its Member States. In response to these developments, domestic courts have sometimes reacted by asserting the power to control decisions of the international organisation that interfere with individual, 'fundamental' as they will be called throughout the text, rights. In other cases, domestic courts have deferred to the fundamental rights protection system that exists at the level of the international organisation.[1]

* Lecturer in International Law, University of Glasgow School of Law/UCL Faculty of Laws. Many thanks are due to Professors Ole Kristian Fauchald, André Nollkaemper, Erika de Wet, Christian J Tams, and Sam Wordsworth, as well as to Drs Jure Vidmar, Gleider Hernández, Philippa Webb, and to Omer Bekerman, for helpful comments and suggestions. The usual disclaimer applies. This contribution was finalised and reflects the law as at January 2010, though the inclusion of some later developments was made possible during the book's production. Despite the entry into force of the Lisbon Treaty, references to the EC, the EC Treaty, and the Court of First Instance (CFI) have not been changed.

[1] See generally on domestic court reactions to acts of international organisations the contributions in: A Reinisch (ed), *Challenging Acts of International Organizations before National*

Many of these responses, whether resistance or deference, it will be argued, have been based on variations of the *Solange* argument, an argument first articulated by the German Federal Constitutional Court. In the two relevant decisions, the German Court successively asserted its power to review decisions of an international organisation for compliance with fundamental rights guaranteed under the German Constitution, and then decided to defer to the international organisation when it was satisfied that an equivalent level of protection was available within the international organisation's framework. This contribution seeks to trace the development, parameters, and effects of the *Solange* argument. As a first step, it seeks to set the scene in which the *Solange* argument was elaborated and in which it operates: the first substantive part defines the terms 'multi-level governance', that is, the framework for the *Solange* argument, and 'judicial dialogue', that is, the mode of operation of the argument (section II). The next task is to analyse the *Solange* argument, in terms of its message and of the various interlocutors which it seeks to engage (section III). Sections IV and V trace the impact of the argument on various courts in their adoption of a deferential or defiant stance towards the international organisation which exercises conferred governmental powers. Section VI, finally, attempts to draw normative conclusions from the significant impact of the *Solange* argument. It concludes that by using the *Solange* argument, domestic courts, being agents of state practice, assert the existence of a list of 'core' or 'fundamental' rights which must be substantively and procedurally protected at whatever level the exercise of governmental powers takes place.

II. MULTI-LEVEL GOVERNANCE AND JUDICIAL DIALOGUE DEFINED

A. Exercise of Public Powers at Multiple Levels

States are increasingly 'contracting out' some of their powers of regulation, that is, the exercise of their governmental or 'public' authority, to international organisations. De Wet, for example, has noted the progressively intensifying shift of public decision-making away from the state towards such international actors,[2] while Sarooshi speaks of international organisations now exercising 'sovereign powers' which states have

Courts (Oxford, Oxford University Press, 2010) [hereinafter: Reinisch 2010]. See further: A Reinisch, *International Organizations before National Courts* (Cambridge, Cambridge University Press, 2000) [hereinafter: Reinisch 2000]; as well as, more generally: K Wellens, *Remedies Against International Organizations* (Cambridge, Cambridge University Press, 2002).

[2] E de Wet, 'The International Constitutional Order' (2006) 55 *Int'l & Comp L Q* 51, 52 f.

conferred on them.[3] The effect of such power conferrals is that both public and private entities at the national level are subject to regulations stemming from a number of different entities or organs exercising governmental powers, belonging, however, to different levels of governance. Some exist and operate at the national level, others at a regional level – whether in an inter-governmental or in a supra-national configuration – and others at the international level.[4]

Natural persons and legal entities subject to national regulation can usually appeal against or attack state (administrative) acts that affect their rights or legal position (*Rechtsposition*) before the state's courts, at least in the last instance. In fact, the ability of individuals and legal entities under the jurisdiction of a state to seek review of the state's public acts exists nowadays not only before domestic courts, but increasingly before a plurality of international tribunals.[5] This serves only to create an even starker contrast with public acts stemming from other levels of governance, that is, from international authorities largely not subject to review.[6] 'Public' or 'governmental' acts of international organisations, such as EU Regulations and Directives, or UN Security Council Resolutions under Chapter VII of the Charter, are not subject to appeal before domestic courts, with the ensuing result that those 'governed' may find themselves without any means of redress, except perhaps before the acting organisation's own court, if available. This is particularly so because, despite calls for the emergence of 'common institutions at regional levels or universal level to compensate for the losses incurred' by the contracting out of governmental authority,[7] such an evolution has not always been forthcoming. Indeed, in the first instance, most conferrals of governmental authority by states in favour of international organisations take place without being

[3] See generally: D Sarooshi, *International Organizations and their Exercise of Sovereign Powers* (Oxford, Oxford University Press, 2005).

[4] The reference to governance at multiple levels rather than to regulation reaching across different legal orders is deliberate. International organisations exercising 'governmental' powers conferred on them by states may or may not consider themselves as operating within an 'autonomous' or 'separate' legal order, their actions thus having effects across legal orders. The perspective adopted here, however, is that of a unified legal order, which allows the existence of partial, relatively separate, legal orders. These partial legal orders, which may be established by an international treaty, or by a national constitution, exist precisely because the pyramid of validity of the unified legal order so allows. Thus any exercise of governmental powers may be seen as taking place within the same legal order but at different levels of the pyramid of validity, and at the same time as reaching across partial legal orders.

[5] A Mahiou, 'La justice internationale et les droits de l'homme: brèves remarques' in PM Dupuy et al (eds), *Völkerrecht als Weltordnung: Festschrift für Christian Tomuschat* (Kehl, NP Engel, 2006) 227, 243.

[6] Commenting on targeted Security Council sanctions, Cannizzaro speaks of a clear 'asymmetry': E Cannizzaro, 'A Machiavellian Moment? The UN Security Council and the Rule of Law' (2006) 3 *Int'l Org L Rev* 198, 200.

[7] See: C Tomuschat, 'International Law: Ensuring the Survival of Mankind on the Eve of a New Century' (1999) 281 *Recueil des Cours* 1, 42.

accompanied by the implementation of safeguards equivalent to those provided for in domestic law for the control of the exercise of public power.[8]

B. Dialogue and 'Judicial Dialogue' Defined

In circumstances of multi-level governance, that is, governance at various levels and in different configurations, dialogue between the various *loci* of power is hailed as the best (or as the only viable and/or realistic) solution.[9] This has led some to call dialogue – somewhat dejectedly – the 'usual' response to problems of multi-level governance.[10] Dialogue between domestic and international courts figures prominently among the proposed responses.[11] But before it can be determined whether judicial dialogue has served as a solution to problems created by the conferral of powers to international organisations and the ensuing multi-level governance, the term must first be defined.

The main feature of dialogue is the necessity for an exchange of ideas between those engaged in it; otherwise it is rather a *mono*logue. However, there are many different types of dialogue – sometimes the argument one of the interlocutors advances is so convincing as to immediately solicit the agreement of the other, who adopts the argument wholesale.[12] The exchange then can be more precisely defined as *influence* exercised by one interlocutor on the other. In another instance, dialogue can be character-

[8] *cf* CPR Romano, 'International Organizations and the International Judicial Process: An Overview' in L Boisson de Chazournes et al (eds), *International Organizations and International Dispute Settlement – Trends and Prospects* (Ardsley, New York, Transnational Publishers, 2002) 3, 34.

[9] But multi-level governance has also sparked the debate on multi-level constitutionalism, ie on the imposition of legal restraints on authorities acting on the international plane; see: S Kadelbach and T Kleinlein, 'International Law – a Constitution for Mankind? An Attempt at a Re-appraisal with an Analysis of Constitutional Principles' (2007) 50 *GYIL* 303, 329; see generally: de Wet (n 2). See for a discussion on the models and techniques of constitutionalisation, which are centred around models of resistance and deference: J Klabbers, A Peters, and G Ulfstein, *The Constitutionalization of International Law* (Oxford, Oxford University Press, 2009) 31 ff.

[10] See: S Oeter, 'The International Legal Order and its Judicial Function: Is there an International Community – Despite the Fragmentation of Judicial Dispute Settlement?' in *Festschrift Tomuschat* (n 5) 583, 598.

[11] See: V Bore Eveno, 'Le contrôle juridictionnel des résolutions du Conseil de sécurité: vers un constitutionnalisme international?' (2006) 110 *RGDIP* 827, 858.

[12] *cf* eg: AM Slaughter, 'A Typology of Transjudicial Communication' (1994) 29 *U Rich L Rev* 99, 101, stating that 'dialogue' between courts may be more or less interactive depending on the circumstances. But she terms 'monologue' the instance where one court's arguments are adopted by another court, since the former may have little sense of the fact that someone other than the litigants may be listening: ibid 113. However, it should be noted that when a Constitutional Court renders a decision it knows will make waves, there is little to suggest that it may be ignorant of the fact that the decision will invariably be considered by other courts facing similar issues, across borders.

ised by the *reaction* of one interlocutor to the claims of the other. In such an instance, one interlocutor advances a claim, to which the other interlocutor expresses principled disagreement, usually also advancing a counter-claim. It is with these two particular types of dialogue – dialogue as agreement and influence, and dialogue as disagreement and reaction – that this chapter is concerned.

Dialogue can take place between courts belonging to different or the same (partial) legal order,[13] as well as between a court and an executive, be it national, international, or supra-national. The dialogue between two or more courts belonging to different (partial) legal orders clearly qualifies as 'judicial dialogue'.[14] But when the court's message has various intended or unintended recipients, and when these recipients do engage with the court's message, dialogue ensues. This is again 'judicial dialogue' of sorts, as it is the court that enters into dialogue with various other interlocutors.

C. Judicial Dialogue in the Context of Multi-level Governance

As briefly discussed above (in section II.A), a common problem created by conferral of powers to international organisations and the subsequent fragmentation of governance between the national and various international levels will be the fact that acts of public authority which could previously be attacked or appealed before a national court now seem to be immune. Effectively, natural persons and legal entities who could have these acts reviewed, in particular for compliance with their fundamental rights as these are guaranteed under domestic (usually constitutional or

[13] The distinction between a 'domestic' and an 'international' court is relative. eg, the German Federal Constitutional Court is undoubtedly a domestic court; in its *Solange* engagement with the European Court of Justice (ECJ), the ECJ can be seen as an international court. However, the ECJ positions itself as a domestic court in its own *Solange* moment, the 3 September 2008 *Kadi* judgment (Joined Cases C-402/05 P and C-415/05 P [2008] ECR I-6351). From the point of view of general international law, the position of the 'domestic' court could be assumed by any judicial organ of a partial legal order in its interaction with the general international legal order (see also n 4 above).

A similar approach could advocate that most international courts – if not all, with the sole exception of the International Court of Justice (ICJ) – are parts of specific (international) legal regimes, whose function is intertwined with that of the regime; *cf* Y Shany, 'One Law to Rule Them All: Should International Courts be viewed as Guardians of Procedural Order and Legal Uniformity?' in this volume, ch 2. In a similar vein, they could be described as organs of 'functional (sectoral) constitutional regimes'; *cf* de Wet (n 2) 53. They can thus be seen as undertaking a sort of 'defence' of the partial legal order, ie of the specific regime, not only against other specific regimes, but also against the overarching general international legal order.

[14] 'Judicial dialogue' is 'the most common characterization of transnational interactions among courts', see: RB Ahdieh, 'Between Dialogue and Decree: International Review of National Courts' (2004) 79 *NYU L Rev* 2029, 2045 and 2050 ff.

'domesticated' international)[15] law, no longer have access to a court to request such a review. The international act will usually not be reviewable at the national level. At the international level, even if there is – utterly exceptionally – a court which individuals can access to seek review, that international court may not be able to review the act for compliance with a list of fundamental rights comparable to those guaranteed at the national level.

National courts, being the guarantors of the rule of law (*Rechtsstaat; état de droit*) and the organs of the state most sensitive to the respect of fundamental rights, will probably at some point react to such a state of affairs;[16] or they may perceive themselves as being required to react under domestic (constitutional) law – which at the very least allows individuals to access them. If this justification for domestic court reaction sounds implausible or utopian, there is another one: domestic courts will not just sit idly by while they are being stripped of jurisdiction they previously possessed. Experience shows that they will react when they see their powers of review over the exercise of governmental power diminishing.[17] The real reason for their reaction probably lies somewhere in between these two extremes; one could plausibly claim that courts may fear breaching their constitutional obligations if they relinquish jurisdiction in favour of an international organisation.[18]

What matters most, however, in terms of the development of judicial dialogue, is the relationship that then emerges between the reacting court

[15] See on the blurring of the dividing lines between international and domestic norms: A Tzanakopoulos, 'Domestic Courts in International Law: The International Judicial Function of National Courts' (2011) 34 *Loy LA Int'l & Comp L Rev* (forthcoming; available at http://ssrn.com/abstract=1861067, last visited 1 June 2011) section II.

[16] Murray calls their role in this respect 'constitutionally sensitive' in '*any* legal system'; JL Murray, 'Fundamental Rights in the European Community Legal Order' (2009) 32 *Fordham Int'l LJ* 531 (emphasis added).

[17] See: A Reinisch, 'Verfahrensrechtliche Aspekte der Rechtskontrolle von Organen der Staatengemeinschaft' (2005) 42 *Berichte der Deutschen Gesellschaft für Völkerrecht* 43, 81 f. *cf* with respect to national bureaucracies resisting transfers of powers to the EC: HG Schermers, 'Comment on Weiler's *The Transformation of Europe*' (1991) 100 *Yale LJ* 2525, 2527; and with respect to the 'erosion' of the jurisdiction of the European Court of Human Rights (ECtHR) because of increasing transfers of powers by States to the EC: Murray (n 16) 545.

[18] *cf* Shany (n 13) for a similar argument in the context of interactions between international courts (which may refuse to engage in jurisdiction-regulation for fear of breaching their mandate). See further: WTO AB Report, *Mexico – Tax Measures on Soft Drinks and Other Beverages* (6 March 2006) WT/DS308/AB/R, paras 52–53, where the WTO Appellate Body clearly finds that it is not open to a Panel to refuse to exercise established jurisdiction, as this would 'diminish' the right of a complaining member to seek redress for a violation of an obligation under the Dispute Settlement Understanding (Understanding on Rules and Procedures Governing the Settlement of Disputes (DSU), Marrakesh Agreement Establishing the World Trade Organisation, Annex 2, Legal Instruments – Results of the Uruguay Round (1994) 33 ILM 1123). Rather, the member is 'entitled' to a decision.

and the state of which it is an organ,[19] as well as the international organisation towards which the reaction is directed. This relationship can be seen as one of courteous dialogue; or as one of mounting pressure; or even as one of outright threat and conflict. When discussing the relationship that emerges from the domestic court reaction, attention should be paid in particular to the form of this reaction and the inspiration that courts of different states and even regional international courts draw from previous reactions of other courts towards international organisations in streamlining their own.

III. THE *SOLANGE* DIALOGUE AND ITS INTERLOCUTORS AND ADDRESSEES

A. The *Solange* Jurisprudence of the German Federal Constitutional Court

The most vocal reaction of a domestic court to the transfer of powers to an international organisation is that of the German Federal Constitutional Court (*Bundesverfassungsgericht*) in the celebrated 1974 *Solange I* decision. Not dwelling on the many intricacies of the case, one could describe in broad strokes the judicial line of defence: as long as the European (Economic) Community (EC), as it then was, does not offer protection of fundamental rights at least equivalent to that guaranteed in the German Constitution (the Basic Law; *Grundgesetz*), while at the same time it has been given power to adopt decisions that are binding on Germany, and even directly applicable in the domestic legal order,[20] the Constitutional Court will guarantee the protection of fundamental rights under the German Constitution by reviewing itself the acts of the organisation for compliance with the provisions of the German Constitution on fundamental rights.[21]

Irrespective of the correctness of the legal reasoning or the analytical perspective of the Constitutional Court in the instance, the defensive argument – and at the same time the claim directed at the Community – is clear: either take up the task of protecting fundamental rights when

[19] Thus to which its (re)action is attributable: see art 4 of the ILC Articles on the Responsibility of States for Internationally Wrongful Acts (2001) UN Doc A/56/10; II(2) *YBILC* 26.

[20] See for an argument extending the reasoning of the Court to cover not only Regulations, which are directly applicable, but also other Community binding acts, such as Directives, which are in the first instance not directly applicable but must be transposed, the means of transposition being left to the discretion of the Member State: C Tomuschat, 'Aller guten Dinge sind III? Zur Diskussion um die Solange-Rechtsprechung des BVerfG' (1990) 25 *Europarecht* 340, 342 f.

[21] See: 37 *BVerfGE* 271, 285.

claiming the power to make law;[22] or we will do it for you. The message is sent on multiple fronts: it is sent to the EC as an international organisation, urging political initiatives to plug the legal holes. It is, however, also sent specifically to the European Court of Justice (ECJ), urging it to expand its activism from simply appropriating powers in favour of the Community,[23] to actually taking up the burdens that (should) go with them. The German executive is also an addressee: it is urged to bring political pressure to bear in order to ensure the protection of fundamental rights at Community level; it is told that it cannot hide behind the Community. There is finally a fourth addressee of the Constitutional Court's message: this is the membership of the organisation at large, including particularly the domestic courts of other members, to which the reasoning of the German Constitutional Court is most likely to appeal.

In 1986, the German Constitutional Court revisited the issue in *Solange II*.[24] 'Constitutional' developments in the meantime had seen the Community – acting mainly through the ECJ – stepping up its protection of fundamental rights, by solidifying the approach that these rights constituted general principles of Community law, informed by the 'common constitutional traditions' of the Member States and the European Convention of Human Rights, to which all Community Member States were also parties. The Community, in particular through the ECJ, had to some extent addressed the reaction of the German Constitutional Court.[25] It had responded. In its own response then, the Constitutional Court established a *doctrine of equivalence* between the protection of fundamental rights offered by the German Constitution and that offered by Community law as reflected in the jurisprudence of the ECJ.[26]

Based on this doctrine of equivalence, the Court stated in *Solange II* that, as long as the Community did offer equivalent protection of fundamental rights, the Constitutional Court would refrain from reviewing Community acts for conformity with the German Constitution. Again, a number of complex issues are raised by the decision, most prominently whether there is in fact any equivalent protection: some arguments have been made as to the need for a *Solange III*, repealing *Solange II*, due to the lack of

[22] 'Making' law is used here in the Kelsenian 'dynamic' sense of establishing new, lower ranking, more specific rules in compliance and in accordance with the prescriptions of higher-ranking, more general rules ('Rechtsdynamik'; 'der Stufenbau der Rechtsordnung'); see generally: H Kelsen, *Reine Rechtslehre*, 2nd edn (Wien, Franz Deuticke, 1960) 228 ff.

[23] The German Federal Constitutional Court later put this impression in no less clear terms than a resounding warning in its *Maastricht* decision, where it cautioned against interpretations of the Treaty on European Union (TEU) which would have effects equivalent to the 'extension' of the Treaty: 89 *BVerfGE* 155.

[24] 73 *BVerfGE* 339.

[25] See: ibid 378, referring in particular to *Nold*, Case 4/73 [1974] ECR 491, 507, and the declaration of 5 April 1977 in [1977] OJ C 103/1.

[26] 73 *BVerfGE* 378.

equivalence.[27] But there are many important features of the *Solange II* judgment aside from such substantive questions of actual equivalence. The decision constitutes a further step in the dialogue between the ECJ and the German Federal Constitutional Court; or, from another angle, an acceptance of the truce offered by the ECJ; or, from yet another angle, the only possible conclusion of the politically unsustainable situation created by *Solange I*.

B. The Various Interlocutors in the Original *Solange* Dialogue

In effect, the *Solange* jurisprudence of the German Federal Constitutional Court pressured the EC to adopt adequate standards of fundamental rights protection, compliance with which in the exercise of public power was monitored by a court. *Solange* was the tale of a power-struggle between two courts; but effectively also between two international persons, a state and an international organisation. Who were then the various interlocutors of the German Federal Constitutional Court in its *Solange* jurisprudence? And how was the dialogue between them configured?

1. *Addressing a Competing Locus of Authority*

In *Solange I*, the Constitutional Court addressed the EC at large and the ECJ in particular. It told them that their assumption of public powers without putting in place adequate safeguards for their exercise was unacceptable from a legal perspective; it was an affront to the most fundamental principles of the German constitutional order. More should be done to address the German concerns over the protection of fundamental rights, lest the Constitutional Court assume review of EC acts directly. Both the EC and the ECJ in particular responded to the German Federal Constitutional Court's concerns. The latter, in *Solange II*, accepted their response as adequate, putting an end to the confrontation, but also reserving its right to revisit the issue should the agreement reached deteriorate in the future.

2. *Addressing the Domestic Executive*

The *Solange* dialogue can also be cast in a more complex light. It was also a dialogue (or struggle) between the Constitutional Court and the German

[27] See, eg: R Scholz, 'Wie lange bis "Solange III"?' (1990) 43 *NJW* 941; H Gersdorf, 'Funktionen der Gemeinschaftsgrundrechte im Lichte des Solange II-Beschlusses des Bundesverfassungsgerichts' (1994) 119 *AöR* 400. Others still see the *Maastricht* judgment of the German Federal Constitutional Court (89 *BVerfGE* 155) as being in effect *Solange III*; eg: N Lavranos, 'The *Solange*-Method as a Tool for Regulating Competing Jurisdictions Among International Courts and Tribunals' (2008) 30 *Loy LA Int'l & Comp L Rev* 275, 318 ff.

executive. Effectively the Court forced Germany to be in breach of its Community obligations, which from the perspective of international law are international obligations stemming from a treaty (the EC Treaty). Germany was forced, after *Solange I*, either to defy its obligations under the Treaty of Rome or to defy its Constitutional Court – an impossible situation to be in if ever there was one. In effect thus the Court forced Germany to undertake its own dialogue with the European Community to resolve the impasse.

3. *Addressing (Implicitly) all Other Courts Similarly Positioned*

Quite apart from the more or less direct interlocutors of the German Federal Constitutional Court in *Solange*, that is, the EC and its Court, and the domestic executive, the Constitutional Court's reasoning, in and of itself, had (and has) a certain appeal and entails the possibility of being applied in numerous situations involving the conferral of governmental powers from one level of governance to another, without a corresponding establishment of (adequate) control mechanisms at the new *locus* for the exercise of the conferred power. The *Solange* argument allows those previously charged with controlling the exercise of power to either re-assert their power to control it at the new *locus* (*Solange I*) or to relinquish it in favour of any control mechanisms at the new *locus*, holding on only to residual (and exceptional) power of control (*Solange II*).

The *Solange* line of argument is thus (implicitly) addressed to whoever is willing to listen and be persuaded that this is a good way to control conferrals of powers to another level of governance: not only to the other EC Member States and in particular their courts, who are most likely to be persuaded to adopt a similar line of argument, but also to any other court potentially facing the same issues arising from the complexity of multilevel governance. As Tomuschat argued in 1990, 'every *principled disobedience* of Community law constitutes in itself a precedent that will invariably find imitators'.[28] The focus here should be on the argument that *principled* disobedience of law will find imitators.

And indeed, both the principled disobedience in *Solange I*, but also the deferential approach in *Solange II*, did find 'imitators'. It is to this influence of the *Solange* reasoning that the rest of this contribution turns.

IV. DEFERENCE: *SOLANGE II* IN OTHER COURTS

The German Federal Constitutional Court's message did not fall on deaf ears: Member States' courts did listen; and some were in fact convinced.

[28] Tomuschat (n 20) 343 (author's translation, emphasis added).

A line of argument similar to that in *Solange II* was adopted by the Italian Constitutional Court (*Corte costituzionale*) in its consideration of the relationship between the Italian and the EC legal order.[29] The *Solange* reasoning still seems very appealing as far as the relationship between the Community and its Member States is concerned. It is not only continuously re-cast and refined by its creator,[30] but it has been adopted in one way or another by some of the courts of states that acceded in 2004.[31]

But the *Solange* argument did reach far beyond the issues of the relationship between the Community and its Member States. The *Solange II* reasoning can be seen as a way for courts to defer to existing control mechanisms for the exercise of public authority at *loci* of power 'outside' the partial legal order in which the court in question operates. Just as the German Federal Constitutional Court deferred to mechanisms for ensuring respect for fundamental rights at the EC level in *Solange II*, so other courts have deferred using similar reasoning – based on the doctrine of equivalence or some variation – and only reserving some residual power of review in the exceptional instance that equivalence is no longer present or the presumption of equivalence is overturned. In this sense, the reasoning of *Solange II* can be qualified as an instance of comity.[32] It has been employed by the European Court of Human Rights (ECtHR),[33] as well as by national courts in their interactions with international organisations other than the EC.

The ECtHR is well-versed in engaging with other courts and tribunals, as well as with the executives of states parties to the European Convention on Human Rights. Dialogue between the ECtHR and domestic courts of states parties, for example, is – in a sense – institutionalised: the relationship between the international tribunal and domestic courts can be described as one of 'division of labour' (*Arbeitsteilung*).[34] Still, the ECtHR has faced problems of coping with multi-level governance when exercising its function of monitoring the application and implementation of the European Convention, as it was eventually confronted with applications claiming Convention violations in the implementation by states parties of international obligations imposed by international organisations. It responded by employing the *Solange II* doctrine of equivalence, as an analysis of its jurisprudence shows.

[29] *Frontini v Ministro delle Finanze* (27 December 1973) (1974) 47 *Rivista di diritto internazionale* 130. *cf* A La Pergola and P Del Duca, 'Community Law, International Law and the Italian Constitution' (1985) 79 *Am J Int'l L* 598, 610 f; Cannizzaro (n 6) 219.

[30] See: the exposition by Lavranos (n 27) 316 ff.

[31] See generally: W Sadurski, '"Solange, chapter 3": Constitutional Courts in Central Europe – Democracy – European Union' (2008) 14 *Eur LJ* 1.

[32] See, eg: Lavranos (n 27) 276, 324.

[33] See: Reinisch (n 17) 61.

[34] *cf* C Grabenwarter, 'Das mehrpolige Grundrechtsverhältnis im Spannungsfeld zwischen europäischem Menschenrechtsschutz und Verfassungsgerichtsbarkeit' in *Festschrift Tomuschat* (n 5) 193.

When a state has undertaken an international obligation to implement a decision of an international organisation,[35] and in particular in circumstances where there is no discretion left to the state with respect to such implementation,[36] an alleged violation of the European Convention on Human Rights necessarily complicates the situation. The implementing state party can do nothing but implement the binding decision as it is, being thus precluded from considering its compatibility with the European Convention. At the same time, it has undertaken the obligation to guarantee Convention rights to 'everyone within [its] jurisdiction'.[37] If the binding obligation is susceptible of necessitating non-compliance with the European Convention on Human Rights, theoretically the ECtHR should find a breach of the Convention on the part of the implementing state. However, there would be little that the state could then do to assume compliance with the Convention, except of course breaching its international obligation to implement the international organisation's decision.[38]

It was the European Commission of Human Rights that was first faced with this situation in *M & Co v Germany* in 1989. When an applicant complained that the implementation of a decision of the European Court of Justice by Germany (for which the latter had no margin of discretion) resulted in the violation of Convention rights, the Court adopted the basic idea of the *doctrine of equivalence* articulated by the German Federal Constitutional Court in *Solange II*:[39] the Commission found that the transfer of powers to an international organisation is allowed under the Convention as long as within that organisation Convention rights will receive *equivalent protection*.[40] This was accepted to be the case within the EC.

[35] Which is tantamount to saying that the decision of the international organisation is binding on the state. Since only binding decisions entail an international obligation for the state to implement them, it is only binding decisions of international organisations that are discussed in this chapter.

[36] *cf* eg the distinction drawn by the EC Court of First Instance (CFI) in Case T-315/01 *Kadi* [2005] ECR II-3649, para 258 (Case T-306/01 *Yusuf* [2005] ECR II-3533 is identical in substance; reference is always to *Kadi*) and Case T-228/02 *OMPI* [2006] ECR II-4665, paras 100–02.

[37] European Convention on Human Rights, art 1.

[38] ie the only other thing that the ECtHR could do would be to impose on the state party an obligation to review the internationally binding decision for compatibility with the European Convention on Human Rights (and thus, by necessity, not to implement it if it is so incompatible, thereby obviously breaching the international obligation to comply); *cf* G Cohen-Jonathan and J-P Jacqué, 'Activités de la Commission européenne des droits de l'homme' (1989) 35 *AFDI* 512, 517. It has thus been commented that a state may be effectively trapped between the 'rock' of Community Law and the 'hard place' of obligations under the European Convention on Human Rights, see: Murray (n 16) 539.

[39] *cf* Cohen-Jonathan and Jacqué (n 38) 515.

[40] *M & Co v Federal Republic of Germany* (Commission Decision, Admissibility) 64 *Decisions and Reports* 138, 145.

The ECtHR has confirmed this approach in its *Bosphorus* judgment,[41] coming even closer to *Solange II* than the Commission had done in 1989. The ECtHR found that the EC offers equivalent protection to rights guaranteed under the European Convention on Human Rights, both substantively as well as procedurally. As such, EC acts are *presumed* to be in conformity with the European Convention. This presumption is rebuttable – the ECtHR reserves the possibility of reviewing an EC act or the domestic implementing act for conformity with the European Convention if the protection offered by the EC is *in casu* 'manifestly deficient'.[42] A similar – and similarly narrow – reservation was in fact also adopted by the German Constitutional Court in *Solange II*.[43]

It appears thus that the ECtHR and the ECJ have found a certain *modus vivendi* based on mutual deference and respect. The ECJ, spurred on by the German Constitutional Court in *Solange I*, will review Community acts for compliance with the European Convention on Human Rights, which reflect general principles of Community Law.[44] The ECtHR in turn will defer to the protection of fundamental rights offered by the Community through the ECJ in appropriate cases. Both Courts have thus resolved to interpret the law they apply in a manner harmonious with each other's 'constitutional' documents.[45] The influence of the German Federal Constitutional Court in the emergence of this ECJ-ECtHR relationship is apparent when one considers that it was *Solange I* that spurred the ECJ to be more assertive in the protection of fundamental rights and *Solange II* that offered the ECtHR the framework for formulating its own *doctrine of equivalence* between the European Convention protection and EC protection of fundamental rights.[46]

[41] With some slight but nonetheless important variations, which however do not necessarily fall within the scope of the chapter and for which see: A Haratsch, 'Die Solange-Rechtsprechung des Europäischen Gerichtshofs für Menschenrechte – Das Kooperationsverhältnis zwischen EGMR und EuGH' (2006) 66 *ZaöRV* 927, 932 f.

[42] *Bosphorus Hava Yolları Turizm ve Ticaret Anonim Şirketi v Ireland* (Grand Chamber, Judgment) App No 45036/98 (2005) para 156.

[43] *cf* Tomuschat (n 20) 340. The difference being that unlike the German Federal Constitutional Court in *Solange II*, the ECtHR reserves the right to confirm the equivalence of protection *ad hoc* in any case before it. In fact, however, the presumption will be next to impossible to rebut; *cf* A Ciampi, 'L'Union Européenne et le respect des droits de l'homme dans la mise en oeuvre des sanctions devant la Cour européenne des droits de l'homme' (2006) 110 *RGDIP* 85, 98 ff.

[44] Subsequently also codified in TEU, art 6(2). The entry into force of the Lisbon Treaty famously opened the way for EU accession to the European Convention on Human Rights.

[45] *cf* Haratsch (n 41) 933.

[46] M Milanović, 'Norm Conflict in International Law: Whither Human Rights?' (2009) 20 *Duke J Comp & Int'l L* 69, 102 ff discusses the concept of equivalent protection from the perspective of norm conflict in international law. At 112 ff he analyses the concept of equivalent protection as a conflict avoidance technique as employed by the ECtHR, and at 113 f he argues that *Solange* differs from the jurisprudence of European Convention on Human Rights organs since the latter does not involve norms belonging to (allegedly) *different*, but rather to the *same* legal order, that of public international law. But from the perspective of different levels of governance the distinction between (self-proclaimed) separate legal orders

What is particularly noteworthy, however, is that in *Bosphorus* the ECtHR completely ignored the more remote source of the obligation that Ireland was implementing, arguably precisely in order to be able to apply the doctrine of equivalence: had the ECtHR acknowledged that Ireland was in fact implementing an obligation under a Security Council Chapter VII Resolution (which it was, in effect), then it would have had to argue that equivalent protection of fundamental rights of individuals existed at the UN level, which was (and is) not the case. Finding equivalence in the protection of fundamental rights at the level of the EC and that of the European Convention on Human Rights is noticeably easier, as demonstrated in the previous paragraph. However, an argument could be made that powers on the part of Ireland had been conferred on the UN *before* that state became a party to the European Convention on Human Rights, and thus at the time of conferral were not subject to Convention guarantees.

The *Nada* case currently pending before the ECtHR brings this matter forcefully into focus:[47] here Switzerland is implementing directly a Security Council Chapter VII Resolution which arguably forces it to breach its obligations under the European Convention. There is no intermediate EC act in implementation of the resolution, and thus any equivalence will have to be found between the protection at European Convention and at UN level. Even more interestingly, issues of intertemporal law seem rather more straightforward: Switzerland became a UN member only in 2002, *after* it had become a party to the European Convention on Human Rights. It clearly conferred powers on the UN that were subject to Convention obligations; Switzerland should thus have ensured the existence of equivalent protection of Convention rights with respect to the exercise of the powers conferred. It remains to be seen whether the ECtHR will stick to the *Solange II* approach and defer to the UN, or will switch to a *Solange I* reasoning following the ECJ and the United Kingdom (UK) Supreme Court,[48] or will opt for some other solution in dealing with governance at the UN level.

The European Court of Human Rights has used the *Solange II* reasoning to defer to international organisations other than the EC and its Courts. In *Waite and Kennedy*, the ECtHR was faced with a complaint that Germany, in according through its domestic courts immunity to the European Space Agency, had violated the applicants' right of access to a court under Article 6(1) of the European Convention on Human Rights. The ECtHR accepted that states parties can establish international organisations and vest them with immunity from jurisdiction – in effect vesting them also with final say over internal matters, such as private law disputes involving staff

becomes blurred: any partial legal order can be seen as separate from any other, even if it has not proclaimed itself to be so (which it may still do): see the discussion in nn 4 and 13 above.

[47] *Nada v Switzerland* (Grand Chamber, pending) App No 10593/08.

[48] See: section V below.

members – as long as these international organisations offer reasonable alternative means of protection of rights under the Convention.[49] In the Commission's words – with which the Grand Chamber agreed in its decision – 'judicial or *equivalent* review could be obtained',[50] and thus the right of access to a court was not impaired. The influence of *Solange II* and of the doctrine of equivalence is implicit but clear in these decisions.[51]

It should be noted that in cases involving similar facts, national courts have adopted the same reasoning, though there have been occasions where the national court has rejected the existence of equivalent protection on the level of the international organisation and has proceeded to deny it immunity and review the organisation's actions. In *Ms Siedler v Western European Union*,[52] the Brussels Labour Court of Appeal found that the internal procedure of the Western European Union (WEU) did not offer guarantees of fair and equitable process as far as the settlement of administrative disputes was concerned. This was ostensibly in violation of the general principle that there should be no denial of justice, and of the right to a fair trial of every person consecrated in Article 6(1) of the European Convention on Human Rights and Article 14(1) of the International Covenant on Civil and Political Rights, and as such the WEU was made to submit to national jurisdiction, its immunity being denied.[53]

The influence of *Solange II* and of the deferential doctrine of equivalence has been adopted by national courts even beyond questions of immunity of international organisations. In *Rukundo v Federal Office of Justice*,[54] the Swiss Federal Tribunal was faced with a claim that transfer of accused to the International Criminal Tribunal for Rwanda (ICTR), an obligation assumed by Switzerland by virtue of the Federal Decree of 21 December 1995, should not take place as the procedure before the Tribunal was not in conformity with the provisions of the European Convention on Human Rights and the International Covenant on Civil and Political Rights. The Swiss Federal Tribunal stated that Switzerland would not lend its support to processes that did not guarantee a minimum protection of fundamental rights as defined in the European Convention and the International Covenant,[55] but went on to presume the conformity (or, one could say, *equivalence*) of ICTR procedures to that standard, a presumption which had not been rebutted in this instance.[56]

[49] *Waite and Kennedy v Germany* (Grand Chamber, Judgment) App No 26083/94 (1999) paras 67–73. *cf Beer and Regan v Germany* (Grand Chamber, Judgment) App No 28934/95 (1999) paras 57–63, which is almost identical.

[50] *Waite and Kennedy* (n 49) para 66 (emphasis added).

[51] See also: A Reinisch's comment on the decisions in (1999) 93 *Am J Int'l L* 933, 936 f and *cf* A Reinisch, 'Introduction' in Reinisch 2010 (n 1) 1, 11 f.

[52] *Ms Siedler v Western European Union*, ILDC 53 (BE 2003); [2004] *Journal des tribunaux* 617.

[53] See: ibid para 40.

[54] *Rukundo v Federal Office of Justice*, ILDC 348 (CH 2001).

[55] ibid para 3(a).

[56] ibid para 3(b).

What is notable in this brief survey of relevant judicial practice, both at the international and at the national level, is the fact that courts will resort to *Solange II* reasoning without necessarily having gone through a *Solange I* phase. In some instances thus, when they consider that there is adequate or 'equivalent' protection of fundamental rights at the new *locus* of exercise of power, they will immediately defer. Another notable feature is the standard against which equivalence is measured. In the case of the ECtHR the standard is that of the European Convention on Human Rights, or what could be called the ECtHR's 'domestic' law (in the sense of the law of its own partial legal order). National courts, however, seem to refer to standards embodied in the European Convention on Human Rights and the International Covenant on Civil and Political Rights rather than their own domestic (constitutional) law. Of course this could be simply because these two bodies of law (international and constitutional) overlap in the area of fundamental rights. In the next two sections, these two points will be taken up in turn.

V. RESISTANCE AND DISOBEDIENCE: *SOLANGE I* IN RESPONSE TO UN 'INTRUSION'

A. Re-inventing *Solange I* in Response to UN Security Council Targeted Sanctions

The *Bosphorus* case, in which the ECtHR applied reasoning similar to *Solange II* and established a doctrine of equivalence of fundamental rights protection at the EC and European Convention levels, had in fact its source in a UN Security Council decision under Chapter VII of the UN Charter. The Irish act that led to a complaint before the ECtHR in that instance was an act in implementation of an EC Regulation, which had been adopted to give effect to a Security Council Resolution imposing sanctions on the Federal Republic of Yugoslavia under Article 41 of the Charter.[57] The introduction of this consideration adds yet another level of governance, and thus yet another level of complexity. This additional level was largely ignored by the ECtHR in *Bosphorus*, arguably because the ECJ had already dealt with the justification of the implementation of the relevant Security Council Resolution in its own *Bosphorus* judgment.[58] However, the domestic measures adopted in implementation of certain Security Council Resolutions under Article 41 of the Charter have given rise to cases in which both the ECJ and national courts have employed a line of resistance and disobedience largely influenced by the *Solange I*

[57] See: SC Res 820 (1993).

[58] Case C-84/95 *Bosphorus* [1996] ECR I-3953, paras 22–23.

reasoning. The *Nada* case, referred to earlier and currently pending before the Grand Chamber of the ECtHR,[59] may offer yet another example of *Solange* reasoning.

In imposing measures under Article 41 of Chapter VII with a view to the maintenance of international peace and security, its primary responsibility,[60] the Security Council has adopted targeted sanctions against individuals and legal entities that are deemed as being associated with terrorist organisations. The relevant sanctions regimes[61] interfere to a significant – though varying – degree with individual rights by introducing asset freezes, travel bans and arms embargoes.

The obligations imposed on UN Member States under certain Security Council Chapter VII Resolutions, in particular those under the 1267 regime, can be characterised as strict, in the sense of denying the addressee states any measure of discretion in their implementation. This is because the Security Council determines, through a Sanctions Committee (the '1267 Committee'), the individuals and legal entities that are to be subjected to restrictive measures, by including them in a 'blacklist' (the Consolidated List). By contrast, under the 1373 regime, Member States are the ones to determine those against which the restrictive measures will be imposed.[62] Under the 1267 regime thus, Member States are left with no discretion at all in the implementation of the measures – they simply have to freeze the assets of the specified persons or be found in breach of the relevant Resolutions and Article 25 of the Charter; not to mention risk becoming themselves a possible target of Security Council Article 41 measures.

At the same time, those designated by the Security Council under the 1267 regime find themselves subjected to severe sanctions. At first this was without any possibility of challenging their designation at the UN level, although some avenues for limited challenges have now been established by the Council. Originally, targeted individuals and entities could only resort to their state of nationality or residence and ask it to request their de-listing; later, they were allowed to submit individual petitions to the 1267 Committee to that effect (through the Focal Point).[63] However, the Committee would decide on the basis of *consensus*, *in camera*, and without any obligation to give reasons for rejecting a de-listing request.[64]

[59] See: text at nn 47–48 above.

[60] UN Charter, art 24(1).

[61] Namely the regimes set up under SC Res 1267 (1999) (the '1267 regime') and SC Res 1373 (2001) (the '1373 regime').

[62] The distinction was clearly drawn by the CFI in *OMPI* (n 36) paras 100–02; see also text at n 36.

[63] SC Res 1730 (2006) para 1. This was superseded by the establishment of an Office of the Ombudsperson by SC Res 1904 (2009) para 20, on which see further below.

[64] See: *Guidelines of the* [1267] *Committee for the Conduct of its Work* (9 December 2008) 6, para 7(a); 2, para 3(a); 7, para 7(g)(vi)(c); 8, para 7(h)(iii); 1, para 2(b). The guidelines have subsequently been amended in the wake of SC Res 1904 (2009) (on which more below), the

The lack of any redress for blacklisted persons at UN level expectedly created a predicament for both national courts as well as for the courts of the European Community, since implementation of the Council measures was taking place on both levels. National and EC courts did in fact engage with the situation. In effect, the conferral of powers to the UN to take measures affecting fundamental rights of individuals under Article 41, and the exercise of that power by the Security Council in particular under the 1267 regime without putting in place any mechanism for those affected to appeal against such severe restrictions became fertile ground for a dispute between courts of various partial legal orders and the UN as to the exercise of control over that power.

B. Court Resistance and Enforced Disobedience

Most courts will consider that they lack jurisdiction *ratione personae* to entertain a direct attack on a Security Council Resolution;[65] but they will, in the first instance, necessarily entertain an attack on a domestic measure, even if it is implementing a Council Resolution. However, when that implementing measure is simply a transposition of the Council decision imposing a strict obligation and leaving the implementing state no discretion in its implementation, then any review of the domestic measure will constitute – if indirectly – a review of the Council measure for compatibility with domestic law standards;[66] in particular with domestic fundamental rights standards. Courts have accordingly adopted a number of evasive tactics in seeking to avoid confrontation with the Security Council, as well

latest version (of 26 January 2011) providing similarly with respect to meetings being closed and decision-making by consensus (3, para 3(b); 4, para 4(a)), but requiring that a summary of reasons for listing be made available on the Committee's website (7, para 6(k)) as well as an updated summary in cases where de-listing is refused (9, para 7(k)). The current version of the Guidelines is available at www.un.org/sc/committees/1267/pdf/1267_guidelines.pdf (last visited 1 June 2011).

[65] See, eg: the position of the Croatian Constitutional Court in *Bobetko Report* (Review of Constitutionality and Legality) (12 November 2002) ILDC 383 (HR 2002) para 3. *cf* also: *Dubsky v Ireland and ors* (13 December 2005) ILDC 485 (IE 2005) para 91; *Croatia v N-T* (13 October 1999) ILDC 384 (HR 1999) paras 11, 16, 18. This applies not only to direct attacks against Security Council Resolutions, but also to any action that a court (rightly or wrongly) attributes to the UN; see, generally: *Behrami & Behrami v France* and *Saramati v France, Germany & Norway* (Grand Chamber, Admissibility) App Nos 71412/01 and 78166/01 (2007) and implicitly The Hague District Court following in *HN v The Netherlands* (10 September 2008) ILDC 1092 (NL 2008) paras 4.12.3 and 4.15.

[66] These 'domestic law standards' are meant here not necessarily in the sense that they will exclusively refer to municipal law; they may also refer to international law, depending on the latter's position and applicability as prescribed by the domestic legal order. *cf* AR Brewer-Carías, *Judicial Review in Comparative Law* (Cambridge, Cambridge University Press, 1989); and: H Mosler, 'Supra-National Judicial Decisions and National Courts' (1980) 4 *Hastings Int'l & Comp L Rev* 425, 457 ff; as well as n 15 above.

as with their own executive branches.[67] The evasive tactics of the Community courts (the Community being considered tantamount to a domestic legal order in the sense of a partial legal order) deserve particular mention in this connection, as they have been much imitated.

In a number of instances, the Community courts avoided the issue of violation of fundamental rights by Security Council Resolutions and their implementing legislation by adopting an excessively deferential review of the Community implementing acts (and indirectly the Council measures necessitating them). In *Bosphorus*, the ECJ found that the objective of maintaining international peace and security was so fundamental as to justify far-reaching interference with fundamental rights, applying thus a low level of scrutiny by employing a broad proportionality test.[68] In *Kadi*, the European Court of First Instance (CFI) considered that as long as the Security Council measures (and thus the Community measures) did not violate *jus cogens*, they were justified in otherwise interfering with fundamental rights.[69] These decisions, in particular the *Kadi* decision of the CFI, had significant influence on various domestic courts, even those of non-Member States of the EC: the Swiss Federal Tribunal in *Nada* adopted an approach similar to the CFI in *Kadi*,[70] and the Turkish Council of State deferred to the Security Council as well.[71] But this deferential approach was reversed by the ECJ when it considered the *Kadi* case on appeal.

1. *The ECJ's Message in* Kadi

In *Kadi*, the ECJ annulled the EC measures adopted in implementation of the 1267 regime. In so doing, the ECJ declared boldly – though implicitly – that unless the UN and its Security Council ensure, in their exercise of sovereign powers, protection of fundamental rights which is equivalent to that offered by the European Community (which is itself at least equivalent to that offered by the German Basic Law, according to the German Federal Constitutional Court in *Solange II*), it will continue to exercise its

[67] See for a short overview of 'avoidance doctrines' adopted by domestic courts to circumvent review of international treaties: E Benvenisti, 'Exit and Voice in the Age of Globalization' (1999–2000) 98 *Mich L Rev* 167, 188 f and relevant notes and *cf* 193 f. See also generally: Reinisch 2000 (n 1) especially 391 for a summary.

[68] *Bosphorus* (n 58) para 26.

[69] *Kadi* (n 36). A long discussion could be had of course on whether the CFI in *Kadi* also adopted the *Solange* argument in its *Maastricht* incarnation, by stating that 'as long as' the SC did not violate *jus cogens* the EC Courts would not activate their jurisdiction over implementing acts. However, the distinguishing feature here would be that the 'red line' drawn, that of *jus cogens*, is a 'red line' under international, rather than under domestic constitutional, law.

[70] *Nada gegen SECO* (14 November 2007) ILDC 461 (CH 2007) para 5.4.

[71] Reversal on appeal of the annulment of Turkish implementing measures in *Al-Qadi*: Decision No 115/2007 on App No 2824/2006 (22 February 2007) available at www.danistay.gov.tr (Council of State sitting as a Court of Appeal) (in Turkish) and forthcoming as ILDC 311 (TK 2007).

review power over EC implementing acts (and thus indirectly over Council Resolutions) without deference. This can be seen when the Court states that the re-examination procedure within the UN system cannot give rise to 'generalised immunity from jurisdiction' within the legal order of the Community.[72] But this is because that re-examination procedure 'does not offer guarantees of judicial protection'.[73] 'From that follows', continues the Court, 'that the Community judicature must ensure full review'.[74] The cumulative effect of paragraphs 321 to 322 of the judgment is to indicate that the only way for Security Council measures to be exceptionally 'immunised' from review within the Community legal order would be for the re-examination procedure at UN level to offer 'the guarantees of judicial protection'.[75]

The ECJ thus left open the possibility of a reversal of its position along the lines of *Solange II*: should the UN put in place a procedure offering adequate (if not necessarily equivalent) judicial protection, then the ECJ seems to indicate that it will retreat and defer to internal UN review.[76] In this sense, even the ICJ could be considered an addressee of the message of *Kadi*; but, unlike the ECJ in the original *Solange* situation, there is little the ICJ can do to remedy the shortcomings of fundamental rights protection in the Security Council's exercise of powers under Chapter VII.[77]

[72] *Kadi* (n 13) para 321.

[73] ibid para 322. See further criticism of the UN re-examination procedure at paras 324–25. *cf* S Griller, 'International Law, Human Rights and the European Community's Autonomous Legal Order: Notes on the ECJ Decision in *Kadi*' (2008) 4 *Eur Const L Rev* 528, 549.

[74] *Kadi* (n 13) para 326.

[75] Some authors have noted that 'reasonable minds can disagree about the precise import of these . . . paragraphs', and indeed they do: D Halberstam and E Stein, 'The United Nations, the European Union, and the King of Sweden: Economic Sanctions and Individual Rights in a Plural World Order' (2009) 46 *CM L Rev* 13, 60 f argue that the ECJ rejects a *Solange*-type deference because it says the UN re-examination procedure 'cannot' give rise to generalised immunity from jurisdiction – instead of saying it 'does not give rise in this particular case'. But the fact is that the ECJ adds that such immunity is unjustified because the re-examination procedures do not offer 'guarantees of judicial protection' (*Kadi* (n 13) para 322). Indeed the ECJ rejects a *Solange*-type *deference*, ie *Solange II*; but as such it applies a *Solange I* approach, leaving open a possibility to defer, and intimating what the UN ought to do to avail itself of such deference. See: B Kunoy and A Dawes, 'Plate Tectonics in Luxembourg: The *ménage à trois* between EC Law, International Law and the European Convention on Human Rights following the UN Sanctions Cases' (2009) 46 *CM L Rev* 73, 81 f; and: L van den Herik and N Schrijver, 'Eroding the Primacy of the UN System of Collective Security: The Judgment of the European Court of Justice in the Cases of Kadi and Al Barakaat' (2008) 5 *Int'l Org L Rev* 329, 335 ff, for opinions similar to the one presented here. See nn 79 ff below for further confirmation of the position here adopted.

[76] Also: R Kolb, 'Le contrôle de Résolutions contraignantes du Conseil de sécurité des Nations Unies sous l'angle du respect du jus cogens' (2008) 18 *RSDIE* 401, 408.

[77] See – among others – in detail: E de Wet, *The Chapter VII Powers of the UN Security Council* (Oxford, Hart Publishing, 2004) chs 1 and 2; D Akande, 'The International Court of Justice and the Security Council: Is there Room for Judicial Control of Decisions of the Political Organs of the United Nations?' (1997) 46 *Int'l & Comp L Q* 309; and A Tzanakopoulos, *Disobeying the Security Council: Countermeasures against Wrongful Sanctions* (Oxford, Oxford University Press, 2011) ch 4.

Thus, *Kadi* is the ECJ's *Solange I*, its response to the UN's exercise of governmental authority without adequate fundamental rights safeguards. It expresses principled disobedience, and at the same time sets forth what must be done for normalisation to ensue. In leaving open the future application of the doctrine of equivalence, it prepares the ground for its own future repeal. But this will only be forthcoming when the objective has been (to a degree to be determined by the ECJ) achieved.

It should be noted that, following the adoption of fresh EC measures against *Kadi*, and the adoption by the Security Council of Resolution 1904 (2009), which established an 'Office of the Ombudsperson' to assist the 1267 Committee in dealing with de-listing requests,[78] the CFI, now renamed the General Court of the EU, had to consider a new challenge to the relevant Community measures by *Kadi*. The General Court expressed some disquiet about the ECJ's reasoning in *Kadi*,[79] but 'grudgingly' applied it,[80] as 'in principle it falls not to [the General Court] but to the Court of Justice to reverse the precedent'.[81] It then went on to review the Community measure giving effect to Security Council Resolutions, as this must remain the case 'at the very least, *so long as* [= *Solange*!] the re-examination procedure operated by the Sanctions Committee clearly fails to offer guarantees of effective judicial protection'[82] and to strike it down anew.

2. *The Interlocutors of the ECJ and the Addressees of the Kadi Message*

The *Kadi* judgment of the ECJ is first of all a direct response to the CFI's handling of the issue. But in constituting a decision on appeal from the CFI it lacks perhaps the elements of voluntariness of engagement, bi-directionality, and lack of superiority that characterise genuine 'judicial dialogue' and in that it should be better qualified simply as 'appellate review'.[83]

The ECJ judgment in *Kadi* is also a *Solange I* moment; even though there are obvious differences to the German Federal Constitutional Court's *Solange I* jurisprudence, it is the *spirit* and the *basic framework argument* that are the same. *Kadi* is a *Solange I* moment not solely in that it engages in dialogue with multiple interlocutors. Most importantly it is a *Solange I* moment in that it issues an ultimatum, creating an unsustainable situation that necessitates response.

[78] On SC Res 1904 (2009) and the impact of the establishment of the Office of the Ombudsperson see further below: text at nn 105–15.

[79] Case T-85/09 *Kadi v Commission* (30 September 2010) paras 113–21.

[80] See for the expression: T Stahlberg, 'Case T-85/09, Kadi II' [2010] ECJBlog.com (26 October) available at www.ecjblog.com (last visited 1 June 2011).

[81] *Kadi* (n 79) para 123.

[82] ibid para 127. See for brief comment: A Tzanakopoulos, '*Kadi II:* The 1267 Sanctions Regime (Back) Before the General Court of the EU' [2010] *EJIL:Talk!* (16 November) available at www.ejiltalk.org (last visited 1 June 2011).

[83] See: Ahdieh (n 14) 2042 ff.

It is however also a 'call to arms' for other (national) courts:[84] it provides them with a theoretical framework in which to challenge themselves implementing measures within their (partial-national) legal order by asserting the importance of fundamental rights. It remains to be seen to what extent other courts will accede to the implicit call for disobedience of the ECJ. The truth is – and that is one of the most important limitations of the *Solange I* doctrine – that the adoption of such a disobedient stance, even if principled, requires a strong (or 'constitutionally confident')[85] court.

In similar cases, for example, the Swiss Federal Tribunal echoed the CFI and did not adopt a *Solange I* approach,[86] and neither did the Turkish Council of State, opting for a much more cautious position.[87] It remains to be seen to what extent the ECJ's *Kadi* judgment, which came after these two decisions, will bolster the constitutional confidence of national courts. Indeed, some developments in the aftermath of *Kadi* do seem to indicate that other courts may be taking up, if implicitly, the *Solange I-Kadi* reasoning.

The decision of the UK Supreme Court of 27 January 2010 deserves special mention in this connection. The Supreme Court considered jointly appeals against decisions of the Court of Appeal,[88] and the High Court,[89] in cases involving challenges to the validity of Orders in Council under section 1 of the UN Act 1946, which allows for the implementation of Security Council measures under Article 41 of the Charter.[90] The impugned Orders were in implementation of measures imposed both under the 1267 and under the 1373 regime.

The Supreme Court decided to quash, in part, the domestic implementing measures for both sanctions regimes. In particular, the Order implementing the 1267 regime was quashed in part because it denied designated individuals access to an effective remedy. It is important to note that under UK domestic law, an Order in Council, which is made by the executive rather than by parliament, cannot deny a person the fundamental right of access to a court. For this, an act of parliament is required. Since section 1 of the UN Act 1946 was not seen as having indeed removed the right of access to a court, the executive could not, by introducing a regime

[84] The decision has been characterised as 'somewhat rebellious': van den Herik and Schrijver (n 75) 330. This is rather an understatement.

[85] See for the expression: T Tridimas and JA Gutierrez-Fons, 'EU Law, International Law and Economic Sanctions Against Terrorism: The Judiciary in Distress?' (2008–09) 32 *Fordham Int'l LJ* 660, 698.

[86] See n 71.

[87] See n 72.

[88] *A, K, M, Q and G v HM Treasury* [2008] EWCA Civ 1187.

[89] *Hay v HM Treasury* [2009] EWHC 1677 (Admin) (QB); ILDC 1367 (UK 2009).

[90] *HM Treasury v Mohammed Jabar Ahmed and ors (FC); HM Treasury v Mohammed al-Ghabra (FC); R (on the application of Hani El Sayed Sabaei Youssef v HM Treasury* [2010] UKSC 2 [hereinafter: *Ahmed*].

through an Order in Council, remove that right. Of course, the Law Lords did recognise that all the Order did was to faithfully implement the 1267 regime;[91] that is, it was the regime imposed by the Security Council rather than the executive that did in effect remove the right of access to a court.

Still, the Supreme Court decided to quash the Order. As Lord Hope stated, and with whom Lord Walker and Lady Hale agreed, what a designated person needed, if he or she were to be afforded an effective remedy, would be a means of subjecting the 1267 listing to judicial review.[92] 'This is something that', Lord Hope continued, '*under the system that the 1267 Committee currently operates, is denied to him*'.[93] It is crucial that this statement comes in the 'operative paragraph' as it were, that is, in the paragraph where Lord Hope, with Lord Walker and Lady Hale, decide that the 1267 applicants should succeed in having the Order quashed. Taking this point further, Lord Mance implied that the situation would be different if designated persons were given 'means by which to challenge the justification for treating them as [associated with Al Qaida or the Taliban] before *any* judicial tribunal or court, at a domestic *or international level*'.[94]

In reaching this decision, the Law Lords seem to have been fully cognisant that they were in effect forcing upon the UK a breach of its international obligations under the Charter and the relevant Resolutions: Lord Brown clearly states that there is no alternative to freezing under the 1267 regime, lest the UK flagrantly violate the UN Charter,[95] while Lord Hope, with Lord Walker and Lady Hale, recognise that requiring parliament to assent to the Orders would put the UK in breach of its international obligations under Article 25 of the Charter *if an Order was not approved*.[96] Like the ECJ in *Kadi*,[97] the Lords suspended the effect of their decision for a limited time, to allow the Treasury to consider its next steps.[98] All this demonstrates that the Court knew it was taking a radical decision.

It cannot be said of course that the UK Supreme Court adopted wholesale either *Solange I* or *Kadi*. However, the similarities are striking: in all three cases an international obligation (in the case of the EC an international obligation binding on its Member States at any rate) was disregarded by reference to domestic law, in particular by reference to the protection of fundamental rights. This was, again in all three cases,

[91] ibid para 64 (Lord Hope, with whom Lord Walker and Lady Hale agree); *cf* para 197 (Lord Brown).

[92] ibid para 81.

[93] ibid (emphasis added); *cf* also: para 82.

[94] ibid para 249 (emphasis added).

[95] ibid para 204.

[96] ibid paras 47–49.

[97] See n 13 paras 373–76; but crucially unlike the CFI in Case T-318/01 *Othman* [2009] ECR II-1627, paras 95–99.

[98] *Ahmed* (n 90) para 84.

coupled with a reference to the inadequacy of protection of the fundamental rights in question at the *locus* – outside the partial legal order of the court – where the relevant power was being exercised. In all these cases then – whether explicitly or implicitly – the courts left it open that they may reconsider if adequate or equivalent protection is instituted at the *locus* of exercise of the powers: that is, at the particular level of governance which is outside of the direct reach of the court.

It further remains to be seen what the reaction of the ECtHR will be, both to the *Kadi* decision and to the UK Supreme Court's *Ahmed* judgment. The ECtHR has shown particular aversion to reviewing UN action under Chapter VII;[99] could it possibly claim that the UN establishes a system of equivalent protection so as to sidestep applications against European Convention on Human Rights States parties?[100] This would imply that the 'general principles of EC law' and UK domestic law provide more protection to fundamental rights than the European Convention on Human Rights does.

Returning to *Kadi*, the decision is, further, a direct (and binding) message to the 'executive' of the Community and to the executives of all 27 Member States: in annulling (in part) the EC implementing measure, it forces the Community, as well as its Member States, to negotiate with the UN Security Council with a view to resolving the fundamental rights impasse that led to the judgment or risk finding themselves in violation of their international obligations under the UN Charter.[101] The UK Supreme Court sends a similar – and even clearer – message to the UK executive, imposing on it a duty to either try and pass legislation through parliament that explicitly removes the fundamental right of access to a court[102] (something that the sovereign parliament can do under UK law), or to negotiate access to an effective remedy on the international level,[103] or to suffer being in breach of UK international obligations under the UN Charter.[104]

But most importantly – though implicitly – the ECJ through *Kadi* and the UK Supreme Court through *Ahmed* address the UN and its Security

[99] See generally: *Behrami* (n 65).

[100] Especially now that the question is definitely coming before it, after the Swiss Federal Tribunal's decision in *Nada* (n 70); see: text at nn 47–48 and n 59.

[101] Unless it is accepted that in the absence of Community implementation states can unilaterally implement sanctions, which is very much disputed (at least from the perspective of Community law): see the Opinion of the Advocate-General in *Kadi* (n 13) para 30; and *cf* Tridimas and Gutierrez-Fons (n 85) 702 ff. For another view along the lines that *Kadi* may constitute a means to generate the political will needed to achieve a solution at UN level, see: van den Herik and Schrijver (n 75) 331. A modest amount of such will is evident in UN Doc A/6/887 – S/2006/331 (2006) and A/62/891 – S/2008/428 (2008).

[102] *cf Ahmed* (n 90) para 76 (Lord Hope with Lord Walker and Lady Hale) and *Hay* (n 89) para 46, which is not overturned on this point by the Supreme Court.

[103] *cf Ahmed* (n 90) paras 81–82 (Lord Hope with Lord Walker and Lady Hale); para 249 (Lord Mance).

[104] *cf* ibid para 84 (Lord Hope with Lord Walker and Lady Hale); para 204 (Lord Brown).

Council in particular.[105] They suggest that by introducing procedures for de-listing that offer judicial guarantees and provide effective remedies for designated persons, the Security Council would earn deference and avoid the disobedience that these courts can impose on their respective executives. It is up to the Council to heed that call – and it seems to be moving, however reluctantly, in that direction. In Resolution 1904 of 17 December 2009, the Security Council established an Office of the Ombudsperson to receive de-listing requests directly from persons designated under the 1267 regime, to gather information, to engage in dialogue with them, with relevant states, and with the 1267 Committee, and to submit a 'Comprehensive Report' to the Committee setting out the arguments on the de-listing request.[106] All this is to be done 'in an independent and impartial manner' on the part of the Ombudsperson, who is to be 'an eminent individual of high moral character, impartiality and integrity with high qualifications and experience in relevant fields, such as legal, human rights, counter-terrorism and sanctions' appointed by the Secretary-General 'in close consultation with the Committee'.[107]

This is an attempt by the Council to respond to the challenge of the ECJ in *Kadi*, as well as decisions of other domestic courts,[108] such as the Canadian Federal Court in *Abdelrazik*,[109] and the English courts in *A, K, M, Q and G* and *Hay*.[110] This is clear when the Council states in the preamble to the Resolution that it is '[*t*]*aking note* of challenges, both legal and otherwise, to the measures implemented by Member States'.[111] This is arguably the reason for the establishment of an Office of the Ombudsperson – to appease courts of Member States or regional organisations and earn their deference.

However, it seems that the Ombudsperson will not be enough to earn the Security Council an acknowledgment by the reacting courts that it is now offering adequate or equivalent protection. An Ombudsperson will not be enough to earn the Council a *Solange II* deference, that is. The ECJ has not had the opportunity to comment yet, but it is unlikely that it will consider this move as offering 'guarantees of judicial protection'.[112] The

[105] As did, in less powerful terms, the CFI's *Kadi* decision; see: U Haltern, 'Gemeinschaftsgrundrechte und Antiterrormaßnahmen der UNO' (2007) 62 *JZ* 537, 541. See for a similar threat in the *OMPI* case (n 36) para 104: Haltern (this note) 545.

[106] SC Res 1904 (2009) para 21 and Annex II.

[107] ibid para 20.

[108] See generally: A Tzanakopoulos, 'Domestic Court Reactions to UN Security Council Sanctions' in Reinisch 2010 (n 1) 54 ff.

[109] *Abdelrazik v Minister of Foreign Affairs & Attorney General of Canada* T-727-08 [2009] FC 580, para 53. See for comment: A Tzanakopoulos 'United Nations Sanctions in Domestic Courts: From Interpretation to Defiance in *Abdelrazik v Canada*' (2010) 10 *J Int'l Crim Just* 249.

[110] See n 88 and n 89 respectively. See for comment: A Tzanakopoulos, 'Stepping Up the (Dualist?) Resistance' [2009] *EJIL:Talk!* (9 October) available at www.ejiltalk.org (last visited 1 June 2011).

[111] SC Res 1904 (2009) 9th Preamble para.

[112] *cf Kadi* (n 13) para 322.

General Court of the EU, for one, did not so find.[113] And the UK Supreme Court has already rejected the introduction of an Ombudsperson as a radical step towards creating a regime that would deserve its deference. While the move 'is to be welcomed',[114] the Law Lords still considered that the 1267 regime does not offer any access to effective judicial remedies.[115] More must obviously be done on the part of the Council to address the courts' concerns over the protection of fundamental rights.

But the question then emerges: which are these fundamental rights that deserve protection to such an extent that courts will force their respective states to disobey international obligations in order to protect them? The rights guaranteed by the domestic constitution? That would be indefensible under international law.[116] Or rather internationally protected human rights? It is to this question that we must now turn.

VI. FUNDAMENTAL RIGHTS AND HUMAN RIGHTS

A distinction between 'human rights' and 'fundamental rights', if indeed there is one, does not seem to be easy to draw. Sometimes the two terms are used interchangeably,[117] while other times 'fundamental rights' is used as an umbrella term, encompassing the two leading systems of protection, namely constitutional law and international human rights law.[118] The ICJ has occasionally 'merged' the two terms into 'fundamental human rights',[119]

[113] *Kadi* (n 79) para 128.

[114] *Ahmed* (n 90) para 78 (Lord Hope, with Lord Walker and Lady Hale).

[115] ibid. See further: para 181 (Lord Rodger) and para 239 (Lord Mance).

[116] See: Articles on State Responsibility, art 3, and Vienna Convention on the Law of Treaties, art 27.

[117] See, eg: Murray (n 16) especially 531 f; *cf* also the US submission in *LaGrand* [2001] ICJ Rep 466, 493, para 76, that 'treatment due to individuals under the [Vienna Convention on Consular Relations of 1963] . . . does not constitute a *fundamental right or a human right*' (emphasis added). *cf* T Meron, 'On a Hierarchy of International Human Rights' (1986) 80 *Am J Int'l L* 1, 5.

[118] See, eg: GL Neuman, 'Human Rights and Constitutional Rights: Harmony and Dissonance' (2003) 55 *Stanford LR* 1863, especially 1865. The term originated in national constitutions and 'inspired' the development of international human rights: Meron (n 117) 8; *cf* D Schindler, 'The International Committee of the Red Cross and Human Rights' (1979) 19:208 *Int'l Rev Red Cross* 3, 5 ff.

[119] See, eg: *Namibia* [1971] ICJ Rep 16, 57, para 131. For a more recent instance of the use of the term 'fundamental human right' by the Court see *Avena* [2004] ICJ Rep 12, 60, para 124; and note that Mexico's submission actually referred not to a 'fundamental human right' but to a 'fundamental due process right, and indeed, a human right': ibid 32, para 30. In *Barcelona Traction (Second Phase)* [1970] ICJ Rep 3, 32, para 34, the Court referred to 'principles and rules concerning the *basic rights of the human person*' (emphasis added), but *cf* also the French text of the decision, which refers to 'principes et . . . règles concernant les *droits fondamentaux* de la personne humaine' (emphasis added). It is a bit perplexing why the term 'droits fondamentaux' was translated as 'basic' rather than 'fundamental rights'. In *Armed Activities (DRC v Uganda)* [2005] ICJ Rep 168, the Court, in response to the DRC's submission that Uganda perpetrated a number of violations of 'fundamental human rights' (see, eg: 232, para 181) finds indeed a number of violations of 'international human rights law and international humanitarian law' (239 ff, paras 205 ff).

while the European Convention is on *Human* Rights and *Fundamental* Freedoms. It could be argued that the term 'fundamental human rights' as used by the ICJ seems to denote those internationally protected rights that have achieved at least *erga omnes* status,[120] while Meron has noted that fundamental (or basic) human rights and peremptory (*jus cogens*) human rights are 'two sometimes overlapping notions'.[121] But regarding the two terms separately, they are either to be perceived as synonymous (or at least equivalent) or as in competition with each other.

The distinction between, say, constitutionally protected 'fundamental' rights and internationally protected 'human' rights might have been meaningful for present purposes if the discussion was centred on competition because of conflict or dissonance and divergence between the two regimes.[122] However, *Solange I* was not an argument in favour of the German constitutional regime of fundamental rights protection over a competing EC regime of rights protection. The point was that *there existed no EC regime of rights protection* for the German constitutional regime to compete with. There was, rather, a complete lack of fundamental or human rights protection in the EC legal order. The aim was thus to force the introduction of at least an *equivalent* fundamental rights protection regime in the EC legal order to fill in the gap. Only in the interim, and for as long as the Community failed to respond positively to this demand for gap-filling, would the German Federal Constitutional Court give precedence to its own (the only!) rights protection regime. In the ECJ's *Kadi* judgment, the implicit claim is, again, not to substitute the EC rights regime for the competing UN Security Council rights regime, but to correct the ostensible lack of a rights protection regime in the exercise of Security Council powers under Chapter VII of the Charter. One can detect a similar undercurrent in the opinions of the UK Law Lords in *Ahmed*.

Conversely, potential conflicts or divergences between 'competing' regimes at different levels of governance are accommodated through the introduction of the *doctrine of equivalence* in *Solange II*. This allows for deference of the German constitutional rights protection regime to that of the Community. The adoption of the *Solange II* argument by the ECtHR has allowed a similar deference on its part to the rights protection regime of the EC. In *Kadi* and *Ahmed*, one can detect the willingness of the ECJ and the UK Supreme Court to potentially defer to the Security Council, should it introduce a means of protection with judicial guarantees for individuals targeted by the Council through sanctions.

[120] *Namibia* (n 119) 57, para 131; *Barcelona Traction (Second Phase)* (n 119) 32, para 34. However, as Meron (n 117) 9 notes, this is a *consequence* rather than a *cause* of a right's fundamental character.

[121] See: n 117, 3.

[122] Which is the topic of Neuman's discussion (n 118).

In this sense, the terms 'fundamental' or 'human' or 'fundamental human' rights can be treated as synonymous,[123] at least in the present context. This, however, denotes a more remote, but very significant implication of the *Solange* argument: which are the rights that qualify as 'fundamental rights' and that must be guaranteed at national, international, and supranational level, enough so that national courts will force upon their own executives the breach of an obligation to comply with the decision of an international organisation that does not offer 'equivalent' protection?

The reaction of domestic courts to the complete lack of fundamental rights protection at the international level will in all probability be based on what the national court is most well-versed in: its own constitutional law. As the *Solange* dialogue between the German Federal Constitutional Court and the EC and ECJ suggests, the reaction will be based on a need to ensure the protection of those principles that are most fundamental for the constitutional order of the reacting state.

One should not, however, be too quick to mount claims of 'constitutional imperialism', 'hegemony',[124] or even 'local constitutional resistance',[125] or to summarily reject the general applicability and appeal of the domestic courts' reaction.[126] At the very least, 'the international human rights regime now forms part of the *context* of national constitutional regimes', while at the same time 'many of the rights contained in human rights treaties have long enjoyed recognition' at least in the 'transatlantic constitutional tradition'.[127] Again, the *Solange* jurisprudence suggests that the fundamental rights whose protection is sought refer to a hard core of basic rights,[128] which have claimed global application through their inclusion in almost universally ratified international treaties, such as the International Covenant on Civil and Political Rights, and through their crystallisation in customary international law.[129] Indeed it has been maintained that there is no inherent preponderance of the fundamental rights protected in the Basic Law of Bonn (whose equivalent protection at Community level was the question in the two instances of *Solange*), but rather that their radiance

[123] See also: Meron (n 117) 5.

[124] Tridimas and Gutierrez-Fons (n 85) 729.

[125] Halberstam and Stein (n 75) 67 f. *cf* ibid 62 ff where the authors argue that the cutting of the umbilical cord with the Grundnorm of international law is a necessary step in the Union's constitutional integration, and that the ECJ 'behoves' the UN to make way for the 'European protection of Europe's particular version of rights'.

[126] *cf* the concerns of Bore Eveno (n 11) 848, who, in discussing the CFI's *Kadi* decision, is worried that the Court's attempt to state the law ('dire le droit') with respect to *jus cogens* has considerable (unfavourable or unwelcome) implications for the coherence of the international legal order.

[127] Neuman (n 118) 1880 (emphasis added) and 1882 respectively.

[128] *cf* 73 *BVerfGE* 387.

[129] *cf* Kolb (n 76) 407 f.

stems from their 'wholehearted' embrace of the basic value system of the Universal Declaration of Human Rights.[130]

In this connection, fundamental rights have been seen as being in an 'almost intrinsic relationship' with (the concept of) *jus cogens*,[131] a 'constitutionalizing force', normatively if not institutionally,[132] and as having a 'radiation' and 'reforming effect' on various fields of public international law.[133] An argument could be that even though *Solange I* arguments are based on domestic law, they have equally a footing in international law, which – in substance – guarantees the same rights.[134]

Are the fundamental rights guaranteed within the European Union legal order not of the same radiance as those guaranteed by the Basic Law of Bonn and those enshrined in the Universal Declaration? They should be, at the very least since they constitute equivalent protection to that offered by the German Constitution, viz the Universal Declaration. As such, there should be nothing 'particularistic' or 'Euro-centric' about claiming their protection at UN level.[135] Significantly, the General Court of the EU in *Kadi* adopts criteria elaborated by the ECtHR on the application of Article 5(4) of the European Convention on Human Rights and proceeds to apply them.[136] While this is not groundbreaking with respect to

[130] See for the argument: T Rensmann, 'The Constitution as a Normative Order of Values: The Influence of International Human Rights Law on the Evolution of Modern Constitutionalism' in *Festschrift Tomuschat* (n 5) 259, 261. *cf* also generally: T Buergenthal, 'Modern Constitutions and Human Rights Treaties' in JI Charney et al (eds) *Politics, Values and Functions – International Law in the 21st Century: Essays in Honor of Professor Louis Henkin* (The Hague, Martinus Nijhoff Publishers, 1997) 197 (commenting on the rank of human rights treaties in domestic legal orders).

[131] A Bianchi, 'Human Rights and the Magic of *Jus Cogens*' (2008) 19 *Eur J Int'l L* 491.

[132] ibid 494 and fns 15–16.

[133] See: T Meron, *The Humanization of International Law* (Leiden, Martinus Nijhoff Publishers, 2006) xv.

[134] See further: Tzanakopoulos (n 15) section II. This could be seen as an extension of the argument of T Broude and Y Shany, 'The International Law and Policy of Multi-Sourced Equivalent Norms' in T Broude and Y Shany (eds) *Multi-Sourced Equivalent Norms in International Law* (Oxford, Hart Publishing, 2011) 1–15: they argue that the fragmentation of international law has brought to the fore the existence of norms that are equivalent though they stem from different sources of international law or belong to different 'sectoral' international legal regimes. At 3 they note that the existence of equivalent norms is not unique to international law, but also exists 'in a variety of domestic legal settings'. The argument here is that equivalent norms also exist in domestic and international law, and that the focus should be on the substantive (equivalent) content of the relevant norm rather than on its form or immediate or more remote source. See also: G Harpaz, 'EU Review of UN Anti-Terror Sanctions: Judicial Juggling in a Four-Layer, Multi-Sourced, Equivalent-Norms Scenario' in Broude and Shany (this note) 171.

[135] *cf* RA Wessel, 'The *Kadi* Case: Towards a More Substantive Hierarchy in International Law?' (2008) 5 *Int'l Org L Rev* 323, 326 f. As Shany notes, 'the fact that two distinct rules of law belonging to different regimes govern the same transaction or situation, should not necessarily entail the conclusion that cases involving these rules are distinct; it all depends *on the substantive degree of similarity between the contents of the rule*': Shany (n 13) (emphasis added).

[136] See (n 79) 176 f.

the way EC courts understand fundamental rights under primary EC law, it is worth noting that Article 9(4) of the International Covenant on Civil and Political Rights is virtually identical to Article 5(4) of the European Convention on Human Rights. In this, the General Court exemplifies the correspondence in substance between (some) human rights that are both domestically protected and internationally guaranteed. Similarly, the 'constitutional' right to be afforded an effective remedy through access to a court in UK domestic law is a right guaranteed both by the International Covenant on Civil and Political Rights,[137] and under customary international law.

The problem then of course would be to identify precisely the list of rights to be afforded protection at all levels of governance, that is, the list of rights that is guaranteed equally under international and domestic law. This is not an easy task; to refer to 'common constitutional traditions', the European Convention on Human Rights, the International Covenant on Civil and Political Rights, and the Universal Declaration may make a fine rhetorical point, but it is not enough to establish a defined list of fundamental rights that are guaranteed under both domestic and international law and against which every instance of exercise of governmental power – at any level of governance – must be measured.

The *Solange* argument, in particular in its incarnation in the ECJ's *Kadi* judgment and in the UK Supreme Court's *Ahmed* judgment, may be seen as highlighting the special importance of the right to a fair trial, and its various facets, such as the right of access to a court and the right to an effective remedy, in cases where fundamental rights of individuals are restricted. In fact, even the German Federal Constitutional Court's decision in *Solange I* could be cast in the same light. Effectively, all these courts stepped in to offer individuals a *forum* in which to litigate their fundamental rights grievances, when there was no alternative such *forum* available: in the original *Solange* this was the case because the ECJ would not entertain claims of violation of fundamental rights; in *Kadi* and *Ahmed* it is the case because there is quite simply no *forum* at all in which to claim the violation.

It may then be argued that the *Solange* argument underlines the fundamental importance of a right of access to a court in which to argue undue restriction or violation of basic rights. In that, it enshrines this particular facet of the right to a fair trial as a core right. The other rights that belong to this list of core rights are still some way from being fully identified. The full elaboration of this list will have to be made through practice. For the time being, state practice, primarily through domestic courts, seems to be on its way to establishing as such a 'fundamental' or 'core' right the right of access to a court to seek review of governmental action – at any level –

[137] Art 14.

for compliance with this – as yet not fully defined – list of fundamental rights. And that might just be its most important contribution.

VII. CONCLUSION

By using the *Solange* argument, domestic courts have sometimes sought to react to the exercise of uncontrolled governmental power affecting fundamental rights at a *locus* other than that of the partial legal order to which the reacting courts belong (*Solange I*). By using the *Solange* argument again, domestic courts have deferred to the protection of fundamental rights available at that different *locus*, when that protection is equivalent to that of their own legal order (*Solange II*). The *Solange* argument, in its variations, is a tool for regulating the relationship between partial legal orders with respect to the protection of fundamental rights. But in the process of the dialogue that ensues from the deployment of the *Solange* argument, domestic courts, as agents of state practice, entrench the existence of a list of fundamental human rights that must be protected, both substantively and procedurally, on whatever level, and at whatever *locus* governmental power affecting individuals is being exercised. The practice has not yet been extensive enough to fully elaborate and define all the rights that belong to that list. But it has served to underline the fundamental importance that courts attach to the right of access to a court to at least challenge governmental acts affecting the individual's legal position with respect to fundamental human rights.

10

Flux and Fragmentation in the International Law of State Jurisdiction: The Synecdochal Example of Canada's Domestic Court Conflicts over Accountability for International Human Rights Violations

ROBERT J CURRIE AND HUGH M KINDRED*

I. INTRODUCTION

ANY SERIOUS EXPLORATION of unity and fragmentation in public international law must consider the normative basis of one of the fundamental tools of state action on the international plane: jurisdiction. And no better illustration of the fluctuating application of jurisdiction may be had than to take a national sample – such as Canada – of domestic courts' struggles to establish accountability for human rights conduct and abuses abroad. The paradigms of the law of jurisdiction, as with the vast corpus of international law, originally responded to the needs of the traditional verities of a legal system based around the state – states as sovereign, unitary entities, in relationships of mutual respect for their equality, independence and co-existence. The associated principle, recognised by the Permanent Court of International Justice in the *Steamship Lotus* case,[1] that a state was free to exert jurisdiction in the absence of a prohibitive rule, was sufficient in times when national legal systems concerned themselves nearly exclusively with individuals within their territorial or national control. Even as international human rights law flourished in the latter half of the twentieth century, the

* Schulich School of Law, Dalhousie University, Halifax NS Canada.
[1] *France v Turkey*, 1927 PCIJ Ser A No 10.

central idea was that states owed each other obligations to guarantee rights to their own citizens and residents, and so breaches were to be handled internally. The law was premised on police enforcing a state's law within its borders, and residents being able to seek redress before local courts.

This traditional approach is increasingly giving way, as a result of rapid globalisation, to a system of mutual interdependence of states. Sovereignty, it is said, is not as robust as it once was, and accordingly the simple principles of jurisdiction are no longer adequate. States now engage in criminal investigations (enforcement jurisdiction) on a multi-territorial basis, where sovereign exclusivity is a barrier rather than a boon in the fight against transnational crime. And as state activities exceed borders, so too individuals who suffer at the hands of state agents now seek human rights-based remedies in a number of jurisdictions. Driven by these changes, the principles of jurisdiction, like those of sovereignty, are becoming modulated by both state practice and by treaty. In particular, transnational assertions of state jurisdiction and of human rights protections have aroused a contest within international law, in which states struggle to ascertain the scope and limits of their ability to take both public and private law jurisdiction over human rights violations.

As these changes occur, there is an inevitable loss of unity in the traditional principles of state jurisdiction. Fragmentation of the law occurs as state practice shifts, putting customary international law in flux. More certainty is offered by jurisdictional requirements in treaty regimes but these are at best piecemeal because they have only partial membership and deal only with sectoral issues. Indeed, partial treaty regimes tend to concretise the fragmentation of jurisdictional rules. In turn, domestic courts, which must discover the applicable international law on jurisdiction and observe it in disputes before them, encounter a distended body of norms that presents a tension between the traditional rules and the new practices. Court decisions reflect the ongoing fragmentation in the law and, in turn, contribute to the diverse state practice that underlies the splintering of norms and needs.

This chapter will illustrate the flux and fragmentation in the principles of state jurisdiction by examining Canada's treatment of the prevention, punishment and reparation of international human rights law violations. Canadian courts have recently issued a number of decisions that reflect the struggle over jurisdictional issues. In the public law case of *R v Hape*,[2] and subsequent decisions, the Supreme Court of Canada refused to apply Canada's international human rights obligations extraterritorially, argu-

[2] [2007] 2 SCR 292, ILDC 758 (CA 2007). Available at www.canlii.org/en/ca/scc/doc/2007/2007scc26/2007scc26.html (last visited 1 June 2011) All Canadian judgments referred to herein can be found online at the website of the Canadian Legal Institute (www.canlii.org).

ing that to do so would violate the principle of foreign state sovereignty. In *Bouzari v Iran*,[3] a leading appellate court declined jurisdiction in a private law suit involving serious human rights violations that took place abroad, based on traditional readings of the limitations of territorial jurisdiction and the privileges of state sovereignty. In each case, there are international law precedents or instruments that suggest a contrary result, but it cannot be said that there is a solid principle demanding it.

The arguments and reasoning expressed by the Canadian courts in reaching their decisions, in both the public (criminal) and private (civil) law cases, mirror the tensions between unity and fragmentation in the international law of state jurisdiction. For the purpose of this chapter, it is not as important what the courts ultimately decided as their engagement with the conflicting international legal concepts and sources, and the way they wrestled with those materials in their judgments. The leading Canadian cases in both public and private law areas eventually reached decisions in line with principles of sovereignty and thus they support traditional concepts of jurisdiction and the unity of those principles. That those cases may have been wrongly decided in light of other expansive Canadian national jurisprudence in the human rights field is beside the point of the present discussion about the international law of jurisdiction. The significance of the cases for present purposes is that the courts were alert to, and took very seriously, the arguments founded in international human rights law, which would have led them to reach decisions that would tend to fragment the traditional principles of jurisdiction. In this sense, Canadian experience is a synecdoche: the part that illustrates the whole, the specific that elucidates the general. Canadian judicial uncertainty nationally epitomises the growing legal disorder internationally.

In explanation of these assertions, this chapter will review the principles of state jurisdiction as a precursor to exploring first the public law contest and then the private law stand-off in the Canadian courts around the extension of jurisdiction to protect human rights abroad. It will conclude with reflections on the fragmentation of the international law of jurisdiction that this Canadian synecdoche reveals.

II. THE INTERNATIONAL LAW OF JURISDICTION

It is important to ground the discussion of Canadian court practices that follows in the international law of jurisdiction – the latter term understood simply to mean the state's ability to exert power over persons, places, subject matter and things. The discussion taking place here engages all three of

[3] (2004), 243 DLR (4th) 406, 71 OR (3d) 675 (Ont. C.A.), leave to appeal to SCC refused, 25 January 2005, ILDC 175 (CA 2004). Available at www.canlii.org/en/on/onca/doc/2004/2004canlii871/2004canlii871.html (last visited 1 June 2011).

the 'categories' of international law jurisdiction set out in Akehurst's classic article:[4] 'prescriptive' jurisdiction to legislate; 'enforcement' jurisdiction to apply executive authority, for example, investigation or arrest; and 'judicial' jurisdiction to adjudicate matters. Judicial jurisdiction has a central position in this discussion as domestic courts are empowered and required to answer fundamental international law questions regarding the very ability of the state to act on the international plane. This applies in both the civil/private and criminal/public law contexts that are surveyed in this chapter. As well, these decisions on jurisdiction themselves make up part of the state practice upon which putative customary international law norms are assessed.

While the starting point of jurisdiction is the plenary, sovereign authority which states have over their own territories, states have always had extraterritorial interests and recent globalisation has compounded the problems that arise. Any exertion of extraterritorial jurisdiction by a state threatens to collide with the interests of other states, territorial or otherwise; obviously, concurrent jurisdictional claims can and do arise. The starting point is the *Lotus* case[5] which accepted that asserting extraterritorial jurisdiction is not unlawful conduct on the part of states, even in a system based on territorial sovereignty. Rather, extending extraterritorial jurisdiction is not illegal *per se*, but only where it interferes unduly with the sovereign interests of another state.

In addition to the *Lotus* case decided in 1927, the Harvard Research Project, published in 1935, made an important survey of the various ways by which states asserted their interests and entitlement to extend their jurisdiction extraterritorially. The exercise of prescriptive jurisdiction extraterritorially takes the form of the familiar principles of nationality, passive personality, and protective and universal authority.[6] These principles arise most frequently from the criminal and regulatory law and practice of states, and are products of customary international law. They are sometimes employed in treaties, typically those treaties often referred to as the 'suppression conventions'[7] that represent efforts by states to criminalise certain conduct under the laws of a large number of national jurisdictions and to coordinate the exercise of jurisdiction over offenders by prosecuting states.[8]

[4] M Akehurst, 'Jurisdiction in International Law' (1972–73) 46 *BYIL* 145.

[5] See: n 1.

[6] See generally: Harvard Research, 'Draft Convention on Jurisdiction With Respect to Crime' (1935) 29 (Supp) *Am J Int'l L* 480; Council of Europe, *Extraterritorial Criminal Jurisdiction* (Strasbourg, European Committee on Crime Problems, 1990); H Kindred and P Saunders (eds), *International Law: Chiefly as Interpreted and Applied in Canada*, 7th edn (Toronto, Emond Montgomery, 2006) ch 9.

[7] N Boister, '"Transnational Criminal Law"?' (2003) 14 *Eur J Int'l L* 953.

[8] eg: International Convention for the Suppression of Terrorist Bombings (1998) 37 ILM 249; the International Convention for the Suppression of Terrorist Financing (2002) Can TS No 9; and United Nations Convention on Transnational Organized Crime, reprinted (2001) 40 ILM 335.

The latter usage reflects the true nature of the principles of jurisdiction: they are simply tools by which states manage jurisdictional conflicts between them, whether potential or actualised. Specifically, their function is bifurcated: on the one hand, they serve normative purposes by providing rules for courts (both domestic and international) to use in rendering decisions about the legality of actions under international law, as well as a means for executive decision-makers to gauge the legality of extraterritorial actions; but on the other hand their purpose is to provide a functional means by which states can communicate their links to and interests in a particular matter. They help to establish which states have what kinds of connections to a particular matter, in situations of concurrent jurisdiction.[9]

While the principles of prescriptive jurisdiction are relatively expansive, the international law regime regarding extraterritorial enforcement jurisdiction is much more restraining. The cardinal rule is that states are not permitted to undertake any enforcement activities within the territories of other states absent the permission of the territorial state.[10] This limitation is, of course, a function of Westphalian sovereignty.

The gap between these two jurisdictional paradigms is well-understood by international lawyers and easily applied on the purely inter-state level. However, it is in the exercise of judicial jurisdiction by domestic courts, as they are called upon to answer questions of international law jurisdiction, that problems rush in to fill the gap. In particular, as state agents have begun to act more regularly outside the states' borders, the courts are confronted with having to determine whether the state's law (particularly constitutional law) may be extended to their activities, and what impact this can and should have on domestic proceedings that relate to those activities. Conversely, as more refugees from the persecution of their home states seek to litigate their injuries in their host states, the latter's courts are faced with deciding whether they may hear suits about events that occurred outside their territory and/or at the instigation of foreign authorities.

[9] As Vaughan Lowe has pointed out, while jurisdictional questions often lack 'clear theoretical answers', they get answered in a practical sense because states protest excessive claims of jurisdiction, and conflict is resolved – typically by negotiation; see: V Lowe, 'Jurisdiction' in MD Evans (ed), *International Law* (Oxford, Oxford University Press, 2003) 329 ff.

[10] *Lotus* (n 1) paras 18–19. As the Supreme Court of Canada has written, 'The general rule that a state's criminal law applies only within its territory is particularly true of the legal procedures enacted to enforce it; the exercise of an enforcement jurisdiction is "inherently territorial"' (*R v Terry* [1996] 2 SCR 207, para 17).

III. PUBLIC LAW PROTECTION OF INTERNATIONAL HUMAN RIGHTS IN CANADA

Canada is a common law jurisdiction and requires legislation to implement treaties that it has signed. It is a signatory to the International Covenant on Civil and Political Rights, and in terms of implementation the major provisions of the treaty are given domestic effect by the Canadian Charter of Rights and Freedoms,[11] a constitutional bill of rights which mostly came into effect in 1982.[12] The Charter does not expressly implement the International Covenant on Civil and Political Rights, but its provisions clearly draw upon the treaty and it is treated by the government and the courts as the principal means by which Canada's international human rights obligations are given effect.[13] Section 32 of the Charter provides that it applies to all Canadian government entities and their agents, but is silent as to whether it has extraterritorial reach.

The international human rights regimes are also silent about their extraterritorial reach. The relevant provisions[14] describe the Member States' obligations in terms of a state's 'jurisdiction', as in Article 2 of the International Covenant on Civil and Political Rights which provides for applicability to persons 'within [the state's] territory and subject to its jurisdiction'. This kind of prescription has spawned various exercises in treaty interpretation[15] from which may be discerned a clear trend towards extraterritoriality being permissible and even obligatory among states which have entered into treaty-based human rights obligations. Under the International Covenant on Civil and Political Rights, for example, the United Nations (UN) Human Rights Committee decided in two 1981 complaints against Uruguay[16] that a state party could be held 'accountable for violations of rights under the Covenant which its agents commit upon the territory of another state, whether with the acquiescence of the Government of that State or in opposition to it',[17] and that 'it would be unconscionable to so interpret the responsibility under Article 2 of the

[11] Canadian Charter of Rights and Freedoms (Charter), Part I of the Constitution Act, 1982, being Schedule B to the Canada Act 1982 (UK) 1982, c 11.

[12] The equality rights provision (s 15) came into effect in 1985.

[13] M Freeman and G van Ert, *International Human Rights Law* (Toronto, Irwin Law, 2004) 188.

[14] European Convention for the Protection of Human Rights and Fundamental Freedoms (1950) 213 UNTS 221, art 1; International Covenant on Civil and Political Rights (1966) 999 UNTS 171, art 2; American Convention on Human Rights (1969) 1144 UNTS 123, art 1.

[15] See generally: Coomans and Kamminga (eds), *Extraterritorial Application of Human Rights Treaties* (Antwerp, Intersentia, 2004). A sizeable literature also exists; a good sampling can be found in R Wilde, 'Triggering State Obligations Extraterritorially: The Spatial Test in Certain Human Rights Treaties' (2007) 40 *Is L Rev* 503, 506 (fn 7).

[16] *Lopez Burgos v Uruguay*, Comm No R/12/52, UN Doc Supp No 40 (A/36/40), 176; and *Celiberti de Casariego v Uruguay*, Comm No R/13/56, UN Doc Supp No 40 (A/36/40), 185.

[17] *Lopez Burgos*, ibid para 12.3; *Celiberti*, ibid para 10.3.

Covenant as to permit a State party to perpetrate violations of the Covenant on the territory of another State, which violations it could not perpetrate on its own territory'.[18] In the Committee's General Comment 31 it affirmed this interpretation of Article 2 and that it applied even when the individuals in question are not nationals of the state party.[19] This was further confirmed by the International Court of Justice (ICJ) in the *Palestinian Wall* case.[20] Similar findings have been made by the Inter-American Commission on Human Rights regarding the applicability of the Organization of American States Charter and the American Declaration of the Rights and Duties of Man.[21]

The European Court of Human Rights (ECtHR) has wrestled with the permissibility of extraterritorial application of the European Convention on Human Rights on a number of occasions since the early 1990s and has the most well-developed jurisprudence, though one marked by vacillation. Article 1 of the Convention requires Member States to secure the Convention protections 'to everyone within their jurisdiction'. In the 2001 *Banković* case the Court employed the international law principles of jurisdiction as interpretive principles to find that jurisdiction was territorially-based and could only be extraterritorial in exceptional circumstances.[22] However, in the recent cases of *Issa*[23] and *Solomou*[24] the Court took a more robust approach, finding that states can be held liable for violations by officials who are operating in a foreign state, where (i) the state agents are in effective military control of the territory upon which the violation is committed, or (ii) if the individual is 'under the authority or control' of the state agents.[25]

The question of whether the Canadian Charter of Rights applies extraterritorially in the execution of Canadian criminal and other public law powers has been examined a number of times by the Supreme Court of Canada since the 1990s. All of this jurisprudence, until recently, addressed the question of whether evidence gathered in a foreign state should be admitted in criminal prosecutions, or excluded on the basis that it violated certain human rights – either section 8 on privacy (search warrants) or section 10 (rights upon detention or arrest). In none of the Supreme

[18] ibid.

[19] General Comment No 31, CCPR/C/21/Rev.1/Add.13, para 10 (2004). Put another way, the UN Committee interpreted 'and' in the phrase 'within its territory and subject to its jurisdiction' disjunctively so that a state party is responsible towards persons either in its territory or subject to its jurisdiction.

[20] *Legal Consequences of the Construction of a Wall in the Occupied Palestinian Territories, Advisory Opinion*, [2004] ICJ 163, paras 107–13.

[21] See: *Coard v United States*, Report No 109/99, Case 10.951 (29 September 1999); *Alejandre v Cuba*, Report No 86/99, Case 11.589 (29 September 1999).

[22] *Banković v Belgium*, 2001 – XII ECHR 333, paras 59 and 71.

[23] *Issa v Turkey* (2004) 41 EHRR 567.

[24] *Solomou and Others v Turkey*, App No 36832/97, Decision of 24 June 2008.

[25] *Issa* (n 23) para 71; *Solomou* (n 24) para 45.

Court cases have the developments in the international case law around Article 2(1) of the International Covenant on Civil and Political Rights ever been acknowledged, let alone dealt with. Two early decisions refused to apply the Charter to foreign police and consequently would not give effect to Charter rights at trial to the extent that the violations directly implicated foreign police conduct.[26] The 1998 case of *R v Cook*[27] addressed whether the Charter could apply to the actions of Canadian police when they were in a foreign state – in that case, the interrogation of a suspect in New Orleans by Canadian officers who had been invited to do so by local police. The decision of the Supreme Court of Canada was divided, but most of the judges recognised and engaged with the international law issues involved. The majority opinion ultimately decided that the Charter could apply, in part because the nationality principle justified extending Canada's jurisdiction over the actions of its police officers, and because the conduct of the officers created no 'objectionable extraterritorial effect', that is, interference with the foreign state's sovereignty.

In 2007, however, the Supreme Court reversed the *Cook* holding abruptly in the case of *R v Hape*,[28] a money laundering prosecution where Canadian police (in co-operation with local police) had searched premises belonging to the Canadian accused that were located in Turks and Caicos. At his trial in Canada, Hape sought to have the documents seized during the searches excluded on the basis that they did not comply with section 8 of the Charter, even though the searches complied with local law, citing *Cook* in support. However, the Supreme Court held that effect could not be given – at trial in Canada – to Charter rights vis-a-vis police activities in the foreign state.

The Court's starting point was twofold: first, Canada's laws should be interpreted in conformity with international law, unless the contrary was obvious;[29] and second, the distinction between prescriptive and enforcement jurisdiction should be maintained, in that Canada might be free to legislate extraterritorially but had to recognise the limits placed by international law on its ability to enforce its laws extraterritorially. The goal of this aspect of the Charter was essentially to prescribe rules for police conduct that would ensure respect for the accused person's Charter rights, in this case to be free from unreasonable search and seizure. Making Canadian police comply with this Canadian law during their investigations would be essentially an act of enforcement jurisdiction. However, such an act of extraterritorial enforcement jurisdiction would be a viola-

[26] *R v Harrer* [1995] 3 SCR 562; *R v Terry* [1996] 2 SCR 207.

[27] *R v Cook* [1998] 2 SCR 597.

[28] See: n 2. Some of the best recent scholarship on this line of jurisprudence has been done by Professor John Currie (no relation): see John Currie, 'International Human Rights Law in the Supreme Court's *Charter* Jurisprudence: Commitment, Retrenchment *and* Retreat – In No Particular Order' (2010) 50:2 *Supreme Court Law Review* 1.

[29] ibid paras 34–39.

tion of the *locus* state's sovereignty, without consent of that state being given.[30] In this instance, despite the fact that the investigation was a co-operative one, there was no evidence that Turks and Caicos had given permission for Canadian law to be applied. The local law must govern any government activities there, including law enforcement. Therefore any attempt by Canadian officials to act in accordance with the Charter would be illegal, and *ipso facto* no Charter remedy could be given at trial.

One must bear in mind that the Charter is the only human rights law of domestic application that restrains the actions of Canadian state officials. The effect of the majority's decision outlined above is that Canadian police officers and other state officials are essentially immunised from the Charter's application when they are acting abroad. But if only the foreign state's law applied, the Canadian officials might be subject to more lax human rights standards or even none at all, depending upon the foreign state in question. The Court implicitly recognised that this was an unpalatable result, and thus carved out an exception: the Charter could apply where complying with local law would cause Canadian officials to contravene Canada's international human rights law obligations.[31]

Hape has been criticised in the Canadian legal literature and, despite the Supreme Court's valiant attempt to wrestle with the international law issues at play, there are serious methodological problems in the judgment. At the forefront of these is whether, in applying domestic human rights laws to domestic police in a domestic trial before a domestic court, extraterritorial enforcement jurisdiction is even engaged. It is surely true that when they were investigating in Turks and Caicos, the Canadian police were exercising enforcement jurisdiction in that state. If they had tried to comply with Canadian laws instead of local laws in the course of the investigation, that *might* have constituted an illegal act of enforcement jurisdiction. However, as Justice Bastarache pointed out in his separate reasons, the Canadian police had permission to be engaged in enforcement jurisdiction in Turks and Caicos, so no illegality arose from their activities so long as they complied with the local law, which they did.

Moreover, whether a particular act of extraterritorial enforcement is illegal is an international law question that engages state responsibility, and not one that was central to the inquiry before the court. In giving that question such centrality, the Court appeared to be confusing the question of jurisdiction with the question of which law applied to the investigation. Another route was available – apply the Charter to the police actions and deal with the fact that the Canadian police had to conform with local law as part of the constitutional analysis. If there was a conflict between the local law and Canadian law, then this could be factored into a more

[30] ibid paras 83–92, 96.
[31] ibid paras 96–101.

nuanced inquiry as to whether a breach actually occurred, or, at least in criminal cases, as to whether the evidence should be excluded as a result of the breach.[32] This would have allowed the Court to extend extraterritorial jurisdiction over potential human rights violations by Canadian officials outside Canada, as it is arguably bound to do under the International Covenant on Civil and Political Rights, but would have had, in the language of *Cook*, 'no objectionable extraterritorial effect'.[33]

The Court's creation of an exception for when the officials' activities would offend Canada's international human rights obligations is also troubling. This exception draws a false dichotomy between the Charter (a domestic law implementing international human rights law) and the international human rights obligations themselves. Once the international law is implemented in Canadian law then for practical purposes the two bodies of law are integrated; it makes little sense to say that the Charter applies only where international human rights law is engaged.[34] It also isolates the international law regarding jurisdiction from the human rights law. As an example of this, it was clear that Canadian officials would be able to immunise themselves from the Charter when they were acting abroad, simply by ensuring that they were under the authority of a local official and that there was no evidence of consent for the application of Canadian law. Yet, this would not necessarily prevent a finding *at a state responsibility level* that Canada was in breach of its international law obligations under the International Covenant on Civil and Political Rights for failing to ensure its officials complied with them when abroad – a jarring result.

These problems resurfaced soon after *Hape* in the *Afghan Detainees* case,[35] where Justice MacTavish of the Federal Court of Canada presided over a motion by Amnesty International and other interveners to apply the Charter to the actions of Canadian soldiers in Afghanistan. This proceeding had been preceded by significant controversy generated over allegations that detainees handed over by Canadian forces were being tortured and otherwise abused by their Afghan captors. The applicants were

[32] Under Canadian law, exclusion of evidence is not automatic upon the finding of a breach of the human rights provision. Rather, the court should determine whether, in all the circumstances, admission of the evidence would bring the administration of justice into disrepute; see: *R v Grant*, 2009 SCC 32.

[33] *R v Cook* (n 27).

[34] The Court nonetheless applied this exception the next year in *Khadr v Canada (Minister of Justice)*, 2008 SCC 28, ILDC 1031 (CA 2008), where it held that the Charter applied to Canadian intelligence agents questioning Omar Khadr at the Guantánamo Bay detention facility on the basis that the entire regime applied there had been found by the US Supreme Court to violate international human rights law and international humanitarian law. And see *Canada (Prime Minister) v Khadr*, 2010 SCC 3.

[35] *Amnesty International Canada v Canada (Canadian Forces)* 2008 FC 336, affirmed 2008 FCA 401 (Fed Ct of Appeal), leave to appeal to the Supreme Court of Canada denied 21 May 2009. The Federal Court of Appeal restricted its reasons to a review of whether the motions judge had made any errors of law, without any substantial discussion of *Hape* or *Khadr*. All subsequent references are to the motion decision.

seeking the possibility of human rights remedies under the Charter for the detainees. It was clear from the outset that the case would involve an application of *Hape*. The applicants argued that the military context was distinguishable, on both law and facts, from the kind of police cooperation dealt with in *Hape* and called for a different result – in particular because it was more in line with the kinds of cases dealt with by the Human Rights Committee and the ECtHR where extraterritorial jurisdiction was exercised.

Justice Mactavish applied *Hape* to answer the question in the negative. She found on the facts that, while the government of Afghanistan had agreed to allow Canadian forces to engage in certain activities – even enforcement-type activities – on Afghan soil, it had not consented to the application of Canadian law, including the Charter, as would be required to make the Charter applicable.[36] Rather, Canada and Afghanistan had agreed that Afghan law and international law, including international human rights and international humanitarian law, would govern the activities of Canadian Forces personnel. Accordingly, the Charter could not be applicable on this basis, since to apply it would be to violate Afghan sovereignty.

She further dismissed an argument by the applicants that it was accepted under international law that states were entitled to apply extraterritorial human rights jurisdiction over the acts of their officials in situations where there was 'effective military control of the person'. In so doing she made interesting use of the decision of the United Kingdom (UK) House of Lords in *Al-Skeini*,[37] on one hand adopting the finding of various Law Lords that the more conservative position of the ECtHR on jurisdiction from *Banković* was 'better law' than the more recent finding in *Issa*; and on the other hand rejecting the Lords' conclusion that extending extraterritorial jurisdiction to a British prison facility in Iraq was an acceptably modest move. While acknowledging the trend towards positive findings on extraterritorial jurisdiction in the international human rights case law,[38] she ultimately ruled that this position was too unsettled to merit a different application than that dictated by *Hape*.[39]

In part, the latter finding seems to have resulted from falling into the trap laid by the Supreme Court's odd distinction between the Charter and international human rights law in *Hape*, as evidenced in the following passage from *Afghan Detainees*:

[36] ibid para 170.

[37] *Al Skeini et al v Secretary of State for Defence* [2007] UKHL 26. The decision of the European Court of Human Rights in *Al-Skeini* (App No 55721/07, 7 July 2011) was released in July 2011, too late for consideration here.

[38] And considering both General Comment 31 and United Nations Committee Against Torture (*General Commentary No 2: Implementation of Article 2 by States Parties* (23/11/2007, CAT/C/GC/2/CRP.1/Rev.4).

[39] *Afghan Detainees* (n 35) paras 214, 281.

> It should also be noted that the comments of the United Nations Human Rights Committee relied upon by the applicants as supporting a more expansive approach to extraterritorial human rights jurisdiction are made in the context of an examination of the scope of the legal obligations on States Parties imposed by Article 2 of the *International Covenant on Civil and Political Rights*. The comments do not address the extraterritorial reach of the domestic laws of States Parties.[40]

It is important to remember that central to *Hape* was the presumption that domestic legislation is in conformity with international law, unless the contrary is explicit. It would have been just as easy, and more sound methodologically, to say that since the Charter implements the International Covenant on Civil and Political Rights obligations, and the UN Human Rights Committee's views as well as the ICJ's decision in the *Palestinian Wall* case shows that extraterritorial jurisdiction is permissible, if not obligatory, the Charter must be amenable to extraterritorial application – particularly where the remedy is a domestic one and the sovereignty concerns that so motivated the Supreme Court's approach in *Hape* are more illusory than real. This is an unsatisfying result; the important principle of state sovereignty has been used to vanquish a threat to it that did not exist.

As can be seen from the foregoing, the predominantly customary international law of jurisdiction and the treaty-based law of jurisdiction with respect to international human rights co-exist and interact in a state of, if not tension, then uneasiness, and certainly not unity. For many years states have universally accepted that the activities of one state's national in a foreign state can give rise to the home state's right to exercise its public law powers, in the sense of criminal prosecution based on the nationality principle or another acceptable ground of extraterritorial prescriptive jurisdiction. However, increasingly it is the activities of a state official in the foreign state that are being dealt with, activities which are overlain with the prohibition on extraterritorial enforcement jurisdiction. Human rights treaties oblige states to require that their officials and agents comply with human rights norms, and a number of international courts and adjudicative bodies have extended that obligation extraterritorially.[41] However, as *Hape* shows, this perspective is at odds with the conservative approach national courts have traditionally taken to extraterritorial jurisdiction out of reciprocal respect for state sovereignty. What is clear is that the human rights regimes are having at least a stretching effect upon the international law of jurisdiction respecting public law process, though whether it is fragmentation or a nascent sectoral realignment is difficult to tell.

[40] ibid para 240.
[41] See: nn 15–24 and accompanying text.

IV. PRIVATE LAW REMEDIES IN CANADA FOR INTERNATIONAL HUMAN RIGHTS ABUSES

Just as perpetrators of international human rights abuses are subject to condemnation and sanctions, so their victims may expect to receive reparation. Local courts in the territory of abuse are frequently unable to render justice, often because the state, though involved in the violence, is immune from suit or exerts influence or condones corruption that defeats the independence and impartiality of the judiciary. Victims of violence tend to try to escape their tormenters by fleeing abroad and then, after recuperation, they seek redress in their new state of refuge or asylum. Canadian courts have received a number of these claims, of which the *Bouzari* case, mentioned in the Introduction, is a classic example.[42] Unfortunately, all of them to date have been dismissed on the basis of a lack of domestic jurisdiction over the foreign events or a claim of sovereign immunity by the foreign defendant. Arguably, however, the courts have failed to pay appropriate attention to other international legal obligations regarding their international responsibility.

Bouzari v Iran[43] involved horrible and despicable acts of torture. As the Ontario Court of Appeal stated: 'From June 1993 to January 1994 Houshang Bouzari was abducted, imprisoned and brutally tortured by agents of the Islamic Republic of Iran. Shortly after his release, he escaped from Iran and eventually came to Canada as a landed immigrant in 1998. He now seeks to sue Iran for the damages he suffered.'[44] It may be added that Bouzari was approached more than once by the second son of the President of Iran with intimations about a large business deal prior to his physical mistreatment. It should also be noted that, in trying to sue Iran in the Canadian courts, Bouzari did not name any of his tormenters as co-defendants.[45]

In this and similar situations,[46] the claims of the victim of abuse deserve greater judicial attention than they often receive in three respects: i) by

[42] See also: *Arar v Syrian Arab Republic* (2005), 127 CRR (2d) 252, 2005 CanLII 4945 (ON SC), *Kazemi (Estate of) v Islamic Republic of Iran*, 2011 QCCS 196 (CanLII), and Arone's case against Canada, discussed by John Terry, 'Taking *Filártiga* on the Road: Why Courts Outside the United States Should Accept Jurisdiction Over Actions Involving Torture Committed Abroad' in Craig Scott (ed), *Torture as Tort* (Oxford / Portland Oregon, Hart Publishing, 2001) 109, 130.

[43] See: n 3.

[44] ibid para 1.

[45] As occurred in the comparable UK case of *Jones v Minister of the Interior of the Kingdom of Saudi Arabia*, [2004] EWCA Civ 1394, rev'd [2006] 2 WLR 1424, [2006] UKHL 26.

[46] Compare similar claims in various other national courts such as *Filartiga v Pen-Irala*, 630 F2d 876 (2nd Circ 1980) (US, under unique legislation), *Prefecture of Voiotia v Federal republic of Germany* (2001) 95 *Am J Int'l L* 198 (English report by Maria Gavouneli and Elias Bantekas) (Greece, Sup Ct); *Ferrini v Federal Republic of Germany* (2005) 99 AJIL 242 (English report by Andrea Bianchi), (2004) 87 *RDI* 539 (Italy, Court of Cassation), *Jones* ibid, and *Al-Adsani v Kuwait (No 2)* (1996) 107 *ILR* 536 (UKHL).

analogy to the universal jurisdiction over the perpetrator of the criminal abuse, ii) on account of the obligations under international human rights law to provide domestic remedies, and iii) by recalibrating the scope of the exception for state immunity from jurisdiction.

A. Universality of Jurisdiction over International Human Rights Abuses

The refusal of Canadian courts to assert civil jurisdiction over defendant perpetrators within their reach for human rights abuses committed abroad relies on the forum's attitude towards foreign torts and delicts. While ready to exercise remedial jurisdiction over wrongs that are committed within Canada, they are cautious about asserting jurisdiction over activities beyond Canada, except in special circumstances. This is a realistic approach on both practical and legal grounds. Although the international legal principles declared in the *Lotus* case[47] would support an exercise of prescriptive jurisdiction, they would not permit enforcement if that involved breaching the fundamental rule against interfering in the affairs and territory of another sovereign state.[48] Thus, while a Canadian court might grant an order to issue a writ out of its geographic jurisdiction, it could not *sub poena* the defendant or witnesses in the foreign state to attend in Canada. As a result, unless there is a 'real and substantial connection'[49] to Canada, Canadian courts ordinarily declare themselves *fora non conveniens* for suits against foreigners for alleged wrongs committed on foreign soil.

Such an attitude is quite appropriate for ordinary incidents such as accidents and assaults, but violent abuses of international human rights are not ordinary wrongs. They are exceptional human misconduct and their perpetrators are *hostes humani generis*. The most appropriate analogy for international human rights violations is not to torts or delicts but to international crimes.

Torture, such as Houshang Bouzari suffered, is an outright crime under international law.[50] It is also, along with murder, extermination, enslavement, illicit imprisonment, rape, persecution, disappearance, apartheid, and other inhumane acts causing great suffering or serious injury, a crime against humanity when performed as part of a widespread or systematic attack against a civilian population.[51] Canada, as a party to the Convention

[47] See: n 1.
[48] See: n 10 and accompanying text.
[49] The phrase is drawn from the leading Canadian case, *Morguard Investments Ltd v De Savoye* [1990] 3 SCR 77.
[50] Convention Against Torture and Other Cruel, Inhuman and Degrading Treatment and Punishment (1984) 1465 UNTS 85, Can TS 1987 No 36, arts 1–4.
[51] Rome Statute of the International Criminal Court, UN Doc A/CONF 183/9 (17 July 1998) 37 ILM 999, art 7.

Against Torture and the Rome Statute of the International Criminal Court,[52] has accepted the obligation to detain and prosecute any accused found in Canada wherever he or she may have committed these crimes. The Crimes Against Humanity and War Crimes Act[53] explicitly asserts jurisdiction over offences that take place outside Canada and over the perpetrators who are subsequently located within Canada.[54]

Victims of such crimes have a legitimate expectation of a remedy from their perpetrators since the internationally prohibited acts also constitute violent abuses of internationally protected human rights. This legitimate expectation is bolstered in international law by Article 75 of the Rome Statute in favour of reparation to victims and the establishment of a Trust Fund for that purpose. It is supported in Canadian law by analogy to Canada's own victims of crime legislation.[55] Accordingly Canadian courts ought to consider exerting parallel civil jurisdiction as well. International law does not forbid such jurisdiction; indeed, international human rights laws demand that domestic provision be made for effective remedial civil jurisdiction.

Variants of this argument were presented in the *Bouzari* case but the Court dismissed them all. In its view there was no justification for a departure from the ordinary practice of applying the test of real and substantial connection of the unlawful incidents with Canada. In particular, the Court did not acknowledge any customary or conventional international legal obligation that required it to apply a rule of universal jurisdiction in a civil action for torture committed abroad by a foreign state defendant.[56] The fact that the defendant was a foreign state entitled to sovereign immunity before the Canadian court was a decisive factor in this decision. The Court did not make a determination under the real and substantial connection test but it noted that its application in this case was 'not easy'[57] because the allegations of torture were violations of international law and no other forum was open to the plaintiff. The Court's sensitivity to, and respect for, the international human rights at stake even as it applied the international right of state immunity displays the conflicted condition of the international law of jurisdiction. The Canadian Court's uncertainty raises intriguing speculation how the decision in the case might have differed had the perpetrators, rather than the state, been sued. The legal arguments favouring civil court

[52] See: nn 50, 51 respectively.

[53] SC 2000, c 24.

[54] ibid ss 6, 8.

[55] The federal government has appointed an Ombudsman for Victims of Crime (SOR/2007-54) who is charged, *inter alia*, with promoting the Canadian Statement of Basic Principles of Justice for Victims of Crime. Nine out of 10 provinces provide compensation for the injuries of victims of crime: see the Canadian Resource Centre for Victims of Crime, available at www.crcvc.ca (last visited 1 June 2011).

[56] See: n 3 para 28.

[57] ibid para 38.

jurisdiction by analogy to criminal court powers is still sustainable. Indeed, it is supported by an additional obligation of the international human rights laws, which, it will now be argued, applies to domestic courts directly.

B. International Obligations to Provide Remedies for Human Rights Abuses

The obligation to protect the human person is set forth in the strongest terms that international law can muster. Many human rights norms, including those covering violent and other egregious abuse under discussion here, are fundamental, non-derogable, *jus cogens*, and *erga omnes*. Regrettably the concepts and law underlying this statement have not been adequately addressed by, or perhaps even to, Canadian courts petitioned by international human rights victims.

The human rights to life, liberty and security and the corollary freedoms from torture, slavery, servitude and cruel, inhuman and degrading treatment found in the International Covenant on Civil and Political Rights[58] deal with the very existence and integrity of the human person. States are obliged to prevent and remediate abuse of these rights in the strongest terms.[59] Of these rights, freedom from torture, the specific basis of claim in *Bouzari's* case, is more particularly regulated by the Convention Against Torture.[60] This group of rights at least, if not the whole body of human legal protections, have a special legal status. They are obligations *erga omnes*. As the ICJ in the *Barcelona Traction* case declared, *erga omnes* obligations are derived, *inter alia*, 'from the principles and rules concerning basic human rights of the human person'.[61] That means these human rights are treaty obligations owed to the international community as a whole, specifically amongst all signatory states for the benefit of all individuals.

It is often too quickly assumed that these obligations to protect human rights and to redress their abuse have territorial limitations.[62] But human beings migrate, especially after persecution and violent abuse, and they carry their human rights with them. Thus it happens, as *Bouzari's* case illustrates, that a victim of human rights violations in one state flees to another state in search of refuge and remediation. While the state of the abuse ought, in the first place, to remedy the situation and to reparate the victim, the state of refuge arguably also incurs an obligation to ensure

[58] See: n 14 arts 6–8.

[59] ibid art 2.

[60] See: n 50 arts 1, 14.

[61] *Barcelona Traction Light and Power Co Case (Belgium v Spain)* [1970] ICJ Rep 3, para 34.

[62] Attention is drawn to the words of the International Covenant on Civil and Political Rights, art 2(1) obliging the state to ensure human rights 'to all individuals within its territory and subject to its jurisdiction' as supporting an interpretation that limits responsibility for remedying human rights abuses to the state in which the violations occurred.

the means of redress to the victim as soon as he/she is admitted to its territory. This approach to reading the human rights treaties is consistent with the jurisdictional authority of the state over its territory and the people within it.[63] Moreover, it is also gives sensible expression to the *erga omnes* character of these human rights obligations on all states parties.

Such an interpretation of the Convention Against Torture was urged on the Canadian court in *Bouzari's* case, specifically on the basis of Article 14, which states in part:

> Each State Party shall ensure in its legal system that the victim of an act of torture obtains redress and has an enforceable right to fair and adequate compensation including the means for as full rehabilitation as possible.

The appellant, Bouzari, argued that this Article required a state party such as Canada to allow a torture victim, like him, to bring a civil suit for redress in the Canadian courts even though that would involve taking jurisdiction over acts of torture committed abroad. The Court disagreed, declaring that Convention Against Torture only requires Canada to provide a remedy for a claimant for torture committed within its territorial jurisdiction. Three reasons were given. First, the silence of the language of Article 14 on this point was read as 'not necessarily mean[ing] the absence of territorial limitation'.[64] It might equally have been interpreted in the reverse way: the silence of Article 14 implies no jurisdictional limitations.

Secondly, the Court appropriately investigated the state practice around Article 14 but found none. It accepted one expert witness' view of a shared state understanding that Article 14 only demands the provision of civil remedies for torture committed within the state's territory. An interpretive declaration made by the United States (US) at the time of its ratification of Convention Against Torture was referred to in support of this opinion.[65] Arguably the fact that the US felt it needed to make this declaration in the absence of state practice could indicate that the provision of civil remedies for torture committed abroad was at least an open legal issue if not a legal requirement.[66]

Thirdly, the Court considered the *travaux préparatoires* of Convention Against Torture, noting that an early draft of Article 14 had expressly referred to torture 'committed in any territory under its jurisdiction'. It accepted the expert opinion that this clause was ultimately omitted as superfluous because Article 14 was implicitly already territorially limited,

[63] See the interpretation of International Covenant on Civil and Political Rights, art 2 by the UN Human Rights Committee (n 19) and accompanying text.

[64] See: n 3 para 76.

[65] ibid paras 77–79.

[66] Furthermore the US substantially reversed its interpretation of Convention Against Torture, art 14 when it enacted the Torture Victim Protection Act 1991, 28 USC Part IV, ch 85, para 1350.

rather than the opposing expert view that its excision indicated an intention to exclude jurisdictional constraint on the state's obligation.[67]

As just explained, the grounds for finding or refuting a territorial limitation on the state's jurisdiction in fulfilling its definite obligation to provide the means for a civil remedy for torture are decidedly weak.[68] The three interpretive arguments might have been determined either way. Lack of explicit language in the treaty or state practice on the ground results in a silence around the issue that may mean acquiescence in either viewpoint. The fact that each side of the case called upon international law experts[69] to assist the court in its interpretation of Convention Against Torture emphasises the uncertainty around the jurisdiction under the international law that national courts have to apply.

The Court in *Bouzari* also separately considered an argument that *jus cogens* required it 'to permit a civil claim against a foreign state for torture committed abroad'.[70] Undoubtedly some human rights are non-derogable *jus cogens*. The rights to life, liberty and security under discussion here are some of the protections that may not be suspended by the state even in dire times of public emergency.[71] Furthermore, these human rights may be classified as peremptory norms of international law or *jus cogens*. This customary international concept has been broadly defined in the Vienna Convention on the Law of Treaties[72] and has been accepted by the ICJ in the *Nicaragua* case.[73] Its significance lies in its status as a rule of international public order before which any conflicting customary or conventional international law is rendered void and of no effect. Applied in the present context of human rights protections, there is dispute as to the rights that have attained the superior status of *jus cogens*. Legal opinions differ over whether all or only some, and if some, which, human rights norms are *jus cogens*, but there is little doubt that those that are central to human life and existence and are non-derogable *erga omnes* obligations have the force of *jus cogens*. Thus international human rights rules of

[67] See: n 3 paras 80–81.

[68] The UN Committee Against Torture, which monitors the implementation of Convention Against Torture, subsequently expressed concern about Canada's position and recommended review of its interpretation of art 14 'to ensure the provision of compensation through its civil jurisdiction to all victims of torture'. Conclusions and Recommendations of the Committee Against Torture: Canada, UN Doc CAT/C/CR/34/CAN, 49 (7 July 2005). And see: CK Hall, 'The Duty of States Parties to the Convention against Torture to Provide Procedures Permitting Victims to Recover Reparations for Torture Committed Abroad' (2007) 18 *Eur J Int'l L* 921.

[69] Professor Ed Morgan of the University of Toronto and Professor Christopher Greenwood, then of the London School of Economics.

[70] See: n 3 para 84.

[71] See International Covenant on Civil and Political Rights (n 14), art 4 which excepts the rights, amongst others, expressed in arts 6–8.

[72] (1969) 1155 UNTS 331, art 53.

[73] *Case Concerning Military and Paramilitary Activities in and Against Nicaragua* (*Nicaragua v United States*) [1986] ICJ Rep 14, para 190.

jus cogens status are compelling at customary international law everywhere for every state.

The *Bouzari* case appears to be the first time *jus cogens* was made the basis of argument in the Canadian courts.[74] Importantly, the proposition that the prohibition of torture is a peremptory rule of international law was accepted by the litigants, including the Attorney General of Canada, and the Court.[75] But the Court also adopted the view of the motions judge below that:

> An examination of the decisions of national courts and international tribunals, as well as state legislation with respect to sovereign immunity, indicates that there is no principle of customary international law which provides an exception from state immunity where an act of torture has been committed outside the forum, even for acts contrary to *jus cogens*.[76]

This judgment decides that the scope of the *jus cogens* norm prohibiting the use of torture by the state does not inhibit the resort to sovereign immunity by the state when called to account in a domestic court for using torture. The decision severs the right to protection from torture and the right to a remedy for torture. The Court sought to justify the wisdom and policy of its opinion as respect for an equilibrium that has developed to date within international law:

> Both under customary international law and international treaty there is today a balance struck between the condemnation of torture as an international crime against humanity and the principle that states must treat each other as equals not subjected to each other's jurisdiction. It would be inconsistent with this balance to provide a civil remedy against a foreign state for torture committed abroad.[77]

This statement purports to relate three quite different international legal concepts: i) criminal responsibility of the individual, ii) civil liability of the state, and iii) sovereign immunity of the state. It is not evident that these concepts are capable of being balanced since they do not all operate on the same plane. Individual criminal liability is very different from state civil liability: the position of individuals and states are not comparable. While individuals may be held criminally responsible in both national and international courts, states are not. Further, criminal and civil legal processes have different objectives and outcomes. Finally, whether an individual or a state bears responsibility goes to the merits of a claim, whereas immunity affects legal process, that is, it inhibits court jurisdiction even to hear

[74] The concept of *jus cogens* has since been recognised by the Supreme Court of Canada in *Suresh v Canada (Minister of Citizenship and Immigration)* [2002] 1 SCR 3, although the question whether torture is included in it was sidestepped as unnecessary to the decision.

[75] See: n 3 para 87.

[76] ibid para 88. See also: *Arar v Syria* (n 42).

[77] ibid para 95.

the claim. In any case, it seems most unlikely that any kind of 'balance' was either designed or achieved in the development of the international law since the contending principles arose independently from different origins through the operation of different law-creating processes.

Clearly, in its discussion of the scope of the *jus cogens* norm prohibiting torture, as in earlier parts of its judgment, the Court was much concerned about the right to immunity of the foreign state defendant. This is a state right that can so easily overreach a human right if not applied restrictively that it deserves separate attention in the next section of this chapter. At this point, it is appropriate to observe once more how the Court's decision might have been different if the action had been against the torturers rather than their state. Absent sovereign immunity concerns, the Court might have determined that the scope of *jus cogens* around torture included peremptory obligations on the state of prevention, prohibition, prosecution and provision for redress.

The general significance of this discussion about the treatment in the *Bouzari* case of the state's obligations in respect of redress for human rights abuses abroad is that the Canadian Court had to operate in a context of uncertainty over the jurisdictional rules of international law. The Convention Against Torture's open-ended provision on remedial jurisdiction runs contrary to the traditional limits of state powers to persons and events within its territorial control. The Court felt unable to interpret the Convention Against Torture as an exception to its territorial jurisdiction, at least without greater certainty of expression or state practice. The peremptory force of the law about torture was met by the ancient constraint against asserting jurisdiction over a foreign state. Although the Court adopted the concept of *jus cogens*, it did not believe it thereby acquired the scope of authority to overreach the restriction of state immunity on its jurisdiction. It remains to be seen whether the arguments based on the linked protections and remedies for human rights found in International Covenant on Civil and Political Rights would fare any better in a domestic court than the similar ones founded on Convention Against Torture in the *Bouzari* case. What the case surely discloses is that, while the Canadian Court was open to the arguments of the torture victim to entertain his civil claim for redress, it found the international law of state jurisdiction under which it had to operate in considerable uncertainty and disarray.

C. State Immunity from Jurisdiction in Civil Suits for International Human Rights Abuses

The immunity of the state from the jurisdiction of another state's courts is a longstanding principle of customary international law that is central to every state's sovereignty and equality. Immunity from jurisdiction extends to all domestic court processes whether their nature is civil or criminal, public or private. On this general principle Bouzari's claim against Iran was judged to be beyond the jurisdiction of the Canadian Court.

Though traditionally unlimited or absolute, the practice of state immunity is now restrictive. But the scope of the restrictions under customary international law is neither fixed nor certain.[78] A process of development has been taking place over several decades, promoted by national, regional and multilateral law making. Some states, like Australia,[79] Canada,[80] South Africa,[81] and the US,[82] have enacted foreign state immunity statutes while others, such as the members of the European Union, have concluded an inter-state immunity convention.[83] At the United Nations, a Convention on the Jurisdictional Immunities of States and Their Property[84] has subsequently been concluded. These laws exhibit different definitions of significant concepts, such as the scope of a state's identity and its immune constituent entities, the character of non-immune commercial acts, and the extent of territorial connection with the forum state necessary to exclude immunity for torts.[85] The particular issue of state immunity from civil actions in domestic courts is now before the ICJ. Germany instituted proceedings against Italy in December 2008 as a result of the decision of Italy's highest court, the Corte de Cassazione, in the *Ferrini* case[86] that affirmed jurisdiction over a claim 'brought by a person who during World War II had been deported to Germany to perform forced labour in the armaments industry'.[87]

In Canada, the enactment of the State Immunity Act[88] crystallised the customary international rules within Canadian law. Although customary international law is automatically adopted within Canadian law, except in the face of clearly contradictory legislation,[89] and statutes are supposed to be interpreted so far as possible consistently with Canada's international

[78] 'Despite the increasing number of emerging exceptions, the general principle of sovereign immunity remains an important part of the international legal order': LeBel J of the Supreme Court of Canada in *Schreiber v Canada (Attorney General)* [2002] 3 SCR 269, para 17.

[79] Foreign Sovereign Immunities Act (1986) 25 ILM 715.

[80] State Immunity Act, RSC 1985, c S-18.

[81] Foreign States Immunities Act (1981) c 87.

[82] Foreign Sovereign Immunities Act 1976, 28 USC paras 1602–11, (1976) 15 ILM 1388.

[83] European Convention on State Immunity (1972) 11 ILM 470. And see the UK State Immunity Act, UK (1978) c 33 which substantively implemented the provisions of the European Convention in British law.

[84] UN GA Res 59/38 (2004).

[85] See the discussion of state practice in: J Bröhmer, *State Immunity and the Violation of Human Rights* (The Hague, Martinus Nijhoff Publishers, 1997) ch 2.

[86] See: n 45.

[87] Quoted from the German application to the ICJ in ICJ Press Release No 2008/14 (23 December 2008).

[88] See: n 80.

[89] *R v Hape* (n 2); *Bouzari v Iran* (n 3).

obligations,[90] this has not happened with the State Immunity Act, at least not in *Bouzari's* case. The approach of the court was to grant Iran such immunity as is stated in the State Immunity Act and thus to set aside all arguments based on Canada's international obligations that supported a more restrictive interpretation, which might have denied Iran immunity. The differences between the plaintiff's arguments and the court's opinions reveal much about the contending principles of state responsibility and of state immunity within the jurisdiction of the forum state's courts.

The *Bouzari* court's approach to state immunity may be reviewed from two different critical viewpoints: i) in a technical manner, like the court, by exploring the scope of the exceptions to immunity explicitly stated in the statute, and ii) more broadly, by interpreting the statute in light of developments in international law regarding state sovereignty and state responsibility for human rights.

The technical arguments surround the statutory exceptions to the immunity of the foreign state on account of its involvement in tortious 'personal or bodily injury . . . that occurs in Canada'[91] and contractual 'commercial activity'.[92] The court declared both exceptions inapplicable. On the tort claim, it might have denied Iran immunity on the evidence that Bouzari continued to suffer physical and psychological injuries from his torture after coming to Canada. As to the commercial activity claim, the court might have held that Iran had no immunity for its grossly coercive and intimidating tactics to secure a business deal with Bouzari. These interpretations of the State Immunity Act were reasonable alternatives which this court chose not to adopt. Instead, in confirming Iran's immunity from suit, the court reduced the jurisdiction arguably available to it to redress human rights abuses.

It probably would not have been necessary to reach for these exceptions at all if the action had been brought against Bouzari's abusers. Immunity is intended to protect the sovereignty of the state so its scope of application to individuals and institutions is limited. State immunity extends to the 'head of the foreign state or of any political subdivision . . . while acting as such in a public capacity'.[93] The son of the president of Iran and Bouzari's other tormentors would not qualify under this element of the definition. Immunity also protects 'any government of the foreign state or of any political subdivision . . . including any of its departments, and any agency of the foreign state'.[94] Obviously governments operate through officials who are consequently immune when acting on behalf of the state

[90] *Ordon Estate v Grail* [1998] 3 SCR 437, *Canadian Foundation for Children, Youth, and the Law v AG Canada* [2004] 1 SCR 76.
[91] State Immunity Act (n 80).
[92] ibid s 5.
[93] ibid s 2.
[94] ibid.

in a public capacity. The goons who inflicted abuse on Bouzari can hardly be included in this class of immune persons.[95]

A broader approach to application of the State Immunity Act was also open to the court. The contextual method of statutory interpretation that is applied in Canada,[96] together with an interpretive presumption that the legislature, in enacting statutes, does not intend to violate international law,[97] requires Canadian courts to take into account such international law as exists on the matter before them and to strive to interpret the governing legislation consistently with that law.[98] Thus, the responsibility on the courts to provide access to remedies to victims of international human rights abuses, as discussed previously, should have been brought to bear on this court's interpretation of the State Immunity Act. It was not. The court observed: 'Even if Canada's international law obligations required that Canada permit a civil remedy for torture abroad by a foreign state, Canada has legislated in a way that does not do so'.[99] Perhaps Canada has, but equally perhaps those non-derogable *erga omnes* human rights obligations of *jus cogens* status could have informed the court's interpretation of the statutory exceptions to state immunity and thus led to a legitimate application of the State Immunity Act that would also have fulfilled these international responsibilities.[100]

In not pursuing this path, the Canadian court displayed a greater concern for the traditional concept of state sovereignty over the more recent norm of state responsibility to provide judicial remedies for international human rights violations. That said, the court faced a difficult decision constrained as it was, on the one hand, by a longstanding principle of

[95] The fact that Bouzari's torturers may not have been agents of the Iranian government would not relieve the state of Iran from responsibility internationally for failing to prevent violations of human rights laws, or the perpetrators from liability domestically for their egregious and actionable wrongs (torts or delicts).

[96] *2747–3174 Québec Inc v Quebec (Régie des perms d'alcool)* [1996] 3 SCR 919; *Rizzo v Rizzo Shoes Ltd* [1998] 1 SCR 27; *R v Gladue* [1999] 1 SCR 688; *Baker v Canada (Minister of Citizenship and Immigration)* [1999] 2 SCR 817. See also: R Sullivan, *Driedger on the Construction of Statutes*, 3rd edn (Toronto, Butterworths, 1994) 330, and HM Kindred, 'The Challenge of Internalizing International Conventional Law: The Experience of Australia, England and Canada with Ratified Treaties' in CPM Waters (ed), *British and Canadian Perspectives on International Law* (Leiden, Martinus Nijhoff Publishers, 2006) 393.

[97] *Daniels v White and the Queen* [1968] SCR 517, 541; *National Corn Growers Assn v Canada (Import Tribunal)* [1990] 2 SCR 1324, 1371; *Ordon Estate v Grail* (n 90). See also: G van Ert, *Using International Law in Canadian Courts*, 2nd edn (Toronto, Irwin Law, 2008) ch 5.

[98] See the cases in n 90.

[99] *Bouzari* case (n 3) para 67. See also: *Arar v Syria* (n 42). *cf Jones v Saudi Arabia* (n 45).

[100] *cf* the division of opinion along these lines in *Al-Adsani v UK* [GC] No 35763/97 ECHR 2001-XI (2002) 34 EHRR 273, in which the ECtHR, in interpreting the right to a fair trial under art 6(1) of the European Convention on Human rights, upheld Kuwait's claim to immunity by nine votes to eight. See also: E Bates, 'The *Al-Adsani* Case, State Immunity and the International Prohibition Against Torture' (2003) 3 *Hum R L Rev* 193; and K Bartsch and B Elberling, '*Jus Cogens* versus State Immunity, Round Two: The Decision of the European Court of Human Rights in the *Kalogeropoulou et al v Greece and Germany* Decision' (2003) 4 *Ger LJ* 477.

state immunity from jurisdiction, which was confirmed by an explicit restatement in the governing legislation, and urged, on the other, by a newer obligation of affirmative action on human rights. The court's predicament exposes the conflicted character of the jurisdictional principles at stake. The development and imposition of international human rights obligations within the national arena has not been accompanied by the necessary accommodation and reform of the restraining principle of sovereign immunity from national jurisdiction. Domestic courts have been left to find a way through this confusion. It is not surprising if courts in different countries reach different, even opposing, solutions. The allowance of state immunity in the *Bouzari* case in Canada may be contrasted with its disallowance in the *Ferrini* case in Italy. The disparity of interpretive views in *Bouzari*, which received weight and veracity from the contemporary yet contrary decision in *Ferrini*, points up the disarray and disunity in the practice of state immunity. The rules of foreign state immunity from jurisdiction are no more certain and unified than the rest of the international law regarding the assertion of state jurisdiction.[101]

V. REFLECTIONS AND CONCLUSIONS

Speaking generally, the principles of state jurisdiction and state immunity have been adopted as customary international law for a very long time. As concepts, they have been broadly accepted and understood. But more particular rules introduced in more recent times – such as the provisions of international human rights treaties – have cut deeply into the domestic jurisdiction of states. As a result, their judicial systems, for example the Canadian courts, have become unsure about the scope of their jurisdiction. In Canada the courts are particularly puzzled about the degree of jurisdictional deference they should accord to foreign sovereigns in the face of obligations to assert jurisdiction to protect international human rights and to remediate their violations.

As the previous discussion has shown, there is jurisdictional uncertainty in both public/criminal and private/civil cases. In the public law area tensions exist between the sovereignty of the foreign state in its own territory and the international human rights obligations carried along by Canadian officials who go to work there. In the private law field the pressures are between the immunity of the foreign state in Canadian territory, especially from Canadian court jurisdiction, and the international human rights requirements on Canada to assert remedial jurisdiction.

[101] The fact that Germany and Italy have engaged in litigation before the ICJ over the customary law rules of immunity from foreign state jurisdiction (n 87) corroborates this observation.

So when does foreign state sovereignty trump the permissive powers, or even the mandatory responsibilities, of domestic jurisdiction? These are big issues which national court systems cannot resolve individually. Their decisions do add to the corpus of state practice from which customary international law may, perhaps, grow. But such cumulative state practice as exists at present around these jurisdictional issues is too indefinite within particular domestic court systems and too various between different national legal systems to found customary international law norms.

In a sense, domestic courts should not be blamed for this disunity since they do not directly create international law by their individual decisions but only seek what it is in order to apply it. Most of international law is made as well as administered by the executive, that is, the government, of the state. However, the rules of jurisdiction and immunity are pre-eminently examples of international law that fall to the judicial organ of the state, that is, the domestic courts, to apply in the course of their work. Consequently, their performance bears witness to the condition of this law. Moreover, in an era of increasing inter-judicial dialogue between the courts of different states, how one court makes its finding on the current state of international law can affect others. In the Canadian context, this was illustrated in *Afghan Detainees* by the Federal Court of Canada's use of the Law Lords' decision in *Al-Skeini*, discussed above. In this sense, then, national courts can be prime movers towards either unity or fragmentation of this body of international law, since the views expressed by national courts can affect the findings of other courts, and all of them contribute to a matrix of state practice that, as a result, may trend towards consistency or confusion.

The state of the rules on jurisdiction is, in part, the consequence of the piecemeal process of creation of international law in this area. The concepts of state jurisdiction and foreign state immunity from jurisdiction developed slowly by inter-state actions and reactions into customary international law. They have produced legal conflicts at times over particular actions in specific sectors of state interests where one state considered another had overstepped the legitimate limits of these general principles. For instance, when the US courts developed the 'effects' doctrine to claim jurisdiction in anti-trust (competition) cases over foreign corporations on account of very indirect and far from proximate effects of their foreign commercial activities on US trade, Europe and Canada, amongst others, responded politically with strong representations about interference with their sovereign jurisdiction, and legally with nullification and 'claw back' legislation to prohibit compliance and enforcement of US court judgments.[102]

[102] See, eg: Canada's Foreign Extraterritorial Measures Act, RSC 1985, c F-29.

In general, however, states have in the past managed to operate the traditional principles of state jurisdiction and foreign state immunity from jurisdiction in a co-operative manner. They have largely stayed within their territorial limits and deferred, out of comity, to the foreign state's authority in those infrequent instances when a potential clash of national powers arose. Thus, notwithstanding the permissiveness of the jurisdictional principles declared in the *Steamship Lotus* case, territorial jurisdiction has been the primary practice of states, as to both prescription and execution of law, except in respect of visiting foreign sovereigns and their property and representatives, when so-called 'absolute' immunity from the local jurisdiction was granted. But the introduction of restrictions on immunity and of obligations to protect international human rights in the second half of the twentieth century has inevitably altered state practice and raised the problems discussed in this chapter.

Although some restrictions on state immunity are now nearly universally accepted as a proposition, the actual limits are uncertain. The variety in national state immunity statutes attests to the lack of consensus amongst states on the degree of jurisdictional deference they should accord each other domestically. Added to this disorder are the impacts of the relatively new conventional and customary laws in respect of international human rights. Their provisions reach far into the state's domestic jurisdiction with stringent and specific obligations. As domestic courts wrestle with the resulting problems over when to assert and when to defer their authority, it is noticeable that all these new international rules have been made without adequate, if any, reference to the traditional customary international law of state jurisdiction. No wonder there is confusion that is mirrored in national court practice.

Is the Canadian courts' experience synechdochal? Are the *Hape*, *Bouzari* and *Afghan Detainees* cases a micro-level illustration of the overall state of the international law of jurisdiction? They certainly indicate that Canadian courts are resisting treaty-based developments because they feel constrained by more traditional international jurisdictional principles. While *Afghan Detainees* and *Bouzari* contained laudatory first efforts at dealing with the international developments regarding extraterritorial jurisdiction in the public and private law spheres respectively under the International Covenant on Civil and Political Rights regime, Canada's highest court has yet to engage this jurisprudence on interpretation of the human rights treaties. On the surface it appears that while some of the world is attempting to explore the parameters of how and when human rights obligations may apply extraterritorially, Canada has fallen back on the restraining principles of sovereignty as the dominant rule, without adequately factoring in the new and dynamic international human rights jurisdictional norms. The Supreme Court continues to use the broader contours of the international law of jurisdiction without inquiry into how these apply in the context of human rights. Put this way, it might be said simply that the Supreme Court is swimming against the tide. More significantly, recent Canadian case law as a whole is an example of state practice that reflects, even contributes, to fragmentation in the international law of jurisdiction – ironically, this is because Canadian courts, as in the *Afghan Detainees* case, view that law as being fragmented.

11

Immunities and Human Rights: Dissecting the Dialogue in National and International Courts

PHILIPPA WEBB*

I. INTRODUCTION

THE LAW ON immunity, a legal subject with a long history, is in transition. Specifically, the extent to which state officials accused of committing international crimes are entitled to immunity from jurisdiction is the subject of intense dialogue and some conflict among national and international courts. 'Dialogue' is used here to refer to the citation, discussion, application, or rejection of decisions of other courts by a judge or judges. Those decisions may be placed before the court by counsel or may be referred to the court on the initiative of the judge.[1]

The field of immunities is special in that national courts play a prominent role in applying and, occasionally, developing customary international law. As former President Higgins of the International Court of Justice (ICJ) has stated:

> Domestic courts have long been acknowledged as playing a very particular role in the field of immunities. Typically, when one State believes itself, or a high official, to be immune from the jurisdiction of the courts of another State, it

* Visiting Assistant Professor of International Law, Leiden University and independent legal consultant. Former Special Assistant and Legal Officer to President Rosalyn Higgins, International Court of Justice (2006–09) and Associate Legal Adviser to Prosecutor Luis Moreno-Ocampo of the International Criminal Court (2005–06). I am grateful to Ben Batros, Gleider Hernandez, and Amal Alamuddin for their comments on earlier drafts. The views expressed in this chapter are the author's own.

[1] See the concept of 'dialogue' in Canadian constitutional law: PW Hogg and AA Bushell, 'The Charter Dialogue Between Courts and Legislatures (Or Perhaps The Charter of Rights Isn't Such A Bad Thing After All)' (1997) 35 *Osgoode H LJ* 75, 81 f; PW Hogg, AA Bushell Thornton, and WK Wright, 'Charter Dialogue Revisited – Or "Much Ado About Metaphors"' (2007) 45 *Osgoode H LJ* 1, 45 ('Dialogue occurs where a judicial decision striking down a piece of legislation for inconsistency with a Charter right or freedom is followed by some action by the competent legislative body').

challenges the purported exercise of that jurisdiction in the courts of the forum State. This has created a substantial body of national jurisprudence on this aspect of international law.[2]

National courts have not been able to rely on clear codifications of the law on immunity: relevant treaties are very specific in nature and may not be in force;[3] national legislation, where it does exist, tends to focus on civil rather than criminal cases.[4] National judges therefore often turn to customary international law, examining state practice and *opinio juris* to determine the legal rule to settle the dispute before them. International judges, too, are engaged in the same exercise and may turn to the decisions of national courts for evidence of state practice.

Dialogue plays an important role in that courts look to each other's practice to determine the current state of the customary international law on immunities. This judicial dialogue can serve to strengthen (by following another court's position) or weaken (by rejecting another court's position) state practice. By studying this dialogue we can identify factors that encourage interaction, discourage exchange, or have a neutral effect. This chapter is not concerned with the state of customary international law on immunities as such, but rather uses this substantive area of law to explore how international and national courts communicate through their decisions.

The dialogue surrounding the law on immunity has been motivated by a number of developments: states have been expanding the jurisdictional reach of their laws; growing attention is being paid to crimes of universal concern with an attendant drive against impunity for such crimes; the statutes of international criminal tribunals provide that official capacity is not a bar to the exercise of jurisdiction;[5] there are treaties creating excep-

[2] Speech by HE Judge R Higgins, President of the International Court of Justice, 'The Changing Position of Domestic Courts in the International Legal Order' First International Law in Domestic Courts Colloquium, The Hague, 27 March 2008.

[3] See, eg: UN Convention on Jurisdictional Immunities of States and Their Property (not yet in force), adopted by UN GA Res 59/38, Annex, UN Doc A/59/49; Vienna Convention on Consular Relations (24 April 1963) 596 UNTS 261, Vienna Convention on Diplomatic Relations (18 April 1961) 500 UNTS 95.

[4] Foreign States Immunities Act 1985 (Australia); Foreign Sovereign Immunities Act 1976 (USA); State Immunity Act 1978 (UK).

[5] Art 7 of the Charter of the Nuremberg Tribunal, art 6 of the Charter of the Tokyo Tribunal, art 7(2) of the ICTY Statute, art 6(2) of the ICTR Statute, art 27 of the ICC Statute all provide that official capacity shall not exempt a person from criminal responsibility. Schabas makes the point that there is a distinction between the removal of the official capacity defence and immunity; a distinction which is clear in the two parts to art 27 of the ICC Statute: WA Schabas, 'The Special Tribunal for Lebanon: Is a "Tribunal of an International Character" Equivalent to an "International Criminal Court"?' (2008) 21 *Leiden J Int'l L* 526 ff. Indeed, the Statutes of the ICTY and ICTR provide that 'official capacity does not exempt from *responsibility*' – but if immunity is a bar to *jurisdiction* rather than *responsibility* (see para 61 of the ICJ's judgment in the *Arrest Warrant* case), then the provisions are silent as to jurisdiction. Interestingly, the Statute of the Special Tribunal for Lebanon (STL) is silent as to official capacity and the Tribunal will thus have to decide this issue in accordance with customary international law.

tions to immunity at regional and international levels;[6] and work on this topic is being undertaken by the *Institut de Droit International* and the International Law Commission.[7]

How do immunity issues arise in the various courts? States may be parties to treaties where jurisdiction over international crimes is expressly envisaged.[8] A number of states have passed legislation allowing the exercise of jurisdiction over a limited category of offences of universal concern, irrespective of the *situs* of the offence and the nationalities of the alleged perpetrator and the victim.[9] Cases also arise when there is a link to the forum state (for example, territoriality, nationality, passive personality).[10]

[6] See, eg: 1975 Convention against Torture, art 5; 1948 Genocide Convention, art IV; 1972 European Convention on State Immunity.

[7] The *Institut de droit international* created in 1995 the Third Commission (Rapporteur: Lady Fox QC) to examine 'The Fundamental Rights of the Person and the Immunity from Jurisdiction in International Law'. The ILC decided in 2007 to include the topic 'Immunity of State officials from foreign criminal jurisdiction' in its programme of work and appointed Mr Roman A Kolodkin as Special Rapporteur for the topic.

[8] See Convention Against Torture and Other Cruel, Inhuman or Degrading Treatment or Punishment, UN GA Res 39/46, 39 UN GAOR Supp (No 51), UN Doc A/39/51 (1984) art 5(2); First Geneva Convention, 75 UNTS 31 (12 August 1949) art 49; Second Geneva Convention, 75 UNTS 85, 12 August 1949, art 50; Third Geneva Convention, 75 UNTS 135, 12 August 1949, art 129; and Fourth Geneva Convention, 75 UNTS 287, 12 August 1949, art 146. Universal criminal jurisdiction exists over crimes against humanity that were recognised in art 6(2)(c) of the Nuremberg Charter of the International Military Tribunal, 8 UNTS 279, 8 August 1945, including murder, extermination, enslavement, deportation, and other inhumane acts. Compare with the more limited terms of art VI of the Convention on the Prevention and Punishment of the Crime of Genocide, 9 December 1948: 'Persons charged with genocide or any of the other acts enumerated in Article 3 shall be tried by a competent tribunal of the State in the territory of which the act was committed, or by such international penal tribunal as may have jurisdiction with respect to those Contracting Parties which shall have accepted its jurisdiction' (*cf* interpretation in *Prosecutor v Ntuyahaga* ICTR-90-40-T (18 March 1999); *Prosecutor v Tadic*, IT-94-1-AR72, para 62 (2 October 1995). 'Universal jurisdiction' is not the same as the principle *aut dedere aut judicare* whereby parties agree to prosecute or extradite an alleged offender found on their territory. Universal jurisdiction, properly understood, allows a state to exercise jurisdiction over a limited category of international crimes, irrespective of the *situs* of the crime and the nationalities of the perpetrator and victim.

[9] A major study by Amnesty International conducted in 2001 concluded that approximately 125 countries had legislation allowing the exercise of criminal jurisdiction without requiring 'a constructive and effective link' between the crime and the forum state, although as a matter of due process most of those states excluded trials *in absentia*: Amnesty International, *Universal Jurisdiction: The duty of states to enact and enforce legislation*, AI index: IOR 53/002-018/2001, September 2001. Since then, Belgium and Spain, two of the most active users of universal jurisdiction, have moved to repeal or amend their universal jurisdiction laws to make them more restrictive: L Reydams, 'Belgium Reneges on Universality: the 5 August 2003 Act on Grave Breaches of International Humanitarian Law' (2003) 1 *J Int'l Crim Just* 679; Centre for Justice and Accountability, 'Spanish Congress Enacts Bill Restricting Spain's Universal Jurisdiction Law' 4 November 2009.

Some States permit civil claims based on torts committed abroad: see, especially for Europe, Brief of the Amicus Curiae the European Commission Supporting Neither Party, *Sosa v Alvarez-Machain*, No 03-339, US Supreme Court, 23 January 2004.

[10] Some states will exercise criminal jurisdiction only when the defendant is within the state's custody, thereby limiting the scope of universal criminal jurisdiction, as well as the scope of civil actions attached to such jurisdiction. Since jurisdiction exists at the time of the commission of the alleged offence, the presence of the defendant on the state's territory

While Judges Higgins, Kooijmans, and Buergenthal, in their Separate Opinion in the *Arrest Warrant* judgment of the ICJ, saw in the United States' (US) Alien Tort Statute 'the beginnings of a very broad form of extraterritorial jurisdiction' in the civil sphere, they also noted that the US' assertion of such jurisdiction in that statute had 'not attracted the approbation of States generally'.[11]

These trends in treaty practice and within national jurisdictions have been having a knock-on effect in international courts. The European Court of Human Rights (ECtHR), for example, has had to decide whether immunities offered by national courts to high state officials violate Article

after the commission of the alleged offence does not turn universal jurisdiction into jurisdiction based on territoriality. Cases cited in the Brief of the Amicus Curiae the European Commission Supporting Neither Party: *Sosa v Alvarez-Machain*, No 03-339, US Supreme Court, 23 January 2004): eg *France,* Law No 95-1 of 2 January 1995, art 2, implementing Security Council Resolution 827 establishing the International Criminal Tribunal for the former Yugoslavia, in *JORF* 71; 3 January 1995; French Law No 96-432 of 22 May 1996, art 2, implementing Security Council Resolution 955 establishing the International Criminal Tribunal for Rwanda, in *JORF* 7695; 23 May 1996; Cour de Cassation, Decision of 16 January 1998, 102 *RGDIP* 825, 827 (1998) (suspect must be present for exercise of universal jurisdiction for genocide and crimes against humanity); *Netherlands,* Dutch Hoge Raad [Dutch Supreme Court] (Hoge Raad der Nederlanden), No 749/01 (CW 2323) para 8.5 (18 September 2001), available at www.rechtspraak.nl (exercise of jurisdiction over torture committed abroad requires presence of accused). But see: Germany, Federal Code of Criminal Procedure, art 153f (2), No 3 and 4, as amended by art 3, No 5 of the Law introducing a Federal Code on Crimes against international law (Völkerstrafgesetzbuch) (26 June 2002), in *Federal Official Journal, BGBl,* pt I, 2253, 2259 (jurisdiction may be exercised over suspects not present but prosecutors allowed to close investigation if suspect not present and no presence expected). Moreover, in deciding whether to bring or maintain a prosecution, public officials may consider whether another state is better equipped to exercise jurisdiction, or has a greater interest in exercising jurisdiction, because the act occurred on its territory or involved its nationals as perpetrators: eg, *Belgium,* Code of Criminal Procedure, art 12a, No 4, as amended by the law of 5 August 2003 on grave violations of international humanitarian law, in *Moniteur belge* (Official Journal) (7 August 2003), available at www.just.fgov.be (prosecutor will request a magistrate to investigate a complaint unless interests of justice or international obligations require that the matter be brought before an international tribunal or tribunal of another state, provided the alternative tribunal is competent, independent, impartial and fair); *Germany,* Federal Code of Criminal Procedure, art 153f (2) No 4 (prosecutor may decide not to investigate if jurisdiction based on territoriality or nationality of victim or suspect exists elsewhere); *Spain,* Spanish Supreme Court, No 327/2003 (25 February 2003), reprinted in 42 ILM 686, 698 (2003) (deference given to courts in the place where the act committed unless authorities of that state impede prosecution or directly participated in crime).

[11] *Case Concerning the Arrest Warrant of 11 April 2000 (Democratic Republic of the Congo v Belgium)* Judgment, ICJ Reports 2002 3, para 48 Joint Separate Opinion of Judges Higgins, Kooijmans and Buergenthal. In the judgment in the same case, the ICJ pointed out that 'rules governing the jurisdiction of national courts must be carefully distinguished from those governing jurisdictional immunities: jurisdiction does not imply absence of immunity, while absence of immunity does not imply jurisdiction. Thus, although various international conventions on the prevention and punishment of certain serious crimes impose on States obligations of prosecution or extradition, thereby requiring them to extend their criminal jurisdiction, such extension of jurisdiction in no way affects immunities under customary international law' (para 59). The *Arrest Warrant* case examined whether the immunity *ratione personae* of the Minister for Foreign Affairs of the Democratic Republic of the Congo was violated by an international arrest warrant issued by a Belgian court for crimes against humanity.

6 of the European Convention on Human Rights on the right to a fair trial.[12]

Traditionally, a state that believes itself, or its officials, to be immune from the jurisdiction of another state, enters appearance in the court of the state concerned to protest its lack of jurisdiction. That is not a waiver of immunity. But in several instances the aggrieved state has come directly to the ICJ, elevating the matter to an inter-state dispute.[13] Unlike in cases of diplomatic protection, there is no requirement regarding the exhaustion of local remedies. All a state needs to show is that there is a dispute between the parties.

The way the *substance* of the law on immunity is being shaped, splintered or unified through dialogue is not the subject of this chapter. Yet, it is important to bear in mind that courts are grappling with the balance to be struck between the condemnation of serious human rights violations and the principle that states must treat each other as equals not to be subjected to each other's jurisdiction.[14] The nature and extent of the dialogue they engage in affects this balancing act.

After a brief description of the methodology used, this chapter considers how national courts are engaged in dialogue on immunities, examining the circumstances that encourage a high level of dialogue and those that discourage it. The chapter then turns to the dialogue among international courts, including their use of national decisions to identify international custom. The chapter concludes with a discussion of emerging patterns in the dialogue among courts in immunities cases.

II. METHODOLOGY

This chapter is based on a survey of 34 cases involving immunities in national and international courts.[15] The cases were initially selected based on a search of the *Oxford Reports on International Law*. Additional cases were identified through references made to them in academic articles and in judgments.

[12] *McElhinney v Ireland,* App No 31253/96; *Al-Adsani v UK,* App No 35763/97; *Fogary v UK,* App No 37112/97 2001. For the purposes of this chapter, the ECtHR is considered an international court.

[13] *Arrest Warrant* case; *Certain Questions of Mutual Assistance in Criminal Matters (Djibouti v France)* Judgment of 2008; the withdrawn *Certain Criminal Proceedings in France (Republic of the Congo v France)*; and Rwanda's Application against France (not yet on the General List due to the absence of France's consent to jurisdiction under art 38(5) of the Rules of Court).

[14] See Court of Appeal of Ontario in *Bouzari v Islamic Republic of Iran* (2004) 71 OR (3d) 675, para 95.

[15] The focus is on cases involving immunities of state officials, but there are some cases on state (sovereign) immunity in the study due to the relevant discussion of the law on immunity in these cases. The chapter covers developments up to December 2009.

The national courts covered by this survey comprise (in alphabetical order): the Austrian Supreme Court, the Belgian *Cour de cassation*, the Dutch *Hoge Raad*, the French *Cour de cassation*, the Greek Supreme Court, the Italian *Corte di Cazzazione*, the Ontario (Canada) Court of Appeal, the Sierra Leone Supreme Court, the Swiss Federal Supreme Court, the United Kingdom (UK) House of Lords and the Bow Street Magistrates' Court, and the US Second, Fourth, Seventh and District of Columbia Circuit Courts. The international courts covered in the study are: the International Court of Justice (ICJ), the International Criminal Tribunal for the Former Yugoslavia (ICTY), the European Court of Human Rights (ECtHR) and the Special Court for Sierra Leone (SCSL). The focus is on cases decided in the past decade.

In examining each case from national or international courts, I consider both quantitative and qualitative aspects: whether cases from other jurisdictions are cited; if so, which jurisdictions tend to be referred to and for which legal issues; to what end are these external citations made (to reinforce a point, to assess the state of customary international law, to distinguish the facts); and what patterns of convergence and divergence are emerging.

III. DIALOGUE ON IMMUNITIES IN NATIONAL COURTS

This section examines the citation, discussion and possible application by national judges of the decisions of other national courts or of international courts.

National jurisdictions characterised by a high level of judicial dialogue on the law on immunity, such as the UK and Italy, tend to not only cite cases from other jurisdictions, but also to engage in in-depth, critical analysis, drawing on a wide range of cases for a variety of points of law. For example, the UK House of Lords judgment in *Jones v Saudi Arabia*[16] refers to cases from Canada, Germany, the US, Ireland, Italy, and Greece as well as the decisions of international courts such as the ICJ, ICTY and ECtHR. The *Ferrini* judgment of the Italian *Corte di Cazzazione* includes references to case law of international courts (ICJ, ICTY and ECtHR) and national courts (UK, Canada). Further, the citations are not merely to the holding of the judgment, but include references to specific opinions and lower court decisions.[17]

This variety of citations (even of unreported cases) is a product of the interest and ability of counsel to conduct comparative research and include

[16] *Jones and ors v Ministry of Interior (Saudi Arabia) and ors* [2006] UKHL 26, 14 June 2006.

[17] See, eg: reference to Ontario Court of Appeal Judgment in the *Bouzari* case as well as the reference to the Ontario Superior Court of Justice judgment.

such material in their submissions to the court.[18] The counsel in *Jones* indeed went beyond case law to draw the House of Lords' attention to comments made by the Committee against Torture on periodic reports by Canada and state practice in the ratification of the Convention against Torture.

Even more important to the level of dialogue than the role of counsel, however, is the attitude of judges to the case law of other jurisdictions. This, in turn, is to a large extent a product of the legal culture of the jurisdiction in question. The House of Lords demonstrates great comfort with engaging in dialogue, even to the point of qualifying and shading their use of external sources in previous judgments. In the following passage from the leading Opinion of Lord Bingham in *Jones v Saudi Arabia,* he enters into a dialogue not only with the ICTY *Furundzija* case, but also with his own use of it in an earlier judgment:

> In the course of my opinion in *A v Secretary of State for the Home Department (No 2),* above, para 33, I quoted with approval a long passage from the judgment of the International Criminal Tribunal for the Former Yugoslavia in *Prosecutor v Furundzija,* above. The passage quoted included para 155 where the tribunal, discussing the possibility that a state might authorise torture by some legislative, administrative or judicial act, said:
>
>> 'If such a situation were to arise, the national measures, violating the general principle and any relevant treaty provision, would produce the legal effects discussed above and in addition would not be accorded international legal recognition. Proceedings could be initiated by potential victims if they had locus standi before a competent international or national judicial body with a view to asking it to hold the national measure to be internationally unlawful; or the victim could bring a civil suit for damage in a foreign court, which would therefore be asked inter alia to disregard the legal value of the national authorising act.'
>
> I do not understand the tribunal to have been addressing the issue of state immunity in civil proceedings; but if it was, its observations, being those of a criminal tribunal trying a criminal case in which no such issue arose, were, on that issue, plainly obiter, as was my citation of them.[19]

The House of Lords in *Jones* did not merely cite cases from other jurisdictions to illustrate or support a point of law. Rather, the Opinions of Lords Bingham and Hoffman engage in dialogue with cases decided in national and international jurisdictions. Lord Bingham cast a critical eye over the *Ferrini* judgment of the Italian *Corte di Cazzazione*, examining which cases it relied upon and which cases it distinguished; he suggested that 'the decision was influenced by the occurrence of some of the unlawful

[18] See reference to: *Syrian Ambassador (Former) to the German Democratic Republic,* unreported, 10 June 1997, Federal Constitutional Court, Case No 2 BvR 1516/96 in *Ex p Pinochet Ugarte (No 3)* [1999] 2 All ER 97, [2000] 1 AC 147.

[19] *Jones and ors v Ministry of Interior (Saudi Arabia) and ors* [2006] UKHL 26, 14 June 2006, para 21.

conduct within the forum state' despite the Italian Court's closing statement to the contrary.[20] Lord Bingham even entered into comparisons between Italian and Canadian decisions, noting:

> The *Ferrini* decision cannot in my opinion be treated as an accurate statement of international law as generally understood; and one swallow does not make a rule of international law. The more closely-reasoned decisions in *Bouzari v Islamic Republic of Iran* (2002) 124 1LR 427, (2004) 71 OR (3d) 675 are to the contrary effect.[21]

In a similar vein, Lord Bingham noted that he did not need to examine in detail the US case law cited by the claimant because the cases did not 'express principles widely shared and observed among other nations'.[22] To reinforce this conclusion, he cited the Joint Separate Opinion of Judges Higgins, Kooijmans and Buergenthal in the *Arrest Warrant* case.[23]

For the House of Lords in *Jones*, dialogue included critical analysis. Lord Bingham's comments on the ECtHR's *Al-Adsani v UK* case included an observation that it was 'a narrowly split decision' and a confession that he had difficulty accepting the view that Article 6 of the European Convention on Human Rights was engaged by the grant of immunity of Kuwait, given that a state cannot be said to deny access to its court if it has no access to give.[24]

Lord Hoffman's analysis of the Greek cases is striking in that he looked into the dialogue that occurred between Greek and German courts in the *Distomo Massacre* case. Noting that the original judgment of the Greek Court of Cassation was 'coldly received' by the German Supreme Court when the claimants sought to enforce it directly in Germany, he gave little weight to the Greek case law.[25]

Even lower down in the court hierarchy of the UK, there is a visible engagement with the case law of other courts. Decisions of the UK Bow Street Magistrates' Court on immunities do not merely cite other cases, but also analyse the text of decisions.[26] Moreover, cases from a variety of jurisdictions are referred to. The *Re Mugabe* judgment cites cases by the ICJ, the Belgian *Cour de cassation* and the French *Cour de cassation*.[27] Nonetheless there are some signs of slippage, of mistakes in terminology, which perhaps reveal a discomfort or confusion with the foreign and

[20] *Jones and ors v Ministry of Interior (Saudi Arabia) and ors* [2006] UKHL 26, 14 June 2006, para 22.

[21] ibid.

[22] ibid para 20.

[23] *Democratic Republic of the Congo v Belgium (Case concerning Arrest Warrant of 11 April 2000)* [2002] ICJ Rep 3, para 48, cited in ibid para 20.

[24] ibid para 14.

[25] ibid para 62.

[26] See the discussion of the words 'such as' used in the ICJ *Arrest Warrant* case in *Re Mofaz* (12 February 2004) ILDC 97 (UK 2004) (UK Bow Street Magistrates' Court).

[27] *Re Mugabe*, first instance, unreported decision, 14 January 2004.

international case law. In the *Re Mofaz* case, the single judge inaccurately referred to 'State immunity' as regards the ICJ *Arrest Warrant* case whereas what was at issue there was immunity *ratione personae*.[28]

The UK House of Lords' willingness to engage in in-depth dialogue and critical analysis may be explained by the fact that the UK legal system sees itself as part of larger entities; the Commonwealth and, more recently, the European Union. The leadership of certain judges, such as the late Lord Bingham, with a strong interest in international and comparative law has also been important. As for Italy, the *Ferrini* judgment itself contains an explanation for its engagement in dialogue: legal norms should not be interpreted in isolation because they 'complete and integrate each other and condition each other's application'.[29] Italian judges deciding immunity cases have also engaged in selective citation of separate or dissenting opinions. The judgment in *Germany v Mantelli and ors*[30] cites the dissenting opinion in the ECtHR's *Al-Adsani v UK* case[31] and *obiter dictum* in the *Kalogeropoulou and ors v Greece and Germany* case[32] to support its point that there is the emergence of a customary rule denying immunity where the defendant state is accused of crimes against humanity. Interestingly, the series of Italian cases on the state immunity of Germany, especially *Ferrini*, triggered the decision of Germany to bring a case to the ICJ against Italy in December 2008, alleging that 'Through its judicial practice . . . Italy has infringed and continues to infringe its obligations towards Germany under international law'.[33]

Historical links between jurisdictions can also lead to high levels of dialogue. In the New Zealand case of *Fang and ors v Jiang and ors*, the judge reserved his decision until the House of Lords had handed down its decision in *Jones v Saudi Arabia* since the plaintiffs had relied heavily on the Court of Appeal decision in that case in their pleadings.[34] Once the House of Lords' judgment was delivered, reversing the Court of Appeal, the judge in the New Zealand case followed its finding that state officials enjoyed immunity *ratione materiae* from civil proceedings even if accused of torture.[35]

[28] See analysis of Roger O'Keefe in the *Oxford Reports in International Law*'s report on this case.

[29] Italian Court of Cassation, *Ferrini v Germany*, Appeal decision, no 5044/4, 11 March 2004, para 9.2 of translation by *ORIL*.

[30] Italian *Corte di Cazzazione/Germany v Mantelli and ors*, Preliminary Order on Jurisdiction, No 14201/2008, 29 May 2008.

[31] *Al-Adsani v UK*, App No 35763/97, 21 November 2001 (Dissenting Opinion).

[32] *Kalogeropoulou and ors v Greece and Germany*, App No 59021/00, 12 December 2002.

[33] Application of Germany: www.icj-cij.org/docket/files/143/14925.pdf (last visited 1 June 2011).

[34] *Fang and ors v Jiang and ors*, ex parte application for leave to serve statement of claim and notice of proceeding outside New Zealand, High Court of Auckland [2007] NZAR 420; ILDC 1226 (NZ 2006).

[35] The judge also made reference to cases by the ECtHR, the ICJ, *Bouzari* judgment of the Ontario Court of Appeal, and the House of Lords judgment in *Pinochet III*.

In national jurisdictions with a low level of judicial dialogue, such as the US and Switzerland, the reluctance to cite cases from other jurisdictions usually originates with counsel. This leads to an inward-looking jurisprudence, with judgments tending exclusively to cite domestic case law.[36] This is in part dependent on whether foreign and international cases are being cited in the parties' pleadings as US judges traditionally do not look beyond the parties' submissions to determine applicable (or foreign) law.[37]

During 2004, cases were filed in the US and the UK against Robert Mugabe, President of Zimbabwe, alleging serious human rights abuses. The decision of the US Second Circuit Court of Appeals was issued nine months after the decision of the UK Bow Street Magistrates' Court,[38] but made no reference to the earlier case.[39] There are several possible reasons for this restraint on dialogue between the courts. First, the UK case was unreported and thus may not have come to the attention of the US court. Second, the US case focused on statutory interpretation of the Alien Tort Statute and the Torture Victim Protection Act rather than the current state of the international law of immunity for Heads of State. Third, in the US case the Federal Government filed a 'suggestion of immunity' that perhaps deterred further inquiry into the case law of other jurisdictions.[40] On the rare occasions when US courts have cited case law from other jurisdictions in immunities cases, brief reference has been made to the 'classic' cases: the ICJ *Arrest Warrant* case (for its statement on the immunities of Heads of State and Ministers for Foreign Affairs)[41] and the ICTY *Furundzija* case (for its characterisation of torture as a violation of *jus cogens*).[42]

The one case in this field decided in Switzerland displayed a similar approach to the US case law in its hesitancy to cite case law from other

[36] See, eg: the US Fourth Circuit Court of Appeals, *Yousuf v Samantar,* 8 January 2009; Seventh Circuit Court of Appeals, *Wei Ye v Jiang Zemin*, 383 F3d 620 (2004), 8 September 2004. See also: the earlier case in the DC Circuit, *Princz v Federal Republic of Germany* (1994), in which the majority made reference to the Nuremberg Trial judgment but not other cases and Judge Wald (in dissent) made reference to the German Federal Constitutional Court and *Barcelona Traction Light & Power Co (Belgium v Spain)* 1970 ICJ Reports, 4. It should be noted that some US judges have spoken strongly in favour of using foreign case law, including Justice Ginsburg and Justice Wald, who see foreign decisions as 'a pool of potential and useful information and thought that must be mined with caution and restraint'. (Ruth Bader Ginsburg, Assoc Justice, US Supreme Court, Address Before South African Constitutional Court (7 February 2006) (transcript available at www.concourt.gov.za/site/ginsberg.html)).

[37] M Damaska, *The Faces of Justice and State Authority: A Comparative Approach to the Legal Process* (New Haven, Yale University Press, 1986) 139.

[38] UK Bow Street Magistrates' Court, *Re Mugabe*, first instance, unreported decision, 14 January 2004.

[39] *Tachiona v United States*, 386 F3d 205, 6 October 2004.

[40] See also: the suggestion of immunity filed in *Wei Ye v Jiang Zemin*, 383 F3d 620 (2004), 8 September 2004.

[41] See Seventh Circuit Court of Appeals/*Enahoro and ors v Abubakar*, 408 F3d 877 (23 May 2005).

[42] See DC Circuit Court of Appeals, *Belhas v Ya'alon*, 515 F3d 1279, 15 February 2008.

jurisdictions. This may nonetheless be explained by the fact that Swiss courts traditionally cite scholarly writing in textbooks or journal articles rather than case law. Indeed, Swiss courts are held by law to focus on 'the established scholarship and interpretation'.[43] In *Adamov v Federal Office of Justice*, the Swiss Federal Supreme Court confirmed the principle that a former Minister of Atomic Energy of the Russian Federation enjoyed immunity from jurisdiction for official acts during his time in office without citing any cases in support of this proposition.[44] In particular, one would have expected a reference to the ICJ *Arrest Warrant* case.

Sometimes a national court will make a conscious effort to discern the view of the 'international community', yet only engage in dialogue regarding specific cases to a limited degree. This may be due to a legal tradition of citing scholarship rather than case law or due to the brevity of the judgments themselves. In *W v Prince of Liechtenstein and ors*,[45] the Austrian Supreme Court noted a discernable trend in international law towards restricting the principle of absolute immunity. In the court's view, this trend was not necessarily limited to criminal prosecution, but might also extend to civil claims. It observed that as regards the immunity of (former) Heads of State:

> [T]he international community increasingly calls for a limitation of this privilege and it has been declared irrelevant by courts and judicial authorities in the event of aggravated violations of public international law . . . which cannot be encompassed under the official acts of a Head of State (and also must not be encompassed under such acts).[46]

The Court cited not the UK *[Ex parte] Pinochet (No 3)* judgment[47] itself, but rather an article in German on the case.[48] In this way, the dialogue between the courts was mediated through academic scholarship. Indeed, in Austria the tradition is to cite leading textbooks rather than case law.[49]

The judgment of the French *Cour de Cassation* in the *Qadhafi* case[50] is less than two pages in length. The brief style of judgment, in which names are not mentioned, renders it difficult for the Court to engage in substantive

[43] Art 1, para 3 of the Swiss Civil Code, cited in Marc Forster, 'Functions and Practice of Legal Citing: Towards a Uniform International Quotation System', *Int'l J Legal Info* (1995) 153.

[44] Appeal Judgment, No 1A 288/2005, 22 December 2005.

[45] Final Appeal/Cassation, 7 Ob 316/00x; ILDC 1 (AT 2001). The case was concerned with family status, but the Court engaged with debate on immunity and human rights.

[46] ibid para 13.

[47] The *Pinochet* case concerned the immunity *ratione materiae* of the former Head of State of Chile, specifically whether he could be extradited to Spain to face charges of torture.

[48] Wirth, *Staatenimmunität für internationale Verbrechen – das zweite Pinochet-Urteil des House of Lords*, Jura2 2000/2, 11 [12] cited at para 11 of the judgment in *W v Prince of Liechtenstein and ors*.

[49] NG Foster, *Austrian Legal System and Laws* (Routledge Cavendish, 2003) 54 ff, 86 (on academic opinion as source of supplementary doctrinal law).

[50] Arrêt no 1414, 13 March 2001.

dialogue. Nonetheless, the judgment reveals a concern for the developments in other jurisdictions, referring to 'this stage of the development of customary international law', 'international custom' and 'general principles of international law'. The brevity of the judgment meant that the Court did not specify which type of immunity (*ratione materiae* or *ratione personae*) was at issue.

In some jurisdictions, the court engages experts who bring relevant national and international case law to the attention of the judges. In the *Bouterse* case, the Amsterdam Court of Appeal sought an expert opinion from a Professor of Leiden University on the international law aspects of the case.[51] In the *Bouzari* case,[52] the Superior Court of Justice of Ontario heard expert evidence from a Professor of the University of Toronto called by the claimant and a Professor from the London School of Economics called by the Attorney General of Canada, who had been granted leave to intervene with respect to international law and Charter issues. The judgments of both the Superior Court of Justice and the Ontario Court of Appeal draw on the evidence of these experts. The judgments display a deep understanding of the UK *[Ex parte] Pinochet (No 3)* judgment, delving into the individual opinions of the Law Lords and the distinctions between them. This dialogue was most likely facilitated by the expert evidence.

In some national jurisdictions attempts to engage in dialogue have created confusion and uncertainty. Belgium is a jurisdiction that tends to be outward-looking; it has a legal culture that is comfortable with international law, and is active in invoking it on the world stage.[53] The Court of Cassation in the *Re Sharon and Yaron* case[54] claimed that the ICJ *Arrest Warrant* case held that international law conferred absolute 'functional immunity' for Ministers of Foreign Affairs, when in fact the ICJ judgment was limited to immunity *ratione personae*. This apparent slippage in terminology is due to the fact that in Belgium, functional immunity is interchangeable with immunity *ratione personae*.[55] The judgment went on to base itself on the *Qadhafi* judgment of the French *Cour de cassation* rather than the ICJ's *Arrest Warrant* case, even though the ICJ case made the same point of law and Belgium was the Respondent.[56] This perhaps indicates a misunderstanding of the scope of the ICJ's case. It may also be because the

[51] The Court of Appeal did not follow Professor Dugard's opinion on each point. See: E de Wet, 'The Prohibition of Torture as an international norm of jus cogens and its implications for national and customary law' (2004) 15 *Eur J Int'l L* 97, 116 ff.

[52] *Bouzari v Islamic Republic of Iran* (2002) 124 1LR 427, (2004) 71 OR (3d) 675.

[53] See, eg: the international arrest warrant at the core of the *Arrest Warrant* case *(Democratic Republic of the Congo v Belgium)*, ICJ Reports 2002, and the 2009 request for the indication of provisional measures in *Questions relating to the Obligation to Prosecute or Extradite (Belgium v Senegal)*.

[54] Final appeal, Cass no p 02 1139 F/1, 12 February 2003.

[55] Arts 101 and 104 of the Constitution of Belgium.

[56] The point being the immunity of Heads of State/Government from the criminal jurisdiction of a foreign state.

Belgian courts prefer to cite cases from a proximate national jurisdiction with civil law traditions, like France.

In the Supreme Court of Sierra Leone, a judgment on Head of State immunity[57] cited the UK *Pinochet* cases and the ICJ's *Arrest Warrant* case but the Court did not discuss immunity *ratione materiae* nor contrast it with immunity *ratione personae*. The Court also conflated the concepts of immunity and criminal responsibility despite the distinction made in the ICJ *Arrest Warrant* case.[58] Finally, the Special Supreme Court of Greece's judgment in *Germany v Margellos*, makes reference to the ICJ *Arrest Warrant* case and the *McElhinney* and *Al-Adsani* cases of the ECtHR. The joint dissent construed *McElhinney* as confirming that there exists in customary international law an exception for torts perpetrated in the territory of the forum by the state itself or persons for whom the state is responsible. However, this construction was based on an incomplete quotation from the judgment, omitting the key phrase 'but this practice is by no means universal'.[59]

In sum, dialogue on immunities in national courts ranges from in-depth, critical analysis to confused or selective citation to the complete absence of reference to the decisions of other jurisdictions. The factors that affect the level of judicial dialogue include the role of counsel, the attitude of the judges, the use of experts, the sources of law traditionally employed and the style of judgment-writing.

IV. DIALOGUE ON IMMUNITIES IN INTERNATIONAL COURTS

Article 38 of the Statute of the ICJ, which effectively states the sources of law for the Court to apply, provides that the Court can look to 'judicial decisions' – not only 'international judicial decisions' – as a subsidiary means for the determination of rules of law. Article 38 also states that the Court shall apply, *inter alia*, 'international custom, as evidence of a general practice accepted as law'. The process of identifying custom may involve a close examination of state practice, including the practice of national courts.

[57] *Sesay and ors v President of the Special Court for Sierra Leone*, SC no 1/2003, 14 October 2005.

[58] See: analysis of Sonkita Conteh in the *ORIL* for this case.

[59] Special Supreme Court of Greece, *German v Margellos*, Petition for cassation, 6/2002, 17 September 2002, para 14 quoting 'there appears to be a trend in international and comparative law towards limiting State immunity in respect of personal injury caused by an act or omission within the forum State (*McElhinney* para 36) – but omitting the remainder. This point was discovered by Maria Gavouneli in her report in the *ORIL*, para A.7. This is not an isolated instance of misquotation: see, eg the analysis in ILDC 855 (GR 2004) at [A4] and [A5] (the court copied the wrong page of the textbook submitted to it); see also the analysis in ILDC 831 (GR 2006) at [A2]–[A5], in particular [A5] where the Greek Supreme Court misconstrues the ECtHR in *Sidiropoulos*.

In his article on the role of domestic courts in the case law of the ICJ, Nollkaemper argues that the ICJ remains an unlikely forum for providing substantive evidence of dialogue.[60] Although its Statute clearly provides for engagement with the practice of national courts, the ICJ's role largely remains confined to traditional inter-state disputes that have little chance of being litigated in a domestic context. He explains that 'Its powers and efficacy depend strongly on consent and support by States; elevating judgments of any single State to a different status from "facts" sits uneasily with this dominant paradigm'.[61]

When analysing the relationship between the ICJ and US courts in the context of the implementation of the *Breard, LaGrand* and *Avena* cases, Nollkaemper observes:

> It thus can be said that the Court sparked 'a judicial dialogue by setting a few minimum requirements and leaving the bulk of the task of implementation to the complete discretion of the United States'. However, it must be added that there is not too much evidence that domestic courts accept a role in the implementation of the judgments of the Court. . . . The refusals by US courts to respect provisional measures issued by the ICJ in the *Breard* and *LaGrand* cases are illustrative. . . . Indeed, Simma and Hoppe conclude that 'there seems to be a lack of judicial dialogue between the ICJ, which is empowered to interpret the Convention, and U.S. courts that face claims under it' and that 'where there are actually signs that such dialogue takes place, we frequently encounter misunderstandings leading to erroneous conclusions'.[62]

Two remarks may be made in this regard. First, Nollkaemper's article and the article by Simma and Hoppe to which he refers[63] were written before the latest instalment in the *Avena* case: the 2008 Request for Interpretation of the Judgment submitted by Mexico along with a request for the indication of provisional measures.[64] These requests were predicated in part on the judgment of the US Supreme Court in *Medellín v Texas*[65] and various decisions taken by Texan courts, including the Court of Criminal Appeals. These cases provide rich material for examining judicial dialogue on implementation between the ICJ and US courts.[66] Second, the field of

[60] A Nollkaemper, 'The Role of Domestic Courts in the Case Law of the International Court of Justice' (2006) 5 *Chinese J Int'l L* 301–22, section IV.

[61] ibid.

[62] ibid section III.C (fnn omitted).

[63] B Simma and C Hoppe, 'From LaGrand and Avena to Medellin: A Rocky Road Toward Implementation' (2005) 14 *Tulane J Int'l & Comp L* 7.

[64] *Request for Interpretation of the Judgment of 31 March 2004 in the Case concerning Avena and Other Mexican Nationals (Mexico v United States of America*, Order of 16 July 2008 on the Request for the Indication of Provisional Measures; Judgment of 19 January 2009.

[65] *Supreme Court Reporter*, vol 128, 2008, 1346.

[66] See, eg: the ICJ's statement at para 36 of the judgment on interpretation: 'The Court notes without necessarily agreeing with certain points made by the Supreme Court in its reasoning regarding international law that the Supreme Court has stated that the *Avena* Judgment creates an obligation that is binding on the United States'.

immunities perhaps gives greater scope for interaction between the ICJ and national courts, rendering the traditional inter-state character of ICJ cases less of an obstacle to dialogue.[67]

National case law played an important role in the ICJ *Arrest Warrant* judgment. The ICJ, so as to discern state practice, looked to national courts and national legislatures to illuminate the position in customary international law as it related to immunities in national courts. The judgment referred to the judgments rendered by the House of Lords in the UK and by the *Cour de cassation* in France in the *Pinochet* and *Qadhafi* cases respectively.[68]

In the 2008 *Djibouti v France* case,[69] one of the issues before the Court was the existence and scope of immunity from jurisdiction of the State Prosecutor and Head of National Security of Djibouti. Both Parties made extensive reference in their pleadings to international and national case law in this regard. Nonetheless, the judgment found that certain legal preconditions – that the acts complained of were the acts of the Government of Djibouti and that the persons in question were its organs, agencies, or instrumentalities in carrying them out – had not been met and made no reference to case law from other jurisdictions.[70]

Instead of an ongoing conversation, the ICJ and other courts appear to be, as President Higgins has put it, 'engaged in a slightly wary *pas de deux*, where national courts watch us and we watch the State practice that their judgments represent'.[71] That state practice is not referred to in the judgments unless the Court is engaged in analysing the current state of customary international law. In other words, the Court appears to turn to the judgments of other courts and tribunals only in the absence of an applicable treaty, a relevant prior pronouncement by the ICJ or as a supplement to other manifestations of state practice (national legislation, General Assembly or Security Council resolutions).

It may be observed that the level of dialogue is more intense and detailed in separate opinions rather than judgments of the ICJ. For instance, in the Joint Separate Opinion in the *Arrest Warrant* case, Judges Higgins, Kooijmans, and Buergenthal analysed state practice, referring to the *Bouterse* case of the Court of Appeal of Amsterdam, all three of the

[67] Nollkaemper suggests the possibility for evolution in the relation between the ICJ and national jurisdictions, stating 'it may well be that in the next 60 years of the Court, the relationship between the Court and domestic courts does take on a more complementary character': A Nollkaemper, 'The Role of Domestic Courts in the Case Law of the International Court of Justice' (2006) 5 *Chinese J Int'l L* 301–22, section IV.

[68] See: para 60.

[69] *Certain questions of mutual assistance in criminal matters (Djibouti v France)*, Judgment, Merits, ICJ Reports 2008.

[70] ibid para 196.

[71] Speech by HE Judge Rosalyn Higgins, President of the International Court of Justice, First International Law in Domestic Courts Colloquium, 'The Changing Position of Domestic Courts in the International Legal Order', The Hague, 27 March 2008.

Pinochet cases in the House of Lords, the *Nulyarimma* and *Polyukhovich* cases in the Australian High Court, the *Cvjetkovic* case in the Austrian Supreme Court, the *in re Javor, Munyeshyaka* and *Qadhafi* cases in the French *Cour d'appel*, and US cases brought under the Alien Tort Statute. Ultimately, they could not deduce – and neither could the majority – that there existed any form of exception in general international law to the rule according immunity from criminal jurisdiction to incumbent Ministers for Foreign Affairs, even where they are suspected of having committed war crimes or crimes against humanity.[72] Unlike judgments of the Court, separate opinions do not require the input of the plenary bench, which thus provides for flexibility in referring to and discussing cases from other jurisdictions.

Given that the issue of immunities is raised in a number of cases on the Court's docket,[73] there will be further opportunities for the *pas de deux* between the ICJ and other courts to develop.

The ICTY has a more regular engagement with the case law of other courts, including in the field of immunities. During a lengthy exchange on the immunities of a Head of State between Judge Robinson and Steven Kay QC during the *Slobodan Milosevic* trial, Mr Kay asserted that 'a national decision doesn't bind an international court', referring in particular to the *Pinochet (No 3)* judgment.[74] Judge Robinson responded with a succinct description of the role of national case law at the ICTY:

> [A national decision] doesn't bind it, but it goes to the question of the development of custom, of a customary rule of law. It is quite clear that decisions of national courts can be considered in determining whether a rule of customary law has developed. That's very evident, and no citation is needed for that. [75]

The references to national and international case law at the ICTY have no doubt been facilitated by the submission of amicus briefs. Thirteen such briefs were submitted in the *Blaskic Subpoena Appeal*[76] and the resulting

[72] *Arrest Warrant of 11 April 2000 (Democratic Republic of the Congo v Belgium), Judgment, ICJ Reports 2002*, 24.

[73] Case between Germany and Italy concerning jurisdictional immunities of the state; Case between Belgium and Senegal concerning the obligation to prosecute or extradite Hissène Habré, former President of Chad; Case between Republic of the Congo and France regarding measures of investigation and prosecution taken in France against the President, Minister of the Interior, Inspector-General of the Armed Forces, Commander of the Presidential Guard (withdrawn in November 2010 at request of the Republic of the Congo); and the Application (not yet acknowledged by France and thus not yet on the General List) by Rwanda against France concerning international arrest warrants issued by French judicial authorities against three Rwandan officials regarding the downing of the aircraft carrying the Heads of State of Rwanda and Burundi.

[74] ICTY Transcript of 29 October 2001 in the *Milosevic* case, exchange between Judge Robinson and Mr Stephen Kay, 43.

[75] ibid.

[76] *Prosecutor v Tihomir Blaskic*, Appeals Chamber, 29 October 1997, Judgment on the Request of the Republic of Croatia for Review of the Decision of Trial Chamber II of 18 July 1997.

judgment on the immunity *ratione materiae* of state officials referred to the position of France in the *Rainbow Warrior* case, the Supreme Court of Israel in the *Eichmann* case, as well as US cases from 1797 and 1840 (*Governor Collott* and *McLeod*).[77]

The ECtHR, by its very nature, is engaged in an ongoing dialogue with national jurisdictions. It is thus unsurprising that its case law on immunities makes extensive reference to national (especially European) case law in an effort to discern trends. In the *McElhinney* case, on the question of immunity for *acta jure imperii*, the Court referred to cases from Austria, France, Germany, Italy, Spain, and Switzerland.[78] In the *Al-Adsani v UK* case, the majority referred the 1999 Report on Jurisdictional Immunities of States and their Property by the working group of the International Law Commission (ILC) as a 'short-cut' to analysing the case law of national jurisdictions.[79] In some cases, national courts had shown sympathy for the argument that states are not entitled to plead immunity where there has been a violation of human rights norms with the character of *jus cogens*, although in most cases the plea of sovereign immunity had succeeded.[80] The working group of the ILC did, however, note recent developments that may give support to the view that a state could not plead immunity in respect of gross human rights violations, including the *Pinochet (No 3)* case. After using the ILC report as a launching pad, the majority engaged in an in-depth analysis of the *Pinochet (No 3)* case, paying attention to what it perceived as the distinction between immunity from civil jurisdiction and from criminal jurisdiction.[81]

The Special Court for Sierra Leone has had one major case in this field concerning the question of the immunity of Charles Taylor, who was President of Liberia at the time criminal proceedings were initiated.[82] The dialogue in the case was limited, with the judgment only referring to the ICJ's *Arrest Warrant* case and the statement of Lord Slynn of Hadley in

[77] Paras 38–41.

[78] *McElhinney v Ireland*, 21 November 2001 (ECtHR) para 27.

[79] *Al-Adsani v UK* App No 35763/97, 21 November 2001, paras 23–24.

[80] It cited (UK) *Al-Adsani v State of Kuwait* 100 International Law Reports 465, 471; (New Zealand) *Controller and Auditor General v Sir Ronald Davidson* [1996] 2 New Zealand Law Reports 278, particularly 290 (per Cooke P); Dissenting Opinion of Justice Wald in (US) *Princz v Federal Republic of Germany* 26 F3d 1166 (DC Cir 1994), 1176–1185; *Siderman de Blake v Republic of Argentina* 965 F2d 699 (9th Cir 1992); *Argentine Republic v Amerada Hess Shipping Corporation* 488 US 428 (1989); *Saudi Arabia v Nelson* 100 *ILR* 544.

[81] Para 34. *cf Ould Dah v France*, App No 13113/03, Decision of the Fifth Section, 17 March 2009, holding that in criminal proceedings for torture, national amnesty laws have no effect. In June 2009, a seven-judge chamber of the ECtHR decided unanimously to follow *Al-Adsani* and *Kalogeropoulou* decisions and uphold sovereign immunity the face of a claim brought by a French national for compensation from Germany for forced labour during the Second World War: *Décision sur la recevabilité de la requête no 14717/06 présentée par Georges Grosz contre la France*, 16 June 2009.

[82] Special Court for Sierra Leone, Appeals Chamber, 31 May 2004, *Prosecutor v Charles Ghankay Taylor*, Case No SCSL-2003-01-I, Decision on Immunity from Jurisdiction, 31 May 2004.

the *Pinochet (No 3)* case. The Court mainly relied on Article 6(2) of its Statute to reach its conclusion that Charles Taylor did not benefit from any form of immunity.

For international courts, dialogue is a means for analysing state practice and thus assessing the status of customary international law on the issue of immunity. Some courts are embedded in co-operative relationships with national jurisdictions (ICTY, ECtHR) and thus engage in a high level of dialogue. The ICJ, on the other hand, only refers to decisions of national and international courts when other sources of law (treaty, custom) are unavailable or uncertain and where the resolution of the dispute before it requires a determination of the current state of the law on immunity.

V. PATTERNS OF DIALOGUE

The above discussion demonstrates that dialogue is occurring to different degrees and taking on different forms in a variety of jurisdictions.

The engagement with case law from other jurisdictions is facilitated by the pleadings of counsel, the submission of amicus briefs, and the knowledge, interest, and personalities of the judges on the Bench.[83] The sheer availability of judgments is also an issue – some judgments are unreported and many are not translated into other languages.

There does not appear to be any connection between the level of dialogue in the field of immunities and the monist/dualist dichotomy. Indeed, the UK, a dualist system, is currently the national jurisdiction that is most engaged in dialogue, whereas the monist systems of the US, Switzerland and Austria – which theoretically consider national and international law as parts of one legal order – demonstrate less engagement with the case law of other jurisdictions, including international judicial decisions.

It is somewhat ironic that it is in common law jurisdictions – traditionally associated with the slow process of developing rules through an accumulation on judgments on similar cases – that immunity rules are being codified,[84] whereas civil law jurisdictions – associated with the systematic codification of rules – generally have no governing code on this topic and still apply customary international law.[85] Does the existence of a Statute

[83] eg, Judge Cassese, former President of the ICTY, had a very strong interest and knowledge of case law from national and international courts. The judgments he was involved in at the ICTY are notable for their extensive reference to national case law, including cases from hundreds of years ago. See, eg: *Prosecutor v Tihomir Blaskic*, Appeals Chamber, 29 October 1997, Judgment on the Request of the Republic of Croatia for Review of the Decision of Trial Chamber II of 18 July 1997.

[84] Foreign States Immunities Act 1985 (Australia); Foreign Sovereign Immunities Act 1976 (USA); State Immunity Act 1978 (UK).

[85] See for an explanation of the machineries of justice of the common law (Anglo-American) and civil law (Continental) systems: M Damaska, *The Faces of Justice and State Authority: A Comparative Approach to the Legal Process* (New Haven, Yale University Press, 1986) 35, 42.

limit the references made to case law of other jurisdictions? In the US cases this appears to be true, but the UK courts demonstrate a strong engagement with national and international case law in addition to close statutory interpretation of their 1978 State Immunity Act.

In terms of international courts, the active engagement in dialogue by the ECtHR and the ICTY is no doubt due to the strong connection that these courts have to national jurisdictions. The former was set up as a mechanism for the enforcement of the obligations entered into by Contracting States in the European Convention on Human Rights, with the ability to handle both inter-state and individual applications. The latter has primacy of jurisdiction over certain crimes committed in the Former Yugoslavia in the 1990s, relies heavily on state co-operation, and works closely with local judiciaries and courts in the region. The ICJ, in contrast, is the principal judicial organ of the UN with its jurisdiction limited to contentious cases between states that come to the Court by consent and advisory opinions requested by certain UN entities. Nonetheless, the special role that national jurisdictions play in the law on immunities has led to some dialogue at the ICJ, and the potential for a more complementary relationship between the Court and national jurisdictions in the future.

There are some cases that enjoy a special status in the dialogue on immunities in international and national courts. The UK House of Lords judgment in *[Ex Parte] Pinochet (No 3)* is widely cited, appearing in more than one-third of the cases in the study.[86] The Appeals Chamber of the Special Court for Sierra Leone referred approvingly to a statement of Lord Slynn of Hadley in the *Pinochet* case even while explicitly declining to discuss national cases in which immunity was invoked before national courts.[87]

In some ways the popularity of the *Pinochet* case is unsurprising in that this was a judgment from a national court of final appeal concerning a former Head of State. The case attracted a high level of attention in the mass media as well as in the academic sphere, with conferences and symposia devoted to analysing its implications. Yet it is undoubtedly a challenging case for trans-judicial dialogue. First, while the members of the six-to-one majority all decided that Senator Pinochet could not benefit from immunity for the specific torture claims, their reasoning varied considerably. It is difficult to identify a common thread for other jurisdictions to follow. Occasionally, one thread may be used selectively by a court.[88]

[86] Twelve cases.

[87] Special Court for Sierra Leone, Appeals Chamber, 31 May 2004, *Prosecutor v Charles Ghankay Taylor*, Case No SCSL-2003-01-I, Decision on Immunity from Jurisdiction, 31 May 2004, para 52.

[88] Lord Slynn of Hadley's Opinion in was cited (in isolation) by the Special Court for Sierra Leone, Appeals Chamber, 31 May 2004, *Prosecutor v Charles Ghankay Taylor*, Case No SCSL-2003-01-I, Decision on Immunity from Jurisdiction, 31 May 2004.

Second, the case is limited to the Convention against Torture, a treaty that contains specific provisions on immunity and jurisdiction. The 'precedent' of *Pinochet* is not so easily transferred to cases concerning, for example, crimes against humanity where no treaty law exists.[89] Third, *Pinochet* concerned the criminal responsibility of an individual state official, not the civil liability of a state.[90] For dialogue to be meaningful, there must be comparable situations before the different courts. The problem with the *Pinochet* case is that its facts are perhaps too narrow to provide a platform for other courts to develop a general 'human rights exception' to immunity *ratione materiae*.

The ICJ's *Arrest Warrant* case is also regularly cited. Interestingly, the Joint Separate Opinion of Judges Higgins, Kooijmans and Buergenthal is often cited alongside the judgment.[91] The citation of the Joint Separate Opinion is perhaps because of its detailed statements on the current state of customary international law based on analysis of national legislation and case law as well as its discussion of possible ways in which immunity may be lifted for human rights violations.

VI. CONCLUSION

The law of immunity is one that crosses national and international jurisdictions, making it a useful area of study for the way courts communicate with each other. Given the absence of a judicial hierarchy or a system of precedent in the international system, as well as the absence of a comprehensive international treaty on immunities, each jurisdiction may contribute to the formation of the customary international law. We are in the realm of what Shany calls 'unregulated interaction' between national and international courts.[92] It is much more fluid and chaotic than the dialogue that takes place within regional systems.[93]

A concomitant of the dialogue on the law on immunity is some confusion, conflict, and uncertainty as to certain legal questions. Should a state or state official accused of human rights violations benefit from immunity from jurisdiction? Does the non-availability of immunity in, for example,

[89] See also: T Rensmann, 'Impact on the Immunity of States and their Officials' in MT Kamminga and M Scheini (eds), *The Impact of Human Rights Law on General International Law* (Oxford, Oxford University Press, 2009) 151.

[90] Court of Appeal of Ontario in *Bouzari v Islamic Republic of Iran* (2004) 71 OR (3d) 675.

[91] *Democratic Republic of the Congo v Belgium*, ICJ Reports 2002, 3. See, eg: *Jones and ors v Ministry of Interior (Saudi Arabia) and ors* [2006] UKHL 26, 14 June 2006, paras 20, 50 and 99.

[92] Y Shany, *Regulating Jurisdictional Relations Between National and International Courts* (Oxford, Oxford University Press, 2007) 39 (saying no international treaty or rule of customary international law provides clear guidance as to when a particular national or international court has the authority in a specific case to exercise jurisdiction over the case).

[93] *cf* A Tzanakopoulos, 'Judicial Dialogue in Multi-level Governance: The Impact of the *Solange* Argument', this volume, ch 9.

the Genocide Convention and the denial of the defence of official capacity in the Statutes of the international criminal tribunals indicate that there is *also* no immunity for such crimes in customary international law? Can there be different answers to these questions according to whether the case before the national court is a criminal or civil case? Does the availability of immunity depend upon the position the defendant holds in government? What is the relationship between state immunity and state responsibility? To the extent that there is conflict and uncertainty, are we waiting for a definitive statement from a leading international court or an accumulation of state practice[94] that matches what is now a significant amount of conventional law? Or will the work of the ILC and/or the *Institut de Droit International* provide the point of convergence?

This chapter has shown that dialogue and conflict is taking place along several axes: national courts referring to other national courts, international tribunals referring to other international tribunals, national courts and international tribunals referring to each other, and the informal interaction among judges, counsel, and academics. The underlying study is of a relatively small number of cases in the realm of immunities. Its findings may nonetheless apply to other areas of international law in that the roles of counsel, judges and experts have a strong impact on the level of judicial dialogue. Moreover, the monism/dualism and common law/civil law distinctions do not appear to explain which courts will view foreign and international case law as a useful resource and which courts will ignore such material. Rather, it is the overall legal culture – including the reliance placed on parties' pleadings, the length and level of detail in the judgments, and the sense of being part of a greater system, whether a community of states or a web of state co-operation agreements – that determines the level of engagement with other national and international courts.

[94] Eric Posner and Cass Sunstein have proposed that the Condorcet jury theorem by which aggregation of successive decisions can, under certain conditions, increase the likelihood that subsequent decisions are correct, may underpin appropriate (if limited) use of comparative and international law in domestic decisions: E Posner and C Sunstein, 'The Law of Other States' (2006) 59 *Stan L Rev* 131, 135; see also: B Keith, 'Seeing the World Whole: Understanding the citation of external sources in Judicial Reasoning' in C Geiringer and D Knight (eds), *Seeing the World Whole: Essays in Honour of Sir Kenneth Keith* (Wellington, Victoria University Press, 2008) 163, 177. But note Posner and Sunstein's view on the lesser (or no) weight to be accorded to decisions of international courts or international treaties (167–68).

12

Transjudicial Dialogue and Consistency in Human Rights Jurisprudence: A Case Study on Diplomatic Assurances against Torture

ARISTOTELES CONSTANTINIDES*

I. INTRODUCTION

A PARALLEL DEVELOPMENT to the multiplication of international dispute settlement mechanisms is the increasing role of national courts in the application of international law and the ongoing 'judicial globalisation'. Judicial globalisation describes the phenomenon of (international, regional, or national) judges entering into a global conversation by referring to and borrowing from each other and by exchanging information at special meetings or summits.[1] There is little doubt that globalisation is also occurring in the process of judging and lawyering,[2] as evidenced by the willingness of judges to accept both the increasing influence of international law and the readiness of lawyers and judges to seek guidance from the experience of other jurisdictions.[3] The phenomenon is also described as transjudicialism, transnational judicial dialogue, inter/transjudicial dialogue or communication, judicial internationalisation, to name but a few.[4] These terms will be used interchangeably in the present chapter.

* Assistant Professor of International Law and Human Rights, University of Cyprus. Many thanks are due to the editors of this book as well as to Erika de Wet and Jure Vidmar for useful comments on a previous draft. The usual disclaimers apply. The chapter discusses case law available as at November 2010.

[1] C Baudenbacher, 'Judicial Globalization: New Development or Old Wine in New Bottles?' (2003) 38 *Tex Int'l LJ* 505.

[2] C L'Heureux-Dubé, 'The Importance of Dialogue: Globalization and the International Impact of the Rehnquist Court' (1998) 34 *Tulsa LJ* 16.

[3] D Williams, 'Courts and Globalization' (2004) 11 *Ind J Global Legal Stud* 66, 68.

[4] See also: S Muller and S Richards, 'Introduction: Globalisation and Highest Courts' in S Muller and S Richards (eds), *Highest Courts and Globalisation* (The Hague, Hague Academic Press, 2010) 4 [hereinafter: *Highest Courts and Globalisation*].

The literature on transjudicial communication was pioneered by Anne-Marie Slaughter who advocated a central role for judges in international governance and suggested that transjudicialism will inevitably lead national and supranational courts to increasingly consider themselves to be members of a larger judicial community, aware of a common enterprise.[5] In her view, we are witnessing 'the gradual construction of a global legal system' with vertical and horizontal networks of national and international judges.[6] Her theory has however been challenged by critical legal scholars who have contested its descriptive validity, normative assumptions and underlying values.[7] Post-colonial views have also cautioned against judicial imperialism[8] and the reduction of the Third World and non-European legal systems to sites of norm consumption and norm internalisation with no impact on norm production.[9]

Until recently the debate had focused mainly on developments in the United States (US),[10] where it is ideologically and politically charged among liberals and conservatives.[11] However, what is absent from much of this theoretical discussion is qualitative and quantitative evidence to support the broader claims put forward. Academic literature on transjudicialism is full of hand-selected 'exemplary' cases which make no more than a shaky empirical foundation of the respective arguments.[12] Most of the existing scholarship tends to focus on a single jurisdiction, or on the dialogue between the European courts and the national courts, and between the European courts.[13] There have been few studies about the treatment of precedent across international courts[14] and little comparative evidence of how frequent judicial borrowing is and what may explain variations amongst courts.[15] Recent attempts to fill the empirical gap have

[5] AM Slaughter, 'A Typology of Transjudicial Communication' (1994) 29 *U Rich L Rev* 127.

[6] AM Slaughter, *A New World Order* (Princeton, Princeton University Press, 2005) 67.

[7] A Mills and T Stephens, 'Challenging the Role of Judges in Slaughter's Liberal Theory of International Law' (2005) 18 *Leiden J Int'l L* 18.

[8] HL Buxbaum, 'From Empire to Globalization . . . and Back? A Post-Colonial View of Transjudicialism' (2004) 11 *Ind J Global Legal Stud* 188.

[9] M Toufayan, 'Identity, Effectiveness and Newness in Transjudicialism's Coming of Age' (2010) 31 *Mich J Int'l L* 314.

[10] See, eg: 'Agora: The United States Constitution and International Law' (2004) 98 *Am J Int'l L* 42.

[11] See, eg: N Dorsen, 'The Relevance of Foreign Legal Materials in U.S. Constitutional Cases: A Conversation Between Justice Antonin Scalia and Justice Stephen Breyer' (2005) 3 *Int'l J Const L* 519.

[12] RC Black and L Epstein, '(Re-)Setting the Scholarly Agenda on Transjudicial Communication' (2007) 32 *Law & Soc Inq* 796.

[13] See eg: L Garlicki, 'Cooperation of Courts: The Role of Supranational Jurisdictions in Europe' (2008) 6 *Int'l J Const L* 509.

[14] See especially: N Miller, 'An International Jurisprudence? The Operation of "Precedent" Across International Tribunals' (2002) 15 *Leiden J Int'l L* 483.

[15] CPR Romano, 'Deciphering the Grammar of the International Jurisprudential Dialogue' (2009) 41 *NYU J Int'l L & Pol* 760.

focused on the dialogue between either national judiciaries[16] or international courts.[17] Transjurisdictional analysis involving international, regional and national courts has been infrequent. True, the precise mapping of interjudicial dialogues around the world is a mad exercise, impossible to take place unless a battalion of comparatists and other jurists are engaged in research on major jurisdictions around the world.[18]

Against the background of such rich theoretical debate but poor empirical evidence, section II of this chapter discusses the main justifications and patterns of transjudicialism. It investigates which factors are conducive to interjudicial dialogue and, also, whether and how such dialogue can lead to consistent jurisprudence, which is a prerequisite for coherence in international (human rights) law. The propositions put forward in the theoretical debate are then tested in a case study on the practice of diplomatic assurances against torture. This practice (briefly presented in section III) involves the return of aliens to their home country on the basis of diplomatic (that is, non-judicial) assurances that the returnees will receive humane treatment, most notably that they will not be subjected to torture. Section IV examines the burgeoning international and domestic jurisprudence on the topic and assesses the pertinence and impact of transjudicialism on the relevant legal rules. Finally, the concluding remarks stress both the positive and negative aspects of transjudicialism, in particular the need not to lose sight of the interests of justice in transjudicial dialogue's quest for consistency.

Diplomatic assurances against torture can make an apposite case study on transjudicial dialogue for the following reasons, which are among the main justifications for transjudicialism, as explained further in section II.C. First, there is no specific instrument regulating this practice. The legal framework governing diplomatic assurances is the principle of non-refoulement enshrined in numerous human rights treaties which are interpreted by the European Court of Human Rights (ECtHR), treaty monitoring ('quasi-judicial') bodies such as the Committee against Torture and the Human Rights Committee,[19] and national courts in Europe and North America where several states use diplomatic assurances. There is thus a regulatory gap that can be filled by courts. Second, diplomatic assurances present similar legal and factual issues. The practice is

[16] H Lambert, 'Transnational Law, Judges and Refugees in the European Union' in GS Goodwin-Gill and H Lambert (eds), *The Limits of Transnational Law – Refugee Law, Policy Harmonization and Judicial Dialogue in the European Union* (Cambridge, Cambridge University Press, 2010) 2.

[17] E Voeten, 'Borrowing and Non-Borrowing Among International Courts' (2010) 39 *J Legal Stud* 547.

[18] L Burgorgue-Larsen, 'De l'internationalisation du dialogue des juges' in R Badinter et al (eds), *Le dialogue des juges. Mélanges en l'honneur du président Bruno Genevois* (Paris, Dalloz, 2009) 119 f.

[19] For present purposes, the Committee Against Torture and the Human Rights Committee are assimilated to judicial bodies and their decisions are treated accordingly.

virtually the same in those countries that use them, with only minor variations not affecting the interpretive issues. As will be seen, a couple of cases even involve identical facts. Third, with the exception of the ECtHR, which was the first to hand down a decision on diplomatic assurances in 1995, all other courts were at some point faced with no precedent of their own to follow. It is therefore interesting to see whether and how they made use – if at all – of the case law of other courts, which of them and for what reasons. Finally, there was active non-governmental organisation (NGO) involvement in some of these cases, which also resulted in detailed *amicus curiae* briefs acquainting judges with the related pronouncements of their counterparts elsewhere.

II. PATTERNS OF TRANSJUDICIALISM AND THE COHERENCE OF INTERNATIONAL LAW

A. The Old and New Transjudicialism: Varying and Changing Patterns

It is well known that there is no doctrine of binding precedents in international law. However, this has not prevented international courts and tribunals from taking each others' decisions into account.[20] This takes place in various forms and uneven patterns which still remain to be thoroughly researched.[21]

On the other hand, the use of international and/or foreign law and jurisprudence in national courts is not a new phenomenon. Suffice it to recall legal transplantation and the role of imperial law in the courts of colonies. It was crucial that all parts of the British Empire interpreted the law as nearly as possible in the same way.[22] Such communication among courts used to be a one-way process where some courts ('givers') impacted others ('receivers').[23]

Beyond the colonial context, traditional comparative law has, at least in certain countries, long been looking for solutions in other jurisdictions. Affinity with foreign sources of a domestic nature is particularly present in Commonwealth courts, due no doubt to the colonial legacy and shared legal cultures, the use of the same language, and a common allegiance, historically, to the Privy Council.[24] It has also been a feature of American

[20] See the preliminary conclusions of Miller (n 14) 498 f.

[21] A more recent study also concludes on the need for further research. See: Voeten (n 17) 573.

[22] Buxbaum (n 8) 184.

[23] L'Heureux-Dubé (n 2) 18.

[24] Lambert (n 16) 2; also: A Lollini, 'Confronting Comparative Methods: Approaches to Using Extra-Systemic Parameters by the Canadian Supreme Court and the South African Constitutional Court' in AS Muller and MA Loth, *Highest Courts and the Internationalisation of Law: Challenges and Changes* (The Hague, Hague Academic Press, 2009) 166 [hereinafter: *Highest Courts and the Internationalisation of Law*].

judging since the founding period.[25] Judges in other juridical families also maintain relationships, facilitated by the same language and the use of the same basic legal concepts.[26]

In the era of globalisation the picture in domestic courts is apparently changing. It is suggested that conversations among courts take the form of a more interactive process where reception is turning to dialogue,[27] making every jurisdiction on the globe, as a matter of principle, eligible as a resource.[28] The point is less to borrow than to benefit from comparative deliberation.[29] The development of human rights jurisprudence, in particular, is increasingly becoming a dialogue.[30] Indeed, some evidence from particular jurisdictions corroborates the changing ways of borrowing.[31] Even British courts show greater willingness to receive and consider the case law of countries outside the common law family, although this trend should not be exaggerated.[32]

B. Transjudicialism and the Coherence of International Law and Jurisprudence

Among the primary tasks of highest national courts is to safeguard the unity of law in their jurisdictions and thus serve basic principles of law such as equality before the law and legal certainty.[33] This is the reason why national judiciaries are organised hierarchically. However, highest national courts see the exercise of their unifying function becoming more complex and demanding with the mounting internationalisation of the law and domestication of international law. Applicable law in domestic cases increasingly includes sources which are shaped in and are shared with other jurisdictions. Moreover, some of these sources of law are based on the case law of international courts such as the European Court of Human Rights.[34] This is however not the case with other international legal sources, even though they were created with the intent to provide

[25] Black and Eppstein (n 12) 794.

[26] G Canivet, 'Trans-Judicial Dialogue in a Global World' in *Highest Courts and Globalisation*, 24.

[27] L'Heureux-Dubé (n 2) 17; AM Slaughter, 'A Global Community of Courts' (2003) 44 *Harv Int'l LJ* 195–99.

[28] Baudenbacher (n 1) 525.

[29] Slaughter, *A New World Order* (n 6) 75.

[30] L'Heureux-Dubé (n 2) 21.

[31] eg: Lollini (n 24) 167.

[32] Lord Bingham of Cornhill, 'The Widening Horizons of Litigation in Britain' in *Highest Courts and Globalisation*, 57.

[33] AS Muller and MA Loth, 'Highest Courts and the Internationalisation of Law: Challenges and Changes' in *Highest Courts and the Internationalisation of Law*, 2.

[34] P Koskelo, 'Modern Challenges for the Judiciary and the Role of Supreme Courts' in *Highest Courts and the Internationalisation of Law*, 131.

for uniform rules across national borders.[35] Thus, the unifying function of highest national courts inevitably extends to rules originating in other legal systems since the need for coherence in the law does not stop at the national border.[36] Highest courts are therefore also called upon to ensure a degree of coherence in relation to other legal systems, including the international legal system.[37] Such coherence cannot however be achieved through the decisions of a single legal institution; other means should be used.[38] Transjudicial dialogue with other national and international courts should be, and is increasingly becoming, such a means.[39]

Contrary to domestic legal systems, there is no equivalent court system with a highest court at the top at the international and transnational level nor is there any formal hierarchy among international courts.[40] Nonetheless, even if the international judiciary does not form a coherent system,[41] international courts have developed doctrines and experiences indicating their will to take the decisions of their peers into account in the pursuit of consistency in international jurisprudence – in this sense it can be said that the international judiciary applies a doctrine of precedent.[42] The debate on the fragmentation of international law has apparently made international judges even more aware of the responsibility they bear for a coherent construction of international law.[43] Whenever possible, they will be likely to frame their judgments in such a way as to minimise the chances of conflict with judgments of other courts.[44] This will help improve the coherence of the international legal system which, in turn, can contribute to the reputation and legitimacy of international law and encourage a better level of compliance with its norms.[45]

[35] M Scheltema, 'The Changing Role of Highest Courts: Concluding Observations' in *Highest Courts and the Internationalisation of Law*, 188.

[36] ibid 189 f; also: E Mak, 'Justice at a New Scale: Introducing a Conceptual Framework for the Analysis of Highest Courts' Role in a Globalised Context' in *Highest Courts and Globalisation*, 119.

[37] Muller and Loth (n 33) 2; see also: Scheltema (n 35) 188 f.

[38] AM Hol, 'Internationalisation and Legitimacy of Decisions by the Highest Courts' in *Highest Courts and the Internationalisation of Law*, 84.

[39] M Delmas-Marty, *Ordering Pluralism: A Conceptual Framework for Understanding the Transnational Legal World* (translated by N Norberg) (Oxford and Portland, Oregon, Hart Publishing, 2009) 19 f, 23; *cf* R Higgins, 'The Changing Position of Domestic Courts in the International Legal Order', 12, available at www.jur.uva.nl/aciluk/object.cfm/24a0465f-1321-b0be-a477aec5c2bedc6b (last visited 1 June 2011).

[40] Y Shany, *The Competing Jurisdictions of International Courts and Tribunals* (Oxford, Oxford University Press, 2003) 109.

[41] ibid 114.

[42] G Ulfstein, 'The International Judiciary' in J Klabbers, A Peters and G Ulfstein (eds), *The Constitutionalization of International Law* (Oxford, Oxford University Press, 2009) 139; M Shahabuddeen, *Precedent in the World Court* (Cambridge, Cambridge University Press, 1996) 8 f.

[43] B Simma, 'Universality of International Law from the Perspective of a Practitioner' (2009) 20 *Eur J Int'l L* 289; Shany (n 40) 127.

[44] Romano (n 15) 766.

[45] Shany (n 40) 118 f.

That said, transnational coherence is not the same as coherence within a national legal system.[46] The latter means the uniform application of the law, guaranteed by the authority of one highest court. In a transnational setting, coherence does not go that far.[47] Depending on the rule and the context, harmonisation should aim at achieving compatibility rather than perfect unity of legal provisions originating in different legal orders.[48] Since overall unity is impossible and perhaps undesirable, the question then is how to reconcile multiple unities in order to reach some form of coordinated diversity;[49] what Delmas-Marty has called 'ordered pluralism', a law that would order complexity without eliminating it.[50]

Besides, the virtues of coherence should not detract from other competing values, most notably the requirements of justice and the related potential for the development and improvement of international norms through divergences in the dialectic process.[51] Thus, when looking for possible arguments in other jurisdictions, it is always a question of whether the arguments found are effective and good. If a court wishes to render a decision that is not consistent with decisions already delivered by other courts, the question is which of the decisions is not in line from the point of view of coherence.[52] In fact, the interests of justice may well warrant the reversal of an unjust ruling. Judicial harmonisation ought not to prevail in all circumstances; ample room should be left for the promotion of other important interests.[53]

In any case, in the absence of mechanisms and procedural principles guaranteeing effective coordination, it is first and foremost in the mind of judges that problems of inconsistency can be solved.[54] It is therefore useful to explore why and how judges make use of the jurisprudence of their international and national counterparts.

C. Motivations for Transjudicial Dialogue

There are several justifications put forward in favor of transjudicial dialogue. However, it has been rightly observed that assuming a

[46] Scheltema (n 35) 191.
[47] ibid.
[48] *cf* Muller and Loth (n 33) 5.
[49] HP Glenn, 'Accommodating Unity' in *Highest Courts and Globalisation*, 97.
[50] Delmas-Marty (n 39) 14.
[51] B Conforti, 'The Role of the Judge in International Law' 1 (2) *Eur J Legal Studies* 5, available at www.ejls.eu/2/20UK.pdf (last visited 1 June 2011); J Charney, 'The Impact on the International Legal System of the Growth of International Courts and Tribunals' (1999) 31 *NYU J Int'l L & Pol* 136.
[52] Hol (n 38) 84.
[53] Shany (n 40) 124.
[54] PM Dupuy, 'The Unity of Application of International Law at the Global Level and the Responsibility of Judges' 1 (2) *Eur J Legal Studies* 2, 21, available at www.ejls.eu/2/21UK.pdf (last visited 1 June 2011).

straightforward relationship between a judicial decision and influencing factors might lead to inaccurate inferences, considering the host of factors that influence judges' decision-making.[55] Judges have an innate reluctance to discuss their own mental processes and the group dynamics that lead to the crafting of a decision.[56]

Transjudicial dialogue, at least in the form of cross-references, is not regulated; it is unbridled and spontaneous.[57] Apart from few institutionalised arrangements (such as the European Court of Justice (ECJ) or the South African Constitution requiring the Constitutional Court to consider public international law), courts speak to each other not because they have to but because they want to.[58] External sources and decisions are cited as persuasive authority (that is, 'authority that *attracts* adherence as opposed to obliging it')[59] rather than as binding authority, which implies that judges have considerable discretion as to what to reject, follow, or ignore.[60]

To begin with, there is the traditional comparative approach that considering and comparing judgments from various jurisdictions makes for better, stronger, more reflective and more informed decisions.[61] Foreign comparisons can be inspiring and broaden the perspectives for decision-making, even if one eventually disagrees with their outcome or reasoning.[62]

Secondly, globalisation has led to homogenisation of legal problems and of legal responses to such problems. In times of globalisation legal problems tend to be compared due to the increased similarity of social debates, which is favoured by advances in global communication.[63] As judges have to deal with the same or similar problems, it is helpful and valuable to share information and discuss approaches.[64] The questions become identical around the world, especially when it comes to fundamental rights.[65] Besides, it is only fair that like cases are treated alike, not only in each country but throughout the world.[66] The threat of international terrorism and the human rights impact of anti-terrorism measures adopted at international, regional and national level – among which is the practice of diplomatic assurances – are *par excellence* among the global

[55] Romano (n 15) 761, fn 17.

[56] ibid 762.

[57] Burgorgue-Larsen (n 18) 116.

[58] Mak (n 36) 121; R Bahdi, 'Globalization of Judgment: Transjudicialism and the Five Faces of International Law in Domestic Courts'(2002) 34 *Geo Wash Int'l L Rev* 558.

[59] HP Glenn, 'Persuasive Authority' (1987) 32 *McGill LJ* 263 (emphasis added).

[60] Slaughter, 'A Typology' (n 5) 124.

[61] L'Heureux-Dubé (n 2) 39; Scheltema (n 35) 187; Slaughter, 'A Global Community of Courts' (n 27) 201.

[62] Hol (n 38) 77.

[63] Baudenbacher (n 1) 505 f.

[64] Koskelo (n 34) 133.

[65] Burgorgue-Larsen (n 18) 120.

[66] J Waldron, 'Treating Like Cases Alike in the World: The Theoretical Basis of the Demand for Legal Unity' in *Highest Courts and Globalisation*, 105 ff.

issues presenting identical legal and other problems anywhere in the world.[67] The availability of identical or similar norms grounded in international and human rights law has facilitated the efforts of national courts to strengthen inter-judicial coordination with a view to jointly addressing these problems.[68]

Furthermore, when facing similar legal issues, courts may need to look at other jurisdictions either because there are no national precedents or because there are well-known strong foreign precedents which are hard to neglect.[69] This is particularly relevant when there is no international legal norm regulating a certain practice – diplomatic assurances against torture are actually such a case. Both international and domestic courts are constantly facing law-making challenges. International legal rules are open-textured and usually broadly formulated, leaving judges ample room for filling lacunae and setting norms (sometimes almost *ex nihilo*)[70] despite the formal, political and structural limits of law-making.[71]

Finally, more than other rules, judge-made rules face legitimacy concerns. Coherence through dialogue can provide such legitimacy. Presenting effective arguments and showing that a decision is consistent with other decisions and fits well in the legal system is a prerequisite of a rational, and therefore, legitimate, decision.[72] In such cases, the echo effect can be significant; in the end, judges might achieve law-making effects through repeated mutual reference, thus reinforcing the precedential value of their decisions.[73] Thus, the search for legitimacy might in some cases be the first and foremost reason to study the decisions of other courts.[74]

D. Modalities (and Obstacles) of Transjudicial Communication

Citing decisions of other courts best exemplifies transjudicial communication. Citations may be passing references, may be simply another authority

[67] *cf* Canivet (n 26) 25 f.

[68] E Benvenisti, 'United We Stand: National Courts Reviewing Counterterrorism Measures' in A Bianchi and A Keller (eds), *Counterterrorism: Democracy's Challenge* (Oxford and Portland, Oregon, Hart Publishing, 2008) 275 f.

[69] Muller and Loth (n 33) 3; L'Heureux-Dubé (n 2) 24; Canivet (n 26) 29; D Maus, 'Le recours aux précédents étrangers et le dialogue des cours constitutionnelles' (2009) 80 *RFDC* 683.

[70] C Rozakis, 'The Interaction Between the European Court of Human Rights and the Other Courts' 2, Speech delivered at the World Conference on Constitutional Justice, Cape Town, 22–24 January 2009, available at www.venice.coe.int/WCCJ/Papers/ECHR_Rozakis_E.pdf (last visited 1 June 2011).

[71] D Terris, CPR Romano and L Swigart, *The International Judge: An Introduction to the Men and Women Who Decide the World's Cases* (Oxford, Oxford University Press, 2007) 104, 127 ff.

[72] Hol (n 38) 78; see also: Simma (n 43) 279.

[73] Romano (n 15) 769–70; *cf* Slaughter, 'A Typology' (n 5) 119.

[74] Hol (n 38) 79.

used to buttress a conclusion already reached, or may reflect extensive consideration of the other court's approach.[75] However, foreign reasoning should not be imported without sufficient consideration of the context in which it is being applied. Solutions developed in one jurisdiction may be inappropriate elsewhere.[76]

Still, borrowing is much more to understand and explore than simple citation practices.[77] It is essential not to equate transnational citations with transnational influence. A study of formal citations may underestimate the extent to which judges are influenced by external decisions.[78] In fact, express citation in international judgments is generally done sparingly, selectively and reluctantly.[79] It may also be that courts are following the solutions of other courts without quoting them.[80] The informality of the borrowing process provides courts with significant leeway that can avert criticism for loss of autonomy, illegitimate judicial activism and arbitrary decision-making.[81]

To address this concern with regard to international courts, it has been suggested that acculturation may explain interjudicial dialogue better than persuasion. Acculturation can be, and often is, unconscious and does not require admission of having been persuaded. An international court might find it difficult to admit having been persuaded because it might then appear to be under the shadow of another court, which would run contrary to the idea of autonomy.[82]

Apart from interjudicial dialogue through their decisions, there are also extrajudicial and less formal cooperative mechanisms between judges, including institutionalised meetings of judges in conferences, exchange of visits to each others' courts, training, etc.[83] Such meetings are becoming quite frequent and are useful for sharing experiences, developing a common understanding of legal questions and fostering mutual professional respect.[84] In addition, there are numerous geographical and subject-specific networks of judges that help maintain and foster ties between them.[85]

Furthermore, developments in information and communication technology have greatly facilitated access to information and connection

[75] L'Heureux-Dubé (n 2) 28.
[76] ibid 26.
[77] Black and Eppstein (n 12) 794.
[78] Voeten (n 17) 550.
[79] Romano (n 15) 758.
[80] C McCrudden, 'A Common Law of Human Rights?: Transnational Judicial Conversations on Constitutional Rights' (2000) 20 *Oxford J Legal Stud* 511; Slaughter, 'A Typology' (n 5) 118. See also the examples given by: Baudenbacher (n 1) 509.
[81] Romano (n 15) 772; for such criticism see, eg: R Alford, 'Misusing International Sources to Interpret the Constitution' (2004) 98 *Am J Int'l L* 57–69.
[82] Romano (n 15) 772.
[83] Canivet (n 26) 33 ff.
[84] Simma (n 43) 289; Bahdi (n 58) 558.
[85] See the long list cited by: Canivet (n 26) 24.

among judges and groups across the world who advocate at the national and international level with reference to international legal standards.[86] A number of legal clinics, advocacy centres and transnational human rights NGOs intervene in domestic cases or support lawyers who wish to include international sources into their arguments.[87] Formal and informal e-mail networks and blogs permit advocates to exchange opinions and strategies with colleagues elsewhere in the world. The exchange inevitably finds its way into arguments made before courts and thus feeds the development of transjudicialism.[88]

On the other hand, there still exist practical obstacles to interjudicial dialogue and communication such as language, differences between legal systems in terms of legal concepts, methods and thought processes,[89] and unfamiliarity of domestic judges with international law.[90]

The remainder of this chapter will examine whether these propositions hold true in the transjudicial dialogue that has developed on the topic of diplomatic assurances against torture. Before doing so, it is essential to present the applicable legal framework and the pertinent legal and interpretive issues.

III. DIPLOMATIC ASSURANCES AGAINST TORTURE IN THE CONTEXT OF NON-REFOULEMENT

Judicial guarantees against the death penalty and/or other ill-treatment have a long history in extradition cases and are often provided in extradition treaties. On the other hand, diplomatic assurances against torture and/or other ill-treatment in relation to other kinds of removal were used less frequently before 9/11 and pose more difficult problems.[91] They have been increasingly and controversially used since 9/11 as a tool in the fight against terrorism with a view to accommodating (or circumventing) state obligations of non-refoulement.[92] Attempts at regulating such assurances

[86] Bahdi (n 58) 558.

[87] ibid; see also: M Tushnet, 'The Inevitable Globalisation of Constitutional Law' in *Highest Courts and Globalisation*, 132–33.

[88] Bahdi (n 58) 558.

[89] Canivet (n 26) 39.

[90] Y Shany, 'How Supreme is the Supreme Law of the Land? Comparative Analysis of the Influence of International Human Rights Treaties upon the Interpretation of Constitutional Texts by Domestic Courts' (2006) 31 *Brooklyn J Int'l L* 396.

[91] E Metcalfe, 'The False Promises of Assurances against Torture' (2009) 6 *Justice J* 64 ff.

[92] The practice has been scrupulously detailed by Human Rights Watch in a series of critical reports: Human Rights Watch, '"Empty Promises": Diplomatic Assurances No Safeguard against Torture', April 2004, available at www.hrw.org/reports/2004/un0404; Human Rights Watch, 'Still at Risk: Diplomatic Assurances No Safeguard Against Torture', April 2005, available at www.hrw.org/reports/2005/eca0405; Human Rights Watch, 'Cases Involving Diplomatic Assurances against Torture – Developments since May 2005', January 2007, available at www.hrw.org/backgrounder/eca/eu0107/eu0107web.pdf (all last visited 1 June 2011).

by establishing minimum standards for their content and use were rejected by the Council of Europe in March 2006 due to, *inter alia*, disagreement among Member States and out of fear of weakening the absolute prohibition against torture and non-refoulement.[93] The United Kingdom (UK) has since led efforts to have diplomatic assurances endorsed by the EU, especially through the G6 group of interior ministers, without any tangible outcome as at the end of 2010.[94] In any case, the practice is maintained in the counterterrorism policies of several states.[95]

In the absence of an international instrument to explicitly prohibit or regulate diplomatic assurances, the principle of non-refoulement remains their governing framework. This principle is firmly established in international treaty and customary law.[96] It was first enunciated in Article 33, paragraph 1 of the 1951 Geneva Convention Relating to the Status of Refugees,[97] albeit not in absolute terms. However, individuals exempted from the scope of protection by virtue of Article 33(2) (namely 'a refugee whom there are reasonable grounds for regarding as a danger to the security of the country in which he is, or who, having been convicted by a final judgement of a particularly serious crime, constitutes a danger to the community of that country') still fall within the protection guaranteed under other, subsequent, treaties as well as customary law.[98] In particular, the protection against refoulement has been expressly articulated in Article 3 of the 1984 Convention Against Torture and Other Cruel, Inhuman or Degrading Treatment or Punishment,[99] which the Committee

[93] Council of Europe, Steering Committee for Human Rights, Group of Specialists on Human Rights and the Fight against Terrorism, Report on second meeting, 3 April 2006, DH–S–TER(2006)005, para 20.

[94] The UK efforts and the EU reaction are documented in Human Rights Watch, 'Not the way forward: The UK's dangerous reliance on diplomatic assurances', 22 October 2008, available at www.hrw.org/en/reports/2008/10/22/not-way-forward-0 (last visited 1 June 2011).

[95] See, eg: Human Rights Watch, Amnesty International, International Commission of Jurists, and Redress Joint Letter, 'Denmark and Diplomatic Assurances Against Grave Violations of Human Rights', 18 June 2008, available at www.hrw.org/en/news/2008/06/17/denmark-and-diplomatic-assurances-against-grave-violations-human-rights; Human Rights Watch, 'Universal Periodic Review of Switzerland: Human Rights Watch's Submission to the Human Rights Council', 5 May 2008, available at http://hrw.org/english/docs/2008/04/07/global18555.htm (both last visited 1 June 2011).

[96] See eg: D Weissbrodt and I Hortreiter, 'The Principle of Non-refoulement: Article 3 of the Convention Against Torture and Other Cruel, Inhuman or Degrading Treatment or Punishment in Comparison with the Non-refoulement Provisions of Other International Human Rights Treaties' (1999) 5 *Buff Hum Rts L Rev* 1–30; R Bruin and K Wouters, 'Terrorism and the Non-derogability of Non-refoulement' (2003) 15 *Int'l J Refugee L* 5–29.

[97] 189 UNTS 150 ('No Contracting State shall expel or return ("refouler") a refugee in any manner whatsoever to the frontiers of territories where his life or freedom would be threatened on account of his race, religion, nationality, membership of a particular social group or political opinion').

[98] J Hathaway, *The Rights of Refugees under International Law* (Cambridge, Cambridge University Press, 2005) 120.

[99] 1465 UNTS 85 ('No State Party shall expel, return ("refouler") or extradite a person to another State where there are substantial grounds for believing that he would be in danger of being subjected to torture').

against Torture has recognised as absolute.[100] The general prohibition of torture in Article 7 of the 1966 International Covenant on Civil and Political Rights[101] has also been interpreted by the Human Rights Committee to be absolute and to include non-refoulement.[102] Likewise, the ECtHR has found the obligation of non-refoulement to be 'inherent' in the general terms of Article 3 of the European Convention of Human Rights (ECHR) which states that 'no one shall be subjected to torture or to inhuman or degrading treatment or punishment'.[103]

The absolute and non-derogable character of non-refoulement has been reaffirmed time and again in the ECtHR jurisprudence in the most unequivocal of terms. With respect to terrorism, it was first stated in *Chahal v United Kingdom*, where the ECtHR held:

> The Court is well aware of the immense difficulties faced by States in modern times in protecting their communities from terrorist violence. However, even in these circumstances, the Convention prohibits in absolute terms torture or inhuman or degrading treatment or punishment, irrespective of the victim's conduct. . . . Article 3 makes no provision for exceptions and no derogation from it is permissible under Article 15 even in the event of a public emergency threatening the life of the nation. The prohibition provided by Article 3 against ill-treatment is equally absolute in expulsion cases.[104]

The *Chahal* principle was unsuccessfully challenged by the UK in *Saadi v Italy*, where a unanimous Grand Chamber explicitly rejected calls for establishing a new test that would balance national security considerations against other relevant concerns, most notably the alleged threat an individual poses to the deporting state.[105] Identical arguments were put

[100] See, eg: *Tapia Paez v Sweden* (Communication No 39/1996, CAT/C/18/D/39/1996), Views of 28 April 1997, para 14.5.

[101] 999 UNTS 171 ('No one shall be subjected to torture or to cruel, inhuman or degrading treatment or punishment').

[102] See: CCPR, General Comment No 31, 'The Nature of the General Legal Obligation Imposed on States Parties to the Covenant', CCPR/C/21/Rev.1/Add.13, 26 May 2004, para 12: 'the article 2 obligation . . . entails an obligation not to extradite, deport, expel or otherwise remove a person . . ., where there are substantial grounds for believing that there is a real risk of irreparable harm, such as that contemplated by articles 6 and 7 of the Covenant'. See with regard to the absolute prohibition of torture: *Mansour Ahani v Canada*, Communication No 1051/2002, CCPR/C/80/D/1051/2002, Views of 15 June 2004, para 10.10.

[103] This was first recognised to apply in extradition cases in the landmark decision of *Soering v United Kingdom*, Judgment of 7 July 1989, Series A No 161, (1989) 11 EHRR 51, paras 87 – 88. In *Cruz Varas and Others v Sweden*, Judgment of 20 March 1991, Series A No 201, (1992) 14 EHRR 1, para 70, the principle was considered to also apply in cases of expulsion.

[104] *Chahal v United Kingdom*, Judgment of 15 November 1996, 23 EHRR 413 (1997) paras 79–80 (citations omitted). These pronouncements have been reaffirmed in numerous subsequent ECtHR judgments (see, eg: *Shamayev and Others v Georgia and Russia*, App No 36378/02, Judgment of 12 April 2005, para 335). *Chahal* was also explicitly relied upon by the Committee Against Torture in *TPS v Canada*, Communication No 99/1997, CAT/C/24/D/99/1997, Views of 16 May, para 15.3.

[105] *Saadi v Italy*, App No 37201/06, Judgment of 28 February 2008, paras 137–42. The UK arguments largely echo the Joint Partly Dissenting Opinion of seven judges in *Chahal*.

forward by the UK, Lithuania, Portugal and Slovakia in *Ramzy v the Netherlands*, which was however struck out of the Court's list in July 2010 due to the applicant's failure to contact his representatives.[106]

It is highly controversial whether diplomatic assurances are reliable at all or can otherwise mitigate the 'real risk' of torture to such an extent that would allow an alien's removal without compromising the absolute prohibition on non-refoulement.[107] Human rights officials of international organisations, including the UN Special Rapporteur on Torture, and human rights NGOs have taken the lead in advocating against the legality of diplomatic assurances.[108] In a series of reports and *amicus curiae* briefs, they have argued that diplomatic assurances should be rejected as a matter of principle for the following reasons: they are not legally binding;[109] they are ineffective in the face of the secret methods of torture and its endemic nature in many receiving states; they are unreliable due to the limits of diplomacy and the reluctance of both sending and receiving states to acknowledge their breach; they are incapable of reducing the 'real risk' of torture; they are unenforceable since post-return monitoring is either non-existent or too weak and ineffective; they have been breached in numerous past instances; overall, they undermine the absolute prohibition of non-refoulement. It makes little difference whether assurances take a more sophisticated form, such as the Memoranda of Understanding (MOU) signed by the UK with Jordan, Libya and Lebanon.

These arguments are convincing, at least with regard to those cases where it is reliably documented that torture is endemic and is practiced

[106] *Ramzy v the Netherlands*, Judgment of 20 July 2010, App No 25424/05.

[107] See for elaborate analysis of the pertinent legal issues: M Nowak, '"Extraordinary Renditions", Diplomatic Assurances and the Principle of Non-Refoulement' in W Kälin et al (eds), *International Law, Conflict and Development: The Emergence of a Holistic Approach in International Affairs* (Leiden/Boston, Martinus Nijhoff Publishers, 2010) 107 ff; L Skoglund, 'Diplomatic Assurances Against Torture An Effective Strategy? A Review of Jurisprudence and Examination of the Arguments' (2008) 77 *Nordic J Int'l L* 319–64; G Noll, 'Diplomatic Assurances and the Silence of Human Rights Law' (2006) 7 *Melbourne J Int'l L* 104–26; M Jones, 'Lies, Damned Lies and Diplomatic Assurances: the Misuse of Diplomatic Assurances in Removal Proceedings' (2006) 8 *Eur J Migration & L* 9–39; A Deeks, 'Promises not to Torture: Diplomatic Assurances in U.S. Courts', *ASIL Discussion Paper Series*, December 2008, available at www.asil.org/files/ASIL-08-DiscussionPaper.pdf (last visited 1 June 2011); M Fornari, 'Garantías Diplomáticas y Lucha Contra el Terrorismo Internacional' (2007) 23 *ADI* 389–406; A Constantinides, 'The Practice of Diplomatic Assurances as Circumvention of the Prohibition on Non-Refoulement' in I Stephanides and C Hadjiconstantinou (eds), *Mélanges Kalliopi K Koufa* (Thessaloniki, Sakkoulas Publications, 2010) 225–42 (in Greek).

[108] See, *inter alia*: Report of Mr Alvaro Gil-Robles, Council of Europe Commissioner for Human Rights, on his visit to Sweden, 21–23 April 2004, CommDH(2004)13, 8 July 2004, para 19; Report of the High Commissioner for Human Rights, 'Protection of human rights and fundamental freedoms while countering terrorism', UN Doc E/CN.4/2006/94, 16 February 2006, paras 22–32; Report of the Special Rapporteur on torture and other cruel, inhuman or degrading treatment or punishment, UN Doc A/60/316, 30 August 2005, para 51.

[109] See also: C Warbrick, 'Diplomatic Assurances and the Removal of Terrorist Suspects from the UK' (2006) 4 *Archbold News* 8; Constantinides (n 107) 232 f.

systematically against certain groups. In such cases, assurances are too weak, precarious and thus meaningless. But even where torture is not endemic, the threshold for establishing that a returnee faces a 'real risk' of torture has been set too high in the first place for external factors, let alone diplomatic assurances, to meaningfully lower it.[110] Once returnees have met the numerous requirements and convinced decision-makers that they do face a 'real risk' of torture, there is little, if anything, in terms of monitoring to prevent torture or ill-treatment from transpiring if they are eventually returned.[111]

Despite such objections, diplomatic assurances are too convenient a tool in the fight against terrorism for numerous governments to abandon them. They have most probably come to stay, as is also shown by the burgeoning international and domestic jurisprudence.

IV. JURISPRUDENCE AND TRANSJUDICIAL DIALOGUE ON DIPLOMATIC ASSURANCES

A. International Jurisprudence

1. *The European Court of Human Rights*

Diplomatic assurances against torture were first rejected in *Chahal*, which set the scene for the jurisprudence that followed. The ECtHR was cautious not to cast doubt on the good faith of the Indian Government and refrained from scrutinising the content of the (vague) assurances, but cautioned against reliance on assurances from a state where torture is endemic or persistent.[112] The reasoning was laconic and tailored to the facts of the case. *Chahal* was relied upon in the deportation case of *Saadi v Italy* where the Court rejected Tunisia's assurances but specified that it had the obligation to 'examine whether such assurances provided, in their practical application, a sufficient guarantee'.[113] Tunisia's assurances were also rejected in the deportation case of *Ben Khemais v Italy* where the Court

[110] This is not the place to dwell at any length on the meaning of 'real risk' of torture in international jurisprudence. See, eg: S Joseph et al, *Seeking Remedies for Torture Victims: A Handbook on the Individual Complaints Procedures of the UN Treaty Bodies* (Geneva, OMCT, 2006) 218 ff.

[111] In the words of Nowak (n 107) 133: 'Apart from providing the person returned with a body guard for 24 hours a day I cannot reasonably conceive of any watertight monitoring mechanism'.

[112] '[T]he violation of human rights by certain members of the security forces in Punjab and elsewhere in India is a recalcitrant and enduring problem. Against this background, the Court is not persuaded that the above assurances would provide Mr Chahal with an adequate guarantee of safety' (para 105). The assurances are reproduced at para 37 of the judgment.

[113] *Saadi v Italy* (n 105) para 148.

gave more credence to reports of Amnesty International than to statements of Tunisia's Advocate General.[114] *Saadi* was also relied upon for rejecting assurances in *Ismoilov v Russia*, which involved the applicant's extradition to Uzbekistan;[115] in *Ryabikin v Russia*, which involved judicial guarantees in a case of extradition of an alleged white-collar criminal to Turkmenistan;[116] and in *Klein v Russia*, which concerned the extradition of an Israeli mercenary to Colombia.[117]

However, assurances were not ruled out altogether in *Saadi*, the ECtHR stating that 'the weight to be given to assurances from the receiving State depends, in each case, on the circumstances obtaining at the material time'.[118] This pronouncement was in line with the much-criticised extradition case of *Mamatkulov and Askarov v Turkey*, where the Grand Chamber of the ECtHR had relied (among other factors) upon assurances given by Uzbekistan's Public Prosecutor and found no violation of Article 3.[119]

In its decisions on diplomatic assurances the ECtHR has not referred to any decision of other courts or treaty bodies. This should come as no big surprise. The ECtHR was the first supranational court to hand down a decision on diplomatic assurances, to which it has steadily adhered. The Court is generally eager to prove that legal security and certainty is one of its merits.[120] The ruling in *Chahal* has set a rather welcome, albeit inconclusive, standard despite efforts by certain governments to overrule it. *Chahal*'s strong reaffirmation and further refinement in *Saadi* was generally welcomed. The decisions of treaty bodies (Committee Against Torture and Human Rights Committee) in the meantime were largely fact-driven and did not go further than the ECtHR, thereby not lending themselves to any meaningful reference. There was equally no decision by any highest national court that the ECtHR could possibly refer to, something it has done in several instances in the past (citing mainly the US Supreme Court and, to a lesser extent, those of South Africa, Canada and New Zealand).[121]

Besides, in terms of citation patterns, the ECtHR is not among the most active participants in the global judicial conversation.[122] The Strasbourg jurisprudence is older, well-established, better known and possesses an undoubted authority.[123] It is for good reason that it is considered one of the

[114] *Ben Khemais v Italy*, App No 246/07, Judgment of 24 February 2009, paras 58–60.

[115] *Ismoilov and others v Russia*, App No 2947/06, Judgment of 24 April 2008, para 127. The case has been referred to the Grand Chamber.

[116] App No 8320/04, Judgment of 19 June 2008, para 119.

[117] App No 24268/08, Judgment of 1 April 2010, para 55.

[118] *Saadi v Italy* (n 105) para 148. See also: D Moeckli, 'Saadi v. Italy: The Rules of the Game Have not Changed' (2008) 8 *Hum R L Rev* 546.

[119] *Mamatkulov and Askarov v Turkey*, App Nos 46827/99, 46951/99, Judgment of 4 February 2005, 41 EHRR 494 (2005) paras 76–77. Three judges filed a dissenting opinion on this issue.

[120] Rozakis (n 70) 5.

[121] ibid 4 f; Voeten (n 17) 559 ff.

[122] Miller (n 14) 498; Baudenbacher (n 1) 512.

[123] Burgorgue-Larsen (n 18) 126.

most important 'givers' of ideas in the context of judicial globalisation.[124] Not surprisingly then, the ECtHR faces no criticism for infrequently citing other courts.[125]

2. *The Committee Against Torture*

In the post 9/11 environment, diplomatic assurances were first rejected in the Committee Against Torture's much celebrated decision in *Agiza v Sweden* (involving the deportation of the applicant and Mohammed Alzery to Egypt) where the Committee held that 'the procurement of diplomatic assurances, which, moreover, provided no mechanism for their enforcement, did not suffice to protect against this manifest risk [of torture]'.[126] This decision came to rectify the Committee's previous unfortunate endorsement of the same Egyptian assurances in *Attia v Sweden*.[127] Hanan Attia was the wife of Agiza and had evaded police custody when her husband and Alzery were deported by a CIA rendition flight to Cairo on 18 December 2001. She challenged the deportation order before the Committee Against Torture, but the Committee held that it was 'satisfied by the provision of guarantees against abusive treatment, which also extend to the complainant and are . . . regularly monitored by the State party's authorities *in situ*'.[128] It also noted that Egypt was 'directly bound properly to treat prisoners within its jurisdiction, and any failure to do so would be a breach of the Convention'.[129] And so it was, as the Committee later came to acknowledge in *Agiza*.

Assurances were also rejected by the Committee Against Torture in *Pelit v Azerbaijan* (concerning extradition to Turkey of a Kurdish activist who was a recognised refugee in Germany) where the Committee interestingly observed that Turkey's assurances were 'an acknowledgment that, without more, expulsion of the complainant would raise issues of her mistreatment'.[130]

In *Agiza* the Committee was presented with an opportunity to develop a robust approach towards diplomatic assurances and to come up with a well-reasoned decision that could clarify the (im)permissibility of diplomatic assurances. It was actually invited to do so by Sweden, which had relied upon *Chahal* and *Mamatkulov* and had urged the Committee to

[124] AM Slaughter, 'A Global Community of Courts' (2003) 44 *Harv Int'l LJ* 201 f.

[125] Voeten (n 17) 572.

[126] *Agiza v Sweden*, Communication No 233/2003, CAT/C/34/D/233/2003, Views of 20 May 2005, para 13.4. For a brief analysis of the case see also: S Joseph, 'Rendering Terrorists and the Convention Against Torture' (2005) 5 *Hum R L Rev* 339–46.

[127] *Attia v Sweden*, Communication No 199/2002, CAT/C/31/D/199/2002, Views of 17 November 2003.

[128] ibid para 12.3.

[129] ibid.

[130] *Pelit v Azerbaijan*, Communication No 281/2005, CAT/C/38/D/281/2005, Views of 29 May 2007, para 11.

adopt a reading of these judgments that would suggest that 'guarantees may be accepted where [unlike in *Chahal*] the authorities of the receiving State can be assumed to have control of the situation'.[131] If the Committee had adopted the path suggested by Sweden it would have engaged in the kind of dialogue that should rather be avoided: one that follows unjust (reading of) precedents for the sake of consistency. To its credit, the Committee avoided this path but it also avoided any discussion of the ECtHR case law altogether, ultimately opting for a more reserved approach by producing a brief reasoning tailored strictly to the facts of the case.

3. *The Human Rights Committee*

Mohammed Alzery suffered the same treatment with Agiza and was subjected to the same diplomatic assurances given by Egypt. In *Alzery v Sweden* the Human Rights Committee found that 'the diplomatic assurances procured were [not] in fact sufficient *in the present case* to eliminate the risk of ill-treatment to a level consistent with the requirements of article 7 of the Covenant'.[132] The main preoccupation of the Committee was with the lack of any monitoring arrangement.

Alzery was a rare case of a treaty body being called upon to decide on identical legal and factual issues previously decided by another treaty body which had been earlier seized by another individual. There could hardly be more favourable circumstances for interaction among the two bodies. Both the applicant and Sweden relied upon the Committee Against Torture's pronouncements in *Agiza*, Sweden having conceded all relevant findings made by the Committee Against Torture. Although the Human Rights Committee noted Sweden's concessions on the basis of the Committee Against Torture's parallel findings in *Agiza*, which were 'made with respect to substantially similar provisions of the Convention against Torture', it did not rely on them and stressed that 'it must nevertheless *independently ascertain* that in the circumstances of the case violations of the relevant provisions of the Covenant or the Optional Protocol occurred'.[133] Indeed, it went on to make its own findings and eventually reached similar conclusions, without, however, any reference to either the Committee Against Torture or any other external source whatsoever.

This reticence is perhaps striking in the circumstances of the case. It is not necessarily so if one looks at the generally low citation patterns of the Human Rights Committee. The Committee is recorded as having adopted similar styles of reasoning to the ECtHR without, for the most part,

[131] *Agiza v Sweden*, para 4.23; see also paras 12.20–12.25 (discussing *Mamatkulov*).

[132] *Alzery v Sweden*, Communication No 1416/2005, CCPR/C/88/D/1416/2005, Views of 25 October 2006, para 11.5 (emphasis added).

[133] ibid para 11.2 (emphasis added).

acknowledging its influence.[134] This is probably due to the universal character of the Committee as opposed to the regional one of the ECtHR and the reluctance of a universal body to attribute particular value to the jurisprudence of some region in the determination of rules of universal import.[135] However, it is difficult to explain such reticence towards another universal treaty body. A possible explanation is the Committee's will to safeguard its institutional autonomy.

The Committee had another opportunity to address diplomatic assurances. In *Maksudov and others v Kyrgyzstan* (concerning the applicants' extradition to Uzbekistan), the Committee stated that 'The existence of assurances, their content and the existence and implementation of enforcement mechanisms are all elements which are relevant to the overall determination of whether, in fact, a real risk of proscribed ill-treatment existed'.[136] Citing *Alzery*, it reiterated that 'at the very minimum, the assurances procured should contain such a monitoring mechanism and be safeguarded by arrangements made outside the text of the assurances themselves which would provide for their effective implementation'.[137] There was no reference to any other decision.

B. Domestic Jurisprudence

1. *UK Courts*

In the UK, assurances based on the Memorandum of Understanding (MOU) with Libya were the only ones rejected by the Special Immigration Appeals Commission (SIAC), which was created in 1997 in the wake of *Chahal* in order to provide an effective remedy against immigration decisions involving national security considerations. In *DD & AS v Secretary of State*, the SIAC cast doubt on Libya's reliability to adhere to the assurances for a number of reasons, including the unpredictability of Colonel Qadhafi, the ineffectiveness of the Qadhafi Development Foundation tasked to monitor the assurances, the absence of a civil society in Libya, etc.[138] However, assurances were not considered irrelevant and were only

[134] Slaughter, 'A Typology' (n 5) 106; Voeten (n 17) 550. There are of course some important exceptions such as the Committee's discussion of the death row phenomenon in *Kindler v Canada*, Communication No 470/1991, CCPR/C/48/D/470/1991, Views of 30 July 1993, where the Committee endorsed Canada's narrow reading of the ECtHR's decision in *Soering*.

[135] *cf* L Helfer and AM Slaughter, 'Towards a Theory of Effective Supranational Adjudication' (1997) 107 *Yale LJ* 376–77; Voeten (n 17) 556; Romano (n 15) 775.

[136] *Maksudov and others v Kyrgyzstan*, Communication Nos 1461/2006, 1462/2006, 1476/2006 and 1477/2006, CCPR/C/93/D/1461, 1462, 1476, 1477/2006, Views of 31 July 2008, para 12.5.

[137] ibid.

[138] *DD & AS v Secretary of State*, SIAC, Appeal No SC/42/2005 and SC/50/2005, 27 April 2007, paras 333 ff, www.siac.tribunals.gov.uk/Documents/siac_sc_42_50_2005.pdf (last visited 1 June 2011).

dismissed on the facts of the case. Indeed, the constant jurisprudence of the SIAC is that 'diplomatic assurances are legally relevant and capable of reducing the risk which would otherwise be faced to a level at which return would no longer breach the UK's obligations'.[139] The SIAC has thus endorsed diplomatic assurances given by Jordan in *Omar Othman (aka Abu Qatada) v Secretary of State*[140] and by Algeria in *Y v Secretary of State*, *BB v Secretary of State* and *U v Secretary of State*.[141] The pertinent findings on the relevance of assurances were upheld by the Court of Appeal and the House of Lords.

In relying on assurances, the SIAC correctly read the Strasbourg jurisprudence as not ruling them out ('there is no ECtHR authority which suggests that assurances are in principle to be ignored in deportation or extradition cases')[142] and has repeatedly referred to both *Mamatkulov* and *Chahal* as 'authority . . . that reliance can lawfully be placed on such assurances; the weight to be given to them depends upon the circumstances of each case'.[143] Rejection of assurances in *Chahal* has been read as showing 'no more than that they may not always be effective'.[144]

The SIAC has only once discussed any non-Strasbourg decision in the context of diplomatic assurances. This was done in *Omar Othman (aka Abu Qatada) v Secretary of State*, where it emphasised 'the crucial differences' between the Egyptian assurances in *Agiza* and the (admittedly more sophisticated) Jordanian ones contained in the MOU with the UK.[145]

The Court of Appeal clarified in *MT, RB and U v Secretary of State* that the legal issue was whether the treatment found would fall within the terms of Article 3 of the ECHR, which would have to be decided according to the Strasbourg jurisprudence.[146] The Court of Appeal also referred

[139] ibid para 317. See also: *Youssef v The Home Office*, Queen's Bench Division, 30 July 2004, [2004] EWHC 1884 (QB) para 69 ('it was reasonable to seek the assurances from the Egyptian Government').

[140] *Omar Othman (aka Abu Qatada) v Secretary of State*, Appeal No SC/15/2005, 26 February 2007, available at www.siac.tribunals.gov.uk/Documents/QATADA_FINAL_7FEB2007.pdf; *Y v Secretary of State for the Home Department*, Appeal No SC/36/2005, 24 August 2006, available at www.siac.tribunals.gov.uk/Documents/Y%20%20%20OPEN%2016%20Aug.pdf (both last visited 1 June 2011).

[141] *BB v Secretary of State for the Home Department*, Appeal No SC/39/2005, 5 December 2006, available at www.siac.tribunals.gov.uk/Documents/SC_39_2005%20BB%20Open%20Judgement%20Nov%2006.pdf; *U v Secretary of State for the Home Department*, Appeal No SC/32/2005, 14 May 2007, available at www.siac.tribunals.gov.uk/Documents/sc_32_2005.pdf (both last visited 1 June 2011).

[142] *Y v Secretary of State* (n 140) para 390.

[143] *Omar Othman (aka Abu Qatada) v Secretary of State* (n 140) para 494. See also: *Y v Secretary of State* (n 140) para 390; *BB v Secretary of State* (n 141) para 4 (referring also to *Shamayev v Georgia and Russia*).

[144] *Omar Othman (aka Abu Qatada) v Secretary of State* (n 140) para 496.

[145] ibid paras 496, 512.

[146] *MT (Algeria), RB (Algeria) and U (Algeria) v Secretary of State for the Home Department*, Cases Nos: T1/2006/2624, T1/2006/2669 and T1/2007/9505, 30 July 2007, [2007] EWCA Civ 808, para 97.

to *Chahal* as demonstrating that 'the legitimacy of acceptance of assurances depends on the facts of each case'.[147] It did so in order to rebut the argument put forward by the appellants that the decision of the Federal Court of Canada in *Sing v Canada* was an authority suggesting that assurances should not be resorted to in circumstances where there is a consistent pattern of gross, flagrant or mass violations of human rights, or of systematic practice of torture. The Court of Appeal relied on the SIAC's findings that there was no such situation in Algeria.[148] Interestingly, it also referred to *Sing v Canada* with respect to the required features of monitoring the assurances, but relied again on the SIAC's findings that practical verification of the Algerian assurances was feasible and would occur.[149]

The House of Lords upheld unanimously all these findings in *RB (Algeria), (FC) and another v Secretary of State*.[150] In his discussion of diplomatic assurances, Lord Philips of Worth Matravers referred to *Chahal* as the starting point and relied on *Mamatkulov, Shamayev* and the Committee Against Torture's *Attia* as cases treating assurances as part of the matrix that had to be considered when assessing the risk of torture.[151] He also considered *Saadi, Ismoilov* and *Ryabikin*, relied upon by the appellants, but concluded that 'these decisions [did not] establish a principle that assurances must eliminate all risk of inhuman treatment before they can be relied upon'.[152] He further cited with approval *Sing v Canada* on the proposition that diplomatic assurances give rise to issues of fact and concluded that 'the only ground upon which those conclusions can be attacked on an appeal restricted to questions of law is irrationality', which the study of the SIAC's lengthy and detailed reasoning did not disclose.[153] Relying on *Saadi*, Lord Hoffmann agreed that 'the question of whether assurances obviate the risk [of torture] is a question of fact, to be decided in the light of all the evidence'.[154] Finally, Lord Hope of Craighead held that *Sing v Canada* was not in support of the proposition that assurances were objectionable in principle.[155]

The jurisprudence of UK courts shows their heavy reliance on Strasbourg case law. Although British courts enjoy discretion under the 1998 Human Rights Act as to how much weight to give to the ECtHR

[147] ibid para 127.
[148] ibid paras 125–26.
[149] ibid paras 130–31.
[150] *RB (Algeria), (FC) and anor v Secretary of State for the Home Department, and joined case*, Appeal judgment, 18 February 2009 UKHL 10; ILDC 1250 (UK 2009).
[151] ibid para 112.
[152] ibid para 113. Lord Philips, however, cautioned that 'assurances should be treated with scepticism, if they are given by a country where inhuman treatment by State agents is endemic' (para 115).
[153] ibid paras 117, 126.
[154] ibid paras 186–87. See also para 236 (per Lord Hope of Craighead).
[155] ibid para 238.

decisions (which they are only required to 'take into account'),[156] the House of Lords did not make use of this space, showing loyalty to the ECtHR and following its case law in most cases, including in politically highly sensitive judgments.[157] A plausible explanation is that the Strasbourg jurisprudence empowered the Lords to extend the reach of their review powers beyond what was previously possible under the common law, and defend their newly acquired authority against legitimacy challenges.[158]

In any case, the British jurisprudence on diplomatic assurances shows great willingness to take part in the transjudicial dialogue on the topic by referring to, relying on and distinguishing from decisions of their counterparts in the ECtHR, the Committee Against Torture and Canada. In itself, this is a proper exercise of dialogue. However, one may be critical of the outcome of these cases and the reliance on deplorable decisions such as *Mamatkulov* and *Attia*, which brings us back to the tension between the competing values of coherence and justice.

2. *Other Domestic Courts in Europe*

Other domestic courts in Europe have also relied on the Strasbourg jurisprudence in deciding cases on diplomatic assurances. Diplomatic assurances were endorsed by the Swiss Federal Tribunal in *X v Bundesamt für Justiz*,[159] an extradition case to Russia, where the court relied on *Mamatkulov* as authority for allowing assurances and also interpreted *Chahal* to the same effect.[160] It then directed the Ministry of Foreign Affairs to request more precise assurances from the Russian authorities, which would allow extradition without violating Switzerland's obligations under the ECHR.[161]

On the other hand, assurances were rejected by the Dutch Supreme Court (relying on *Chahal*) in the extradition case of *Nuriye Kesbir* to Turkey;[162] the Constitutional Court of Slovakia (relying on *Chahal* and *Saadi*) in the extradition case of *Mustapha Labsi* to Algeria;[163] and the

[156] McCrudden (n 80) 503 f.

[157] N Krisch, 'The Open Architecture of European Human Rights Law' (2008) 71 *Modern L Rev* 203.

[158] ibid 204 f.

[159] Decision of 18 December 2007. I am grateful to Andreas Ziegler for pointing out this case to me.

[160] Paras 6.5.1 and 6.9.

[161] Paras 6.14–6.15.

[162] Decision of 15 September 2006. I am grateful to André Nollkaemper for locating this decision for me.

[163] Decision of 7 August 2008. See: Amnesty International, 'Slovakia: Constitutional Court Upholds the Absolute Prohibition of Torture', AI Index: EUR 72/005/2008 (Public), 27 June 2008, available at www.amnesty.org/en/library/asset/EUR72/005/2008/en/dbc9ab8e-4467-11dd-a853-cb8a3d8264d3/eur720052008eng.html (last visited 1 June 2011).

Administrative Court of Düsseldorf in January 2009 in a case concerning deportation to Jordan,[164] and in March 2009 in a case concerning deportation to Tunisia,[165] both relying on *Chahal* and *Saadi*.

The March 2009 decision of the Administrative Court of Düsseldorf provides an extensive discussion of diplomatic assurances with several references to reports of international organisations and NGOs and goes beyond existing case law in finding that diplomatic assurances are not legally binding. This decision shows that domestic courts in Europe can still be loyal to Strasbourg and go beyond its jurisprudence to offer better protection. It remains to be seen whether higher courts in Germany will follow the same commendable path.

An important part of the role of European highest national courts towards the ECtHR is to ensure that the law within their jurisdiction is interpreted and applied in a consistent manner and in compliance with the Convention.[166] With regard to diplomatic assurances domestic courts fulfilled this role, even though they reached different outcomes. This happened due to the inconclusiveness of some of Strasbourg's case law. Finally, it is noteworthy that none of them cited any non-Strasburg decisions, although there are references to other international sources.

3. *Canada*

In Canada, an extradition to China (*Sing v Canada*)[167] and a deportation to Egypt (*Mahjoub v Canada*),[168] both based on diplomatic assurances, were blocked by federal courts. In *Mahjoub* the Court ruled that the executive had reached a 'patently unreasonable' decision by disregarding the bulk of evidence from a multitude of sources that cited Egypt's non-compliance with assurances.[169] In *Sing*, one of the most critical decisions towards diplomatic assurances, the Court emphasised 'the flaws and pitfalls inherent in diplomatic assurances'[170] and 'the growing consensus that diplomatic assurances should not be sought when the practice of torture is sufficiently systematic or widespread'.[171] In discussing diplomatic

[164] Verwaltungsgericht Düsseldorf, 21 K 3263/07.A, 16 January 2009. I am grateful to Helmut Aust for pointing out this case to me.

[165] Verwaltungsgericht Düsseldorf, 11 K 4716/07.A, 4 March 2009. I am grateful to Helmut Aust for locating this judgment for me.

[166] WME Thomassen, 'The European Convention on Human Rights (ECHR) and the Position of the National Judge' in *Highest Courts and the Internationalisation of Law*, 119.

[167] *Sing v Canada (Minister of Citizenship and Immigration)*, 2007 FC 361, 5 April 2007, available at http://decisions.fct-cf.gc.ca/en/2007/2007fc361/2007fc361.html (last visited 1 June 2011).

[168] *Mahjoub v Canada (Minister of Citizenship and Immigration)*, 2005 FC 156, 31 January 2005, available at http://reports.fja.gc.ca/eng/2005/2005fc156/2005fc156.html (last visited 1 June 2011).

[169] ibid paras 84–97.

[170] *Sing v Canada* (n 167) para 132.

[171] ibid para 136.

assurances, *Sing* referred extensively to reports of the UN Special Rapporteur on Torture but not to international or foreign jurisprudence. *Mahjoub* also referred to abundant international non-judicial sources but reliance upon international or national jurisprudence was limited to criticising the executive for not relying on the Committee Against Torture's findings on Egypt's diplomatic assurances in *Agiza*.[172]

The absence of citations of foreign decisions in these two cases should not be taken as indication of any broader reluctance of Canadian courts to engage in transjudicial dialogue. It is probably a consequence of the Supreme Court's approach to diplomatic assurances as a factual issue in *Suresh v Canada*,[173] which is binding authority for lower courts in Canada. On the contrary, the Supreme Court of Canada is generally praised as being an active participant in the global conversation among courts, particularly in constitutional and human rights law.[174]

4. *The US Case of* Khouzam v Hogan

Litigation concerning diplomatic assurances has been limited in the US, even though US federal legislation explicitly allows for their use.[175] However, *Khouzam v Hogan*, the only US judgment on diplomatic assurances, is throughout an exercise in interjudicial dialogue and presents a rare instance of such dialogue by lower courts in the US.[176] This was probably consequent on significant NGO involvement in the proceedings and it was even praised by avowed opponents of transjudicialism.[177] The case involved the applicant's deportation to Egypt. The District Court of Pennsylvania ruled that 'it is not unreasonable to utilize appropriate diplomatic assurances to avoid violating [the FARRA, that is, the implementing legislation of the Convention against Torture]. That a particular country may have a record of torture does not mean that a diplomatic assurance will never have sufficient indicia of reliability'.[178]

The Court made extensive reference to both international and domestic jurisprudence in discussing two issues: whether the Convention against Torture and the FARRA categorically prohibit reliance upon diplomatic

[172] *Mahjoub v Canada* (n 168) paras 71 and 94.
[173] *Suresh v Canada (Minister of Citizenship and Immigration)*, [2002] 1 SCR 3.
[174] Baudenbacher (n 1) 522.
[175] 8 CFR para 208.17 (c), providing, *inter alia*, that 'The Secretary of State may forward to the Attorney General assurances that the Secretary has obtained from the government of a specific country that an alien would not be tortured there if the alien were removed to that country' and 'once assurances are provided . . ., the alien's claim for protection under the Convention Against Torture shall not be considered further by an immigration judge, the Board of Immigration Appeals, or an asylum officer'.
[176] R Alford, 'Lower Courts and Constitutional Comparativism' (2008) 77 *Fordham L Rev* 657.
[177] ibid 658 f, 661.
[178] *Khouzam v Hogan*, 529 F Supp 2d 543, 557 (MD Pa 2008).

assurances in removal cases to countries with a consistent record of engaging in torture and whether the US policy of not disclosing the assurances violated the applicant's due process rights.

In dealing with the first issue, the Court discussed the relevance of pronouncements by treaty bodies, such as the Committee Against Torture, and held that, although not binding, such pronouncements may afford significant guidance in interpreting the language of treaties to which the US is a party. It also stated that a treaty's *travaux preparatoires* and the post-ratification understanding of the parties may be considered by courts as aids to the interpretation of such treaty. Absent any US reservation, understanding, declaration or proviso concerning diplomatic assurances upon ratification of the Convention against Torture, the Court added that:

> [I]t is appropriate to consider pronouncements of international tribunals and foreign courts, as well as the post-ratification conduct of other signatory States, in assessing the non-refoulement obligation of the United States under FARRA.[179]

In doing so, it referred to the UK Court of Appeal's decision in *MT, RB and U v Secretary of State* and in the Federal Court of Canada's decision in *Mahjoub v Canada* in support of the proposition that diplomatic assurances (even if not regarded as sufficiently reliable in specific cases) are not categorically barred by Article 3 of the Convention, and thus rejected Khouzam's facial challenge to the diplomatic assurances.[180]

In its treatment of the second issue, the Court in effect employed transjudicialism in order to remedy the US executive's policy of not disclosing diplomatic assurances by considering it to be in violation of Khouzam's due process rights under the Fifth Amendment. In doing so, the Court first noted that the US was the only government that denied a person subject to removal the right to challenge the reliability and sufficiency of diplomatic assurances against torture before an independent, impartial body – which was a Declaration made by Human Rights Watch. Relying on the US Supreme Court's rulings in *Lawrence v Texas*[181] and *Roper v Simmons*[182] on the use and relevance of international and foreign jurisprudence, it then referred to the Canadian cases of *Suresh* and *Mahjoub*, the UK Court of Appeal's decision in *MT, RB and U v Secretary of State*, and the Committee Against Torture's *Agiza* and *Pelit* as relevant (albeit not having binding effect) in determining 'whether certain action in the United States violates fundamental interests'.[183]

179 ibid para 556.
180 ibid paras 556–57.
181 539 US 558 (2003).
182 543 US 551 (2005).
183 *Khouzam v Hogan* (n 178) paras 565–66.

C. Assessment

At first sight, it would seem that neither the ECtHR nor the treaty bodies spoke to or borrowed from each other or any domestic courts in their decisions on diplomatic assurances. There was no dialogue in the form of express citations. However, one cannot fail to notice that they were all aware of the solutions reached by their counterparts and came to almost identical findings, albeit without any public acknowledgment of outside influence. This affirms that transjudicialism involves more than cross-referencing, which is not necessarily the preferred option even when the circumstances call for it. In the case of diplomatic assurances the issues were virtually identical and the UN treaty bodies did (borrow and) apply the solutions previously given by the ECtHR. However, they fell short of acknowledging such borrowing, most likely due to legitimacy concerns, the ECtHR being a regional court with less inclusive membership than the UN treaty bodies. Indeed, this is among the main factors deterring international courts from citing decisions of regional ones.[184]

The explanation is different for the ECtHR's exclusive reliance upon its own jurisprudence. Legitimacy concerns should have played no role there. The Strasbourg Court was the first to rule on diplomatic assurances and set a welcome, albeit inconclusive, standard in *Chahal*. The reasoning of both the ECtHR and all other international decisions was laconic, tailored to the facts and lacked any analytical strength and rigour. The two UN treaty bodies were proven to be reluctant to take the lead in producing a robust approach. Thus, there was not much to borrow with a view to producing better, more reflective and more informed decisions, which is among the main motivations for transjudicialism.

In terms of substance, international jurisprudence has for the most part reached welcome outcomes, with the unfortunate exceptions of the ECtHR's *Mamatkulov* and the Committe Against Torture's *Attia*. Even though *Attia* was quickly reversed, both decisions have been referred to in domestic case law in the quest to justify diplomatic assurances.

The case law of both highest and lower national courts on diplomatic assurances shows that they have been more prone to explicit forms of inter-judicial dialogue, including citations. With the exception of British courts, domestic courts in Europe have relied exclusively on the ECtHR's rulings, without paying any attention to related judicial developments elsewhere. This did not prevent them from producing different outcomes but, as already noted, this was mainly due to the inconclusiveness of the *Chahal* standard they were applying. Be that as it may, they did play their part in transjudicialism within Europe.

[184] Voeten (n 17) 556.

Their North American counterparts seemed equally willing to engage in transjudicial dialogue in their decisions on diplomatic assurances, but the features and extent of such dialogue depended on the (factual and/or legal) issues they had to deal with. In doing so, they were assisted, indeed propelled, by *amicus curiae* briefs, especially by human rights NGOs. Most significantly, the District Court of Pennsylvania resorted to transjudicialism in an apparent effort to foster the legitimacy of its finding that the US policy of not disclosing the diplomatic assurances to affected individuals was unconstitutional.

In deciding controversial and high-profile cases on diplomatic assurances against torture, courts are faced with a hard choice: to either run counter to the anti-terrorism policies of the executive power or face severe criticism by the human rights movement that they are eroding the principle of non-refoulement. This is a choice they have to make in the absence of a precise rule outlawing diplomatic assurances; courts are tasked to specify a rather vague standard,[185] that is, whether diplomatic assurances can mitigate the risk of torture. In either case, the stakes are high and their decisions are in need of legitimacy. This can further explain why many national courts have resorted to the case law of other international and/or national courts to justify their choice. In this sense, the case study on diplomatic assurances provides some evidence that national and supranational courts are willing to participate in a common judicial enterprise, as suggested by Anne Marie Slaughter. Nevertheless, the patterns and outcome of their dialogue is more in line with Delmas-Marty's more nuanced concept of 'ordered pluralism', which allows for coherence in the sense of compatibility rather than perfect unity.

V. CONCLUDING REMARKS: THE PROMISE AND PERILS OF TRANSJUDICIALISM

There is little doubt that transjudicial communication is commonplace and spreading. This is true both in terms of citation patterns and extrajudicial activities; it takes place through borrowing, cross-references, institutionalised or informal meetings and various networks. Courts show willingness to consider and take the decisions of their counterparts into account, even though they are not always prepared to acknowledge it in the form of citations. Dialogue is even more likely to take place when favourable conditions are present: gaps in the legal framework; lack of precedent; identical or similar legal issues; transnational nature of the problem; effective advocacy; strong interest on the part of transnational social networks and civil society. Such dialogue leads to more interaction,

[185] See on the distinction between clear rules and vague standards: Benvenisti (n 68) 276.

better coordination, consistency in jurisprudence and more coherence in the law. The relevance and contribution of transjudicial communication in fostering these important values is to be acknowledged and welcomed, and following this path in the future is to be encouraged and supported.

That said, not all assumptions and propositions put forward with regard to transjudicial dialogue stand the test of empirical findings. The assumption that dialogue makes for more reasoned judgments has not been proven in the case study on diplomatic assurances. Much depends on the merits of the specific 'precedents' followed and the ways courts make use of them. For example, the *Chahal* standard, which was the influential starting point, was categorical in its result but laconic in its reasoning and inconclusive in normative terms, and hence its application has given rise to different outcomes. Relying on it did not make other decisions more reasoned. On the other hand, the effective use of interjudicial dialogue by lower courts in the US and Germany shows that making proper use of the right decisions for the right problem can give the right answers and welcome solutions. One only hopes that this path will be followed by the higher/est national courts in those countries and elsewhere.

Similarly, the assumption that dialogue produces better outcomes is also an unwarranted generalisation. Whether transjudicialism always makes for better judgments is question-begging (and, of course, subjective) and depends on the approach taken on the substantive questions on a case-by-case basis. Following a 'bad' precedent such as *Mamatkulov* or *Attia* may reproduce deplorable outcomes and does not make a decision any better. More nuanced conclusions are warranted, based on empirical evidence rather than on ideologically-based and other assumptions.

This case study has shown that abstract propositions put forward in the unity-or-fragmentation debate need and require more empirical verification. The case study on interjudicial dialogue in the limited context of diplomatic assurances against torture has exposed both the promise and perils of transjudicial dialogue. On the one hand, courts may be inspired by decisions of other courts and feel empowered to follow a settled jurisprudence beyond their jurisdictional confines with a view to reaching welcome and innovative solutions to issues new to them. On the other hand, a unified judicial approach and unitary interpretations may yield objectionable solutions and outcomes. For example, transjudicial dialogue has contributed to some extent in maintaining the flawed practice of diplomatic assurances – in vain anticipation of improving it – which risks eroding a fundamental principle of international human rights law. Transjudicialism has a great potential in contributing to the unity and coherence of international law and jurisprudence. But such unity should not be an end in itself nor the end of the story.

13

Racial Discrimination in Japan: Unity, Diversity and International Law

TIMOTHY WEBSTER*

I. INTRODUCTION

UNITY AND FRAGMENTATION have recently emerged as central themes, if not tightly defined concepts, in international legal theory. Fragmentation, the more frequently discussed of the pair, refers alternatively to distinct legal subsystems in the international arena, such as trade, human rights, environmental law, investments;[1] the threat of conflict between subsystems;[2] the proliferation of international courts, tribunals, and institutions;[3] and the related possibility that they will contradict each other.[4] There would seem to be fragmentation in the very idea itself. Unity too is defined variously, as 'cross-fertilisation' among these competing legal regimes,[5] the emergence of similar interpretive principles across different international systems,[6] or the consistent application of

* Lecturer-in-Law and Senior Research Scholar, Yale Law School; Senior Fellow, China Law Center. I appreciate the comments of Professors André Nollkaemper and Ole Kristian Fauchald on earlier drafts of this chapter.

[1] International Law Commission (ILC), Fragmentation of International Law: Difficulties Arising from the Diversification and Expansion of International Law (ILC Fragmentation Report), UN Doc A/CN.4/682 (2006) (finalised by Martti Koskenniemi) 8.

[2] ibid para 6.

[3] E Benvenisti and GW Downs, 'The Empire's New Clothes: Political Economy and the Fragmentation of International Law' (2007) 60 *Stan L Rev* 595.

[4] B Simma, 'Fragmentation in a Positive Light' (2004) 25 *Mich J Int'l L* 845.

[5] A Cassese, *International Law*, 1st edn (Oxford, Oxford University Press, 2001) 45 ('The gradual interpenetration and cross-fertilization of previously somewhat compartmentalized areas of international law is a significant development: it shows that at least at the normative level the international community is becoming more integrated and – what is even more important – that such values as human rights and the need to promote development are increasingly permeating various sectors of international law that previously seemed impervious to them').

[6] PM Dupuy, 'The Danger of Fragmentation or Unification of the International Legal System and the International Court of Justice' (1999) 31 *NYU J Int'l L & Pol* 791 (Dupuy notes that the international legal order possesses two kinds of unity: formal unity and substantial unity. Formal unity, following HLA Hart's secondary rules, refers to rules of change that

international law by domestic courts.[7] Unity likewise is not a unified concept, but susceptible to multiple meanings.

This chapter focuses on the concepts of unity and fragmentation as they emerge in the application of international human rights law (IHRL) by the courts of one country: Japan.[8] Unity refers to relatively strong adherence to the letter of international treaty law, as well as relatively close conformity with the legal practices of other courts around the world. In the absence of such unity, one faces fragmentation of international law, when domestic practice deviates significantly from international practices or trends. Both elements – unity and fragmentation – are critical to understanding Japan's engagement with the international normative community, for the judiciary's response to these norms and obligations has been *mixed*. International criminal justice standards have had an impact on Japanese conceptions of certain trial rights, for example. But there is less consistency on issues such as the right to equality and minority rights.[9]

Since ratifying the International Covenant on Civil and Political Rights[10] and International Covenant on Economic, Social and Cultural Rights[11] in 1979, Japan has ratified many of the major many IHRL treaties, including the Refugee Convention (1982), Women's Convention (1980, entered into force in 1985), the Racial Discrimination Convention (1995), and others.[12] In the ensuing decades, Japanese courts have had hundreds of occasions to apply, deny, or otherwise shape the forms that IHRL takes in Japan.[13]

permit public international law to create, modify, extinguish and adjudicate international norms. Substantial unity, on the other hand, refers to rules that have obtained broad support across a number of treaties or legal regimes, such as prohibitions on genocide or the use of force, and the establishment of an unspecified corps of basic rights. See: ibid 793 ff.).

[7] S Wittich, 'Domestic Implementation and the Unity of International Law' in A Zimmerman and R Hofman (eds), *Unity and Diversity in International Law* (Kiel, Duncker und Humblot, 2006) 342, 347.

[8] ibid 347.

[9] See for more on the impact of international law on criminal justice and minority rights: T Webster, 'International Human Rights in Japan: The View at Thirty' (2010) 23 *Colum J Asian L* 241.

[10] International Covenant on Civil and Political Rights (19 December 1966) 999 UNTS 171 (entered into force for Japan on 21 September 1979).

[11] International Covenant on Economic, Social and Cultural Rights (16 December 1966, 999 UNTS 3 (entered into force for Japan on 21 September 1979).

[12] In addition to the International Covenant on Civil and Political Rights and International Covenant on Economic, Social and Cultural Rights, Japan ratified the Convention Relating to the Status of Refugees in 1982, the Convention on the Elimination of All Forms of Discrimination against Women in 1985, the Convention on the Rights of the Child in 1994, the International Convention on the Elimination of All Forms of Racial Discrimination in 1995, and the Convention against Torture in 1999. See generally: Y Iwasawa, *International Law, Human Rights and Japanese Law* (Oxford, Oxford University Press, 1998) 2 f.

[13] A search for cases that cite the Convention to Eliminate All Forms of Racial Discrimination, International Covenant on Civil and Political Rights and International Covenant on Economic, Social and Cultural Rights in TKC Law Library Database – one of Japan's most comprehensive catalogues of case law – reveals 19, 369 and 169 cases, respectively.

To narrow the task, this chapter focuses on one particular norm – non-discrimination (or anti-discrimination) – that surfaces across several treaties. In particular, we look at antidiscrimination lawsuits that reference Japanese law and provisions of three international instruments ratified by Japan: the International Covenant on Civil and Political Rights, the International Convention on Economic, Social and Cultural Rights, and the International Convention to Eliminate All Forms of Racial Discrimination.[14] These treaties outlaw discrimination, but in quite different ways. The International Covenant on Civil and Political Rights makes a blanket statement that 'All persons are equal before the law', and in effect calls on states to ensure equality through domestic legislation:

> [T]he *law* shall prohibit any discrimination and guarantee to all persons equal and effective protection against discrimination on any ground such as race, colour, sex, language, religion, political or other opinion, national or social origin, property, birth or other status.[15]

Under the International Covenant on Economic, Social and Cultural Rights, on the other hand, signatories 'undertake to guarantee that the rights enunciated in the present Covenant will be exercised without discrimination of any kind as to race, colour, sex, language, religion, political or other opinion, national or social origin, property, birth or other status'.[16] That is, states need only guarantee that the rights enshrined in the International Covenant on Economic, Social and Cultural Rights are implemented equally, arguably a lower standard than the one in the International Covenant on Civil and Political Rights, which requires the affirmative proscription of discrimination. Finally, under Article 2(1)(d) of the Convention to Eliminate All Forms of Racial Discrimination, states 'shall prohibit and bring to an end, by all appropriate means, including legislation as required by circumstances, racial discrimination by any persons, group or organization'.[17] The Convention to Eliminate All Forms of Racial Discrimination thus urges states to pass anti-discrimination laws, and in particular to target racial discrimination by *private* actors. Breaching the private sphere suggests a higher level of government activity to conform to the Convention to Eliminate All Forms of Racial Discrimination, including legislation. Since the early 1980s, Japanese judges have grappled with the implementation of the International Covenant on Civil and Political Rights and the International Covenant on

[14] International Covenant on the Elimination of All Forms of Racial Discrimination (21 December 1965) 660 UNTS (entered into force for Japan on 14 January 1996).

[15] International Covenant on Civil and Political Rights, art 26 (emphasis added). By requiring 'the law' to prohibit discrimination, it seems the treaty is referring to the domestic law of the signatory.

[16] International Covenant on Economic, Social and Cultural Rights, art 2(2).

[17] Convention to Eliminate All Forms of Racial Discrimination, art 2(1)(d).

Economic, Social and Cultural Rights, and since 1999 with the implementation of the Convention to Eliminate All Forms of Racial Discrimination.

Domestic courts applying international treaties decide which provisions to incorporate into domestic jurisprudence, and which to rebuff at the border. Subject to appropriate guidance from the political branches, domestic courts have a fair amount of leeway to decide how and whether to apply international law. Implementing international law is seldom a matter of simply applying clear language of a particular provision. When it is, courts have a straightforward task.[18] But more ambiguously phrased provisions, or conflicts between international legal provisions and domestic ones, require the exercise of interpretive powers. The results further vary by the nature of the case, and the actors involved. Variations across court decisions may signal internal debates about how best to effectuate a provision's language, or highlight tensions between international law and domestic jurisprudence – areas of disharmony between the two normative regimes.

Over time, court application of the international law of discrimination has evolved into canons of interpretations. With regard to the International Covenant on Civil and Political Rights and the Convention to Eliminate All Forms of Racial Discrimination, courts consistently hold that private actors can be liable for private acts of discrimination, but they do not find government bodies liable for failing to pass antidiscrimination law. Since 1999, judges have found a wide swathe of discriminatory conduct illegal in areas such as shopping, housing, public facilities, and other economic transactions between two private persons, or between a person and an organisation.[19] Repeated decisions, over time and space, reinforce the prohibition of racial discrimination in various types of private relationships.

But not every act of discrimination amounts to an illegal violation of international law, as Japanese courts' experience with the International Covenant on Economic, Social and Cultural Rights suggests. For the past three decades, courts have adjudicated numerous disputes over the social and economic rights of resident Koreans,[20] Japan's largest minority population. In lawsuit after lawsuit, resident Koreans use IHRL to plead for access to social benefits enjoyed by Japanese citizens, but not resident aliens. The Japanese judiciary has repeatedly ruled that Japan's allocation

[18] See: n 69.

[19] See generally: T Webster, 'Reconstituting Japanese Law: International Norms and Domestic Litigation'(2008) 30 *Mich J Int'l L* 211.

[20] Brought to Japan, involuntarily and voluntarily during its colonial period (1910–45), the Korean minority has posed a series of human rights problems in Japan ever since. From the 1910 annexation of Japan until the issuance of a circular by the Ministry of Justice on 19 April 1952, resident Koreans were regarded as Japanese citizens. Since denationalisation, resident Koreans have waged a number of legal battles to assert various human rights. See generally: Y Iwasawa, 'Legal Treatment of Koreans in Japan: The Impact of International Human Rights Law on Japanese Law' (1986) 8 *Hum Rts Q* 131.

of social benefits – whatever their particular configuration – pass constitutional muster, and do not contravene international law. In such cases, judges have ruled that international obligations, such as the right of social security in Article 9 of the International Covenant on Economic, Social and Cultural Rights, is to be 'achieved progressively', at some indefinite point in the future.[21] Thus, in a given lawsuit, a plaintiff cannot expect to realise the right to social security guaranteed by international law. This interpretation probably violates international law,[22] suggesting fragmentation from the international community. Yet the Japanese judiciary largely defers to the political branches when reviewing legislation and social policy.

Judges thus shape the ways international law is experienced by people and organisations in Japan. Unity, or uniform application of international law, represents one pole of domestic implementation. Fragmentation, the breach or selective application of international legal provisions, marks the other end of this continuum. Indeed, courts can deny the direct effect of international law, and arrive at any number of different results. Fragmentation thus represents not simply a breach of international obligation, but the variety of interpretations that results when a judge understands that he is not bound by provisions of a particular treaty. Both unity and fragmentation surface throughout the three decades in which Japan has domesticated international law, revealing both adherence and deviation from the global international human rights system.

This chapter proceeds in three parts. Section II addresses the dialogue between Japanese courts and foreign or international law, showing that Japan does participate in cross-jurisdictional dialogues, even if it does not always conform to generally agreed upon international practice. Section III outlines the position of international law in the Japanese legal system, and offers a general framework for understanding judicial application of treaties. Section IV investigates several courts' applications of three international treaties, paying particular attention to the International Covenant on Economic, Social and Cultural Rights and the Convention to Eliminate All Forms of Racial Discrimination. A brief conclusion follows.

[21] See below section III.

[22] This probably violates the very language of International Covenant on Economic, Social and Cultural Rights, art 2(2) of which prohibits discrimination on grounds of nationality. International Covenant on Economic, Social and Cultural Rights, art 2(2). Moreover, General Comment 19 provides that 'All persons should be covered by the social security system, especially individuals belonging to the most disadvantaged and marginalised groups, without discrimination'. The right to social security, UN Doc E/C.12/GC/19 (4 February 2008) para 23. Likewise, General Comment 3 places limits on progressive realisation, noting that various obligations – including the right not to be discriminated against – are immediately effective. The nature of states parties obligations (art 2(1)), UN Doc E/C.12/GC/3 (14 December 1990) para 1.

II. JAPANESE COURTS AND INTERNATIONAL LEGAL MATERIAL

Japanese judges, on occasion, cite the opinions of foreign courts,[23] and comments and interpretations of United Nations (UN) bodies, such as the Human Rights Committee. Japanese courts use these decisions and comments to mold their own understanding of topics such as degrading treatment, the right to counsel, equality and discrimination. Since Japan has not signed the First Optional Protocol to the International Covenant on Civil and Political Rights, nor recognised the competence of international committees to receive individual complaints, litigation offers the most prominent, and arguably most effective, arena for challenging conduct that violates human rights norms.[24] Though not bound by this type of international legal material,[25] Japanese judges absorb it in various ways. International materials have not significantly influenced Japanese jurisprudence, but a few cases pushed the Japanese judiciary at least to recognise that the underlying behavior was illegal, even if it did not offer a remedy.

Two examples reflect this modest, but undeniable, influence. In the first, a resident Korean plaintiff challenged the fingerprinting requirement for resident aliens. When the suit was filed in 1989, Japan still required resident Koreans and Taiwanese, many of them born and raised in Japan, to be fingerprinted when renewing their resident alien certificates. For many, this was a potent symbol of discrimination, given the criminal connotations of fingerprinting. Yun Chang-yol claimed that the fingerprinting system violated his constitutional rights, as well as Articles 7 (degrading treatment) and 26 (non-discrimination) of the International Covenant on Civil and Political Rights. The Osaka High Court found the fingerprinting system constitutional, even though the Diet had abolished the system in 1991. Under international law, however, the Court modestly suggested 'there was room to suspect' the system was illegal, at least as applied to resident Koreans and Taiwanese.[26]

[23] One index of the Japanese judiciary's dialogue with foreign courts is look at citations to the Inter-American Commission on Human Rights, and the European Convention on Human Rights, as well as their respective courts. The author searched for these four terms in the TKC Law Library, a leading Japanese database of court opinions. Japanese courts cited the European Convention 27 times, the European Court 14 times, the Inter-American Convention 10 times and the Court once.

[24] Iwasawa (n 12) 118.

[25] See: M Masanao, 'Saibansho ni yoru jinken joyaku no tekiyo ni kansuru shomondai' (Various problems relating to the application of human rights treaties in courts) in Buraku Kaihô Jinken Kenkyûsho (Buraku Liberation and Human Rights Research Center) (ed) *Kokusai Jinken Kiyaku to Kokunai Hanrei* (*International Human Rights Covenants and Domestic Jurisprudence* (Tokyo, Liberation Press, 2004) 8, 23.

[26] *Yun Chang-yol v Japan & Kyoto* (Osaka High Ct, 28 October 1994) 1513 Hanrei jihô 1513, (1995) 38 *Japanese Ann Int'l L* 118.

In arriving at this conclusion, the Osaka High Court referenced a significant amount of international legal material, including the *Tyrer* decision from the European Court of Human Rights (ECtHR),[27] the *East Africa* case of the European Commission of Human Rights, and many Views and General Comments of the Human Rights Committee.[28] These materials described various judges' and international experts' views on degrading treatment. The *Tyrer* decision defined degrading treatment as involving a 'certain level of humiliation', beyond the shame felt from criminal conviction, but below that of torture.[29] This proved helpful to the Japanese Court's conception of degrading treatment. Likewise, General Comment 20 includes 'acts that cause mental suffering' in its description of degrading treatment, which also triggered a response from the Japanese Court.[30] In the end, the Osaka High Court defined degrading treatment as 'conduct which, under the positive or negative commitment of a public official, inflicts physical or *mental suffering* on an individual and whose degree of suffering *reaches a certain level*, albeit not to a degree evaluated as torture or cruel and inhuman punishment'.[31] From this formulation of degrading treatment, the appellate court relied heavily on foreign and international concepts to arrive at this definition. The Court did not find that fingerprinting in fact reached the 'certain level' of mental suffering necessary to constitute degrading treatment, but it arrived at this conclusion on sound comparative terms.

In a second case, the Takamatsu High Court grappled with a prisoner's right to counsel. The trial court had found that the prison warden had violated the prisoner's rights by limiting his time with counsel, and requiring a prison guard to be present during the lawyer's visit. As the prisoner was bringing a civil lawsuit against the prison abuses, such interference was quite inimical to his cause. On appeal, the Court examined the issue of the right to equality before courts and tribunals guaranteed in Article 14(1) of the International Covenant on Civil and Political Rights.

Among the international materials surveyed by the Court were two decisions by the ECtHR, and a Resolution of the UN General Assembly. Based on the ECtHR decisions – *Golder v UK* and *Campbell & Fell v UK* – the Court established that the right to a fair trial (as guaranteed in Article 6(1) of the European Convention) included both a prisoner's right to

27 *Tyrer v United Kingdom*, App No 5856/72 (ECtHR 25 April 1978) para 4.

28 Yun (n 26) 1518.

29 In *Tyrer*, the ECtHR found that birching the bare bottom of a Manx boy amounted to 'degrading treatment' under art 3 of the European Convention. In order to qualify as degrading treatment, the ECtHR held, 'the humiliation or debasement involved must attain a *particular level* and must in any event be other than that usual element of humiliation [inherent in conviction]' ibid 6 (emphasis added).

30 Human Rights Committee, General Comment No 20, art 7(5), UN Doc HRI / GEN / 1Rev.1 (1994).

31 38 *Japanese Ann Int'l L* 130 (emphasis added).

contact and consult with an attorney to prepare a civil suit (*Golder*), and that prison officials should not be present for such meetings (*Campbell & Fell*).[32] The Resolution likewise established a detainee's right to communicate and consult with legal counsel, and further that he should enjoy adequate time and facilities, and some degree of independence from prison officials.[33]

As to the actual interpretation of these various materials, the Court consulted Article 31(3) of the Vienna Convention,[34] which deals specifically with the parties to a treaty, and their subsequent agreements, practices and relationships. But since Japan is not a party to the European Convention, the Court found that none of the principles in Article 31 could apply to Japan. The Resolution, likewise, was not a subsequent practice under the Vienna Convention. The Court did, however, find that the case law and Resolution could 'serve as a guide to the interpretation of Article 14(1) of the [International Covenant on Civil and Political Rights]'.[35] In other words, and as Japanese courts have held in other decisions,[36] international legal material can be used as 'supplementary means of interpretation' to define or guide the meaning of treaty terms. The Vienna Convention specifically proposes that courts refer to 'supplementary means' when treaty terms are 'ambiguous or obscure'.[37] While terms like 'degrading treatment' and 'fair trial' are relatively comprehensible, reference to international legal materials can help Japanese courts draw the line between fair and unfair, or degrading and merely derogatory, while ensuring they stay abreast of recent trends and developments in the rest of the world.

III. THE MECHANICS OF INTERNATIONAL LAW IN JAPAN

The Constitution of Japan provides that treaties 'shall be faithfully observed'.[38] The conventional view concerning the effect of international law in Japan is that, upon ratification and publication by the Diet, inter-

[32] (1998) 41 *Japanese Ann Int'l L* 87, 89.

[33] UN General Assembly, Body of Principles for the Protection of All Persons under Any Form of Detention or Imprisonment (9 December 1988) UN Doc A / RES / 43 / 173. The Resolution states that interviews 'may be within sight, but not within the hearing, of a law enforcement official.' ibid Principle 18.

[34] Vienna Convention on the Law of Treaties (23 May 1969) 1155 UNTS 331.

[35] (1998) 41 *Japanese Ann Int'l L* 89, 90.

[36] See, eg: Yun (n 26) 1513 Hanrei jihô 87. 'General comments and views of the Human Rights Committee should be relied upon as supplementary means of interpreting the ICCPR [International Covenant on Civil and Political Rights]. Furthermore, contents of international conventions like the European Convention of Human Rights, or its jurisprudence, can also be treated as supplementary means of interpreting the ICCPR'.

[37] Vienna Convention, art 32(a).

[38] Kenpô, art 98(2).

national treaties have 'domestic legal force in Japan'.[39] But it would be more correct to say that the effect of such treaties is *contextual*, dependent upon at least four factors: (1) the existing state or absence of Japanese law; (2) the precision of the treaty obligation; (3) the judge's individual commitment to international human rights law; and (4) the self-executing nature of the treaty.[40]

First, judges consider whether existing law covers the particular act. If there is law in point, judges typically try to reconcile the treaty language with that of prevailing domestic law. According to the Japanese legal hierarchy, the Constitution is the supreme law of the land. International law ranks second, and statutory law, administrative regulations and other ordinances third.[41] When possible, Japanese courts read constitutional obligations as coterminous with those of international treaty law.[42] The antidiscrimination provisions of Article 14 of the Constitution and Article 26 of the International Covenant on Civil and Political Rights, or the right to a fair trial in Article 37 of the Constitution and Article 14 of the International Covenant on Civil and Political Rights, are understood as creating the same basic rights. Were an international treaty to clash with the Constitution, Japan would defer to the Constitution.[43] In practice, it is difficult to imagine such a conflict.[44]

Second, the language of the treaty is scrutinised. A clearly stated provision of international law is most likely to overturn an inconsistent statutory law. For example, the guarantee of the International Covenant on Civil and Political Rights of 'the free assistance of an interpreter'[45] in a criminal trial convinced an appellate court to waive a trial court's imposition of translator's fees after convicting a foreign defendant.[46] The trial court, pursuant to the Criminal Procedure Law, was well within its rights to impose translator's fees. But since the International Covenant on Civil and Political Rights has very clear language – services must be *free* – the

39 Iwasawa (n 12) 29.

40 See: T, Webster (n 19) 237 f.

41 Iwasawa (n 12) 95.

42 See, eg: nn 92–95 and accompanying text.

43 A Japanese representative told the Human Rights Committee in 1993 that in the event of a conflict, 'the Constitution would prevail'. See: Iwasawa (n 12) 8.

44 The Convention to Eliminate All Forms of Racial Discrimination requires State parties to pass laws banning hate speech in art 4(a), but this would probably violate the right to free speech found in art 21 of the Japanese Constitution. This would suggest that the Constitution would prevail over the Convenrtion's affirmative obligation to pass a law. Before acceding to the Convention to Eliminate All Forms of Racial Discrimination, the Government of Japan attached a reservation that it would only fulfil this provision to the extent it is not guaranteed with other constitutionally guaranteed rights (such as assembly, association and expression).

45 International Covenant on Civil and Political Rights, art 14(f) provides that persons facing criminal charges shall 'have the free assistance of an interpreter if he cannot understand or speak the language used in court'.

46 See: Judgment, *Gaikokujin hanzai saibanreishû* [Record of Criminal Cases of Foreigners] 55, 55 (1994) (Tokyo H Ct, 2 February 1993).

Court of Appeals found that Japanese statutory law violated international obligations, and hence rescinded the translator's fees. In most cases, courts attempt to harmonise international treaty law with domestic law.[47]

Third, a judge's disposition towards international law influences the ultimate adjudication. In their opinions, judges can signal openness to international law by citing, analysing and interpreting the treaty's provisions. Sometimes they may discourse at great length about the evolution of human rights.[48] Or the opinion may include detailed analyses of *travaux préparatoires*, recent developments of the ECtHR, or pronouncements from UN bodies.[49] In other cases, judges omit discussion of the treaty altogether, even if referenced by the plaintiff.[50] This omission may stem from what Murakami Masanao refers to as 'judges' resistance to international law'.[51]

Fourth, the nature of the treaty weighs heavily in the decision. Judges in Japan have concluded that the International Covenant on Civil and Political Rights has direct effect,[52] while the International Covenant on Economic, Social and Cultural Rights does not.[53] This difference stems from language in the International Covenant on Economic, Social and Cultural Rights that the rights it recognises are to be achieved 'progressively',[54] which judges interpret to mean at some indefinite point in the future (but not in the present case). No such language qualifies the

[47] See: Judgment, 811 Hanrei taimuzu 76, 87 (Tokyo H Ct, 3 March 1993), translated in (1994) 37 *Japanese Ann Int'l L* 129, 131 ('The specific intent of the parties to a treaty is, of course, an important element, but the [treaty] provisions must be precise. In particular, when an international rule imposes on states an obligation to act, when it involves appropriation of national expenditure, or when a similar system already exists in domestic law, then harmony with the system must be fully taken into account').

[48] See: *Bortz v Suzuki*, 1045 Hanrei taimuzu 216 (Shizuoka D Ct, 12 October 1999); T Webster, 'Bortz v. Suzuki: A Translation and Introduction' (2007) 16 *Pac Rim L & Pol'y J* 631 (the district court judge wrote a lengthy history of the concept of human rights from Confucius to the twentieth century). Subsequent references will cite the Japanese reporter and the English translation.

[49] See below section II.

[50] See: *McGowan v Narita*, Wa No 11926 (Osaka D Ct, 30 January 2006); T Webster, 'Case Note and Commentary: McGowan v. Narita' (2008) 9 *Austl J Asian L* 346 (the plaintiff raised a claim based on the Convention to Eliminate All Forms of Racial Discrimination, but the judge did not discuss the treaty).

[51] See: Murakami (n 25) 24. Murakami refers specifically to judges who resist direct application of international law over applicable domestic law, but instead opt for indirect effect, with its less controversial mode of using international law as an interpretive aid or standard. There is, then, room to consider an individual judge's attitude towards international law.

[52] Judgment, 1597 Hanrei jihô 115, 127 (Tokushima D Ct, 15 March 1996) ('[The International Covenant on Civil and Political Rights] has direct effect as domestic law, and moreover the effect of prevailing over statutes.').

[53] Judgment, 1055 Hanrei jihô 9, 18 (Tokyo D Ct, 22 September 1982) ('[The International Covenant on Economic, Social and Cultural Rights] only obligates the States Parties to actively promote the social security policy. One cannot interpret it to accord concrete rights to aliens.').

[54] International Covenant on Economic, Social and Cultural Rights, art 2(2).

right guaranteed in the International Covenant on Civil and Political Rights, which obligates states 'to respect and to ensure to all individual within its territory and subject to its jurisdiction the rights recognized in the present Covenant'.[55] On occasion, judges have given it direct effect, as seen in the above case on translator's fees, and other cases involving the rights of criminal defendants.[56]

With respect to the Convention to Eliminate All Forms of Racial Discrimination, judges have concluded that it does not have direct effect between private parties and the state, at least in the circumstances presented to courts. Plaintiffs repeatedly cite Article 2(1)(d) of the Convention to Eliminate All Forms of Racial Discrimination, which provides that state parties 'shall prohibit and bring to an end, by all appropriate means, including *legislation as required by circumstance*, racial discrimination by any person, group or organization'.[57] Litigants cite this Article to support the claim that Japanese government bodies are obligated to pass laws to proscribe private acts of racial discrimination. But Japanese courts interpret this obligation as a 'political obligation', not a legal one.[58] In the words of one court, this Article 'should not be interpreted to impose a clear and uniform obligation to prohibit and bring to an end specific acts of racial discrimination by enacting laws for individual citizens'.[59] Instead, since the content of the provision is 'general and abstract, it cannot lead inexorably to only one kind of law or policy that a state party must take'.[60] And since the text of the Convention to Eliminate All Forms of Racial Discrimination itself provides that the legislation is required 'by circumstance', it does not create a direct and absolute obligation to pass a law.[61] In sum, a private person cannot canvass Japanese government bodies to pass antidiscrimination law, and then sue them when the body does not do so. It is unclear which provisions of the Convention to Eliminate All

[55] International Covenant on Civil and Political Rights, art 2(1).

[56] Criminal procedure is one area where the effect of the International Covenant on Civil and Political Rights has been particularly noticeable. Detained prisoners have successfully sued their detention facilities when they limited or disrupted the prisoners' access to counsel. Each prisoner relied on the guarantee of the International Covenant on Civil and Political Rights for 'adequate time and facilities for the preparation of his defence and to communicate with counsel of his own choosing', International Covenant on Civil and Political Rights, art 14(3)(b). See: 1597 Hanrei jihô 115 (Tokushima D Ct, 15 March 1996), partially translated in (1997) 40 *Japanese Ann Int'l L* 118; 858 Hanrei jihô 79 (Osaka D Ct, 9 March 2004), partially translated in (2005) 48 *Japanese Ann Int'l L* 164.

[57] Convention to Eliminate All Forms of Racial Discrimination, art 2(1)(d) (emphasis added). See, eg: *Bortz*, 1045 Hanrei taimuzu 219, 16 *Pac Rim L & Pol'y J* 636.

[58] *Arudou v Earth Cure*, 1150 Hanrei taimuzu 185, 194 (Sapporo D Ct, 11 November 2002); T Webster, 'Arudou v. Earth Cure: Judgment of November 11, 2002, Sapporo District Court' (2008) 9 *Asian-Pac L & Pol'y J* 297, 310. Future references will cite both the Japanese reporter and the English translation.

[59] ibid.

[60] See: Judgment, 2000 Hanrei jihô 79, 83 (Osaka D Ct, 18 December 2007).

[61] ibid 83.

Forms of Racial Discrimination could be directly applied against the state.[62]

Courts have likewise held that the Convention to Eliminate All Forms of Racial Discrimination does not apply to private parties. But that has not prevented them from ordering compensation to numerous victims of racial discrimination. Instead of directly applying the Convention to Eliminate All Forms of Racial Discrimination, courts assume the more cautious legal posture of 'indirect application'[63] when claims are levelled against private actors. By using the Convention to Eliminate All Forms of Racial Discrimination as a reference or 'interpretive standard' against which to evaluate defendant's conduct under domestic law, judges channel international norms into Japanese society. Beneath this judicial modesty lies strong adherence to international law. Judges may say that they are not directly applying international law, but by providing remedies for private acts of discrimination, they effectuate Article 6 of the Convention to Eliminate All Forms of Racial Discrimination, which tasks 'competent national tribunals' with repairing victims for the damages suffered as a result of (racial) discrimination.[64]

IV. DOMESTIC IMPLEMENTATION OF INTERNATIONAL LAW: CASES

Japanese courts increasingly resort to international human rights law. Since ratifying the International Covenant on Civil and Political Rights, and the International Covenant on Economic, Social and Cultural Rights in 1978, Japan has warmed to the influence of international law in the domestic sphere. In the intervening decades, Japanese courts have seen more and more cases claiming international law. The International Covenant on Economic, Social and Cultural Rights, for instance, has been cited more in the 10 years from 2000 to 2010 than in the first 22 years after it was in effect.[65]

[62] The Government of Japan told the Convention to Eliminate All Forms of Racial Discrimination Committee that direct application of treaty provisions is 'judged in each specific case, taking into consideration the purpose, meaning and wording of the provisions concerned'. Japan, Second periodic report, 26 September 2000, UN Doc CERD/C/350Add.2, para 5.

[63] See, eg: *Bortz,* 1045 Hanrei taimuzu 225, 16 *Pac Rim L & Pol'y J* 652.

[64] Convention to Eliminate All Forms of Racial Discrimination, art 6.

[65] The author conducted a keyword search for International Covenant on Economic, Social and Cultural Rights (in Japanese) in the Lex/DB Database, and discovered that, as of January 2010, there have been 369 court cases that cite the International Covenant on Civil and Political Rights, and 119 that cite the International Covenant on Economic, Social and Cultural Rights. 154 of the International Covenant on Civil and Political Rights citations took place between 2001 and 2010, and 60 of the International Covenant on Economic, Social and Cultural Rights citations. In other words, citation to international law has increased in the recent past.

While Japan has signalled its commitment to human rights at the inter-state level, the effect on the ground has been more contested. While scholars have characterised the Japanese judiciary's awakening to international human rights law as a 'revolution',[66] the process has actually been gradual, contested, and incremental. Indeed, the revolution is still unfolding. In the 1980s, Japanese courts largely dismissed claims that cited international human rights law. In the 1990s, they started to apply international treaties in cases involving the rights of criminal defendants and ethnic minorities.[67] In the new millennium, judges apply international law through the relatively cautious pose of 'indirect effect', even as their rulings fulfil Japan's obligations under international law. There is, on the whole, relatively robust implementation of international human rights norms and obligations, but under the guise of judicial modesty.

In the 1980s, judges expressed some hesitation about claims brought under the International Covenant on Civil and Political Rights, the International Covenant on Economic, Social and Cultural Rights, and other international human rights treaties. They typically got rid of international claims under any number of avoidance techniques. Saitō Yoshitaka has enumerated several ways by which courts denied the direct effect of international treaties during this period, including avoiding reference to the treaty altogether, assuming international treaties are coterminous with constitutional protections, and deciding that the treaty is not self-executing.[68] During this period, courts did not actively grapple with the possibilities of direct, or even indirect, effect of IHRL. Indeed, judicial application of international law was largely unexplored until well into the 1990s.

In the 1990s, Japanese judges used international treaties in a new way, directly applying their provisions to fill in for gaps in legislation, but only in a limited number of circumstances. For instance, in the interpreter's fees case, noted briefly above, the Tokyo High Court recognised that the International Covenant on Civil and Political Rights had 'self-executing effect', and directly applied one of its provisions to correct a contradictory domestic law.[69] A trial court had assessed translation fees to a convicted criminal, pursuant to Article 181 of the Code of Criminal Procedure. On appeal, the defendant challenged this assessment, noting that the

[66] KL Port, 'The Japanese International Law "Revolution": International Human Rights Law and Its Impact in Japan' (1991) 28 *Stan J Int'l L* 139.

[67] See: T Webster (n 9) 242.

[68] S Yoshitaka, *Kokusai Jinken B Kiyaku no Wagakuni Saibansho ni okeru Tekiyô* [*Applications of the International Covenant on Civil and Political Rights by Japanese Courts*] in Sumiyoshi Yoshihito (ed) *Gendai Kokusai Shakai to Jinken no Shosô: Miyazaki Shigeki Sensei Koki Kinen* [*Aspects of Contemporary International Society and Human Rights: Commemorating the 70th Birthday of Professor Miyazaki Shigeki*] (Tokyo, Seibundô, 1996) 55, 75 ff.

[69] Judgment, Gaikokujin hanzai saibanreishû (n 29) 55. See for an analysis of the case: T Webster (n 9) 254.

International Covenant on Civil and Political Rights guarantees 'the free assistance of an interpreter' in criminal cases.[70] The appeals court agreed with the defendant that international law did, in fact, guarantee free translation services, reversing the trial court's assessment. This was the first time that international law had been deployed against a contravening domestic practice. The Court stated that 'the right to the assistance of an interpreter . . . had not previously been known in Japanese law'.[71]

In another case, a court directly applied international law upon finding that a prison director violated international law when he impeded a lawyer's access to his detained client. Among other things, the director limited client interviews to 30 minutes, rejected requests for interviews, interrupted meetings, and required the presence of prison staff for meetings between lawyer and client.[72] The Court found that these acts of interference, collectively, violated the detainee's right to 'adequate time and facilities for the preparation of his defence and to communicate with counsel of his own choosing', as guaranteed under Article 14(3)(b) of the International Covenant on Civil and Political Rights.[73] These decisions forced the judiciary to grapple with Japan's international human rights obligations in a more substantive way.

The 2000s continue this trend of more fulsome applications of IHRL, at least in certain areas. On the one hand, Japanese courts maintain their relatively deferential stance towards government bodies, holding that government bodies do *not* violate international law by not passing laws to target ethnic or racial discrimination in the private sphere. But they are quite uniform in holding *individual citizens* liable for their private acts of discrimination. The 'personalisation' of international law introduces a new phase into Japan's adaptation process. Several lawsuits suggest that private actors – stores, bars, real estate agencies, people, golf clubs – may not discriminate against ethnic or racial others. Courts draw this conclusion by recourse to domestic and international standards. An analysis of the case law shows that the Convention to Eliminate All Forms of Racial Discrimination plays a key role in this process of proscription.

In the following section we analyse numerous applications of international law. The findings suggest that there is relatively strong court adherence to the obligations assumed under the International Covenant on Civil and Political Rights and Convention to Eliminate All Forms of Racial Discrimination,[74] but somewhat less so of the obligations assumed under

[70] International Covenant on Civil and Political Rights, art 14(3)(f).

[71] Judgment, Gaikokujin hanzai saibanreishû (n 29) 55.

[72] Judgment, (Tokushima D Ct, 15 March 1996) 1597 Hanrei jihô 115, 123, aff'd (Takamatsu H Ct, 25 November 1997); partially translated in (1998) 41 *Japanese Ann Int'l L* 87, 90.

[73] 1597 Hanrei jihô 123, 41 *Japanese Ann Int'l L* 90.

[74] Plaintiffs challenging racial discrimination in the private sphere cite both the International Covenant on Civil and Political Rights and the Convention to Eliminate All Forms of Racial Discrimination. Accordingly, we take the International Covenant on Civil

the International Covenant on Economic, Social and Cultural Rights. Judges seem to agree that treaties have domestic legal force in the Japanese judicial system, but each treaty individually has had a very different impact on human rights in Japan. Accordingly, we examine the jurisprudence on a treaty-by-treaty basis.

A. International Covenant on Economic, Social and Cultural Rights

Since the early 1980s, when plaintiffs first began to bring claims under the International Covenant on Economic, Social and Cultural Rights, Japanese courts have repeatedly held that the International Covenant on Economic, Social and Cultural Rights does not have direct effect.[75] They arrive at this conclusion by reading one particular provision of the International Covenant on Economic, Social and Cultural Rights, which obligates state parties to 'take steps . . . with a view to *achieving progressively* the full realization of the right recognized [herein]'.[76] Japanese judges read this provision to mean that certain rights are 'by nature not immediately realizable', 'but rather entrusted to the discretion of the legislative authorities to determine'.[77] In other words, a Japanese judge cannot implement the rights contained in the International Covenant on Economic, Social and Cultural Rights *in this particular lawsuit*, and so must defer implementation of the right altogether. The problem is that, three decades after ratifying the International Covenant on Economic, Social and Cultural Rights, courts continue to interpret the International Covenant on Economic, Social and Cultural Rights 'progressively'.

Japanese courts are not unique in reading International Covenant on Economic, Social and Cultural Rights obligations as lacking direct effect.[78]

and Political Rights and the Convention to Eliminate All Forms of Racial Discrimination as one track, and the International Covenant on Economic, Social and Cultural Rights as another.

[75] See, eg: *Shiomi v Japan* (Osaka H Ct, 19 December 1984) 1145 Hanrei jihô 3, paras 25–26 (noting that the International Covenant on Economic, Social and Cultural Rights was directly applicable, and only had to be realised progressively).

[76] International Covenant on Economic, Social and Cultural Rights, art 2(1) (emphasis added).

[77] *Kang Bu-jung v Governor of Osaka*, 1718 Hanrei jihô 30, 42 (Osaka H Ct, 15 October 1999).

[78] eg, German courts deny that the International Covenant on Economic, Social and Cultural Rights has direct effect in domestic litigation. See: B Simma, DE Khan, M Zöckler and R Geiger, 'The Role of German Courts in the Enforcement of International Human Rights' in B Conforti and F Francioni (eds), *Enforcing International Human Rights in Domestic Courts* (The Hague, Martinus Nijhoff, 1997) 71, 78. Dutch courts have taken a more nuanced approach. In one case involving social security rights, the Central Appeals Court held that the 'material rights contained in the [International Covenant on Economic, Social and Cultural Rights] do not in general have direct effect. The Court feels, however, that it would be wrong to assume that a provision such as Article 7(a)(i) can never as a matter of principle have direct effect.' Judgment (Central Apps Ct, 3 July 1986), (1988) 19 *Neth YB Int'l L* 427, 429.

Indeed, many legal systems agree that economic and social rights are weaker than civil and political rights.[79] But the International Covenant on Economic, Social and Cultural Rights maintains that all the rights that it guarantees 'will be exercised without discrimination of any kind as to race, colour, sex, language, religion, political or other opinion, *national or social origin*, property, birth or other status'.[80] This does not require a state party to eliminate all forms of discrimination in society, just to ensure that the rights contained in the International Covenant on Economic, Social and Cultural Rights are guaranteed without discrimination.

In Japanese domestic litigation, the International Covenant on Economic, Social and Cultural Rights has been invoked repeatedly to handle various forms of discrimination against resident Koreans. In particular, resident Koreans invoke the International Covenant on Economic, Social and Cultural Rights to bolster claims to social security benefits that local government agencies have denied them, such as disability pensions,[81] old age pensions,[82] and military pensions.[83] How do courts justify denying pensions to these people in light of the unambiguous prohibition on discrimination in the International Covenant on Economic, Social and Cultural Rights?

The first case, *Shiomi v Osaka*, moved up and down Japanese courts for decades.[84] Born to Korean parents in 1934 in Osaka, Shiomi Hide was originally a citizen of the Japanese Empire, as were all persons born within the jurisdiction of Japan during imperial times (which included Taiwan from 1895, and Korea from 1910). After the Second World War, however, the 1951 Peace Treaty with the Allied Powers denationalised all non-ethnic Japanese, including those who remained in Japan. Accordingly, Ms Shiomi lost her Japanese citizenship. In 1970, Shiomi married a Japanese man and was naturalised, once again becoming a Japanese citizen. In 1972, she applied for a disability pension because she was blind, but her claim was rejected because she was not a Japanese citizen when the pension law passed in 1959. She sued the Governor of Osaka for refusing her application, losing at the trial, appellate and supreme courts.

[79] C Krause and M Scheinin, 'The Right Not To Be Discriminated Against' in TS Orlin et al (eds), *The Jurisprudence of Human Rights Law: A Comparative Interpretative Approach* (Turku, Institute of Human Rights Abo Akademi University, 2000) 254.

[80] International Covenant on Economic, Social and Cultural Rights, art 2(2) (emphasis added).

[81] *Shiomi v Governor of Osaka*, 31 Gyôsaishû 216 (Osaka D Ct 29 October 1980) aff'd 35 Gyôsaishû 2220 (Osaka H Ct, 19 December 1984) aff'd 1363 Hanrei jihô 68 (S Ct, 2 March 1989).

[82] *Hyon Sun Im v Governor of Kyoto*, 1993 Hanrei jihô 104 (Kyoto D Ct, 23 February 2007).

[83] *Kang*, 1718 Hanrei jihô 42.

[84] Shiomi first applied for a pension in 1972, but her application was rejected. She sued the Governor of Osaka in 1973, but the Osaka District Court dismissed her case in 1981. She filed another lawsuit in 1985, after Japan changed its pension laws. This suit was dismissed by the Osaka District Court in 1994, the Osaka High Court in 1996, and the Supreme Court in 2001. See: 'Top Court Rejects Blind Ex-Korean National's Pensions Claim' Kyodo News Agency, 13 March 2001.

Shiomi cited the International Covenant on Economic, Social and Cultural Rights, which unambiguously states 'The State Parties to the present Covenant recognize the right of *everyone* to social security, including social insurance'.[85] But the Court focused on another provision of the treaty, found in a different section altogether, about progressively achieving the rights found in the treaty:

> [Based on Article 2(1)] it is clearly expected that the full realization of the rights will be achieved progressively. In order to fully realize the rights contained in the Covenant, State Parties should take legislative measures (including, of course, amendments of laws already in force). The various provisions contained in the Covenant do not become standards by which to judge the State Parties' laws already in force, or decisions based on those laws.[86]

The Osaka High Court avoided the issue of judging the wisdom or comprehensiveness of the Government's provision of pensions to resident Koreans. But a lawsuit would surely be an appropriate venue for this kind of review. In 1982, upon acceding to the Refugee Convention, Japan revised its laws to nullify the nationality requirements for pensioners. But the revisions still excluded many persons. Resident aliens over 35 in 1982 were effectively barred, because they would be unable to make 25 years of payments by the time they would qualify for old age pensions at age 60.[87] Though an interim measure was later passed to cover these people, others remain ineligible for pensions. Persons over 60 years of age in 1986 could receive old age pensions, and persons over 20 years of age in 1982 could not receive disability pensions.[88] It is difficult to conclude that such exclusions are rational, but Japanese courts have refrained from reviewing the rationality of these measures because of the International Covenant on Economic, Social and Cultural Rights's language about progressive achievement.

Resident Koreans have raised similar arguments in cases regarding old age pensions. With respect to the former, five Korean women – aged 78 to 89 – are presently appealing a trial court decision that it was not 'unjust discrimination' for the Government to deny their application for a pension.[89] Judge Yamashita Hiroshi explained that the 'progressive achievement' language of Article 2(1) qualifies the rights guaranteed in both Article 9 (guaranteeing social security to 'everyone') and Article 2(2) (prohibiting discrimination based on 'national or social origin' among

[85] International Covenant on Economic, Social and Cultural Rights, art 9 (emphasis added).

[86] *Shiomi*, 35 Gyôsaishû 2282. *cf* 31 Gyôsaishû 216 (Osaka D Ct, 29 October 1980) *with* 35 Gyôsaishû 2220 (Osaka H Ct, 19 December 1984).

[87] See: Iwasawa (n 12) 172.

[88] ibid 172.

[89] See: 'Kyoto court dismisses Korean residents' claim over denial of pension' Japan Econ Newswire, 23 February 2007.

others).[90] 'Accordingly, since Article 2(2) and Article 9 are neither self-executing nor justiciable, they cannot be used to evaluate whether Japan's laws or legislative omissions are illegal.'[91] In this way, upon finding that *one* provision of the treaty was not meant to have immediate applicability, the Court denied the possibility of direct effect for the treaty *in toto*.[92]

Once again, the combination of progressive achievement and legislative deference led the Court to arrive at a conclusion that fragments from the clear anti-discriminatory intent of international law in general, and the International Covenant on Economic, Social and Cultural Rights in particular. The Japanese judiciary has thus consistently deviated from international standards in cases involving the pension rights of resident Koreans, many of whom were former citizens of Japan. Even as the Japanese Diet has changed the standards for receiving pension benefits, courts have consistently upheld the legislature's formulation. This is questionable as a matter of policy, and problematic as a matter of international law, such as the presumption that international law should be interpreted in conformity with domestic law. One final judgment rounds out the discussion, and shows that judges can evince a more unified stance toward international law, even while adhering to canons of interpretation that deny direct effect.

Finally, litigants have also cited the International Covenant on Economic, Social and Cultural Rights to challenge the Government's refusal to provide veterans pensions. Resident Korean Kang Bu-jung applied for a pension to cover an injury sustained while he served in the Japanese Navy during the Second World War.[93] Kang was a Japanese citizen when he sustained the injury, but lost this status with the denationalisation of all Koreans in 1952. That meant he was no longer applicable to receive a military pension under the Assistance Law.[94] He applied for a pension in 1993, but was turned down because of the nationality requirement of the 1952 Assistance Law.

On appeal, the Osaka High Court noted that the right to equality enshrined in Article 26 of the International Covenant on Civil and Political Rights and Article 2(1) of the International Covenant on Economic, Social

[90] *Hyon*, 1993 Hanrei jihô 132.

[91] ibid.

[92] Simma et al have noted that German courts dispose of International Covenant on Economic, Social and Cultural Rights claims in a similar way. See: B Simma et al (n 77) 86. They instead advise 'courts should understand that each specific norm . . . must be tested separately for its self-executing character. With regard to the "progressive realization" of economic and social right [in art 2(1)], courts should note that some norms of such treaties, for example, non-discrimination clauses, might very well possess the necessary concreteness to be accepted as self-executing', ibid.

[93] See: *Kang*, 1718 Hanrei jihô 42; *Nonpayment of war pensions to Koreans unconstitutional*, Asian Pol News, 18 October 1999.

[94] The 1952 Law for Assistance to War Victims and Their Bereaved Families required that recipients of assistance hold Japanese citizenship. See: Iwasawa (n 12) 176.

and Cultural Rights was coterminous with that enshrined in Article 14 of the Japanese Constitution, which guarantees the right to equality.[95] The Court further determined that the International Covenant on Economic, Social and Cultural Rights was not binding on Japanese courts, due to its language about progressive achievement, and hence its anti-discrimination provisions could not support the finding of an illegal violation.[96] It did state, however, that the Assistance Law's exclusion of Kang, based on his nationality, 'may have violated Article 14 of the Constitution and Article 26 of the [International Covenant on Civil and Political Rights]',[97] both of which guarantee the right to equality. The Court further 'requested the Diet to take legislative measures to correct the legal treatment of these people'.[98]

While the Court specifically rejected the notion that the International Covenant on Economic, Social and Cultural Rights could have direct or indirect effect in this case, it nonetheless fused the normative force of international law (the binding International Covenant on Civil and Political Rights) with domestic constitutional law to suggest that domestic law *may have been* illegal. While this conclusion is not as strong as, say, an outright finding of a violation, it nonetheless represents progress in the ongoing domestication of the norms of international law.

B. Convention to Eliminate all Forms of Racial Discrimination

Japan ratified the Convention to Eliminate All Forms of Racial Discrimination in 1995. When signing the treaty, the Cabinet of Japan (executive branch) attached a reservation to the treaty, such that the fulfilment of obligations under the Convention to Eliminate All Forms of Racial Discrimination 'is compatible with the guarantee of the rights to freedom of assembly, association, and expression and other rights under the Constitution of Japan'.[99] In essence, the Cabinet froze the constitutional limits of these various rights, immunising them from the influence of international law. At the same time, the Diet did not take any steps to revise Japanese domestic laws to ensure conformity with the new treaty obligations posed by the Convention to Eliminate All Forms of Racial Discrimination. The Diet did not expand protections into the private sphere, as it did after ratifying the Women's Convention, nor revise acts with a discriminatory hue.[100] In the 15 years since ratification, the Japanese

[95] *Kang*, 1718 Hanrei jihô 48.
[96] ibid 50.
[97] ibid.
[98] ibid.
[99] See: *Bortz*, 1045 Hanrei taimuzu 224, 16 *Pac Rim L & Pol'y J* 651.
[100] The issue of whether various minority populations in Japan are sufficiently protected suffuses this discussion. See: Comm on Elimination of Racial Discrimination, Summary Record of the 1444th Meeting: Japan, UN Doc CERD/C/SR.1444, paras 28, 30 (11 June 2001).

judiciary has taken the lead in implementing the obligations imposed by the Convention to Eliminate All Forms of Racial Discrimination. Indeed, with each new racial discrimination lawsuit, Japanese judges draft the 'law' against racial discrimination.[101]

Over the years, courts have come to a general consensus about the proper application of the Convention to Eliminate All Forms of Racial Discrimination. Between private parties, judges ostensibly deny that the Convention has *direct* applicability, opting instead for *indirect* application. Courts use the Convention to Eliminate All Forms of Racial Discrimination as an 'interpretative standard' by which to determine whether certain conduct runs afoul of domestic law, as filtered through these international norms. In this way, they can effectuate the treaty's prohibition and elimination of racial discrimination by private actors.[102] When it comes to cases brought against state actors, however, Japanese courts have not clearly determined whether the treaty has direct effect. But courts uniformly determine that Japanese government bodies do not violate international law, even if they do not pass legislation that would seem to be required by the treaty.

Various court decisions show that the Convention to Eliminate All Forms of Racial Discrimination does, in fact, penetrate to private relations.[103] In these cases, real persons (racial minorities of one type or another) sue legal persons (stores, bars, bathhouses) for some type of racial exclusion. Judges consistently find that stores, bars, and public facilities – and their employees – cannot exclude someone simply because of his race or ethnicity. Nor can entities deny services simply on account of the race of the client. Viewed collectively, these suits permit judges to regulate private conduct in the fields of housing, providing goods and services, public facilities, financial sector, and so on.

But courts are less demanding of state actors. In cases where defendants have sued local municipalities for not passing ordinances that ban racial discrimination,[104] courts have come down on the municipalities' side, essentially holding that they can pass – or not pass – laws as they see fit. This reflects the generally deferential attitude toward legislation that the Japanese judiciary has traditionally maintained.

The Shizuoka District Court first applied the Convention to Eliminate All Forms of Racial Discrimination to private relations in a 1999 decision. Hamamatsu, Japan contains a large Brazilian population, including many

[101] The Japanese Constitution prohibits racial discrimination in the public sphere. Kenpô, art 14. But no laws ban racial discrimination in the private sphere. See: T Webster (n 19) 217.

[102] Art 2(1)(d) of the Convention to Eliminate All Forms of Racial Discrimination prohibits 'racial discrimination by any persons, group or organization'.

[103] See generally: T Webster (n 19) 216 ff (discussing various cases where plaintiffs have cited the Convention to Eliminate All Forms of Racial Discrimination when suing for private acts of racial discrimination).

[104] See: ibid 222 ff.

Japanese Brazilians, who work in industrial and manufacturing jobs with special visas from the Government. In this particular incident, a Japanese jewellery store employee shooed away a customer, Ana Bortz, upon discovering that she was Brazilian (and not French as he initially thought).[105] He pointed to a sign on the wall that said 'foreigners are strictly forbidden', and asked her to leave the store.[106] When she refused, he called the police. After an hour and 40 minutes of angry charges, remonstrations, and threats to sue, Ms Bortz left the store with her husband. She made good on her threat, which elicited a strong rebuke by the Shizuoka District Court, and a 1.5 million yen ($12,500) damages award.

As one of the first decisions to invoke the Convention to Eliminate All Forms of Racial Discrimination, the Court grappled with the interrelationship between international and domestic law at some length. Judge Soh Tetsuro explained that Japan is a monist country, and iterated the conventional view that '[the Convention to Eliminate All Forms of Racial Discrimination] is beneath the Constitution, but still has effect in this country as domestic law'.[107] But he was more concerned about the fact that Japan had not passed a law to ban racial discrimination:

> CERD [Convention to Eliminate All Forms of Racial Discrimination] goes one step farther [than the Universal Declaration of Human Rights] by requiring signatories to take legislative and other measures to deal with individual and group acts of racial discrimination.
>
> If an act of racial discrimination violates a provision of CERD, but the state or local body did not take the measures that it should have, then one could, in accordance with Article 6 of CERD, at the very least seek compensation for damages, or take other measures for relief, from the state or local body for the omission.[108]

Article 6 of the Convention to Eliminate All Forms of Racial Discrimination guarantees victims of racial discrimination 'effective protection and remedies, through the competent national tribunals'. Japan did not pass anti-discrimination legislation, either nationally or locally,[109] but this absence cannot inoculate against racist behaviour. To fill in the gap, Judge Soh used the Convention to Eliminate All Forms of Racial Discrimination's prohibition of 'racial discrimination by persons, group or organization' to determine that shooing away Ms Bortz because she was foreign constituted an illegal act of racism. The Court cited international law as a yardstick, or 'interpretive standard',[110] by which to hold that the discriminatory behaviour was illegal.

[105] *Bortz*, 1045 Hanrei taimuzu 217, 16 *Pac Rim L & Pol'y J* 633.
[106] ibid.
[107] *Bortz*, 1045 Hanrei taimuzu 225, 16 *Pac Rim L & Pol'y J* 652.
[108] ibid.
[109] To this day, Japan has not passed a law at either national or local levels. See: T Webster (n 19) 250.
[110] *Bortz*, 1045 Hanrei taimuzu 225, 16 *Pac Rim L & Pol'y J* 652.

The Convention to Eliminate All Forms of Racial Discrimination bans discrimination in the private sphere in several ways. One provision requires states parties to 'prohibit and bring to an end, by all appropriate means, including legislation as required by the circumstances, racial discrimination by any persons, group or organization'.[111] Another guarantees the 'right of access to any place or service intended for use by the general public, such as transport, hotels, restaurants, cafes, theatres and parks'.[112] When the jewellery store drove Ms Bortz away for being foreign, it violated her right of general access. As the Court noted, 'managers who run stores like the defendants' do not have the freedom to restrict customers, place restraints on who may enter, limit people who receive introductions, or form a completely exclusive association'.[113] Stores open to the public must remain open to the public, even an increasingly international and racially different one.

In providing Bortz with an 'effective remedy' for this violation, the Shizuoka District Court gave effect to international law in novel ways. It provided a relatively large (by Japanese standards) damages award, meant to compensate for her emotional distress and to cover legal fees.[114] It also required an apology from the defendant for the injury to the plaintiff's dignity.[115] But most important, the ruling set a precedent for future litigants who experience racial discrimination. Subsequent verdicts have also used the Convention to Eliminate All Forms of Racial Discrimination as an 'interpretive standard', channelling international law into the social fabric of Japanese private relations.

One foreigner particularly moved by the Bortz story was Arudou Debito, né David Aldwinckle, a self-styled human rights activist. In the late 1990s, Arudou noticed several bathhouses in northern Japan had posted 'No foreigners' signs to their front doors. In September 2000, he arranged for a group of foreigners (American, Chinese, German) and Japanese to enter the Yunohana bathhouse to see if it would enforce the 'Japanese Only' policy.[116] The bathhouse turned away the white foreigners, but let in the other Asians, including a Chinese woman. It allowed in one of Arudou's biracial daughters (the more phenotypically Asian one), but denied the other daughter, who more closely resembled her Anglo-American father.

Arudou tried again a month later, after he had become a naturalised Japanese citizen. Now legally Japanese, Arudou assumed he would be able to gain entrance. But he was again rejected. The manager explained

[111] Convention to Eliminate All Forms of Racial Discrimination, art 2(d).
[112] ibid art 5(f).
[113] *Bortz*, 1045 Hanrei taimuzu 225, 16 *Pac Rim L & Pol'y J* 652.
[114] ibid.
[115] *Bortz*, 1045 Hanrei taimuzu 231, 16 *Pac Rim L & Pol'y J* 666.
[116] *Arudou*, 1150 Hanrei taimuzu 187–88, 9 *Asian-Pac L & Pol'y J* 300.

that other customers would not understand that he was Japanese, and his presence would still discomfit them. Concern for a putatively xenophobic clientele prevented Arudou's entrance. Together with two other white *refusés* (one American, one German), Arudou filed a lawsuit in February 2001. He sued the bathhouse for racial discrimination, and the Otaru Municipal Government for not taking adequate measures to ban racial discrimination.

The Sapporo District Court found against the bathhouse, but not the city. As in *Bortz*, the Court applied the Convention to Eliminate All Forms of Racial Discrimination in substance, even while denying its direct effect as between private persons:

> Article 14(1) of the Constitution, the ICCPR [International Covenant on Civil and Political Rights], and CERD [Convention to Eliminate All Forms of Racial Discrimination] do not apply directly to relations between private persons. But if private conduct specifically violates, or risks violating, another person's basic rights or equality, these *provisions* can be used to evaluate *social norms*. Articles 1 and 90 of the Civil Code,[117] among others, generally regulate private autonomy, and protect an individual's interests against illegal infringements of basic rights and equality. Thus, Article 14(1) of the Constitution, the ICCPR, and CERD can serve as a *standard* to *interpret* the above provisions of private law.[118]

The Sapporo District Court finessed the constitutional right to equality and international proscription of racial discrimination as 'interpretive standards' by which to judge private acts. Even as the Court refused to apply international treaties 'directly to relations between private persons', it used international standards to evaluate Japanese social norms.

The Court considered the bathhouse's rationale for not admitting foreigners, but determined that it lacked the necessary rational basis. The defendant protested that rowdy Russian soldiers had previously driven away many Japanese customers, and that a blanket ban of foreigners solved the problem in uniform way. That is, it did not discriminate against certain foreigners because *all* groups of foreigners were banned. But the Court found fault with the bathhouse's over-inclusiveness, banning plenty of well-mannered foreigners who knew how to take baths.

Against the city, the Court held the city was under no 'clear and uniform obligation' to pass anti-discrimination law.[119] The Convention to

[117] Art 1 of the Civil Code requires that rights and obligations shall be 'performed in good faith'. Minpô, art 1. Art 90 proscribes acts that are 'contrary to public policy or good morals'; Minpô, art 90. The latter provision is commonly used in cases where a person discriminates against another, eg, on the basis of gender.

[118] *Arudou*, 1150 Hanrei taimuzu 193, 9 *Asian-Pac L & Pol'y J* 317 (emphasis added). The Court went on to note that Yunohana's conduct amounted to 'discrimination based on race, skin color, descent, ethnic origin or racial origin. In light of Article 14(1) of the Constitution, Article 26 of the International Covenant on Civil and Political Rights and the Convention to Eliminate All Forms of Racial Discrimination, these amount to private acts of racial discrimination that ought to be eliminated'.

[119] *Arudou*, 1150 Hanrei taimuzu 195; 9 *Asian-Pac L & Pol'y J* 320.

Eliminate All Forms of Racial Discrimination does provide that 'Each State Party shall prohibit and bring to an end, by all appropriate means, including legislation as required by circumstances, racial discrimination by any person, group or organization'.[120] But the Court held that Japan's current circumstances did not 'require' legislation by the city of Otaru.

In a certain sense, the Court inverted the traditional view of who is subject to international law. It held a private person liable for violating international law, even while claiming that international law does not apply against private actors. But it determined that a state actor, ostensibly bound by international law to pass legislation in 'appropriate circumstances', was not liable for failing to legislate against racial discrimination. To be sure, the Court also referenced domestic legal standards in arriving at these conclusions, such as the constitutional right to equality, and the Civil Code's proscription of acts contrary to public policy. But in providing a remedy for an act of racial discrimination, in the absence of a clear legislative mandate proscribing such behaviour, it effectuated the clear language of the Convention to Eliminate All Forms of Racial Discrimination.

V. CONCLUSION

Understanding a country's implementation of international law requires attention to those areas where it both adheres to and deviates from the letter of the law. Here, the focus has been on Japanese courts' application of two treaties that do not *stricto sensu* impose binding obligations on Japan. Of course, the conclusion that these treaties do not bind is itself a legal conclusion that courts have derived, and not necessarily a component of the treaty itself.

The above discussion shows that Japanese courts recognise interpretations of international legal provisions as put forth by other countries' courts and international organisations' views and opinions. Such 'dialogue' would lead one to expect greater conformity with the interpretations of these foreign bodies, and Japanese courts fulfil this expectation to a limited degree. But there is still 'room to suspect' that Japanese courts could further align their judgments to international best practices, particularly with regard to their treatment of the resident alien population.

Within the subject matter of anti-discrimination, there are diverging approaches to the roles that courts play in addressing acts of public and private discrimination. The primary difference between court analysis of public versus private acts lies not so much in the treaty itself, but rather the nature of the underlying dispute. That is, whether a court applies or devi-

[120] Convention to Eliminate All Forms of Racial Discrimination, art 2(1).

ates from international law depends largely upon the nature of the actors, and the action itself. When it comes to state action (in the form of legislation over social security), or state inaction (in the form of failing to pass anti-discrimination laws), courts do not strictly effectuate international legal obligations. It is clear that the Japanese Diet's exclusion of resident Koreans from social security benefits violates the non-discrimination language of the International Covenant on Economic, Social and Cultural Rights. But courts avoid this conclusion by claiming that the treaty itself does not have direct effect by virtue of language on 'progressive' achievement. In the 1999 *Kang* decision, the Court noted that excluding resident Koreans from pensions 'may' violate both constitutional and international law, but went on to find that the exclusion was legal. While international law can help plaintiffs point out human rights violations of the Japanese Government, courts typically do not use international law to reveal the defects or inconsistencies of the political branches.

But courts show a much more united front when it comes to private actors. In case after case, courts have denied that the Convention to Eliminate All Forms of Racial Discrimination has direct effect between private parties. Yet in case after case, they apply the Convention to Eliminate All Forms of Racial Discrimination indirectly to give effect to its provisions banning racial discrimination by persons or groups, and requiring national courts to provide remedies in such instances. Courts closely adhere to the letter of the Convention to Eliminate All Forms of Racial Discrimination, even if they claim not to be bound by it.

The experience of Japanese courts' implementation of international human rights law suggests the very real risk that international law can fragment. While there is a high degree of adherence to the letter of international law with respect to private actors, the judiciary is largely unwilling to call government action or inaction that fails to meet universally accepted standards illegal or contrary to international law. It would be difficult, of course, to expect all countries to implement international law in the same way. But it is still surprising that a country like Japan – which acknowledges the experiences of other countries' courts, as well as the expert opinions and comments of international organisations – strays from widely recognised standards.

14

Subtle but Enduring – The Role of Domestic Courts in the Shaping of International Economic Law through Proper Interpretation of Domestic Law: The WTO Agreement before Swiss Courts

ANDREAS R ZIEGLER*

I. INTRODUCTION

THE ESTABLISHMENT OF the World Trade Organization (WTO) in 1995 and the entry into force of its comprehensive set of trade agreements has considerably changed the importance of international trade rules in the domestic legal orders of WTO members, including Switzerland. The fact that WTO law is increasingly going beyond mere 'negative integration' and is setting substantive rules regarding domestic administrative law (including procedure) has led to important changes in the relevance of WTO law for domestic decision making of administrative and adjudicatory bodies. This is particularly evident in the new areas covered by comprehensive trade regulation, including trade-related intellectual property rights as covered under the Agreement on Trade-Related Aspects of Intellectual Property Rights, and government procurement as treated under the WTO's plurilateral Government Procurement Agreement.[1]

* Professor at the Faculty of Law and Criminal Sciences of the University of Lausanne (Switzerland) and Visiting Professor at the University of New South Wales (Sydney, Australia), the Swiss Federal Institute of Technology (Zurich, Switzerland) and the University of St Gallen (Switzerland).

[1] The GPA is a plurilateral agreement, ie not all WTO members are parties to it. For Switzerland this agreement entered into force on 1 June 1995 like the rest of the WTO agreements (on the accession see below section II).

Today, more and more cases are brought before the WTO touching upon a variety of subjects and thus exceeding classical trade law issues; *cf* the trade and environment debate to name only one example. In the political debate in Switzerland this development is sometimes seen as an intrusion of international regulation into national sovereignty, but at the same time it is understood that this system guarantees market access and non-discrimination for Swiss companies abroad. The increasingly important discussion has in recent years been mirrored by a slowly augmenting number of cases touching upon WTO law discussed before Swiss adjudicatory bodies. However, absolute numbers of cases remain relatively low in comparison to other areas of international economic agreements, such as the case law related to Switzerland's bilateral economic integration agreements with the European Union (EU). In the 1960s and 1970s the General Agreement on Tariffs and Trades (GATT) had only been of relevance in three cases before the Swiss Supreme Court;[2] nowadays there are several cases each year, whereby the relevance of the goods- and services-related agreements is less marked than the case law including a reference to the Agreement on Trade Related Aspects of Intellectual Property Rights (TRIPs Agreement) and the Government Procurement Agreement (GPA).

This contribution looks at the treatment of WTO law as public international law before domestic courts. It uses the case law of the Swiss Federal Supreme Court in order to show that, as in the past, domestic courts in most states remain reluctant to use WTO law as a legal basis for their decision. At the same time, this contribution argues that they seem to be more and more open to prefer an interpretation of domestic law that is compatible with a state's WTO obligations to one that leads to incoherence.[3] While this may seem normal in order to create coherence between different levels of multilayered governance it is in sharp contrast to the older practice in many states. It seems that slowly the concept of multilayered governance[4] is being accepted by the courts (at least in certain states) but that interpretation of domestic sources in coherence with existing obligations is still preferable in many instances to giving priority to international obligations over domestic obligations.

[2] See also: L Engelberger, *Die unmittelbare Anwendbarkeit des WTO-Rechts in der Schweiz* (Bern, Peter Lang Publishing, 2004) 164. The cases BGE 86 I 312 (1960); BGE 104 Ib 429 (1974); and BGE 104 Ib 412 (1978) will be analysed in detail in this chapter. 'BGE' stands for the German 'Bundesgerichtsentscheide', a short form of 'Entscheide des Bundesgerichts', in French 'Arrêts du tribunal federal', ie 'ATF'; they are published both in a written form and on the internet).

[3] See for another recent example of the much more studied case law of the EU: MC Bronckers, 'From "direct effect" to "muted dialogue"' (2008) 4 *J Int'l Econ L* 11, 885; JH Jackson, 'Direct effect of treaties in the US and the EU, the case of the WTO' in A Arnull, P Eeckhout and T Tridimas (eds), *Continuity and change in EU law – Essays in Honour of Sir Francis Jacobs* (Oxford, Oxford University Press, 2008) 361 ff.

[4] See, eg: T Cottier, 'Multilayered governance, pluralism, and moral conflict' (2009) 2 *Ind J Global Legal Stud* 16, 647 ff.

II. LEGAL EFFECTS OF GATT AND WTO MEMBERSHIP

The relationship between international law (including international trade law) and domestic law is an easy one from the perspective of international law, but often a difficult one from the perspective of domestic law.[5] From the perspective of international law, primacy of international law is well established, superseding national and local rules as a matter of logic. States are bound by their international commitments (*pacta sunt servanda*), which is equally true for trade as for any other field of international law. WTO dispute settlement has overall been remarkably successful in ensuring adherence to its rulings. From the perspective of domestic law, the relationship between international law and domestic law is difficult, and the burden of finding a way to bring together a country's international commitments and domestic rules is basically a challenge to the states and their domestic legal systems. Key approaches have been proposed in the doctrines of monism and dualism, the former making international law part of the law of the land without formal transition, and the latter requiring an act of formal enactment of international law into domestic rules. While monism may be seen as a pragmatic, internationally law-friendly approach, dualism underlines the national sovereignty and the supremacy of national parliaments.[6]

Switzerland is traditionally considered to have a monist legal system regarding the relationship between treaty law and domestic law. This is true insofar as treaties achieve immediate validity and become part of the Swiss legal order upon their entry into force. This principle is normally derived from Articles 5.4 and 191 of the Federal Constitution although these provisions are not very specific. Normally treaties take precedence over domestic law.[7]

However, as in other systems there exists a discussion in the case law and legal writing as to whether in certain cases the courts remain bound to apply domestic law approved by parliament that is contrary to international treaties when parliament has done so intentionally.[8] The Court held in its leading case regarding this question:

[5] T Cottier, 'A Theory of Direct Effect in Global Law' in A Bogdandy (ed), *European Integration and International Co-ordination. Studies in Transnational Economic Law in Honour of Claus-Dieter Ehlermann* (The Hague, Kluwer Law International, 2002) 305 ff.

[6] ibid 310.

[7] See eg: AR Ziegler, *Einführung in das Völkerrecht* (Bern, Stämpfli Publishing, 2006) 121 ff. See also: VPB (Verwaltungspraxis der Bundesbehörden) 54.53 (1990), Joint statement of the Federal Office of Justice and the Directorate of International Law (26 April 1989) analysing the Swiss legal practice and doctrine; more recently VPB 64.20, Statement of the Directorate of International Law (4 March 1998). Since 1987 (VPB 51) theses reports are also available at www.vpb.admin.ch (last visited 1 June 2011).

[8] See for details: Ziegler (n 7) 121 ff; and the leading case *re Schubert* by the Swiss Federal Supreme Court (BGE 99 Ib 43 ff); later confirmed in BGE 112 II 1, 13; BGE 111 V 201, 203.

> The possibility of a conscious departure by the legislator (the highest national authority) allows the reduction of hardships and the safeguarding of important interests in practice. Such a conscious departure certainly cannot change the rights and obligations of a state under international law, but it is authoritative in the domestic sphere and binding upon the Supreme Court.[9]

It is held that if parliament was conscious that a decree could raise concerns as to its compatibility with international law, then the Supreme Court would not be entitled to examine this aspect, and would be obliged to apply the Federal Decree in question according to Article 190 of the Federal Constitution.[10]

In most cases courts can avoid such incoherence by simply interpreting domestic law in a way that makes the domestic legislation consistent with the country's international treaty obligations.[11] This doctrine is widely known today, and practiced in many countries including the United States (US) and Switzerland.[12] In the US, it is based on the Charming Betsy canon as known by US courts.[13] Although being a mere canon of construction, it results in an indirect application of the international treaty rule in question and it thus constitutes an important legal tool to bring about coherence between a country's international treaty obligations and domestic law.[14] As will be shown below, interpretation of domestic law in lines with international treaty obligations is a legal technique that is also increasingly important for matters of WTO law before Swiss courts.

The entry into force of the treaty obligations remains an obvious prerequisite for the application of any international treaty according to the rules of the Vienna Convention on the Law of Treaties (VCLT).[15] Once an international treaty has been ratified; it enjoys automatic validity. According to the adoption theory, a transformation into national law is not required.[16] In Switzerland international treaties are ratified by the Federal Council (the executive) upon their approval by the Swiss Parliament.[17] This

[9] Translation provided by the author.

[10] See: Ziegler (n 7) 122 ff.

[11] See: below section V.C on interpretation.

[12] T Cottier (n 6) 99 ff.

[13] The Charming Betsy Canon is normally restated as 'Absent express language to the contrary, a statute should not be interpreted to conflict with international obligations'. See, eg: *Hyundai Electronics Co v United States*, 53 F Supp 2d 1334, 1343 (1999); 'It has also been observed that an act of congress ought never to be construed to violate the law of nations, if any other possible construction remains', *Murray v Schooner Charming Betsy*, 6 US (2 Branch) 64 (1804).

[14] See: Engelberger (n 2) 20, with further references; *cf* also: VPB 70.18 (2006) and VPB 67.67 (2003).

[15] SR 0.111 (SR = Systematische Sammlung des Bundesrechts = Systematic Collection of Swiss Law).

[16] See: Ziegler (n 7) 113 ff.

[17] The Federal Parliament has two Chambers, the House of Representatives and the Senate, which have equal powers, as stated in art 148 II of the Federal Constitution.

approval does not take the form of a law, but of a Federal Decree.[18] With the exchange of ratifications deeds, the treaty becomes binding.

After the Second World War Switzerland was not among the 23 founding Members of the GATT but it acceded to this Agreement on a provisional basis on 22 November 1958[19] – the GATT officially entered into force for Switzerland on 1 August 1966.[20] The accession negotiations had been rather difficult in view of the high level of protection for the farm sector in Switzerland. It was particularly the influence of Hans Schaffner, the responsible Government Councillor (*Bundesrat, Conseil fédéral*), that led to a rather generous exception for his sector and thus an acceptable outcome of the negotiations for Switzerland at the Ministerial Meeting on 21 May 1963.[21]

When the GATT was transformed from a quasi-international organisation into today's form, the well-established WTO, Switzerland acceded to the newly created organisation on 1 June 1995. The reason for Switzerland's not being among the original members of the WTO is only due to the fact that domestic procedural steps (possibility of a popular referendum) has to be respected, which did not allow for the ratification of the Marrakesh Agreement in due time for membership to start on 1 January 1995.

In principle the monist tradition in Switzerland means that no specific law is needed to implement an international treaty. The approval by parliament, and possibly by the people in a referendum, is not a law but purely a decision to approve the treaty ratification by the Government. With regard to the accession to the GATT only minor changes in the domestic legislation were made. When Switzerland joined the WTO, however, a number of amendments to existing laws were undertaken and well commented in the Message by the Federal Council regarding accession to the WTO. These changes of existing laws were necessary in order to avoid

[18] See: Federal Constitution, arts 163, 166, and 184. The Federal Constitution requires a referendum before the ratification of certain categories of international agreements, which are deemed to be the most important ones, in order to safeguard democratic rights. In this event, there is a public vote regarding the parliamentary approval. See also: Federal Constitution, arts 140, 141, and 141a. In the case of the WTO Agreements there was a facultative referendum according to art 141 para 1 no 2 of the Constitution, because the treaty provided for the entry into an international organisation (the plurilateral agreements in Annex 4 were no subject to this referendum); see Message by the Federal Government relating to the planned accession to the WTO (GATT-Botschaft 1994) vol I of 19 September 1994, Bundesblatt (BBl = Official Journal) 1994 IV 136, 422.

[19] Declaration of 22 November 1958 relating to the provision accession of Switzerland to the Genera Agreement, reprinted in Official Journal (Amtliche Sammlung = AS) 1959 1741, 1962 1044, 1965 546. See also: Message by the Federal Government relating to the planned accession to the GATT (GATT-Botschaft) 1959, BBl 1959 I 647.

[20] Protocol relating to the accession of Switzerland to the GATT, signed in Geneva on 1 April 1966, approved by the Federal Assembly on 30 June 1966; entry into force 1 August 1966 (SR 0.632.211.1, AS 1966 964; BBl 1966 I 713 (original drafted in French).

[21] GATT-Botschaft 1966, BBl 1966 I, 715; and Engelberger (n 2) 77 f; as well as A Weitnauer, *Rechenschaft – Vierzig Jahre im Dienst des schweizerischen Staates* (Zurich, Artemis Publishing, 1981) 166.

any conflicts between existing laws and the new treaty obligations. They are not referred to as specific WTO legislation but have the objective of implementing specific obligations under international law into domestic rules. With regard to highly specific and technical treaties such as the WTO Agreement, this way of adapting the domestic legal order to new, international obligations has become quite typical in recent times. An illustrious example of a law very much inspired by the WTO obligations is the Swiss Law on Public Procurement which was needed in order to prepare the federal government level's procurement practice for the new requirements under the WTO Government Procurement Agreement as entered into by Switzerland.[22]

III. ROLE OF THE COURTS IN THE APPLICATION OF INTERNATIONAL TREATIES

A direct connection between the doctrine of monism and the doctrine of 'direct effect' exists. According to the notion of direct effect, in case of an explicit conflict between domestic and international rules, a private person may challenge the domestic law provision by directly relying on the international law provision. Direct effect may be explicitly prescribed or prohibited by an international agreement or domestic rule. Regularly, however, it is left to the judge to assume a direct effect of a certain rule and grant it in a certain case, or to reject direct application of international agreements.[23] The fact that international treaties become 'part of the law of the land' upon their entry into force thus leads to a special role for the courts and the administration. Courts have over time developed a theory that the provision of international treaties does not always lead to direct applicability and that certain norms contained in international treaties can thus not be invoked by individuals before domestic courts and in administrative proceedings. In Switzerland, it is normally held that a treaty norm must be justiciable, that is, its content must be sufficiently precise and clear to constitute the basis for a decision in a specific case.[24] In addition, it is generally held that such a provision must contain rights or obligations relevant to the individual and that it is meant to direct the authorities or the judge to give effect to the norm. In Switzerland the question whether a specific international treaty rule has direct effect is hardly separated from the question whether it can be invoked by an individual.

[22] See: below section V.C on the GPA.
[23] See: Cottier (n 12).
[24] See, eg: BGE 124 III 90, 91, BGE 118 Ia 112, 116 f, BGE 106 Ib 182, 187. See generally: AR Ziegler (n 7) fn 274.

As in the US the Swiss authorities and courts often use the term 'self-executing character' of a norm to distinguish it from a rule that needs domestic implementation by a specific law to become applicable. Programmatic norms in particular lack this sufficient degree of preciseness. It is also lacking in norms that regulate a matter only in rough outline, that leave a substantial scope of interpretation or that contain only guiding principles, that is, norms that are directed at the legislator. A clear statement regarding the possibility for individuals to rely on self-executing provisions of international treaties before the Swiss Federal Supreme Court is contained in Article 95 Letter b of the Federal Law on the Federal Supreme Court.[25]

Swiss courts are normally relatively open to accepting that specific treaty provisions have direct effect in the domestic legal order. Swiss courts have been relatively generous in recognising the direct effect of human rights. The norms of the European Convention on Human Rights[26] are largely considered to be self-executing, as well as some provisions of the UN Convention on the Rights of the Child[27] and other UN Human Rights Treaties. While the International Covenant on Civil and Political Rights is considered to be, in large part, directly applicable, the authorities and courts have been more reluctant to grant direct application to the economic and social rights contained in the International Covenant on Economic, Social and Cultural Rights.[28]

The principles regarding the direct applicability or direct effect also hold true for international law stemming from trade agreements such as the GATT 1947 and other parts of the WTO legal framework. In its message to parliament regarding the WTO Agreements, the Federal Council stated that direct effect of certain dispositions could not be excluded. But a general assessment would not be possible, as the question was up for decision by relevant jurisprudence on a case-by-case basis.[29]

However, as in other countries, the judiciary and the authorities in Switzerland have been particularly reluctant to give direct effect to international treaty norms liberalising international trade.[30] WTO law itself does not give any indication about its effect and character in domestic legal systems. In national law it is first of all for the executive and especially the courts to decide about the character of a certain international

[25] Supreme Court Statute (BGG = Bundesgerichtsgesetz), SR 173.110; entry into force 1 January 2007. Previously, the same solution could be found in art 84 para 1 lit c OG.

[26] See: SR 0.101; BGE 117 Ib 367, 370 f; BGE 125 II 417, 424 f.

[27] See: SR 0.107; BGE 124 III 90, 91 f; whereas BGE 124 II 361, 367 and BGE 126 II 377, 392 denied direct effect.

[28] See: SR 0.10.3.2, SR 0.10.3.1 and BGE 120 Ia 1, 11; BGE 126 I 240; BGE 130 I 113, 123.

[29] GATT Message 1 (1994), BBl 1994 IV 1 ff, 418.

[30] See for an early overview on the problems and arguments: EU Petersmann, M Hilf (eds), *National Constitutions and International Economic Law* (Deventer, Kluwer, 1993); R Brand, 'Direct Effect of International Economic Law in the United States and the European Union' (1996–97) *Nw J Int'l L & Bus* 17, 556 ff.

law norm.[31] For Switzerland, judges have shown a tendency to accept the statements made by the executive regarding the nature of specific obligations, particularly in politically sensitive areas such as international trade.[32] With regard to the Convention establishing the European Free Trade Area (EFTA)[33] and the bilateral Free Trade Agreement between Switzerland and the European Community[34] the Swiss authorities and courts have also been criticised for denying too often direct effect where treaty norms were intended to liberalise trade between the Parties and to entitle individuals to rely upon theses norms.

Several authors, including the author of this chapter, have held that the reluctance of the Swiss courts to give direct effect to rules liberalising international trade in regional and global trade agreements stems from the courts' fear of interfering in an illegitimate way with the executive branch of the country. As with regard to foreign policy in general, courts fear that they might harm the interests of the country and lack legitimacy to give effect to rules that would grant market access to foreign exporters and service suppliers. This has been criticised as a mercantilist and protectionist attitude but certainly corresponds to the traditional attitude of judges in most countries, including the major trading powers.[35]

IV. DEVELOPMENT OF CASE LAW RELATING TO THE GATT BEFORE 1995

The decision *BGE 86 I 312 of 2 December 1960, Bosshard & Co v Swiss Federal Ministry of Economic Affairs*, is the first judgment of the Swiss Federal Supreme Court which makes an explicit reference to the GATT 1947, although still under the provisional application as negotiated in 1958. The case concerned an administrative decision of 1960 not to admit the import of certain textiles from Japan by a private importer. The measures were part of trade measures against imports of cheap textiles to protect the Swiss textiles sector. The Government argued that these measures had been taken in a way fully compatible with the GATT. As the claimant had not used this argument himself the judges did not need to consider the role and function of the GATT in this respect. The claimant eventually won his case as the Government had not respected domestic procedural requirements.

Similarly, in the Case BGE 100 IB 429, Judgment of 28 June 1974 *re Denner AG v Swiss Ministry of Economic Affairs*, the Federal Supreme Court

[31] Ziegler (n 7) 119.
[32] eg: BGE 120 Ia 1, 10 ff.
[33] See: SR 0.632.31; BGE 98 Ib 385, 388.
[34] See: SR 0.632.401, BGE 105 II 59, BGE 112 IV 53, BGE 114 Ib 168, VPB 63.54 (1999).
[35] See: Cottier (n 12) and several authors in: Petersmann, Hilf (eds) (n 30).

avoided properly addressing the legal character of the GATT under Swiss law. The case concerned the denial of an import licence for red wine by a retail company. The Swiss Federal Supreme Court mentioned as an *obiter dictum* that due to the binding effect of the agreement, Switzerland could not impose customs duties going beyond the bound rates under the GATT. The plaintiffs had further argued that requiring them as retailers to pay an additional duty for the import of red wine as a compensation measure for not buying a corresponding amount of Swiss wine would be an infringement of the GATT. The Court did not address this issue as the retailer had not even been offered this opportunity.[36]

Also in its decision BGE 104 Ib 412 of 22 December 1978 *re Coop Schweiz, Migros-Genossenschafts-Bund and Others v Swiss Ministry of Economic Affairs*, the Swiss Federal Supreme Court did not explicitly address the legal effects of the GATT for the Swiss legal order. The case concerned a duty levied on imported oil for human consumption. The claimants had argued the amount of the duty was higher than the admissible amount under the bound rates in the GATT. This argument was, however, not sufficiently substantiated by the claimants and thus the Court did not address it.

In an unpublished decision of 19 March 1982 *re Firma F v High Customs Commission*[37] the Federal Customs Appeals Commission dealt also with the GATT under Swiss law. The appeal concerned an extraordinary customs duty that the customs authorities had applied to imports of peaches and grapes. The appellant had argued that the extraordinary customs duty was as an emergency action incompatible with Article XIX GATT. The Federal Customs Appeals Commission analysed the duty under Article XIX but also under Article VI:3 GATT (antidumping measures and countervailing duties) and came to the conclusion that it was probably not justified under either of theses provisions as the measure was not necessary as requested under these rules. The Commission came to the conclusion that the measure was not proportionate and hence unlawful under Swiss law. This decision seems to rely – at least implicitly – on the direct application of GATT provisions by domestic authorities but it had no effect on the later decision by the Supreme Court.[38]

Only in its landmark decision BGE 112 Ib 183 of 2 September 1986 *re Maison G Sprl v Swiss General Customs Directorate* did the Swiss Federal Supreme Court decide explicitly on the direct applicability of the GATT by Swiss courts. The case concerned a duty levied on heavy transport vehicles transiting Switzerland. This levy was part of a general tax system to foster goods transports by railway. The claimant argued that such a duty was incompatible with Articles V:3 and VIII GATT. This claim was rejected by the Court with the argument that the GATT was only

36 See: Consideration 8 of the judgment.
37 Reprinted in VPB 46:71 (1982) 463.
38 See: Engelberger (n 2) 99 ff.

concerned with the rights and obligations of states towards each other and could not be invoked by an individual. This argument was not explained in detail but merely corroborated by a sketchy reference to two contributions[39] in the literature.[40] When one looks at the quoted references, it becomes clear that in one case the author merely talks about decisions taken by the *contracting parties* under Article XXV and does not address the legal effects of the GATT as such in the domestic legal order.[41] With regard to the second quote, the author equally underlines merely the absence of any sanctions regarding the non-respect of decisions by the GATT organs.[42] Here, it seems that the Court has not fully understood the difference between the absence of sanctions relating to the non-respect of decisions taken under the GATT and the binding commitments as such.[43] However, this basic statement haunts the questions relating to direct applicability of GATT and WTO law in Switzerland to the present day.[44] Interestingly, at the time, the judgment – and indeed, the legal effects of the GATT 1947 in general – did not attract much attention from legal scholars. It was only in 1990 that Thomas Cottier, a former GATT negotiator for Switzerland, commented on the decision.[45] Similarly, Ernst-Ulrich Petersmann, a former legal adviser at the GATT, referred to this decision in his writings on the constitutional functions of international trade law in a journal article published in 1990.[46] Later several authors commented negatively on the decision.[47]

[39] See also the criticism by Engelberger (n 2) 95.

[40] See: R Senti, *GATT, System der Welthandelsordnung* (Zurich, Schultess, 1986) 45 and O Long, 'La place du droit et ses limites dans le système commercial multilatéral du GATT' 182 *Recueil des Cours* 83.

[41] See: Senti (n 40) 45. It should also be mentioned that my remarkable colleague Richard Senti is a highly respected trade economist and not a legal scholar.

[42] See: Long (n 40) 83.

[43] See also: Engelberger (n 2) 95.

[44] See the references in the cases before the Federal Supreme Court in *Kingston-Bier,* party published in: VPB 63:54 (1999) 54, 512 and *Bresaola,* Judgment 2A.496/1996 of 14/7/1997 E. 4b), unpublished, partly reprinted in: T Cottier, M Wagner, 'Grundzüge der Weltwirtschaftsordnung' in JP Müller, L Wildhaber, *Praxis des Völkerrechts,* 3rd edn (Bern, Stämpfli Publishing, 2001) 895, 938. See also the newspaper reports in Neue Zürcher Zeitung (NZZ) 1997 no 177, 11; Engelberger (n 2) 168.

[45] T Cottier, 'Die Bedeutung des GATT im Prozess der europäischen Integration. Eine Untersuchung aus schweizerischer Sicht' in O Jacot-Guillarmod, D Schindler and T Cottier (eds), *EG-Recht und schweizerische Rechtsordnung* (This booklet is published as one of a series under the title 'Beihefte zur ZSR': (1990) 10 *Beihefte zur ZSR* 139 ff (fn 94)).

[46] See: EU Petersmann, 'Die Verfassungsentscheidung für eine völkerrechtskonforme Rechtsordnung als Strukturprinzip der Schweizer Bundesverfassung' (1990) *Archiv des öffentlichen Rechts* 115, 537, 560.

[47] See: WE Andrich, *Die Wirtschaftsfreiheit im schweizerischen Aussenwirtschaftsrecht,* Diss St Gallen 1995, 73; M Schlatter, *Die Sicherung der wirtschaftlichen Freiheits- und Gleichheitsrechte durch völkerrechtliche Verträge und deren Verhältnis zum nationalen Wirtschaftsverfassungs- und Wirtschaftsverwaltungsrecht, – Untersucht am Beispiel der Umsetzung der GATT/WTO-Übereinkommen (Uruguay-Runde) in das schweizerische Recht,* Diss St Gallen 2000, 211. Both were doctoral students supervised by EU Petersmann. See also: PE Holzer, *Die Ermittlung der innerstaatlichen Anwendbarkeit völkerrechtlicher Vertragsbestimmungen* (Zurich, 1998) 76 (fn

V. APPLICABILITY OF WTO LAW IN SWITZERLAND AND THE PRACTICE OF THE FEDERAL SUPREME COURT

A. GATT 1994

After 1995, there were expectations that the enhanced legal framework of the WTO and the existence of the dispute settlement understanding might influence the treatment of GATT and WTO rules in Switzerland. In its first decision regarding the GATT after 1995 (the unpublished decision of 9 June 1998 *re Kingston-Bier*),[48] the Swiss Federal Supreme Court dealt with a claim brought by importers of beer which had contained added levels of alcohol since 1993. This case resulted from an appeal against a decision by the Swiss Federal Alcohol Appeal Commission (*Eidgenössische Alkoholrekurskommission*) of 20 March 1997 to levy a duty on the base of the higher alcohol content which would not have been the same had the beer been of domestic production. Although the claimants had not invoked the GATT, this Commission had itself addressed the issue whether the amount charged was compatible with the national treatment (NT) obligation under Article III:2 GATT. The Appeals Commission had come to the conclusion that the levy was discriminatory (different taxation of imports and domestic production) and that this constituted a violation of the GATT, but that this violation had no legal consequence in light of the existing case law indicating a lack of direct applicability of the GATT as resulted from the precedent set by the Federal Supreme Court.[49] The Swiss Federal Supreme Court confirmed the judgment and its own decision of 1986 in its final judgment of 9 June 1998.[50] Interestingly, the Swiss Federal Supreme Court also referred to the WTO Agreement in this case by explicitly stating that it had not to rule on the direct applicability of this new Agreement as it was not (yet) applicable in this case. It should also be noted that the law that was found to be incompatible with the GATT in this particular case had in the meantime been modified by the authorities in order to avoid any future incompatibilities.

In its decision BGE 122 II 411 of 27 September 1996, *Swiss Federal Ministry of Economic Affairs v Appeals Commission for the Swiss Federal Ministry of Economic Affairs and Vilaclara Jr & Co*,[51] the Swiss Federal

329); this doctoral thesis was supervised by T Cottier. See also: D Thürer, 'WTO-Teilordnung im System des Völker- und Europarechts' in D Thürer, S Kux (eds), *GATT 94 und die Welthandelsorganisation* (Zurich, Schulthess Publishing, 1996) 41, 52.

[48] See: n 44.

[49] See: *Re Maison G Sprl v Swiss General Customs Directorate*, BGE 112 Ib 183, Judgment of 2 September 1986 Consideration 3c.

[50] Decision not officially published but reprinted in 1998 ASA 69, 366 ff.

[51] See: BGE 122 II 411.

Supreme Court dealt with the allocation of a tariff quota for white wine. The importer had considered that it was not permissible under the GATT to ask importers to provide a bank guarantee when they applied for imports under a tariff quota. The Court held that this was a question of domestic procedural law as the WTO Agreement contained no rule whatsoever that governed this aspect.[52]

In an unpublished decision of 14 July 1997 *re A SA v Federal Office for Agriculture and Appeals Commission for the Swiss Federal Ministry of Economic Affairs*,[53] the plaintiff was an importer of dried meat (Bresaola). Following the Uruguay Round, the allocation of certain tariff quotas for such dried meat had been subject to an auctioning system. This auctioning system seemed to the plaintiff incompatible with Article 4:2 of the Agreement on Agriculture and Article 3 of the Import Licensing Agreement. The Court recognised that the WTO Agreement was intended to create greater legal certainty, especially with regard to those provisions of the GATT that now were dealt with in more specific agreements, such as the one on import licensing. At the same time the Court reiterated that many provisions under the WTO were just as vague as under the GATT 1947 and that on the whole the Parties still enjoyed considerable discretion with regard to the exact measures to be adopted, a fact that could jeopardise the direct application of these provisions by domestic courts. All these considerations, however, were without direct relevance for the case as the Court found the measures at stake to be in full compliance with the quoted provisions. It is interesting to observe how the Court used this first relevant case under the newly created WTO legal framework to develop its views on the character of the WTO Agreement under Swiss law in view of its existing case law regarding the GATT 1947. As in many later cases the Court left open the question as to whether a provision of the WTO Agreements is directly applicable or not and concluded that, in any case, the domestic legislation was compatible with the international rules. Although the judgment was not published in the official case reports, the decision was reprinted (partly) in various books as well as in several articles in law journals,[54] and also reported in the major economic newspaper of the country which can be taken as a significant sign that the public perception of the WTO also in Switzerland has changed in comparison to the former GATT.[55]

[52] ibid 419.
[53] See: n 44.
[54] See: Schlatter (n 47) 221 f; D Wüger, 'Die direkte Anwendbarkeit staatsvertraglichen Rechts' in T Cottier et al (eds), *Der Staatsvertrag im schweizerischen Verfassungsrecht* (Bern, Stämpfli Publishing, 2001) 247.
[55] See also: Engelberger (n 2) 105.

B. GATS

Regarding the GATS, the attitude of the Swiss courts is similar to the one developed with regard to the GATT 1947 and the GATT 1994. In its decision BGE 125 II 293 of 7 May 1999 *re Sunrise Communications AG, diAx mobile and Orange Communications SA v Federal Communication Commission*,[56] the Supreme Court held that the GATS only creates duties and rights for Parties, which does not create directly applicable rights for individual service suppliers, which could be invoked by telecommunications companies before the authorities and the Court.

In its unpublished decision 2P.243/2000 of 14 March 2001 *re B v Public Health Directorate of the Canton of Zurich*, the claimant had tried to invoke Article VII GATS on the recognition of diplomas in order to be admitted to practice as a specialist for homoeopathy. The Court held that Article VII did not require WTO Members to automatically recognise a foreign diploma but simply encouraged Parties to facilitate such recognition, for example, through the conclusion of bilateral agreements. In the absence of such an agreement the GATS did not contain any individual rights for service suppliers.

In unpublished decision 2A.503/2000 of 3 October 2001 *re Commcare AG Communications and Networks v Swisscom AG*[57] the Swiss Federal Supreme Court held that Articles II, III, VI and VIX GATS in connection with Article 5 b) ii) of the Annex on Telecommunications did not confer a right to unbundling or interconnection of service suppliers. The question whether this provision had direct effect was explicitly left open.[58] However, despite this outcome, the Federal Government decided in 2003 to introduce the unbundling in the telecommunications sector requested by the claimants in the case at stake. The decision by the Supreme Court was criticised for two reasons: one group of authors considered that the requirement to unbundle the telecommunications sectors was sufficiently precisely contained in the GATS and its annexes.[59] A second group criticised the

[56] See: BGE 125 II 293, 305; Engelberger (n 2) 170.

[57] Decision 2A.503/2000 of 3/10/2001, unpublished, reprinted partially in (2002) ZBl 103/2002, 244; and in: Zeitschrift für Immaterialgüter-, Informations-und Wettbewerbsrecht – sic! 2002, 18; as well as in: RDAF 2003 I, 595; and reported by Engelberger (n 2) 171f.

[58] Consideration 9c) *in fine*.

[59] See: CB Graber, '"Lost Highway" – Bleibt KMU der Zugang zur Breitbandkommunikation verbaut – Wege zur Marktöffnung nach schweizerischem und internationalem Recht', Jusletter of 16 June 2003, para 6; also published in: D Girsberger, J Schmid (eds), *Rechtsfragen rund um die KMU* (Zurich, Schulthess Publishing, 2003) 217 ff, para 35 ff; T Poledna, 'Unbundling – Stolpersteine auf der "letzten Meile"' (2002) *AJP* 334 ff, 338 f; P Csoport, C von Zedtwitz, 'Verhandlungsanalyse zur Interkonnektion – Wertschöpfungsstrategien für Ex-Monopolisten der Telekommunikation' 2003 *AJP* 1189; as well as in: R Rhinow, 'Stellungnahme zum Gutachten von Andreas Kley zur Frage, ob das Völkerrecht oder das Fernmelderecht eine genügende gesetzliche Grundlage für eine Verpflichtung zur Entbündelung im Anschlussnetz bieten', Zurich, 7 February 2001, unpublished but quoted

general attitude of the Federal Supreme Court in failing to accept the direct applicability of the GATS.[60]

In its decision BGE 131 II 13 of 30 November 2004 *re Swisscom Fixnet AG v TDC Switzerland AG and Federal Communications Commissions* the Supreme Court dealt with the criticism regarding its earlier decision. But it refused to change its position regarding the alleged requirement that Parties had to unbundle their telecommunications sector. In particular, the Court referred to the official position of the Federal Government in this respect and the fact that the respective annexes had not been submitted for approval by parliament which implicitly confirmed that the Government was of the opinion that no individual rights were created by theses annexes.[61] The Court ultimately admitted that the GATS and its Annexes created certain expectations regarding the unbundling of the sector but left open whether such expectations were of a purely political nature or had a legal foundation in the agreements. In any case the Court refused to accept that an individual right had been created.[62] Finally, in another decision relating to the telecommunications sector, BGE 132 II 47 of 22 November 2005 *re TDC Switzerland AG v Swisscom Fixnet AG and Federal Communications Commission (ComCom)* the Court again refused to interpret the GATS and its telecommunications Annex as creating a specific right to unbundling and interconnection.

C. TRIPs

The TRIPs Agreement as adopted in 1995 is different from the GATT and the GATS insofar as it creates a wide range of harmonisation rules that must be taken into account by domestic authorities and the legislature when regulating intellectual property rights. As such, it has direct implications for individuals in situations of possible conflict of norms. This clear link between the scope of regulation and the individuals has an important legal significance: quite evidently, a direct effect of the TRIPs Agreement on individuals can be established, and has also partially been accepted by domestic courts internationally.[63]

by: A Kley, 'Enthält das WTO-Recht eine Verpflichtung zur Entbündelung des Fernmeldeanschlussnetzes' (2003) *SZIER* 508, 513.

[60] See: Engelberger (n 2) 89 ff; M Oesch, 'Gewaltenteilung und Rechtsschutz im schweizerischen Aussenwirtschaftsrecht' (2005) *ZBl* 105/2005, 314 ff.

[61] See: BGE 131 II 13, 41 ff.

[62] Consideration 9.

[63] Courts of several EU Member States have accepted a direct effect of certain provision of the TRIPs Agreement, particularly for TRIPs arts 9 and 13; see: P Van den Bossche, *The Law and Policy of the World Trade Organization – Text, Cases and Materials*, 2nd edn (Cambridge, Cambridge University Press, 2008) 68.

The Swiss Federal Supreme Court applied the TRIPs Agreement for the first time in its decision BGE 122 III 469 of 23 October 1996 *re Chanel SA Genève and Chanel SA v EPA AG*. The claimant argued that the authorities should not have allowed parallel imports of his products in view of a proper interpretation of the domestic law on trademarks in light of Article 16.1 TRIPs. The Court mentioned that Article 16 TRIPs did not prohibit parallel imports *per se*, but for the rest did not address the question of direct applicability of this provision of the agreement as a whole as the claim had not been sufficiently substantiated.[64]

In its decision BGE 124 III 277 of 24 March 1998 *re Quarz AG, Campomar SL and Nike Sports Cosmetics SA v Nike International Ltd*, the Federal Supreme Court was asked whether Article 4 TRIPs (MFN) could be invoked by the claimants to defend their trademark rights. The Court held that Article 4 TRIPS was only applicable with regard to the treatment resulting from international treaties concluded after the coming into force of the TRIPs Agreement for Switzerland (1 June 1995) and thus did not affect claims based on a treaty concluded prior to this date.[65] The Court did not address the question as to whether Article 4 was of direct effect as the fact that it did not convey the rights suggested by the claimant had pre-empted its application.

In its decision BGE 124 III 321 of 20 July 1998 *re Imprafot AG v Nintendo Co Ltd and Waldmeier AG* the Swiss Federal Supreme Court stated that no provision of the TRIPs Agreement could be interpreted as to create a right to parallel imports and thus did not allow interpreting Article 12 of the Swiss Copyright Act in a specific way. The question of direct applicability of the TRIPs Agreement or a specific provision contained in it was thus again avoided.[66] The Swiss Federal Supreme Court was asked in BGE 126 III 129 of 7 December 1999 *re Kodak SA v Jumbo Markt AG* whether Articles 6 and 28 TRIPs created a right to parallel imports. The Court denied that these provisions could be interpreted in a way that created such a right. The question regarding the direct applicability of these provisions was not discussed.[67] Similarly, in its decision 131 III 76 of 4 October 2004 the

[64] See: BGE 122 III 469 Consideration 5g bb), 480; see also: Engelberger (n 2) 114.

[65] See: BGE 124 III 277, 284; see also: Engelberger (n 2) 115 f.

[66] See: BGE 124 III 321 E. 2 f, 330f; see also: Engelberger (n 2) 116 f; T Cottier, R Arpagaus, 'Einleitung' in T Cottier, R Arpagaus (eds), *Schweizerisches Aussenwirtschafts- und Binnenmarktrecht*, (Basel / Frankfurt am Main, Helbing & Lichtenhahn, 1999) 33.

[67] See: BGE 126 III 129 E 3b, 137f; see also: Engelberger (n 2) 117; E Bollinger, 'Die Regelung der Parallelimporte im Recht der WTO' Zeitschrift für Immaterialgüter-, Informations-und Wettbewerbsrecht - sic! 1998, 541 ff; R Hilty, 'Verbot von Parallelimporten – Heimatschutz oder Schildbügerstreich' Zeitschrift für Immaterialgüter-, Informations-und Wettbewerbsrecht - sic! 2000, 231ff; W Stieger, '"Kodak" – Eine Momentaufnahme des Schnittbereichs vom Immaterialgüter- und Kartellrecht aus helvetischer Sicht' Zeitschrift für Immaterialgüter-, Informations-und Wettbewerbsrecht – sic! 2001, 89 ff; R Zäch, 'Parallelimporte patentrechtlich geschützter Güter nach Massgabe des Kartellgesetzes' Zeitschrift für Immaterialgüter-, Informations-und Wettbewerbsrecht - sic! 2000, 275 ff.

Court came to the conclusion that the domestic law was fully compatible with Article 3.1 TRIPs Agreement and thus did not have to qualify its character in any further way.[68]

Until the creation of a central Federal Administrative Tribunal in 2004 several specialised commissions heard appeals at first instance against decisions by federal bodies. In this context decisions by the Swiss Intellectual Property Institute were regularly challenged before the Appeal Commission for Intellectual Property.[69] This Commission rendered two decisions in relation to the TRIPs Agreement. In its decision of 22 September 1997 *re The Beatles*[70] the Commission decided that Article 16.2 TRIPs did cover trademarks with regard to goods and services and thus created a right for the owner of a well-known trademark in the area. Whether Article 16.2 TRIPs simply informed the correct interpretation of Articles 3.1 and 2 b of the Swiss Trademark Act or was as such the source of this right was not addressed properly.[71] The same reasoning was applied by the Commission in its decision of 17 November 1997 *re The Joyride*.[72]

Several regional courts have addressed the issue of the direct applicability of the TRIPs agreement. In a decision of 1 October 1997 the High Court of the Canton of Basel-Land decided that Article 50.2 TRIPs did not go beyond what was contained in Article 77.2 of the Swiss Patent Act and thus decided to leave open the question whether the TRIPs Agreement was of direct application.[73] In a decision of 21 May 2001 the Appeals Court of the Canton of Bern considered that a reference to international treaties in the Swiss Copyright Act did not lead to the applicability of the TRIPs Agreement.[74] The Court was criticised for failing to address the relevance of the TRIPs agreement in this context.[75]

D. Government Procurement Agreement

Another agreement under the WTO that regularly comes to the attention of Swiss courts is the Agreement on Government Procurement (GPA).

[68] See: BGE 131 II 76 E.4.2.

[69] In German: 'Rekurskommission für das geistiges Eigentum'.

[70] Published in: Zeitschrift für Immaterialgüter-, Informations-und Wettbewerbsrecht – sic! 1997, 581 ff.

[71] Consideration 4, 581. See: Engelberger (n 2) 117 f.

[72] Published in: Zeitschrift für Immaterialgüter-, Informations-und Wettbewerbsrecht – sic! 1998 51 ff; see: Engelberger (n 2) 118.

[73] See: Entscheid des Obergerichts Basel-Landschaft of 1 October 1997; published in: Zeitschrift für Immaterialgüter-, Informations-und Wettbewerbsrecht – sic! 1998 78 ff; see also: Engelberger (n 2) 118 f.

[74] See: Entscheid des Appellationsgerichtshofs Bern of 21 May 2001; published in: Zeitschrift für Immaterialgüter-, Informations-und Wettbewerbsrecht – sic! 2001 613 ff with comments by Reto Hilty.

[75] See: Engelberger (n 2) 119 f.

Similarly to the TRIPs Agreement it contains detailed procedural rules that must be implemented at the domestic level. The GPA is one of four original plurilateral agreements contained in Annex 4 of the WTO Agreement. According to the Swiss Federal Council in its Message relating to the accession to the WTO, the GPA contains both self-executing norms as well as principles needing concretisation, for example, the dispositions regarding the creation of an appeal procedure.[76]

Due to the federal structure of Switzerland and its tradition of local autonomy regarding procurement decisions, the obligations of the GPA were implemented in Switzerland in a great number of laws at different levels. It can be said that government procurement law in Switzerland is extremely compartmentalised and thus the reference to the central principles contained in the GPA are of great importance for the coherence of the Swiss legislation.

In an *obiter dictum* to its decision of 20 November 1998 re *Groupement G2IR3 v Conseil communal de La Chaux-de-Fonds* the Swiss Federal Supreme Court decided that the correct interpretation of Article 9 of the Swiss Internal Market Act and the Intercantonal Treaty on Public Procurement in light of Article XX of the Government Procurement Agreement was that a procurement decision of a local authority could be challenged before a court.[77] In two later decisions, BGE 125 I 496 and BGer 2P.42/2001 of 8 June 2001 (unpublished), this interpretation was confirmed. In its decision BGE 125 I 209 of 26 April 1999 *re JC Decaux Mobilier Urbain Genève Sa* and *Decaux SA v Ville de Genève, Etat de Genève and Société Générale d'Affichage*, the Court came to the conclusion that the proper interpretation of the GPA did exclude the claims at stake from its applicability.[78] A similar attitude regarding Articles XII and XIII:4 of the GPA can be found in the Court's unpublished decision BGer 2.274/1999 of 2 March 2000.[79]

In a decision of 2 March 2000 *re ARGE X v ARGE Y, Regierungsrat and Verwaltungsgericht des Kantons Thurgau* the Court considered that the scope of the GPA and the domestic implementing Act (Intercantonal Treaty on Public Procurement) were identical and thus no analysis of the former was required. However, in its decision 2P.151/1999 of 30 May 2000 *re ARGE X v Kanton Wallis* the Court reiterated the statement contained in the Government's message regarding Switzerland's accession to the

[76] See: GATT Message 1 (1994) 421 and GATT Message 2 (1994) 1171.

[77] BGE 125 II 86 E.2-6; Engelberger (n 2) 122; E Clerc, *L'ouverture des marches publics: Effectivité et protection juridique* (Fribourg, Editions Universitaires Fribourg, 1997) 364 ff; T Cottier, B Merkt, 'Die Auswirkungen des Welthandelsrechts der WTO und des BGBM auf das Submissionsrecht in der Schweiz' in R von Büren, T Cottier (eds), *Die neue schweizerische Wettbewerbsordnung im internationalen Umfeld* (Bern, Stämpfli Publishing, 1997) 35, 75ff; AR Gadola, 'Rechtsschutz und andere Formen der Überwachung der Vorschriften über das öffentliche Beschaffungswesen' 1996 *AJP* 967 ff.

[78] See: Consideration 6, 212 ff; and Engelberger (n 2) 122 f.

[79] See: Engelberger (n 2) 123.

WTO, namely that the GPA contained both directly applicable norms and mere hortatory language and thus in certain cases could be invoked by private parties. This led in the decision at stake to the direct application of Article XIII: 1 b) of the GPA. The Court found, however, that there was no violation of this provision in this case.[80] Similarly in its decision of 26 June 2000 *re ARGE X v Regierungsrat des Kantons Basel-Landschaft* the Court considered that the transparency principle of the GPA could be invoked but was not violated in the case before it.[81] In the unpublished decision BGer 2P.299/2000 of 24 August 2001 the Court concluded however, that the transparency principle under domestic law as concretised by Article XII: 2 h of the GPA was violated.[82]

At the federal level government procurement decisions could be challenged at first instance before the Federal Appeals Commission for Public Procurement until the Federal Administrative Tribunal took over in 2006. This Commission rendered an important number of decisions in which the scope and function of the GPA were addressed. Similarly to the case law established by the Federal Supreme Court, the Commission usually considers alleged violation of the GPA simultaneously with the corresponding violations of the domestic legislation. Due to the implementing character of the domestic legislation in this field it is difficult to distinguish the interpretation of domestic law in the light of the GPA from an autonomous application of the GPA in the domestic order.[83] Similarly, regional courts have made reference to the GPA in the same manner, albeit not always in a very convincing way.[84]

VI. INFLUENCE OF REPORTS BY PANELS AND THE APPELLATE BODY

Apart from the question of the application of the WTO agreement and its Annexes by domestic courts, the influence of the case law as developed under the Understanding on Dispute Settlement (DSU) seems to be of major interest. In view of the often vague character of the covered agreements it is generally held that the reports prepared by dispute settlement panels and especially the Appellate Body may have an important role in providing guidance for the correct interpretation of the covered agreements.

In its government message, the Swiss Federal Council stated explicitly that it considered that Panel and Appellate Body reports were only bind-

[80] See: Consideration 3b; and Engelberger (n 3) 123.
[81] BGer 2P.4/2000, published in: (2001) ZBl 102; Consideration 1d.
[82] See: Engelberger (n 2) 124.
[83] See also: ibid 125.
[84] See the comments by: ibid 127 ff.

ing upon Contracting Parties and that individuals could never invoke them directly as it was for the Parties concerned to decide upon the proper implementation of these reports.[85] To the present day, Switzerland has rarely been involved in dispute settlement proceedings at the WTO and has never been the defendant in proceedings before a Panel or the Appellate Body. There are therefore no Dispute Settlement Body (DSB) reports directly addressed to Switzerland as a Party and no court has ever had to articulate a judgment on the effect of such a decision in Swiss law.

In its decision H-2004-174 of 20 October 2005[86] *re Preferential Treatment of Domestic Newspapers* the Appeals Commission for Infrastructure and the Environment had to deal with the claim that the preferential prices charged by the Swiss Postal Services for the delivery of domestic newspapers as opposed to foreign newspapers was unlawful. One of the claimants' arguments was that the preferential treatment constituted a forbidden discrimination under Article III GATT. The Commission avoided applying Article III GATT directly[87] but held once again that Article 15 of the Postal Act had to be interpreted in a way that made it consistent with the international obligations of Switzerland, that is, Article III GATT. The Commission came to the conclusion that a preferential treatment was in violation of Article III: 4 GATT and could not be justified by the exception contained in Article III: 8 letter b GATT. With regard to the proper interpretation of this latter provision the Commission relied heavily on its interpretation by the WTO Appellate Body in its report WT/DS31/AB/R of 30/6/1997 *Canada – Certain Measures Concerning Periodicals*.[88] Whether the reading of the report by the Commission was accurate remains questionable, but for our purposes it is interesting to see that the Commission used the WTO Report as an authoritative means for interpreting the meaning of the WTO obligations and thereby indirectly to interpret domestic law in a treaty-consistent manner.

In its decision BGE 131 III 76 of 4 October 2004 *re X A/S v Y AG* the claimants alleged that the treatment by the authorities was discriminatory under Article 3.1 TRIPs and referred to a WTO Panel Decision of 7 November 1989 United States – section 337 of the Tariff Act of 1930 (BISD 36S/345). This case concerned the reduced availability of a choice of forum under Article III: 4 GATT. The Court erroneously spoke of a 'GATT Panel of 1998' but did not take a position on the relevance of this Panel Report for the case at stake as it considered the domestic law to be in full compliance with the TRIPs Agreement in view of the contained reference to exceptions in the Paris Convention.[89]

[85] See: GATT Message 1, BBl 1994 IV 1 ff, 418.
[86] Partly published in: VPB 70.18 (2006).
[87] See: Consideration 13.3.
[88] See: Consideration 13.4.2.
[89] See: Consideration 2.

Local and specialised authorities also seem inclined to refer to GATT and WTO Dispute Settlement Reports, although this often seems to depend on whether the claimant refers to such reports and/or whether the law clerks involved are familiar with WTO law. This is particularly common in the area of government procurement.

A very interesting example is the reference by the Administrative Tribunal of the Canton of Zurich to the case law relating to processes and production methods (PPMs) with regard to Articles I, III and XX (b) GATT, in particular the *Tuna/Dolphin* and *Shrimps/Turtles* cases, when asked whether Article XXIII: 2 of the GPA allowed the authorities to request bidders to provide wood only from sustainable forestry.[90]

Another example is the reference to the Panel Report Korea – Measures Affecting Government Procurement, WT/DS163R adopted on 15 June 2000 in a decision by the Federal Appeals Commission for Public Procurement CRM 7/01 of 28 September 2001 *re Skyguide*.[91] Here the Swiss authorities had to decide whether a public body was controlled by the state and thus subject to the disciplines of the GPA or whether it was sufficiently independent to be considered as a separate entity. The authorities tried to apply the same test as had been developed by the WTO Panel in order to interpret the scope of the implementing legislation in conformity with the GPA. It even referred to a second Panel Report also prepared under the GATT 1947, namely US – Sonar Mapping System, Government Procurement Agreement.DS1/R of 23 April 1992 which was never adopted. Despite the fact that this second report was never officially adopted by the Parties, the Federal Appeals Commission for Public Procurement considered that it had led to the negotiations of the current Article I: 3 GPA and thus should be used for its proper interpretation.[92]

VII. CONCLUSION

Many authors, including this one have criticised the Federal Supreme Court and other tribunals and administrative bodies for denying in a general way direct effect to the GATT 1947. Most of them have also criticised Swiss courts' refusal to address the question of the direct effect of the GATT 1994 and the other agreements of the WTO after 1995. In particular with regard to the trade liberalising provisions under the GATT and the GATS, it remains the case that the Supreme Court has never openly admitted that they could be of direct effect.

[90] Decision by the Administrative Tribunal of the Canton of Zurich VG Zürich VB1998.00369 Considerations 3c and 4 as reported in P Galli et al, *Praxis des öffentlichen Beschaffungsrechts vol I: Landesrecht*, 2nd edn (Zurich, Schulthess Publishing, 2007) 260.

[91] Reprinted in: VPB 66:5 (2002) 57 ff.

[92] Consideration 3c) ee.

Nevertheless, it can be seen that the Swiss courts and especially the administrative bodies at first instance have been very creative in interpreting domestic legislation in a way that led to the fulfilment of, or adherence to, the international obligations. The treaty-consistent interpretation of domestic law has thus led to a high indirect effect of WTO law on the Swiss legal order. Importantly this includes WTO jurisprudence, that is, reports by Panels and the Appellate Body, even if not adopted. The question of whether Swiss judges are sufficiently prepared to apply these treaties and the respective case law is a valid one, but it is also true that on the whole there have been few incoherent decisions in recent years.

This development is particularly true for the new generation of agreements under the WTO. The case law regarding the TRIPs Agreement and the GPA show clearly that the respective specialised judges are used to the sprit and language of these agreements and take them fully into account when interpreting the domestic legislations in this field. This task is also made easier by the fact that legislature has adopted specific legislation or amended existing laws in order to satisfy the requirements of these agreements leading to some kind of positive integration as opposed to the negative integration through liberalisation of the GATT, and in parts of the GATS.

Avoiding a clear answer as to the direct effect of WTO law in Swiss jurisprudence, the matter of consistent interpretation of Swiss law with WTO law not only brings with it the necessary legal consistency, but also has positive effects on the construction of domestic law. As has been shown, particularly in areas in which international trade rules are of a detailed, elaborate nature and may constitute an example to follow for the establishment of an efficient legal framework, WTO rules can be of utmost importance to domestic law. Regularly, they will not set aside domestic rules, but rather support the interpretation of broad and open-textured domestic law by offering explicit and detailed legal text. This important interaction between international law and domestic rules is nicely evidenced by the Swiss experience: subtle but enduring consistent interpretation of domestic rules with WTO law by Swiss courts brings closer together domestic and international economic law.

15

Conclusions

OLE KRISTIAN FAUCHALD AND ANDRÉ NOLLKAEMPER

IN THE INTERNATIONAL legal order a certain degree of fragmentation is inevitable and, moreover, fulfils important functions. States have to respond to a multitude of challenges that vary with subject area and over time. Given the essentially decentralised nature of the international legal system, and the fact that priorities are defined by different political systems, fragmentation is an inevitable consequence of the positive function that international law fulfils for varying constellations of states.

While international tribunals largely are in the hands of states and thus reflect such fragmentation, and thereby can further the positive functions of fragmentation, they have also recognised that they function in a system that is wider than the specific jurisdiction or treaty regime by which they were established. Their practices contribute incrementally to a relatively coherent structure of international law. Indeed, they provide some evidence for the following prediction by Georges Abi Saab:

> Can there be a 'judicial system' without a centralized 'judicial power' invested in it, and with the jurisdiction of its components remaining in general ultimately consensual? I answer in the affirmative. Such a system can develop through the 'cumulative process' of international law, of which custom is the most visible, but not the only, example. This process would progressively condense and crystallize the different particles of consensual or authoritative jurisdictional empowerment into a certain structure.[1]

One aim of this book was to contribute to our understanding of the extent to which, and the ways in which, national and international courts contribute to the 'de-fragmentation' in the international legal order and, thereby, to the development of the 'structure' referred to by Abi-Saab.

Based on the chapters in this volume, in this concluding chapter we shall first consider how and through what principles and procedures *international tribunals* seek to counteract fragmentation and contribute to a

[1] GM Abi-Saab, 'Fragmentation or Unification: Some Concluding Remarks' (1999) 31 *NYUJ Int'l L & Pol* 919, 926 f.

coherent approach to international law (section I). Thereafter, we shall discuss principles and techniques that *national courts* have applied to counteract fragmentation of international law as applied in domestic legal systems (section II). We end with some concluding observations on the normative and empirical aspects of the subject matter of the book (section III).

I. THE PRACTICE OF INTERNATIONAL TRIBUNALS

The chapters in this volume have helped to clarify three issues. First, we will assess whether international tribunals have developed common approaches to treaty interpretation (section II.A). This will focus in particular on the application of the principles contained in Articles 31 to 33 of the Vienna Convention on the Law of Treaties and on how different characteristics of tribunals may influence the way they rely on the Vienna Convention. The underlying hypothesis is that to the extent that international tribunals follow the rules set out in the Vienna Convention, and/or attach weight to methods of interpretation used by other tribunals, in particular the International Court of Justice (ICJ), this may counteract to some extent fragmenting effects of tribunals that are organised by separate regimes.

Second, we will assess the evidence concerning the communication among international tribunals (section II.B). The underlying hypothesis here is that communication among international tribunals to some extent counteracts fragmentation resulting from the lack of centralised law-making institutions in international law. International tribunals could thus, through communication, contribute actively to the coordination of substantive rules of international law. This hypothesis thus focuses on norm-harmonisation from the perspective of substantive rules.

Third, we reflect on the need to develop a methodology for coordinating conflicting or competing functions of international tribunals and the possibility of doing so (section II.C).

A. Approaches to Treaty Interpretation

Some treaties have addressed the interpretive methods that international tribunals are to apply. In most of these cases such methods are those that are commonly used in international law,[2] sometimes with certain specifi-

[2] One example is the WTO Understanding on Rules and Procedures Governing the Settlement of Disputes (1994) (DSU) art 3.2, see: Gruszczynski, this volume at 37f.

cations.[3] Apart from these situations, international tribunals basically have two options. First, they can assume that states that concluded treaties had the implicit intention that the interpretive method to be applied is the method that applies as a matter of general international law. Given that this method remains fairly open-textured, international tribunals would be left with considerable discretion.[4] Secondly, international tribunals can assume that the interpretive method to be applied falls within its discretionary power as established by the treaty regime in question; the tribunal should develop its own methodology in light of the characteristics and functions of the treaty regime in question.

In practice, these two options may not be far removed from one another. When we assess the practice of international tribunals,[5] the main differences between these options can probably be traced by examining the extent to which tribunals rely on the Vienna Convention, general rules of treaty interpretation, and the practice of other tribunals, in particular the ICJ. In any case, all the treaty regimes examined in Part One of this book rely on the Vienna Convention and corresponding general rules of treaty interpretation.

Within this common approach, approaches of tribunals to treaty interpretation may differ depending on their nature and characteristics. Shany distinguishes between three categories of tribunals: inter-state arbitration tribunals that focus on settling disputes between states (the arbitration tribunals examined by Paparinskis could be placed in this category), tribunals that primarily sustain co-operative relations among their member states (the WTO dispute settlement mechanism examined by Gruszczynski and Zimmermann is part of this category), and tribunals that primarily promote state compliance with specific treaty norms (the European Court of Human Rights (ECtHR), discussed by Nordeide falls into this category).[6] Shany observes that 'a regime's goals, structures, and procedures, shape and control the judicial functions of international courts belonging to that regime to a considerable extent.'[7]

As to the first category, Paparinskis explores the extent to which investment tribunals respect the Vienna Convention on the Law of Treaties and associated customary rules in the context of bilateral treaties. While investment arbitration panels extensively refer to the Vienna Convention

[3] See: art 6 of the Agreement on the European Economic Area (1993) as further elaborated in art 3 of the Agreement between the EFTA States on the Establishment of a Surveillance Authority and a Court of Justice (1992).

[4] See: Gruszczynski, this volume at 38.

[5] Constantinides, this volume at 276, questions the extent to which one may rely on statements by international tribunals: 'A study of formal citations may underestimate the extent to which judges are influenced by external decisions. In fact, express citation in international judgments is generally done sparingly, selectively and reluctantly.'

[6] Shany, this volume at 19f.

[7] ibid 20.

and the case law of the ICJ,[8] Paparinskis critically examines whether their use of interpretive arguments can be justified under the Vienna Convention or other general principles of treaty interpretation. His view is that investment tribunals in general go further in taking into account interpretive materials than they are authorised to under general international law. He also observes that such approaches cannot be justified on the basis of state consent, as there is a lack of practice among states to reform the normative framework for investment tribunals' use of interpretive arguments.[9]

As to tribunals that primarily sustain co-operative relations among their Member States, Gruszczynski points to the extensive use of general rules concerning treaty interpretation in the jurisprudence of the WTO, in accordance with Article 3.2 of the WTO Dispute Settlement Understanding (DSU).[10] His general conclusion is that:

> [T]he analysis of WTO practice shows a clear tendency on the part of the dispute settlement bodies to interpret WTO provisions in accordance with the methods established by the Vienna Convention on the Law of Treaties. Deviations from its model are not very frequent and appear to be less visible in the more recent case law. Future WTO jurisprudence will show whether this is a permanent trend.[11]

Nevertheless, on the basis of a limited but representative assessment of the WTO jurisprudence, he identifies two areas where there is a lack of compatibility between the practice of the WTO and the Vienna Convention: the WTO dispute settlement mechanism is relying on overly textual methods, and it is limiting the role of non-WTO rules in the process of interpretation.[12] Hence, while Paparinskis observes that investment arbitration tribunals generally take into account too broad a range of interpretive materials, Gruszczynski observes that the WTO dispute settlement mechanism is too restrictive in its application of interpretive materials.

As to tribunals that primarily promote state compliance with specific treaty norms, Nordeide points to characteristics of the ECtHR – the special nature of human rights law and the limited regional scope of the ECtHR – that might explain why the ECtHR has developed a method-

[8] OK Fauchald, 'The Legal Reasoning of ICSID Tribunals – An Empirical Analysis' (2008) 19 *Eur J Int'l L* 301.

[9] Paparinskis, this volume at 113f: 'even though practice sometimes goes further than the traditional understanding of sources and interpretation, it has not resulted in an underlying normative shift of the meta-rules. Most instances of State practice and case law confirm the traditional understanding of sources and interpretation, and the explicit and implicit attempts to change the traditional approaches are neither widespread nor consistent enough to change the VCLT and customary rules on treaty interpretation'.

[10] Gruszczynski, this volume at 41–46.

[11] ibid 56.

[12] ibid 38f and 41.

ology distinct from the methodology of general international law.[13] While the ECtHR at a general level seems to adhere to the methodology of the Vienna Convention on the Law of Treaties, its application in practice seems to be unsettled.[14] Nordeide finds that:

> [T]he Court's approach might therefore be described as an openness to the ILC's articulation of the rationale of systemic integration, but a reticence towards engaging in the finer details of the legal technique the ILC identified in Article 31(3)(c) of the Vienna Convention on the Law of Treaties. This would seem to stand in contrast to the approach taken by other international courts.[15]

We may thus observe that previous practice of the ECtHR would be in accordance with Shany's expectations for this category of tribunals, namely that they would 'focus their energies on promoting state compliance' with the norms.[16] However, as emphasised by Nordeide, recent developments in the case law of the ECtHR, including also its increasing use of general principles of international law,[17] indicate that the Court may be headed towards redefining its approach to international rules concerning methodology,[18] with more attention being paid to jurisdiction-regulation and norm-harmonisation.

It thus appears that while all international tribunals examined in Part One attach weight to the Vienna Convention on the Law of Treaties, the way in which of Articles 31 and 32 of the Vienna Convention are applied differs significantly. Indeed, they show that the Convention in itself is too open textured to be a significant force in the determination of processes of (de-)fragmentation, and that factors specific to the treaty regime, and the outlook of particular international courts, carry more weight.

Nonetheless, Part One of this book also demonstrates the problems of predicting the interpretive approaches of international tribunals on the basis of their characteristics. Further research is needed to determine which characteristics of international tribunals would be particularly significant for their methodological approaches.

Moreover, research is needed regarding less 'objective' factors affecting the approaches of tribunals. It can be argued that the impact that international tribunals' characteristics have on their approach to interpretation depends on the perception that the members of the tribunals have of such

[13] Nordeide, this volume at 118, 122f and 132.
[14] ibid 121 and 134, respectively.
[15] ibid 134.
[16] Shany, this volume at 20.
[17] Nordeide, this volume at 126–28.
[18] Nordeide, this volume at 137 finds that 'the three judgements in 2001 regarding sovereign immunity marked a turning point; a point where the Court made a choice of principle as regards the influence of other international law.' He also remarks that the methodology developed over the years by the ECtHR 'appear[s] to sit uncomfortably with how the technique of systemic integration is articulated in Article 31(3)(c) of the Vienna Convention on the Law of Treaties' (ibid).

characteristics. Such subjective elements may change over relatively brief periods of time.[19] In particular, we would call for research into how international tribunals develop perceptions of themselves and their relationship to other international institutions, and the influence of such perceptions on interpretative practices.

B. Communication among International Tribunals

The chapters of this volume[20] allow us to formulate tentative conclusions on the question of whether communication among international tribunals may to some extent counteract fragmentation resulting from the lack of centralised law making institutions in international law.

Communication among international tribunals may either take the form of formal communication through citation, discussion, application, or rejection of decisions of other courts by a judge or judges;[21] or informal communication, especially through exchanges of personnel, joint meetings, and coordinated participation at seminars, conferences and workshops. This book has focused on formal communication.

What are the factors determining whether a tribunal is likely to refer to the case law of other tribunals? A long list of potential factors could be mentioned, including those characteristics that Shany mentions as a basis for classifying international tribunals.[22] Additional factors that may be significant include the extent to which the tribunal is specialised, whether it is a permanent institution or established *ad hoc*, whether it is global, regional or bilateral, and whether the parties to disputes are likely to invoke case law from other tribunals.

The ECtHR is the only regional tribunal that has been studied in some detail here. Nordeide's study indicates that the tribunal's geographical scope and its identity as a human rights tribunal have been very significant for the methodological approaches it has taken.[23] The practice of the ECtHR is far from settled when it comes to its relationship with other areas of international law. So far, there are few references to case law of other international tribunals, but there are indications that this may change.[24] One factor that may significantly affect the extent and way in which the

[19] It can be argued that many tribunals are currently experiencing such shifts in their 'characteristics'. One example is the recent developments in the jurisprudence of the ECtHR as exposed by Nordeide in this volume. Another example is the changing 'characteristics' of *ad hoc* investment tribunals as exposed by Paparinskis.

[20] In addition to the chapters in Part One, the contributions of Webb and Constantinides are of relevance here.

[21] Webb, this volume at 245. See also: Constantinides, this volume at 275–77 [section II.D of contribution].

[22] Shany, this volume at 19f.

[23] Nordeide, this volume at 118.

[24] See: ibid 127f, where he refers to the *Mamatkulov* case.

ECtHR refers to case law from other tribunals is its increasing recourse to general principles of international law.[25] We may assume that increased attention to general principles as well as to customary law[26] will lead to increased communication with other international tribunals.

As to the role of arguments of the parties, Gruszczynski notes that the 'WTO case law shows only small number of instances where the need to take extraneous treaty rules into account was argued by the parties'.[27] He confirms the general observation that the WTO dispute settlement mechanism rarely refers to case law from other tribunals.[28] Little empirical work seems to have done on the extent to which communication among international tribunals is related to or dependent on the claims and arguments brought forward by the parties to the disputes. This is an area that could benefit from further research

Communication among international tribunals concerns both norm-harmonisation and jurisdiction-regulation. Norm-harmonisation aspects of communication among international tribunals are closely related to the prevention of conflicting case law. Such communication may also induce international tribunals to import concepts and norms that are foreign to their regime, and to export their own concepts and norms to other regimes. Depending on the stakeholders' viewpoint, there may thus be advantages and disadvantages associated with such communication.

Paparinskis discusses in depth one situation in which there might be good reasons to caution against norm-harmonisation: where case law is developed by *ad hoc* tribunals in relation to individual bilateral treaties.[29] He describes the underlying situation within investment law as follows: 'The historical record . . . shows a 30-year long process of bilateral treaty-making creating a considerable number of similarly worded rules, with the adjudications beginning at the stage when a large number of binding rules (that would be complicated to change) already existed with considerable uncertainty about their content'.[30] He is critical of the norm-harmonisation that is taking place among investment arbitration tribunals due to its lack of state endorsement.[31] The tension between inter-tribunal communication with the purpose of norm-harmonisation and state control over the norm-harmonisation process can surely be generalised

[25] ibid 123f and 129.
[26] Webb, this volume at 257–62.
[27] Gruszczynski, this volume at 51.
[28] ibid.
[29] See: Paparinskis, this volume at 89, where he specifies the situation as one where there is a 'case-by-case fleshing out and refinement of presumptions, criteria and sub-criteria'.
[30] ibid 95.
[31] ibid 113: 'Whatever view one takes about the merits of these changes in treaty practice, they appear to indicate strong dissatisfaction with the overly flexible interpretative practices, rejecting particular criteria, criticising broader normative foundations and searching for more appropriate approaches in other legal regimes and systems'.

to other situations, though there may be differences in the degree of autonomy that states have granted to international courts.

Zimmermann's chapter on WTO-IMF relationships provides a case-study of jurisdiction-regulation aspects of communication among international tribunals (and institutions). According to Zimmermann, the

> IMF-WTO relationship is an interesting illustration of policy-coordination and resolution of jurisdictional issues between two international organizations of which only one (the WTO) disposes of a highly elaborated and widely respected dispute settlement system whereas the other (the IMF) relies on a quite unique set of institutional mechanisms for overseeing compliance with the underlying treaty framework.[32]

The core of the case is an unclear obligation to consult with the IMF (Article XV of GATT). The case law of the WTO and the political follow up of the provision show reluctance to make use of the consultation mechanism, also casting doubt on an alleged development in the direction of an obligation to consult.[33]

The chapter has wider relevance. Even if there are several proposals that jurisdictional overlaps could be dealt with through consultation mechanisms, there are few examples of such mechanisms.[34] Zimmermann's contribution illustrates the many complex and sometimes politically sensitive issues that need to be resolved when setting up a co-ordination mechanism.[35] Given the significant difficulty of predicting the outcomes, the primary interest in the WTO-IMF context seems to have been to seek a flexible approach through addressing the issues at an administrative level within the framework of a Co-operation Agreement.[36]

This volume has identified a number of unresolved and under-investigated issues pertaining to formal communication among international tribunals. There is a need for better knowledge regarding the factors that determine whether a tribunal is likely to refer to the case law of other tribunals, the legitimacy of formal communication, as well as the design of formalised mechanisms for communication in order to appropriately address jurisdiction-regulation and norm-harmonisation needs. Against this background, we conclude that the chapters in this volume not so much lead us to draw general conclusions regarding the question whether increasing communication among international tribunals counteracts fragmentation, but rather point to further questions for research.

It should be noted that while this book has focused on formal communication, various forms of informal communication among international

[32] Zimmermann, this volume at 58.

[33] ibid 64f.

[34] The most advanced systems have been established within the EU and the EEA, see: Shany, this volume at 21.

[35] Zimmermann, this volume at 60–67 [section II of the contribution].

[36] ibid at 63.

tribunals have become increasingly frequent.[37] In light of the above tentative assumption that the perception within tribunals of their role is likely to affect their approach to methodology (section I.A), we encourage further research on various forms of informal communication among international tribunals as well as on the effects that such communication has for the tribunals' self-perception.

C. Developing a Method to Reconcile Tensions?

In chapter one, Shany calls for a method that reconciles tensions between the competing functions of international tribunals and that offers guiding principles for determining when certain functions should prevail over other functions.[38] As he observes, the resort to norm-harmonisation and jurisdiction-regulation may interfere with core tasks of the tribunal, such as prompt and effective dispute resolution, advancement of the specific goals of the regime, and limit its flexibility to find solutions appropriate to the case in question.[39] The question is when, and in what situations, courts should give priority to norm-harmonisation and jurisdiction-regulation, and how conflicts between these interests should be settled.

The case studies included in this volume paint a rather complex picture of the factors that determine whether and how international tribunals contribute to norm-harmonisation and jurisdiction-regulation and how they reconcile these interests with their task to settle disputes. Shany rightly argues that courts are primarily loyal to the regimes under which they operate (in the case of regime courts) or to parties to the dispute (in the case of international arbitration tribunals). Broader 'systemic welfare' interests must be legitimised through appeal to the more specialised interests of the specific regime and parties.[40] The case studies also demonstrate that emphasis must be placed on factors other than those identified by Shany as primary factors. For instance, this approach of international tribunals is not only determined by their formal functions, but also by subjective factors (the tribunals' 'self-perception').[41]

A key element in this context is the extent to which international tribunals are dependent on the views and interests of key stakeholders,[42] and the relative weight and role of the perception by tribunals of their own role. The range of stakeholders differs among the regimes, and there may

[37] Constantinides, this volume at 276.

[38] Shany, this volume at 15–34.

[39] ibid 16.

[40] ibid 32.

[41] Shany acknowledges issues relating to self-perception in some places, see: ibid 27 and 30.

[42] ibid 29f.

be fundamental differences in opinion regarding which stakeholders are relevant and important (for example, are environmental non-governmental organisations (NGOs) among the relevant key stakeholders in relation to the WTO?). Moreover, the views and interests of the key stakeholders are likely to vary over time, and thus add an element of dynamism (for example, how is the WTO perceived among stakeholders, essentially as 'bilateral' and 'contractual' or as 'law-making'?).[43] The matter is further complicated as some stakeholders indeed may have an interests in a broad reading of the function of tribunals in the wider international legal order, whereas others attach overriding weight to regime-specific factors.

Against this background, we conclude that a method to reconcile tensions between the competing functions of international tribunals will have to involve the characteristics of the international regimes, the 'self-perception' of international tribunals, and the views and interests of key stakeholders. Whether it will be feasible to develop such a method remains highly questionable. But a first step surely is to expose the methods currently used and the role of underlying factors – in this respect the chapters in this volume have provided a useful contribution.

II. THE PRACTICE OF NATIONAL COURTS

Part Two of this book has focused on the practice of national courts and their role in mitigating fragmentation of international law. It can be assumed that because of the combination of, first, the control by national law and, second, the differences in national legal systems and national legal cultures, there is a significant possibility that interpretations of international law differ across courts and across states – thus, contributing to the phenomenon of fragmentation.

As we noted in the Introduction to this volume, while most authors have limited the term 'fragmentation' to refer to horizontal fragmentation between institutions and functional regimes within the international legal order, there is no need to confine the concept of fragmentation to this meaning. In view of the interplay between domestic and international law, and the engagement of national courts in the international legal order, national judicial practice is a central factor for the level and characteristics of the fragmentation of international law.[44] The fragmentation caused by divergent national receptions of international law is 'an ephemeral reflec-

[43] See: Gruszczynski, this volume at 50f.

[44] See examples given in: P Trimble, 'Review Essay: International Law, World Order, and Critical Legal Studies' (1990) 42 *Stanford L Rev* 811, 836 f. The connection between the role of national courts and fragmentation is noted by: A Kunzelmann, 'Australian International Law: The Impact of Australian Courts on the Fragmentation of International Law' (2008) 27 *AustlYBIL* 225, 248.

tion of a more fundamental, multi-dimensional fragmentation of global society itself'.[45]

Such differences are not necessarily a matter of non-compliance with international obligations. They also can result from different constructions and interpretations that may even go beyond what is required by international law. To give one example from the book: a Japanese court held that a bathhouse in Osaka was liable for not admitting foreigners, basing that liability in part on the UN Conventions on the Elimination of Racial Discrimination.[46] That is a construction that is far removed from how the Convention operates at international level, and how it has been received in different states.

The chapters in this book have reviewed how courts sustain or mitigate the fragmentation that may result from the separation of legal orders. They examined particular approaches that national courts can take, discussed the potential and limitations of such approaches, and provided examples of how courts have actually made use of such approaches, or where they have been limited in doing so.

In this section, the main trends that emerge from these chapters are reviewed and commented upon. After commenting on specific issues relating to the divide between the international and the national legal order (section II.A), we will examine the same topics as in the preceding section: the practice of interpretation (section II.B) and communication between courts (section II.C). Finally, we will provide some thoughts on the limits to national courts' contribution to defragmentation of international law (section II.D).

A. The Separation between Legal Orders

A key cause of the differing ways in which national courts interpret and apply rules of international law is the formal separation between the international and the national legal order. A critical question thus is to what extent, in the practice of national courts, this separation is sustained or mitigated, and what the consequences thereof for the process of fragmentation may be. The practices of states and courts under this heading can be considered in terms of 'jurisdiction-regulation'.[47]

Obviously, the possibility of courts overcoming the separation between the international and the national legal order is determined by the (constitutional) legislature. The rule that international law is part of the law of the land, allows courts to apply international law directly, undistorted by

[45] VJ Jackson, *Constitutional Engagement in a Transnational Era* (Oxford, Oxford University Press, 2010) 50 f.
[46] Webster, this volume at 295–319.
[47] Shany, this volume at 15–34.

transformation. For the states considered in this book, this was for instance the case for Japan[48] and Switzerland,[49] but not for Norway and the United Kingdom (UK).[50]

The differences between these situations can be significant, but need not be. First, the principle that international law is the law of the land may be a precondition for the application of international law as such, without transformation. This may mitigate fragmentation resulting from the domestic application of international law. But it clearly is not a sufficient condition. As observed by Webster, while the conventional view concerning the effect of international law in Japan is that, upon ratification and publication by the Diet, international treaties have 'domestic legal force in Japan', 'it would be more correct to say that the effect of such treaties is *contextual*, dependent upon at least four factors: (1) the existing state or absence of Japanese law; (2) the precision of the treaty obligation; (3) the judge's individual commitment to international . . . law; and (4) the self-executing nature of the treaty'.[51]

This means that while courts may apply some treaties as such, they will not be able to give effect to other treaties. Thus, in Japan, judges have concluded that the International Covenant on Civil and Political Rights (ICCPR) has direct effect, while the International Covenant on Economic, Social and Cultural Rights (ICESCR) does not.[52] Also the practice of the application of WTO law in Switzerland illustrates the barriers that may and often do exist that hinder the application of international law and that thus do in effect disallow national courts to apply international law at all.[53]

Second, even if courts do give effect to a rule of international law, in particular in monist states, that in itself says nothing about the key question whether they do so in a way that conforms to the understanding of that rule in the international legal order. The meaning given to a particular obligation then depends on the principles and practice of interpretation – examined below in section II.B.

Third, in all cases, whether international law is law of the land or not, the principle of consistent interpretation allows courts to apply a rule of national law in conformity with international law. In most cases courts can avoid incoherence between international and national law by interpreting domestic law in a way that makes the domestic legislation consistent with the country's international treaty obligations.[54] As noted by Ziegler: 'WTO rules can be of utmost importance to domestic law.

[48] Webster, this volume at 295–319.
[49] Ziegler, this volume at 321–49.
[50] Harbo, this volume at 167–83, who notes that the domestic legislature had a decisive influence on the national courts' relationship with the ECtHR.
[51] Webster, this volume at 303.
[52] ibid 304.
[53] Ziegler, this volume at 57–85.
[54] D'Aspremont, this volume at 141–65.

Regularly, they will not set aside domestic rules, but support the interpretation of broad and open-textured domestic law by offering explicit and detailed legal text'.[55] He also observes that 'Swiss courts and especially the administrative bodies at first instance have been very creative in interpreting domestic legislation in a way that led to the fulfilment of, or adherence to, the international obligations. The treaty-consistent interpretation of domestic law has thus led to a high indirect effect of WTO law on the Swiss legal order'.[56] Whereas the principle of international law as law of the land as such does not say much about the phenomenon of fragmentation, the principle of consistent interpretation in fact can achieve a high level of consistency between an international obligation and the way in which that obligation is interpreted at the national level.

B. Approaches to Treaty Interpretation

In cases where national courts can give effect to a rule of international law, whether 'directly' or through the principle of consistent interpretation, the question arises whether they do so in a way that somehow conforms to the meaning of that rule in the international legal order (presuming that a relatively unequivocal meaning exists in the international legal order). The practices of states and courts under this heading can be considered in terms of 'norm-harmonisation',[57] though they may directly reflect, and have direct consequences for the regulation of jurisdiction between national and international legal orders, and the separation between these two categories clearly is not a sharp one.

One obvious strategy to achieve relative consistency between the meaning of a rule at national level and the meaning of a rule at international level is to rely on the same international principles of interpretation that guide interpretation in the international legal order, that is: the principles contained in the Vienna Convention on the Law of Treaties.

The chapters in this volume have provided only few examples of instances where courts relied on the principles of the Vienna Convention. Webster notes that a Japanese court consulted Article 31(3) of the Vienna Convention, but since Japan is not a party to the Convention, the court found that none of the principles contained in Article 31 could apply to Japan. The court did, however, proceed to consult case law as a guide to the interpretation of Article 14(1) of the ICCPR.[58]

Outside the small sample of cases researched in this book, there is substantial practice from courts that have indeed resorted to the Vienna

[55] Ziegler, this volume at 341.
[56] ibid.
[57] Shany, this volume at 15–34.
[58] Webster, this volume at 301f.

Convention or to corresponding principles.[59] That practice recognises that international obligations, also when these have been made part of national law, should be given the meaning ascribed to them by the system in which they originated.[60]

The scope and effect of this practice and its impact on (de-)fragmentation has hardly been researched, however. It can be expected that there is considerable variation across states. Though the way in which the international norms have been made part of national law need not be decisive, it can be a relevant factor. When states have incorporated an international obligation into national law, based on a general rule of reference, such as is the case in the United States (US)[61] or the Netherlands,[62] that obligation will generally remain recognisable as such and can be subjected to rules of treaty interpretation, though it can also be expected that within this category there will be significant variation.

The situation may be different when states opt for transformation. In these cases the original international quality may go unrecognised, and it cannot be presumed at all that interpretation is subject to international rules of treaty interpretation. A comparative review of practice of interpretation would provide useful insight in the degree and way in which national courts maintain a connection with the interpretation of rules of international law at international level.

A related question that also would benefit from comparative research is to what extent the international principles of treaty interpretation actually are able to exert a significant influence over treaty interpretation, compared to national principles of statutory and constitutional interpretation.

[59] See eg: *King v Bristow Helicopters Ltd, Re M (CM)* [2002] UKHL 7; ILDC 242 (UK 2002) [80]; *NEC Semi-Conductors Ltd v Inland Revenue Commissioners* [2003] EWHC 2813; ILDC 260 (UK 2003); New Zealand, Supreme Court, *Attorney–General v Zaoui and Inspector-General of Intelligence and Security* (2005) NZSC 38; ILDC 81 (NZ 2005) [25]; Argentina, Supreme Court of Justice, *Office of the Public Prosecutor v Lariz Iriondo*, L.845.XL, vol 328; ILDC 125 (AR 2005); Belgium, Court of Cassation, *Sabanci v Erdal*, Case No P 05 1491 N [2006] Journal des Tribunaux 642; ILDC 592 (BE 2006); see further: R Gardiner, *Treaty Interpretation* (Oxford, Oxford University Press, 2008) 128 ff; See also the examples given in: E Criddle, 'The Vienna Convention on the Law of Treaties in U.S. Treaty Interpretation' (2004) 44 *Va J Int'l L* 431.

[60] See eg: *R (Al Fawwaz) v Governor of Brixton Prison* [2001] UKHL 69; ILDC 234 (UK 2001) (forthcoming) [39] (in which Lord Slynn states that 'to apply to . . . treaties the strict canons appropriate to the construction of domestic statutes would often tend to defeat rather than to serve [their] purpose'); see also: J Wouters and M Vidal, 'Non-Tax Treaties: Domestic Courts and Treaty Interpretation' in G Maisto (ed), *Courts and Tax Treaty Law* (Amsterdam, IBFD, 2007) 3, 5 f.

[61] Such as art VI of the US Constitution, providing that '[t]his Constitution, and the laws of the United States which shall be made in pursuance thereof; and all treaties made, or which shall be made, under the authority of the United States, shall be the supreme law of the land; and the judges in every state shall be bound thereby, anything in the Constitution or laws of any State to the contrary notwithstanding'. CM Vazquez, 'Treaties as Law of the Land: the Supremacy Clause and the Judicial Enforcement of Treaties' (2008) 122 *Harv L Rev* 599.

[62] JG Brouwer, 'The Netherlands' in JG Brouwer (ed), *National Treaty Law and Practice: Dedicated to the Memory of Monroe Leigh* (Leiden, Martinus Nijhoff Publishers, 2005) 483.

It seems obvious that the terms and categories of interpretation differ across states. But it is also to be recognised that the international principles are open-textured, and it seems a plausible working hypothesis that it is not so much the formal principles of interpretation that are decisive as the normative choices, and that the question whether national or international principles are used for interpretation is of secondary relevance. We return to this theme below.

C. Communication among Courts

The practices of national courts that engage in communication with other courts can be grouped in two categories: practices that attribute weight to decisions of international courts whose interpretative competence they have accepted (section III.C.1) and practices that attribute weight to decisions of other courts, whether international or national.

1. *Weight of Decisions of Competent International Courts*

National courts may mitigate fragmentation by giving effect to decisions of international tribunals with the competence in regard to the interpretation of a particular treaty.[63] The fact that international decisions, strictly speaking, are not binding on states other than the parties to the dispute does not negate that they are legally relevant and, indeed, often critical for determining the state of the law as binding on the courts.

Constantinides shows that the practice of English courts on diplomatic assurances shows a heavy reliance on the jurisprudence of the ECtHR. 'Although British courts enjoy discretion under the 1998 Human Rights Act as to how much weight to give to the ECtHR decisions (which they are only required to 'take into account'), the House of Lords did not make use of this space, showing loyalty to the ECtHR and following its case law in most cases, including in politically highly sensitive judgments'.[64] Other

[63] See, generally: M Bedjaoui, 'The Reception by National Courts of Decisions of International Tribunals' (1995–96) 28 *NYU J Int'l L & Pol* 45; CH Schreuer, 'The Authority of International Judicial Practice in Domestic Courts' (1974) 23 *Int'l & Comp L Q* 68; H Mosler, 'Supra-National Judicial Decisions and National Courts' (1980–81) 4 *Hastings Int'l & Comp L Rev* 425, 464 (discussing how national courts have made reference to principles, rules and legal arguments in the reasoning of international judgments, when the national courts are confronted with the same legal questions); TM Franck and GH Fox (eds), *International Law Decisions in National Courts* (Irvington-on-Hudson, Transnational, 1996); HD Jarmul, 'The Effect of Decisions of Regional Human Rights Tribunals on National Courts' (1995–96) 28 *NYU J Int'l L & Pol* 311; R Lefeber, 'The Last Judgment: Legal Effects of Decisions of International Courts and Arbitral Tribunals in the Proceedings of National Courts' in N Blokker (ed), *The Netherlands in Court: Essays in Honour of Johan G. Lammers* (Leiden, Martinus Nijhoff Publishers, 2006) 165; Y Shany, *Regulating Jurisdictional Relations between National and International Courts* (Oxford, Oxford University Press, 2007).

[64] Constantinides, this volume at 287f.

national courts in Europe have also relied on the ECtHR jurisprudence when deciding cases on diplomatic assurances.[65]

In Switzerland, a commission charged with the task of applying the WTO Agreement relied heavily on its interpretation by the WTO Appellate Body.[66] Ziegler observes that:

> Whether the reading of the Report by the Commission was accurate remains questionable . . . for our purposes it is interesting to see that the Commission used the WTO Report as an authoritative means for interpreting the meaning of the WTO obligations and thereby indirectly to interpret domestic law in a treaty-consistent manner.[67]

The acceptance of interpretations by international tribunals is not mechanical, however. Harbo's analysis of the reception of the case law of the ECtHR on proportionality in English and Norwegian courts shows that there is considerable reluctance to do so.[68] Harbo notes that the ECtHR is hardly receptive to opinions and practices at the national level, which in turn may limit the willingness of national courts or other organs to faithfully follow whatever comes out of the ECtHR.[69] In the *Bøhler* case, the Norwegian Supreme Court stated that it would apply the same methodology as the ECtHR.[70] However, it further stated that when Norwegian courts interpret the Convention, they may also take into account traditional Norwegian value judgments. Still, '[t]aking a proactive approach, the Court stated that the Norwegian courts should seek interaction with the ECtHR in order to influence its practice.'[71]

The lack of willingness and/or ability of national courts to give effect to decisions of international tribunals may be enhanced in view of the recent discussion on lack of trust in and legitimacy of international tribunals. This ties in with the 'Solange argument' considered by Tzanakopoulos.[72] He observes that in light of concerns over the legitimacy of international tribunals, national courts have sometimes reacted by asserting the power to control decisions of the international organisation that interferes with individual 'fundamental' rights.[73] This is not simply a matter of protecting individuals against decisions of the Security Council that may outright interfere with individual rights, it may in a much more subtle way come down to a differ-

[65] ibid 288f.
[66] See: Consideration 13.4.2.
[67] Ziegler, this volume at 339.
[68] Harbo, this volume at 167–83.
[69] ibid 168f.
[70] Rt 2000: 996 (*Bøhler*).
[71] Harbo, this volume at 178.
[72] Tzanakopoulos, this volume at 185–215.
[73] See generally on national courts' reactions to acts of international organisations the contributions: A Reinisch (ed), *Challenging Acts of International Organizations before National Courts* (Oxford, Oxford University Press, 2010).

ence of opinion between an international tribunal and a national court about the way individual rights should best be protected. The increasing recognition of the differences in such opinions leads to a pluralistic outlook on the relationship between international and national courts.[74]

Portraying the relationship between international and national courts in a hierarchical manner in which international tribunals can curtail fragmenting effects of domestication, as long as national courts faithfully follow what international tribunals prescribe is too simple. It can be expected that national courts often contest what is the better interpretation of a particular norm in a particular context. This may also lead to divergence in interpretation between states. It is also possible that international tribunals incorporate domestic practices in their future judgments, leading to continuous adjustments.

This is an area with major research questions. On what grounds do national courts follow or contest decisions of international tribunals? Are these essentially related to an equivalence of the protection of fundamental rights, or are there broader legitimacy concerns at issue and, if so, what are these? Do the grounds on which national courts contest decisions of international tribunals differ between states and, if so, how does this affect processes of fragmentation? And how do international tribunals respond to such contestation – do they recognise this as legitimate checks and balances and do they allow it to influence future judicial decision making, or do they insist on their hierarchal position, thereby consolidating the opposition between the international and the national normative sphere?

2. *Communication with Other Courts*

Apart from attributing weight to decisions of international tribunals that have been given the competence in regard to interpretation of particular treaties, there is a wide-ranging practice of communication with other national and international courts. Such communication is often referred to in terms of 'dialogues', and concerns the citation, discussion, application, or rejection of decisions of other courts by a judge or judges.[75] Constantinides refers in this context to 'transjudicial communication'.[76] The distinction with the previous point is that here we are concerned with international tribunals that do not formally have interpretive competence in regard to a particular treaty, but whose interpretation a national court somehow does find relevant for its own interpretation.

Many chapters in this book provide empirical material which shows that such communication indeed takes place. Noteworthy examples can

[74] Nico Krisch, *Beyond Constitutionalism. The Pluralist Structure of Postnational Law* (Oxford, Oxford University Press, 2011).

[75] Webb, this volume at 245.

[76] Constantinides, this volume at 267–94.

be found in Webb's treatment of the development of the law of immunities. In particular, the extent to which state officials accused of committing international crimes are entitled to immunity from jurisdiction 'is the subject of intense dialogue and some conflict among national and international courts'.[77] She observes that states characterised by a high level of judicial dialogue on the law on immunity, such as the UK and Italy, 'tend to not only cite cases from other jurisdictions, but also to engage in in-depth, critical analysis, drawing on a wide range of cases for a variety of points of law'.[78]

Japanese courts too recognise interpretations of international legal provisions as put forth by foreign courts and international tribunals, including the ECtHR and the Inter-American Court of Human Rights. Webster observes that '[s]uch dialogue would lead one to expect greater conformity with the interpretations of these foreign bodies, and Japanese courts fulfil this expectation to a limited degree'.[79]

Constantinides illustrates that the British case law on diplomatic assurances shows great willingness to take part in the transjudicial dialogue on the topic by referring to and relying on not only international tribunals and institutions (the ECtHR and the Committee against Torture) but also courts in Canada.[80] However, there are considerable differences between states. Apart from British courts, 'domestic courts in Europe have relied exclusively on the ECtHR's rulings, without paying any attention to related judicial developments elsewhere'.[81]

The nature and impact of citations or discussions varies widely.[82] They may be passing references, 'may simply be another authority used to buttress a conclusion already reached, or may reflect extensive considerations of the other courts' approaches.'[83] Also, the dialogue on immunities in national courts ranges from in-depth, critical analyses, via confused or selective citation, to the complete absence of reference to decisions from other jurisdictions.[84]

It appears that in many of these cases one cannot really speak of any 'dialogue'; rather, there is more of a one-way communication.[85] Indeed, there are huge differences in the degree to which citation and references actually are part of what could be labelled a dialogue. Tzanakopoulos writes that the main feature of dialogue is the necessity for an exchange of

[77] Webb, this volume at 245.
[78] ibid 250.
[79] Webster, this volume at 318.
[80] Constantinides, this volume at 267–94.
[81] ibid 292.
[82] RC Black and L Epstein, '(Re-)setting the Scholarly Agenda on Transjudicial Communication' (2007) 32 *Law and Social Inquiry* 791.
[83] Constantinides, this volume at 275f.
[84] Webb, this volume at 245–65.
[85] Harbo, this volume at 167–83.

ideas between those engaged in it; otherwise it is rather a *mono*logue.[86] This is for example the case when the argument of one international or foreign court 'is so convincing as to immediately solicit the agreement of the other, who adopts the argument wholesale'.[87] The exchange then can be more precisely defined as *influence* exercised by one interlocutor on the other.[88]

The chapters offer various explanations of why national courts do in fact engage in communication with other courts. The degree of accessibility of domestic jurisprudence clearly is a factor. Available examples of transnational judicial communication remain selective, and they overemphasise developments in some regions and not in others. Most information on 'court-to-court' dialogue still comes from Western Europe, North America, and Australia; there is limited access to developments in Central and Eastern Europe, Asia, or Africa. As a consequence, the communication between a few dominant countries and its potential for shaping the rule of law may seem hegemonic and overly one-sided.

However, lack of accessibility is certainly not the only reason why some courts hardly ever enter the transnational judicial debate. For example, the US Supreme Court is very reticent in referring to decisions of international courts such as the ECtHR, or to the courts of other countries – even in instances when those decisions are readily available. In contrast, the South African Constitutional Court, or courts in India and Canada, have a very liberal practice in this regard and routinely refer to decisions of courts from other regions. In view of such differences, clearly availability of information is not a decisive factor. Possible explanations are cultural links between states (and courts); and the prestige of some courts (courts seem to refer more to courts that they (rightly or wrongly) deem prestigious, such as the US Supreme Court or the German *Bundesverfassungsgericht*, rather than courts from developing countries).

Webb offers a range of explanations that are of wider relevance than her discussion of the case law on immunities. For one, the variety of citations 'is a product of the interest and ability of counsel to conduct comparative research and include such material in their submissions to the court'.[89] Conversely, in national jurisdictions with few references to foreign courts, such as the US and Switzerland, 'the reluctance to cite cases form other jurisdictions usually originates with counsel.'[90] Another factor is the attitude of judges to the case law of other jurisdictions. Webb observes that this 'is to a large extent a product of the legal culture of the jurisdic-

[86] Tzanakopoulos, this volume at 188, citing AM Slaughter, 'A Typology of Transjudicial Communication' (1994) 29 *U Rich L Rev* 99, 101.
[87] ibid.
[88] ibid.
[89] Webb, this volume, at 250f.
[90] ibid 254.

tion in question.'[91] Other relevant factors may be historical links between jurisdictions,[92] the use of experts, the style of judgment-writing,[93] and the availability of foreign judgments.[94]

On this latter point, the *lack of access to* the decisions of national courts is a serious practical obstacle to judicial dialogue. This also has implications for the extent to which national courts use international law. There is a very uneven distribution of available data across and within different regions, not to mention language barriers. Whereas most decisions of international tribunals, such as the ICJ, the International Criminal Tribunal for the Former Yugoslavia, or the ECtHR, are available online in English (and mostly also in French), this is not the case with decisions of national courts. As a result, a vast majority of national court decisions are available – if at all – only to persons who speak a certain language and are familiar with finding court documents in a particular domestic legal system.[95]

Constantinides points to relevant favourable conditions, such as gaps in the legal framework, lack of precedent, identical or similar legal issues, transnational nature of the problem, effective advocacy, and strong interest on the part of transnational social networks and civil society.[96]

Webster points to the relevance of a 'judge's disposition towards international law'. In their opinions, judges can signal openness to international law by citing and analysing decisions of international and foreign courts. But judges also omit discussion of the treaty and any relevant foreign or international decisions altogether, even if referenced by plaintiff, reflecting a resistance to international law.[97]

The chapters reveal certain factors that are, perhaps contrary to what is commonly thought, less relevant. For instance, there does not appear to be any connection between the level of dialogue in the field of immunities and the monist/dualist dichotomy. Webb observes that a dualist system like the UK is the national jurisdiction that is most engaged in dialogue, whereas 'monist' (or in any case more open) systems like the US, Switzerland and Austria show significantly less examples of dialogues.[98]

While communication between national courts and other (national or international) courts is often thought of as leading to a certain co-

[91] ibid 251.
[92] ibid 253.
[93] ibid 256f.
[94] ibid.
[95] In addition, the practice of some states, of which Norway is one example, to 'outsource' databases on court decisions to self-funding institutions that depend on being paid for searches in their databases, significantly reduces the availability of such decisions.
[96] Constantinides, this volume at 293.
[97] Webster, this volume 300 [FN 25] citing M Masanao, 'Saibansho ni yoru jinken joyaku no tekiyo ni kansuru shomondai' ('Various problems relating to the application of human rights treaties in courts') in *Kokusai Jinken Kiyaku to Kokunai Hanrei* (*International Human Rights Covenants and Domestic Jurisprudence*) (Tokyo, Liberation Press, 2004) 24.
[98] Webb, this volume at 262.

ordination and uniformity in interpretation and reception of international obligations, this is by no means the only effect. Indeed, it may well lead to disconnection between the international and the national sphere. Tzanakopoulos observes that the *Solange* argument is

> (implicitly) addressed to whoever is willing to listen and be persuaded that this is a good way to control conferrals of powers to another level of governance: not only to the other EC Member States and in particular their courts, who are most likely to be persuaded to adopt a similar line of argument, but also any other court potentially facing the same issues arising from the complexity of multi-level governance.[99]

He cites Tomuschat who observed already in 1990 that 'every *principled disobedience* of Community law constitutes in itself a precedent that will invariably find imitators'.[100] Decisions that refuse to follow particular interpretations of international tribunals provide other courts 'with a theoretical framework in which to challenge themselves implementing measures within their (partial-national) legal order by asserting the importance of fundamental rights. The practice after the *Kadi* case indeed shows examples of this form of communication.'[101]

Communication between courts is thus a complex phenomenon that can lead both to co-ordination and some form of coherence, but can also easily lead to fragmentation. Despite a substantial body of literature on dialogues, the topic as a whole remains under-researched. What is absent from much of the theoretical discussion is qualitative and quantitative evidence to support the broader claims put forward. Academic literature is full of hand-selected 'exemplary' cases which make no more than a shaky empirical foundation of the respective arguments.[102] Most of the existing scholarship tends to focus on a single jurisdiction, or on the dialogue between the European courts and the national courts, and between the European courts.[103] There is more need for studies such as those undertaken by Webb in the field of immunities and by Constantinides in regard to diplomatic assurances, systematically analysing patterns of dialogues and their effects.

[99] Tzanakopoulos, this volume at 194.
[100] C Tomuschat, 'Aller guten Dinge sind III? Zur Diskussion um die Solange-Rechtsprechung des BVerfG' (1990) 25 *Europarecht* 340, 343.
[101] Tzanakopoulos, this volume at 363.
[102] RC Black and L Epstein, '(Re-)setting the Scholarly Agenda on Transjudicial Communication' (2007) 32 *Law and Social Inquiry* 791.
[103] See, eg: L Garlicki, 'Cooperation of Courts: The Role of Supranational Jurisdictions in Europe' (2008) 6 *Int'l J Const L* 509–30.

D. Limits to National Courts' Contribution to Defragmentation of International Law

The question underlying the preceding sections somehow presumes that a relatively unequivocal meaning of a rule of international law can be discerned in the international legal order. However, it is apparent from the chapters in Part One of this volume that this cannot at all be assumed. To the extent the international legal order itself is fragmented, it can hardly be expected that national courts somehow try to mitigate or resolve that fragmentation. In such situations, the question concerns not so much whether national courts connect the meaning and application of a rule of international law to the meaning of that rule in *the* international legal order, but to a particular meaning given to that rule in a particular part of the international legal order. Indeed, the practice of national courts can only reflect the fragmentation at international level.

In this volume, this point is argued by Currie and Kindred. They observe that the doctrine and principles of jurisdiction and human rights protection at the international level are in a difficult and often conflicting relationship. The principles of jurisdiction are becoming modulated, but there will remain a gap between the principles of jurisdiction and what is required from the perspective of human rights. Contradictions at the international level are reflected at the national level: 'Court decisions reflect the ongoing fragmentation in the law and, in turn, contribute to the diverse state practice that underlies the splintering of norms and needs.'[104] Currie and Kindred observe that the Canadian courts 'were alert to, and took very seriously, the arguments founded in international human rights law, which would have led them to reach decisions that would tend to fragment the traditional principles of jurisdiction'.[105] They add: 'Canadian judicial uncertainty nationally epitomises the growing legal disorder internationally'.[106]

However, national courts are not entirely powerless in this situation. D'Aspremont explores the relevance of the principle of systemic integration (see section I.A above) in national courts, by which national courts will attempt to interpret rules of international law in the light of other rules, in order to optimise the coherence between them. Despite the fact that international law must be regarded as a separate legal order from the perspective of national courts, he finds, on the basis of limited practice, that 'domestic judges are in a position to use the principle of systemic integration and carry out a very integrationist interpretation of inter-national

[104] Currie and Kindred, this volume at 218.
[105] ibid 219.
[106] ibid.

law'.[107] In light of our observations above concerning communication among national courts, there are apparent problems associated with such initiatives. As also highlighted by d'Aspremont, 'the use of the principle of systemic integration by domestic judges can simultaneously yield contradicting interpretations, for each domestic court . . . can carry out various systemic integrations of international law.'[108] In particular, he sees the potential for a dialogue between national courts and legal scholars that might be conducive to de-fragmentation of international law.

Even if we may expect national courts to, at least to some extent, model their resort to systemic integration on the practice of international tribunals, contributions to this volume show that international tribunals are far from having developed a consistent approach to Article 31(3)(c) of the Vienna Convention on the Law of Treaties (see section I.A above). Moreover, as is also pointed out by d'Aspremont, the risk of diverging systemic integrations of international law is higher at the domestic level than at the international level.[109]

There is clearly a need for more knowledge about the extent to which domestic courts in fact merely reflect fragmentation in international law. Research is needed regarding the explicit or implicit application of the principle of systemic integration within domestic legal systems: by courts, by the legislature, and by administrative authorities. While nothing would formally prevent actors within domestic legal systems from making use of the principle of systemic integration, there are, as we have hinted at above, significant barriers that must be overcome before international tribunals will make effective and systematic use of the practice of national legal systems. Research as called for above could improve the ability and willingness of international tribunals to take into account such practice.

III. SOME CONCLUDING OBSERVATIONS

The discussion of rather specific techniques applied by international and national courts to counteract fragmentation, has to be placed against a series of fundamental normative questions that are raised by the phenomenon of fragmentation. In most of this book these normative aspects have been left aside. For a fuller understanding of the role of international and national courts in regard to the process of fragmentation this question obviously needneeds to be considered, not only because the perceived positive and negative aspects of fragmentation are likely to influence judicial practices, but also for our external evaluation of such practices.

[107] D'Aspremont, this volume at 160f.
[108] ibid 142.
[109] ibid 161.

The universalist aspirations of much of international law[110] and a perceived need for consistency and coherence may drive the application of techniques that counteract fragmentation, as described in the various chapters in this volume, and indeed may lead one to positively assess such application. However, that perspectives needs to be balanced with the value of grounding interpretation and application of the law in a localised expression (as far as the practices of national courts are concerned)[111] and the need to protect the specific nature and aims of specialised regimes (as far as courts that operate within treaty regimes are concerned). International law may lose some of its uniform meaning in this process, yet may gain national and regional relevance.[112] Indeed, the possibility and permissibility of variations is generally a condition underlying the acceptance of these obligations in the first place. In this respect, the very indeterminacy that fosters processes of auto-interpretation and differences between states is 'not a scandal or a structural deficiency', but 'an absolutely central aspect of International Law's acceptability'.[113] The same holds to some extent for differences in interpretations between particular treaty regimes. Indeed, the 'respect of legitimate difference inherent in such a pluralist conception may actually enhance the effectiveness of international law by increasing the legitimacy and political acceptability of international legal rules'.[114]

Further research on the role of international tribunals and national courts in connection with the fragmentation of international law can build on the case studies provided in this volume, and should take as its starting point the normative complexities of the above perspectives.

It follows from the above that despite an abundance of literature on fragmentation, both normative and empirical factors remain underdeveloped. As to the latter, we acknowledge that the precise mapping of interjudicial dialogues around the world is a challenging exercise. We observe that ideology and political preferences are likely to remain essential to the future debate on fragmentation of international law, and consider that such factors should be taken into account in future empirical research of the topic.

[110] On the importance of uniform interpretation: P Pescatore, 'Conclusion' in FG Jacobs and S Roberts (eds), *The Effects of Treaties in Domestic Law* (London, Sweet & Maxwell, 1987) 282.

[111] ME Adjami, 'African Courts, International Law, and Comparative Case-Law: Chimera or Emerging Human Rights Jurisprudence' (2002) 24 *Mich J Int'l L* 164.

[112] K Knop, 'Here and There: International Law in Domestic Courts' (2000) 32 *NYU J Int'l L & Pol* 501, 504.

[113] M Koskeniemmi, *From Apology to Utopia: The Structure of International Legal Argument*, 2nd edn (Cambridge, Cambridge University Press, 2006) 591.

[114] WW Burke-White, 'International Legal Pluralism' (2004) 25 *Mich J Int'l L* 963, 978. See also: SR Ratner, 'Regulatory Takings in Institutional Context: Beyond the Fear of Fragmented International Law' (2008) 102 *Am J Int'l L* 475.

Despite these challenges, the usefulness of further empirical research to the main stakeholders in international and national legal systems is in our view unquestionable. This book has contributed to the empirical basis for debates concerning fragmentation and pluralism in international law, and it is our hope that it will inspire further empirical and normative exploration of fragmentation and pluralism in the interface between different regimes, and between international and national law.

www.ingramcontent.com/pod-product-compliance
Lightning Source LLC
Chambersburg PA
CBHW071246180926
51613CB00007B/268/J
* 9 7 8 1 8 4 9 4 6 2 4 7 1 *